THE SINO-SOVIET CONFLICT
1956–1961

ORIGINALLY PUBLISHED BY
PRINCETON UNIVERSITY PRESS

THE
SINO-SOVIET
CONFLICT
1956-1961

BY DONALD S. ZAGORIA

WITH A NEW PREFACE

ATHENEUM   NEW YORK
1969

Published by Atheneum
Reprinted by arrangement with Princeton University Press

First Atheneum Printing September 1964
Second Printing June 1966
Third Printing April 1967
Fourth Printing April 1969

To my parents

PREFACE

IT IS A PLEASURE to acknowledge the assistance I have had in the preparation of this book. Research on it began in the fall of 1958. In the early stages of my work, I received valuable advice, stimulation, and criticism from Paul S. McPherson, a pioneer in the still relatively unexploited area of systematic content analysis of Communist communications, and one without whom a whole generation of analysts of Communist communications would have been much poorer. I benefited greatly as well from the published work of Doak Barnett, Zbigniew Brzezinski, A. M. Halpern, Alice Hsieh, Richard Lowenthal, Roderick MacFarquhar, Victor Zorza and many others. Some of their contributions to the study of Soviet and Chinese politics are listed in the bibliography.

In the later stages of research, I owe an immeasurable debt to Allen S. Whiting, who read the entire manuscript several times, made many valuable comments, generously offered me the use of his files, and provided many illuminating insights into the nature of the Sino-Soviet relationship. I am also grateful to numerous analysts and friends in various agencies of the United States Government who helped to shape this book. In addition, I have profited from the advice of many colleagues at The RAND Corporation, particularly Myron Rush, Arnold Horelick, Nathan Leites, Marshall Shulman, and Alexander George. This book does not, however, necessarily represent the opinions of any agency or individual. Some of those cited above would certainly disagree with interpretations and analysis I have stubbornly clung to.

Anita Magnus helped trace many of the elusive sources. The assistance of my wife, Janet, who generously took time off from more active interests in another continent, was indispensable, and I can only marvel that she played the roles of drone and critic with unfailing grace. Maureen Grace, Leona Levine, Lucille Goldsen, Natalie Wilcoxen, Bonnie Lieb, Anne Redmond, and Lilita Dzirkals typed the numerous drafts of the manuscript. I should like to thank the editors of *Problems of Communism, The China Quarterly*, and *Asian Survey* for their permission to reproduce here portions of articles I wrote for their publications. I should also like to thank Ian Graham for helping to make intelligible and literate what otherwise might not have been so. If the style of this book leaves something to be desired, I can only plead that any work which includes numerous extracts from Communist media is not likely to be poetic.

My primary purpose in writing this book was to subject the Sino-Soviet conflict to close analysis. Another almost equally important purpose, however, was to try to demonstrate the value of the Communists' own stream of communications as raw material for penetrating through the dialectical fog to the political calculations and conflicts which lay behind it. The "Kremlinologist"—or whatever one chooses to call the analyst of Communist communications—has been a shadowy figure in conventional academic and government circles for a number of reasons. Some of those who pioneered in the field were not sufficiently rigorous in their discipline or cautious in their interpretation. As Robert Conquest has pointed out, the work of Franz Borkenau would be quite acceptable if only he had added here and there a few qualifying phrases to show that his interpretations were just that and not confirmed conclusions. For my own part, I would readily concede that interpretations different from my own are sometimes possible and I have used a substantial number of extracts from Communist media in part to enable the interested reader to form his own interpretations. Throughout this book, it would have been quite appropriate to insert qualifying phrases such as "the above suggests that," "it is likely that," and so on, but such qualifiers would soon become tiresome. Let me make it clear, therefore, that while all or most of the material cited in this book is of political significance, the reader is at liberty to make his own judgment of what that significance is.

Sometimes, too, it must be conceded the Kremlinologist weaves a web of interpretations on too fragmentary evidence. Like the psychoanalyst who takes one or two dreams and analyzes them to death, the plier of this trade sometimes makes too much of too little. When the analyst backs up the conclusions he reached on the basis of one dream with evidence from thirty dreams, however, then we must begin to sit up and take notice. The task for the Kremlinologist is to sample a great deal of symbolic evidence from Communist media, to try to fit this evidence into a meaningful pattern, to be prepared to drop one hypothesis and substitute another in the face of new evidence, and, above all, to be committed not to any one particular explanation but only to the technique itself.

The Kremlinologist, in his passion for exegesis, has sometimes disparagingly been called a Talmudist. What the critic seems to forget is that it is the Communists who are the Talmudists and that to understand their scriptures, exegesis is indispensable. As Czeslaw Milosz wrote a decade ago in *The Captive Mind:* "Whoever would take the measure of intellectual life in the countries of Central or Eastern Europe from the monotonous articles appearing in the press or the stereotyped speeches pronounced there, would be making a grave error. Just as theologians in periods of strict orthodoxy expressed their views in the rigorous language of the Church, so the writers of the people's democracies make use of an accepted special style, terminology, and linguistic ritual. What is important is not what someone said but what he wanted to say, disguising his thought by removing a comma, inserting an 'and,' establishing this rather than another sequence in the problems discussed. Unless one has lived there one cannot know how many titanic battles are being fought, how the heroes of Ketman are falling, what this warfare is being waged over." I have tried in this book to take the measure of one of the titanic battles of the Communist world and to determine just what it is that this warfare is being fought about. In doing so, I have found it necessary to penetrate behind the linguistic ritual that Milosz describes.

As an indication of the special style of political language employed in the Communist world, consider the following two passages which appeared in Communist media in June 1960, the first in the Chinese Communist Party journal *Hung ch'i,* the second in a speech by Khrushchev:

"A wolf is a wolf, and its man-eating nature does not change. An ancient Chinese fable about the Chungshan wolf tells the story of Schoolmaster Tungkuo, who once found a wolf wounded by hunters and saved it by hiding it in his bag. After the hunters had left, he released the wolf from the bag. Instead of showing gratitude, the wolf wanted to devour him. Fortunately a peasant came along who understood well the man-eating nature of the wolf. He lured it back into the bag and beat it to death, and thus Schoolmaster Tungkuo was saved." (June 16, 1960)

"It is common knowledge that a wolf is just as bloodthirsty as a lion or a tiger, but he is much weaker. That is why a man fears less meeting a wolf than meeting a tiger or lion. Of course, small beasts of prey can also bite; essentially they are the same, but they have different possibilities. They are not as strong and it is easier to render them harmless." (June 21, 1960)

I do not suppose that any reader would be content to stop at the conclusion that the Chinese Communists believe that wolves are more dangerous than Khrushchev believes they are. If we substitute "U.S. imperialism" for "wolf," and "Comrade Khrushchev" for "Schoolmaster Tungkuo," and "Mao Tse-tung" for the "peasant who came along," we find that this particular allegory conveys a great deal about the difference between Chinese and Soviet thinking about the West, and about Mao's estimates of Khrushchev's personal diplomacy. It would not be too much of an exaggeration to say that every issue of *Hung ch'i* and every speech of Khrushchev contains similar semantic devices, not always allegory, to transmit political messages to Communist-Talmudists throughout the world. If we add to *Hung ch'i* and Khrushchev's speeches all the other Soviet and Chinese Party journals and newspapers, the speeches of other leaders, and the mass media, we might in fact soon come to the conclusion that the Talmudic scholar had a much easier time of it than the Kremlinologist.

Some final caveats are in order. First, this book does not purport to be a study of the Sino-Soviet relationship in its entirety. It confines itself largely to the elements of conflict in that relationship. I have tried at various points throughout the book, and particularly at the end, to put the conflict into the larger perspective of the relationship as a whole. Second, when this book was originally conceived, the task was to trace a Sino-Soviet conflict the existence of which many analysts in government and academic circles questioned. Therefore, I have introduced a great deal of material to support my analysis. Now that the conflict itself has become apparent to any observer, it would be fruitful to explore more fully than was possible here the underlying causes of conflict. Equally fruitful would be a study of this relationship after it has taken a somewhat more stable form than it had at the end of 1961, when this book went to press.

PREFACE TO
THE ATHENEUM EDITION

PREFACES TO SECOND EDITIONS are customarily designed to demonstrate how farsighted and omniscient the author was and how peevish and petty were his critics. The usual assertion is that although some time has passed and some new evidence is available, nothing has appeared which would force the author to revise any of his principal conclusions or to change substantially any of his chapters. I shall not depart from this tradition.

I would have liked to substitute for my last chapter an article I subsequently wrote for *Foreign Affairs,* had it been feasible. My principal reason for wanting to make this substitution is that my last chapter was written with a sense of caution that is no longer in order. There is no longer any possibility of a papering over or a reconciliation of the Sino-Soviet dispute. It is irreparable. The more perceptive communists themselves are well aware of this fact. Recently a British correspondent asked an Italian communist leader whether there would be any point in holding a new world communist meeting. He was answered with a story:

> "A few centuries ago it was learned in an Italian village that the Patriarch of Constantinople was saying mass in a new way. The faithful were dismayed but an optimist said: 'it doesn't matter. The Pope and Patriarch will get together, discuss the whole question and after a time reach an agreement, because after all they both believe in the same god.' As you know, they are still talking."

Both the Russian and Chinese parties have also given indication of a belief that the split is irrevocable, particularly so long as the present leaderships remain. A joke going the rounds in Moscow these days is that no improvement in Sino-Soviet relations can be expected until there is a "Maosoleum." Perhaps a better indication of the Russians' attitude is reflected in their abortive effort in the fall of 1963 to excommunicate Peking and its Albanian and North Korean allies from the international communist movement, a development I shall return to subsequently. Peking, for its part, has issued a number of programmatic statements indicating that it would not surrender principle for the sake of unity. In one of the most important of these in

October, 1963, a prominent Chinese Communist leader, Chou Yang, undertook to explain the split in dialectical terms, arguing that Marxism has always bred revisionism and that everything tends to divide itself in two. Chou accused the Russians and all their allies in Europe, North America and Australasia of "singing the tune of social democracy" while claiming that the revolutionary movement in Asia, Africa and Latin America now stands in the "front line." Moreover, Chinese claims to authority in the international movement are now unlimited. Not only have they criticized the Italian party for its theory of "structural reform," but they have broadly attacked Khrushchev's internal policies as well, arguing that his political and economic reforms indicate a degeneration of the Soviet party and system. Meanwhile economic relations continue to deteriorate, both sides are taking precautionary measures along the inflammable Sinkiang border with Soviet Central Asia, and the struggle for power in the international communist movement and for influence with nationalist governments in underdeveloped areas intensifies.

I have often been asked whether I intend to bring this book up to date. I have no such intention for several reasons. First of all, I am not a journalist and therefore feel under no obligation to keep the reader informed of the latest news. This book was intended as an inquiry into the origins of the Sino-Soviet dispute. Second, I see no particular value in issuing bi-annual status reports on the rift. The interested reader will find no shortage of current articles on the latest developments. More important, the basic issues, in my opinion, remain the same and much of the tactical maneuvering that has gained the headlines in recent months will not be worth recalling by the time this edition appears in print.

There are nevertheless some points to be made on the basis of developments since this book was published that are likely to have enduring consequences.

As far as the Soviet Union is concerned, the fact that the anti-China campaign has been carried down to the entire party apparatus and to the Russian masses has several important implications. It places severe inhibitions on Soviet foreign policy. There is a deep-seated urge for peace in Russia which no sensitive traveller can fail to observe. In part this urge accounts for the enormous popularity of the late President Kennedy in Russia and the deep and genuine grief provoked by his assassination, a reaction I was able to measure personally as I travelled in the Soviet Union at the time. Khrushchev has exploited and even stimulated this widespread and profound sentiment for peace in condemning the Chinese leaders as irresponsible and callous warmongers while arrogating to himself the role of the peacemaker who is acutely aware of the horrendous consequences of a nuclear war. By committing himself in this manner to keeping peace and thereby to providing for the Russian people the good things of life which they are beginning to expect and to gain, Khrushchev severely limits his ability to adopt an aggressive foreign policy. This is not to say that it would be impossible for Khrushchev or his successor to renew or to intensify the cold war. So long as the Soviet Union remains a highly developed totalitarian society, such a shift is not impossible. But it could only be accomplished at great cost to internal stability. In the succession crisis that will probably follow Khrushchev's death, no Soviet leader is likely to want to take such a risk. For this reason, the potential successors to Khrushchev are not likely to "campaign" on a platform of seeking a rapprochement with China unless the Chinese themselves make a radical change in their own policy.

Particularly among the Russian technical intelligentsia, who are well entrenched in positions of power both in the party and state bureaucracy, there is widespread support for Khrushchev's stand against China. Many of these people are in fact opposed to making concessions to China because they fear that such concessions could only be accompanied by undesirable retrogressions both in Soviet foreign policy and in Soviet internal policy. European-oriented in their outlook, they believe that the wider the split with China, the closer Russia draws toward Europe.

In the last analysis, the split with China is forcing on the Russian ruling circles and people alike a realization that there is a profound conflict between building up the Soviet economy and raising the standard of living on the one hand and supporting foreign communist parties on the other. The Soviet party has by no means resolved this dilemma by renouncing the international communist movement, a move that would threaten the very legitimacy of communist party rule in Russia. But it has certainly given priority to Russian "national" as opposed to "revolutionary" interests.

The contradiction between these two was always latent in Soviet foreign policy. But under Stalin, the international communist movement automatically accepted his assumption that the interests of the Soviet motherland and all other communist parties were identical. Now that it has been made abundantly clear that this is not the case, each communist party is likely to act increasingly out of self-interest. The Russians will try to direct and to channel these competing communist interests, sometimes with success but often with failure. The long-range effect of this on the Soviet party can only be to strengthen the force of nationalism and to weaken the force of ideology. Already the Soviet man in the street is inclined to atttribute the recent bread shortage to the fact that the USSR is shipping wheat to Cuba. While members of the Soviet Central Committee are not likely to share this farfetched view, they may have more sophisticated doubts about "proletarian internationalism." Thus one wonders whether some members of the Soviet élite are beginning to have second thoughts about the wisdom of heavy investments in foreign communist parties such as the Cuban which are emotionally closer to Peking, costly to support and risky to defend. Or, to take another example, will the Soviet party enthusiastically support a pro-Chinese communist party in Indonesia in overthrowing the Indonesian government when it is much more likely to have greater influence on the Indonesian government itself? There are already some indications the Russians are aware of this dilemma and prefer the status quo. In a word, the expansion of communism is no longer automatically identical with Soviet interests and in the long run this realization will have profound effect on the Soviet party.

The effect of the split on China has been equally profound. At the risk of some oversimplification, it can be stated that the Chinese leaders began their assault on Soviet policy primarily because they hoped to force Khrushchev away from a détente with the United States and towards more militant support for their own pressing national goals, particularly in Asia. They hoped to utilize the strength of the Soviet Union and the international communist movement in order to compensate for their own national weakness. A militant Soviet foreign policy, they believed, could gradually force the withdrawal of American power from the Western Pacific, enable China to complete its civil war by annexing Taiwan, and eventually enable it to become the dominant power in Asia and one of the great powers in the world. Now that this policy has failed, the Chinese have increasingly turned their backs on the Soviet bloc in Europe and are seeking to forge a coalition of communist and radical nationalist movements in Africa, Asia and Latin America which they hope to utilize for promoting their goals. The fact that most of the communist parties of Asia and important segments of the Fidelista movement in Latin America are already aligned on their side is an early indication that they may have success in molding an alliance of the more radical and militantly anti-imperialist elements in the "third world." Increasingly then, China can be expected to try to transform the East-West struggle into a North-South struggle. This cannot help but have much influence on the world scene in the years to come.

Since the "third world" itself cannot supply China with the machinery, oil and industrial raw materials which it urgently requires to resume its frantic drive towards industrialization, Peking can at the same time be expected to look for trading partners and temporary allies in Western Europe and Japan. Its wooing of French, German, Italian and Japanese business interests will almost certainly continue and a wholesale reorientation of its trade westward will follow. (Communist China's trade with non-communist countries in 1963 was reportedly 75% of its overall foreign trade.) So long as the Western allies are unable to agree on a common trading policy towards China, the Peking leaders will be able successfully to play the Western nations against each other.

The Sino-Soviet alliance itself has been transformed by the split from an offensive into a defensive alliance. Russia and China will no longer be able to coordinate foreign policy and in many areas of the world they will be directly in conflict with one another. Nevertheless, the military alliance is likely to remain in effect and any attempt by the Western powers to roll back the "socialist camp" by military or other means will be jointly resisted. This means, for example, that Russia would come to China's aid if there were an attempted invasion of the Chinese mainland from Formosa. It would also mean that an invasion of North Vietnam, Cuba or any other "socialist" country would be opposed by both Russia and China although probably without coordination.

The split has already had a dramatic effect on the international communist movement. At first there was confusion and a refusal to believe that the rift was permanent. Increasingly, however, the communist parties of the world are coming to realize that the period of the single-centered communist movement is over and a new era is beginning. There is still nothing like a consensus of views on what should be the relations among communist parties in the new period of diversity and fragmentation of power. The Italian communists are at the forefront in attempting to work out liberal guidelines. They believe that each party must be autonomous in determining its own domestic policy and that neither the experience nor the general line of any one party can be binding on another. They assert that no party is above criticism by another. They believe also that contacts between parties should be increasingly bilateral while at the same time there should be periodic regional meetings of parties faced with similar problems. They obviously hope to play a leading role in determining the future policies of the communist parties in Western Europe. The effectuation of such views would of course result in an institutionalization of pluralism in the communist world. These views are much too extreme for the "centrists" in the communist world, who still cling to the hope that a compromise can be reached by Russia and China at a new international meeting.

The most significant development of the past two years within the international communist movement, however, has been what might be called the initial flowering of independence. In the early fall of 1963, Moscow decided to hold an international conference of communist parties for the purpose of formally rallying the majority of parties to its side of the dispute with Peking. Soviet publications during that period reflected a Kremlin conviction that Peking would have to be excommunicated and that two-thirds of the world parties would support Moscow. The 1963 edition of the *International Yearbook of Politics and Economics,* published by the Moscow Institute of World Economy and International Relations, went so far as to exclude Albania, Communist China and North Korea from the family of socialist countries. The yearbook was passed for printing in the period September 12 through 24, that is, at the very time that the Russians began their verbal offensive to excommunicate Peking. Shortly thereafter, however, the Italian communist party issued a formal declaration opposing an international conference on the grounds that it could lead only to a formal split or to a meaningless compromise. There were also reports of a meeting of several of the West European parties which arrived at a similar conclusion. Moreover, few of the East European parties, supposedly Khrushchev's most loyal allies, joined in the Soviet-led efforts to call such a conference. Khruschev's most faithful supporters in this abortive excommunication effort were, in fact, the two largest "Stalinist" parties in the international movement, the French and the East German.

Initially the Russians reacted to this opposition by indirectly denouncing the Italian party in an esoteric communication recalling Lenin's struggle against delegates to the third Comintern Congress who did not want to "decisively attack . . . leftist stupidities" which would condemn the communist movement to destruction. But when —sometime in mid-November—it became clear to Moscow that the majority of the world movement would not support excommunication of the Chinese, Albanians and North Koreans, the Russians began to take a more conciliatory line. Another international conference may yet be held but it is unlikely to take up the issue of excommunication.

This ability of the international movement to defy Moscow on an issue of such importance as a showdown conference with Peking is only one of several examples of the rapidly changing nature of the communist international. Rumania's ability successfully to resist Khrushchev's plans for integrating the Rumanian economy into an East European version of a Common Market is another. Recently the Rumanians have voted against the rest of the communist bloc in the United Nations and have discontinued dissemination of a Rumanian-language version of *New Times,* a Russian journal designed to spread the Soviet line on international affairs. More recently, Rumania has entered into broad economic negotiations with the United States, a move that will show other East European communist countries that Moscow can be defied with impunity. It is hard to imagine that Rumania would have achieved such a degree of independence from Moscow so soon if there had been no Sino-Soviet split.

These developments mean not only that the smaller parties are no longer completely subservient to Moscow's wishes. They suggest that the degree of autonomy of the smaller parties is already much greater than many Western specialists realize. Moreover, the fact that the most "liberal" of the parties, namely the Italian and the Polish, have been leading the resistance to exclusion of Peking from the communist international, suggests a conscious desire to preserve their autonomy. For, the Italians and the Poles are undoubtedly fearful that excommunication of Peking would be followed by a Soviet tightening of the reins on the remaining Soviet-led part of the movement. Such a tightening, on the other hand, is precisely what the more Stalinist parties like the French and the East German want, and this explains the paradoxical situation in which the parties most ideologically opposed to China nevertheless refuse to support a showdown with China while some of the European Stalinist parties, which share some of Peking's views, are in favor of such a showdown.

Since this book was first published, new information has come to light on some aspects of Sino-Soviet relations in the period from 1956 to 1961. In the heat of their polemical exchanges with Moscow, the Chinese have provided some clues concerning one of the least known aspects of their relationship, namely the military. Peking has accused the Russians of defaulting on a 1957 agreement to provide it with a prototype atomic bomb and assistance in its own nuclear weapons program. The Chinese claim that the Russians made unreasonable demands (not specified) in 1958 and then tore up the agreement a year later shortly before Khrushchev went to Camp David to see President Eisenhower.

The precise nature of the original agreement remains unclear, as do the circumstances surrounding its abrogation. My own guess is that the Russians may have agreed in 1957 to give the Chinese short-range missiles and some information on producing an atomic bomb. A high-level Chinese military mission was in Moscow in the fall of 1957. I would further speculate that the precise arrangements for control of the missiles were never agreed upon and that the offshore island crisis in 1958 gave the Russians pause about the entire arrangement, and led to their reneging a year later. The Chinese have suggested that the Russians made unwarranted demands on their sovereignty. The charge suggests that the Soviets asked for complete control of the missile installations. These developments must have played a very important role in exacerbating the conflict in its early stages. The Russians were unwilling to allow their Chinese allies a weapons capability that could provoke a war in the Pacific which might drag the Soviet Union against its will into a major war. The Chinese, on the other hand, were confirmed by this in their growing suspicion that the Soviet Union had little interest in supporting Chinese goals in Asia or in treating them as a full-fledged partner.

The split between Russia and China has progressed more rapidly than I anticipated in 1961. My lack of foresight in this regard can be traced to two factors. First, I attributed too great a degree of rationality to both the Russians and the Chinese. Since both parties had so much to lose and little to gain by this confllict, I assumed that rationality would triumph in the end. Secondly, the common ideology which I expected to set limits on the conflict operated rather to sharpen it. Indeed, one of the lessons to be drawn from this dispute is that ideologically oriented powers such as Russia and China have much greater difficulty in harmonizing differences of view and interest than do the more pragmatic non-communist powers which are accustomed to having and to adjusting conflicting interests.

CONTENTS

CONTENTS

THE SINO-SOVIET CONFLICT
1956–1961

"At the present time there is no statute which could regulate relations between parties. . . . It is not possible for leadership over socialist countries and Communist parties to be exercised from any center at all. This is neither possible nor necessary."

—Khrushchev's report on the Moscow Conference. (Soviet Home Service, January 19, 1961.)

"The existence of factions leads to the existence of a number of centers, and the existence of a number of centers connotes the absence of a common center of the Party, the breaking up of the unity of will, the weakening and disintegration of discipline, the weakening and disintegration of the dictatorship."

—Stalin, *Foundations of Leninism,* 1924.

INTRODUCTION

EVENTS of recent years within the Communist world have raised a serious question in the West concerning relations between the two leviathans of Communist power—Russia and China. Discussed with especial fervor since the Moscow Conference of Communist parties in November 1960, this question has become the subject of something on the order of a national debate in the United States, conducted actively in the press and covering the vast range of Sino-Soviet relations within and without the world Communist movement.

Up to now, three general schools of thought have emerged. The first of these schools—exemplified perhaps most clearly by certain members of Congress and certain academic groups—holds that conflict between Russia and China, to the extent that it exists, is of little consequence. It maintains that the two Communist powers have a single overriding aim in common—the conquest of the non-Communist world—and that they pursue this aim relentlessly and in cooperation. Any differences of national outlook or temperament, any power rivalries, any differences over ideology are subordinated to this central and overriding aim. Such differences cannot be of great import for the West and, some would go so far, to explore them too closely can even be dangerous.[1] If the Russians and the Chinese are not deliberately trying to dupe the West, they will in any case close ranks in the face of an effort to exploit differences between them.

A second school holds that a break between the Soviet Union and China is inevitable. This school, made up of members drawn both from the press and from some academic quarters, argues that the interests of the two Communist partners are essentially and ultimately incompatible. Depending on the importance accorded to the place of ideology in Russian motivation, members of this school may hold one of several viewpoints, not always distinct one from the other. One view holds that Russia is increasingly becoming a "status quo" power, anxious to retain the gains of the past, to preserve its modern industrial society, and to avoid the costs and destruction of modern war; conflict with China arises from the fact that its interests necessarily diverge from those of a partner whose population pressure and revolutionary fervor

3

drive it to expand at all cost. Another point of view maintains that the "national interests" of the two countries conflict and that competition for control over such border areas as Outer Mongolia must lead them to dispute and ultimately to split. Finally, some within this school contend that because the Communist system demands absolutely centralized power and because neither Russia nor China will relinquish its claim to power, rupture between them is inevitable.

Proponents of the above two schools have tended to dominate public debate until recently. Now, however, a third school is becoming distinguishable. It contends that while there are serious differences of interest and outlook between Russia and China, the overriding common aims of both, their joint commitment to an international revolutionary process which they believe is historically inevitable and which they believe it is their duty to aid, their shared determination to establish Communism throughout the world, set limits on conflict between the two. The outermost limit, most within this group argue, is a break-up of the Sino-Soviet alliance; conflict and competition between the partners to the alliance will continue and may even lead to a radical deterioration of relations, the argument follows, but this will proceed within a self-limiting framework of basic struggle against the West.

To state my own position clearly at the outset, I cannot agree with either of the first two schools. It is apparent to me that the first of these is either unaware of the evidence of serious conflict or determined to disregard such evidence in favor of preconceived views unsusceptible to change. To the extent that some within this school are merely unaware of the evidence, I hope that this book will lead them to reexamine their views. For the rest, it seems to me they mistakenly attribute to the Communist world a monolithism which, if it ever actually existed, clearly has not existed since the death of Stalin. Their preoccupation with what is undoubtedly the very real challenge of international Communism has prevented these proponents of the first school from crediting the evidence: first of Tito's break with Stalin, then of the discord between Gomulka and Khrushchev, and finally of the Sino-Soviet conflict. Their fear of a lowering in the Western guard has led them to deny the development of pluralism in the world Communist movement and prevented them, I believe, from making the sound assessment of the strengths and weaknesses of that movement which is essential to maintenance of the Western guard. In short, I think their stance plays them false, and on their own terms.

Proponents of the "split" school fail similarly, I believe, to examine the evidence on the question of Sino-Soviet relations. Were they to do so, it seems to me they could not conclude, as some of them do, that the commitment to world revolution does not count for much in the Communist world, that it counts for almost nothing at all in Russia, which is becoming a "status quo" power with an increasingly "mature" society led by a leader much more interested in building up the Russian economy than in spreading his power abroad. To believe that Communist Russia is interested largely in its own security and not in spreading its power and hegemony; to believe that Khrushchev and Mikoyan are "realists" like their Western opposites and do not take their revolutionary ideology very seriously; to believe that some kind of territorial stabilization with the USSR can be achieved in the fashion of 19th century balance-of-power politics[2]—to believe all this is to misunderstand the phenomenon that is international Communism and therefore to be incapable of understanding the Sino-Soviet conflict. For this conflict in large measure derives from the fact that although both partners are committed to worldwide revolution under Communist leadership, they often disagree on the strategy and tactics for pursuing that goal.

Perceiving that the Sino-Soviet conflict is a direct result of the ideological commitment to worldwide revolution and of differences on how to promote it, some members of the "split" school argue not that the "national interests" of the two powers are mutually incompatible but that China and Russia will be unable to divide their revolutionary domains in any stable fashion. They say that the Communist system itself demands one leader, therefore China and Russia could not resolve their differences without one accepting subordination to the other. If, for purposes of argument, the two partners were willing and able to divide up the world into spheres of influence, they would, in this view, "quickly find themselves embroiled with each other in hundreds of places, cancelling out each other's power."[3] The evidence of such embroilment in many parts of the world is already substantial. Yet it does not seem to me

5

that it is necessary to conclude from this that a total and irreparable break is inevitable.

There is a possibility, and it is no more than that, that sheer necessity may force the two Communist powers to work out a relationship of equality unique in the history of world Communism, a relationship which would recognize the inability of either power to impose its will, the impossibility of avoiding or suppressing differences of view and interest, and the overriding need to maintain a common front against the West. Such a relationship might take many years to work out and it might not be stable. Yet it seems to me that it is the direction in which the two partners will try to move. In any event, I believe that the possibility of such a relationship must enter our thinking, that we must explore the important middle ground covered by this third school.

I would place myself in the third school, recognizing that there are within it those who minimize the possibility of an open schism between Russia and China. Particularly after the 22nd Party Congress developments, I would hold that there are a number of circumstances which could at any time within the next five years lead the long-smoldering Sino-Soviet conflict, into open but not total break.[4] Such a break need not be permanent, it need not involve gravitation by the USSR or China to the West, it need not make less serious the challenge presented by the Communist world to the West.

It is my purpose in writing this book to present the evidence of Sino-Soviet conflict in recent years and to explore the middle ground between the first and second schools described above. In doing so I hope to demonstrate that the Sino-Soviet conflict is far-reaching in scope and profound in depth, but that it need not lead to a permanent rupture. I also hope to show that a careful, serious, and continuing study of the evidence is essential to understanding the conflict and to avoiding many of the oversimplifications about it prevalent in the West. In this connection, it is one of my principal intentions to show that overt Communist communications, if analyzed rigorously, can greatly enrich our knowledge of otherwise obscure aspects of Communist politics. Finally, I propose to draw some tentative implications of the conflict for American policy.

The book covers the period between the 20th Congress of the Communist Party of the Soviet Union (CPSU) in 1956 and the

22nd Congress in 1961. I have chosen the 20th Congress as my starting point in the story of Sino-Soviet conflict for a number of reasons. First, the Congress defined Soviet policy on precisely the three issues of strategy on which the Sino-Soviet differences have subsequently centered: the way to build "socialism" and Communism in states already ruled by Communist parties, the nature of the relationship among Communist parties, and the way to pursue the struggle against the West. Second, the Chinese Communists themselves, in heated private exchanges with the Russians, allegedly trace their differences with Khrushchev to the 20th Congress. Finally, and not least important, it was after the Congress—and the impact on the Communist world of Khrushchev's secret speech about Stalin—that China first began to intervene in East European Communist affairs and to speak and act as a separate source of doctrine and strategy for the Communist world. At this time were raised the questions which have since haunted the Sino-Soviet alliance and the world Communist movement. What happens if the two most powerful and autonomous partners in the Communist alliance cannot agree on basic issues of principle and policy? Can the Sino-Soviet alliance and the alliance of a number of Communist states be maintained if the right of the leading state to interpret the ideology and define the strategy is not recognized by all?

The 22nd Congress is my terminal point. The depth of the Sino-Soviet conflict became apparent to the entire world at that Congress when Chinese Communist Premier Chou En-lai publicly disagreed with Khrushchev's attack on the Albanian Communist Party. The issues dividing Russia and China were, of course, much more complex than Soviet policy toward Albania. The tiny Balkan country was merely the immediate problem in a struggle over policy and authority that goes back several years. At the time that this book went to press in December 1961, it was too early to judge whether the dispute over Albania would be confined to that issue, whether it could be papered over, or whether, touching off other issues long in controversy, it would precipitate the type of partial break to which I have alluded.

Whatever the years ahead portend, Sino-Soviet conflict in the years 1956 to 1961 cannot be understood without reference to a wider perspective. This perspective must encompass the very broad elements which bind Russia and China together, elements which might all too easily be lost sight of in the course of concentration on Sino-Soviet conflict. It must cast a long look back into history to the soil in which the Sino-Soviet relationship of recent years was nourished. It must look outside the events within the given period to the explanations for conflict, in all their dimensions.

The Ties That Bind

One cannot stress too much that the partners to the Sino-Soviet alliance are dedicated to a common purpose and bound together by a common ideology.[5] Charter members, one might say, of the same Church, whose Bible is *The Communist Manifesto* and whose holy books include the works of Marx, Engels, Lenin, Stalin, and Mao, Russia and China share a way of looking at the world that distinguishes them from the non-Communist world and ties them together. They see the world in terms of class conflict, of imperialist oppression, of capitalist crises, of "national liberation movements," of "just and unjust wars," of the ultimate and inevitable triumph of Communism throughout the world.

The common commitment of Russia and China involves a number of common beliefs that can be derived from the eight "general laws" subscribed to by the twelve ruling Communist parties in the November 1957 Declaration. These "laws," presumably applicable to the revolution that had already taken place in countries ruled by the Communists and to the revolution due to take place eventually in all countries, specified the following.

There would be, first, a "proletarian revolution in one form or another" which would result in the establishment of "one form or another of the dictatorship of the proletariat," i.e., a dictatorship of the Communist Party; second, an alliance of the working class with the bulk of the peasantry; third, an abolition of capitalist ownership and the establishment of public ownership of the basic means of production and a gradual "socialist reorganization of agriculture"; fourth, a planned development of the national economy "with the aim of building socialism and Communism"; fifth, a "socialist revolution in the sphere of ideology and culture and the creation of a large intelligentsia devoted to the working class" and the cause of "socialism"; sixth, elimination of "national oppres-

8

sion"; seventh, a defense of the "achievements of socialism against encroachments by external and internal enemies"; eighth, solidarity of the working class of a given country with the working class of other countries—proletarian internationalism."[6]

Elsewhere in this Communist declaration of principle, the ruling parties rejected the views of the "revisionists" who denied the "historical necessity" of a proletarian revolution and the dictatorship of the proletariat during the period of transition from capitalism to socialism, the leading role of the Communist Party in this revolution, the principle of proletarian internationalism, and the Leninist principles of party organization and democratic centralism.

In addition to the means and goals to which Russia and China are equally and unequivocally committed, much in their views of the historical and socio-economic forces at work in the 20th century, their ways of looking at the world, ties them together, particularly as their actions, policies, and expectations are closely related to these views. In the underdeveloped areas, both see the same sharpening of tensions between the developed imperialist metropolises and their former or present colonies, the same seedbeds of agrarian revolution, the same exploitable contradictions between what they call the "comprador bourgeoisie" serving the interests of foreign imperialism and the "national bourgeoisie" seeking to gain political and economic independence. Both see the same enemy, United States "imperialism," standing in the way of national, "democratic," and finally "socialist" revolution, the ushering in by local Communist parties of Communist dictatorship.

In the advanced capitalist countries, both see the same sharpening contradictions between the bourgeoisie and the working class; the same potentialities for manipulating fears of war, capitalizing on trade rivalries, and encouraging anti-Americanism. Both believe that the Western economic system must sooner or later lead to a succession of revolutionary phases whose concluding chapter will be the Communist succession to power.

Even leaving ideology aside, there have been built up between Russia and China over the past years a web of relations— economic, political, military, and other—which tend to tie them together. Both have provided and continue to provide the other with support and assistance that would be difficult to obtain elsewhere.

The Russians, for their part, have provided the Chinese with considerable military assistance, including some help in developing a nuclear weapons program. They have provided large-scale and indispensable assistance to China's industrialization drive by supplying capital equipment, raw materials, technical aid and training. During the past decade Sino-Soviet trade has expanded from small beginnings to the impressive total of some $2 billion.[7] The USSR is China's principal supplier of petroleum, a basic raw material for her industrial and military buildup. By a thirty-year Treaty of Friendship, Alliance, and Mutual Assistance, the Russians are committed to come to China's support if she is attacked by Japan or "any state allied with it," a euphemism that was clearly intended to mean the United States.

For her part, China has provided the Russians with food and raw materials that have enabled the Russians to concentrate their resources elsewhere. She has not only helped shield the Soviet frontier from the Pacific to the heart of Asia, but she has rendered considerable assistance in extending Soviet power into south and southeast Asia.

For any number of reasons, then, there are strong ties between the partners to the Sino-Soviet alliance, and it would be dangerous to disregard them and suppose that the Sino-Soviet relationship is characterized simply by disagreement and conflict.

The Historical Roots
of Conflict

The story of Sino-Soviet conflict in the years 1956–1961 necessarily draws the student of that conflict back into history. For example, one of the persistent problems at issue between Russia and China in recent years has been the question of Communist cooperation with nationalist parties in the underdeveloped areas. In general, the Russians are prepared in the short run to cooperate with such nationalist parties and leaders and to instruct local Communist parties to remain relatively quiescent. This is because the short- and middle-range Soviet goal is to eliminate Western political and economic influence from these areas, not to acquire them as satellites. The Chinese, on the other hand, urge a much more activist revolutionary policy even at the risk of breaking alliances with the Nassers, Nehrus, Kassims, etc. They fear that if the Communists do not take the initiative in many of these areas soon, they will in the long run be overwhelmed by the nationalists.

Such a dispute is not new to the Communist movement. As early as the Second Comintern Congress in 1920, Lenin and M. N. Roy, the Indian Communist, engaged in argument over the extent to which, if at all, the Communists should cooperate with nationalists in what the Communists call the "colonial and semi-colonial countries." The argument has in fact never really been settled by the Communists, who have in the course of their history alternated between two divergent policies vis-à-vis the nationalists, sometimes cooperating with them while casting a wary eye to the future, sometimes fighting against them while wondering whether or not such a fight was premature.

Nor is the dispute new to Sino-Soviet relations. The Chinese Communists' fear that cooperation with "bourgeois nationalism" may lead to disaster has roots in their own revolutionary experience, particularly in the fateful year of 1927. In that year, the Kuomintang, the Chinese Nationalist party with whom the Chinese Communists had been allied, turned on them and virtually decimated the Party. This experience has undoubtedly colored to a very large extent the Chinese Communist views on prolonged cooperation with nationalist parties and leaders.

The disaster of 1927 having been a direct result of Stalin's policies in China, these policies, and their failure, are indispensable background for understanding the Sino-Soviet relationship as it has developed in subsequent years. A few words about them, therefore, are in order.

In the mid-1920's, Soviet policy in China was dominated by fear of a possible British-Japanese alliance which would strangle the Chinese revolution then in progress and, worse still, threaten the security of the Soviet Union. In addition, the Russians feared the *rapprochement* then taking place between Germany and the Western powers victorious in World War I. Stalin's purpose therefore was not to foment Communist revolution in China, which he thought, in any case, had little chance of success, but to build up a strong "anti-imperialist" China which would serve as a Soviet ally against a British-Japanese or British-German axis.

The vehicle chosen for Stalin's China policy was the Kuomintang, the Nationalist revolutionary organization modelled on the

Russian Communist Party but maintaining, as Moscow well knew, a much different political and ideological perspective from that of the Communists. To strengthen the Kuomintang, Stalin, via the Comintern, ordered the Chinese Communists to merge with it and to subordinate their own social and political aspirations temporarily to those of the Nationalists.

On April 12, 1927, the leader of one element of the Kuomintang, a young nationalist general trained in Moscow, Chiang Kai-shek, annihilated the Chinese Communist Party in Shanghai and thus dealt a disastrous blow to Stalin's China policy and an almost fatal blow to Chinese Communism. Refusing to believe that the Kuomintang could not be utilized as a vehicle for Soviet policy in spite of their policies toward the Chinese Communists, and increasingly bound up with a struggle against Trotsky in which he could ill afford to concede his mistakes, Stalin pursued his policy of unity with the Nationalists. In the Wuhan ports, as in Shanghai, the Kuomintang again proceeded to devour its Communist "allies." The Chinese Communists went underground. Remnants of the Party were rescued by Mao Tse-tung, who led them to the hills, where they remained for many years until, in the mid-1930's, they made the long march to the north to lay the foundations for their ultimate seizure of power. From 1927 on, as George Kennan has suggested, Moscow had in the Chinese Communists "an ally but not a satellite."[8]

In 1936, by which time Mao had succeeded in piecing together the scattered remnant of the Chinese Party, there is fair evidence to suggest that Stalin once again ordered the CCP to strike a bargain with Chiang Kai-shek that they would have preferred to avoid.

The final and by no means the least of Stalin's mistakes regarding the Chinese Communists occurred on the very eve of their long-awaited triumph. In the years immediately after World War II, it seems, Stalin advised Mao against what he regarded as premature attempts to overthrow Chiang Kai-shek. To the Chinese Communists he must surely have seemed more interested in dividing the "imperialists" than in taking the risks of supporting a Chinese Communist seizure of power. In any event, they ignored Stalin's advice and went on to conquer mainland China.[9]

We cannot know, of course, whether the Chinese Communists believed that in all these instances Stalin simply miscalculated or whether they believed he sacrificed the Chinese Communist Party on the cross of Russian interests as he perceived them. Whichever the case, it is apparent that such repeated experience with Soviet directives, which seemed to serve Soviet rather than Chinese interests, which appeared to make of China a pawn in the power struggle in the Kremlin, and which in any event proved to be wrong, has had a permanent impact on the Chinese Communist leadership.

It is hardly to be wondered at that in recent years, as the Sino-Soviet conflict has blossomed, the Chinese Communists have begun to allude to Soviet miscalculations in China with thinly veiled scorn and bitterness. Liu Shao-ch'i, Mao's heir-apparent, has referred to "erroneous tendencies" during the period of China's "democratic revolution" from 1921–1949 and he made it plain that these "tendencies" were of Russian origin.[10] In 1960, one Chinese Communist publication referred to "some people" who in 1946 had lacked sufficient belief in "our ability to defeat the enemy" and who were afraid to risk war with the United States.[11] Again, it left little doubt it was referring to Stalin.

A review of this early experience of the Chinese Communists with their Russian allies contributes to an understanding of the present Sino-Soviet conflict in several respects. First of all, it makes plain why Mao has been determined to maintain much greater independence from Moscow than the Russians have been willing to concede. Second, it gives reason for the Chinese Communists to believe that the Russians are repeating today in many colonial and semi-colonial countries the very same error they committed in China in the 1920's and 1930's—sacrificing local Communist parties to Soviet interests. Finally, the sorry Soviet record in China has strengthened the strong elements of national self-esteem in Chinese Communism and has made its leaders more reluctant to compromise with a partner which, it probably believes, has little comprehension of the revolutionary process in underdeveloped countries.

The Factors Making for Conflict

Having in mind the cohesive factors in the Sino-Soviet alliance and some of the historical ground of conflict, we would do well now, I think, briefly to look into the divisive factors in that conflict.

First of all, there is the factor which might be called Maoist chauvinism, the claim made explicitly by Mao that he is the Asian Marx, his evident desire to go down in history as one of the prophets of rather than a disciple of Communism. To what extent such claims can be traced to a Chinese feeling of superiority to the "barbarians" in the outside world and thus to deep roots in Chinese history is a problem which can only be suggested here. But it is clear that such pretensions once troubled Mao's relations with Stalin and that they have increasingly troubled his relations with Khrushchev.

As early as the spring of 1946, in an interview of extraordinary importance, Liu Shao-ch'i told Anna Louise Strong that Mao had discovered an Asiatic form of Marxism, that Marx and Lenin were Europeans and therefore, by implication, not very much interested in or capable of solving Asiatic problems, that Mao was the first to succeed in adapting Marxism to China, and that Mao's revolutionary theories charted a path to power not only for the Chinese people "but for the billion folk that live in the colonial countries of southeast Asia." The passage deserves reproduction in full:

"Mao Tse-tung's great accomplishment has been to change Marxism from a European to an Asiatic form. Marx and Lenin were Europeans; they wrote in European languages about European histories and problems, seldom discussing Asia or China. The basic principles of Marxism are undoubtedly adaptable to all countries, but to apply their general truth to concrete revolutionary practices in China is a difficult task. Mao Tse-tung is Chinese; he analyzes Chinese problems and guides the Chinese people in their struggle to victory. He uses Marxist-Leninist principles to explain Chinese history and the practical problems of China. He is the first that has succeeded in doing so. Not only has he applied Marxist methods to solve the problems of 450 million people, but he has thus popularized Marxism among the Chinese people as a weapon for them to use. On every kind of problem—the nation, the peasants, strategy, the construction of the party, literature and culture, military affairs, finance and economy, methods of work, philosophy —Mao has not only applied Marxism to new conditions but has given it a new development. He has created a Chinese or Asiatic form of Marxism. China is a semi-feudal, semi-colonial country in

14

which vast numbers of people live at the edge of starvation, tilling small bits of soil. Its economy is agricultural, backward, and dispersed. In attempting the transition to a more industrialized economy, China faces the competition and the pressures—economic, political, and military—of advanced industrial lands. This is the basic situation that affects both the relations of social classes and the methods of struggle towards any such goal as national independence and a better, freer life for the Chinese. There are similar conditions in other lands of southeast Asia. The courses chosen by China will influence them all."[12]

From 1949 to 1951, the two years following the Chinese Communist seizure of power, Mao's claims to ideological autonomy and the persistent Chinese insistence that they had discovered a model to be followed in other colonial and semi-colonial countries was the cause of considerable friction with Stalin. A well-documented survey of the period shows:

1. Chinese propagandists explicitly claimed that Mao's theories on revolution were independently arrived at, while the Russians consistently endeavored to show Mao's complete theoretical dependence on Stalin.

2. The Chinese asserted that Mao's writing on the Chinese revolution embodied an ideology—the "ideology of Mao Tse-tung"; there was no recognition of such an ideology in Soviet writings.

3. Between 1949 and 1951 the Chinese viewed their revolution as the model to be followed in other underdeveloped countries and they referred to this model revolutionary path as "Mao's road"; such themes were absent from Soviet writings, which conceded only that the Chinese revolution had "inspired" the peoples of backward countries in their own revolutionary movements.[13]

In 1951 such claims disappeared, probably because Mao's economic and military dependence on Stalin forced him to greater caution and modesty. But in 1958 these claims were revived and, in fact, were extended. There was increasing reference to "the Mao Tse-tung ideology" (an ideology which the Russians have never acknowledged). It was stated that Mao had "solved" the problem of socialist construction for a backward country with a large peasantry (a claim never acknowledged by the Russians). The Chinese model, it was said, was of "significance" for other Communist states and even to some extent of "international

15

significance." Mao was called one of the most outstanding Marxist-Leninist theoreticians of the modern era and, inasmuch as no others were given this honor, the implication was that he was the most outstanding. Every aspect of Chinese life—political, social, economic, or military—apparently had had fundamental contributions made to it by Mao.

The political significance of such claims is difficult to exaggerate. First of all, however, they suggest that Mao has always viewed himself on a level not with Stalin, let alone Khrushchev,[14] but with Marx and Lenin, the founding fathers of Communism. In the light of this image, Mao's scorn and contempt for the brash peasant who now sits on top of the world Communist movement are easy to imagine. Second, the claims imply that Mao has never reconciled himself to taking orders from Moscow with regard to either Chinese domestic or foreign policies. Third, they suggest that Mao has always considered himself the leader of the revolution in all underdeveloped areas, including Asia, Africa, and Latin America.

A second important factor relating to the Sino-Soviet conflict of recent years is the great difference in the revolutionary experience of the Russian and Chinese Communist parties. The Russian Bolsheviks came to power almost overnight; they took over the major cities and only then expanded their power base to the countryside; inheriting a modern national army from the old regime, they received little experience in guerrilla warfare;[15] they came to give legal revolutionary methods a premium, believing that revolutionary "opportunities" would arise during a time of national crisis, perhaps induced by war, in which the ruling classes would have become so weakened that they would topple almost of their own weight; they had less experience in dealing with the "national bourgeoisie" and more in overthrowing a landed aristocracy. The Chinese, by contrast, came to power after a struggle lasting more than two decades; they established bases in rural areas and only then encircled and strangled the cities; their revolutionary experience was almost entirely based on protracted guerrilla warfare; they came to believe that the way to take power was through arduous armed struggle over an extended period of time, a struggle in the course of which the army could be demoralized and the peasantry gradually won over to the side of the revolution; they gave a great deal of attention to the correct handling of the

16

"national bourgeoisie." The different revolutionary perspectives which emerge from such divergent Russian and Chinese experiences necessarily lead to differences in assessment concerning the revolutionary process elsewhere, for each Party tends to view the revolutionary process in other countries in terms of its own.

Differences in the political environment of Communist Russia and Communist China give rise to further divergence of outlook. The island of Taiwan, with a formally constituted rival Chinese regime, for instance, threatens the very legitimacy of the Chinese Communist revolution and stands in the way of its final consolidation. There is no parallel to this phenomenon in the Soviet environment. The extent to which the Chinese Communist leaders feel that the Nationalist regime is a threat to their survival is difficult to judge, but the sense of insecurity on the part of the Communist leaders should not be underestimated. They see the world in an ideological perspective in which the danger of "imperialist" intervention and restoration is persistent, and it is instructive that not until 1958 did Khrushchev feel secure enough to call the triumph of "socialism" in the Soviet Union "final and complete," i.e., incapable of being reversed from without. This kind of perspective is, for the Communists, empirical and by no means abstruse or "theoretical." To say that socialism is "final and complete" is on the same level as saying that grain production increased last year. In the case of China itself, several Westerners in conversations with Chinese leaders have noted the passion with which they speak of their determination to reincorporate Taiwan into China. One of these, a British Member of Parliament who had a three and one-half hour conversation with Chinese Communist Foreign Minister Ch'en Yi in December 1960, for example, reports that "for a long time Marshal Ch'en would talk of nothing but Formosa" and its "illegal" occupation by the American "imperialists."[16] It seems reasonably certain that the Chinese are prepared to take considerable risks to "liberate" Taiwan and that this goal makes for friction with their Soviet ally, whose military power they require for such a venture but whose leaders are reluctant to take large risks on behalf of a cause which is not central to their own ambitions.

China's political environment also involves her relative isolation in the world. Recognized by only a handful of states, excluded from most major world organs, she finds her position far from that of the Soviet Union, a world power with far-flung interests. The isolation of China does not mean, as some suggest, that China's leaders are ignorant of the outside world in general[17] or of the potential consequences of a nuclear war in particular and that an end to their isolation would soften their militancy. The factors which produce Chinese Communist militancy are more complex than that. But isolation from the world community does mean that in some areas China can pursue a policy that is forbidden to the USSR because of its worldwide commitments and interests. Thus, while Communist China can support extremist nationalist or insurgent groups in Latin America, where few countries recognize her, the Soviet Union must be more cautious. A similar generalization holds for other countries in which the Russians have, while the Chinese do not have, diplomatic representation. This difference is particularly applicable to their relations with the United States, the major enemy of both. While both Communist powers regard the United States as the main enemy, it is only the Russians who can negotiate with us, a factor undoubtedly contributing to Chinese Communist suspicions and fears that their Russian allies will strive to reach a bargain with the U.S. that will sacrifice Chinese interests. Much of Chinese Communist militancy in recent years is attributable to their fears of an East-West *détente* at their expense.

A fourth factor of conflict is economic. The Chinese Communists' primitive agriculture barely manages to keep ahead of population growth; enormous industrial strains are produced by their headlong efforts to outstrip some advanced capitalist countries in the space of a few decades; their economy is greatly dependent on outside trade for sources of critical raw materials. China is a so-called "have not" country. The Russians, on the other hand, have a developed economy which, while weak in certain areas, nonetheless does not generate the kinds of tensions and strains which any country in the midst of industrial revolution must undergo. Russia is becoming a "have" country. This is not to argue that the Chinese Communists adopt a militant foreign policy in order to divert their peoples' attentions from domestic economic strain; but there are interesting parallels in Communist history which suggest there sometimes may be a relationship between domestic upheaval and militancy abroad.

A fifth factor giving rise to Sino-Soviet conflict is military. The Chinese Communists have no atomic or nuclear weapons and little hope of acquiring more than a token nuclear capability in the near future. Even if they should test an atomic device in the near future, it will probably take at least a decade for them to perfect ample modern delivery vehicles. This means that China cannot use its own military to advance its political goals except in a very limited sense. For achieving its major political goals—absorption of Taiwan, for example—it must rely on Soviet military power, which is not always at Chinese disposal.

Still another basic factor making for differences between the two Communist allies might be called their separate revolutionary interests. I speak of "revolutionary interests" rather than "national interests" because, although the latter concept is not irrelevant to an explanation of conflict between the two, it is not wholly adequate. It fails to take account of the urge to expedite the revolutionary process so central to both Russian and Chinese actions. While the pursuit of this goal is influenced by national viewpoints, the goal of international revolution itself goes beyond such traditional goals of nation states as security and survival. In the perspective of both Russia and China, the world is in revolutionary ferment and ultimately destined to become Communist. But in the process of hastening this process, differences of priority, of sectionalism, and of timing arise. For example, the Chinese want to fan revolutionary flames more vigorously in the Asian and African underdeveloped areas, where they expect to guide the revolution, than in Europe, where they are willing for the most part to leave the job to the Russians. The Russians, on the other hand, in charting a revolutionary line for the underdeveloped areas, probably believe that the advanced Western countries are their primary target, and that weakening them may require greater flexibility in policy toward the underdeveloped areas. This is probably the principal reason, for instance, why Khrushchev has done so little to support the Algerian rebels. For Khrushchev, to split De Gaulle away from the Western alliance would be a much bigger prize than a free Algeria, even an Algeria under Communist domination. But for Mao, an Algerian insurrection, supported with Chinese arms and advisers, would be the gateway to North Africa.

Until the death of Stalin, Russian and Chinese "revolutionary interests" did not clash to a very large extent because Stalin's policy was not, as is Khrushchev's, worldwide. Stalin's goal after 1949, when the Chinese Communists took power, was not so much

one of expanding the Communist empire as it was one of consolidating the gains made immediately after World War II. It is
true that Stalin sought to exploit real or apparent opportunities, as
in Korea, but the opportunities he sought to exploit were in areas
geographically contiguous to the Communist Bloc. Stalin was not
much interested in areas he could not reach with Russian bayonets,
a fact which helps to account for his inflexible attitude toward the
neutrals.

For this reason also, Communist parties in non-Communist
countries were, for Stalin, largely a weapon for preventing an attack on the Soviet Union, not for "exporting" revolution to the
West, a possibility for which Stalin had little hope in the postwar
years. To be sure, Communist parties in these areas were employed,
as Khrushchev employs them, to weaken and disrupt the West. But
in Stalin's day the motivation was largely defensive; in Khrushchev's day, when the Soviet Union can take a far bolder view than
Stalin of its revolutionary horizons because of its tremendous accre-
tions of power, the motivation is largely offensive. As one observer
has put it, Soviet policy in the post-Stalin era can be compared to
the earlier awakening of the United States from isolationism to a
conscious acceptance of worldwide responsibilities.[18] The Soviet
counterpart of this change has been the more deliberate acceptance
of its "duties" to worldwide revolutionary movements. "Proletarian
internationalism" in Khruschev's day has come to involve Soviet
responsibilities to as well as demands upon foreign Communists.[19]

To the extent, and it is a large one, that post-Stalin Soviet
policy began to exploit worldwide opportunities and to act like a
world power, conflicts of priority and hegemony with China increased. Is Berlin more important than Taiwan? Should the revolutionary movement in Asia, Africa, and Latin America receive
priority over the opportunities for splitting the Western alliance
system? What happens when there is a conflict between Soviet
policies in one part of the world and Chinese policies in the same
or another part?

The Immediate Causes
of Conflict

The reasons that have thus far been advanced for Sino-Soviet
conflict are all of a rather high level of generalization which does

not always adequately explain why things happened at certain times rather than others. To one extent or another, most of the factors mentioned so far have been inherent in the Sino-Soviet relationship since the Chinese Communists first came to power in 1949. Yet it is a fact that until 1956 the relationship was relatively untroubled, or, at least, the troubles were well hidden. What, then, are the more immediate factors which have, when wedded to the longer range factors, produced tensions of such a serious kind?

Since 1956 the Chinese Communists have become increasingly disillusioned with Khrushchev's leadership of international Communism. This disillusion has been all the more marked because it was the Chinese who in all likelihood contributed greatly to Khrushchev's triumph over Malenkov in 1954.[20] Mao's gamble on Khrushchev must have looked to the Chinese leader after 1956 as an extremely bad bet. As we shall have occasion to see, Khrushchev's handling of de-Stalinization and of the Polish and Hungarian developments in 1956 met with varying degrees of derision and contempt from Mao.

The major blow must have come in 1957, however, when the Russians made a significant weapons breakthrough with the sputnik and ICBM. The CCP (to anticipate the argument of this book) believed that these weapons developments led to a decisive change in the balance of power between East and West and at last afforded the opportunity to achieve long-denied foreign policy gains behind the Soviet deterrent shield. The "good neighbor" policy practiced by the Chinese in Asia after the Bandung conference in 1955 had not resulted in any appreciable payoffs in terms of weakening the Western alliance system in Asia, of gaining increased recognition, or of solving the problem of Taiwan. Yet when Mao advocated a stepped-up assault against the "imperialists" in the wake of the Soviet weapons development, Khrushchev held back and argued for a more cautious strategy envisioning negotiations and carefully controlled risks in foreign policy initiatives.

Increasingly frustrated with Soviet policies, the Chinese Communists increasingly sought to modify them. The challenge to Soviet ·policies soon became a challenge to Soviet leadership of world Communism, not that China wants at this time to replace the Russians at the helm, a task for which they are well aware they are not yet sufficiently powerful, but in the sense that Peking demands a position of parity in the leadership and a recognition of its special prerogatives regarding both the conceptualization and execution of Bloc policy, particularly for the colonial and semi-colonial areas over which Mao claims a proprietary role.

It is the author's contention, in a word, that the conflict became acute in recent years because some basic potentialities for conflict were brought to life by a series of developments within and without the Communist world to which Moscow and Peking had different answers and different needs. To look at the conflict against the background of these various factors which contribute to it, and to be aware of the intensity with which it has been waged in recent years, is to recognize at once that no amount of "papering over," such as occurred at the November 1960 meeting in Moscow, is likely to eliminate the causes of dispute.

The Limits of Conflict

At the same time, the framework I suggest for analyzing the Sino-Soviet conflict is one in which it is recognized clearly that Communist China and Communist Russia have much more in common with each other than with the Western world, which both view as a decaying social order doomed to the dustbin of history. This means that there are rational limits to the conflict between them.

One obvious such limit is that the two Communist powers cannot change partners in the world struggle. There is nothing but self-delusion in some Western talk about the possibility of a Soviet-U.S. alliance, brought about by Russia's fear of China. There is even less chance of wooing China away from the USSR. Another such limit is that, however much pressure the Russians decide to bring to bear on Peking to gain compliance with their policies, they will not apply any sanctions or take any actions that would seem likely to jeopardize the existence of a Communist regime in China. The struggle between Russia and China will thus take place within the confines of a common commitment to Communism, even if both partners disagree on how to achieve that ultimate goal. Talk of a war between Russia and China, or of a population explosion of the "yellow hordes" into Soviet Asia, is, in my opinion, premature.

There are some conditions under which a partial break could occur. Mao may come to believe that a temporary split is necessary

22

to help overthrow Khrushchev, or he may regard such a split as preferable to following a mistaken Soviet policy. Khrushchev, for his part, may believe that he must discipline the Chinese Party sooner rather than later, for, with the passage of time, as China acquires a nuclear capability and enters the ranks of the great powers, the balance of power between Russia and China must gradually change. Khrushchev and Mao may miscalculate each other's intentions, each believing that the other is bluffing and not prepared to be the first to go over the brink. A third party in the international Communist movement, such as Albania, may serve as a catalyst to bring about a split that neither side wanted. This could happen, for example, if both sides' prestige came to be heavily engaged in a test of strength. Finally, in a totalitarian world where much depends on the personal whims of two powerful leaders, the element of irrationality cannot be discounted. It is quite likely that the personal relations between Mao and Khrushchev are already strained close to the breaking point.

In sum, while the Sino-Soviet conflict must be viewed within the context of a common ideological commitment, it is difficult to state with precision its outermost limits. The future course of events will depend to a great extent on the success or lack of it which Russia and China have in working out a new and unique relationship, on whether Khrushchev dies before Mao, on the policies of the new leaders who replace Khrushchev and Mao, on the success or lack of it of Soviet and Chinese domestic and foreign policies, and on a myriad of other factors which cannot presently be assessed.

Because I believe it is hazardous in the analysis of Communist politics to project past trends into the future, this book ends with a question mark and not with a prophecy. Not being a Marxist-Leninist, I can offer no sure guide to the future. If I will have provided the reader with some insight into the origins and evolution of the Sino-Soviet conflict and some feeling for the complex forces at work in the anomalous Sino-Soviet relationship, I shall have fulfilled my central purpose.

A NOTE ON METHODOLOGY

THE SOURCES employed in this book are largely open Communist communications, particularly the speeches of leaders and articles in important Party journals and newspapers. There is an erroneous popular impression in the West that all public or open communication in the Communist world is "propaganda" and that the "real" discourse of the Communist movement is conducted in private communications. Such a simple dichotomy between open and private communications, I feel, does a great injustice to the many-faceted structure of discourse in the Communist world. Restricted channels of communication, as it happens, do not meet all the requirements of either the Soviet Union or the international Communist movement. The requirements of control and of political action force the Communists to use open channels, however guardedly, to supplement strictly private ones. A vast empire, comprising almost one billion citizens, millions of Communist party members, and thousands of Party activists cannot be effectively guided on the basis of secret channels of communication alone. For this reason, serious study of those portions of public communications which are intended largely for Communist audiences can provide valuable and fruitful insights into Communist behavior. Even those portions of public communications intended for non-Communist audiences can be employed to determine Communist propaganda strategy and the political estimates and assumptions on which the strategy is based.

Since the time five or ten years ago when systematic analysis of Communist communications was dismissed as "Kremlinology," Western students have developed a considerable amount of sophistication in using these sources. Although this approach is still regarded in some circles as a black art, there can be no reasonable doubt that a rich body of work has grown up which provides important insights into various aspects of Communist politics.[1] This work is testimony of the fact that open Communist publications can provide the basis for serious study of Communist politics.

The reasons for this are many. First of all, because factionalism and open airing of differences have been proscribed, Communists are forced to differ with one another through the employment of what has come to be known to some in the West as "esoteric communication," or Aesopian language. As often as not, differences over policy or strategy alternatives are heavily veiled in doctrinal exegesis. Yet behind the seemingly arid doctrinal polemics lie real and serious political problems.

Particularly in the post-Stalin era, such veiled conflict has increased. The death of Stalin led to a gradual erosion of Soviet authority within the international Communist movement. It is not enough in Khrushchev's day, as it was in Stalin's, for the Soviet press to give a signal to the worldwide Communist movement for a change in line. Khrushchev must not only signal a change; he must defend the change, demonstrate its advantages over other possible courses of action, argue with doubters or with those whose interests would be harmed by the change, and prove that he is not betraying the basic ideology. When there is opposition to his policy either at home or in foreign parties, he must, through veiled communication, try to induce defection from his opponents and to secure the support of neutrals. The "fraternal" parties often argue back. They do not customarily attack Soviet policies openly any more than Moscow attacks them openly, and so they too resort to "esoteric communication." Thus, Communist communication— which in Stalin's day was a one-way proposition—now flows in two directions. By 1960 the world had seen evidence of a veiled dialogue over policy alternatives not only between Khrushchev and Mao but also between the USSR and tiny Albania. By 1961, the Soviet-Albanian dialogue had ceased to be esoteric and had become public. In today's Communist world, deviants not only may exist; they are an inevitable outgrowth of the erosion of Stalinist controls and of their replacement by more subtle, voluntary, and permissive controls. The concomitant of this erosion is increasing public communication between one Party and another, and between various Communist parties and the Soviet center.

Since the death of Stalin, and the simultaneous end of complete centralization in the international Communist movement, there has been greater give-and-take between the Soviet and other parties; there is, in fact, bargaining. Yet the other Communist parties, rightly feeling that the process of bargaining with the center puts them at serious disadvantage, cannot limit their protests to secret Party documents and meetings. If they did so, the Russians, and the "mechanical majority" which the Russians wield, could

25

easily ignore or overrule them. Deviant parties must increasingly resort to veiled polemics in open media, in an effort to convince the world Communist movement of the correctness of their views. In this effort, they cannot merely argue that their own interests are being shunted aside by the Russians. They must elevate the argument to the theoretical plane, for it is only by such an argument that they can appeal to other Communist parties with different interests. This is one of the principal reasons why Peking has been forced to use veiled public communications to recriminate with the Russians.

There is a particular reason why open communications—particularly those relating to doctrine—are valuable in understanding the Sino-Soviet conflict. The conflict between the two parties since 1956 has centered on questions of strategy and tactics for building socialism-Communism at home, for stabilizing the relationships within the Communist Bloc, and for expanding the power of Communism abroad. Strategy, for the Communists, is the link between theory and action. The theory, or ideology, defines the ultimate goals and indicates the action needed to arrive at those goals. Because of this symbiotic relationship between theory and strategy, the former must be revised when there is a change or adjustment in the latter. If one Party objects to Soviet revisions of theory, the objection may be not to changes in theory per se, but to changes in revolutionary strategy which the new theory reflects. In other words, differences over strategy are frequently expressed on the level of theory. We thus have the spectacle of the Russians and Chinese conducting veiled public dialogues over ideological niceties such as "the strength of imperialism" or the "character of the present epoch." When one Communist accuses another of "overestimating imperialist strength," he is generally doing so because he wishes to undertake a bolder strategic course than his opponent. To justify such a course he argues that the imperialists are not as strong as the opponent believes. The ideology is not cynically manipulated to justify a particular strategy. The very fact that the Communists feel obligated to make periodic revisions in their ideology indicates that it is, in their eyes, a living organism that must be adapted to new conditions. The fact that the same basic body of doctrine is utilized to justify divergent strategies means only that the ideology is general enough to be susceptible to vary-

26

ing interpretations and that these interpretations will vary according to the specific needs, interests, expectations, and evaluations of particular Communist parties. The task of the serious student of intra-Communist conflict, therefore, is to penetrate the dialectical exegesis to discover the divergent estimates and expectations behind it.

Behind divergent views on ideological fine points lie divergent prescriptions for action. What has been called the "action program," the application to new situations of the "operational code,"[3] is monthly and weekly being re-examined against the flux of events and shaped to fit new circumstances. Behind the tactical adjustments to the twists and turns of history lies an overall design. A close and systematic examination of changes in Communist doctrine, as reflected in open media, can reveal adjustments in tactics and can provide important clues to the grand design. More important for our purposes, it can provide important clues to the differences over strategy and tactics between one Party and another.

Embedded in Communist communications is an obscure but vast world of meaning, part of which is accessible to those with certain necessary tools.[4] Chief among these is a knowledge of the intellectual heritage of the Communist world: Communist ideology and the changes in it and the revolutionary history of the Soviet, Chinese, and other Communist parties. Another prerequisite is knowledge of the protocol of Communist media. What is customary practice and what is not? Does a given ideological formulation modify or contradict earlier formulations? Does a given version of Communist history modify an earlier version, and, if so, what is the likely political explanation? Where, in short, is political grain most likely to be hidden in the chaff of Communist communications? Such knowledge, applied to an analysis of Communist communications on a given topic, and, of course, supplemented by as much information about the specific situation at hand as is available through whatever other sources exist, can produce rewarding results.

In the post-Stalin era, for reasons explained above, the appearance of political "grain" in open communications has greatly increased. The author would assert as a working hypothesis that most of the major political problems of the Communist world in the post-Stalin era have, like icebergs, protruded above the surface.

This is true of the Stalin succession crisis; the Soviet-Yugoslav controversy, which spans the entire period since Stalin's death; the fissures in the Communist world produced by Khrushchev's secret speech; the Soviet-Polish strains in 1956–57; and the Sino-Soviet tensions since 1956. On these and other important issues, there have been more or less open dialogues between the elites and sub-elites of one Party, or between the elites of different parties. For instance, when Malenkov announced publicly in 1954 that another world war would mean the destruction of world civilization, this was a reflection of a dialogue begun in 1954 over the adequacy of Soviet deterrent power, the likelihood and consequences of war, and the desirability of some kind of accommodation with the West. On some of these interrelated questions, the dialogue continues even today.

The veiled dialogues in public Communist media can be viewed as a third outermost layer of communication in the Communist world. The Western world has only occasional access to the second layer: secret Party documents, diplomatic correspondence, and similar sources. Even more rare are the occasional reports of the first layer: notes of actual conversations among Communist leaders, minutes of Presidium meetings, and other intimate records. Yet the correspondence between the third layer and those portions of the second which have become public has often been surprising.[5] Either some of the published portions of alleged secret letters exchanged between Peking and Moscow are very well-conceived frauds, or the Russians and Chinese argue in private much as they argue in public,[6] disputing such questions as "the nature of the present epoch," the "inevitability of war," and the possibility of "peaceful transformation to socialism." Ideology and reality have become so interconnected in the Communist mind, it seems, that discussions about reality are never free from ideological assumptions and terminology. The methodological implications of this correspondence between these two layers—open doctrinal dialogue and secret party documents—are considerable.

From lengthy private conversations with Soviet and East European defectors and Yugoslav Party members, I am convinced that the Communists themselves read their own communications with a full awareness of the vast world of meaning within them for the practiced eye. Seweryn Bialer, a former Polish Communist, has described the great study devoted by Polish *apparatchiki* to key speeches and articles in *Pravda*. They have learned through experience that politically significant articles generally appear on inside pages, particularly at or near the bottom. They can separate grain from chaff merely by looking at the title of an article, or by watching for certain initials at the end of an article which indicate its authoritative origin. When Khrushchev or other Soviet leaders make an important speech, Polish *apparatchiki* sometimes take several hours off from other duties, no matter how pressing, to study the speech carefully for clues as to shifts in the Soviet line.

In this way, partly, foreign Communist parties attune themselves to the subtle tactical changes in Soviet policy.

The collection of "esoteric" evidence is, for a Westerner, a time-consuming and arduous task. The detective-scholar must scan hundreds of articles in Communist media, constantly searching for indicators of political significance. When *Pravda* and *Izvestiya* conduct a debate over the priorities to be accorded light versus heavy industry, as they did in the late months of 1954, as likely as not the debate is conducted on the bottom of inside pages and in the text of articles replete with routine and familiar formulae. When Mao and Khrushchev presented divergent strategic views to the November 1957 Moscow conference, their divergence was virtually unknown in the West. Yet a careful and systematic comparison of Soviet and Chinese Communist media in the few months following the conference afforded a considerable amount of insight into the nature of these differences. Of course, the collection and evaluation of "esoteric" evidence is a delicate business, more of an art than a science, and it is possible to make educated guesses that are wrong. But such guesses, it is maintained, are worth more than uneducated ones, particularly to the extent that they permit systematic testing and improvement.

The collection and evaluation of this particular kind of evidence is made time-consuming, too, by the fact that the significance of what is said often lies in how it departs from precedent. The task then is to sift enough documentary material to establish what past behavior has been. When Malenkov said in 1954 that war would destroy world civilization, no exhaustive search of the speeches of Communist leaders was required to reveal that never before had a Communist made such an assertion. But when Mao said in November 1957 that "the strength of socialism exceeds the strength of imperialism," it was difficult to recall precisely what he had previously said on this critical subject, what Khrushchev and the Soviet leaders had said, and how in general the balance of forces between East and West had been evaluated in the Communist world, an evaluation central to Communist conduct in the international arena. To estimate the novelty of Mao's phrasing required an exhaustive search through Communist documents for all material bearing on the question of the relationship of forces between East and West.

It is not my purpose to try to state systematically the "rules" for interpreting Communist communications—a task which would be extremely difficult and could be done only partially. Rather I am asserting (a) that there are theoretical and empirical grounds for believing that useful analysis is possible; (b) such analysis has proved useful and accurate in the past; (c) such analysis is not a wholly intuitive and subjective enterprise by any means, but has a rigorous, if largely implicit, methodology; and (d) such analysis is not merely a means of developing interesting hypotheses—which in itself would be useful, since some of them could be checked by other kinds of data or by events themselves—but the technique also includes means of enabling the analyst to evaluate or "test" to some extent the hypotheses it uncovers.

There are several kinds of clues in open Communist media which help unravel the political mysteries of the Communist world. First of all, there is the polemical tone. On August 8, 1958, after Khrushchev had just left Peking, where he had doubtless discussed the Middle East crisis with Mao, the Chinese Party paper, *Jen-min jih-pao* (People's Daily) wrote that *"some soft-hearted advocates of peace* naively believe that in order to relax tension at all costs the enemy must not be provoked. . . . *Some groundlessly conclude* that peace can be gained only when there is no armed resistance against the attacks of the imperialists and colonialists . . . " [italics supplied].[7] Such language invites the question: Who are the "some"? In this particular case, the answer seemed apparent. Soviet newspapers, unlike those of the Chinese, were failing to call for "armed resistance" to "imperialist" attacks. Throughout the Lebanon crisis, Soviet communications had diverged from Chinese on the advisability of a political versus a military response to the Western intervention.

To take another example from the Sino-Soviet dialogue: in April 1960, *Hung ch'i* (Red Flag) wrote that "it is *absolutely impermissible* for us to mistake certain tactical changes on the part of imperialism for changes in the very nature of imperialism" [italics supplied].[8] The language clearly suggests that someone, and someone in a position of authority, was doing precisely what *Hung Ch'i* said was impermissible. In this case, the "someone" seemed to be Khrushchev. In the same article the author wrote that *"we must see* that even though imperialism does not unleash a world war, it may start local wars in certain areas where opportunities arise" [italics supplied]. The polemical tone suggested the author thought some Communists did not "see" the point.

Examples of polemical language can be drawn from dialogues other than the Sino-Soviet. A dialogue within the Chinese Communist Party over the pace of the great "leap forward" and the scope of the communes, for instance, was clearly evident in articles and speeches surrounding the tenth anniversary of the CPR (Chinese People's Republic) in October 1959. Liu Shao-ch'i's speech was punctuated with references to "some people" who believed that the communes had been set up too fast and who had described China's great cause as being "in an awful mess."[9] It can be assumed generally that in Communist parlance "some people" or "some comrades" is a euphemism which refers to opposition at the very highest levels of the Party.

Another favorite polemical device of the Communists in dialogue is the use of the formula, "of course . . . but. . . . " The first half of the sentence is a bow in the direction of the opponent's argument; the second is the reply or refutation. Thus, in the same speech, Liu Shao-ch'i said, clearly with the underdeveloped Communist countries in mind: "Of course, revolution and construction in China have features peculiar to this country. But it is also possible that some of these important special features may reappear in some other countries."[10] In 1957, Khrushchev had used the same formula to rebut the views of the East European autonomists. "Of course" we must take national peculiarities into consideration, he said, "but" all Communists must abide by the universal laws of socialist construction.

A second clue that a dialogue over policy is under way in Communist media lies in divergent emphasis given to a particular point by different leaders in the same Party, different papers in the same country, or different parties. Thus, throughout the early stage of the post-Stalin succession crisis, Malenkov more frequently referred to the Government as opposed to the Party than did Khrushchev or other Soviet leaders. This led several observers to the conclusion that he was basing his bid for power on the Government apparatus rather than the Party apparatus. I have already referred to the divergent emphasis in *Pravda* and *Izvestya* on heavy versus light industry in late 1954. Throughout the Soviet-Yugoslav dialogue in 1956–1957 there were divergent emphasis on such questions as the relationship among fraternal parties, the Soviet leading role, and the desirability of cooperation with Western socialists. Throughout the Sino-Soviet dialogue there has been divergent emphasis on local wars: The Chinese say they are inevitable, the Russians say they are increasingly deterrable. Sometimes divergent emphasis comes close to outright contradiction, as in 1959, when the Chinese said the Communist parties must grasp leadership in the early stages of the revolution in underdeveloped countries, while the Russians said that "the bourgeoisie assumes the role of hegemony."[11]

A third indication of a dialogue is omission. In the fall of 1956, when Gomulka first came to power, *Pravda* published only brief reports on Gomulka's major speeches, in contrast to the usual practice of publishing in full all major speeches of the top leaders of other fraternal parties. Gomulka himself, for many months after he came to power, did not repeat publicly a routine formula about the Soviet leading role in the Bloc. In 1956, when the Chinese first produced the "contradictions" argument to rationalize Stalin's crimes, *Pravda* deleted several paragraphs from an otherwise verbatim reproduction of the article. Omissions of this type in the Communist world are likely to be politically significant.

Distortion can be indicative of political differences. In 1958 the Bulgarian newspapers reproduced the Soviet October Revolution slogans with one significant change. While the Russian slogans had all the satellites and China "building socialism," the Bulgarian translation of the Russian slogans had China alone "completing the building of socialism."[12] This was an obvious distortion in China's favor, one of the earliest indications of the Bulgarian flirtation with Peking. Similarly, in 1958, when the Soviet press published an article by a Chinese leader quoting the commune resolution, it distorted a critical passage in the resolution to read that "communes" rather than "Communism" would be realized in the not distant future. [13] This seemed to reflect Soviet sensitivity over Chinese claims of discovering a shortcut to Communism.

A fifth clue to divergencies is selective reporting or interpretations of developments in the West. On Februrary 3, 1960, President Eisenhower intimated at his press conference the possibility that the United States might share nuclear weapons with its European allies. Moscow's reportage stressed the difficulties of such a step and implied it was unlikely; Peking's implied that such a step would soon be taken.

Still another indication of importance is a highly differentiated pattern of response. Thus Communist China was the only other Bloc country to come out with an authoritive public endorsement of East Germany's threat of January 26, 1959, to "request its allies to place rocket weapons at its disposal" if the atomic armament of West Germany continued.[14] In 1958, Albanian, East German, and Bulgarian spokesmen were much more sympathetic to the Chinese communes and the "leap forward" than Polish, Hungarian, and Rumanian spokesmen. These divergent responses provided important clues: first, to possible Bloc pressure on Moscow for nuclear sharing and, second, to the amount of Bloc support for Chinese programs.

Finally, a sudden change in routine formulae is often a sign of policy difference, and may help to throw light on them. In October 1958, the CPSU October Revolution slogans contained a seemingly routine slogan to the effect that China was, like all other satellites, "building socialism." Such a formula was not significant except when compared with previous slogans. A check of May Day and October Revolution slogans for the two previous years showed that the Chinese had been described in past slogans not as "building socialism," but as "builders of socialism." No other Communists had been so described. The subtle distinction implied that China was closer to achieving socialism than other Bloc countries. (At the 21st Congress of the CPSU, the Russians described themselves as "builders of Communism." This did not mean that they had *built* Communism, but that they were nearer full Communism than before the Congress. In short, "builders of" is a term denoting a higher stage than "building.") Thus, until October 1958, the

CPSU slogans had followed a systematic pattern which discriminated in favor of Chinese efforts at socialist construction and against efforts by the rest of the satellites. Suddenly in October 1958 the distinction was dropped and China was relegated to a position of parity with all other satellites. The author inferred at the time that this was an early, perhaps the earliest, indication of Soviet disgruntlement over Chinese claims to have found a fast road to Communism via the communes. The fact that the Bulgarians deliberately chose to distort that particular slogan was still another concrete indication of its political significance. Alteration of any rigidly observed formula is usually made for a particular political reason. While analysts may disagree on the reason for change, they generally do not deny that it is politically significant.

The above examples of clues to political divergencies within Communist media are merely a few out of hundreds that might be cited. Such evidence is often revealing; in analyzing Bloc policy, it is indispensable. And until such time as the Communists publish proceedings of their inner councils, it is unlikely that better evidence on contemporary Communist problems will be available.[15]

The reluctance of many in the West to credit such evidence with much significance stems from the fact, pointed out by Myron Rush, that "men whose understanding of political reality has been formed by a free society find it difficult to suppose that piddling with stereotyped formulas can be an important mode of political behavior for powerful leaders. Even in default of the customary data used in political analysis, they are understandably reluctant to accept far-reaching conclusions drawn from this elusive evidence. Yet the fact remains: these minutiae—no less than purges and policy debates—are the very stuff of Soviet politics."[16]

The use of evidence drawn from "symbolic" or "esoteric" communication has hitherto been confined, for the most part, to studies of power relationships within the Soviet hierarchy. The present study hopes to demonstrate that such evidence can and must be employed in the examination of other critical areas of Soviet and Chinese behavior. While I have used all available evidence from whatever source to illuminate the problems examined in this study, I have followed the practice of not crediting a hypothesis until satisfactory evidence, even if indirect, could be found for it in the Communists' own stream of communications. For example, in

1960, there were rumors of border incidents between Russia and China. I suspended judgment until some kind of indirect confirmation in Soviet or Chinese media was available. When a Soviet historical journal suddenly and gratuitously criticized unprovoked Chinese assaults on undefended Russian borderlands in the 17th century, I found the rumors had gained in credibility.[17]

What I have tried to do in this Note on Methodology is to provide the reader some notion of what I am up to in this book and how I propose to go about it. Such a note must be very brief. A major work remains to be written on the particular method for analyzing Communist communications that I have tried to sketch.

PART ONE

THE SEEDS OF CONFLICT:
1956–1957

CHAPTER 1

THE DEBATE OVER DE-STALINIZATION
AND INTRA-BLOC RELATIONS

IN 1960, polemics from Peking and Moscow, thinly veiled by doctrinal exegesis, revealed growing disunity between the two Communist giants over a range of issues covering the entire spectrum of strategy and tactics in the world revolution. Privately, Khrushchev was reported to have made bitter personal attacks on Mao before stunned onlookers from the international Communist movement. According to an authoritative account, Mao attacked Khrushchev for revisionism, for mishandling de-Stalinization, for blundering responses to the Polish and Hungarian crises, and—worst of all from Peking's viewpoint—for sacrificing Chinese interests in pursuit of a chimerical Soviet-American détente. Khrushchev allegedly replied in kind, likening Mao's behavior to that of Stalin, accusing him of being detached from the realities of the modern world, and—perhaps the worst crime for a true Marxist-Leninist—of ignoring the interests of world revolution for the sake of China's national concerns.[1]

Was this the end to the long-vaunted unity of the two most powerful partners of international Communism? Or was it merely dialectical discourse, in Mao's terms, "Unity-criticism-unity"? How far back did the dispute go? Where might it end?

In the broadest perspective, the dispute might be traced back to the Second Comintern Congress of 1920, to the divergences between Lenin and M. N. Roy, the Indian Communist, on strategy for the underdeveloped countries of Asia, and to the strains between Comintern policy and Chinese Communist preferences in the 1920's. More conveniently, the Sino-Soviet dispute might be examined from the inception of the Chinese People's Republic (CPR) and the lengthy negotiations between Mao and Stalin in the winter of 1949–1950, when, for the first time, the two leaders confronted one another as self-made national leaders and as possible competitors in the world Communist movement. For our purposes, however, it will be most useful to begin with the 20th Congress of the Communist Party of the Soviet Union (CPSU) in February 1956. Here, as Peking was later to contend in its private polemics, were sown the seeds of discord that bore such bitter fruit in 1960.

The 20th Party Congress represents the major turning point in Sino-Soviet relations in the post-Stalin era. That Congress set the stage for several of the major elements of conflict that have since appeared: differences over global strategy, over intra-bloc relations, over the pace and scope of de-Stalinization, over the permissible diversity of methods used in building socialism and Communism, and over the fundamental question of socialist-camp leadership.

Soviet Global Strategy

With regard to Soviet foreign policy and global revolutionary strategy, Khrushchev introduced at the 20th Congress three new axioms. First, he professed that peaceful coexistence was not a mere tactical expedient but a "fundamental principle" of Soviet foreign policy, based on "our certainty" of the victory of Communism in peaceful competition. Moreover, there was no alternative to peaceful coexistence: "either peaceful coexistence or the most destructive war in history. There is no third way." Second, Khrushchev modified the Marxist-Leninist dogma that wars are inevitable as long as capitalism survives, concluding that "war is not a fatalistic inevitability." This new evaluation stemmed from the existence of "mighty social and political forces" which possessed formidable means to prevent the imperialists from unleashing war. Finally, Khrushchev said there was increasing possibility of a non-violent transformation to socialism in a number of capitalist countries.[2]

These doctrinal modifications have rightly been regarded with suspicion in the West. The Bolsheviks had long professed a belief in "peaceful coexistence"; there was considerable ambiguity in Khrushchev's assertion that war was no longer "fatalistically inevitable"; and the proclaimed belief in non-violent transformation of capitalist society was accompanied by critical qualifiers which seemed to imply that violence would ensue if the capitalists resisted the "inevitable" course of history and tried to prevent a Communist revolution.

In short, there was no justification for interpreting the 20th Congress modifications as the beginning of a new era in East-West relations or of the waning of Bolshevik worldwide revolutionary impulses. On the contrary, it could be argued that these doctrinal modifications represented the culmination of the adaptation of

Bolshevism to a new and unique setting—a world with thermonuclear weapons, a process that was manifestly well advanced by
1954, when Malenkov blurted out that a world war would destroy
civilization.

The advent of the thermonuclear era had forced the Bolsheviks
to re-appraise the strategy and tactics of the pre-nuclear era. In relation to strategy and tactics for the "world revolution," the 20th
Congress modifications meant essentially that fundamental aims
could and must be pursued with a minimum of violence, a minimum
of risk-taking. In the nuclear age it was no longer possible to think,
as Lenin did, of a series of bloody clashes with the imperialists.
Nor was it possible to believe that the Soviet Union could indiscriminately push history along, by inciting and supporting armed
rebellions and civil wars throughout the capitalist world, without
inviting a nuclear response from the West. But if nuclear weapons
imposed restraints on the Bolsheviks, they would also impose
restraints on the West. An attack on the USSR would be increasingly unlikely, particularly after the Russians successfully tested
an intercontinental missile in 1957. Moreover, the West would
be increasingly unlikely to intervene in the crucial contested areas
throughout the world, where Communist parties could push local
insurrections and thus gradually erode the Western position. Thus,
if the nuclear era imposed restraints on the Russians, it also brought
about unprecedented opportunities for spreading worldwide revolution behind the Soviet deterrent shield.

The Bolsheviks have never believed in the decisiveness of military power or technology; they have believed rather in the primacy
of economic and social factors. Another overriding element in their
strategic calculations, therefore, as reflected in the 20th Congress,
was a belief that they would in the foreseeable future surpass
the West in economic production. Increasingly Soviet economic
power could be used to push forward the world revolution by
alienating the underdeveloped countries from the West, by courting
the neutrals, by disrupting the capitalist world market. A Western
economic crisis on the scale of 1929–1932, they believed, was inevitable in any case. In the not-distant future, such an event, or a
series of such events, combined with Soviet economic might, would
accelerate the impending crisis of world imperialism.

In a word, the 20th Congress doctrinal modifications, translated into strategic calculations, meant that it was both necessary and possible to realize the triumph of world Communism without resort to an armed holocaust. Such an overall calculation implied a delicate and subtle flexibility in tactics. On the one hand, the West must not be pushed to the point of initiating global nuclear war; on the other hand, there was increasing opportunity to push the West by a variety of means not involving large risks of war.

Understanding of this calculation is essential to an understanding of the Sino-Soviet polemic. When in 1958–1960 the Chinese Communists took sharp issue with the Soviet strategic outlook, they were saying in effect that the limits Moscow imposed on herself and the Bloc, because of the fear of all-out war, were too severe, and that the opportunities available as a result of Soviet military and economic power and Western weakness were not being sufficiently exploited. Peking began to voice this objection, however, in 1958, not at the time of the 20th Congress. Whether or not they harbored doubts in 1956 about the global strategic line enunciated at the Congress, the Chinese endorsed the major doctrinal innovations offered by Khrushchev: peaceful coexistence, the no longer fatalistic inevitability of war, and the increasing possibility of non-violent transition to socialism. It was not until two years later, when they began to change their own global perspectives, that the Chinese retrospectively attacked the 20th Congress line. More will be said about this later.

On other questions, however, the 20th Congress did provide an immediate turning point in the Moscow-Peking relationship. The two most prominent issues were those of de-Stalinization and the nature of relations among fraternal parties. On both these issues, the differences between Moscow and Peking were to become apparent within a few months of the Congress.

Peking and de-Stalinization

In a secret letter to the Soviet Party dated September 10, 1960, the Chinese Communists are alleged to have stated that the "real differences" between themselves and Khrushchev began when, in his secret speech to the 20th Congress, Khrushchev denied Stalin's positive role without any previous discussion with the other Communist parties.[3] It is quite likely that, just as the Chinese allegedly charged, Khrushchev had undertaken the assault on Stalin without informing the Chinese and other Bloc parties beforehand. The Chinese delegate to the Congress, Chu Teh, mentioned Stalin favorably in a speech given to the Congress, an indication that Peking either did not know of the impending developments or was seeking to head them off. Peking now apparently offers the former explanation rather than the latter, and there is no reason to think it is not the true one.

The dismay created in Peking by Khrushchev's abrupt unveiling of Stalin's crimes and megalomania is suggested by the fact that, from February to April 1956, Chinese Communist media virtually ignored the question of de-Stalinization, a question that was already being bitterly debated throughout the Communist world and that had already resulted in mass defections from Communist parties.

Further proof of Peking's annoyance was forthcoming in April 1956 in the form of a long analysis in *Jen-min jih-pao* of the Stalin era, "based on discussions of an enlarged meeting of the Political Bureau" of the Central Committee of the Chinese Communist Party—that is, discussions by the top thirty or forty CCP leaders.[4] The article had four main purposes with regard to the implications of Khrushchev's secret attack on Stalin: first, to limit that attack so that it could not be expanded, as it later was by the "revisionists," to a full-scale attack on the Communist system in general; second, to put Khrushchev's revelations in a theoretical context that would explain to a deeply troubled Communist world how such "mistakes" could have occurred; third, to protect Mao from the charge that he was following in Stalin's footsteps; and, finally, by putting de-Stalinization in such a context, to establish Peking as a source of doctrinal guidance for the entire Communist movement.

Peking's first purpose—to limit the attack to Stalin himself and to qualify the allegations against him—was apparent from the manner in which it conceded that Stalin had committed some "serious mistakes," and then went on to give Stalin credit for "an ineffaceable share" in carrying out Lenin's principles. Stalin, the Chinese contended, for all his "mistakes," was an "outstanding Marxist-Leninist fighter" who had defended Lenin's line of industrialization and collectivization against the enemies of Leninism—the Trotskyites, Zinovievites, and other "bourgeois agents." Stalin was a figure whose contributions and whose errors, mostly committed in the latter part of his life, must be weighed against each other with a view to profiting from both.[5] The motive behind this analysis was evidently to be sure that the Communist baby would not be thrown out with the Stalinist bath water. The very fact that the CCP felt compelled to publish such an analysis is some indication of the dismay with which Khrushchev's attack on the dead *vozhd* must have been greeted in Peking. Limiting the attack on Stalin was a reflection of Peking's felt need to defend its own adaptation of Stalinism to Chinese conditions. Like Stalin, Mao too had pursued a policy of industrialization and rapid collectivization. Peking wished to ensure that Khrushchev's attack on Stalin did not lead to a widespread domestic reaction against Maoism.

Peking's desire to limit the attack on Stalin, however, should not be taken to mean that the Chinese were, or are, Stalinists. There was much in the April article that must have made the Soviet dictator turn over in his grave, particularly the assertions that "contradictions" were inevitable even under Communism and that Communist societies must seek a balance between centralism and "democracy." To identify the Chinese leaders, at that time or now, as inflexible Stalinists is to miss the point. The Chinese correctly anticipated in Khrushchev's violent attack on Stalin the opening of a Pandora's box that could cause great confusion in the entire Communist world, including China. Their effort to limit the attack on Stalin was a symptom, not of Peking's admiration for Stalinism, but of its fear that grave consequences would ensue from Khrushchev's attack.

The second aim of the CCP was to put Khrushchev's revelations in theoretical perspective and thus to head off the tidal wave of centrifugal forces within the Communist movement that it correctly anticipated. In June, the Italian Communist Party leader Togliatti.was to ascribe Stalin's "mistakes" to a "degeneration" of the Soviet system which the Soviet leaders were duty-bound to investigate and put right.[6] "Revisionists" in Poland, Hungary, and throughout the Communist world were to go further and contend that a repetition of Stalin's crimes could be avoided only by drastic changes in the nature of the Communist system—changes in the direction of increasing democratization and checks and balances on the exercise of absolute power.[7] The CCP answer to such charges, even before they were made, was that "mistakes" were inevitable in the building of socialism but, "whatever the mistakes," the dictatorship of the proletariat was "always far superior to all dictatorships of the exploiting classes."

The foundation for Peking's rationale of Stalinism was its famous theory of "contradictions." "To deny the existence of contradictions," said the April article in *Jen-min jih-pao*, "is to deny dialectics." Society in fact developed through "continual contradictions." "Viewed in this light, the existence of contradictions between the individual and the collective in a socialist society is nothing strange."[8] If socialist and even Communist society must expect "continual contradictions," it followed that one must not become overly upset with any particular "contradiction." What was necessary was to try to minimize and to avoid them, not to deny that they exist.

In republishing the Chinese article almost verbatim, *Pravda* deleted the remarks cited above.[9] Khrushchev had been arguing and would continue to argue that Stalin's mistakes had nothing to do with "socialist" society and therefore could never reappear in the future.[10] Stalin's mistakes were merely the result of a particular personality at a particular historical period. Such an attitude must have seemed to the wily Chinese the height of political short-sightedness: first to unveil the real Stalin before the Communist world and then to try to brush under the table any questions or doubts that would inevitably arise! Mao had offered Khrushchev a way out: to concede that Stalin's "mistakes" *might* reappear in the future, that *some* corrective actions needed to be taken in all Communist countries, and that even in a Communist society there could be injustice and conflicts of interest between the leaders and the led. The Russians probably rejected this part of the CCP analysis because they did not anticipate the scope of the convulsions that were to shake the Communist world. Also, there may not have been a consensus of the leaders on the limits of de-Stalinization.

Peking's third aim was to protect Mao from the possible charge that he was following in Stalin's footsteps. Significantly, Mao's name was not mentioned once in the entire Chinese analysis. Indeed the *Jen-min jih-pao* article was based on the discussions of an "enlarged meeting of the Political Bureau" and thus came under a collective imprimatur. A collectively created article on basic doctrine had been unknown in China since the early days of the Communist regime. Implicitly, then, the very form of the article was suggesting that in China there was no "cult of the individual." There was also strong internal evidence to suggest that the article was designed in part to protect Mao. It pointedly noted that not all "leaders of Communist parties" inevitably made the same mistakes. "Leaders of communist parties and socialist states" had a duty to "reduce mistakes, avoid serious ones, endeavor to learn lessons from isolated local and temporary mistakes . . . be most prudent and modest, keep close to the masses. . . . " If "leaders" did this, they would not fall into the trap that Stalin fell into when, "in the later years of his work," he became conceited, imprudent, and subjective.[11] In short, if "leaders" such as Mao did *not* make the same "mistakes," they would not run the same danger.

Moreover, the article continued, one could not deduce from Stalin's mistakes that "leaders" play an unimportant role in history. "To deny the role of the individual, the role of the vanguard and of leaders is completely wrong." A leader begins making serious mistakes only when "he loses overall penetrating insight into the affairs of the country." In China, the implication was clear, there was no danger of this. All errors ascribed in the article to the CCP were assigned to the period before 1936, when Mao assumed control of the Party. In the period from 1927–1936, it was stated "some of our comrades crudely applied . . . Stalin's . . . main-blow formula. . . . " Other mistakes of "Right opportunism" in the period from 1924 to 1927, and mistakes of "Left opportunism" in the period from 1931 to 1934, were noted. Thus, suggested the Chinese analysis, there had been no "mistakes" in the CCP line since 1936, presumably because Mao, unlike Stalin, had not fallen victim to the "cult-of-personality"; he had not lost touch with the masses and become conceited and arbitrary.

The Chinese Formula: Lessons of the Stalin Era

The first three purposes behind the CCP's April analysis were essentially defensive: to limit the attack on Stalin, to explain to a troubled Communist world how such crimes could have gone unchecked for so long, and to protect Mao. Peking's fourth purpose was more self-seeking. By putting de-Stalinization in a theoretically oriented context, the Chinese were suggesting to the Communist world that they were better Marxist-Leninists than the Russians with their brash peasant leader. Throughout the April article there were passages which seemed to suggest that, if Moscow had not thought the problems of de-Stalinization through, Peking had.

Moreover, the nature of the April article indicated that it was addressed to the entire international Communist movement. Specific passages reinforced this impression. "Leaders of Communist parties and socialist states" one of them said, "have the duty to do their utmost, to reduce errors, avoid certain serious ones. . . . " To do this, "every leader" must be modest and circumspect. The CCP was doing more than rescuing Khrushchev from himself and asking the world Communist movement to continue to trust blindly in Soviet leadership; it was in effect speaking *in place* of the Russians. It was filling a gap created by Khrushchev's own theoretical barrenness.

Yet the Chinese Communists were not merely cynically seeking to advance their own influence and power at the expense of Moscow. The problems raised by Khrushchev's secret speech were real and acute. If what Khrushchev said about Stalin was true, what were the implications for socialist society, indeed for the very nature of Communism? Were there any lessons to be learned from the Stalin era? Did Communist dictatorship need to be liberalized? By not offering any theoretical framework for de-Stalinization, the Russians were acting as if change were unnecessary. Khrushchev would later argue that Stalin's mistakes had nothing to do with the nature of Soviet society, not a response that could satisfy the Togliattis and Titos, let alone the revisionists throughout the Communist world who now saw the opportunity to press for a genuine democratization of the Communist system.

Peking appreciated clearly that Khrushchev's secret speech about Stalin demanded an answer to the burning questions: how many of Stalin's crimes can be attributed to the very nature of Communist totalitarianism? What must be done to avoid repetition of his mistakes? In the April article Peking was offering a formula to rid Communist societies of those aspects of Stalinism no longer feasible or desirable, while insuring the continued dictatorship of the Communist parties. In short, Peking was seeking a balance between coercion and permissiveness. The principal lesson of the

Stalin era, it averred, in effect, was that Stalin had overstressed the coercive elements of Communist rule at the expense of the permissive: "To defeat powerful enemies, the dictatorship of the proletariat requires a high degree of centralization of power. This highly centralized power must be combined with a high level of democracy. When there is an undue emphasis on centralization, many mistakes are bound to occur."[12] The rigid Stalinist system, Peking was saying, could not be continued in any Communist state without the danger of creating another Stalin. It was necessary to avoid "complacency" and "rigidity" of outlook. It was necessary for all leaders to maintain close contact with the masses, as the Chinese Party chiefs had done. It was necessary, as the CCP also had done, to combine collective leadership with individual responsibility, to combine democracy and centralism. Reforms such as the workers' councils in Yugoslavia were reforms in the right direction. Although the April article did not specifically refer to the Yugoslav experiment, other articles in the Chinese press in the fall of 1956 were to give the Yugoslavs credit for it. Moscow, for its part, still condemned the workers' councils as anti-Marxist.

The Chinese, it appears, were seeking a middle road out of the dilemma raised by Khrushchev's indictment of Stalin. Peking never went as far as Togliatti and others later did in condemning the Stalinist system as "degenerate" and in advocating wholesale reforms. But it went halfway to meet the revisionists in arguing that Stalin's excessive centralism must be corrected.

These incipient differences between Moscow and Peking on the proper balance to be maintained between permissiveness and coercion in Communist societies were again to be reflected in divergent analyses of the Poznan riots in Poland in mid-July. Moscow and all the satellites, with the significant exception of Poland and Hungary, insisted that the disturbances were organized by Western provocateurs. Warsaw and Budapest argued that the absence of redress for legitimate working class grievances were largely responsible. Peking agreed that "imperialist agents" provoked the demonstrators but pointed out that the "imperialists" could not have succeeded if there had been no weakness to exploit. It saw the riots as the April article had seen Stalin's errors: as a storm warning. "We must solve the difficulties of the working people in good time," wrote the Chinese Communist Party paper, "allowing no loophole for enemy agents."[13]

Again in November, Peking, unlike Moscow, saw a lesson in the Hungarian rebellion. It shared Tito's concern over the implications of the fact that "there is more than a small number of counterrevolutionaries in Hungary." If it unhesitatingly approved Moscow's brutal suppression of the revolution, it also recognized that the conditions which created the insurrection could appear in other Communist states. Communist regimes, Peking wrote at the time, must establish a "dictatorship over the enemy" and "*at the same time* a democracy for the people" [italics supplied]; a "one-sided view" favoring one at the expense of the other would be incorrect.[14]

In Mao's eyes, Khrushchev in his "secret" speech had thrown open the gates to attacks on the entire structure of Communist society, while at the same time crudely denying that there were any lessons to be learned from the Stalin era. How could Peking maintain confidence in a Soviet leader who would undertake such a major initiative without prior consultation with other Communist parties and apparently without a plan to meet foreseeable adverse consequences?

If Khrushchev had created problems for Mao, the Chinese leader had reciprocated. By offering the CCP as a source of doctrinal guidance and wisdom for the entire Communist movement, Peking was already, however subtly, asserting its role as a co-partner in the camp leadership. Khrushchev's blunder offered Mao an unparalleled opportunity to increase his prestige and influence in Eastern Europe and in the Communist world—even within the CPSU itself. While it would be misleading to trace every facet of the Sino-Soviet conflict to Khrushchev's abrupt and inept handling of de-Stalinization at the 20th Congress, there can be little doubt that his action there left a bitter taste in Mao's mouth. Nor can there be much doubt that Mao skillfully made the best of a bad situation and exploited the opportunity to build up his influence at Khrushchev's expense. The Communist world could not have two Romes. If this issue was not fully apparent until 1960, it was already dimly apparent in 1956.

Moscow and Intra-Bloc Relations: How Many Roads to Socialism?

The death of Stalin was the death of Stalinism in intra-bloc relations. The Communist camp could no longer be governed by an imperial dictator with viceroys in each satellite capital and an elaborate police network. The chronic problem that has beset the Russians since the death of Stalin has been to establish some pattern of intra-bloc relationships which would ensure unity and yet tolerate diversity.[15] In Stalin's day the problem was simple because —except for the Sino-Soviet relationship—it was avoided. No diversity was tolerated; the slightest glimmer was suppressed in its infancy. Stalin governed the Communist Bloc in this manner, not because he was unaware of the pressures for autonomy and national distinctiveness, but in order to suppress them. In his view, the way to keep the lid on was to seal it tightly.

Khrushchev's problem, the problem of any successor to Stalin, was to govern the international Communist movement so as to ensure unity and, at the same time, to allow for the differing national perspectives and interests of the various Communist states and parties, which he saw could not indefinitely be suppressed. To balance these two objectives was to recognize the need for diversity but to set limits on it. This raises the questions at the heart of intra-bloc relations since 1953. How much independence can each Communist Party have in formulating its own domestic policies? Are all parties equal or are some "more equal than others"? How much of Soviet experience and of the Soviet model is universally valid and how much is a historical peculiarity that need not be repeated elsewhere? Are there multiple paths to socialism?

At the 20th Congress, Khrushchev himself took a big step toward setting loose the very forces of polycentrism and diversity that he subsequently tried to contain. He cited China's "creative Marxism in action" and Yugoslavia's "specific forms of economic management and organization of the state apparatus" as examples of "much that is unique in socialist construction."[16] Moreover, in his eagerness to woo Tito back into the Bloc, Khrushchev in 1956 assented to "a multiplicity of forms of socialist development," agreed not to "impose" Soviet opinion, and to base Soviet-Yugoslav relations on "complete voluntariness and equality. . . . "[17] The aftermath of the 20th Congress and Tito's June 1956 visit to Moscow confirmed the worst fears of the unreconstructed Stalinists in the Soviet ruling circles. Throughout the Communist world, which was shaken by Khrushchev's unveiling of Stalin's crimes, there arose tremendous pressures for greater independence from

Moscow.[18] Khrushchev was thus caught in a dilemma of his own making. He wanted an "independent" Yugoslavia back in a monolithic Bloc that would greatly restrict Tito's freedom of action. At the same time, he wanted to demonstrate to those uncommitted countries he was seeking to wean away from the West that there was nothing incompatible between independence and membership in the "socialist family."

Khrushchev's first reaction to the pressures for polycentrism was to continue the ideological *rapprochement* with Tito while being careful to restrict the formulas of "equality" and independence to Yugoslavia alone. In the period following Tito's June 1956 visit to Moscow, there was a notable discrepancy between Yugoslavia's attempt to generalize the concept of independence so as to include all Bloc parties and the Soviet attempt to limit the concept to the Soviet-Yugoslav relationship. Moscow rejected the contention of the Yugoslav and Italian parties that Stalin's errors demonstrated the need for a sweeping change in intra-bloc relations.[19] The CPSU saw no need for any change in the relationship then existing between Moscow and the fraternal parties—a change demanded by Tito and Togliatti, who were soon to be joined by Gomulka and Kadar. Throughout this initial period of ferment, from February to October 1956, Soviet propaganda and official statements emphasized that only in monolithic unity could there be genuine independence.[20]

It was not until the Soviet Government declaration of October 30, issued in the midst of the Hungarian rebellion, that the CPSU reluctantly came to concede the importance of "equality," "mutual respect," and "independence" in Bloc relations.[21] A week later, Suslov, in his October Revolution anniversary speech, introduced the idea that the unity of the Bloc countries was directly proportional to the degree to which the principles of "equality" and "mutual respect" were observed: "The nature of mutual relations of the countries of socialism is such that the more strictly they adhere to principles of equality and mutual respect of the interests and rights of each other, the stronger is the friendship between the peoples of these countries, and the more monolithic the entire socialist world."[22] This statement reversed the emphasis in Soviet statements before the Hungarian revolution, which had insisted not that equality guaranteed unity but rather that unity created the

51

conditions for equality. But in November 1956, while granting the importance of "equality," the CPSU at the same time indicated the limits beyond which the urge for independence must not go. To this end, Suslov spelled out "laws" of socialist revolution and construction. He was conspicuously silent about Yugoslavia, a silence which was notable because the formal October Revolution speech is traditionally the vehicle for elaborating the major developments of the preceding year. Tito's visit to Moscow a few months before had been one of the highlights of Soviet diplomacy. The silence about Yugoslavia was soon to give way to open hostility. On November 18, at the Polish Embassy reception for Gomulka, Khrushchev made an indirect attack on the Yugoslav leader.[23] On November 23 *Pravda* openly rebutted Tito's Pula speech, which had reiterated Yugoslav demands for greater equality between all Communist parties.[24]

At about the same time, Khrushchev stepped up the campaign against "national Communism" which had begun in July. In a New Year's reply to questions submitted by the Czech Party organ, *Rude pravo,* the Soviet leader warned that undue emphasis on national characteristics and on "special paths" to socialism could harm both socialist construction in the particular country and the whole family of socialist nations.[25]

A week before, *Pravda* had attacked the Polish "pro-thaw" organ, *Nowa kultura,* for its unsatisfactory definition of proletarian internationalism, the first independent Soviet criticism of the Poles since Gomulka came to power.[26] Both *Nowa kultura* and Belgrade had begun to define intra-bloc relations in terms of "coexistence," the same concept used to define the Bloc's relations with the "imperialist" West. At the same time, a Warsaw-Belgrade axis was being built up on the basis of a common desire to resist undue Soviet interference in their internal affairs. On December 29, a joint Yugoslav-Polish communiqué declared that "under the present conditions bilateral inter-party relations constitute the most correct form of cooperation between the Communist and Workers parties."[27] In short, both parties were resisting any efforts to recreate organizations such as the Cominform or Comintern which could be used to impose the Soviet will on member parties.

A Cautious Retreat after the Purge of
the Soviet Anti-Party Group

In the wake of the purge of Malenkov, Molotov, and other members of the "anti-Party" group, in June 1957, there were several indications that Khrushchev was moving cautiously back toward the abortive 20th Congress approval of "different roads to socialism." *Izvestiya* conceded that there were "a great variety of concrete forms and methods of building socialism in the various countries depending on the historic, national, and other peculiarities in each country."[28] Two days later, Khrushchev, in a speech in Czechoslovakia, reaffirmed the idea of building socialism in accord with national peculiarities.[29] Speaking to Czech agriculturalists later, he made the unprecedented statement that, although he was in favor of collective farms, "when to establish them and in what manner" were "exclusively your own affair."[30] On July 12, a *Pravda* editorial on creative Marxism, attacking the "dogmatism" of the ousted leaders, said the Marxist theory was by no means "something finished and untouchable" and that "it provides only general guiding principles which are being applied in a different way under the conditions of each separate country." Meanwhile, a Soviet-Czech communiqué in July, the first joint statement to be signed after the purge, called the struggle against dogmatism "equally necessary" with that against revisionism.[31] This was the first time in any Soviet or satellite Party document that the dogmatist had been classed with the revisionist.

This striking shift in Soviet emphasis is open to several interpretations. On the one hand, Khrushchev could have been trying to use the anti-Party group as a convenient scapegoat for the "hard" line on intra-bloc relations adopted by the Russians in late 1956 and early 1957. The problem with this explanation is that Khrushchev himself had clearly identified himself with this line. A more likely explanation is that the anti-Party group applied a brake on Khrushchev's Bloc policy and forced him to be tougher than he really wanted to be. Additionally, there is the possibility, which does not exclude the first two, that the increasing stabilization of the situation in Eastern Europe by mid-1957 allowed a softer line on Bloc relations. In any case, the Soviet shift to a more flexible policy and the increasing professions of loyalty from Warsaw combined to make possible a genuine compromise at the Moscow summit meeting in November 1957.

The Soviet-Chinese Differences
on Intra-Bloc Relations

The differences that arose between Moscow and Peking on intra-bloc relations in 1956–1957 were essentially a product of differing views on how best to combat the centrifugal forces that Khrushchev's own policy had created—in other words, how to achieve unity in diversity. The Chinese, as we have suggested, were probably appalled at the crudity with which Khrushchev first removed the veil from Stalin's crimes, humbled himself before Tito, and then expressed surprise when these policies resulted in pressures for polycentrism. Peking's article of April 1956 already contained the seeds of an approach to intra-bloc relations midway between the demands for polycentrism voiced by Togliatti and the denial from Moscow that any changes in intra-bloc relations were necessary.

In June, Togliatti argued: "The experience accomplished in the building of a socialist society in the Soviet Union cannot contain instructions for resolving all the questions which may present themselves today to us and to the Communists of other countries. . . . Thus various points or centers of development and orientation are established. There is established . . . a polycentric system, corresponding to the new situation. . . . The solution which today probably most nearly corresponds to this new situation may be that of full autonomy of the individual Communist parties and of bilateral relations between them."[32]

This was an explicit call for the removal of the CPSU from the center of the international Communist movement, and for a new arrangement in which all the Communist parties would be equal and would have bilateral relations, one with another, rather than being collectively subordinated to Moscow. The absence of unilateral dictation by Moscow would thus inhibit any desires on the part of more powerful parties to dictate to weaker parties. Polycentrism would also mean much greater independence for Communist parties throughout the world to establish policies in accord with local conditions.

54

The CCP's April article had stopped short of recognizing polycentrism or the corollary of polycentrism, multiple paths to socialism. Moreover, it had cited the CPSU as the center of the Communist camp. On the other hand, the article had explicitly criticized Stalin's effort to impose direct Soviet control on the Yugoslavs: "Stalin," it said, "gave certain wrong advice on the international Communist movement, and, in particular, made a wrong decision on the question of Yugoslavia" [italics supplied].[33] Also, in cautioning against a dogmatic application of Stalinist tactics, the article was already suggesting what was later to become an explicit contention—that each Communist Party must be given greater leeway in developing its own domestic policies. Finally, in contending that any Communist Party might continue to make mistakes in the future, the April article was clearly suggesting that the CPSU was not infallible. The implication followed that it should not seek to impose its views.

Peking Supports Gomulka
against Moscow

The Hungarian revolution was not a real test of the Sino-Soviet differences over tolerable diversity because it was clearly intolerable to both sides. But the ascendancy of Gomulka in Poland provided such a test. Gomulka was obviously a loyal Communist: he had no independent foreign policy; he professed the utmost loyalty to the socialist camp; his single "aberration" was that he believed he must be given a free hand in "building socialism" in Poland, that Soviet methods could not be blindly copied, that there were "special problems" which required peculiarly Polish solutions.

As early as September there were signs that Mao was urging the Poles to develop their own brand of socialism. In that month, Edward Ochab, first secretary of the Polish Party, was in Peking for the Chinese Party Congress. According to Flora Lewis, whose information came from unidentified Polish Party sources, Mao, in conversations with Ochab, "showed sympathy for the Polish liberal faction and for Gomulka."[34] At one point, when Mao and Ochab were discussing Molotov's ouster as Soviet Foreign Minister, Mao is alleged to have said: "It seems that China and Poland have been keeping company for some time already without even knowing it.

It is good company and we are glad of it."[35] Mao's attitude encouraged Ochab to speak out about Poland's troubles with Moscow. Ochab, in the presence of Soviet delegate Anastas Mikoyan, allegedly described difficulties with the Russians over trade and domestic autonomy. Mikoyan at another point reacted strongly to Ochab's moderate appraisal of the Poznan riots. Ochab retorted that the Poles knew more about what was going on in Poland than the Russians, adding "our people will no longer tolerate taking orders from abroad."[36] At this point Mikoyan exploded and Ochab silently shook hands with Mao and left the room. Mao turned and followed Ochab, ignoring Mikoyan. According to Miss Lewis, Mikoyan, piqued at this incident, "boarded a plane the same day and returned to Moscow although the Congress had not closed."[37]

In October, Mao reportedly advised Moscow against armed intervention "if the Polish revolution got out of hand."[38] Whether or not Moscow intended to use force against the Polish Communists, who had just installed Gomulka as First Secretary, there seems little doubt that Peking lent support to Gomulka in his political battle with Moscow—support bitterly resented by the Russians.

From the opening in late October of the Polish Party's eighth plenum, at which Gomulka outlined his program, Peking's enthusiasm for the Gomulka regime was in stark contrast to Soviet and satellite hostility. The very first Chinese news dispatch on the Polish eighth plenum indicated that many people "spoke enthusiastically" about it. The Polish people, it went on, considered the plenum "the most significant political event in the past ten years."[39] The Chinese dispatch also pointedly linked accounts of armed workers in Warsaw factories with "concern about the visit of the CPSU Central Committee delegation headed by N. S. Khrushchev." It pointed to a "most touching article" in *Trybuna ludu* which hailed the new Gomulka leadership as one that would "lead us to the realization of correct and just plans." Most important, it sought to convey the idea that Poland was not attempting to secede from the Bloc but only to follow a distinctive path to socialism. It did this by quoting selectively from an open letter of the Warsaw University of Technology, which said *inter alia:* "We are convinced that unity with the Soviet Union, China, and all People's Democracies should be the fundamental principle for the foreign and economic policies of our country. However, such a unity and alliance, under any circumstance, must not hinder the exercise of sovereignty of any one country and its own choice of the road leading to socialism."[40] In this obvious attempt to reassure his readers that the Poles were not seeking to overturn the Communist system, the NCNA correspondent said that the Polish people "were careful to see that . . . reactionaries could not utilize the confusion to create incidents" and that the "complete realization of socialist democracy" would not be confused with steps toward "bourgeois democracy."

The Chinese portrayal of a spontaneous popular movement for socialist democracy and national sovereignty, under the control of the Polish leaders and involving nothing that the USSR need fear, was essentially the same one presented in the Polish press and Gomulka's speeches, particularly his first major speech of October 20. Tass dismissed this speech in one sentence: "The first to speak was Comrade Wladyslav Gomulka." Peking published it in full on October 27.

In their statement of November 1 on intra-bloc relations, the Chinese swiftly applauded the Soviet Government's statement of October 30, which for the first time conceded the need for "equality" in relations among all Communist parties.[41] At the same time, China came out formally on Gomulka's side in his quarrel with Moscow. The CPR Government, the statement said, had noted the Polish people's demands that "democracy, independence, and equality be strengthened and the material well-being of the people be raised," and had concluded that "these demands are completely proper." It implicitly cautioned Moscow not to confuse Gomulkaism with reaction, noting "with satisfaction" that the Polish people and their leaders were aware of the danger from reactionary elements which wanted to undermine the socialist system and the unity among socialist countries. It is "absolutely necessary," said the Chinese Government "to appreciate this fact" and not to confuse the "just demands of the broadest mass of the people" with the conspiratorial activities of "an extremely small number of reactionary elements." The statement concluded with a warning against "big power chauvinism," which "inevitably results in serious damage to the solidarity and common cause of the socialist countries." Later that month, Chinese comment on the Soviet-

Polish talks in Moscow made the same point. Although big power and small power chauvinism were both dangers, "the main thing" was to avoid the former.[42]

In late November and early December, the Russians began openly, if indirectly, to criticize Polish policy through leaders of two of the satellites which most feared liberalization: Czechoslovakia and East Germany. On November 27 the editor of the East German paper *Neues deutschland* attacked the Polish press, and on December 5 Czech First Secretary Novotny attacked Polish agricultural policy.[43] Both statements were rebroadcast by the Russians, but ignored by Peking.

Peking Takes Middle Ground in the Soviet-Yugoslav Debate

The summer and fall of 1956 had witnessed a steady cooling off in the Soviet-Yugoslav *rapprochement*. On November 11, Tito, speaking at Pula, warned that the Soviet leaders had not drawn the proper conclusions from the Hungarian revolution and in effect demanded a "democratization" of the Communist Bloc.[44] On November 23 a *Pravda* editorial rebutted the Pula speech. At the same time, Soviet media played up Yugoslav National Day on November 29, reaffirming Soviet-Yugoslav solidarity and their ability to settle differences amicably. The anniversary was given unprecedented publicity for a non-decennial year. The Russians would have none of Tito's ideological program, implicit in which was a challenge to Soviet hegemony in the Communist world, but they nevertheless wanted to continue good state relations.

On December 11 Peking entered the Soviet-Yugoslav debate for the first time by releasing a 4,000-word summary of the main issues in the controversy. The summary included the core of Tito's Pula speech and some supporting statements from foreign Communist leaders including Togliatti, the principal advocate of polycentrism. At the same time, it recapitulated *Pravda's* rejoinder and some echoing statements by satellite spokesmen, but offered no comment. On December 12 the entire Peking press published the text of Tito's Pula speech, previously published in full only in Poland and Hungary. On December 13 the Peking papers carried the full text of *Pravda's* rebuttal.

This pose of "objectivity" should not be confused with sympathy for Tito. There had been a marked coolness in the relations between Peking and Belgrade for many years. Since the beginning of Khrushchev's *rapprochement* with Tito in 1955, Peking had been unenthusiastic. Tito's 1956 visit to Moscow had drawn more than 1,000 commentaries from the Moscow radio but only 37 from the Peking radio. On Yugoslav National Day in 1956, an occasion blown up by Moscow as a vehicle for emphasizing Soviet-Yugoslav friendship, Peking marked the event in two commentaries and in meager NCNA reportage on a Yugoslav Embassy reception attended neither by Mao nor by Liu Shao-ch'i.

Behind Peking's objective pose lay an avowed belief that "contradictions" were inevitable in the socialist world and that the only way to get rid of them was not to suppress them but to undertake a genuine exchange of views.

Perhaps the best illustration of the Chinese formula for overcoming socialist disunity was contained in a 15,000-word statement of December 29.[45] For the first time, Mao extended his theory of "non-antagonistic contradictions" to include the inevitability of such "contradictions" between socialist countries and even between Communist parties. Such contradictions, however, were "not basic"; they were not a "fundamental clash of interests . . . but conflicts between right and wrong opinions. . . . " They were contradictions whose solution must "first and foremost be subordinated to the overall interests of the struggle against the enemy." As to Tito's Pula speech, which Peking now commented on for the first time, it contained some correct statements, but the Yugoslav comrades were "going too far." Even "if some part of their criticism of fraternal parties is reasonable, the basic stand and method they adopt infringes upon the principles of comradely discussion." The statement went on to seek to draw the limits of tolerable diversity from Soviet experience and Soviet leadership.

What the *Jen-min jih-pao* statement of December 29 seemed to be suggesting was, first, that domestic variations from Soviet experience were permissible if they did not depart from the "fundamentals" of Soviet experience. These fundamentals were: (1) a Communist party taking Marxism-Leninism as its guide to action; (2) seizure of power by the proletariat from the bourgeoisie by means of revolutionary struggle; (3) a post-revolution dictatorship of the proletariat which nationalizes industry and carries out a step-by-step collectivization of agriculture; (4) a planned development of socialist economy; (5) firm adherence by the state to the principles of proletarian internationalism. These derivatives of Soviet experience, said the Chinese, were of "fundamental" and "universal" significance. The "other part"—i.e., whatever Soviet experience is not included above—"is not of universal significance." It was in this sense that each country had "its own specific path of development." Indeed, the universal truth of Marxism-Leninism manifested itself "only through the medium of specific national characteristics."[46]

A mere glance at the above list of "fundamentals" indicates how general they are and what a large and important sphere is left open to the influence of "national characteristics." What is essential is that a Communist party controls state power, allies itself to the Bloc, and conducts a program of nationalization of industry and collectivization of agriculture. What is not essential is that the methods and pace of the program be everywhere the same or that they be modeled on the practices in the USSR. In short, there was considerable scope in the Chinese formula for domestic variation from Soviet experience within an overall framework of Communist power and common ideological orientation.

The second major point, so far as permissible diversity was concerned, was that there could be less diversity on international than on domestic matters. Independent foreign policies could not be tolerated, and intra-bloc differences must always be subordinated to the struggle against imperialism. Peking would defend Gomulka's right to pursue a slow road to collectivization and to compromise with the Polish church, but would not tolerate neutralism in the struggle with the West. While all Communist parties should be treated as genuine and not merely nominal equals, this equality was in a "framework of international union." In the interests of the common cause, it was necessary to strengthen international solidarity in the Communist Bloc "with the Soviet Union at its center." The imperialists were trying "in a thousand and one ways" to make use of "narrow nationalist sentiments" in order to wreck this solidarity. The "class struggle on a world scale" must limit all internecine quarrels and differences over national variation and intra-bloc relations.[47]

Even when it had said all this, Peking seemed willing to be

more permissive than Moscow concerning the limits of foreign policy diversity. In late 1956, the question of American aid to Poland loomed large. According to the *New York Times* correspondent in Warsaw, Gomulka was treading cautiously on the matter of aid at that time so as not to stir up Russian fears,[48] which presumably had been expressed during Gomulka's trip to Moscow in November. Yet no Chinese statements then warned of the dangers of U.S. aid, as they were to do a year later in the onslaught against Tito. It seems likely that at this time the Chinese were willing to gamble with the consequences of a socialist state taking aid from the "imperialists," while the Russians were not. Thus, even the Chinese formula for restoring the authority of the Bloc's center offered some scope for international differences—so long as these differences did not involve an erosion of the common front against the West. In defining the outer limits of this common front, Peking was evidently willing to take greater risks than the Russians.

Chou En-lai as Mediator

In early 1957, Chinese Communist Premier Chou En-lai visited the Soviet Union, Poland, and Hungary. His purpose was clearly to restore some of the badly shattered unity of the Communist world. In all his speeches in Moscow, Budapest, and Warsaw, his overriding theme was that in the past there had indeed been "mistakes" in the mutual relations between Bloc countries, that these mistakes "should be corrected," but that "the fraternal relations of mutual assistance and cooperation between the socialist countries are incontestably of greater importance."[49] Everywhere he applauded the Soviet Government statement of October 30, 1956, as a harbinger of Soviet "determination to eliminate certain abnormal features that existed in its relations with other socialist states."[50] All problems between socialist countries could be solved "through amicable consultation."[51] Back in Peking, he stated the Chinese formula concisely: differences were to be expected; they should be resolved through "comradely discussion and consultation"; if they could not be, they should be minimized and the solidarity of the camp upheld.[52]

Chou's formula continued to sanction domestic diversity but, in accord with the December 1956 CCP article, stressed the importance of not letting quarrels over diversity obscure the more important battle against the West. Above all, the situation could not be allowed to deteriorate to a point where a Communist country such as Hungary might desire to leave the Communist Bloc. Diversity had to be stopped at the point where it threatened Bloc disunity or created opportunities for the West. It was for this reason that Chou En-lai, throughout his tour of Poland and Hungary, continually appealed for recognition of Soviet leadership of the Bloc, while at the same time he may have privately assured Kadar and Gomulka that China would oppose undue Soviet interference in Hungarian and Polish internal affairs.

The Chinese Formula: A Confederative Approach to Unity[53]

The moderate Chinese Communist position in 1956 on intra-bloc relations was motivated by several considerations. First and foremost, the Chinese feared a disruption of international Communist unity. This unity had been seriously impaired by Khrushchev's secret speech to the 20th CPSU Congress and by the Hungarian and Polish developments in the fall of 1956. A tidal wave of centrifugal forces threatened the monolithic unity of the Communist world. Peking's primary goal was to restore unity, but to restore it on terms which could provide a realistic framework for the maintenance of genuine as opposed to nominal unity.

As one student of these events has put it,[54] Peking sought what might be called a flexible, confederative approach to Bloc relations, as contrasted with the unitary approach insisted upon by Moscow. This confederative approach implied that there should be limits to Soviet prerogatives vis-à-vis other Bloc countries; that deviations from the Soviet model of socialist construction were not necessarily harmful; that honest differences of view should be settled by genuine and frank discussion through intra-party channels and not in public; and, above all, that such honest differences, which inevitably arise, must be subordinated to the overriding common goals of all concerned—particularly to the struggle with the West.

The reasons for Peking's interest in restoring the authority of the center are evident. The main one concerned China's strategic security. Chinese comment on the Hungarian revolution demonstrated a very urgent concern about any weakening of the Warsaw

Treaty alliance or the collective security of the Bloc. If the alliance faltered, there would be a real danger that "the countries in the camp of socialism will . . . be picked off one by one by the forces of Western imperialism. . . . " The unity of the socialist countries in Europe was "the most powerful guarantee of world peace as a whole."[55] Along the same lines, the important Chinese Communist theoretical journal, *Hsueh-hsi* wrote: "The aggressive forces of imperialism . . . are not afraid of one Poland, one Hungary, or one China. What they fear is the unity of the socialist countries headed by the Soviet Union."[56]

Second, China's economic development could be seriously impaired by the dislocations produced in Eastern Europe. In fact, this appears to have happened. The assistance to Poland and Hungary given by the Soviet Union in 1957 seems to have adversely affected its ability to supply China with badly needed capital goods.

Third, the Chinese leadership undoubtedly believed that the Russians, in making their radical break with Stalinism, had gone too far too fast. If Russian leadership was inadequate, as it must plainly have seemed from Peking, it was necessary for Mao to step in and fill the vacuum. At the same time, Mao must have been delighted to have an opportunity to increase his prestige and influence in Eastern Europe.

Finally, alongside all China's devout protestations about unity with the socialist camp and the Soviet Union, there had been— ever since the Chinese Communists came to power—recurrent indications of fear of excessive Soviet intervention in China's internal affairs. A comparison of the principal Russian and Chinese writings on the Stalin-Tito break of 1948 shows a reluctance on the part of Peking to accept Stalin's accusation against Tito of "revising Marxist-Leninist teachings."[57] The focus of the Chinese attack on Tito was that he adopted an "anti-Soviet position," not that he sought to revise Marxism-Leninism. The importance of this distinction is apparent. Mao did not wish to put himself into the position of conceding that anyone who disagreed with Stalin was a heretic. A fine line had to be drawn between anti-Sovietism and heresy, for already Peking must have been concerned about the day when Stalin or his successors might accuse the Chinese of revising Marxism-Leninism.

In sum, then, the Chinese had a very real stake in the battle between the centralists and the autonomists. On the one hand, they did not want to let the autonomists get out of hand and damage Bloc unity on which Peking so vitally depended; on the other hand, they did not want the centralists to be able to suppress domestic adaptations of Soviet experience. If Belgrade and Warsaw were now on the Soviet list for Soviet chastisement, Peking could be next.

The East European autonomists were well aware of the Chinese dilemma and sought throughout 1956–1957 to play off Peking against Moscow. Moreover, Khrushchev himself recognized Chinese sensitivity on this score. On July 11, 1957, he told a Czechoslovak audience that the idea of building socialism in accord with national peculiarities applied to all socialist countries and "especially to China."[58] On July 12, *Pravda* even agreed that Mao's speech about "contradictions," published in June, contained several tenets of "general" significance for Marxist-Leninist theory, a reaction in marked contrast to the coolness with which Moscow had first received Peking's theory of "contradictions." This Soviet deference to Chinese "creativity" was, to be sure, not unprecedented. In September 1956, Mikoyan had in fact made some of the strongest statements ever made by any Soviet leader in support of the Chinese right to build socialism in their own way. At the same time, he called for common approaches to the "most important" things.[59] Soviet deference was thus not without its limit. Indeed, the oscillations in the Soviet line on this question have been a useful barometer of the state of relations between Peking and Moscow.

The Winds of Change

As late as April 1957 there was evidence of Peking's continued efforts to secure a confederative approach to Bloc unity. An April 11 joint communiqué signed by a Polish Government delegation and the CPR,[60] after a visit to Peking by Polish Premier Cyrankiewicz, refrained from singling out the Soviet Union as the leader of the socialist camp—a departure from Chinese practice which was clearly in deference to Polish wishes. At the same time, Peking media, in praising the joint accord, made little reference to the dangers of revisionism.[61] One may conclude from this that as of April 1957 there had been no basic change in the Chinese Communist approach to the problems of camp unity preoccupying the Bloc since early 1956. Suddenly there was such a change. Whether it can be dated to the summer or early fall of 1957 is problematic. What is certain is that by November 1957 the Chinese dialectical pendulum had swung 180 degrees. Overnight, the CCP deserted the Poles and became the staunchest foe within the Bloc not of "dogmatism" but of revisionism.

The major clue to this switch came in the summer, when Mao abruptly called off his scheduled visit to Warsaw.

What had transpired in the summer of 1957 that could account for this sudden change in Chinese policy? If we are to understand the Sino-Soviet conflict as it subsequently developed, we must investigate this period.

CHAPTER 2

THE PEKING PENDULUM SWINGS TO THE LEFT: JUNE–NOVEMBER 1957[1]

THE period between June and November 1957 was one of the most fateful and obscure periods in recent Chinese Communist history. Sometime within those six months, Chinese Communist domestic and external policy underwent a radical transformation from Right to Left.[2] From the defenders of Gomulka and the advocates of a confederative approach to Bloc unity, the Chinese Communists became by November 1957 the most vigorous opponents of Right-wing "revisionism" and the leading advocates of a strict centralist approach to Bloc unity. Their cautious domestic program, based on the Soviet model, was scrapped and in its place there appeared the early outlines of a distinctively Chinese economic and social model, which was to be based on ideological as well as material incentives, mass movements more than rationalization and regularization of work processes, "native" as well as modern techniques, small and medium as well as large-scale industrial plants, speed more than balance, and intense application of labor more than of capital to industry. By September, when the CCP Central Committee met in plenary session, it was apparent that these and other major changes in domestic economic policy had been decided upon. These changes were the early outlines of a program that would by 1958 embody the bold "leap forward" and the communes. On the foreign policy front there was also a radical swing to the Left in CCP thinking. By November 1957 it was apparent that the Chinese Communists were considering abandoning the cautious, consolidating, Bandung-spirit, Right strategy, in effect since 1954, and that they were laying the groundwork for a forward surge.

The beginning of the swing to the Left can be dated to mid-June. At that time, the "blooming and contending" period, in which the Communist rulers invited their subjects to criticize the regime, came to an abrupt halt. The period of a "hundred flowers" —Mao's phrase—had lasted but a scant six weeks. Undoubtedly Mao and the Party were astonished by the forceful and bitter attacks on Party policies from all segments of the population.

66

These were suggestions for an abolition of one-party rule and its replacement by a coalition government representing all democratic parties; the journalists complained about lack of freedom of the press; scholars argued that Marxism as the guiding ideology was bound to become static and that no doctrine could embody the whole truth; students declared that society was in a "mess" and that another "revolution" was necessary, and they organized demonstrations on the streets and raised what was subsequently described as an "anti-Party storm"; writers and artists appealed for creative freedom; in some provinces, there were wholesale defections of the peasants from collective farms; trade union leaders sought to assert a policy independent of the Party and there developed what the regime called a "crisis" in trade union work.[3]

The "hundred flowers" period must have been a traumatic experience for Mao. It is very unlikely that he had set a trap for his dissident subjects—as is maintained by some students of Communist affairs. It is much more likely that the Chinese leader was the victim of his own ideas and illusions. For years he had carefully fostered the idea that the Communist Party represented the broad interests of the Chinese masses, and that it was a genuinely popular party. He studiously avoided describing Communist China as a "proletarian dictatorship" and called it instead a "people's democracy." This ideological deviation from Moscow was of great psychological and ideological importance. It reflected Mao's belief that the ostensible representation of non-Communist parties in the Government was an expression of genuine unity between Chinese Communists and non-Communists. Mao probably believed that he could be a benevolent dictator, that he could avoid Stalin's mistakes, and that he could ameliorate the conflict between rulers and ruled.[4]

But traumatic as the "blooming and contending" period may have been for Communist China's rulers, it was not in itself sufficient to cause their wholesale revamping of domestic and foreign policy. That was brought about as well by the domestic economic crisis which, by early fall, was being attacked through radical economic policies designed to retrieve a desperate situation. The economic situation in the summer of 1957 was bleak. There were appeals to coal miners to give up some of their Chinese New Year holiday in order to ensure that factories, railways, and ships might not have to cease operation. There were reports of cutbacks in development plans all along the line, and of cuts in the cloth and pork rations. There were also reports of national calamities.[5] Most serious of all, collectivization had failed to produce the expected agricultural expansion. For a nation still overwhelmingly agrarian, such shortfalls in food production must have caused considerable concern.

Several key statements by China's economic planners during this period indicated that the CCP was not expecting much assistance from the Soviet Union in resolving the economic dilemma. Already in May, Li Fu-ch'un had warned: "We should rely on our own strength as far as possible."[6] Po I-po told the National People's Congress in June that China must reduce her "reliance upon foreign countries."[7] Plans to develop medium and small as well as large-scale enterprises, later to become the hallmark of the commune program and "leap forward," were justified in terms of reducing China's dependence upon Soviet exports.

The economic crisis had to be faced without massive Soviet aid. But what, then, was the solution? It seems apparent in retrospect that the Chinese Communist Party divided roughly into two opposed schools of thought at the time. The Left wing of the Party, which gained the ascendancy in the summer and fall of 1957 after the dramatic failure of the hundred flowers experiment, advocated a breakneck pace of economic development as the "only way out." It believed that "objective" difficulties could be overcome by exhortation and ideological fervor, that—as Liu Shao-ch'i was to say in 1958—Marxism could produce grain and steel.[8] It believed that speed and balance were not incompatible and that, even if they were, speed was more important in the short run.[9] It was this wing of the Party which conceived the "great leap forward" and the communes. It had an almost mystical faith in the power of the masses if properly mobilized. It believed that China could actually pull itself up by its own bootstraps if proper policies were adopted. If, as it believed, the Soviet model on which China's first Five Year Plan had been based had proved inadequate for China's distinctive problems, then the Soviet model must be scrapped and replaced by one which maximized the one resource that China had in abundance—labor power.

The Right wing of the Party stood for a "reasonable," sound, and balanced approach to economic development. Its watchwords were regularization, rationalization, planning, and balance. It had a pragmatic outlook based on an awareness of objective limitations, on the importance of incentives in increasing production, and on the danger of speed at the cost of balance. As was to be revealed later, it opposed the great leap forward and the communes as premature. While recognizing that China's first Five-Year Plan had proved inadequate for China's distinctive problems, and that the situation was critical, it believed that the solution lay not in massive mobilization of labor power and the arousing of ideological fervor, but in a limited decentralization of the economy and a partial restoration of the free market. It sought to borrow experience from wherever it could, including the West, in order to meet China's problems. Reflections of the Right's thinking were to appear in November, after the Left had gained the ascendancy and begun to attack its views. Thus, on November 3, the journal *Hsueh-hsi* railed against "certain people" who denied the importance of Soviet experience, wanted to "learn from all," and believed there should be "free competition and fluctuation of prices." The journal denounced such views as "preposterous"; it said they would "obliterate the basic differences between socialist and capitalist economy."[10] Making necessary allowance for the exaggeration and distortion of a defeated view, we can infer that the Right advocated some type of New Economic Policy (NEP) for China, which would have involved the same kind of massive retreat undertaken in similar adverse circumstances by the Soviet Union in 1921. Such a retreat would probably have been marked, as it was in the USSR, by temporary concessions to private traders and by a temporary restoration of "capitalism" in certain spheres of activity.

The battle between the Left and Right approaches to economic construction was probably decided sometime between June, when the pragmatists were still in control, and September, when outlines of the Left economic policy were becoming visible.[11] Liu Shao-ch'i admitted as much when he said to the CCP Congress in May 1958 that there had been a struggle between "two ways of carrying on socialist transformation and construction"—one which would do it "faster and better," and another "slowly and not so well"—and that this "struggle" was "not fully decided" until the launching of the anti-Rightist campaign, i.e., the summer of 1957.[12]

The chief spokesmen of the "go slow" school to which Liu refers have been identified by MacFarquhar as Chou En-lai, Deputy Premier Ch'en Yi, and most of the top economic planners. These last would include Li Fu-ch'un (Chairman of the State Planning Commission), Li Hsien-nien (Minister of Finance), and Po I-po (Chairman of the State Economic Commission).[13] The chief spokesmen of the Left would seem to have been Liu Shao-ch'i and Teng Hsiao-p'ing, the rapidly rising Party secretary. The role of Mao is something of an enigma. It is most likely that he was and remains the adjudicator between the two opposing schools; that, like Stalin, he plays one off against the other; and that in times when he decides on a policy of revolutionary upsurge he calls on the Left to lead it, while in periods of revolutionary retreat and consolidation he calls on the Right. Until a thorough and detailed study of the Chinese leadership is undertaken, however, this hypothesis must be cautiously advanced.[14]

At the National People's Congress in June 1957, there was evidence that the Right was still in control. Chou En-lai announced that capital investment in 1957 would be 20 per cent less than in 1956 and that budgetary expenditure would be cut by 4 per cent.[15]

The period between June and September was one of frantic juggling between the two schools. By September, the ascendancy of the Left wing was clear. The best evidence for this was the revival at the Central Committee plenum in that month of the twelve-year agricultural program which had been implicitly disparaged by Chou En-lai a year earlier at the Party Congress. Chou had said there was a tendency on the part of officials to try to do everything at once, ignoring actual conditions and "recklessly running ahead." He added pointedly: "Such a tendency recurred at the beginning of 1956 following the publication of the Draft Program for Agricultural Development. . . . "[16] This agricultural program was now significantly revived by T'an Chen-lin, who in 1958 was to become the regime's chief spokesman on argicultural policy and the communes.[17] Further evidence of an intra-party dispute over the program was Liu Shao-ch'i's specific criticism in May 1958 of those who had "misgivings" about it.[18]

The revival of the twelve-year agricultural program, is not the only evidence that the Left emerged triumphant from the September 1957 plenum. Another indication was that, after the plenum, the CCP press began to indicate that the policy of material incentives would now be supplemented with "ideological incentives." *Jen-min jih-pao* wrote, for instance, that: "In our wage policy in the past . . . we have also overemphasized the importance of material incentives, while inadvisably relaxing our political and ideological work among the workers and employees."[19] It was but a minor step from such a position to the assault on material incentives in the hectic autumn of 1958.

A still further indication of a Left victory was the stress by Chinese journals following the plenum on the abundant labor supply in the countryside. Thus the Chinese leaders were already thinking of the basic premise of the commune: that proper organization and mobilization of labor was the remedy for badly lagging agricultural development. By December 1957, the triumph of the Left economic policy was announced in a *Jen-min jih-pao* editorial which said. "We have to hasten the tempo of construction by adopting a policy of industry and thrift in order *to move it forward with gigantic and rapid strides. No other paths are open*" [italics supplied].[20]

In sum, throughout the summer and early fall of 1957, there appears to have been a struggle between two opposing schools of thought within the Chinese Communist Party. These schools had existed for some time. One was a pragmatic, conservative group dominated by "realistic" economic planners. The other, led by Liu Shao-ch'i, believed that it was necessary and feasible to build socialism at a rapid pace. What brought the latent struggle between the two wings of the Party into the open was a combination of crises, the usual cause of Communist intra-party conflict. First there was the crisis of the "hundred flowers," which could easily have been employed by the Left as a weapon against the Right for being too tolerant of "bourgeois remnants." Although the Left probably avoided direct attacks on Mao, it may have sought to convince him that he had been misled by Rightist views. The second and probably more decisive crisis was economic. The regime believed that, in order to overcome the serious problems it faced, it had the choice of radical retreat or radical advance. The Left-wing solution of a radical advance won the day.

What did all this mean for Chinese intra-bloc and foreign policy? Can the Left-Right struggle over domestic economic policy be projected into the international arena? Was the Right advocating caution against the desire of the Left to undertake a radical revision of China's foreign policy? It must be said immediately that there is little empirical evidence to support such a view. Once the Left gained the ascendancy, there was persistent criticism of Right-wing economic views but virtually no criticism of Right-wing views on foreign policy. It is therefore possible that the intra-party dispute was confined to domestic policy.

On the other hand, it is difficult to believe that, in the worldview of the Chinese Left, there is not an intimate connection between solutions for domestic and foreign problems. In 1959, the slogan of the Left was "permanent revolution" both on the domestic and foreign fronts. Moreover, an abrupt shift to the Left in intrabloc and foreign policy occurred in November 1957. (We shall discuss these changes in subsequent chapters.) It seems unlikely that it was a mere coincidence that the shift to a centralist intrabloc policy and a bold foreign strategy occurred almost at the same time as the Left became the dominant voice in the Party and adopted a bold new domestic policy. It is of course possible that changes in CCP external policy would have occurred no matter who was in power in Peking and no matter what the domestic solution turned out to be. But if the Right economic strategy had prevailed at home, and if Rightist leaders had remained in the ascendancy, it seems more than likely that the change in external policies would not have been so abrupt.

This is not to say that there is a direct relationship between Communist domestic and external policies under all conditions. There have certainly been periods in Communist history when a Left-wing domestic policy was pursued alongside a Right-wing external policy. But radical convulsions at home are generally reflected in policy abroad. There is in fact an interesting comparison between developments in China in the summer and early fall of 1957 and those in the Soviet Union in 1928. At that time, the Russians forced the pace of industrialization and launched collectivization against the background of an internal factional dispute. Simultaneously, they undertook a Left swing in foreign policy which was to last until 1934.

It is not that the Communists deliberately create foreign policy crises in order to conceal domestic difficulties, but rather that the dynamics of Communism are such that internal convulsions accompanied by factional disputes are likely to be reflected in the foreign policy arena. Thus, paradoxical as it might seem, Peking's abrupt shift to Left-wing internal policies coincided with the end of the Sino-Soviet dialogue that had begun in 1956, and the beginning of a new one. It ended the 1956 dialogue because the CCP was no longer championing in late 1957—as it was in 1956 and early 1957—the cause of the East European autonomists. In November, indeed, the Chinese were to desert Gomulka abruptly, and to startle much of the Communist world by asserting the need for unqualified loyalty to Soviet leadership. The shift began a new dialogue which resulted from the fact that Peking, beginning in the fall of 1957, sought to push Soviet intra-bloc policy to the Left, that is, to make it less tolerant of regimes that were Rightist in domestic policy or inclined to seek independent ties with the West; in 1956, on the other hand, Peking had sought to push intra-bloc policy to the Right, that is, to make it more tolerant of Rightist regimes. Added to this variation on an old theme were two new and critical issues. One, which we shall consider in the next chapter, was the question of a distinctive Chinese path to socialism-Communism. In 1958 this particular dialogue would center on the Chinese "leap forward" and the communes. The other was the question of global strategy, which we shall consider in detail at a later stage.

In all three areas, the essence of the conflict was that Peking wished to pursue a bolder or more forward strategy than the one advocated or deemed advisable by the Russians. This was more than a question of divergent evaluations of opportunity and risk, and it is not sufficient to explain it merely on the basis of the ascendancy of the Left wing of the CCP. What it demonstrated was that the power imperatives of the Chinese Communists may frequently differ from those of the Russians.

In 1956 and early 1957, a "liberal" intra-bloc policy was a corollary of China's "liberal" domestic policy and conservative foreign policy. In the fall of 1957 and in 1958, a "tough" intra-bloc policy was the corollary of her domestic convulsion and of her growing desire to achieve some of her long-denied foreign policy goals. Conversely, in the former period, the Soviet leadership was divided and was unable to experiment with a policy of great tolerance toward the East European regimes, especially since these were at times emboldened to oppose Moscow's authority. In the latter period, the USSR had already stabilized its leadership, the situation in Eastern Europe itself was stabilized, and so the Russians were better able to tolerate Rightist policies which they now were confident they could prevent from getting out of control.

The earliest element in the new phase of Sino-Soviet conflict was the dispute over the communes and the distinctive Chinese path to Communism. It is to this that we now turn.

PART TWO

THE DISPUTE OVER COMMUNES:
1958–1960

"The speed of construction has been the most important question confronting us since the victory of the socialist revolution. The aim of our revolution is to expand the social productive forces as quickly as possible. . . . Karl Marx prophesied that the proletarian revolution would usher us into a great epoch when '20 years are concentrated in a day.' If in past revolutionary struggles we experienced such great times, then is not our present socialist construction another great time again?"

—Liu Shao-ch'i's report to the 8th CCP Congress, May 5, 1958[1]

"The revolutionary spirit signifies not only the desire to go ahead, but also a sober assessment of the opportunities, both objective and subjective. If everything depended solely on the wishes of the Communists and on their revolutionary zeal, then, of course, Communist ideals would have been realized long ago. But in addition to wishes there are such objective factors as, say, the inadequate level of the productive forces, of the consciousness of the masses, and the existence of elements who resist the new and progressive. Consequently, the Party is merciless to 'revolutionary' phraseology or adventurism, substituted for the genuinely revolutionary spirit, as well as to applying measures for which the time is not yet ripe. . . . One can imagine the difficulties that would have arisen if the CPSU had followed this wishful thinking, if it had acted rashly and had not taken cognizance of the real state of affairs."

—Problems of Peace and Socialism, April, 1959[2]

. "The purpose of building socialism is to prepare actively for the transition to Communism. It seems that the attainment of Communism in China is no longer a remote future event."

—Chinese commune resolution, August 29, 1958[3]

CHAPTER 3

THE DISPUTE OVER COMMUNES AND
THE ROAD TO COMMUNISM

"The claims of the contemporary 'Left-wingers' in the international Communist movement that when you have power in your hands, Communism can be introduced immediately, bypassing definite historical stages of development, are wrong. Such claims contradict Leninism. Lenin taught that to try to anticipate in practice the coming results of a fully developed, fully consolidated and constituted, fully grown and matured Communism is the same thing as trying to teach mathematics to a four-year-old."—*Pravda,* June 12, 1960

THE conflict over the communes and the "transition to Communism" cannot be viewed as a marginal element of the overall Sino-Soviet conflict. Nor can it be viewed merely as an added irritant that intensified growing strains in the alliance only in conjunction with "real" problems (e.g., China's desire for a nuclear capability and its demands on Taiwan). To minimize the importance of the dispute over the communes is to miss some of the basic factors producing conflict.

The commune controversy was and is a contest over power, over economics, over the pace of domestic revolutionary advance, and over basic ideology. It is a contest for power because the Chinese Communist Party has strongly suggested that Mao has solved the problem of building Communism in an underdeveloped country with a large peasant population and that this solution is valid for all underdeveloped countries. For the Russians to concede this would be tantamount to conceding to Peking the leadership of the revolution in Asia, Africa, and Latin America.

The commune controversy is a contest over economics because the Chinese "general line"—of which the commune and the "leap foward" are component parts—is based on an economic conception radically different from that governing the Soviet Five Year Plans, and indeed China's first Five Year Plan.

Introduced in 1958, this "general line" stresses the intensive application of labor as well as capital to economic development; small and medium-sized as well as large-sized industrial enterprises; "native" or "traditional" techniques as well as modern technology; and the overriding importance of subjective factors such as "Communist spirit" as compared with material incentives. It represents a carefully considered conclusion by the Chinese that their economic problems cannot be solved by following the Soviet model, that China in fact has to develop a new and unique model for socialist and Communist construction. It stands thus as a challenge to basic Soviet economic planning.

The commune dispute is, thirdly, a contest over the pace of domestic revolutionary advance. The Chinese believe that the Soviet road to the ultimate Communist society is unnecessarily long and tortuous and that there is real danger of losing momentum and ideological fervor along the way. They hope, via the communes, to speed the transition to Communism and, coordinately, to sustain popular enthusiasm.

Finally, the dispute is one of basically different ideological perspectives. Adapting general Marxist-Leninist principles on the construction of a Communist society to the specific framework of Chinese society, Mao has produced a Chinese variant of Marxism-Leninism. By 1960, Chinese journals were once again, as in 1949–1951, claiming that Mao had "sinified" Marxism-Leninism. This contention is true. What is now referred to in the Chinese press as "the Mao Tse-tung ideology" is a peculiar blend of Marxism, Stalinism, Trotskyism, and pragmatism, based on a number of conditioning social and economic factors never or no longer relevant in the Soviet Union. It would not be going too far to say that Mao and Khrushchev no longer look at their own worlds, much less the outside world, through the same Marxist-Leninist spectacles.

Among the issues involved in the conflict over the communes and the road to Communism, some are obviously more important than others. Are the Russians more concerned, for instance, about the Chinese ideological challenge than they are about their differing economic strategy? How important is the power factor? What are the Chinese really after? This section seeks to provide the basis for answering such questions. It analyzes the Sino-Soviet polemic over the Chinese communes since its development in 1958, along with related political and ideological questions; it reviews Soviet theory on the "transition to Communism," and thus seeks to clarify the extent of the Chinese revision in 1958; and it briefly reviews the early Soviet experience with agricultural communes as a guide to Soviet thinking today.

The Revival of Permanent Revolution

If one were to search for the best single guide to Chinese Communist ideology and practice in the turbulent period since late 1957, the period when the Sino-Soviet conflict began to blossom, it could be found in the Maoist theory of "permanent revolution."[4] It is not accidental that Khrushchev, in the fall of 1959, obliquely compared Mao to Trotsky. Several Western analysts too have insisted on seeing in Maoist theory a revival of Trotskyism. The question, however, is not what Maoism has in common with Trotskyism or what Mao's theory of "permanent revolution" has in common with Trotsky's.[5] It is rather what is the meaning given to Mao's theory by the Chinese: that is, what is its precise political and philosophical connotation, what is the peculiar Chinese reality that it reflects, how does Mao's use of the term "permanent revolution" differ from the orthodox Soviet usage, and why has Mao's development of a new theory connected with this term, never acknowledged by the Russians, been so obnoxious to Moscow.[6]

As employed by Chinese spokesmen and theoreticians since early 1958, when it was first introduced, the concept has three applications. Two of these concern Chinese revolutionary strategy in non-Communist countries and will be treated in that context. What we will take up here is the application of the theory to the process of socialist and Communist construction in a country already ruled by a Communist Party.[7]

In this area, the Chinese usage of the term is unique. Neither Marx nor Lenin nor Trotsky nor Stalin ever used the term to describe the domestic revolutionary process that would take place *after* the Communists had seized power. For all of them, the term denoted a concept associated with the revolutionary process in a given country *before* the Communists took power.

The first use of the term by a Chinese Communist Party leader to characterize Peking's own domestic revolutionary process was made by Liu Shao-ch'i in his extremely important report to the second session of the 8th Party Congress in May 1958. In Liu's brief remarks on the subject, the operative idea was that "uninterrupted revolution" meant that there could be no "halfway halt" in the advance toward Communism: "Marx, Engels, and Lenin often pointed out that the watchword of the working class should be 'uninterrupted revolution.' In putting forward new revolutionary tasks in good time, so that there is no halfway halt in the revolutionary advance of the people, the revolutionary fervour of the masses will not subside with interruptions of the revolution, and Party and state functionaries will not rest content with the success won and grow arrogant or apathetic, the Central Committee of the Communist Party and Comrade Mao Tse-tung have always guided the Chinese revolution by this Marxist-Leninist theory of uninterrupted revolution."[8]

As a guide to the considerations which prompted the sharp turn to the Left in Chinese domestic policies in late 1957 and early 1958, there is no better source than this speech by Liu to the Party Congress. In it he launched a violent attack on the Right wing of the Party, which wanted "to go slower rather than faster," which believed it was better to slow down the tempo, and which was pessimistic about China's economic revival. In this speech he mapped out the "general line" that has since guided the Party. The key to this general line was that it was geared to "build our country, *in the shortest possible time,* into a great socialist country" [italics supplied].[9]

In October 1958 a more extensive exposition of the Maoist variant of permanent revolution appeared in *Hsueh-hsi,* the theoretical journal now superseded by *Hung ch'i.* In this article, Mao's theory was presented as a "creative development" of the Marxist-Leninist theory of permanent revolution. It specifically indicated that Mao's theory had relevance for the entire revolutionary process from the "new democratic revolution" to Communism, and it was indirectly revealed that there were "some" who did not understand the relevance of the theory in a "socialist" society and who were "alarmed:"

"Chairman Mao did not restrict the application of this Marxist-Leninist theory of uninterrupted revolution to the one point of democratic revolution changing into socialist revolution but . . . fully extended the application of this theory in order to guide the complete revolutionary movement of our country, including the new democratic revolution, socialist revolution, socialist construction and the transition from socialism to Communism.

"There are some who ask in alarm: when you advocate uninterrupted revolution in a socialist society, what is the object of the revolution? *Actually, viewed from the standpoint of Marxists, the objects of revolution always are the production relations and the superstructure, which at the time are lagging behind the development of the productive forces and therefore interfering with the development of the productive forces.* . . . Marxists must not conceal contradictions and also must not shun revolution. . . . Whoever understands these general truths will not think it strange that it is still necessary to advocate uninterrupted revolution in a socialist society . . . " [italics supplied].[10]

This extremely significant passage was more than a rejection of gradualism in the advance toward Communism, a gradualism which, as we shall see, was essential to Soviet theory and practice. It also flew in the face of Stalin's dislike, particularly in his last years, for sharp breaks in economic and social development, a dislike that his heirs have clearly shared. And it suggested, quite heretically, that advances in the "superstructure" could take place without prior development of the productive base. In Soviet, as in Marxist thinking, social relations and social institutions reflect the level of development of the productive base. The superstructure cannot move faster than the base. Complete collectivization is impossible until the technical revolution in the countryside makes it feasible. Complete Communism is impossible until there is an abundance of material goods.

The principal reason for this Maoist ideological sleight of hand was the felt need of the Chinese leadership to introduce a radical institutional reform on a backward technological and productive base. There are, in this connection, interesting parallels with the Russia of 1928. During the first Five-Year Plan in Russia, as in China during the "great leap," a weak agricultural sector threatened to retard if not to stagnate industrialization. As Mao now called for "uninterrupted revolution," so Stalin in 1928 called for

81

revolution from above. As the Chinese were in 1958 inflating statistics and seeking to inculcate revolutionary zeal in the masses, so did the Russians in the early 1930's.

Indeed, not until 1950, after Russia had entered into a stage of self-sustaining economic growth, did Stalin rule out "sudden leaps" in the building of Communism and emphasize, not revolution, but consolidation. Precisely this emphasis, maintained by Stalin's successors, the Chinese found to be incompatible with their present stage of economic development. So, while the Russians accused them of trying to skip stages, the Chinese replied with equally good Marxist reasoning that the Russians were bringing the revolution to a premature standstill. Thus, in 1958, one Chinese writer said: "*According to some,* the victory of the proletariat and the advent of a socialist society mean the end of the social revolution, after which there will be all sorts of phenomena of crystallization, ranging from economic matters to the superstructure, and tendencies toward absoluteness, *all resulting in interference with the development, by leaps forward, of the forces of production*" [italics supplied].[11]

And in 1960, Lu Ting-yi, member of the CCP Politburo, criticized "a kind of theory" which holds that ". . . there is no need to develop the socialist system, but only to consolidate it, and even if it is to be developed, to go forward to Communism, still there is no need to undergo a struggle and to pass through a qualitative leap; and thus the process of the uninterrupted revolution of human society goes up to this point and no farther."[12]

It is difficult to avoid the impression from such polemics and counter-polemics that the nub of the matter is that while China is not yet at a stage of self-sustaining growth, the Soviet Union is. Thus, the Russians understandably think in terms of consolidating their own system while the Chinese are with equally good reason still trying radical institutional experiments.

The Maoist theory of permanent revolution cannot then, be explained outside the context of the frenetic pace of domestic social and economic change accompanying the great leap forward and the communes. But neither can it be explained wholly by that. And no ideological variant, least of all one by Mao, can be localized in the Communist world, given the symbiotic relationship between power and ideology and given Mao's unique position. Thus, once the Chinese became proselytizers as well as ideologues, the theory of permanent revolution came to represent a critical threat to the USSR. For one thing, it appeals to those numerous Communists throughout the world, particularly in the underdeveloped countries, who want to move faster. The Chinese capacity to endorse more radical policies and theories than those endorsed by Moscow has always been and will continue to be a primary source of leverage in the Communist world. For many of these Communists in underdeveloped areas, there is already a suspicion of the steady weakening in the Soviet Union of the revolutionary and ideological impulse and the steady growth of the impulse for security, welfare, and national interest. To them, Maoism, permanent revolution, and their own revolutionary aspirations have much in common.

A corollary of the theory of permanent revolution is that of "permanent contradictions," or the existence within society, from non-socialist to "socialist" to "Communist," of a never-ending series of internal contradictions. Mao had been fascinated with the concept of "contradictions" since the late 1930's, when he wrote his first work on the subject. Now, it found its place in the permanent revolution theory, which called for solution of social problems by unceasing struggle and experimentation.

For the Russians, who have been conspicuously silent about Mao's theory of permanent revolution, it is a heresy worse even than the communes. For, while the communes and the great leap can and have been discounted as products of peculiarly Chinese conditions, the concept of permanent revolution poses a fundamental philosophical challenge to the entire corpus of Soviet dogma on the "transition to Communism," which stresses gradualism and rules out sudden or qualitative leaps.

The Soviet View: Gradual Pace of the Transition to Communism

As early as 1950, Stalin presented a philosophical rationale for a gradualist approach to Communism. In his essay on linguistics,[13] he spelled out a theory of development for "socialist" societies that had the effect of sanctifying the concepts of "gradualness" and "evolution" in the development of these societies. Prior to 1950, Marxist theory had rested on the assumption that *any* transition from "quantitative" to "qualitative" changes of development implied a breach of continuity and took place by means of a leap.[14] Stalin's opus on linguistics differentiated between "explosions" (*vzryv,* literally an explosion or violent upheaval) and evolutionary changes in social development. He said that *only* in non-socialist societies (i.e., societies where Communist parties were not in power) did the transition from one stage of development to a higher stage take place by means of an "explosion." In Soviet or "socialist" society, change was produced by an accumulation of elements of the new quality and a dying-away of the old, not, as Party "textualists and Talmudists" thought, by quick leaps.

Again in 1952, in his essay on "Economic Problems of Socialism in the USSR," Stalin criticized those who wanted to move too fast toward Communism. It was necessary, he said, to prepare "a genuine, not a declarative transition to Communism." The statement is one Khrushchev might well have repeated to his Chinese allies six years later. For, Khrushchev like Stalin, has emphasized the gradualist approach to the building of Communism. At the 20th Congress of the CPSU in 1956, for example, he criticized "hotheads" and "dreamers" who "disregarded reality" and appealed "for more immediate realization of the principles of Communist society at the present stage."[15] His language strongly suggested that a high-level group within the Soviet Party wished to advance much faster toward the ultimate Communist goal than he deemed advisable. Pressures from this group, coupled with pressures from elsewhere in the Communist world, may in part have led Khrushchev in 1957 to announce that Communism was "no longer a remote goal" in the USSR.[16] The theses issued in connection with the 40th Anniversary of the October Revolution added that Communism was the "immediate practical aim" of the Soviet people, the first such statement in Soviet history.[17]

Despite these statements, there was little indication in 1958, on the eve of the Chinese commune program, that for the Soviet leaders the "transition to Communism" was much more than a final goal to which they periodically paid lip service. There was little discussion of Communism. There were no indications of impending moves to introduce free distribution of any of the principal goods and services, to move towards genuine equalitarianism in wage payments, or to introduce any of the classical goals held out by the founding fathers of Communism.

Origins of the Communes[18]

The Chinese Communist decision to launch the commune program in the summer and fall of 1958 concerned Sino-Soviet relations in several important ways. First, the communes were a radical institutional response to economic problems that by the fall of 1957 were acute and for which the Soviet model of development supplied no ready answers. The single most important of these problems was the rapidly growing population. There was also relative stagnation in food production, dwindling food reserves, and mounting disaffection among the peasantry and rural cadres.[19] These critical problems led the CCP to abandon the Soviet cooperative model and to choose a path to Communism radically different from the Soviet model. The new path, it was explicitly stated, would accord with the "special conditions" in China. These conditions, specified by Mao and others and explicitly distinguished from conditions in the USSR, were: a large territory, a large population coupled with a relatively small amount of arable land, a predominantly agrarian economy, and a low level of mechanization.[20] The basic decision in the novel Chinese Communist economic solution was the decision to utilize on an unprecedented scale the one resource abundant in China: its manpower. It was concluded that the key to China's agricultural development was the proper organization of labor power and that the key to industrial development was the expansion of labor-intensive rather than capital-intensive industry. This solution, it has been suggested, bore much greater similarity to Japanese than to Soviet precedent.[21]

The second important factor affecting Sino-Soviet relations was that the commune program—as we have seen—was conceived by the Left or radical wing of the CCP which, by the early fall of 1957, had gained the ascendancy. The Left wing had an almost mystical faith in the "masses," in "native" and traditional techniques, in improvised solutions, in the power of ideology to serve as incentive, in the possibilities of mass mobilization. The Right wing of the Party never subscribed to the communes, to the great leap forward, or to the entire general line introduced at the Party Congress in May 1958. This group preferred a slower and less radical approach to China's acute economic problems, an approach based on careful planning, on improving technology, and on utilizing wage incentives. While it evidently called for a Chinese NEP, at the same time it did not want to abandon so precipitately the tried and tested Soviet model of economic development, no matter what its shortcomings when superimposed on unique Chinese conditions.

The deep divisions within the CCP were conceded by Liu Shao-ch'i in his speech to the Party Congress in May 1958. They were to emerge in the open again in the fall of 1959 when the general line had demonstrated serious inadequacies and when the Left wing was consequently forced to take a defensive position. The importance of this division within the CCP for Sino-Soviet relations in the period from 1957–1961 cannot be exaggerated. The ideological and economic perspectives of the Russians were much closer to the Right than to the Left wing of the CCP. Thus the very fact that the Left had gained the ascendancy introduced into Sino-Soviet relations an element of discord that to this day has not been resolved. Moreover, the division within the CCP afforded the Russians a certain amount of leverage. Although we do not know to what extent, there seems little doubt that Moscow sought to influence the intra-party struggle on behalf of the Right.

The Sino-Soviet conflict in the years with which this study deals takes its form largely from the fact that the Left wing of the CCP has been in command since the fall of 1957.[22] This is not to say that no conflict would have occurred if the moderates or pragmatists in the CCP had been in control. It can certainly be argued that the dispute on global and intra-bloc strategy would have occurred in any event. In their international outlook, the Right and the Left wings of the CCP probably have more in common with each other than either has with the Soviet leadership. Yet there seems good reason to believe that, if the Right had been in control, the form and the scope of the Sino-Soviet conflict would have been considerably different. We shall return to this thesis throughout the discussion.

A third factor of outstanding importance when considering the communes in the light of Sino-Soviet relations is the lack of Soviet economic aid. In the fall of 1957 it probably seemed to the CCP Left wing that the only alternative to a radical institutional response to China's economic problems was a massive dose of Soviet aid. Yet it soon became apparent that such aid was not forthcoming. It is true that the USSR was the supplier of equipment and technical assistance which was indispensable to Chinese economic progress. But, as one economist who has studied the problem indicates, "it is in this sense—and only in this sense—that one can validly talk of Soviet assistance at all. China has had for years . . . no Soviet assistance in the ordinary sense of the word, i.e., in the sense of financial support. The same applies to the most recent arrangement which pledged the USSR to provide equipment by 1967 for about eighty additional industrial projects; they will have to be paid for in counter-supplies of Chinese commodities. There is some inexorable arithmetic which condemns the Soviet Union's financial aid to insufficiency."[23]

There is doubtless some validity in that school of thought among Western analysts which places heavy emphasis on China's unwillingness to mortgage itself to a Soviet aid program. The fact remains that there has been an apparent Soviet refusal to extend economic credits to Peking since 1954.[24] Moreover, in 1956–1957, when the CCP's agonizing reappraisal was taking place, the USSR was heavily committed to bailing out Eastern Europe from the effects of the Hungarian revolution. The Chinese had a pretext for telling the Russians that the radical departure from Soviet experience was a necessary corollary of insufficient Soviet help, and they probably did so.

The first step on the road toward the communes was taken in September 1957 at a CCP plenum which decided that an increase in agricultural productivity was indispensable to China's economic well-being. At about that time, the distinctive Chinese policy of "simultaneous development of industry and agriculture" was first announced. The plenum also evidently concluded that the key to agricultural development was the massive mobilization of labor power. Mao's speech to the plenum was never published, but shortly afterward Chinese journals began to emphasize the abundant labor force in the countryside and to call for an agricultural mechanization program adapted to the conditions of the country.[25] Immediately after the plenum, a peasant labor army of some 100 million was organized to undertake a gigantic program of water conservancy construction and fertilizer accumulation which would dwarf such previous efforts in the countryside.[26] The greatly augmented labor effort would have to be secured without material incentives, which were ruled out in order to maximize savings and investment for future growth.

The former British chargé in Peking recalls the first big program there involving mass mobilization techniques. It was some time in the winter of 1957; outside of Peking, the task was to construct the Ming Tombs reservoir: "The project was completed in rather over six months, by relays of workers, students, political leaders, and even distinguished visitors, coming out from Peking (about 25 miles away) and camping on the site. . . . Work was done almost entirely by hand, spade, and basket . . . it was rather as if 20,000 good-humored 'Supers' were let loose at the shooting of some Biblical film under the auspices of Cecil B. deMille. . . . As a spectacle and propaganda demonstration the show was impressive; I am prepared to believe that many of those present had volunteered for their job without too much pressure and that they enjoyed it. Moreover, a large dam was built by economically inefficient methods in a short time; such is the power of human hands."[27]

As larger and more important labor-intensive projects were initiated throughout the countryside, it became imperative to devise a mechanism to coordinate and control the labor supply. This was probably the single most important factor leading to the commune.

A second vital step on the path which led to the communes was the decision in March 1958 to embark on a greatly enlarged local industry program involving the construction of thousands of small-scale industrial installations in rural areas. The objects here were several: first, to exploit the underemployed labor force of the cooperatives; second, to decentralize industry and thus to decrease the dependence of local industries on the larger industrial complexes of the northeast. Such a program necessitated a larger unit in the countryside than the producer's cooperative.

It is beyond the scope of this inquiry to analyze the calculations and miscalculations behind the Chinese commune program and the related great leap forward. Nevertheless, it is necessary to stress that the common denominator of these calculations was the felt need to accelerate rapidly the pace of economic (particularly agricultural) development, and the fervent belief that this acceleration could be accomplished largely with human labor power and native ingenuity. Several examples of this Leftist faith in the "masses," native techniques, and the power of ideology can be offered.

In September 1958, the towing-cable machine, a system of cables and winches used to tow various kinds of plows was introduced and publicized by T'an Chen-lin at a national conference in Kiangsi Province. A *Jen-min jih-pao* editorial wrote of these machines: "The appearance of the towing-cable machine removes the mystic viewpoint of the people toward the mechanization and electrification of agriculture. It makes them see that agricultural mechanization and electrification is not an unattainable aim, nor is it a thing of the remote future. *We can do it now, with our own hands.* Agricultural mechanization and electrification can be realized without those complicated big machines (i.e., tractors) which are hard and expensive to produce. The extensive popularization of the towing-cable machine, simple and economical, is a short cut to . . . agricultural mechanization and electrification under the concrete conditions of our country" [italics supplied].[28]

In 1959, the towing-cable machine, along with locally produced baby tractors and mass-produced ball bearings, was almost to disappear from Chinese Communist discussions of agricultural mechanization.

A second revealing insight into the almost mystical estimates and calculations of the Chinese leadership, or at least of Chairman Mao, can be gleaned from the following quotation ascribed to him in a June issue of *Jen-min jih-pao:* "At a Supreme State Conference in February this year, Chairman Mao mentioned a criticism made by a friend against the Communist Party, saying that the Communist Party 'loves grandeur and achievement, wants quick results and profit, belittles the past, and believes blindly in the future.' Chairman Mao, replying to the criticism, said the Communist Party was just like that, that it loved the grandeur of socialism, wanted quick results in socialism, belittled the past, and believed blindly in the future."[29]

A final example of the grandiose expectations which the regime leadership had in 1958 was the fantastic prediction in the Chinese Party newspaper for October 1, 1958, that China's food problem, basically solved in 1958, would be "completely solved" in 1959.

Mao himself is on record in the November 16 issue of *Hung Ch'i* as having made the even more extreme prediction that grain production would double not only in 1958 but also in 1959. After surveying the economic scene, *Jen-min jih-pao* was moved to comment: "Judging from these figures, a happy prosperous life of abundant food and clothing is no longer a remote ideal and can be realized *within two or three years*" [italics supplied].[30]

Such statements cannot be dismissed as propaganda for the Chinese people. No Communist regime makes idle promises to its own people without some expectation of paying them off. To do otherwise would reduce the credibility of the regime's promises. This statement, and others like it in the fall of 1958, rather suggest that the Chinese Communist leadership was badly misinformed both about the state of its own economy, particularly the size of the 1958 harvest, and about the potentialities for future growth by sheer exploitation of human labor. It was this gross miscalculation that helps to explain the revolutionary over-optimism of the Chinese leadership that was to play its part in the Sino-Soviet conflict.

Soviet Lack of Information on the Communes

Before we examine the commune resolution and the subsequent Chinese controversy with Moscow, it is necessary to ask how much advance information the Communist Party of the Soviet Union had on this radical switch in CCP policy.

In 1957–1958 Soviet journals were closely following economic developments in China. Important articles assessing those developments appeared in *Voprosy ekonomiki*, the principal economic journal, and in *Sovetskoye Kitayavedeniye*.[31] These articles approved as an "objective necessity" Mao's 1957 decision to develop industry and agriculture simultaneously. In view of the serious lag in Chinese agriculture, they hailed the decision as a creative development of the theory of socialist industrialization. They wrote also that the construction of medium and small enterprises alongside large-scale enterprises and the rural industrialization program were of major importance for capital expansion under the conditions existing in China, because such projects demanded only a little capital, were capable of speeding up productivity, allowed a rational and maximum use of resources, and would improve the living standards of the peasantry.[32] Further, Soviet articles approved of the mass use of labor power for the construction of irrigation and other facilities in the countryside, seeing in this another peculiarly Chinese response to capital shortage. One article spoke of the "colossal successes" of the Chinese peasantry in irrigation construction at the end of 1957 and the beginning of 1958.[33] Thus, Soviet journals seemed to approve of the new Chinese economic policies which ultimately led to the communes—despite the fact that these policies varied considerably from past and present Soviet economic practice.

Chinese economic policies made almost inevitable some new form of agricultural organization which could unite the efforts of many cooperatives in large-scale construction projects, particularly for irrigation and rural industrial construction. It was not inevitable, however, that the new organizations take the spectacular form of the communes, and Moscow may well have estimated that the Chinese agricultural reorganization would stop at some sort of enlarged cooperative similar to the giant cooperatives formed in 1958 in Bulgaria, or that it would lead to cooperative unions similar to those being formed in the USSR itself.[34]

In any event, it is doubtful that Moscow knew of Peking's precise plans even as late as June 1958, when the commune experiment was already underway. Soon after the Chengtu Party Conference in March, a campaign to merge small collectives was undertaken in two pilot provinces. Some of these "large cooperatives" amalgamated twenty to thirty existing cooperatives. Many features of the later communes appeared in these early prototypes.

In April, Mao wrote an article—not published until June— in which he implied that the Chinese intended to move into a more advanced stage of "production relations."[35] Mao said: "The former exploiting classes are reduced to mere drops in the ocean of the working people and they must change whether they want to or not. There are undoubtedly some who will never change and would prefer to remain wooden-headed till their dying day, but this does not affect things in general. All degenerate modes of thought and other unsuitable parts of the superstructure are daily crumbling. It still takes time to clear this refuse away completely but there is no doubt that these things will break up. Apart from their other

91

characteristics, China's 600 million people are: first of all poor and secondly 'blank.' This seems a bad thing, but in fact it is a good thing. *Poor people want change, want to do things, want revolution. A clean sheet of paper has nothing on it, so that the newest and most beautiful words can be written and the newest and most beautiful pictures painted on it"* [italics supplied].

Mao went on to say that "throughout the country the Communist spirit is surging forward."[36] Retrospectively, it may be assumed that he already had the communes in mind at this time. In the same month, twenty-seven small cooperatives in Honan province were amalgamated to form the Sputnik Joint Cooperative,[37] the prototype of the communes to follow.[38] Although there were no public references to them at the Chinese Party Congress in May, Chinese journal articles suggest that they were almost certainly under discussion there. Thus, although the communes were not formally unveiled until July, there are indications that as early as March, April, and May the top CCP leadership was actively considering and making preparations for a nationwide commune program.

If the Russians had had ready access to the thinking of Chinese Party leaders, they would have received indications of the coming commune program during that early experimental period. The evidence available suggests, however, that they did not have inside information. In June 1958, Khrushchev told the Bulgarian Party Congress: "The creative development of Marxist-Leninist theory is a task for the entire international Communist movement. . . . It is known, for instance, what an enormous contribution to the theory and practice of the socialist revolution is being made by the Communist Party of China, which is masterfully combining the universal truth of Marxism-Leninism with the concrete practice of revolution and of building socialism in its country."[39]

In the same speech, Khrushchev specifically praised the CCP for having "found original forms to implement Lenin's cooperative plan." In view of Khrushchev's coolness toward the communes after they were formally launched, it is highly unlikely that he would have made such a statement, particularly to a forum of Bloc leaders, if he had been fully aware of the commune program at the time.

Similar praise for Chinese "creativity" was voiced in June

1958 by the Soviet theoretician M. B. Mitin at the Academy of Sciences conference on the theoretical problems of building Communism in the USSR: "The example of socialist construction in China is a striking demonstration of the way the Chinese Communist Party adapts its program to the peculiar conditions of the country and, at the same time, furthers the creative development of Marxism-Leninism."[40] Aside from Mitin's remarks, there were no other references to Chinese socialist construction.

There are other indications that the Soviet Party was less than well informed about the commune plans in general and the proceedings of the Chinese 8th Party Congress in particular. Foreign Communist observers evidently had not been invited to the Congress, despite the importance of the subjects discussed, and second-hand reports on it in the Soviet press gave no indication of awareness of an impending transformation of rural society. Even the most highly specialized of Soviet journals—those published by and for Soviet Sinologists—seemed to be uniformed.

A feature article in one of these, which, judging from its documentation, was written in June or later in the summer, even discussed "The Triumph of Leninist Ideas in China."[41] The brunt of the article was the importance of Leninism and Soviet experience to the successes of the Chinese revolution. "To march along the Russian road," said the article, "was the conclusion of the outstanding representatives of China." The Chinese revolution was a continuation of the Great October Revolution. The Chinese successes in agriculture were due in no small account to the fact that the Chinese were following "the Leninist cooperative plan and the experience of kolkhoz construction in the Soviet Union." Yet, the very term "people's commune"—Peking has since said—was adopted in June by Mao and the CCP central committee,[42] and on July 1 Ch'en Po-ta formally and publicly unveiled the term "people's commune" for the first time in *Hung ch'i*.

On July 31 Khrushchev arrived in Peking to confer with Mao. Two weeks previously Ch'en Po-ta had published a second *Hung ch'i* article which discussed the commune concept in detail and eulogized Mao more extravagantly than ever before in recent years as a Marxist-Leninist theorist.[43] Chen's article provided a theoretical justification for the communes, arguing that Marx and Engels had pointed out only the "general direction of the struggle" and that they had not pretended to "write out a prescription for each nation." Ch'en quoted Lenin to the effect that "special conditions unknown to the European countries" appeared in the East. He further attributed the commune concept expressly to Mao. It is unlikely that Ch'en would have spelled out such an elaborate and provocative justification for a special and unique Chinese road to socialism and Communism if the commune decision had not been firm by this time.

If the Soviet Embassy in Peking had been attentive and had understood the great significance of this article, Khrushchev's attention might have been called to it prior to his departure. It is dubious, however, whether Khrushchev was briefed on the communes at all, or whether this was one of the topics he came to discuss. The gravity of the Middle East situation at the time and the imminence of a new Chinese Communist venture in the Taiwan Strait would seem to have justified a top-level meeting, even without a critical development in Chinese domestic policy. And there was nothing in the ensuing joint communiqué or in press comment on the meeting to suggest that the internal affairs of either country had been under discussion.

Soviet Comment on the Eve of the Commune Resolution

The Soviet Party, even if it had only open Chinese sources to work from, must surely have been able by some time in August to deduce that a reorganization of the Chinese countryside was in the offing and that this reorganization would introduce a new form to be called the "people's commune." Although it was clear by August, however, that a fundamental rural reorganization involving communes was coming, the precise nature of these communes was not yet clear. There is the possibility, of course, that Moscow had not yet had time properly to evaluate what information it had on the commune program, and therefore had not formulated a clear line on it.

In any event, articles in Soviet journals throughout August and even early September continued to say that the Chinese co-operative system was viable and had enormous possibilities for development, emphasized that China was following the tested Leninist cooperative plan and tested Soviet experience, and continued to congratulate the Chinese on their creative application of Marxism.

On August 5, 1958, a journal of the Central Committee of the CPSU, *V pomoshch' politicheskomu soobrazovaniyu*,[44] contained a feature article on the success of the Chinese Communist Party in the construction of socialism. The article included a quotation from the Mao-Khrushchev communiqué issued on August 3 and was thus written, in part at least, after the meeting. It began by asserting that the Chinese Communist Party creatively combined the general truths of Marxism-Leninism with the concrete revolutionary struggle in China. It continued: "The Chinese people have achieved huge successes in the implementation of the Party's general line in agriculture. In an exceptionally short period, in only one Five Year Plan, the gigantic task of the voluntary uniting of many millions of the peasantry into agricultural production cooperatives has been solved. . . . "[45] The best Chinese Party cadres, the article went on, had explained to the peasantry "the experience of collectivization and the successes of the kolkhoz regime in the USSR." From year to year, it said, the Chinese Communist Party "increases aid to the cooperative movement."

In late August an article on the "great upsurge in agriculture in China" by V. Sidekhmenov, a Soviet expert on China, appeared in the principal Party organs of five republics.[46] The article said that in the course of the twelve-year period beginning in 1956 Chinese agricultural production cooperatives would achieve enormous grain yields, and it continued: "The task is posed, in the next three to five years, to make all peasants, *united in cooperatives, prosperous*" [italics supplied].[47]

On August 18, one month after the Chinese press had first publicly unveiled the commune, two weeks after the Mao-Khrushchev meeting, and seven days after the New China News Agency (NCNA) reported that it was Chairman Mao's "guiding idea" to organize Chinese society into "large communes to form the basic units of Chinese society," a *Pravda* editorial could still say: "This year, China will surpass the USA in gross output of wheat by at least two million tons, and this is not a limit. In their recent meetings with Chairman Mao Tse-tung, the Chinese peasants spoke with enthusiasm about the great possibilities inherent in the cooperative system. . . . The CPR is striding with gigantic steps toward the complete triumph of socialism."[48] The "recent meetings" referred to by *Pravda* were the very meetings in which Mao had initiated the mass campaign to organize communes throughout China. He had visited a cooperative in Hopei on August 4 and extolled the virtues of the commune organization and of communal life, and on August 9 he had been in Shantung, where—it was subsequently disclosed—he issued the commune directive.[49]

On September 4, a Soviet expert on China, M. Kapitsa, author of a recent work on Soviet-Chinese relations, published in *Krasnaya zvezda* (Red Star) a eulogistic article on the great leap forward. "The Communist Party of China," he wrote, "has been guided by the most important Marxist-Leninist theses in every stage of socialist construction." On September 6, four days before the commune resolution was published, the official Soviet government organ *Izvestiya* wrote of staggering rice yields in China and concluded that "the great successes in the Chinese countryside are a reflection of the creative application of Marxist-Leninist teaching and the concrete practice of socialist construction."

The evidence adduced above is subject to varying interpretations, all of which must be tentative and, to some extent, speculative. It is inconceivable that Moscow had no advance knowledge of the Chinese commune program. On the basis of Soviet journals, however, it seems evident that the Russians did not have early, frank, and complete information on the communes and the ideological claims that would surround them. Such information, in the light of the strain evident in Sino-Soviet relations *after* the full scope of the Chinese initiative was made public, would doubtless have caused considerable official alarm, which would probably have been reflected in the press. Moreover, if the Soviet leadership had been fully aware of the impending Chinese initiative, it probably would have begun to take some preemptive ideological action well before the time it actually began to do so in November 1958.

It is possible, of course, that some alarm was prevalent in higher Soviet Party circles without being reflected in the Party press, but it is hard to believe that the reactions of the leadership would not have been reflected in a journal normally so sensitive to them as *Pravda*. It might also be argued that the Soviet leaders, aware of Chinese intentions, published references to the viability and great potential strength of the cooperatives as a subtle warning to the Chinese not to go too far. Such covert warnings, however, would be difficult to reconcile with the simultaneous praise for Chinese creativity.

In sum, the evidence suggests that the Soviet Party had less advance information on the Chinese communes than one would expect if there had been a close working relationship between the two parties.

The Commune Resolution

The first paragraph of the commune resolution of August 29, 1958, announced that the communes would "accelerate socialist construction, complete the building of socialism ahead of time, and carry out the gradual transition to Communism." The sixth paragraph was even more euphoric concerning the possibilities for Communism in China. It did not use the word "gradual" at all: "The primary purpose of establishing people's communes is to accelerate the speed of socialist construction and the purpose of building socialism is to prepare actively for the transition to Communism. It seems that the attainment of Communism in China is no longer a remote future event. We should actively use the form of the people's communes to explore the practical road to transition to Communism."[50]

The communes would be the "basic social units of Communist society." They would be raised from collective to public ownership in three or four years in some places and five or six years or "even longer" elsewhere. With the completion of this process, communes would still be "socialist" in character. They would not become Communist until the next stage: "After a number of years, as the social product greatly increases, as the Communist consciousness and morality of the entire people are raised to a much higher degree, and as universal education is instituted and developed, the differences between workers and peasants, town and country, and mental and manual labor . . . will gradually vanish, and the function of the state will be limited to protecting the country from external aggression and will play no role internally."[51] At such a time, Chinese society would "enter the era of Communism."

If there was still a note of caution and gradualism in the

resolution itself, this is not so in some of the contemporary pronouncements on it. Politburo member Lu Ting-yi, referring to the 110-year-old Communist Manifesto, claimed that of Marx's ten preconditions for Communism the CPR had already carried out eight. All that remained, said Lu, were (1) the combination of agriculture with manufacturing and (2) the combination of education with industrial production. Indeed, Lu claimed that both of the remaining preconditions were already "beginning to be carried out."[52] In short, Peking was suggesting that it had discovered a short-cut that might bring China to Communism before its Russian ally, which had a 32-year headstart.

The Free-Supply System: "To Each According to Need"

None of the elements in the Chinese communes aroused Soviet misgivings so much as the so-called free-supply system. In rejecting the communes, Khrushchev and Soviet spokesmen persistently referred to the impossibility of creating an "equalitarian" society before the time was ripe. On pragmatic grounds Khrushchev undoubtedly believed that a system of distribution independent of incentives to labor would ultimately falter. On ideological grounds he feared that the CCP plan could be construed to imply that the Soviet Union was lagging on the road to Communism.

It is impossible to separate the pragmatic from the ideological in Khrushchev's motives for opposing the supply system. It is clear, however, from the reforms he had instituted in the Soviet Union that he had few illusions about "socialist consciousness." To increase production, Khrushchev knew very well that he had to increase incentives. The problem was how far he could go without restoring vestiges of capitalism. In fact, it is not too gross an oversimplification to suggest that the battle over domestic policy between Khrushchev and some of the anti-Party group (Kaganovich and Molotov) was to a large degree over the problem of incentives. After the purge of the anti-Party group, Khrushchev consistently maintained that his beaten foes had not realized the importance of incentives. In July 1957, shortly after the purge of the opposition, he even went so far as to suggest that Stalin himself had had an erroneous view of this problem. Describing the Stalinist .

era, he said: "The principle of material incentives for collective farmers and all agricultural workers in increasing the output of agricultural produce was grossly violated. I will quote the following example: Soon after the end of the war, I went to the village where I was born to see my cousin. She had an orchard. I told her, 'You have wonderful apple trees.' She replied, 'I will cut them down in the autumn.' I asked her why. 'Heavy taxes have to be paid,' she said, 'so it is not profitable to have an orchard.' I mentioned this talk to Stalin and reported that the collective farmers were cutting down orchards, to which he replied that I was a Narodnik, that I had a Narodnik attitude, and that I was losing the proletarian touch."[53] Later in the same speech, Khrushchev said that without incentives, "you will not go far." He criticized "hardheads" who were incapable of understanding this.

In Khrushchev's first implicit attack on the communes, he singled out the supply system. Doubtless he felt that the CCP Left wing, like his own anti-Party opponents, would never "go far" in building socialism with an anti-incentive program. In his November 14 "Theses" on the Soviet Seven Year Plan, Khrushchev inserted the following polemical passage: "Vladimir Ilyich Lenin has taught that without material incentives it is impossible to lead tens and tens of millions of people to Communism. The founders of Marxism-Leninism underlined the importance of the principle of material interest of all toilers in the growth of communal production for the creation of an abundance of products which would ensure the transition to Communism; and, in their time, they criticized the attitude of equalization in distribution."[54]

Similarly, in Khrushchev's first specific criticism of the communes, he emphasized to Senator Humphrey that it was the egalitarian aspect of the commune which would not work. He told Humphrey on December 1 that the Russians had experimented with communes after the revolution and they did not work because "you can't get production without incentive." To Humphrey's suggestion that this sounded rather capitalistic, Khrushchev replied, "call it what you will, it works." In more refined theoretical language, Khrushchev made the same pragmatic point in his speech to the 21st Party Congress: "Egalitarian communism would lead to the eating away of accumulated means and would make impossible further successful development of the economy and expanded reproduction."[55] In Khrushchev's view, the CCP was putting the cart before the horse. It was trying to solve the distribution problem before it had even begun to approach the problem of creating abundance.

Soviet Theory on Distribution
According to Need

It is important to note here how deeply engrained in Bolshevik writing was this aversion to a premature introduction of Communist distribution, that is, of what has been classically held out as the ultimate goal of Communist societies: distribution according to "need." Lenin himself wrote in *State and Revolution* that in the lower development stage preceding full Communism, namely socialism, society was not yet capable of eliminating the injustice resulting from distribution of goods according to work performed. In the socialist state, said Lenin, although exploitation of man by man is eliminated, unjust differences in wealth persist. These differences, said Lenin, are a "defect," but an unavoidable one during the socialist stage, because people are not yet psychologically prepared to work for the good of society without material incentives. "If we are not to fall into utopianism," wrote the founder of Bolshevism, "we cannot imagine that, having overthrown capitalism, people will at once learn to work for society. . . . "[56]

Only from 1917 to 1921, because of the disruption caused to the economy by the civil war, did the USSR temporarily deviate from the principle of more pay for more work and adopt an emergency policy of equalization of consumption. This distribution system, practiced during the period of what is commonly called "War Communism," has always been treated by the Russians as a temporary aberration forced on them by adverse circumstances, particularly the shortage of food and industrial goods. In an obvious allusion to the distribution system in effect in the Chinese communes, Khrushchev in his 21st Party Congress speech pointedly emphasized that the War Communism system of "equal distribution" could "not constitute a normal economic system."[57]

How far the Russians were moving from the concept of egalitarian distribution was to be made evident at a conference of Soviet social scientists in 1958.[58] K. V. Ostrovityanov, a leading Soviet theoretician, charged that free supply of various important products would "undermine" the stimulating role of "the socialist principle of distribution," the entire system of commodity exchange between town and country, and the cost-accounting base of Soviet industry. The gradual transition to distribution according to "need," he implied, would take place not via a free supply system, but rather through raising the real wages of low-income groups. He explained that the Communist principle of distribution "does not signify egalitarianism and leveling of consumption but a full satisfaction of the variegated and rising needs and tastes of the members of society."[59] Thus, in the Soviet view, distribution according to "need" had to await a much higher level of Communist society.[60]

It is important to recognize that this very same distribution problem was a contentious one in the CCP itself. The existence of conflicting schools of opinion was reflected throughout October and November 1958 in the pages of the Chinese Communist press. The extreme Left wing of the Party contended that it was necessary to go over to a 100 per cent automatic supply system—i.e., to eliminate wage payments completely. It recalled with pride the glory of China's own period of War Communism, referred to the wage system as a "vestige of bourgeois concepts," and remarked contemptuously on expectations of "more pay for more work."[61] The moderates took the view that the wage system had a historically progressive function and could not be eliminated overnight.[62]

The view which prevailed was a compromise. Its outlines were already distinct on October 22 when a *Jen-min jih-pao* article appeared under the title, "The Best Form of Distribution During the Transition to Communism: A Treatise on the Distribution System *Combined* of Part Wages and Part Supply" [italics supplied]. The author contended that the part-wage, part-supply system was "an important find in Marxism" discovered by Mao.[63] Other articles in the Chinese press soon condemned the wholly automatic supply system as a Left deviation and the unalloyed wage system as a Right deviation.

A CCP resolution in December adopted this middle position. It decreed that the division between wages and supply would be decided by each commune in the light of its own conditions. It cautioned that the element of supply should not be too great and contended that the wage element, for the present, should rise faster than the supply element.[64]

Whether such a compromise can or cannot be attributed to Soviet pressure, the fact remains that the compromise was unsatisfactory to the Russians, who—even after December—scarcely mentioned the mixed system of wages and handouts in their rare commentaries on the communes. What must have been particularly hard for the Soviet leaders to bear was the continuing Chinese defense of their compromise supply system as a "budding sprout of Communism."

Radicalism, Chauvinism, Evangelism

The ideological challenge presented by the CCP to the CPSU can be conveniently discussed under the three divisions of the above heading. By "radicalism" we mean the conscious and explicit attempt of the Chinese Communists to justify their accelerated march to Communism, not within the framework of contemporary Soviet or even Stalinist doctrine, but rather by harking back to the classics of Marxism-Leninism.

In September and October 1958, various Chinese spokesmen claimed that their views on labor under Communism were similar to those expressed in Marx's *Critique of the Gotha Program*. Liu Shao-ch'i, implicitly attacking labor specialization on September 16, cited Mao, Marx, and Engels as his authorities. In articles about the proper form of distribution in both socialist and Communist societies, *Jen-min jih-pao* throughout October and November appealed almost exclusively to the authority of Marx and Engels. In seeking to justify the "emancipation" of women, writers cited Engels' *Origin of the Family, Private Property and the State*. Communal mess halls, nurseries, and kindergartens were justified by citations from Lenin's 1919 work, *The Great Beginning*. In articles on education under Communism, authority was sought from Engels' *Principles of Communism*. In not one case, from the promulgation of the commune directive in early September through November, did the Chinese press refer to recent Soviet experience or doctrine.

Chinese Communist chauvinism was another element characteristic of the period from August to November 1958. Li Hsien-nien, writing in the October 16 *Hung ch'i,* called the introduction of the supply system "a great event without parallel in history" and "an event of world significance."[65] Vice Chairman Chu Teh said on September 9 that communes were "a major event not only in Chinese history but in world history."[66] Such references seemed calculated to invite invidious comparisons with the USSR, the only country in the world whose history would make it susceptible to such comparison.

A much more significant facet of Chinese chauvinism was the cult of Mao Tse-tung that began early in 1958. Mao was described as a "great prophet" (*Jen-min jih-pao,* October 1, 1958). The expression "great" (*wei-ta*) was applied both to the Party and to Mao. Whereas a standard reference had formerly been "The Communist Party of China under the leadership of Chairman Mao Tse-tung," now frequent reference was made to the leadership of "The Chinese Communist Party *and* Chairman Mao Tse-tung."[67] Mao was called "one of *the most outstanding* Marxist-Leninist revolutionaries, statesmen, and theoreticians of our age" [italics supplied].[68]

By the end of 1959 and early 1960, Mao's ideology was being increasingly equated with Marxism-Leninism and sometimes given priority over it. Thus Tao Chu, the influential leader of the Kwangtung Party, said in October 1959: "Marx did no more than point out to us the general direction of the struggle. Lenin added to Marxism but did not provide a concrete solution to all our problems. . . . Our Party, under the guidance of Comrade Mao Tsetung, creatively applied Marxism-Leninism . . . and enabled our country to achieve such tremendous successes in socialist revolution and socialist construction."[69] The Vice President of Peking University, Hu Hsi-kuei, asserted that "we must study Marxism-Leninism *as well as* the Mao Tse-tung ideology" [italics supplied] —implying that the latter comes first.[70] *Chung-kuo ch'ing-nien* (China Youth) finally drew the ultimate conclusion: Mao Tsetung's writings are Marxism-Leninism.[71] More modest but equally significant, one Chinese paper said on February 1, 1960, that "Mao Tse-tung's thought is Chinese Marxism."[72] The idea that Mao had sinified Marxism-Leninism was also stated by *Jen-min jih-pao* in early 1960.[73]

For Sino-Soviet relations, the implications of the growing cult of Mao were obvious. Mao was once again, as in 1949–1951, being portrayed as an independent source of authority and strategy, who had adapted Marxism to China and whose theories were relevant for all colonial peoples. (See Introduction.)

It was Chinese Communist missionary zeal, which—wedded to the cult of Mao—represented the most potentially explosive element in Sino-Soviet relations. This one may call "Maoist evangelism." Such evangelism, moreover, was not to be restricted to underdeveloped countries. Signs of Chinese proselytizing were noticeable, for example, when several East European satellite delegations visited China in the fall of 1958 to tour the country and inspect the communes. Polish Labor Minister Zawadski, who headed a delegation to China in December, was reported as having said on December 15 that his delegation would "widely recommend the experience of this movement [the communes] to the Polish people."[74] No such remark was attributed to Zawadski in Polish media reporting the same event. In October, Chinese media attributed to Bulgarian Deputy Premier Chervenkov explicit praise of the communes as a condition for the transition to Communism; Bulgarian media, reporting the very same event—a farewell banquet in Peking—contained no reference to the communes in their reports of Chervenkov's remarks.[75]

In the comment surrounding the original commune resolution, furthermore, Peking did not always take care to restrict the applicability of the commune system to China. The resolution itself described the commune as the "best form of organization for the attainment of socialism and the gradual transition to Communism." In some cases, Peking did specify that the commune was the best organizational form for China. That the qualifier was not used rigidly or consistently suggests that the CCP was not seriously concerned to mute this crucial ideological point.

Indeed, at least with respect to Asia and the rest of the underdeveloped world, it seemed the Chinese were intent on making the point. This was implicit in their claim that Mao had solved the problems of socialist and Communist construction for these areas as well as for China, a claim which was suggested in the first extended discussion of the communes to appear in a Chinese Communist publication. An article by Ch'en Po-ta, the editor of *Hung ch'i*, and one of the most prominent CCP theoreticians, in the July

16 issue of *Hung ch'i* significantly titled "Under the Banner of Chairman Mao," contended in effect that Mao had discovered a special road enabling China to accelerate socialist construction and to realize Communism "in the not distant future."[76] Mao had done this in accordance with Lenin's injunction to the countries of the East to "creatively develop" Marxist theory "in the light of special conditions unknown to European countries . . . realizing that the peasants are the principal masses." Ch'en contended that Marx and Engels had pointed out only "the general direction of the struggle" and had not pretended to "write out a prescription for each nation" to realize Communism. The implications were clear: the path to Communism in the East would differ considerably from that in Europe, and Mao had discovered the special path for the East.[77] Although Ch'en's article was the most outspoken claim of this sort since 1949, Chinese journals two months earlier, after the secret CCP Congress in May,[78] had called the Chinese "general line" adopted at the Congress "a new development of Marxism on the question of socialist construction" and, as such, "significant . . . for the other fraternal states engaged in building socialism."[79]

It would be difficult to exaggerate the political significance of such contentions. If Mao had solved the problems of socialist and Communist construction for countries of the East, it was not improbable that Chinese experience was more relevant for these countries than Soviet experience. Did it not also follow that Peking should be accorded leadership of the revolutionary movement in these areas?

There is, of course, one ellipsis in this chain of reasoning. In effect, the Chinese Communists were claiming in 1958 that Mao had discovered a special path for building Communism in backward countries once the Communists had taken power. As yet, they had not renewed the earlier claims of 1949–1951 that the Chinese road to power was also relevant in those countries. In 1959 they were to fill this gap, and to carry their claims to their logical conclusion. Mao knew best how to make the revolution, how to consolidate it, and how to proceed toward Communism. To put it baldly, the CCP was claiming leadership over the revolutionary movement in all underdeveloped areas in Africa, Asia, and Latin America.

Soviet Vulnerability to
Chinese Initiative

Before we undertake a discussion of the ultimate Soviet response to Chinese initiative on the communes, it is important for us to consider a number of vulnerabilities to which many Communists may have felt the Soviet position was subject.

Under the best of circumstances, Khrushchev was vulnerable to an ideological attack from Mao. He did not have the prestige of the Chinese leader. It was Mao, not he, who had provided the rationale for explaining the Hungarian revolution in 1956 by developing a new theory of relations between socialist states and the theory of "contradictions" between leaders and masses. It was Mao's theoretical stature, not his, that had been recognized by the entire Communist world even during Stalin's lifetime. It was also Mao who, even in Soviet journals, was an "outstanding Marxist theoretician," an honorific that no other Bloc leader was accorded at the time of Stalin's death. In 1959, Western reporters in East Berlin quoted a young Communist philosopher: "Khrushchev is just an economic pragmatist, but Mao is a thinker, a theorist." Another said: "You can say what you like, but we need ideals, and the only place you can get them today is from Mao Tse-tung . . . not from Nikita Khrushchev."[80] Such attitudes were probably not uncommon in international Communist circles.

The charge of practicism, a term of derogation in Communist circles meaning disdain for theory, was certainly rekindled by Khrushchev's agricultural reforms in 1958. At that time, Khrushchev dissolved the machine-tractor stations (MTS) and sold their machinery to the collective farms, a step specifically ruled out as "backward" by Stalin in 1952. The MTS, inasmuch as they were state-owned, had always been regarded as a much "higher" form of property than the collectively owned cooperatives. The MTS were, moreover, the advanced posts of the Party in the countryside. Khrushchev's defense of the reform, when he introduced it in March 1958, was replete with preemptive attacks against "some comrades" who held that with the MTS reform "unclarities will arise in some theoretical questions" and who feared that the reform would weaken national property.[81] The reform was followed by a "countryside discussion" in which noted Soviet theoreticians railed against "dogmatically thinking persons . . . [who] do not feel the breath of life."[82]

Khrushchev's agricultural policy contained still another "backward" step when viewed against the Stalinist testament. Stalin had indicated that organized barter should gradually replace "commodity turnover," the production of goods for the market, and that the market system should gradually disappear. Khrushchev was moving in an opposite direction; he justified the retention of "commodity turnover" for an indefinite period during the transition to Communism. Moreover, Khrushchev's refusal to launch a frontal assault on the private plot of land and the private cow made him vulnerable to the charge of coddling the peasantry at the expense of the urban population.

Thus, at precisely the time when Khrushchev was open to Leftist criticism in his agrarian policy, Mao introduced a dramatic Left-wing reform which must have seemed to many Bloc Communists a revolutionary step forward.

And it was not only agrarian policy on which Khrushchev was, so to speak, vulnerable. By the fall of 1958 the whole concept of the "transition to Communism" had been for many years hardly more than a slogan in the Soviet press. With the exception of the Academy of Sciences conference in June, serious discussions of the hows and whens of the transition were virtually non-existent.[83] Discussion centered instead on the need to raise economic production. Khrushchev was, as he confessed on several occasions, not so much interested in theory as in this.[84] The Chinese, by contrast, made the unprecedented assertion that they had discovered in the commune the basic unit of the future Communist society, a unit for which the Russians were still groping. They asserted that some characteristics of the new Communist man had already appeared in China. By moving toward the abolition of all private property, the Chinese seemed to be moving much closer to the classical Communist goal than was the Soviet Union, which still tolerated private garden plots, privately owned cows, and privately owned implements of production. By instituting a system of "free supply" in the communes the Chinese created the impression of moving closer to the ultimate Marxist goal of distribution according to "need," a goal which the USSR disregarded even in theorizing about the future. Other unique Chinese programs seemed to be more in harmony with the egalitarian tradition of the Communist fathers than were those of the Soviet Union. Thus, when the Chinese required all Party and state bureaucrats to do manual labor and all army officers to serve in the ranks, this practice recalled the Communist Manifesto itself in which Marx and Engels called for the "equal liability of all to labor."

Most of the classical Communist works which the Chinese cited in the fall of 1958 as justification for their views on the transition to Communism had been ignored for many years in the Soviet Union. In fact, close examination of many of these classical works would have proved embarrassing to the pragmatic Soviet leadership. The Chinese commune program, by offering a firm path to Communism, must have seemed to many Communists a solution to problems long evaded in Moscow.

Left-wing groups throughout the Bloc who wanted to move more speedily toward socialism, but who had been forced to move within the limits set down by the Russians, must have greeted the announcement with enthusiasm. In October, for example, the Natolinist faction in Poland cited Chinese precedents and views in a full-scale attack on the gradualist economic policies of the Gomulka leadership. In East Germany, where there were several indications of a dispute in the leadership over the proper pace of construction, the Left-wing elements in the Party seized upon the Chinese leap forward as an example of the bold revolutionary thinking needed in their own country.[85] The former Stalinist dictator, Vulko Chervenkov, seemed to be the head of a "go faster" China lobby in Sofia.[86] Throughout Communist history, the question of the pace of advance toward the final goal has been a chronic problem that has consistently divided the Right from the Left. The Chinese ideological and economic initiative thus came as a valuable weapon to the Left.

Finally, the Russians were also open to criticism from the Right. Throughout 1957 and 1958 they had been busy combatting "revisionism," which had as its common denominator the demand for autonomy and recognition of national distinctiveness. "Revisionists" could argue that if Chinese "special conditions" were special enough to justify such a radical departure from Soviet experience as the communes, why could not other countries also offer more distinctive paths to socialism-Communism? While this was certainly not a line the Chinese wished to encourage, it nonetheless was an effect produced by their shift in policy.

In short, for a variety of reasons, the Chinese initiative could have been and was exploited by groups throughout the Bloc. Stalinists who believed that Khrushchev had betrayed them; Leftwingers who wanted to speed up the pace of development in their own countries; Asians who saw similarities between their own problems and those of China; "autonomists" who would exploit any opening that could be used as a sanction for "separate roads." The Chinese ideological challenge, therefore, could not be waved away or localized.

Early Soviet Reaction to the Chinese Initiative

The early Soviet reaction to the multiple Chinese challenge was varied. First, the Soviets began a revival and intensification of Moscow's own ideological claims, highlighted by the inauguration in November of two new mass movements portrayed as "cells of the future Communist society."[87] Second, they largely ignored, distorted, or minimized the communes and particularly the ideological claims for them. (The specific reaction to the communes will be discussed separately.) Third, the Soviet press began subtly to increase its stress on the enormous material and technological prerequisites for Communism and the impossibility of tampering with the "superstructure" before a radical increase had taken place in production "forces." Finally, they began polemically to stress the importance of material incentives in building Communism and the impossibility of introducing distribution according to "need" until the highest phase of Communism had been reached.

The extraordinary 21st CPSU Congress, to be hailed in Soviet media as the congress of "builders of Communism," was convoked for February 1959 on September 5, one week after the Chinese commune resolution had been adopted but before it was made public.[88] A regularly scheduled Party Congress was not mandatory until 1960, and it seems unlikely that such an extraordinary Congress was necessary merely—as was claimed—to discuss and to ratify Khrushchev's new Seven Year Plan.[89] The 21st Party Congress was, it seems, convoked in large measure because Khrushchev believed that he had to reply to the Chinese challenge in the highest forum available to him. Indeed, the Congress proceedings cannot be properly evaluated outside the context of the budding Sino-Soviet conflict.[90]

Authoritative articles in the Soviet press gave clues to the pre-emptive ideological strategy Khrushchev had in mind. A *Kommunist* editorial, signed to the press on September 9, revived Khrushchev's line of November 1957—subsequently ignored—that Communism was not remote in the USSR: "It is necessary to evaluate the significance of the forthcoming XXI Congress of the CPSU. Our country is in the process of a great upsurge. The higher phase of Communism is already not a remote aim; the completion of the construction of socialism and the realization of the gradual transition from socialism to Communism is the basic content of the contemporary stage of development of Soviet society."[91]

On October 16, there appeared in Soviet journals two articles that seem to have been the opening guns in the Soviet counter-attack. *Voprosy ekonomiki* (Problems of Economics), in an article ironically titled "Great China Builds *Socialism*" [italics supplied], made it clear that China's low level of industrialization precluded any rapid advance to Communism. In countries such as China, which had been economically underdeveloped in the past, the Soviet journal wrote, it was not sufficient in building socialism to bring about a victory of socialist methods of production; a "certain level of development of production forces is also needed." Since the level had not been reached in China, "it follows from this that the transition period [to socialism] has not been completed in the CPR."[92] Moreover, the article significantly called the communes "higher type cooperatives."[93]

The other article, in *Voprosy Filosofii* (Problems of Philosophy), by T. A. Stepanyan, the prominent Soviet philosopher and expert on "the transition to Communism," was even more pointed in rebuffing Chinese claims concerning the imminence of Communism in China. Stepanyan put forward a "new law" of socialist development providing that socialist states would reach Communism in groups, each group constituting an "economic zone" which would reach the final goal in accordance with the level of its regional economic development. From this, it was clear the Soviets believed that the European Bloc countries would reach Communism first: "It must be assumed that the European socialist countries, which are united in an economic council for mutual aid, constitute a special economic zone and will be the first to enter Communism. The Asian socialist countries, which have much in common as regards their economic and cultural development, constitute another regional zone and will also *jointly* enter Communism" [italics supplied].[94] China would have to wait until North Korea, North Vietnam, and the Mongolian People's Republic had become fully industrialized and collectivized before it could begin the process of Communist construction!

Two days later, on October 18, Moscow took the next step toward heading off the Chinese claims. The CPSU's October Revolution anniversary slogans not only ignored the Chinese communes but used a subtle semantic device to downgrade China to a position of parity with the East European and Asian satellites in the building of socialism. For the first time since 1956, the careful distinction drawn in the Chinese favor between their level of socialist construction and that of the other satellites was abruptly dropped.[95] (See Table 1.)

In early November Pavel Yudin, the Soviet Ambassador to China, returned to Peking after an extended stay in Moscow. Although Yudin's prolonged absence from his post in Peking may be explainable on grounds unconnected with the budding Sino-Soviet conflict, it seems likely that he returned to Peking when he did largely in order to convey Soviet objections. It is also likely that Yudin held a series of conferences in Moscow with top Soviet Party officials in order to fill them in on Chinese thinking and to receive instructions for his future conversations with Chinese leaders.

Yudin's two public speeches in Peking on November 6 and 7, the latter the anniversary of the October Revolution, were an important turning point in the conflict.[96] The beginning of the Chinese retreat can be dated from shortly after Yudin's return. In his two public speeches, Yudin completely ignored the communes, sustaining the pattern of the Soviet leaders' total silence on the subject.[97] He avoided any implication that the CPR might be advancing toward Communism at a pace faster than that of other Bloc countries. He restated the Soviet position that Communism in any country required a comprehensive material and technical foundation, developed to a point where the most advanced capitalist countries would be overtaken in per capita production. By empha-

TABLE I
Soviet Slogans on Socialist Construction

CHINA	SATELLITES
May 1954 (no reference to building of socialism)	(no reference to building of socialism)
Oct. 1954 successfully struggling for . . . construction of the foundations of socialism	successfully struggling for . . . construction of a socialist society
May 1955 successfully struggling for . . . construction of the foundations of socialism	successfully struggling for . . . construction of socialism
Oct. 1955 successfully struggling for . . . construction of the foundations of socialism	struggling for . . . the construction of socialism
May 1956 *successfully realizing* a socialist transformation	*struggling for* . . . the construction of socialism
Oct. 1956 *successfully building* socialism	*struggling for* . . . the construction of socialism
May 1957 *builder of* socialism	*building* socialism
Oct. 1957 *builder of* socialism	*building* socialism
May 1958 *builder of* socialism	*building* socialism
Oct. 1958 *building* socialism	*building* socialism

In October 1956 the CPSU introduced the practice of greeting each Bloc country in a separate slogan. Prior to that time, a single slogan had been used to greet the people's democracies collectively. The satellites have consistently been described in identical language in their respective slogans, except for (1) North Vietnam (not promoted from "building a new life" to "building socialism" until October 1958) and (2) Hungary in the May 1957 slogan that came after the Hungarian rebellion.

In Soviet slogans since October 1957, only China has been differentiated as to status: China comes first, followed by the other Communist countries in Russian alphabetical order.

sizing per capita production, Yudin was describing the preconditions for Communism in precisely those terms which most strikingly underlined the weakness of the CPR's claims to be leading 650 million people to Communism.

Soviet Reaction to the
Communes Themselves

To evaluate the Soviet reaction to the Chinese commune experiment, it is essential to divide the problem into three parts, one economic, another ideological, and a final, historical. It is not true that the Russians completely ignored the communes. All top leaders ignored the communes, but there was, particularly in specialized Soviet journals, a minimal discussion. Nor is it easy to say, as we have already indicated, that Khrushchev was not at all concerned about the economics of the communes but was exclusively concerned about their ideological implications.

A close examination of the Soviet reaction to the communes suggests, first, that Khrushchev was not concerned so much about the Chinese adopting a *different* agrarian policy as about the unviable aspects of that policy. He probably thought, like the Right wing in the Chinese Party itself, that the communes were premature and would do more harm than good, and perhaps he may have been concerned that if the commune program led to serious shortfalls in the Chinese economy, the Russians would have to do the bailing out.

On the economic side, there is a considerable body of evidence to suggest that Moscow was fully aware of and sympathetic to the manifold, serious, and distinctive economic problems facing the Chinese leadership in 1957. Moscow in effect endorsed the agonizing reappraisal of fundamental policies which began at that time and which ultimately led to the communes. For example, in July 1958, *Voprosy ekonomiki* wrote approvingly of the Maoist decision in February 1957 to pursue the distinctive policy of simultaneous development of industry and agriculture: "The course of simultaneous development of industry and agriculture on the basis of preferential development of heavy industry advanced by the Central Committee of the CCP in 1957 represents a creative development of the theory of socialist industrialization as applied to the concrete and specific conditions of People's China where agricultural development continues to predominate in the national economy."[98]

Although the Maoist emphasis on local industry and the construction of medium- and small-sized enterprises ran contrary to Soviet experience, the Soviet journal also applauded that: "It should be emphasized that the correct solution of the problem of the combined construction of large, medium and small sized enterprises is of major importance for capital expansion under the conditions existing in the CPR. In the CPR, the development of local industry is now given much attention. The all-out development of local industry is not only of economic but political significance."[99]

The Soviet journal further defended the upgrading of agricultural priority in the Chinese economy by contending that "if a more correct relationship between the development of industry and agriculture were not provided, this would doubtless have a negative effect in the not too distant future on the overall economic position of China." The Chinese Party's Central Committee, it wrote, had corrected this situation "in ample time."

Similar and more extensive Soviet discussions of the new Maoist economic policies can be found in other Soviet journals of the period. Thus, articles in *Problemy vostokavedeniya* (Problems of Eastern Studies), Nos. 2 and 3, 1958, stressed, as did Peking, that the central problem in Chinese agricultural development was that of extending the use of China's one major resource —labor power. Kurbatov, in *Sovetskoye kitayavedeniye* (Soviet Chinese Studies), No. 3, 1958, wrote that because China's peculiar problems "preclude supplying the countryside with the required amount of technique and fully mechanized agriculture within the next few years," it was necessary to develop a mass movement for perfecting farm techniques and machinery.[100]

Even after the communes were formed, some Soviet publications continued to justify them—without explaining much about them—on the very same ground advanced by Peking: that the tasks facing Chinese agriculture made the smaller cooperatives obsolete. Thus, in *Sovetskoye kitayavedeniye*, No. 4, 1958, Meliksetov wrote that the Chinese economy had been "hindered by the narrow organizational limits of the cooperatives": "The small number of cooperatives did not answer the needs of the changed situation and were not capable of capital construction or mechanization and electrification on a large scale or contributing to the growth of local industry. The construction of irrigation facilities, the creation of local industry, forest planting, etc., demanded a unity of cooperatives of several volosts (*hsiens*) and even uezds (*hsiangs*). This is why in the summer of 1958 there began the movement for the creation of multi-faceted large people's communes and the inclusion in them of all local industry."[101]

Again in the very same article in *Voprosy ekonomiki* which sought to deflate Chinese pretensions about building Communism ("Great China Builds Socialism"), it was contended that the communes facilitated the process of capital construction. Broad masses of peasantry were now able to collaborate "on a large scale, breaking through the cooperative . . . and other boundaries." Moreover, the author held that, "under the conditions prevailing in the CPR, the people's commune is the best organizational form" and even a "necessary basic course" for accelerating the construction of Communism.[102] It is true that much of this commentary can be explained simply on the grounds that the communes were a fact and that something had to be said about them, particularly in the more specialized Soviet economic and sinological journals. It is also true that it was far more significant that the communes were completely ignored in the speeches of Soviet Party Presidium members and largely ignored in Soviet propaganda for mass consumption. Nevertheless, the sympathetic reaction of the more scholarly journals does suggest that if the Chinese had chosen to call the "communes" by some other name, if they had made no ideological claims for them, and if they had not pushed the "egalitarian" aspect of the experiment as far as they did, the communes would not have caused the considerable friction in Sino-Soviet relations that they did.

The Russians probably calculated that the Chinese Communists, overenthusiastic as they were, would be forced by domestic pressures to modify substantially the more extreme levelling aspects of the communes. Thus *New Times* wrote pointedly in January 1959 that the communal structure "had not taken final shape."[103] Mikoyan, during his tour of the United States in the same month, remarked that the USSR had gone through similar experiences in its initial phase of development but that it had "outgrown" this phase. Khrushchev, too, may also have calculated that the Chinese comrades themselves would soon find out that the commune experiment had done more harm than good.

While the Russians were disturbed about the economics of the communes, they were probably more disturbed by the ideological challenge implicit in them. We have seen how some Soviet journals called them "higher type cooperatives," a deliberate distortion of what the Chinese claimed. While the Chinese suggested that communes were relevant for other backward countries, the Russians stressed that they were born under peculiar Chinese conditions and could not be duplicated elsewhere. While the Chinese insisted that they were a vehicle for the accelerated transition to

Communism, the Russians contended that they could help only in accelerating the achievement of socialism. To this end they even tampered with Chinese articles appearing in the Soviet press. On Chinese National Day, October 1, 1958, an article by Chinese Politburo alternate member Po I-po, in *Izvestiya,* quoted the commune resolution which had said that the "attainment of Communism" in China was no longer a remote future event. In *Izvestiya,* the phrase "the establishment of communes" was substituted for "the attainment of Communism." Since it is unlikely either that Po himself would deliberately have misquoted the CCP commune directive or that this was merely a typographical error, it can be taken to indicate a deliberate distortion on the part of *Izvestiya's* editors reflecting Soviet distaste for the Chinese ideological claims.

The best single indicator of Soviet reservations, however, was the almost complete avoidance of the subject of the communes in ceremonial speeches or messages and in mass propaganda (as distinguished from the specialized journals). Thus, in 1958, Khrushchev's National Day telegram to Mao referred three times to the CPR's efforts in socialist construction and avoided the communes completely.[104] A. Andreyev, CPSU Central Committee member and chairman of the Sino-Soviet Friendship Society, similarly ignored the communes in his Hall of Columns speech on the eve of CPR National Day.[105] *Pravda's* Peking correspondent, V. Orchenikov, in a front-page story on CPR National Day, wrote of Chinese agricultural successes without once mentioning the communes.[106] The subject was avoided even by Soviet official spokesmen in Peking when responding directly to remarks in which their Chinese counterparts lauded the communes. Soviet radio propaganda for mass consumption also virtually ignored the communes. Although CPR National Day is a traditional occasion for review of Chinese Communist progress in all spheres of domestic activity, Radio Moscow managed to broadcast 215 commentaries about China without discussing the communes in more than three.[107]

The Soviet Experience with
Agricultural Communes

One final element that must be taken into consideration in evaluating the Soviets' cool response to the Chinese communes is their own unsuccessful experiment with agricultural communes in the period immediately after the 1917 revolution. The Russians found within a few years that such a drastic form of socialization—in which all private property was eliminated and became the collective property of the commune—was unfeasible. By 1920 the Bolsheviks were actively encouraging two other forms of agricultural cooperative which allowed the peasants varying degrees of private ownership. The "lower" cooperative form, the TOZ (Society for Joint Land Cultivation), was simply a production cooperative in which the peasants joined together at certain times to work their land and to buy and use expensive machinery. The means of production were socialized, that is, used in common, *only* during the time of field work. But each peasant retained his rights to his own private property, to the harvest of his land, and to his own livestock and tools.

The other form of agricultural cooperative was one step "higher" than the TOZ—that is, it had a greater amount of collectivity—but was still not completely socialized like the commune. This was the "artel." In the artel, most production was carried on collectively and most means of production were owned by the artel. But considerable private production was carried on separately in private garden plots owned by each member family, and each family owned some agricultural capital. The peasant thus received both a collective and a private income. In the Party's thinking, as it evolved in the 1920's, the artel was to be a "school" in socialism. It would prepare the peasants for passage to the higher form of socialist enterprise: the commune.

During the massive Soviet retreat in the face of economic adversity in 1921, known as the New Economic Policy, both the commune and the artel suffered considerable decline as greater scope was allowed to private initiative in the countryside as well as in the city. In order to keep the cooperative spirit alive during this period of retreat, the Party encouraged the spread of the TOZ, the form of cooperative least objectionable to the peasantry. By 1929, on the eve of the massive collectivization drive, the number of TOZ's represented roughly 70 per cent of the still meager collectivized sector.[108]

When Stalin launched the forced collectivization drive in the fall of 1929, he was well aware that the difficulties in herding the peasantry into communes might prove insurmountable. Therefore, he made the artel—the halfway house between TOZ and commune —the almost exclusive form of cooperative. The communes would have to wait for a "later time."[109] By 1932, with mass collectivization virtually complete, the artels constituted 95.9 per cent of the total number of cooperatives and the communes but 2 per cent. Meanwhile, the few communes that remained were in effect transformed into artels. By a government order in 1933, the members of the communes—like those in artels—were permitted the private ownership of one cow, some small livestock, and poultry. Likewise, increasing emphasis was put on piecework (payment according to individual output) as opposed to the egalitarian distribution of the communes. Thus, at an early point in its history, the Soviet Union turned its back on the very kind of distribution system that was to be seized upon by Peking in the late 1950's. The egalitarian or levelling aspect of the Chinese communes was one of the most important sources of discord between Moscow and Peking after 1958.

The Bolsheviks, having had experience of their own with "egalitarianism" based on an extremely low over-all output, realized that such a program of what amounted to concealed rationing was not conducive to productive effort. For all the Bolshevik excesses in implementing their forced collectivization program in the hectic 1930's, they did not make the mistake of instituting a system of rationing scarcity and calling such a system a sprout of Communism.

Stalin's only major pronouncement on the agricultural communes occurred in his report to the 17th Party Congress in 1934. But the attitude he expressed has remained the Bolshevik attitude towards agricultural communes to this day. He ascribed their failure to three factors: underdeveloped technology, a shortage of products, and a premature egalitarianism that had been forced on the communes by conditions of scarcity: "The present agricultural commune arose on the basis of an underdeveloped technology and a shortage of products. *This really explains why it practiced egalitarianism and showed little concern for the individual, everyday interest of its members*—as a result of which it is now being compelled to assume the status of the artel, in which the individual and public interests of the collective farmers are rationally com-

118

bined. . . . Practice has shown that the communes would certainly have been doomed had they not abandoned egalitarianism" [italics supplied].[110] Stalin realized that compulsory levelling was not the way to educate the peasantry in the "school of socialism."

While Stalin ruled out the commune for the foreseeable future, he did not rule it out forever. It could arise, he said, only "out of developed and prosperous artels": "The future agricultural commune will arise when the fields and farms of the artel are replete with grain, with poultry, with vegetables, and all other produce; when the artels have mechanized laundries, modern dining rooms, mechanized bakeries, etc.; when the collective farmer sees that it is more to his advantage to receive his meat and milk from the collective farm's meat and dairy department than to keep his own cow and small livestock. . . . The future commune will arise on the basis of a more developed technology and of a more developed artel, on the basis of an abundance of products. When will that be? Not soon, of course. But be it will. *It would be criminal to accelerate artificially the process of transition from the artel to the future commune. That would confuse the whole issue and would facilitate the work of our enemies* [italics supplied]. The transition from the artel to the future commune must proceed gradually, to the extent that *all* the collective farmers become convinced that such a transition is necessary [italics in original]."[111]

It would be difficult to exaggerate the political significance of the comments emphasized in this passage. Although the statement was made twenty-four years before the Chinese Communists introduced their communes, it could easily have appeared in 1958, so typical is it of the historic Soviet aversion toward premature establishment of communes. When Stalin said, as he did, that it would be "criminal" to accelerate the transition to the commune and that such a speed-up would help the "enemy," he meant that premature communization could lead to mass dissidence. Khrushchev himself was to make much the same point in a 1959 speech in which he warned that excessive speed in socialist construction could "be exploited by enemies of Communism."[112] It is against the background of such a realistic understanding of the tenacity of the individualistic instincts of the peasantry—an attitude deeply engrained in Bolshevik theory and practice—that one must evaluate the Soviet reaction to the Chinese commune experiment.

As late as 1939, after the Bolsheviks had announced their entry into a new stage of construction—the period of gradual transition from socialism to Communism—they continued to warn that the commune was still a distant goal. Molotov told the 18th Party Congress in March 1939 that the entry into the transition period had "caused confusion" in the minds of some overzealous members who wanted right then and there to begin setting up model communes, a move which he warned would "lead us astray."[113]

In Stalin's last years, in fact, the commune seemed to have almost disappeared from Bolshevik thinking as a feasible short-term solution to the agricultural problem. Stalin's essay on the "Economic Problems of Socialism in the USSR," published on the eve of the 19th Party Congress in October 1959, nowhere even mentioned the commune. Rather, Stalin decried any "simple" solutions to the problem of how to achieve Communism.

The Soviet Attitude toward Communes after Stalin's Death

There was no change in the unfavorable Soviet attitude toward communes in the years after Stalin's death, right up to the very eve of the Chinese commune decree in the fall of 1958. The *Bolshaya sovetskaya entsiklopediya* (Large Soviet Encyclopedia), Vol. 22, signed for the press on September 9, 1953, six months after Stalin's death, devoted only two paragraphs to the commune and concluded that it was a "less vital form" than the artel. In 1958, the Chinese Communists would defend their communes by arguing that the artel-type cooperative had not proved "vital" enough.

Khrushchev's radical agricultural reforms in early 1958 led to renewed discussion in the Soviet press on the problem that had long faced the Soviet regime—what organizational forms would be provided for agriculture as Soviet society moved further towards the ultimate Communist society. Because Khrushchev's reforms seemed to many Communists a step backward on the road to Communism, Soviet ideologists were given the task of rationalizing them. In the course of this dialogue, in the spring of 1958, there was general agreement that although the precise institutional form for agriculture during the period of transition to Communism had not yet been found it would certainly not be the commune. Thus, the dean of Soviet economists, Academician S. G. Strumulin, wrote in *Literaturnaya gazeta* (Literary Gazette) on March 25, 1958, that transformation of the artel into a commune "has been precluded in practice for an entirely indefinite period." Strumulin amplified his objections to the current realization of the commune in a longer article in *Voprosy ekonomiki*.[114] There he ruled out the commune on three grounds: first, because the Communist principle of distribution presupposed "inexhaustible sources of abundance," so that to try to realize the commune in the backward Soviet *kolkhoz* village would be "absurd." Second, Strumulin pointed out that the collective farms differed greatly in economic prosperity, a fact which was inevitable for some time to come. It would be equally "absurd," he wrote, to envisage a situation in which rich communes would compete with backward communes. Finally, he objected to the decentralization and dispersal of communes as incompatible with the necessity for one master to guide production. Such a dispersal of authority he called a "reactionary utopia."

Another Soviet writer in the spring of 1958 seemed to rule out the agricultural commune not only during the transition to Communism but forever.[115] Glotov, a Soviet economist, contended that communes were "unlikely" under socialism because conditions were not yet ripe. Even under Communism, he said, they would be "obviously senseless."

We argued earlier that evidence in Soviet media prior to the Chinese commune declaration, published in September 1958, strongly suggested little awareness of the Chinese intention to go ahead with communes. The evidence cited above from the Soviet press in the spring of 1958 might be interpreted as an indication that the Russians *did* have advance knowledge of the Chinese commune program and were warning them against implementing it. Such a theory seems untenable for several reasons. First, Soviet articles in the spring of 1958 on the subject of communes were not consistent with one another. Some writers seemed to hesitate about whether communes were possible in the USSR at some future date, while others seemed to rule them out unequivocally. If the articles had been intended to serve as a warning to Peking, they would probably have taken a unanimous approach to the problem. Moreover, Moscow would not have left the task of heading off the Chinese to academicians like Strumulin and Glotov; such a task would very probably have been undertaken—as it was in November 1958—by Khrushchev himself.

Second, and perhaps most pertinently, the Soviet articles vetoing communes in the spring of 1958 can be explained on the basis of Soviet internal developments, notably Khrushchev's radical Machine Tractor Station (MTS) reform a few months earlier. It had long been Soviet dogma, as we have seen, that the "higher" agricultural commune would one day replace the "lower" artel. Presumably, such a transformation would take place as the USSR moved closer to Communism. Khrushchev's MTS reform in January 1958 seemed to reverse this progressive trend toward a "higher" form of agricultural organization. The property of the "higher" state-owned MTS was sold to the "lower" cooperative *kolkhozy*. As is evident from Khrushchev's speeches defending the move, many Soviet economists and ideologues—and probably some in the ruling circles—interpreted this reform as a retrograde step. The move seemed particularly dubious, from an ideological point of view, because it came at a time when Khrushchev himself had just indicated during the 40th anniversary celebrations that the USSR might soon enter a new stage of Communist construction. Moreover, Stalin had dismissed the sale of the MTS to the *kolkhozy* as "reactionary" and unfeasible. Khrushchev was thus faced with the task of explaining how he could move into a "higher" stage of the transition to Communism by strengthening a "lower" form of agricultural organization. To do this required some fancy ideological footwork and some explanation of the future direction of agricultural organization during the transition to Communism. Specifically, were communes to be established in place of the artels, as Soviet dogma had long indicated? Since Khrushchev had no intention of abandoning material incentives or forcing premature communization on the countryside, he had to dismiss the agricultural commune, at least during the period of transition to Communism. His theoreticians were called upon to discuss and to explain this development.

The Future of the Soviet Artel

It seems likely that Khrushchev and the present Soviet leadership are moving away from the idea of transforming the present artel-type cooperatives into communes at some future date. By various gradual steps—economic rather than political or organizational—Khrushchev intends to wipe out the still considerable private economic activity in the village. Ever since the early postwar years, he has envisaged the transformation of Soviet villages into "agricultural cities," an idea for which he was once criticized. These urbanized villages would contain communal bakeries, dining halls, schools, clubs, and so on. Khrushchev has said also that private production and private ownership in the artels will be reduced at the same time as the peasants realize that the communal sector can and will satisfy their needs. He seeks to make vegetable production on private plots economically unprofitable through the establishment of vegetable *sovkhozes* around large cities to specialize in vegetable production, bring down production costs, and eventually reduce the market price below what the individual peasant can afford to sell at. Furthermore, future expansion of capital investment in the *kolkhoz* economy is to be effected by increasing the share of collective farm income which is devoted to the "indivisible fund," that part of the collective farm's resources not subject to distribution among its members. At the same time, there will be increasing emphasis on large-scale inter-*kolkhoz* cooperation in industrial projects, such as building electric power stations and producing construction materials, which will aid in rural development and be a major step toward establishing a mixed industrial-agricultural economy in the countryside.

In short, Khrushchev intends to wipe out private economic activity and ownership in the Soviet village, but in the course of time and through envelopment tactics rather than a headlong institutional reform. Khrushchev's agricultural policies remain evolutionary. The present Soviet village is to change only slowly as the increasing industrialization of agriculture raises productivity, as the peasants themselves become convinced that their needs can be satisfied by the communal sector, and as the material and psychological prerequisites for village urbanization are achieved. No firm target date has been set for the completion of the village reconstruction program, and there are warnings against haste and haphazard planning. Although there is encouragement to the peasants to surrender private livestock to the artel, there are also warnings against using force.

123

Finally, there is no indication that Moscow intends to implement any form of so-called "free supply," or distribution according to "need," in the foreseeable future. On the contrary, Khrushchev's policies in the village, as well as in industry, are heavily laced with material incentives designed to spur productivity. Thus, inequality in distribution will be preserved.

The Chinese Retreat:
November–December 1958

Signs of a Chinese retreat on the communes were evident, as has been indicated, as early as the October Revolution anniversary on November 7, immediately after Soviet Ambassador Yudin returned from an extended stay in the Soviet Union.

Authoritative CCP spokesmen and central press comment at the time of the anniversary acknowledged that the CCP was still in the stage of "socialist construction" and refrained from any striking predictions about the attainment of Communism in China. For the first time since August, they also referred generously to recent Soviet achievements in building Communism. CCP Vice Chairman Chu Teh at the Soviet Ambassador's reception of November 7, said that the Chinese people "have the confidence to accomplish socialist construction in a very short historical period and, further, to pass on to Communism."[116] Thus Chu conveyed the idea that the period needed for completing socialism was short only in the perspective of history. He also separated Communism from socialism and relegated the former to an indefinite future.

Two weeks later on November 21, it was again Chu, who, in a speech to a conference of young activists, warned them against "behaving like Utopians," and went out of his way to stress that China was still building socialism, that industrialization and the "highest world levels in science and culture" were prerequisites for Communism, and that a "hard struggle" was still needed to complete socialist construction.[117] "Our achievements so far," said Chu, "are still far behind what is needed to complete the building of socialism." He referred to communes but did not relate them to progress toward Communism, and he said nothing about the free-supply system.

A day later, *Jen-min jih-pao* affirmed in very strong and polemical terms that during the socialist stage "no other way" of distribution was possible than distribution according to work.[118]

The December Resolution

The resolution on communes adopted by a CCP plenum on December 10 formalized the Chinese retreat on the transition to Communism in various respects. First, it indicated that much time would pass before the completion of socialist construction: " . . . it will still take a fairly long time to realize, on a large scale, . . . the building of a socialist country with a highly developed modern industry, agriculture, science, and culture. This whole process will take fifteen, twenty, or more years to complete, counting from now."[119]

The August resolution had offered no kind of time limit for the completion of socialism and had suggested that the two processes of building socialism and Communism could be merged. By allowing "fifteen, twenty, or more years" for the completion of socialist construction alone, the Chinese were being more conservative than they had been before the communes were instituted. The *Jen-min jih-pao* editorial on January 1, 1958, had contended that it would "still require ten to fifteen years to build a modern industrial and agricultural foundation in our country" and thus to "fundamentally complete" the building of socialism. The "ten to fifteen years" figure was significantly the one used by Moscow in the third edition of the textbook *Politicheskaya ekonomiya uchebnik* which appeared in September.[120]

Second, the December resolution emphasized the wage principle rather than the automatic supply system. A negation of the "pay according to work" principle, it warned, could dampen labor enthusiasm. For this reason, that principle "must occupy an important place over a long period." Any attempt to institute the principle of distribution according to "need" prematurely was "undoubtedly a utopian concept that cannot possibly succeed."[121]

Third, the resolution conceded that Chinese productive capacity was "still very low" and that the transition to Communism depended on a development of production forces.[122]

Fourth, the resolution introduced a qualification of the theory

125

of permanent revolution. While affirming that theory, it pointed out: "We are at the same time advocates of the Marxist-Leninist theory of the development of revolution by stages; we hold that different stages of development reflect qualitative changes and that these stages different in quality should not be confused."[123] Just how the two theories of "permanent revolution" and "revolution by stages" were compatible was a problem left to Chinese dialecticians to solve in the subsequent months. But this ideological modification —implying a slowdown in the revolutionary advance—was one of the most important results of the plenum. The *Hung ch'i* editorial on the December resolution said: "To unify the theory of uninter- rupted revolution with the theory of the development of revolution by stages—this was the fundamental starting point of the 6th plenary session. . . . "[124] *Hung ch'i* added that the transition from collective to national ownership of the communes could not be "impetuous." There should be no groundless declarations that the communes would achieve national ownership suddenly or that China would "enter Communism immediately." Such statements would "greatly lower the standards of Communism in the minds of the people, distort and vulgarize the great ideal of Communism."

What motivated the Chinese retreat? It is likely, in retrospect, that some aspects of the commune—particularly the supply system —were not achieving the hoped-for results, that the CCP had dis- covered by late November that Marxism could not produce grain, and had concluded that it had overreached itself in its initial revolu- tionary fervor. It is also quite likely that the USSR made formal protestations through intra-party channels or through Ambassador Yudin personally when he returned to Peking, as well perhaps as through other channels, to convey its concern. Khrushchev's sar- castic remarks to Senator Humphrey on December 1, to the effect that "you can't get production without incentives" and that the communes were "reactionary," were probably made with the full awareness that they would find their way back to Peking.

Another possible factor involved in the Chinese retreat is worth consideration. One of the implicit demands in Peking's radical ideological formulations in the summer and early fall of 1958 was an acceleration not only of its own pace toward the ultimate Communist goal but also of the pace of the entire Bloc. The Chinese may have believed that their views were being adopted in Europe. The beginnings of an acceleration of political and economic activity throughout the European satellite Bloc can be traced to the fall of 1958 and early 1959. This acceleration was sanctioned at the 21st CPSU Congress. The Bulgarian press indicated as early as October 1958 that Bulgaria intended to finish its third Five Year Plan earlier than anticipated, that to accomplish this task it must mobilize its "inexhaustible labor reserves," a strong indication it had been impressed by the Chinese example.[125] After the CPSU Congress, Hungarian leaders announced that "we will complete the building of socialism sooner than planned" and Czech leaders discussed ways of stepping up the growth of Communist "shoots." Rumanian leaders looked forward to completing the building of socialism in broad outline.

In many of these countries, there was a corresponding stepup in the pace of industrialization and collectivization. Hungary doubled its collectivized sector in January and February 1959;[126] Rumania began cracking down on *kulaks* and announced in October that collectivization would be completed by 1965.[127]

Some of the satellites, moreover, began introducing egalitarian measures clearly modelled on Chinese lines. Party and government bureaucrats began doing physical labor and army officers began serving periods of time in the ranks. The Albanian Party Central Committee in its November 3–4, 1958, plenary meeting adopted a decision requiring all state and Party officials, including members of the Central Committee, to engage in physical work. This was the first such decree by any European satellite and it was given wide publicity by the Chinese NCNA on November 12.[128] In a sense, then, the Chinese pressures for a return to the radical revolutionary traditions of Marxism had found a response, if they had not actually been anticipated, in Europe.

The single most important consideration influencing the Chinese retreat, however, seems to have been the economic payoff expected from the USSR. The Soviet doctrine of "more or less simultaneous" transition to Communism, announced at the 21st Party Congress in February, carried with it the corollary—spelled out at the Congress by none other than Ambassador Yudin himself—that the more developed countries would help the lesser developed countries, so that all would move faster "in a single front" toward Communism.[129] Moreover, on February 7, 1959, shortly after the

Congress, the USSR announced that it would supply China with 78 new heavy industrial enterprises worth 5 billion rubles.[130] Finally, the trade figures for 1959 show a sharp upswing in "turnover." They were 60 per cent above the 1957 trough, and 37 per cent above the 1956 peak.[131]

The upswing in 1958 alone of 18 per cent was probably far in excess of a modest expansion envisaged by the trade "protocol." The primary factor evidently was the urgent Chinese import needs generated by the "big leap." The experience of 1958 was repeated in 1959. There was a sharp increase in Chinese imports of Soviet machinery and equipment to 2.4 billion rubles, nearly twice the peak imports of 1958. This rapid acceleration of trade must have brought home to the Chinese leaders their dependence on Soviet support in any effort to accelerate their rate of industrialization. Even more important, it made clear how valuable it was to have a supplier like the USSR, which was willing to provide support at short notice, even at considerable inconvenience to its planners and industrial managers.

The Chinese could not have expected the Russians to "bail them out" in this fashion without a reciprocal payoff. The payoff, it would seem, was the temporary ideological retreat.

The 21st CPSU Congress

At the 21st CPSU Congress in February 1959, the "Congress of Builders of Communism," Khrushchev took upon himself the unfamiliar mantle of prominent Marxist-Leninist theoretician and delivered the most complete statement on the transition to Communism offered by any Soviet leader since Stalin's programmatic article on "Economic Problems of Socialism" in 1952. His remarks on the transition were included in a section of his report titled "New Stage in Communist Construction and Some Problems of Marxist-Leninist Theory."[132] Congress speakers and the Soviet press and radio claimed that Khrushchev's report was a major contribution to, indeed the incarnation of, "creative Marxist-Leninist teachings."[133] *Izvestiya* went so far as to say it provided a program for expanded Communist construction illuminating the all-triumphant theory of Marxism-Leninism.[134] Many speakers stressed that Khrushchev's theoretical propositions were of "colossal importance" for the entire Communist movement,[135] while Pavel Yudin pointedly remarked that "now everybody who wants to understand what Communism is, must study, besides the works of the classical writers of Marxism-Leninism, the works of the 21st CPSU Congress."[136]

It was clear from all this that the 21st Congress proceedings were intended to be the Soviet contribution to the dialogue on future Communist society that Mao had provocatively begun a year earlier. More, the Congress was to provide the forum in which Khrushchev would attempt to regain the ideological initiative from Mao, to establish himself as a lawgiver for the entire bloc, and to codify Soviet thinking on the transition to Communism.

In his report, Khrushchev advanced three basic propositions which were calculated, on the one hand, to expose the weakness of some of the Chinese positions advanced in 1958 and, on the other, to find some common ground with Peking without radically altering the basic Soviet gradualist approach. Khrushchev's first proposition was that, in order to make the transition from capitalism to Communism, it was necessary to pass through a socialist phase of development which could not be "violated or bypassed at will." Progress toward Communism must be made "step by step," by creating the material and spiritual prerequisites for a "methodical transition" to Communism.[137] Khrushchev was in effect sharpening the long-held Soviet doctrine that the transition must be gradual.

The second proposition was double-edged. Despite differences between the stages of Communism and socialism, said Khrushchev, there was "no wall" between them. Communism grows from socialism. It would not emerge suddenly. Soviet society, for example, already had many "tangible features of Communism." There would be no particular moment when "we shall shut one door and announce 'the building of socialism is completed' and open another door with the announcement 'we are now in Communism.' . . . In fact, we are already opening the door into Communist society. . . ."[138] This masterful stroke of dialectics conceded what the Chinese had insisted on: the continuity between socialism and Communism. Peking's December Resolution had anticipated Khrushchev's very language when it contended that "no 'Great Wall' exists or can be allowed to exist between . . . socialism and Communism."[139] Its Chinese version of "permanent revolution" and its unique Chinese formula "socialism-Communism" had also been intended to stress the continuity of development. At the same time, the way in which Khrushchev expounded the concept of continuity pointed up the enormous progress that the USSR had already made on the road to Communism. Khrushchev could boldly announce, "We are already opening the door to a Communist society," despite the fact that forty-two years after the Bolshevik revolution there had still been no announcement of the completion of "socialist construction."

Khrushchev's third and final proposition was a masterpiece of equivocation. The transition to Communism, he said, could not be understood as "a decelerated movement," yet it could be accelerated only on the basis of a development of material production. One could not rest on one's laurels, as this would lead to stagnation; yet "there must be no undue haste, no hurried introduction of measures that have not yet matured."[140] The Soviet leader was charting a very fine course between the Scylla of haste and the Charybdis of stagnation.

As if to fend off criticisms of the USSR's slow road to the good society, Khrushchev, in addition to delivering these three "laws" on the transition, went into a detailed explanation of the Soviet timetable for building Communism. When the USSR had caught up with the United States in per capita production, he said, a task which would take twelve years or less (i.e., until about 1971), the USSR would have completed the "initial phase" of Communist construction. (Here was the first indication that the construction of Communism, like the construction of socialism, would be divided into stages.) The completion of this initial stage, continued Khrushchev, would be merely a "midway station" on the road to Communism. Afterward, it would still be necessary for the Soviet Union to leave the United States behind and "push ahead." In the "coming period," emphasis would be laid on "the building of the material and technical base of Communism."[141] In short, the CPSU was making considerable progress toward the achievement of Communism, but the goal depended largely on a vast increase in material wealth.

Khrushchev's most significant doctrinal concession to Peking came in the reversal of a "law" elaborated only four months earlier by a Soviet philosopher. As we have seen, Stepanyan had written in October that the European Bloc countries would enter Communism as a group and well before the Asian Bloc countries.

130

Khrushchev now announced that all Bloc countries would make the transition to Communism "more or less simultaneously."[142]

This new canon seemed intended to remove the competitive elements from the race between Moscow and Peking for Communism. Moreover, it implied, a commitment of aid from the more to the less developed Bloc countries, on condition, as Yudin made clear at the Congress, that there was increased Bloc economic coordination and specialization, something that Peking had balked at for several years. Yudin said: *"The more the economic plans of these [Bloc] countries are coordinated* and the more the developed countries help the lesser developed countries, the faster will all, in a single front, move toward Communism" [italics supplied].[143] In effect, Khrushchev was telling Mao, "We'll give you more help, if you'll coordinate with the Bloc economically and stop trying to achieve autarchy."

In the same vein, when discussing the "more or less simultaneous transition" formula, Khrushchev's theoreticians put their stress on the "more or less." Thus, only two months after Khrushchev's doctrinal "concession," *Kommunist* warned against any overly literal interpretation of the formula and stressed that there could not possibly be "absolutely equal development" toward the final goal. Some countries would be more equal than others. This meant, *Kommunist* strongly implied, that the USSR would continue to set the pace on the road to Communism: "The experience of the USSR indicates that objective conditions which allow the beginning of the direct tasks for the establishment of the transition to Communism arise *only after* the socialist stage of development has been passed through. *Of course,* already at this stage, particularly at its concluding part, Communist shoots appear. However, only a full socialist society, possessing a corresponding material base and socialist production relations, begins the gradual transition to Communism" [italics supplied].[144]

Since it would take fifteen to twenty years or more to complete the building of socialism in China, the periodical held, the Chinese could not be competitors in this area for at least that length of time. By the end of that period, moreover, according to Khrushchev's Congress calculations, the USSR would have completed the "initial stage" of Communist construction and would be well on its way toward full Communism. The likelihood was thus that Moscow would continue to set the pace toward Communism for the foreseeable future, the "more or less simultaneous" transition theory notwithstanding.

On the question of communes and the related question of distribution, Khrushchev at the 21st Congress came down hard on the Chinese. The collective-farm, cooperative form of production relations, he said, without mentioning communes, has not only not exhausted its possibilities, but "serves and can go on serving for a long time the development of the productive forces of agriculture." Moreover, "in articles and lectures, some scientific workers" had advocated "prematurely" the introduction of the Communist principle of distribution according to need. Such "levelling would mean not transition to Communism, but the discrediting of Communism."[145] He emphasized what he had told Senator Humphrey two months earlier,[146] that early Soviet experience with equal food distribution under War Communism was not voluntarily adopted but was a "temporary measure" introduced because of "an acute shortage of food and consumers' goods." This method of distribution "could not be regarded as normal." Its defects came to the surface immediately. Without "material incentives," he said, "there could be no question of . . . leading the millions forward to Communism."[147]

Yudin reiterated Khrushchev's oblique lecture to the Chinese on these points and added: "We must observe the principles of Leninism and must not have the slightest manifestation of utopianism when we decide the conditions and methods of Communism."[148] Yudin also conveyed a more subtle warning to the Chinese by recalling that the Yugoslavs, those "so-called Marxist-Leninists," did not give any importance to the fact that "it is impossible for a single nation to enter a Communist society [alone] during the present stage of the world socialist system." This was a neat reminder to Peking of its practical dependence on the USSR.

On balance then, the 21st Congress reply to the Chinese had, in the typical Khrushchev manner, elements of both carrot and stick. It sought to maintain Soviet prestige and doctrinal authority while at the same time making some concessions. It promised Mao more economic help if Mao would cooperate in Khrushchev's specialization plan. It agreed with Mao that the pace toward Communism must be speeded up, but rejected any radical revisions of the Soviet gradualist timetable. It warned the Chinese that their distribution system was unworkable and suggested that the communes had been set up prematurely. Finally, it implicitly reminded China of its economic dependence on the USSR. At best, the Congress laid the groundwork for an uneasy truce on interrelated problems of the "transition to Communism."

Peking's Reaction to the 21st Congress

The Chinese Communist Party paper waited nine days—until February 5—to comment editorially on those portions of Khrushchev's speech dealing with the "transition to Communism."[149] (After the 20th Congress in 1956, it had waited only four days.) On February 16, *Hung ch'i* gave a comprehensive review of the Congress.[150]

The single most notable thing about the Chinese reaction was the fact that only one of Khrushchev's propositions—the "more or less simultaneous" transition to Communism—was treated as a "creative" addition to Marxism-Leninism. Both *Hung ch'i* and *Jen-min jih-pao* summarized all of Khrushchev's other propositions—his condemnation of "egalitarian Communism," his warning against impetuousness, his insistence on material prerequisites for Communism. Both esteemed the value of Soviet experience; *Hung ch'i* reiterated Mao's formulation of November 1957—a formulation that had been missing from Peking propaganda for some time—that the socialist camp must have a leader and that the leader was the Soviet Union. But on the communes and the Chinese path to Communism, Peking did not give way. In fact *Hung ch'i* went out of its way to indicate that the Soviet solution to the agrarian problem— the gradual merging of collective and state property—was valid only for the USSR: "The Communist Party of the Soviet Union has mapped out a path for developing and bringing closer together the two forms of Soviet socialist ownership—collective farm ownership and ownership by the whole people. *It held* that the merging of the two forms of ownership is the solution to the profoundly significant question of overcoming the essential differences between the rural and urban areas" [italics supplied].[151]

Peking's unenthusiastic response to Khrushchev's theoretical propositions on the transition to Communism seemed to reflect a

133

desire neither to press the controversy further nor to give in. A compromise, but a tenuous compromise, had evidently been achieved. As we shall see, this compromise was soon shattered.

The Truce Breaks

Khrushchev's speech in Poland on July 18, 1959, tore the 21st Congress truce to shreds.[152] Speaking to the Plawce producers co-operative in Poznan on how "The Cooperative Way is the Surest Way for the Peasant," Khrushchev strongly implied that the Chinese, in setting up communes, had a "poor understanding" of how to build Communism. Referring to the early Soviet experience with communes, he said they were a dismal failure because neither the material nor political prerequisites for them existed. Those "people" who wanted to set them up in the USSR, he said, "had a poor understanding of what Communism is and how it is to be built." Dismissing the War Communism experiment—and, by implication, the Chinese one—he said that "nothing came of many of these communes."[153]

Khrushchev's indirect but unmistakable attack on the Chinese communes was clearly premeditated and carefully executed. Bloc media gave no hint that Khrushchev's Poznan speech contained a passage on communes until three days after the speech had been delivered. An extensive summary of the speech carried by the Polish Home Service on July 18 omitted all reference to the commune passage. It was not until July 21 that *Pravda, Trybuna ludu,* and the Moscow Radio Home Service carried similar versions of the speech, including the passage on communes. This unusual delay and tight coordination suggest a very carefully planned maneuver.

Khrushchev's attack on the communes was his first direct public reference to the idea of communes since the experiment had been launched almost a year earlier. In private statements to Senator Humphrey in December 1958 he had scoffed at the communes, but at the 21st Congress he had in effect denied making such statements. Moreover, Khrushchev's attack sharply reversed the accommodating tone taken by Soviet media after the 21st Congress. Thus, as late as June 2, *Kommunist* (no. 8, 1959) alluded briefly but favorably to the communes.[154] On March 5 a Soviet radio broadcast had called the communes a contribution to the "common fund of practical experience." In the same month, *New Times* endorsed the Chinese contention that the communes were the "best" form for China's socialist construction.[155] Perhaps even more significantly, the first issue of a new journal of Soviet sinologists, *Problemy vostokavedeniya*, signed to the press on March 21, gave considerable attention to the "originalities" of Chinese socialist construction in China and called on Soviet scholars to give more study to those "original" contributions. An article in the second issue of the same journal, signed to the press on April 17, credited the communes with significant economic advantages over their predecessors.

The frontal assault by Khrushchev thus broke a truce that had lasted six months. Soviet media had begun to say some positive things about the Chinese communes, and Chinese media had withdrawn their most extreme claims, for example, that Communism could be achieved at a relatively early date and that the communes were superior to cooperatives as a collective way of life.

Although there are several possible explanations for Khrushchev's bold initiative, the most likely is that he wanted to influence the discussions then in progress within the Chinese Party. An enlarged plenum of the Chinese Central Committee evidently met throughout July and early August in Lushan. A resolution was adopted on August 16 and released on August 26. The plenum's basic preoccupation was with the communes in particular and the entire leap forward program in general. There is good evidence to indicate that this plenum was marked by a severe intra-party battle. There were apparently three schools of thought. The extreme Right, which came under severe fire after the plenum, wanted to disband the communes and to undertake a general retreat from the leap forward and the general line that had been undertaken in 1958. The Left wanted to press on with the communes and the leap forward more or less as originally conceived. A center group, which apparently won the day, wished to continue with the communes and the "leap" but in a more cautious manner.

The August 26 resolution itself suggested the intensity of the conflict that had raged at the plenum. Rightists had accused the leadership of "petty bourgeois fanaticism." This charge, taken directly from Lenin's "Left-wing Communism,"[156] was clearly not one that could or would have been made by lower level cadres against the leadership unless the leadership itself, or at least the

Central Committee, was badly split. Shortly after the resolution was published, slashing attacks on the Rightists began appearing in the Chinese press. These attacks revealed the character of the Rightist criticisms. The communes, said the Right, were "set up too early and too fast"; they were "doomed to failure"; they hindered production and depressed the living standards of the peasantry. The Right was also accused of having launched a general attack on the planning associated with the leap forward, the mass iron and steel campaign, and the reliance on mass mobilization in place of incentives.[157]

The Rightist opposition did not appear overnight. As we pointed out earlier, as early as 1958, Liu Shao-ch'i, in his speech to the Party Congress, had directed a considerable amount of criticism toward this group within the Party which had opposed the line of rapid collectivization in 1955, expressed misgivings about the slogan "greater and faster," and opposed the concept of "uninterrupted revolution." What brought the chronic intra-party controversy to a head was the disastrous state of the Chinese economy by the fall of 1959. The specter of famine haunted the countryside; transportation bottlenecks had appeared; the mass iron and steel campaign had been a failure; earlier expectations had been shown to be illusory.

While we lack evidence to argue that the Rightists represent a pro-Soviet faction in the CCP, it is nonetheless apparent that their pragmatic views are more akin to those of Khrushchev and the Russians than the views of the dominant faction in the Chinese Party. It is the essence of these pragmatic views that they place greater emphasis on the hard facts of economic life and less on such "subjective" factors as the "mobilization of the masses," "permanent revolution," non-material incentives, etc. It is likely, moreover, that the Rightists, in the course of the internal dialogue in China, argued against the communes on the basis of the unsuccessful Soviet experience with agricultural communes in the 1920's. The regime press, in rebutting the Rightists, explained polemically that the Soviet model could not be followed too rigidly because "there are [no] ready patterns" for socialist construction. Moreover, on September 1, 1959, the *Yün-nan jih-pao* (Yunnan Daily) wrote of people who had said "maliciously" that China must study the experience of the Soviet Union, where communes had proved unworkable. Again, on September 22, the *Szu ch'uan jih-pao* (Szechwan Daily) wrote about "some" who were saying that "since the Soviet Union failed in agricultural communes, we should not repeat the attempt."

By the end of September 1959, the intra-party battle in China appears to have reached a point where there was a genuine crisis in the Chinese leadership. This crisis can be inferred from a very important article which appeared in the *Jen-min jih-pao* for September 28, by Liu Lan-t'ao, a member of the CCP Central Committee Secretariat. Liu began by noting that "the life and death struggle between the bourgeoisie and the proletariat will inevitably be reflected in the Party." He said that the bourgeoisie was constantly trying to "find agents within our Party" in order to undermine it from within, "even from inside the Party and its leading nucleus." Some "waverers and unreliable elements" were apt to be influenced by them. He continued: "The attack now launched by the right opportunists against the Party in opposition to the Party's general line for building socialism, the big leap forward and the people's communes is essentially sabotage [of socialism] on behalf of bourgeois interests. It is quite clear that if their anti-Party activities are not thoroughly crushed, the Party cannot . . . firmly hold the leadership of the state. . . . In no case will opportunist *factions* or talk and *activities* calculated to split the Party and usurp its leadership be permitted to exist inside the Party" [italics supplied].[158] The unprecedented language employed here seemed to foreshadow a widespread purge in the Chinese leadership. But there is no evidence that such a purge occurred. Perhaps a word to the wise was sufficient. Perhaps Mao decided at the last minute against any Stalinist bloodbaths. Perhaps the Right was so strong that it could not be purged without a drastic weakening of the Party that none would want. The point is that by the fall of 1959 the Chinese Party leadership had not only the Soviet Union to contend with; it had its own Right-wing opposition.

What is really remarkable is that, in the face of this crisis in the Party leadership and the growing crisis in the relationship with the Soviet Party, there was neither a convulsion in the Chinese Party nor a radical reversal of the Leftist line followed since 1957. In fact, the Lushan plenum in August 1959 signalled another push forward. If the period from December 1958 to the spring of 1959 can be called a period of consolidation and retreat, the fall of 1959 witnessed a new swing forward of the pendulum.

The Tenth Anniversary of the CPR: October 1959

The conflict over the communes showed no signs of dying down by the time of the tenth anniversary of the CPR in October 1959. On that occasion, there was virtually complete Soviet silence on the communes. Neither Khrushchev nor Suslov, who spoke in Peking, nor the Khrushchev-Voroshilov message to the CCP leadership, referred to the communes. The message used the euphemism, "very profound socio-economic transformations."[159] The *Pravda* editorial on the occasion talked about the harvest in the "collective fields."[160] On August 25, 1959, *Pravda* published a report from Peking entitled "On the Fields of China" without once mentioning the communes.

Similarly, the Russians were niggardly with compliments on the CCP general line of socialist construction and the "great leap." Of the tenth-anniversary speeches, only Suslov's made a passing reference to the general line. Khrushchev, in his major speech in Peking, showed little inclination to speak of Chinese economic successes. He twice apologized for not doing so, once because it was such a "short speech" and again because "it is not for me, a guest, to come to China . . . [and] to talk of your successes."[161]

The failure of the Soviet leaders, on the tenth anniversary of the CPR, to mention the communes or to praise at some length the Chinese economic program stands out conspicuously for more than one reason. First, there had already been considerable speculation in the Western press concerning Soviet coolness toward the communes—all the more reason why one would expect the Russians on such an important occasion, one normally used to emphasize Sino-Soviet solidarity, to make some gesture, if only a semantic one, to discourage such speculation. Second, there had been a number of changes in the commune program since its inception in 1958. Because these changes brought the communes closer to the form of the original cooperatives, one might have expected Moscow to come slowly to terms with the communes.

On the other hand, as mentioned, the Lushan plenum had

decided to inject new vigor into the commune program. This decision was reflected in the new hard line initiated by the CCP in September, a line which included a strong defense of the communal mess halls on practical as well as theoretical grounds, and which called for the early reactivation of those that had been dissolved by "mistake." After Lushan, there was a renewed Chinese emphasis on ideological claims which had met with strong Soviet disfavor from the start. Moreover, the CCP leadership even carried its defense of the communes into the pages of the Soviet press, where it vehemently rejected the "Right opportunist" view that the communes were "moving backward" and the "only way out" was to "dissolve them."[162]

Although the CCP withdrew some of the more radical of its ideological claims in 1958, after the Lushan plenum it began again firmly to restate others. These included the revitalized theory of "uninterrupted revolution," the notion that the wages-plus-supply compromise embodied rudiments of Communist distribution, the notion that the communes were the best form for the transition to Communism, and, perhaps most important, the idea that Chinese experience had validity for other socialist countries.[163] At the same time the CCP began to revive the chauvinistic claims for Mao that had been waning in the early part of 1959. Mao was now hailed as "one of the most outstanding" of all the Marxist-Leninist statesmen, revolutionaries, and theoreticians "of our age."[164]

The Communes and the Future of
Sino-Soviet Relations

By 1960 the conflict over the communes and the transition to Communism had receded into the background, to be replaced by the more acute conflict over global strategy. As a continuing and potential source of discord, however, the issue remains. While in their vigorous attacks on Soviet policy in April 1960 the Chinese largely centered their criticism on Soviet global revolutionary strategy, there was continued defiance of Soviet views on the transition to Communism and continued reassertion of the Chinese path and its relevance to underdeveloped countries. The CCP contended that revolutions in Oriental countries would "undoubtedly display even greater peculiarities than the Russian revolution"; they protested against "foreign and Chinese philistines" who had "their heads stuffed with metaphysics" and did not understand the revolutionary dialectics of the general line, the leap forward, and the communes.[165] For their part, the Russians gave little indication that they desired an accommodation on Chinese terms. As of the time when this book is in production (winter 1961), not one Soviet Presidium member has publicly mentioned the Chinese communes.

As a source of continuing Sino-Soviet friction, the conflict over the communes and the path to Communism should not be underrated. If the problem had been one of Chinese distinctiveness alone, it would undoubtedly have been resolved in its infancy. The Russians have not liked, but have come to terms with, earlier Chinese "creative" adaptations of Marxism. Why, then, have they refused to come to terms with the communes? If China's extravagant ideological claims are the reason, or a part of it, why has China made them? Even if it is conceded that the Chinese believed the communes to be a necessary response to peculiar and pressing Chinese economic problems, and the inculcation of revolutionary zeal to be a necessary ingredient of that response, the CCP manifestly went far beyond the limits it could have set. There seems no objective reason why the CCP had to suggest that the commune and the general line were valid for all underdeveloped countries. Nor was there any reason why the commune program had to be justified by a revival of the Marxist classics and by a buildup for Mao that rivalled and continues to rival the cult of Stalin. Finally, the implicit, and often explicit, suggestion that the Chinese were advancing to Communism faster than the Russians was surely a piece of gratuitous chauvinism on the part of Peking.

In sum, the Russians refuse to come to terms with the communes because they correctly perceive in them a deliberate challenge to Soviet hegemony in the Communist world. By emphasizing the "classical" Marxist-Leninist origins of their program, the Chinese suggest that the Russians have abandoned, or at least have deviated from, the original Marxist path. By a chauvinistic buildup for Mao, the Chinese suggest that he is the principal living repository of doctrinal wisdom for the entire Communist world. Finally, the missionary zeal which accompanies Chinese ideology suggests that it is Peking and not Moscow which should lead the revolution in the underdeveloped countries.

If the conflict over the communes, as such, had been an isolated cause of the friction in Sino-Soviet relations since 1958, it could probably have been contained within firm bounds. It will be argued below, however, that the conflict, by early 1958, had spread into the field of intra-bloc relations and global revolutionary strategy. In these areas, too, the CCP was deliberately challenging Soviet policy and strategy. Thus, no single area of conflict should be looked at in isolation. The challenge was a multiple one which arose as much from Chinese frustration over Soviet policies as from a Chinese desire for a greater role in formulating those policies, particularly when they impinged on Chinese interests.

PART THREE

THE ORIGINS OF THE DIALOGUE ON
INTRA-BLOC RELATIONS
AND GLOBAL STRATEGY: 1957–1958

CHAPTER 4

PEKING'S NEW LINE ON INTRA-BLOC RELATIONS:

NOVEMBER 1957

W E HAVE seen how the ascendancy of the Peking Left led in the early fall of 1957 to bold new domestic policies and ideological claims that resulted in conflict with Moscow. We have suggested that this domestic convulsion also resulted in an abrupt change in Peking's external policies and perspectives. In November 1957, when the Communist leaders assembled in Moscow for the 40th Anniversary of the October Revolution and for an important conference on Bloc strategy, this shift in Chinese thinking had already occurred. The November 1957 conference, in fact, may be considered the beginning of the long dialogue between Peking and Moscow on foreign policy that was to culminate in near schism three years later. This chapter illustrates the change in Peking's line on intra-bloc relations as it was reflected in statements by Mao at the November conference. A later chapter examines the same Moscow conference to illustrate the change in Peking's line on foreign policy.

Mao Speaks Up for the
"Centralist" Position

Of the issues that faced the Communist leaders when they assembled in Moscow in November 1957, none was more important or more controversial than the broad complex of questions having to do with intra-bloc relations and permissible diversity. These issues had been at the center of international Communist politics since the 20th Congress of the CPSU. What were the limits of Soviet prerogatives vis-à-vis other Communist parties? To what extent could socialist countries diverge from orthodox Soviet practices in building socialism? Were all Communist parties equal, or were some more equal than others?

The hopes of Gomulka, Togliatti, and Kadar—the most prominent of those who wanted more latitude in pursuing their own liberal domestic policies—depended to a considerable extent on Peking. After all, it was the Chinese who in 1956 and early

1957 had urged on the Russians a more moderate and flexible attitude toward other fraternal parties. It was the Chinese who had argued for a confederative as opposed to a unitary solution to intra-bloc relations. In the light of the past record, these leaders, or some of them, undoubtedly expected to have strong support for their position from Mao.

There seems little reason to doubt that a year or even three months earlier, Mao would have supported them on some issues against the Russians. Yet not only did he fail to do so at the November conference, but he seems to have led the vigilante wing of the conference which sought to expose all "un-Communist" behavior. According to a reliable newspaper account based on Polish sources, Gomulka was deeply disappointed in the results of a three-hour talk with Mao in Moscow, because the Chinese Communist leader had taken a "hard Soviet line in favor of Communist conformity."[1] On all the critical issues involving questions of permissible diversity, Mao took a centralist position. Before we seek an explanation for this sudden change in Chinese behavior, we shall offer some evidence concerning it.

The Soviet Leading Role

On November 17, the eve of the conference, Mao, in a speech at Moscow University, made the strongest and most unqualified endorsement of Soviet leadership of the Bloc voiced by any of the conference participants. "The socialist camp must have a head," he said, "and this head is the USSR." Moreover, "the Communist and workers' parties of all countries must have a head and that head is the CPSU."[2] The *Jen-min jih-pao* editorial of November 25, summing up the conference, said it was "of great significance" that the Moscow meeting pointed out the "central role of the Soviet Union in the solidarity of the socialist countries." The USSR's central position was "an objective reality brought about historically, and not something that someone [had] created artificially."[3]

Chinese stress on the Soviet Union's leading role in the Bloc was not new. In March 1957, Chou En-lai, during and after his tour of Eastern Europe, stressed the leading role of the CPSU in the Communist movement. Chinese ideological formulations had ever since 1949 routinely referred to the socialist camp as "headed by the Soviet Union." What was new in November 1957 was the

146

polemical emphasis. According to Peking, the Soviet Union not only *was* the head of the camp; it *must* occupy that position.

Moreover, it was clear that Mao had upheld Soviet prerogatives in debate with Gomulka, Kardelj (the Yugoslav representative), and Togliatti, who all failed to bow to Soviet leadership of the camp in their post-conference statements. It is quite likely that Chinese rather than Soviet insistence led the Moscow conference to include a strong passage on Soviet leadership in its declaration. For, while the conference was in session, Khrushchev told the American journalist Henry Shapiro that there was "no need for a center which would guide the Communist movement";[4] and in a speech to the East German SED Congress on July 11, 1958, Khrushchev said that the "addition [to the declaration] concerning the role of the USSR and the CPSU was proposed and motivated at the talks themselves, not by the delegation of the CPSU, but by the representatives of other fraternal parties."[5] According to the Yugoslavs, it was Mao's insistence on strengthening the declaration's statements on the need for subordination to Moscow that helped to prevent Yugoslavia from signing.[6]

Not only did Mao take a "hard" line against Gomulka and Tito on Soviet leadership of the Bloc, but he also made a major shift from earlier Chinese policy on Bloc relations by avoiding any reference to the "equality" or "independence" of Bloc members. In his November 6 speech to the Supreme Soviet, Mao spoke only of "identity of interests, mutual respect, confidence, mutual assistance, and inspiration."[7] The previous March, Chou En-lai had declared, "The socialist countries are united by the common ideal and aim of Communism; therefore, their relations are based on the principles of proletarian internationalism. The socialist countries are at the same time independent sovereign states; therefore their relations are based also on the Marxist-Leninist principle of national equality."[8] This theme of equality had been prominent in CCP pronouncements on Bloc relations throughout the fall of 1956.

The Applicability of
Soviet Experience

On the applicability of Soviet experience in building socialism, also a contentious subject at the conference, Mao made another major shift in the Chinese line. He stressed the importance of

147

studying Soviet experience and minimized the role of national characteristics. In his speech of November 6 to the Supreme Soviet, Mao called the Soviet path the "bright common way" for all mankind. He said that although the Chinese national revolution had its own national characteristics, China had always made "full use of the rich experience of the CPSU."[9] Poland, Hungary, and others, he implied, should do likewise: "It is clear that, after the October Revolution, if a proletarian revolutionary of any country should overlook or not seriously study the experience of the Russian revolution and should fail to use these experiences analytically and in a creative way in the light of the specific conditions in his own country, he would not be able to master Leninism . . . and he would not be able to solve the problems of revolution and construction in his own country correctly."[10] True, this statement refers to the need for a "creative" use of Marxism-Leninism. Yet its emphasis and that of other statements in the speech was on uniformity rather than creativity. This emphasis contrasts with the importance attached to "national characteristics" in Peking's statement of December 1956. At that time, it had pointedly noted that "doctrinaries do not understand that the universal truth of Marxism-Leninism manifests itself concretely and becomes operative in real life *only* through the medium of specific national characteristics. They are not willing to make a careful study of the social and historical features of their own countries and nations or to apply in a practical way the universal truth of Marxism-Leninism in the light of these features. . . . there must be a proper method of learning. *All the experience of the Soviet Union, including its fundamental experience, is bound up with definite national characteristics,* and no other country should copy it mechanically" [italics supplied].[11] The passages italicized above had come close to the actual espousal of revisionism.

Now, in November 1957, Mao threw his weight against Gomulka and the autonomists on the subject of revisionism. In his speech to the Supreme Soviet, he declared: "At present the urgent task is to oppose revisionist deviations."[12] He made no mention of dogmatism or of the right of each Party to judge for itself what was the main danger—a right demanded by Gomulka and one that Mao himself would almost certainly have sanctioned a year earlier. No Chinese statement of the preceding two years had called the combatting of revisionism—a euphemism for Marxism that is overly "creative"—"the urgent task." And Mao could not have been referring to the anti-Rightest struggle inside China, which he discussed in a separate portion of his speech.

Whether the upgrading of revisionism to an urgent threat was already signalled by the June 1957 revised version of Mao's speech on contradictions, in which he had called revisionism "even more dangerous than doctrinairism,"[13] or whether it had occurred later, it is beyond dispute that some time shortly before the November 1957 conference the CCP had made almost a *volte-face* in its view toward intra-bloc relations.

It is in fact quite likely that at the November 1957 conference the Chinese successfully forced the Russians to take a stiffer stand against Yugoslav revisionism than the Russians wanted to take. In 1960 the Chinese reportedly told the Indian Communists that the Soviet attitude toward Yugoslavia was "cringing" and that at the November 1957 conference, Peking told the Russians: "If you do not fight revisionism, we will have to take up the battle single-handed against all distortions of Marxism."[14] It was, according to this Indian account, only at this point that the Russians agreed to accept the Chinese amendments to twelve-party draft declaration.

In 1956 and early 1957, the Chinese formula had emphasized the need for genuine discussion rather than *diktat* in resolving differences within the Communist world, and for the importance of distinguishing differences of approach from attempts to subvert. While Peking all along had stressed the need for unity, for following Soviet leadership, for studying Soviet experience, it had put equal stress on the need for tolerance, for avoiding "great nation chauvinism," and for building socialism in accord with national peculiarities. As late as April 1957, Peking was continuing to reassure the Poles of its support. A joint communiqué, signed on April 11 by a Polish government delegation and the CPR after a visit to Peking by Polish Premier Cyrankiewicz, failed to designate the Soviet Union as the leader of the socialist camp.[15] Since this was a departure from normal Chinese propaganda practice, one can only suppose it was in deference to Polish wishes. At the same time, Peking media, in praising the joint accord, largely ignored the dangers of revisionism, dangers which the Russians had been continually stressing in contexts which made it clear they had Poland in mind.

At the November 1957 conference, this Chinese attitude was changed and suddenly Mao polemically defended the Soviet leading role to the point of insisting—over Russian reluctance—that a reference to it be included in the conference declaration. Suddenly he bypassed the need for equality in inter-Communist relations. The importance of national characteristics in building socialism was not so important as the lesson of Soviet experience. Revisionism was an "urgent danger." What was behind this change in Chinese Communist policy? Why had Mao become more royalist than the king?

Toward an Explanation of the CCP Shift in Line

It is important to keep in mind that the shift in intra-bloc policy was only one part of the overall strategic revision that occurred in Peking in the fall of 1957. The CCP Left, which assumed dominance in the late summer and early fall of 1957, made three distinct changes in Chinese Communist policy at about the same time: they moved from a cautious economic policy based on the Soviet model to a frenzied one based on the maximum exploitation of human labor power; they changed from defenders of diversity within the camp to enforcers of unity; and they reversed the cautious, defensive foreign strategy that had characterized Chinese policy since 1954. This new foreign policy called for maximum political and military pressure on the West all over the globe, but particularly in Asia, in the underdeveloped areas in general, and wherever the Bloc had "just grievances," as in Taiwan.

The new attitude required an intra-bloc policy based on unity and strength. Preparing for a radical step-up in political and military pressure on the West under the cover of the Soviet deterrent, Peking's radicals could no longer tolerate in Eastern Europe the relatively diverse policies they had excused during the Bandung period. They needed a Bloc monolithism designed to bolster outward thrust. Thus one Chinese paper wrote in February 1958, shortly before the CCP assault on Yugoslavia: "The greater the solidarity . . . among the socialist countries, the more powerful we shall become. On the other hand, should there be divisive forces among us, our strength would be dissipated. Then, even if we possessed such a powerful weapon as intercontinental ballistic missiles, we would not be able to overwhelm the enemies. We might even be overwhelmed by them."[16] In short, China's exploitation of Soviet weapons developments and of the Soviet deterrent could be maximized only if there were firm unity within the Bloc.

It is not accidental that Yugoslavia became the major target of Peking's venom. In periods of international calm, when the strategy of the Right allows cooperation with socialists, neutralists, and moderates, Bloc relations with Yugoslavia tend to improve. At such times there is no great need for iron discipline within the ranks. Conversely, in periods of international tension, when Left foreign policy is in the ascendant and cooperation with socialists, neutralists, and moderates yields to revolutionary and direct-action tactics, the errant Yugoslavs are the first to feel the burden of the change. At such times, it is necessary for the Bloc to close ranks and unify policy-making. Hence, in the spring of 1958, the beginning of the Sino-Soviet conflict manifested itself in divergent attitudes toward Yugoslavia. The Russians wanted to increase pressure on Tito, but not to the point where the strategy of the Right would be jeopardized. The Chinese, on the other hand, were calling for an abandonment of the strategy of the Right and, consistent with this, for an all-out assault on Yugoslav revisionism. The connections between intra-bloc relations, external revolutionary strategy, and foreign policy are direct. For this reason, to understand the CCP change in intra-bloc policy, it is necessary to understand in all its dimensions the new Left strategy that was unfolding in Peking in the autumn of 1957. It is to this that we now turn.

CHAPTER 5

THE ORIGINS OF THE DISPUTE OVER
GLOBAL STRATEGY: NOVEMBER 1957

The Question of Strategy

No OTHER revolutionary movement in history has been as preoccupied with the question of strategy and tactics as has the Communist. For the Communists, strategy is a science. As Stalin put it in his classic discussion in *The Foundations of Leninism,* "the strategy and tactics of Leninism constitute the science of leadership in the revolutionary struggle of the proletariat." Through strategy and tactics the Communists weave their way "scientifically" through the complicated maze of history and the class struggle, confident that the correct formulation of the strategic line will lead them more quickly to a victory that history has already ordained. At every critical juncture in Communist history, there is a pause for a long hard look at the nature of the epoch, at the contending social forces, at Communist strength vis-à-vis the strength of the enemy, at the dynamics of the capitalist society that is doomed to extinction. There is a pause to answer the questions: What is the nature of the present historical epoch? Who are our potential allies? Who is our main enemy? What is the relationship of our forces to those of the enemy? What ought to be the scope and intensity of our efforts to accelerate change?[1] For it is the answers to these questions that will determine the strategic line.

Of these interrelated questions, one stands out above all others: what is the overall power relationship—political, economic, and military—between us and the enemy? On an accurate assessment of this relationship depends whether a Communist Party takes one step forward or two steps back. The history of Communism is replete with Left- and Right-wing "deviations." Such deviations are produced when some members of the Party see either a more or less favorable correlation of forces than do those members dominating the Party. The Leftist, anxious to move forward, minimizes the strength of the enemy, whether that enemy be the kulak, the bourgeoisie, or Western "imperialism." He believes that the risks of a forward strategy are not so great as the risks of standing still. The

Rightist maximizes the strength of the enemy. He believes that the risks of a forward strategy are too great in the existing historical stage, and that they will jeopardize temporary alliances and unite foes who would otherwise be disunited. To want to move forward when the correlation of forces is unfavorable is the heresy of the Leftist; to want to retreat or to stand still at a time when the power balance is either favorable or dubious is the sin of the Rightist.

The differences between the Communist Left and the Communist Right have never been between those who wanted to arrive at a "permanent" understanding with the enemy and those who rejected any such understanding. There is, in the Communist world view, no possibility of any permanent *détente* with the domestic bourgeoisie or with Western imperialism. The choice is not between peace and conflict, but rather between alternative paces of, and methods for, waging the conflict.

To tread the delicate path between the Leftist and Rightist heresies is easy enough, provided one strong leader within a Party, or one Party within the Communist Bloc, can define the "correct" position. This position, by definition, is the centrist one. If there is such a strong leader, moreover, there is no difficulty in moving from a cautious to a bold strategy in the space of a month, for what was Rightist heresy yesterday can become the centrist position today. Thus, in 1928, Trotsky's policy of rapid collectivization was a Left-wing deviation; in 1929, it was the correct centrist position. The problem of strategy becomes difficult, if not insoluble, however, when two autonomous Communist countries view differently the correlation of forces, and therefore the opportunities for and the risks of revolutionary advance.

It is with such an understanding that a very important part of the Sino-Soviet conflict must be viewed. From the Soviet point of view, Mao is a "Left deviationist" who is urging a premature forward strategy, on the erroneous assumption that the Bloc has the decisive overall power advantage. From the Chinese point of view, Khrushchev is a "Right deviationist" who is acting with unnecessary caution and placing the ultimate victory in jeopardy.

This is not to argue that the Sino-Soviet conflict can be understood exclusively in terms of alternative revolutionary strategies. In the Introduction we have considered some of the basic factors which contributed to and undoubtedly accelerated the conflict.

The important point to establish here is that in the fall of 1957 the conflict took the *form* of a dispute over strategy. We proceed on the assumption that, if we know more about the immediate origins of and stated grounds for the controversy, we shall also know more about the underlying reasons for conflict.

We have seen how the Chinese Communists, in the late summer and fall of 1957, drastically revised both their domestic economic and intra-bloc strategy. In the present chapter we shall see that in the same period there was a radical shift in their global perspectives and strategy. This shift, like the shift in intra-bloc policy, was signalled by Mao's speeches and behavior at the November 1957 conference of Communist parties in Moscow. It was in fact this shift in global perspective that dictated change in intra-bloc strategy, and while it did not necessarily dictate the change in domestic policy, that too was intimately related, for the Left-wing group which gained ascendancy in the CCP in late 1957 viewed Chinese domestic difficulties and foreign policy frustrations in much the same light. The answer to both, in their view, was to push forward with a frenetic "leap forward," to instill new life into the sagging revolution, to make a qualitative jump, and to adopt bold solutions. On the domestic front, this thinking was rationalized by the contention that there was no way out other than through the general line, the leap forward, and the communes. On the foreign policy front, it was maintained that Soviet weapons developments in the fall of 1957 made it possible for the Bloc to move toward a bolder revolutionary strategy abroad.

The Significance of the Soviet Weapons Developments

On August 26 Tass announced that the Soviet Union had successfully tested "an intercontinental multi-stage ballistic rocket." On October 4 Moscow announced the launching of the first earth satellite, on November 3 the launching of the second. Ironically, these dramatic indications of Soviet power accelerated the Sino-Soviet conflict on strategy.

Immediately after the ICBM test, Peking began to emphasize the enormous military implications of the event. The Chinese Party newspaper cited American press commentary which said that the ICBM would greatly alter the balance of power between East and West and called the ICBM "the ultimate weapon."[2] Khrushchev called it "the absolute weapon" three months later.[3]

Chinese comment on the first and second sputniks similarly pointed out the military aspects of these achievements. Commentators stressed that the sputniks had ended American hopes for world hegemony and had dealt a powerful blow to the imperialist "policy of strength."[4]

In mid-November 1957 Mao arrived in Moscow to attend the summit conference of Communist leaders. It seems reasonable to assume that one of the primary purposes of this conference—in addition to discussing intra-bloc relations (see previous chapter)—was to chart worldwide Communist strategy and tactics for the period ahead. In this connection, the answers to several interrelated questions were of critical importance. How did these Soviet weapons developments affect the balance of power between East and West? Was the West now absolutely deterred from the risk of general war? If so, what risks could the Bloc now afford to take? What risks could it not afford to take? Even if it was true that the USSR had narrowed the Western advantage in strategic striking power, did not the West still have at its disposal impressive, perhaps superior, military and economic strength? In the light of such considerations, what kinds of political initiatives should follow? Should the USSR seek to negotiate with the West from a position of strength, now that it was quite possible that the West could be forced into making concessions, or should it forsake negotiations and adopt a more revolutionary policy all over the globe—particularly in those areas where the West was exposed and vulnerable, where revolutionary situations were ripe, where the Bloc had "just" grievances (e.g., in Taiwan), or where the Bloc had local military superiority?

The Khrushchev Evaluation:
The West Is Deterred

For Moscow, the Soviet weapons developments did indeed seem to represent the culmination of the drive for the long-sought absolute deterrent. The adequacy of Soviet deterrent power—and crucial problems such as the level of defense spending and the posture toward the West, which hinged on the assessment of Soviet deterrent power—had been a subject of controversy among the Soviet leadership since 1953.[5] For example, Mikoyan's declaration in March 1954 that the USSR's possession of nuclear weapons meant that the danger of war "has receded to a large extent" was

155

published only in the Yerevan Party newspaper and was deleted from the version of his speech published in *Pravda*.[6] Mikoyan's speech, moreover, was made on the same day that Malenkov made his famous statement that a new world war with present means of warfare would "mean the destruction of world civilization."[7] A month later, at the Supreme Soviet session, Mikoyan again expressed his confidence in Soviet deterrent power when he said that atomic and hydrogen weapons in the hands of the USSR were "tying the hands of those who would want to fight."[8] No other Presidium speaker advanced that idea either at the Supreme Soviet meeting in April or in the year that followed, and Malenkov's formulation was quickly overturned and subsequently rejected.

In 1955 Major General N. Talenskii contended that atomic weapons "by their very nature *enhance* the danger of military adventures" [italics supplied][9]—an indication that there remained those in the Soviet hierarchy who did not yet believe in the adequacy of Soviet deterrent power and who in particular feared a surprise attack. As late as the 20th Party Congress in 1956 there remained a significant difference in the Soviet leaders' formulations on the critical question of deterrence. While Khrushchev, Mikoyan, and Malenkov expressed varying degrees of confidence in Soviet deterrent power, Molotov and Suslov put their stress on the need for a continued alert, and Kaganovich in particular stressed that imperialism was incorrigibly "adventurous." Whatever were the precise lines between factions, there apparently were conflicting views, and Malenkov and Mikoyan seem to have been the early, and premature, spokesman of the mutual-deterrence line.

Khrushchev apparently took a position midway between the optimistic Mikoyan line and the more dire warnings of Kaganovich. He had been confident enough at the 20th Congress to say that "prominent leaders of bourgeois countries frankly admit with increasing frequency that 'there will be no victory' in a war in which atomic weapons are used. These leaders still do not venture to state that capitalism will find its grave in another world war, should it unleash one, but they are already compelled to openly admit that *the socialist camp is invincible*" [italics supplied].[10]

Later, the Soviet ICBM, which Khrushchev was to characterize as the "ultimate" weapon, almost certainly added to his confidence in Soviet deterrent power. In an interview with *Pravda* in September, Marshal K. A. Vershinin, commander in chief of the Soviet Air Force, spoke at length on the theme of the vulnerability of the United States to Soviet strategic missiles.[11] Vershinin's interview, which Khrushchev subsequently said he dictated (he told this to Vice-President Nixon), defined with unprecedented directness the strategic basis of Soviet military strength. It specifically disparaged the possibility of defense against rocket weapons and the military value of bomber forces, aircraft carriers, and U.S. bases abroad. All in all, it presented the most graphic picture ever given by any Soviet spokesman of the military vulnerability of the United States to Soviet strategic power.

In the year that followed the Soviet weapons successes of autumn 1957, Khrushchev became confident enough to claim Soviet superiority in missiles (November 1957);[12] to cast doubt on the American assumption that the United States was militarily stronger than the USSR (January 1958);[13] to throw out the traditional Stalinist concept of capitalist encirclement, because it was "no longer clear who encircles whom" (March 1958);[14] and to contend that the situation was such that the West would "hardly dare to unleash a war against the countries of the socialist camp" (October 1958).[15]

In sum, Soviet weapons developments in the fall of 1957 seemed to resolve the question, long unsettled in Soviet ruling circles, of the adequacy of deterrence. Given Soviet strategic power, only "insane" imperialists would now dare attack the USSR, Khrushchev said in May 1959.[16]

The Soviet ICBM also brought about a revolution in Soviet military writing. This revolution had been anticipated by the Vershinin interview just mentioned. Whereas, prior to the fall of 1957, Soviet military leaders repeatedly stated that nuclear weapons could not by themselves decide the outcome of modern wars, they now began to assert the predominant role of such weapons in any future general war.[17] Second, Soviet military strategists now asserted that the strategic significance of U.S. military bases in Europe had been drastically reduced. Third, the ICBM in Moscow's view had "greatly reduced the role of the air force," the principal weapon in the strategic arsenal of the U.S. military establishment. Finally, the new rocket weapons, according to Moscow, had "radically changed the nature of naval warfare," diminishing

157

the advantages conferred by aircraft carrriers and other surface units.[18]

The Russians also were eager to exploit the political gains which would accrue to them from the ICBM. They contended that there was dawning "a new era in international relations" which would lead to a "radical reappraisal of many ossified concepts of both military and diplomatic strategy."[19] They argued that the sputniks had enormously increased the "moral and political influence" of the Soviet Union, and were convincing proof of the high level achieved by Soviet science and technology. Moreover, said Moscow: "it is not just a matter of an increase in the weight and prestige of one country. *It is a question of a change in the balance of forces between Socialism and capitalism, of the strengthening of the former and the weakening of the latter* [italics in original]. Any change of this kind is naturally of great importance in international relations."[20]

Furthermore, in the Soviet view, the world had entered "a new stage of coexistence," in which coexistence "has become more stable than ever before" because the imperialist policy of "positions of strength" had been undermined.[21]

The enormous military, strategic, and political implications of the ICBM and sputniks had thus not been lost on Moscow. Militarily and politically, the Soviet Union had clearly taken a giant leap forward in the race with the West. The new opportunities for political aggrandizement, rocket-rattling, and pressures on the West were clearly foreseen.

Yet it is essential to note the important limits to Soviet optimism and the perspective in which the weapons developments were viewed. These limits and this perspective become all the more significant in light of Mao's assessments of the same weapons developments. First, and most important, no Soviet spokesman and no Soviet writer then asserted or now asserts that the sputnik-ICBM development had led to such a radical change in the balance of forces between East and West that the East was now *predominant*. The articles cited above, the Moscow Declarations of November 1957 and December 1960, and Khrushchev in all of his speeches said only that the undoubted change in the balance of forces had led to a situation where the East was now *stronger* and the West weaker than before. The Russians did not—and still do not—assert that the overall strength of the Bloc exceeds that of the West.[22] This, as we shall see, is precisely what Mao did and does assert.

Second, Khrushchev did not yet claim in the autumn of 1957 that the USSR had military superiority—let alone overall superiority—over the West. Such claims were not made by the Russians until early in 1960. Chinese journals, on the other hand, have clearly implied since the fall of 1957 that the Russians do have military superiority.

Third, the Russians—in sharp contrast to Peking—continued to pay implicit tribute to Western economic potential and prowess, thus implying that in overall economic-military strength the West was not a "paper tiger."

Fourth, beginning in the fall of 1957, Khrushchev and other Soviet spokesmen began frequently to assert that the USSR, too, would suffer "great damage," "great sacrifices," "great losses," and "no little destruction" in a nuclear war with the West.[23] Such considerations were absent from the speeches of Chinese leaders, which stressed *only* that imperialism would be destroyed in a world war.

Fifth, Moscow left vague the level of damage that the United States might suffer in a general war, a vagueness in sharp contrast to their vivid warning that the European NATO countries could be "wiped from the face of the earth." This could be taken to mean a lack of confidence in their ability to launch a decisive nuclear blow against the United States. Again, the Chinese unqualified insistence that imperialism would be wiped from the face of the earth betrayed a greater confidence in Soviet strategic power than the Russians themselves had.

Thus, if Khrushchev recognized the politico-military revolution brought about by the ICBM, he also recognized that the West was far from beaten. He did not assert that the East was now stronger than the West overall, probably because he did not believe that this was true. He did not yet claim military superiority, probably because he did not believe that he had it. If he was aware of the tremendous damage he could inflict on the United States, he was also aware of the tremendous damage that could be inflicted on the Soviet Union. Finally, he was still much impressed with American economic and military potential, and did not ignore it in estimating the overall balance of forces between the two camps. For if the

U.S. had considerable economic fat, that fat might quickly be converted into muscle.

The Maoist Assessment: The
East Wind Prevails

If Khrushchev's assessment of the strategic change wrought by Soviet weapons developments was as sanguine and moderate as it seems, Mao's assessment was apparently rather different. On November 17 Mao addressed a group of Chinese students who were attending Moscow University. He described the two Soviet sputniks as "a new turning point" and coined the now famous slogan which has since permeated Chinese Communist propaganda: "At present, it is not the west wind which is prevailing over the east wind, but the east wind prevailing over the west wind."[24] Of the entire world's population, he went on, the socialist countries had nearly one billion, the independent, former colonial countries had more than 700 million, and the "imperialists" only 400 million. The implication— not present in Khrushchev's speeches—was that the population advantage was an important factor in the strategic equation.

The very next day, Mao gave a considered estimate of the East-West balance of forces to the assembled Communist leaders from all over the world. The full text of this crucial speech has never been released. But parts of it were made public by the Chinese a year later and other portions can be inferred from Chinese press articles that appeared soon after the Moscow conference. We thus know that Mao told the Communist assembly in unequivocal terms: "I am of the opinion that the international situation has now reached *a new turning-point*. There are two winds in the world today: the East wind and the West wind. . . . I think the characteristic of the situation today is the East wind prevailing over the West wind. *That is to say, the socialist forces are overwhelmingly superior to the imperialist forces*" [italics supplied].[25] The italicized passages were the heart of Mao's famous meteorological formula. It is difficult to exaggerate the importance of the fact that no Soviet leader or journal has *ever* made such an unequivocal statement as the one italicized above. Moscow's standard formulation since the fall of 1957 has been the more ambiguous one that the balance of forces between socialism and imperialism has been altered "in favor of" the former.[26] This formulation, deliberately vague as it is, does not say that the Bloc is stronger than the West but only that the Bloc is substantially stronger than it was. Nor have Soviet spokesmen indicated that the fall of 1957 marked a "turning point" in the balance of forces. The Russians did speak, as we have seen, of a "new era" both in international relations and in world science, but they did not relate this "new era" to a change in the balance of forces between the Communist and Western powers. On the contrary, the Russians have consistently emphasized that the next "turning point" in the East-West balance will occur sometime around 1970, when the USSR outstrips the USA in overall production. Mao's speech of November 17 went well beyond this estimate.

Mao's speech to the Communist summit meeting on November 18 was significant in other regards as well. He recounted to the meeting his conversation with Anna Louise Strong in 1946, at a time when the Chinese Nationalists "began to attack us" and "I myself was also worried." It was at that time that he coined his equally famous term of contempt for an enemy "paper tiger." Although Chiang's forces heavily outnumbered the forces of the Chinese Communists, Mao told the Moscow meeting, "we said Chiang Kai-shek was only a paper tiger; we would certainly win against him."[27] Mao continued:

"In order to struggle against the enemy, we have formed the concept over a long period, namely, that strategically we should slight all enemies, and tactically we should take full account of them. That is also to say, we might slight the enemy as a whole but take full account of him so far as each and every concrete question is concerned. If we do not slight the enemy as a whole, we shall be committing the mistake of opportunism. . . . But on concrete questions and on questions concerning each and every particular enemy, if we do not take full account of the enemy, we shall be committing the mistake of adventurism. In war, battles can only be fought one by one and the enemy can only be annihilated bit by bit. . . . Strategically, we slight the eating of a meal; we can finish the meal. But when actually eating, we do it a mouthful at a time. It would be impossible for you to swallow the entire feast in a single mouthful. This is called one-by-one solution. And in military literature, it is called smashing the enemy one by one."[28]

For the analyst of Chinese Communist international conduct

in the period since the fall of 1957, there is perhaps no more revealing passage than the one quoted above. In his own terms, Mao was charting a fine course between "adventurism" and "opportunism." While the enemy could not be depreciated, he should not be feared. And while in each particular engagement he must be taken seriously, still the Communists would triumph in the long run. What was necessary was to swallow the enemy "one by one." In the light of Mao's view that the East wind now prevailed, it seems reasonable to assume he meant the time to start swallowing had now come. This kind of thinking probably lay behind the offshore island venture the following autumn.

For further indications of what Mao told the Communist leaders at the Moscow conference of November 1957 it is necessary to turn to the Chinese press. A number of important articles on strategy appeared therein after the conference. Taken together, these articles seem to elaborate the points made by Mao in Moscow.[29]

For one thing, most of these articles, unlike Soviet articles of the time, reflected the idea that Soviet weapons developments had led to a new turning point in the balance of power between East and West. Some explicitly stated, like Mao, that the East was now stronger than the West.[30]

Secondly, the articles made the claim, not made in Moscow, that there had been a "qualitative" change in the balance of power between East and West. In Communist terminology, at key turning points in history a number of "quantitative" changes suddenly become "qualitative" and therefore critical. *Kuang-ming Jih-pao* said, on February 9, 1958, that "the qualitative change in the distribution of world power has . . . torn apart the paper tiger of American imperialism and shattered the tale of the 'position of strength.' "[31]

Third, several of these Chinese articles in the post-conference period specifically claimed far more for Soviet military power than the Russians themselves claimed. *Shih-chieh chih-shih* (World Culture), for instance wrote on December 20: "The absolute superiority of the Soviet Union in intercontinental ballistic missiles has placed the striking capabilities of the United States . . . in an inferior position. The Soviet intercontinental ballistic missiles not only can reach any military base in Central Europe, Asia or Africa, but also force the United States, for the first time in history, to a position *where neither escape nor striking back is possible*" [italics supplied].[32]

Implicit in this contention was the view that the United States could not reply to a Soviet first strike, that it would in fact be decisively beaten if the Russians were to strike first. In 1960 Khrushchev would say in effect that neither the U.S. nor the USSR could be put into a position where striking back was impossible.[33]

Fourth, unlike Khrushchev, who specifically held out the possibility that the U.S. might catch up with the USSR in rocketry,[34] the Chinese Communists asserted that the new turning point was irreversible because the United States could never catch up. This was so because the rate of growth of the socialist economies in general, and of the Soviet Union in particular, was greater than the rate of growth of the Western and American economies. Thus, said *Kuang-ming jih-pao:* "The U.S. may achieve fruitful results in future experiments and even come to possess both earth satellites and intercontinental ballistic missiles. But the Soviet Union is advancing at a faster speed than that of the capitalist countries. The U.S. is definitely lagging behind, and *permanently* so" [italics supplied].[35] In the same vein, *Jen-min jih-pao* said that "the United States will try to catch up [in science and technology] but the Soviet Union will be still further ahead."[36]

Fifth, the Chinese journals argued polemically—clearly, it seemed, in response to an alternative argument advanced at the Moscow conference—that the Bloc was superior to the West *in spite of the fact* that the West was still predominant in key industrial indexes. *Jen-min jih-pao* wrote: "Some people who observe things superficially, and do not see the essence of a question, do not believe that socialism is really superior in strength to imperialism. They say the output of iron and steel and the total quantity of many other products in the United States are still much higher than in the Soviet Union, and it will not be long before the United States can also produce its own artificial satellite and intercontinental missile, and so on and so forth."[37]

In the same spirit, *Hsueh-hsi* wrote: "Some people who do not look at the basic nature of questions may still have this kind of doubt. They say that, in spite of the huge population of the socialist countries, their economy is backward, whereas the imperialist camp still commands enormous economic forces, though the size of its population is small. They may even cite an example to illustrate that the output of steel in the United States still doubles that of the Soviet Union and they then ask how can we say that the strength of socialism is stronger than that of imperialism?"[38]

The Chinese Communist reply to this kind of question was that World War II had clearly demonstrated that steel output was not decisive. The Red Army alone and not the combined forces of Britain, the United States, and the Soviet Union, it was held, had defeated Germany.

The criticisms may, of course, have been directed in part at the Yugoslavs and Poles. The Yugoslav press did in fact contend, after the Moscow conference was over, that Western economic power was still a mighty factor to be reckoned with. But there is reason to believe that the statements quoted may have been directed at the Russians as well. The Russians had been consistently respectful of U.S. economic might. Khrushchev himself was to pay implicit tribute to that strength when he announced at the 21st Party Congress that the Bloc would not achieve a "world-historic victory" over capitalism until about 1970, when it would overtake the West in both physical volume of production and per capita output. "Material production," Khrushchev emphasized at that time, "is the decisive sphere of human endeavor."[39]

The sixth reason for Chinese Communist bullishness in calculating the new balance of forces was the apparent Maoist belief that even *before* the Soviet weapons developments in the fall of 1957 there had been dramatic evidence of the swift decline of imperialism. When the Soviet acquisition of the ICBM was added to the history of imperialist decline since World War II, there could be no doubt as to Bloc superiority. The following extensive quotation from *Jen-min jih-pao* illustrates this view:

"The superiority in strength of socialism over imperialism has been demonstrated *before now* in a series of facts. These are: in the Second World War, the main power which destroyed Hitler and triumphed over the Japanese aggressors was the Soviet Union and not the combined forces of the United States and Britain. In the Chinese people's war of liberation, the victor was not Chiang Kai-shek who had the strong support of the United States, but the revolutionary people of China. In the Korean war, the Chinese

People's Volunteers and the Korean People's Army threw the so-called UN forces . . . back from the Yalu river. In Vietnam, the Vietnamese Democratic Republic thoroughly defeated the armed forces of the U.S.-supported French colonialists. In Egypt's struggle to defend its sovereign rights over the Suez Canal, the Soviet Union's warning to Britain, France, and Israel, coupled with the opposition of world public opinion, played a decisive role in halting aggression. . . . In addition, the decline of the imperialist forces has also been strikingly manifested in the withdrawal of Britain from India, Burma, Egypt, and other colonies, the withdrawal of the Netherlands from Indonesia, the withdrawal of France from a whole series of colonies in Western Asia and North Africa.

"It goes without saying that these withdrawals resulted from the double blows to imperialism dealt by the socialist forces and the nationalist forces which oppose colonialism. *The superiority of the anti-imperialist forces over the imperialist forces demonstrated by these events has expressed itself in even more concentrated form and reached unprecedented heights with the Soviet Union's launching of the artificial satellites. . . . That is why we say that this is a new turning point in the international situation"* [italics supplied].[40]

In sum, the entire history of the postwar period was viewed by the Chinese Communists—in retrospect at least—as a period of swift imperialist decline. The Soviet weapons developments in the fall of 1957 could only rapidly accelerate that decline.

The Maoist strategic assessment, presented to the Moscow conference, may now be summed up on the basis of what we know from subsequent versions of Mao's speech itself and from articles in the Chinese press. It held that there had been, as a result of Soviet weapons developments and a rapid prior imperialist decline, a qualitative change in the balance of power. The Communist Bloc had thus become stronger overall than the West, despite the fact that it still lagged behind economically. The West was but temporarily ahead in the economic race. The Soviet military lead was irreversible. The Western camp was, moreover, in a phase of rapid decline accelerated by contradictions of growing intensity. As *Jen-min jih-pao* wrote, probably with an eye to Moscow as much as to the West, "the swiftness of history's advance always outstrips people's estimates."[41]

The Maoist Action Program

If the above is a fair presentation of the strategic assessment given the Communist world by Mao in November 1957, the important question is: what did Mao want to do in order to exploit the new turning point? A close examination of Chinese media of the time supplies pertinent clues.

In the first place, Mao seemed to advocate a stepped-up assault on the imperialists in Africa, Asia, and the Middle East. As *Shih-chieh chih-shih* (December 20) put it: "To the imperialists, the Middle East is exceedingly important economically, militarily, and politically. . . . If the influence of the imperialists were forced out of this area, the repercussions would naturally be felt in other areas, especially Africa."[42] If this stepped-up assault were to meet with Western counteraction, the Bloc should not hesitate to fight local wars because the West, fully aware of Soviet strategic superiority, would not dare raise the ante. Said the same issue of *Shih-chieh chih-shih:* " . . . the march of mankind toward peace and progress is a trend of history that never can be obstructed. . . . This of course does not exclude detouring changes taking place in a certain period of time, *nor does this exclude tensions developing in certain localities or in relation to certain problems"* [italics supplied].[43] In short, given Soviet strategic superiority, the most the West could now hope for would be to offer local resistance which would lead to "tensions" in "certain localities."

This Chinese view—that wars would increasingly and inevitably be local wars—was stated more or less explicitly in a *Shih-chieh chih-shih* article of December 5.[44] This article was one of the few extensive discussions noted by the author in any Communist journal on the alleged American "limited war strategy." It came at a time when the Russians were suggesting, quite to the contrary, that the West was increasingly deterred from local as well as global conflict and that wars of all kinds could be avoided. The article began by noting that the West was increasingly frustrated in its efforts to spark an all-out war. Since 1956, it stated, American publications had pointed out the need of preparing both for large wars "and more especially small war or local war." The American publications, it went on, *"consider that local war will occur more often, have greater possibility, and become more necessary"* [italics

166

supplied].[45] Thus, the U.S. was revising and supplementing its massive retaliation policy. More stress was being placed on tactical weapons, including tactical nuclear weapons. The article cited Secretary of State Dulles and Henry Kissinger as advocates of less reliance on massive retaliation and a greater build-up for limited war employing nuclear weapons. Such a strategy, the article continued, was doomed to failure because "now the superiority in nuclear weapons obviously is in the hands of the Soviet Union." It could not "alter the basic situation arising from the new power balance—the distinct inferiority of the fighting strength of imperialism."[46]

Mao's line on the possibility of tensions "developing in certain localities" as mankind marched toward "progress"—in the context of his insistence on the Bloc's overall strategic superiority—seemed to have two major implications for Bloc strategy in the immediate future. One was that the West would come increasingly to realize that it could no longer threaten or contemplate global war in the pursuit of its objectives and would increasingly resort to limited nuclear and conventional wars in order to maintain or to adjust the status quo in its favor. To Western-initiated local wars the Bloc should respond with force. Moreover, since it no longer had as much to fear from Western strategic power, the Bloc could feel free to ignite and/or support limited revolutionary wars, so-called "wars of liberation."

As Mao and the Chinese Left wing surveyed the world scene, Asia, Africa, and Latin America must have seemed inviting theaters for wars of "national liberation." Chinese interest in these backward areas turned sharply upwards in 1958. A war of "liberation" was already raging in Algeria. The hotter such conflicts became, and the more of them there were, the greater the opportunities for the Chinese to spread their power and influence. The Algerians—and the rebels who would imitate them—would sooner or later be forced to come to Peking or to Moscow for assistance against the imperialists. The United States could clearly not render assistance to colonial rebels because this would deepen the contradictions in the imperialist camp.

The Maoist line on the increasing likelihood of local conflicts must have been contemplated, too, against the background of Chinese claims to Formosa. It must have seemed increasingly unlikely that these aspirations could be realized without the use or threat of local force against American military power in the Taiwan Straits. Mao's view seems to have been that the Bloc could now pursue a policy of "brinksmanship" in selected areas under the cover of the Soviet nuclear shield. If the West employed or threatened to use tactical nuclear weapons, the Russians should reply in kind. Negotiations, while not to be ruled out, were to be given a priority second to direct revolutionary tactics that accepted the risk of local wars.

The Khrushchev Action Program

It seems clear that the Russians had greater confidence than the Chinese in the possibility of making gains by negotiations. The first Soviet calls for a summit meeting came in December 1957, four months after the first ICBM test.[47] At that time, it can be confidently suggested, Khrushchev saw Soviet weapons gains not so much as an opportunity to begin revolutionary assaults on the West throughout the world—assaults which risked local war with the West—but primarily to begin his long climb to the summit. Apparently more realistic than Mao in his estimate of the overall power balance between East and West, Khrushchev seemed less confident that he could push the West around with relative impunity; he seemed more sensitive to and wary of the danger of local wars escalating into a general war. In the fall of 1957, Soviet spokesmen began publicly to assert that "the danger of local military conflicts being converted into a large-scale conflagration has become much more pronounced."[48] Soviet media have persistently continued—in sharp contrast to Peking—to stress this danger. While such statements have an ancillary purpose of deterring the West, it is not unlikely that they also genuinely reflect Soviet fears. Furthermore, Khrushchev may not have been very confident of his own strategic striking power if it came to a nuclear showdown. A look around Western Europe must have convinced him that Western striking power was still formidable. NATO had already taken a decision to establish IRBM bases in member countries and there was talk of distribution of nuclear weapons throughout Western Europe. In retrospect, it seems as if Khrushchev recognized that the West in 1957 still had a considerable strategic advantage.

The incipient strategic differences between Peking and Moscow thus seemed to concern the level of risk that the Bloc could afford to run in the immediate future, the risks the West would run, the tactics to be employed by the Bloc, and the priorities to be attached to negotiations as opposed to direct revolutionary assaults in specified theaters which involved the risk of limited war. While Khrushchev was not unaware of the appreciable military gains he had made, or of the possibility of employing those gains as blackmail against the West in Berlin or elsewhere, he seemed prepared to take only minimal and controlled risks of war—minimal in the sense that there should be no Soviet initiative which could reasonably be expected to provoke either a massive Western response or a local war with the West, and controlled in the sense that there was always an avenue of retreat if the West showed signs of firm resistance.[49] Khrushchev seemed confident that time was on his side and that such risks were unnecessary. Above all, he did not want to run the risk of engaging the West in a local military conflict, which not only might lead to defeat or stalemate, but might also spread, alienate the neutrals, unite the West, and destroy his hopes of making gains peacefully. His great unwillingness to seek local military confrontations with the West was to be clearly demonstrated in his response to the Anglo-American military landings in the Middle East in the summer of 1958.

China and Nuclear Weapons

One final point might be made concerning divergent Sino-Soviet strategic thinking as it evolved in the fall of 1957. The Chinese strategic views, as outlined by Chinese journals in the winter of 1957, seemed to suggest that the new American limited-war strategy would involve increased sharing of nuclear weapons between the Americans and their allies. The *Shih-chieh chih-shih* article of December 5 said that the U.S. and Britain would "jointly manufacture and control atomic nuclear weapons. . . . Stockpiles of nuclear weapons and guided missiles are to be built up in the areas covered by NATO and other military blocs. . . . The U.S. will offer [its allies] more information concerning nuclear weapons but will share with Britain alone the secrets of manufacture."[50] If the U.S. was going to engage in greater nuclear sharing, and if its policy envisaged the increasing use or threat of limited nuclear wars, was this not sufficient reason for the Russians to engage in similar weapons sharing with Peking?

From the Chinese strategic viewpoint, nuclear sharing would have been particularly desirable because a major hurdle that stood between Peking and its immediate objectives in the Taiwan straits was American possession of tactical nuclear weapons. Peking may have believed that unless it had a Soviet commitment to use such weapons against the U.S., or unless it secured such weapons from Moscow, it had little hope of obtaining Formosa or the offshore islands.

Prior to the Moscow conference, a high-level Chinese Communist military delegation suddenly arrived in Moscow without advance publicity. It arrived on November 6, two days after an interview between the Chinese Minister of National Defense, Marshal P'eng Teh-huai, and his Soviet counterpart, Marshal Malinovsky. The mission included the Chinese chief of staff, General Su Yü, as well as Marshal Yeh Chien-ying, who, several years earlier, had publicly called for the import of modern weapons "from foreign countries."[51] Yeh, in fact, seems to have belonged to a group among the Chinese military which advocated a revision of Maoist military doctrine in the direction of a "rapid modernization" of China's armed forces.

That there were strong pressures within the Chinese Communist military for a nuclear build-up was to become evident in the spring of 1958, when Peking began a campaign against the "exclusively military point of view" and its overemphasis on the dangers of surprise attack and the decisiveness of nuclear weapons. At that time also, Chinese marshals began to assert that China would have nuclear weapons only when "its *own* working class and scientists" developed them "in the not distant future" [italics supplied].[52] One Chinese marshal warned against reliance "on outside aid" in trying to solve China's military problems.[53]

It seems likely that one purpose of the sudden dispatch of the Chinese military to Moscow was to confer with Soviet counterparts on the possibility of the Russians' stepping up their assistance to China's nuclear weapons program, assistance which seemed to have been given at a rather deliberately slow pace in the past. It seems likely, too, that the Russians were reluctant to do so. This can be inferred from the following exchange between P'eng Te-huai and Malinovsky on November 27. Marshal P'eng: "During our stay of over 20 days in the Soviet Union, the heroic Soviet Army made a profound impression on us. The Soviet Army is equipped with the latest modern weapons. . . . The Soviet Army is also the best example for the People's Liberation Army of China."[54] Malinovsky: *"The might of our armies is based not only on the fact that they are armed with modern first-class weapons, but primarily on the fact that they are closely linked with their people* and that their leaders and organizers are the Communist Parties of the Soviet Union and China. . . . We *willingly transmit our experience* in the building up of armed forces to our Chinese friends and brothers-in-arms" [italics supplied].[55]

The Russian defense minister may have been telling his Chinese counterpart that he should not be in a hurry to obtain nuclear weapons, that the Russians would, for the time being, limit their assistance to technical help and training. When Chinese propaganda after the Moscow conference, and particularly in the spring of 1958, began to assert that men are more important than weapons, that weapons alone do not decide the outcome of war, and that the American "paper tiger" was beaten in Korea despite the fact that China did not have nuclear weapons, it seemed clear that the Chinese were making the best of a bad situation. Their strategy in the spring of 1958 seemed predicated on the assumption that China would not have a nuclear capability of any sort for some time to come.

The foregoing suggests that the November 1957 conference in Moscow was of *pivotal* importance in the growing Šino-Soviet conflict over strategy. While it did *not* involve a dramatic confrontation between Peking and Moscow, it did involve serious bargaining over strategy and probably over nuclear weapons sharing. Against the background of Soviet weapons developments and Mao's confidence in the swift decline of the West, Mao—and the Chinese Left wing which had assumed control in the fall of 1957—was pushing for a major, if limited, assault on the imperialists. The Russians were evidently holding back to a more cautious strategy. One of three outcomes was possible: Peking would adapt its strategy to that of Moscow; Moscow would move into line with Peking; or the gap would widen.

CHAPTER 6

THE CONFLICT WIDENS: 1958

"Full Steam Ahead"

IT WAS under such a title that an editorial in the official Chinese Communist newspaper, *Jen-min jih-pao,* rang in the New Year of 1958.[1] China's leadership entered 1958, the first year of the second Five Year Plan, on a wave of domestic and global revolutionary hubris. On the domestic front, there began to appear slogans such as, "Overtake Britain in 15 years," "Work hard for three years to change the face of China," and "Strive for better, faster, greater" results in the leap forward. The New Year's Day editorial in *Jen-min jih-pao* for the first time revealed the regime's determination to promote Chinese economic development at top speed. For the first time it published a timetable for the completion of socialist construction and the beginning of the transition to Communism. It would take 10 to 15 years to build a "modern industrial and agricultural base" and thus to "fundamentally complete" the building of a socialist society. In 15 years, China would catch up with and surpass Britain in the output of iron and steel and other important industrial products. After another 20 or 30 years, it would "catch up to and surpass the United States economically and bring about the gradual transition from socialist to communist society." This, the editorial announced, was "the great, glorious, and arduous historical task for our people." In all, it would take China merely 30–45 years to catch up to and surpass the United States in economic production. This was the vision that underlay China's economic "planning" in early 1958!

Revolutionary hubris was also manifest in the regime's global perspectives. The editorial began by announcing that the "crisis of the Free World" was now apparent; it continued:

"People's thinking often lags behind realities, and they underestimate the speed of development of the objective situation. How can we but arrive at such a conclusion as we review the development of the international and the domestic situation in 1957?

"The successful launching by the Soviet Union of the two manmade satellites and the Moscow meeting of the Communist and Workers' parties of various countries, in a matter of a few weeks, changed the whole world atmosphere. . . . The east wind prevails over the west wind, the forces of socialism are stronger than the forces of imperialism and the peace forces are stronger than the forces of war. *If there was still some dispute on this not long ago, even among Communists, now the fact is common knowledge* even in the Western world. What the spokesmen of Western imperialism now talk about is no longer 'the crisis of Communism' and the 'decadence and retreat of the Soviet Union' but the 'crisis of the Free World' and the 'decadence and retreat of the United States' " [italics supplied].[2]

The New Year's Day editorial painted a strategic picture almost identical to the one drawn by Mao a few months earlier. The Bloc now had strategic superiority over the West; the West, particularly the United States, was in a stage of swift decline unimaginable a year earlier; the Western alliance system was crumbling under the impact of Soviet weapons developments; nationalist anti-colonial movements were in a state of incipient revolt throughout Asia and Africa. The conclusion was obvious: the Bloc could now with relative impunity accelerate the inevitable decline of imperialism. The concluding passage of the editorial is worth quoting at some length. Few other passages in Chinese writings of the time better illustrate the perspectives of the Left wing now wielding power in Peking:

"The world is what man makes it to be. Before 1957, people could not have anticipated that in the world and in China, there could have been such rapid and gigantic changes. If we are adept in taking our lessons, then we must first thoroughly rectify that ideological state which lags behind objective realities, we must rouse ourselves to surge upward, to fully promote our revolutionary activism and creativeness, remove pessimism, doubt and conservatism. . . . Our cause is the revolutionary cause, and what we most need is the revolutionary optimism, which in strategy belittles all 'powerful' foes, belittles all 'serious' difficulties and hardships— though in tactics we must attach importance to them, and they must be overcome one by one. . . . We ride with the wind and march forward. Let us ride with the east wind which has overpowered the west wind, ride with the wind of Communism which has overthrown the Rightists, overthrown bureaucratism, and overthrown conservatism."[3]

At this stage of the revolutionary flow, the Peking Jacobins were merely talking of "riding with the wind." In only a few months they would launch the audacious commune program and the leap forward, try to force the Russian hand further in the campaign against Yugoslav revisionism than Moscow wished to go, advocate armed response to Western intervention in the Middle East crisis, and begin a venture in the Taiwan Straits. It would be difficult to isolate any one of these occurrences as *the* major turning point in the Sino-Soviet relationship, the point at which divergent strategic assessments turned into political conflict. Cumulatively, however, there can be no doubt that all these developments soon exercised a greater strain on the Sino-Soviet relationship than it had ever before faced.

Chou En-Lai's Report to the National People's Congress

In February, Chou En-lai delivered the first major policy review of the new year.[4] He began by noting that within the previous half year or more, "a decisive change" in the international situation had taken place, a change which had resulted from Soviet satellite launchings and the unprecedented unity of the Communist world revealed at the Moscow conference. There was, said Chou, a new change in the *"long-standing superiority* of the forces of socialism over those of imperialism . . . a new turning point in the world situation" [italics supplied]. Reiterating Mao's line at the Moscow conference, he said that "everyone can now see that . . . our socialist camp has definitely gained supremacy in population and popular support, in the rate of industrial and agricultural development, and in a number of important fields in science and technology." Even the imperialists realized that they now stood before an "invincible" socialist camp "headed by the Soviet Union" and "stronger and more united than ever before."[5] Suggesting that Soviet deterrent power had been the major reason for the defeat of the Anglo-French attempt to overthrow Nasser in 1956 and for the defeat of the Turkish "armed threat" to Syria in 1957, Chou reflected Peking's increasing confidence in the exploitability of Soviet deterrent power.

He surveyed the prospects of the "national independence movement," said its "vigorous development" in the past six months was "not to be checked." It was making considerable headway in the

Middle East, in Africa, and in Southeast Asia. And while the picture was extremely bright for the socialist camp, the Chinese premier went on, it was unprecedentedly dark for the camp of the imperialists. The West was faced with "serious economic recessions and political crises." The United States was trying to tighten its control over its allies, but the latter had come to see more clearly that the U.S. was not a reliable ally. At the last NATO conference in Paris, contradictions among the Western allies reached the point where it was no longer possible to conceal them. The dilemma before the United States was clear. If it rejected "peaceful coexistence," it would become more isolated; if it grew reckless and sought a way out through war, it would be digging its own grave. The time has come, said Chou, "for the U.S. to do some sober thinking."[6]

Peking saw a world in which the East was now stronger than ever, and the United States faced the dilemma of either going to war or accepting increasing reverses. Assuming that the first alternative did not come about, where would U.S. reverses most likely occur?

Chou pointed first to Korea, contending that the continued presence of U.S. forces in South Korea constituted a threat to peace in the Far East, a state of affairs which the Korean and Chinese peoples "cannot allow to continue." He then turned to Vietnam and declared that Western violation of the Geneva agreements "should not continue." (He was satisfied with the independent development of Laos and Cambodia, since both adhered to a policy of neutrality.)

Next citing Taiwan, Chou twice referred to Chinese Communist determination to liberate Taiwan, ignoring the qualifier "peacefully" which had been normal since 1955. At the same time, he made a virulent attack on the "two Chinas" concept. The "crucial issue" in Sino-American relations, he said, was not that China wanted U.S. recognition, but that the U.S. occupied Chinese territory. This great issue could not be "obscured."[7]

With the advantage of hindsight, it is possible to conjecture that this speech reflected the planning for the Taiwan Straits venture that the Chinese initiated a few months later. Chou's fear of increasing world acceptance of a "two Chinas" solution was well founded. Proposals were being made, both in the West and in the non-Communist East, for various kinds of "two Chinas" solutions which would barter American recognition of Communist China for Chinese Communist recognition of the sovereignty of Taiwan. As Chou said, even some "friends" of China (e.g., India) "naively" thought that by supporting such ideas they were helping Peking gain international acceptance. Chou made it clear that Communist China would never consider relinquishing its claims to Taiwan in exchange for admission to the United Nations and American diplomatic recognition.

Emboldened by the new wave of revolutionary optimism in the CCP, convinced that the West was in a period of decline, and faced with an increasing interest by other countries in a settlement which might force it to recognize the sovereignty of Taiwan, Peking may have decided as early as February 1958 that drastic action would have to be taken to scuttle the "two Chinas" concept.

Peking's Attack on Yugoslavia, May 1958

The relationship between Moscow and Belgrade in the period of the abortive reconciliation—roughly from June 1955 to November 1957—is a tangled skein of Communist intrigue, miscalculation, and false hope. On the basis of inside Yugoslav sources, one scholar has brilliantly traced the evolution of the relationship in this confused period, so far as it is now possible to do so.[8] For our present purposes, it is sufficient to pick up the story in August 1957, a few months before the 40th Anniversary celebrations in Moscow, which were to be used as the ceremonial backdrop for the Moscow conference of Communist leaders from all over the world.

At that time, Khrushchev and Tito met in Bucharest in an effort to reach agreement on issues that had been in public debate for about a year. Evidently the two men agreed to some sort of arrangement which brought the erratic Soviet-Yugoslav *rapprochement* to new heights.[9] In September Tito publicly endorsed the "leading role" of the Soviet Union, and soon afterwards he recognized East Germany, an action which led to considerable outcry in the West and which, from the point of view of Tito's professed "non-aligned" position, contained serious liabilities. Since the second break with Belgrade, Khrushchev has claimed that Tito agreed at the Bucharest meeting to come to the 40th Anniversary celebrations and to sign a joint declaration of Communist principles. This would have marked the triumphant culmination of Khrushchev's two-year effort to woo Yugoslavia back into the Bloc. The Yugoslavs, on the other hand, left the Bucharest meeting under the impression that "they could be more useful to the cause of peace by staying . . . outside the Soviet bloc."[10]

As Lowenthal points out, the two versions are not necessarily in conflict. From the very beginning of the *rapprochement,* each side had been reading different interpretations into the same documents and agreements. Essentially, Tito wanted to return to the fold, but on his own terms; he wanted to continue pursuing an international policy of neutrality outside the Warsaw Pact; he wanted complete internal autonomy; and, moreover, he wanted other Communist countries to "study" Yugoslav experience. Tito was thus both a Communist neutralist and a Communist evangelist. He undoubtedly conjured up an image of a triumphant tour of Russia during the 40th Anniversary celebrations (like the one he received in the summer of 1956) and hoped that the elite of international Communism would pay him homage.

Khrushchev had different ideas. He probably did not believe that he could get Tito to join the Warsaw Pact, but he probably did believe that he could commit Tito to support most of Soviet foreign policy, that he could effectively circumscribe Tito's evangelism and neutralism, and that the wooing of Tito back to the Communist camp would be a major triumph for his own diplomatic policies, which included using Tito to woo the non-Communist neutrals. The problem for Khrushchev was to guarantee that Tito's non-alignment did not become a cancer in the international Communist movement, a danger which lay behind much of the opposition to the Tito *rapprochement* by unreconstructed Stalinists throughout the Bloc. In order to circumscribe Yugoslav freedom of action and demonstrate to the Communist world that the risks of taking Tito back into the Bloc were not so great, Khrushchev evidently decided to step up the pressure against him on the very eve of the Moscow conference. According to Lowenthal's sources, Yugoslavia's new Party program had virtually been shelved after the Bucharest meeting in the interests of a *rapprochement* with Moscow. Now, however, the Russians, "asked to see the draft so that they might suggest amendments even before it reached the Yugoslav Party members!"[11] Such a highhanded request must have made Tito doubt the wisdom of his course, which had all along been a subject of high-level debate within the Yugoslav Party.

Probably the critical turning point came when the Soviet draft of the Declaration to be signed in Moscow on the 40th Anniversary of the Revolution arrived in Belgrade. Although this draft was evidently a milder version of the tough declaration later insisted upon by Peking, and did not yet contain the formula about the Soviet leading role, it was nonetheless a harsh document that implicitly ruled out the possibility of non-alignment and explicitly emphasized the danger of revisionism. It was a document that boded ill for the Yugoslav leader's political objectives. Tito could not but have seen this; at any rate, he came down with a "diplomatic illness" which, it was suddenly announced, would prevent his attendance at the Moscow meeting. The triumphant return of the prodigal son to the fold thus never took place. Tito's gamble, as Lowenthal aptly calls it, was lost. Although Tito had backed the right horse—namely Khrushchev—the animal had balked at the last fence.

At the Moscow conference, Yugoslav representatives Kardelj and Rankovic made it clear from the outset that they would not sign the Communist declaration of principle. It is reliably reported that Khrushchev told them angrily at the time that, if they refused to sign, "we will attack you." Yugoslavia, said Khrushchev, would have to choose between East and West; it could no longer continue to sit "in two chairs."[12]

The developments that soon followed the conference were more or less predictable. The Russians mounted a huge campaign against revisionism, a considerable portion of which was broadcast to Yugoslavia.[13] For the first few months, however, the anti-revisionist campaign did not directly mention Yugoslavia; both sides may have hoped to avoid a second break. Tito apparently made changes in the Yugoslav draft program designed to make it more palatable to Moscow, and the latter, for its part, refrained from attack. Tito still evidently counted on exercising pressure on Moscow through Gomulka and Kadar, who, he believed, would support his desire to limit Soviet hegemony within the international Communist movement. Khrushchev counted on Tito's lowering his price for readmission into the Bloc. At the end of March, however,

Yugoslav overtures to both Kadar and Gomulka, and the receptivity of both, apparently convinced Khrushchev that Tito was trying to form an "autonomist" bloc within the Communist movement. At this point, it seems, he decided to initiate the break in Party relations between the Bloc and Yugoslavia. To this end, the Russians announced on April 5, 1958, that they would not send a delegation to the forthcoming Yugoslav Congress.[14] Their announcement was followed by similar ones from other fraternal parties.

Meanwhile, sometime in March the 230-page draft program of the Yugoslav Communist Party had been circulated for discussion and comment throughout the Communist world.[15] The program, although it contained some minor changes from the original version that had antagonized Moscow, formalized the views which had been the target of a good deal of Soviet fire since the latter part of 1956. It was intolerable to Moscow for a number of reasons. It was the first attempt by anyone to codify a set of "revisionist" principles and then to circulate them throughout the Communist movement. The Yugoslavs adhered to a policy of non-alignment and neutrality and, in fact, they argued that all Communist states should be free to be neutral. This posed a direct threat to the Warsaw Pact. The Yugoslavs also suggested that "progress" could be made by parties other than Communist, particularly socialist parties in the West and in the underdeveloped countries. This implied that Communist parties no longer had a monopoly on wisdom and progress. The Yugoslavs also suggested that much in their own program was deserving of study by other Communist parties, that, in effect, other parties might experiment with decentralization and "democratization" along Yugoslav lines—a suggestion that could hardly have been welcomed by Khrushchev. Above all, the Yugoslav program implicitly denied Soviet prerogatives in the Communist world by arguing that all the parties were equal and enjoyed internal autonomy. Finally, the Yugoslav Party program was a new program of Communist principle which would stand in sharp contrast to the obsolete Russian program which had been written in 1919 but was as yet not updated.

Given the nature of this program, the refusal of Tito to sign the Moscow declaration, and the increasing realization in Belgrade and Moscow that the *rapprochement* had not gained the ends that either Party envisaged, an open Soviet attack on Belgrade was only a matter of time. It came on April 19, three days before the convening of the Yugoslav Congress, when the Moscow *Kommunist* issued a "principled party criticism" of the Yugoslav program. The criticism was severe, although it was more limited, it is important to note, than the Chinese blast that was to follow.

The program, *Kommunist* conceded, "includes . . . quite a few correct generalizations"; "comradely party criticism" must not stand in the way of friendly relations; the Yugoslavs are "continuing to work toward improvement of the draft"; and "we wish" the Yugoslav "comrades" success in this matter.[16] At the same time, the Soviet critic made a rather detailed critique of the Yugoslav propositions outlined before. Nevertheless, two days after the Yugoslav Party Congress opened, Soviet Presidium member Furtseva said in Warsaw: "We have been and we will be friends with Yugoslavia—always."[17] It seemed the Russians were hoping to put sufficient pressure on Tito to force major modifications in the draft program, but had not yet abandoned hope for a *rapprochement* for which they were continuing to ask a higher price than Tito wanted to pay.

Relative Soviet restraint notwithstanding, the Yugoslavs went ahead to endorse most of those passages of the program which had proved offensive to the Russians. On April 23, a strongly worded speech by Rankovic at the Yugoslav Congress led to a walk-out by the Soviet ambassador to Belgrade, who was present as an "observer."

Peking Enters the Scene

It was into this progressively deteriorating but still not hopeless situation that Peking injected its charge of May 5 after the Yugoslav Congress had concluded. A *Jen-min jih-pao* editorial of that date lashed out at the Yugoslavs with an asperity unknown since the days of Stalin.[18] Going far beyond the "principled" criticism of *Kommunist* in April, the Chinese condemned the entire Yugoslav program as "out and out revisionist"; referred to the "leading group" of the Yugoslav Party in such a manner as to appeal to the party rank and file over the heads of the leadership; suggested that the Yugoslav program was put forward at American behest, thus hinting that the Yugoslav leaders were imperialist agents within the ranks of the Communist movement; implied that Tito was motivated by an ambition to spread his own brand of revisionism throughout the Bloc; suggested that refusal by the Yugoslav leaders to revise their views could lead to a break in state relations with Communist countries; and, perhaps most important, charged that the 1948 Cominform resolution against Yugoslavia was still valid.

There were in fact two Cominform resolutions against Tito, one issued in 1948, which confined itself to Tito's ideological heresies, and the other issued in 1949, which linked Tito to Western imperialism and described him as a "murderer."

In the 1955 Soviet *rapprochement* with Tito, the 1949 resolution was withdrawn but the 1948 one was not. This fact was made public by French Party leader Fajon, who stated that the 1949 document had been based on forgeries by Beria and Abakumov, but that the 1948 resolution was still valid. The former Polish Communist Seweryn Bialer has also written, on the basis of secret Party documents available to him, that the 1948 resolution was never withdrawn. The Russians refused to withdraw this resolution probably because Khrushchev desired to maintain a club for use against Tito when the occasion demanded. Up to the point when Peking asserted that the 1948 resolution was still valid, this club had never been publicly used by the Russians. It was now applied with tremendous force by Peking.

Peking's May 5 indictment of the Yugoslav leaders was a call for complete and unconditional Yugoslav surrender. It was undoubtedly made with the awareness that it could never be realized. What the Chinese Communists evidently desired was such a heightening of Bloc-Yugoslav tensions as to put an end once and for all to the erratic Soviet-Yugoslav *rapprochment*.

Enough has already been said to suggest the reasons for Peking's sudden interest in an ultra-orthodox line on Bloc unity and revisionism. In the Chinese view, the forward strategy which they advocated against the background of Soviet weapons developments could not be undertaken if the Bloc was dissipating its energies in internecine quarrels over the limits of Soviet hegemony. The connection between Bloc monolithism and the exploitation of Soviet weapons developments had been made explicit by Peking as early as February 1958, well before the second Bloc-Yugoslav schism. *Kuang-ming jih-pao* then wrote: "The greater the solidarity . . . among the socialist countries, the more powerful we shall become. On the other hand, should there be divisive forces among us, our strength would be dissipated. Then, even if we possessed such a powerful weapon as intercontinental ballistic missiles, we would not be able to overwhelm the enemies. We might even be overwhelmed by them,"[19]

Following the November 1957 conference, Chinese spokesmen, as we have seen, maintained that the Bloc was now more united than ever before. Its greater monolithic unity, along with Soviet weapons developments, was, in fact, a principal reason for the new "turning point" in the world situation. It was to be expected that the Chinese would vigorously attack any—like the Yugoslavs—who threatened to undermine Bloc strength.

The *Jen-min jih-pao* editorial came, significantly, on the eve of a CPSU Central Committee plenum that was called to discuss the new Yugoslav crisis.[20] It is noteworthy that no resolution on Yugoslavia was published after that plenum, an indication either of possible indecision or of a decision not to force matters to a head. While the plenum was still in progress, *Pravda* belatedly published Khrushchev's and Voroshilov's congratulations to Tito on his re-election as President of Yugoslavia. From these clues, it was already possible to deduce that the Russians, although they had promptly republished the Chinese attack, were not as enthusiastic to force matters to a head as was Peking.

Substantiation of this theory came in a *Pravda* editorial on May 9. This editorial was more strongly anti-Yugoslav than the original *Kommunist* article in April, but not as strong as the *Jen-min jih-pao* attack. On the one hand, the Yugoslav leaders were still described as "comrades"; the attack was still limited to "many theses" in the draft program rather than to the program as a whole; and the tone of the attack was much less severe than that of the Chinese. On the other hand, there was a threat that state relations might suffer; economic sanctions were clearly hinted at; and it was suggested that U.S. aid had been given to the Yugoslavs with the obvious intention of promoting disunity within the Bloc. On May 27, economic sanctions became a reality with the receipt in Belgrade of a Soviet note announcing postponement of credit agreements.[21]

On June 1 the Chinese returned to the fray with a slashing attack on the Yugoslav Party by Ch'en Po-ta, a member of the Politburo and a leading CCP theoretician. Ch'en accused Tito flatly of having been bought by the American imperialists, and at a "high

182

price."[22] Again, this charge was stronger than Moscow's. It clearly suggested that the Yugoslavs were conscious traitors to the Communist world; Moscow had stopped short of this, saying only that the Americans were trying to exploit the Yugoslavs.

On June 3 Khrushchev, in addressing the Bulgarian Communist Party's 7th Congress, identified himself with *some* of the CCP's strongest positions. He endorsed the 1948 Cominform resolution for the first time, and accused the Yugoslav leaders of spreading revisionism, accepting bribes from the imperialists, and, implicitly, of acting like a Trojan horse in the socialist camp. At the same time, Khrushchev spoke of the desirability of maintaining state relations and even of "reaching mutual understanding and cooperation on the Party level."[23] The Chinese, on the other hand, were clearly not even interested in maintaining state relations. The Yugoslav ambassador in Peking, recalled in late June, was refused interviews with Chinese leaders, and his farewell reception was boycotted.

On June 15 Marshal Tito spoke in Labin launching a full-scale counterattack. He reserved his severest comments for the CCP, insinuating that the Chinese were using the Yugoslavs as scapegoats for domestic difficulties and charging that Marx, Engels, and Lenin would "turn over in their graves" if they knew how they were being interpreted.[24]

On June 16 the Budapest radio announced the trial and execution of Imre Nagy, an announcement that was to become a vehicle for carrying the campaign against Yugoslavia even further. The announcement concerning Nagy accused the Yugoslav embassy in Budapest of rendering assistance to Nagy's "counterrevolutionary activity."[25]

On June 26 the Chinese replied to Tito's Labin speech by calling him a "traitor" and by suggesting that "the Tito element," in contrast to "neutralists in general," was out to "corrode, disintegrate, and subvert" the Bloc.[26] Tito's crime, in short, was not neutralism but Communist neutralism. In one of the more interesting passages of the attack, Peking said that "some people" did not understand why it was "necessary to drive Tito to the side of the imperialists." The CCP answer to this question, which may have come from Moscow, reflecting a Soviet desire to avoid a complete break, was that Tito would retain his bargaining position between the two camps in any case and that it would do no good to relax the efforts to expose him.

Khrushchev continued, nonetheless, to take a middle-of-the-road line on Tito, or at least to hold out the continued possibility of an understanding. In a speech on July 11 to the East German 5th Congress, he continued to use the Trojan horse analogy to describe the Yugoslavs.[27] On the other hand, he continued to refer to "Comrade" Tito and to the Yugoslav "comrades." These honorifics had long since disappeared from Chinese statements, which now referred only to the "Tito clique." At the same time, Khrushchev said that it would be wrong to pay too much attention to the Yugoslav revisionists and that it would also be wrong to "exaggerate the present conflict" between the CPSU and the Yugoslav leaders. Even in the existing state of relations, said Khrushchev, "it will be good to preserve some spark of hope and to search for acceptable forms of contact on certain questions."[28]

In the months immediately following and in the entire period from spring 1958 to date, the CCP continued to take a more uncompromising line toward Tito than Moscow. The Russians, as Khrushchev had recommended, began more and more to ignore Tito. Peking intensified its attack, going so far as to suggest in September that the views of the "Tito-clique" and of Djilas, the noted political leader imprisoned by Tito, were in fact the same.[29] In the same month, Peking recalled its ambassador in Belgrade and, at the time of writing, he has not yet returned.

Some Conclusions

The following conclusions concerning the second Soviet-Yugoslav schism seem warranted: Khrushchev took the initiative against Yugoslavia in an attempt to restore Bloc discipline, weakened after the Hungarian rebellion, to combat the growth of revisionism, and to offset the danger of an "autonomist" bloc within the international Communist movement. At the same time, he wished to keep the campaign against Yugoslavia within limits because he considered Tito still useful for a number of his diplomatic purposes, he knew that to bring pressure on a Communist neutral country might alienate non-Communist neutral countries, and he did not want to weaken the *détente* elements of his diplomacy. The Russians were pushed by Peking to adopt positions more extreme than they originally intended, but Moscow stopped short of the complete break desired and effected by Peking.[30]

Inquiring into the reasons for China's interest in bringing the Yugoslav issue to a head, we would find, I think, that Chinese insistence, after the fall of 1957, on sharpening the conflict with the West, played a paramount role. In such accentuated conflict it was necessary, in Peking's view, to suppress ideological diversity within the Communist world, particularly diversity which held out the prospect of non-alignment by Communist states in the East-West struggle and rejected the dichotomic world view. A new and more intense struggle against the West could not be mounted if revisionists held out the desirability of an East-West "understanding," of neutralism, and of "equality" within the Communist Bloc. The May 5 *Jen-min jih-pao* editorial presented the rationale for the Chinese view thus: "The world is now at a new historic turning point with the East wind prevailing over the West wind. The struggle between the Marxist line and the revisionist line is nothing but a reflection of the sharpening struggle between . . . the imperialist world and the socialist world. It is impossible for any Marxist-Leninist to escape this struggle. Historical developments will testify even more clearly to the great significance of this struggle for the international Communist movement!"[31] This statement, with its insistence on an inevitably sharpening struggle between East and West, was at odds both with the Moscow declaration of November 1957 and with Soviet propaganda and official statements of the period. The Moscow declaration had asserted that "the Communist parties regard the struggle for peace as their foremost task." Neither it nor unilateral Soviet declarations spoke of a sharpening struggle.

A second and related motivation for the Chinese attack on Yugoslavia was the fear of an impending Soviet-American *détente.* Moscow had been pushing for a summit meeting since the winter of 1957. Although Camp David was still more than a year away, the signs of a Soviet move in this direction were already perceptible. By preventing a Soviet-Yugoslav *rapprochement,* the Chinese probably believed that they could make more difficult a Moscow-Washington *rapprochement.* This is not to say that Peking feared, or that there was any real likelihood of, a permanent or a genuine Soviet-U.S. understanding. But the Chinese correctly feared that even a *détente atmosphere,* an easing of relations between East and

West, would make it increasingly difficult for them to achieve their objectives in the Far East. While Khrushchev could exploit Soviet military power for his political purposes, Peking would have to rely on Soviet military power for achieving its objectives. If Khrushchev improved relations with the West, he would be less willing to use his military power on behalf of Chinese interests. A *détente*, in this sense, could come only at the expense of Chinese objectives.

Thus, in attacking Yugoslav views on the necessity of coexistence, the need to abate the East-West struggle, the possibility of a peaceful transition to socialism, and the need to "modernize" Marxist-Leninist doctrine in accord with the new epoch, the Chinese were aiming at Moscow as well as at Belgrade. The views for which they criticized Tito in the spring of 1958 were in part the same for which they were to criticize Khrushchev in 1960. By ostensibly focusing the attack on Tito, the Chinese apparently hoped to avoid a direct confrontation with the Russians and yet to circumscribe Soviet efforts to achieve a *détente*.

I have devoted so much attention to Peking's vitriolic attack on the Yugoslav Party in the spring of 1958 because it seems to have been the first explicit expression of Mao's disagreement with Khrushchev over Bloc strategy. Khrushchev's middle-of-the-road policy toward Tito reflected his centrist position on global strategy. He was not prepared, in the wake of Soviet weapons developments in the fall of 1957, to mount an all-out, direct, revolutionary assault on the bastions of imperialism. On the contrary, he now saw the opportunity for greater diplomatic flexibility and for greater political exploitation of Russia's military muscles in behalf of Soviet interests. The Chinese Left-wing attitude toward Tito, on the other hand, reflected its Left-wing attitude toward global strategy. They wanted to step up the revolutionary assault on the West in Taiwan, in the colonial areas, and wherever the opportunities seemed most promising.

As I have suggested earlier, it would be difficult to pinpoint these divergent attitudes toward Tito as the beginning of the Sino-Soviet conflict. Chinese dissatisfaction with Russian policies certainly was clear during the Middle East crisis in the summer of 1958, and again in the autumn, when Moscow failed to give strong support to, and may even have opposed, Mao's venture in the Taiwan Strait. It seems idle to try to select any one of these developments as the beginning of the conflict. The seeds of this conflict were sown, as I have shown, at the November 1957 Moscow conference; they certainly must be traced, as I have indicated, to 1956, when Peking first began to speak as a source of guidance and strategy for the entire Bloc. The Yugoslav issue served to illustrate clearly that the incipient conflict was not being resolved.

The Warsaw Pact Meeting

In late May, some weeks after the initial Chinese intervention in the Soviet-Yugoslav dispute, a meeting of the Warsaw Pact members took place in Moscow. Ch'en Yün, a vice chairman of the Chinese Communist Party and the senior Chinese "observer" at the meeting, delivered a lengthy speech to the Political Consultative Committee. His tone and emphasis differed markedly from that of Khrushchev's speech to the same conference. The final Pact Declaration reflected Khrushchev's, not Ch'en's thinking.

Ch'en began, like Chou En-lai a few months earlier, by immediately pointing out (as neither Khrushchev nor the Declaration did) that "tremendous and profound changes" had taken place in the world situation since the first meeting of the Political Consultative Committee in January 1956.[32] Stressing the weakness of the imperialist camp, Ch'en said that while the power and prestige of the socialist camp was growing the United States was sinking into a new and deep economic crisis which was "accelerating the coming of the world economic crisis of capitalism." The class struggle in the imperialist countries was intensifying. Friction was growing among the Western allies. The movements against colonialism were "surging to unprecedented heights." Life had proved that "the seemingly strong U.S. imperialism is only a 'paper tiger' outwardly strong."

Ch'en went on to deliver essentially the same message to Khrushchev that Mao himself had delivered at the November 1957 conference. Note the polemical tone in which one of his passages is couched: " 'U.S. phobia' is entirely groundless. It is *extremely erroneous and harmful* to overestimate the imperialist forces of war and underestimate the forces of peace and socialism. If formerly, for instance, at the time after the October Revolution, Lenin, the Soviet Communist Party, and the Soviet people, confronted with the encirclement of the capitalist world and the armed intervention of

14 countries, were not afraid, *why should there be any fear toward imperialism when the socialist camp has absolute superiority?"* [italics supplied][33]

The Chinese spokesman seemed to be asking how Khrushchev could justify his call for negotiations and a summit meeting, with their possible harmful consequences for the Bloc's global expansion and Chinese national interests, at a time when the Bloc's superiority was "absolute."

In glaring contradiction to the spirit of Khrushchev's relatively conciliatory speech and the Pact Declaration, which claimed that the Warsaw Treaty states were reducing their armed forces and that Soviet troops would be evacuated from Rumania, Ch'en concluded that the Warsaw Treaty alliance must be further strengthened.

Khrushchev's report to the conference, while it contained both threatening and conciliatory statements, seemed to be quite different from Ch'en's in its basic estimates.[34] The Soviet leader began by conceding that a new war could lead to the destruction of "millions of people," that "great cities and industrial centers would be razed from the face of the earth," that "vast territories" would be poisoned with radioactive fall-out. Although the Western powers were stalling on a summit meeting and thus preventing the "so greatly needed turning point" in the development of international events, "the more farsighted political leaders of the capitalist world *already* realized the need for radical changes in method and approach to the solution of international problems." Khrushchev expressed the hope that American leaders might "take a more sober view of things." Although he indulged in a little saber-rattling of his own, he commented that "it is not saber-rattling but meetings between responsible statesmen that will lead to a solution of controversial issues." He held out the prospect to the West of "vast markets" in China, the Arab world, and even the USSR if the cold war ended. He called for "partial disarmament measures," urged the Warsaw Treaty states to speak out for "further unilateral reduction" of armed forces, and called on the NATO countries "to follow suit."[35]

While the speech offered no specific concessions to the Western position, it can be interpreted in retrospect as one of the earliest signs of Khrushchev's long climb to the summit and Camp David.

The Chinese Military Conference:
May–July 1958

On May 27 the Military Committee of the Chinese Communist Party's Central Committee assembled for an unprecedented eight-week session. The conference was addressed by Mao, other top political figures of the regime, and most of the top military leaders. In the brief published reports of the proceedings, it was noted only that the conference reviewed the development of the People's Liberation Army (PLA) and discussed proposals on national defense. The speakers included Mao Tse-tung, Chu Teh, Lin Piao, Teng Hsiao-ping, Liu Po-ch'eng, Ho Lung, Ch'en Yi, Lo Jung-huan, Nieh Jung-chen, and Yeh Chien-ying. P'eng Teh-huai summed up the discussion.[36]

These are the bare outlines of the conference. The background was that the domestic and global strategic revisions made in Peking in the fall of 1957 necessitated new and rather critical roles for the military. On the domestic front, the leap forward and the communes envisaged the establishment of a "people's militia" in the communes and the widespread use of the military in economic construction. On the foreign policy front, the Maoist assessment seemed, as I have indicated, to look forward to the increasing likelihood of local wars. In fact, the conference ended on the very eve of the Taiwan Straits venture, and it seems likely that planning for the undertaking was one of the most important subjects discussed. Beyond this specific task, however, there was the equally important question of China's overall military posture. If the East wind now prevailed, and if the Soviet Union now had decisive strategic superiority over the West, what did this imply for Chinese Communist military strategy? In particular, what did it imply regarding Soviet sharing of nuclear weapons with Peking? The long background of strife between the Party and the professional military in Communist China provides a clue to the way the Chinese answered these questions. Ever since the first Chinese Communist armies were organized in 1927, there had been, as there was in the USSR, a chronic problem regarding the issues of Party control and defense strategy. In the period from 1954 through 1957, several issues divided the Party from the military, and the military within itself.[37] The professional

189

military, or some of them, wanted to increase defense expenditure, to give increased priority to military as opposed to economic outlays, to minimize Party prerogatives in the army, and to minimize the use of the army for tasks of economic construction. On the critical issue regarding what strategy was required to cope with the problems of modern war, one military group evidently shared the Maoist belief that any future war in which China was involved would be a long war of attrition, so that manpower and resources could be mobilized after the war had begun. This group probably placed a great deal of confidence in Soviet deterrent power and minimized the importance of building in the immediate future a modernized Chinese armed force equipped with nuclear weapons. Another group, perhaps not so confident of Peking's ability to secure its own objectives behind the shield of Soviet deterrent power, and not sharing the Maoist belief that the next war would be a long war of attrition, wanted to build a modern military establishment, including a strong air force and an adequate air-defense system. This group probably wanted nuclear weapons sooner rather than later.

These issues had never been fully resolved. When the CCP in late 1957 and early 1958 embarked on a leap forward at home and a bolder strategy abroad, these issues were bound to come to the fore again. The professional military may well have asked how Mao and the Party could reconcile the widespread use of the PLA in tasks of economic construction with a forward revolutionary strategy accepting the risk of local wars. Moreover, they might have asked how Mao could reconcile his extremely high regard for Soviet weapons developments with his simultaneous insistence on a traditional strategy which deprecated the decisiveness of modern weapons, insisted that atom bombs were "paper tigers," and exalted men over weapons.

In the view of some of the professional military, the nature of war had so changed that Mao's military doctrine, elaborated in the pre-nuclear era, was now outdated. There would have to be devised a new doctrine, they felt, in which the role of nuclear weapons would be paramount and in which the professional military would be freed from some of the unnecessary encumbrances of Party control.

The military conference from May to July 1958 was probably,

therefore, the scene of a bitter and protracted debate between the modernizers and the traditionalists. This can be inferred from a plethora of articles which began to appear in the Chinese Communist Party and military press after the conference was concluded. These articles denounced the military-firsters for advocating a revision of Maoist military doctrine, the "decisiveness" of nuclear weapons, a rapid "modernization" of China's armed forces, and "liquidation" of the system of Party leadership in the armed forces. They stressed the importance of economic construction for national defense, thus implying that no shifts in priority were necessary, as the professional military apparently argued.

In a typical denunciation of the views of the military reformers, Marshal Chu Teh declared on the anniversary of the PLA (August 1, 1958): "We are not advocates of the sole importance of arms. . . . People's hearts, not technology, in the final analysis, decide victory or defeat in war."[38] Chu also rapped the tendency to "pay attention only to national defense, but not to the significance of economic construction for national defense"—a clear admonition that modernization of the armed forces, including a nuclear weapons program, must await the prior achievement of China's industrialization goals. The next day the Army's official organ assailed those in the military establishment who were "one-sidedly stressing the role of atomic weapons and modern military techniques."[39] The same article asserted that some in the military "neglected Party leadership and political work . . . , overstressed unification and centralization, and overstressed the individual authority of officers." They also "stood for mechanical application of foreign experience," an indication that this group wished to import from the USSR the new Soviet military strategy predicated on the vastly increased importance of nuclear weapons.

A month earlier, while the military conference was still in session, the Army paper had attacked "purely military views" which "one-sidedly stress the suddenness and complexity of modern warfare . . . , assert the system of Party committees will impede the better judgment and concentration of command . . . [and] even openly advocate liquidation of the system of Party committee leadership."[40] Such views, the paper said, have caused ideological confusion and "weakened the fine tradition of our army in practical work." No matter how technology was modernized, the writer

191

contended, "it will never be outmoded for politics to assume command . . . [and] the system of exercising absolute collective leadership over the army will never be outmoded."

The regime's vigorous rebuttal of the viewpoint of the dissatisfied army group—its persistence in a doctrinal emphasis on human rather than technological resources in warfare, its insistence upon industrialization as a prerequisite to modernization of the armed forces, its depreciation of the importance of nuclear weapons and the value of surprise attack in modern warfare, and its rejection of diminished Party control of the army—clearly reflected adherence to defense planning based on the assumption of Western military superiority for some time to come. This in turn suggests that Moscow had already balked at supplying China with nuclear weapons. Indeed, one critical reason for the regime's continued adherence to the Maoist traditional strategy in the nuclear era may have been Khrushchev's reluctance to assure Mao that Moscow would soon share nuclear weapons with Peking.

In late May, the commander of the PLA Air Force, Liu Ya-lou, clearly implied that China could expect a sizable nuclear capability only *after* it had caught up economically with Britain and the United States: "If we catch up with Britain and then the United States in industrial and agricultural production and in the fields of science and technology, in terms of modernized equipment our army will certainly catch up and surpass them. *China's working class and scientists will certainly be able to make the most up-to-date aircraft and atomic bombs* in the not distant future. By that time, in addition to the political factor in which we always occupy an absolutely predominant position, *we can use atomic weapons and rockets, made by the workers, engineers, and scientists of our country,* in coping with the enemies who dare to invade our country and undermine world peace. By that time, another new turning point will probably be reached in the international situation. The socialist camp will get stronger and the imperialist camp will get weaker. The revolutionary movement in the world in general and Asia in particular will advance with more vigorous steps" [italics supplied].[41]

The passages italicized imply that a Chinese nuclear capability will have to await the time when *Chinese* industry, science, and technology can make them. In another passage of the same article,

Liu seemed to be arguing with those among the professional military who wanted a crash nuclear program which would cut into the resources devoted to the leap forward. He stressed that "economic construction is *closely connected* with defense construction. The building of modern industries is a prerequisite for modernizing our national defense . . . " [italics supplied].[42] The answer to those who advocated a crash nuclear program was that economic construction had to come first.

If there were any lingering hopes among Chinese army officers that the USSR might soon provide China with a nuclear capability, Marshal Ho Lung seemed to dispel them in an August statement warning against reliance on "outside aid" in trying to solve China's military problems.[43]

The strategic revisions made by Mao and the "native radicals" in the fall of 1957 and early 1958 seemed predicated on the assumption that China would not have a significant nuclear capability in the near future. As I have suggested, Khrushchev may have failed to indicate at the 1957 Moscow conference a willingness to step up Soviet assistance to China's nuclear weapons program. If this was the case, the CCP had little choice but to reassert the validity of Maoist military doctrine and its disparagement of modern nuclear weapons. As a corollary, it had to stamp down on professionalism in the PLA and to reject vigorously the warnings from the professionals that subordination of military to economic priorities might seriously endanger China's security. For the only other real alternative to reassertion of the Maoist strategy was to embark on a crash nuclear weapons program, or at least to elevate military expenditures to a much higher priority. This the Chinese clearly chose not to do. On the contrary, their economic decisions in early 1958 seemed based on the opposite assumption, namely, that military priorities would have to take second place, for the next ten years or so, to a rapid acceleration of industry and agriculture. In a very real sense, then, Soviet reluctance to share nuclear weapons may have been one critical reason why the CCP decided to embark on a frenetic leap forward. If the Soviet ally was reluctant to share nuclear weapons, then the Chinese economy had to be raised as quickly as possible to a level where it could itself provide the foundations for a modern military establishment. To dissipate its energies in a modern weapons race, the CCP may have calculated, would be pointless and in the long run might even prove disastrous to the economy. For the next ten years, China would have little choice but to rely on Soviet deterrent power and to seek its goals in limited ventures that would not risk a massive nuclear response from the United States.

It is of course conceivable that Mao did not urge Moscow in November 1957 to step up its assistance to China's nuclear weapons program, that he preferred to concentrate on the leap forward and the pressing economic tasks associated with it. But in the light of Chinese megalomania in late 1957 and early 1958, and of Peking's urgent desire for great power status, this hypothesis seems difficult to credit. Moreover, there were strong indications in early 1959, to be discussed later, that Peking did exert continuing pressure on Moscow for nuclear sharing.

How large a role in the Sino-Soviet conflict should be assigned to Peking's nuclear frustrations is an open question. Moscow may well have resisted Chinese pressures by arguing that nuclear diffusion within the Bloc would lead to nuclear diffusion in the West. It may have insisted that, for the time being, Chinese interests could be guaranteed by the Soviet deterrent. It may have argued that the Communist political campaign for an atom-free zone in Asia would be more credible without diffusion and that such a campaign might soon result in the elimination of American nuclear power from the Western Pacific and Japan. While it is doubtful that Mao would be fully satisfied with such arguments, he could do little but accept them. The critical question in Mao's mind must have been to what extent he could exploit Soviet deterrent power in his own behalf without Moscow's balking at some critical point. As we shall soon see, this was what appeared to happen in the Taiwan Straits in the fall of 1958. From that point on, Mao could hardly have been very confident that Soviet deterrent power could and would be used in his behalf without serious qualification or limitation.

The strain produced by Moscow's reluctance to diffuse nuclear weapons must have added considerably to the strains that were already apparent. Yet worse was to come. When American and British troops landed in Lebanon and Jordan in the midst of the Iraqi rebellion, a critical issue of foreign policy arose to accentuate the incipient conflict.

194

The Middle East Crisis:
Summer 1958

Until the Middle East crisis in the summer of 1958, the Sino-Soviet conflict over strategy had been confined to words. Neither side had yet taken an initiative against the West, or responded to a Western initiative, so as to bring the debate over strategy to the fore. The Iraqi coup on July 13, 1958, and the subsequent British and American landings in Lebanon and Jordan presented the first real test of the divergent strategic views. Here was a development that seemed to fit into the prospectus that Mao had outlined a few months earlier. The "national liberation movement" in the Middle East had led to a point where a revolution in Iraq had ousted a pro-Western government and thus abruptly put in jeopardy the keystone of the Western defense system in that area: the Baghdad pact. As Communist commentators were quick to point out, the Baghdad pact was now without Baghdad.

But the West refused to stand idly by while its position in the Middle East was being threatened. The Communists may well have expected that the Anglo-American landings in the Middle East were intended, not solely to protect Lebanon and Jordan from the spread of revolution, but also to suppress the Iraqi revolt. The situation cannot be better described than in the words of Richard Lowenthal:

"There is little doubt that the Allied landings were at first genuinely viewed by the Soviet and Chinese leaders as preparation for armed intervention against the new Iraqi Government; during the first few days, they were, after all, so interpreted by a great many non-Communists as well. If that expectation had come true, the USSR would have been faced with the choice of using force against American troops, with all the risks involved, or appearing impotent in the face of American intervention in a crucial, contested area.

"To avoid this dilemma, Khrushchev was determined to use every conceivable political pressure to prevent the Western powers from carrying out their supposed intentions while at the same time evading a military commitment of his own. Although he hurried to recognize the new Iraqi government and promised Nasser support in the unlikely event of a Western attack on the UAR, he sent no 'volunteer' fighters and instead issued his appeal for an emergency summit meeting with Indian participation on 19 July."[44]

As this passage implies, Khrushchev's initial reaction to the Western troop landings may have been one of near-panic. On July 23 he accepted the Western counterproposal for a summit meeting within the framework of the UN Security Council, an indication of his urgent desire to get the West to the conference table and so to forestall any potential move against Iraq.[45] Meanwhile, official Soviet statements between July 15 and 23 stressed that the *United Nations* must take decisive, urgent, and vigorous measures to curb the Western aggression.[46] While the specter of unilateral Soviet intervention was raised ("The Soviet Government . . . reserves the right to adopt the necessary measures dictated by the interests of maintaining peace and security") the counterthreat was not as high on the scale as some in the past—for example, during the Suez crisis in 1956.

In this same critical period of July 15–23, the Chinese Communists appeared to be skeptical of both the efficacy and the advisability of appeals to the UN, and of the chances of removing the West by political means. Rather, they seemed to favor a vigorous military response if the West did not withdraw from Lebanon and Jordan and if it attacked the new Iraqi republic.

Jen-min jih-pao editorials of July 20 and 21, for example, did not endorse Khrushchev's July 19 emergency appeal for a summit meeting. The July 20 editorial, significantly titled "The Countries and Peoples of the World Who Love Peace and Freedom Cannot Look On with Folded Arms," may even have dissented from this appeal when it said: " 'Nothing can be saved by yielding to evil, and coddling wrong only helps the devil.' The histories of the aggressive wars launched by Hitler Germany and Japan are still fresh in the memories of the whole world and are sufficient to bring this lesson home. *Consequently, if the U.S.-British aggressors refuse to withdraw from Lebanon and Jordan, and insist on expanding their aggression, then the only course left to the people of the world is to hit the aggressors on the head!* . . . The imperialists have always bullied the weak and been afraid of the strong. *The only language they understand is that of force*" [italics supplied].[47]

The July 21 editorial pointed out that the West was already

making sport of the UN Charter "without meeting with counter-blows." More important, in an analogy between the American war for independence and the current war, it seemed to suggest that the Bloc contribute arms and "volunteer armies" to protect the Iraqi Government and to help oust the Americans from Lebanon.

"What is especially worthy of comparison [between the American war for independence and the present war for independence in Iraq and Lebanon] is that the American war of independence relied greatly on the support of foreign armed forces. The Americans appealed for aid to Canada, Ireland, and France and *obtained important military assistance from France, Holland, and Spain.*

"During the first two and one half years of the [American] independence war, *over 90 per cent of all the arms used were imported,* from Europe, especially from France. The French and Europeans formed volunteer armies and went to America to take part in the war.

"Yet today both the struggle of the Lebanese people and the victory of the Iraqi people depend almost exclusively on their own efforts. We want to ask: 'Why are they not entitled to the international assistance which the American war of independence secured? Who dares to say that the French who supported America in those days were aggressors . . . ?' " [italics supplied][48]

It has been suggested that the above language may have embodied a plea for a united Arab rather than a Bloc military response to the Western initiative. This seems unlikely, however, for several reasons. First, on internal evidence alone, the plea was for "international assistance," suggesting that, even if Arab support were envisaged, the plea was not limited to the Arabs. Second, if the plea had been intended to muster *only* Arab support, it would more probably have been couched in terms of the "unbreakable unity" of the Arab liberation movement and the need for the fraternal Arab peoples to come to each other's aid. Third, the language in these paragraphs was the same kind of Aesopian language which has been characteristic of the Sino-Soviet dialogue since its inception. It is not language intended for the uninitiated or for "bourgeois nationalists" such as Nasser. Finally, it seems highly doubtful that Peking could have believed Nasser's army—which had been incapable of repelling Israeli troops—capable of effectively repelling the British and Americans.

Throughout the crisis in July, there appears to have been a difference between the degree of risk Khrushchev was prepared to accept and the degree Mao wanted to see him accept. In Khrushchev's letter to President Eisenhower on July 19, proposing the emergency summit meeting, he counseled moderation: "We address you not from positions of intimidation but from positions of reason. We believe at this momentous hour that it would be more reasonable not to bring the heated atmosphere to the boiling point; it is sufficiently inflammable as it is. The statesmen of countries must seek solutions not by means of fanning war psychosis but reasonably and calmly."[49]

A *Pravda* editorial on July 21 reiterated that the USSR could not remain indifferent to what was happening on its frontiers, but called for reason and calm on the grounds that both the United States and the USSR had hydrogen and atomic weapons. The next day Khrushchev told a reception in Moscow, after his talks with Nasser, "You can be confident that we shall do everything to ensure that there will not be a war in the Middle East."[50]

Chinese public statements, on the contrary, seemed to contend that, unless Western military action were met with military counteraction, the West would become increasingly cocky and general war would ensue. Moreover, Peking asserted that the Bloc, because of its overwhelming superiority, should not fear war. The first point was made by *Jen-min jih-pao* on July 17: "There cannot be the slightest indulgence or tolerance toward American imperialism's act of aggression. . . . The present situation is an uncommonly grave one. . . . If the American aggressors are permitted to do as they wish, then not only will the people of the Middle East be enslaved, but a new world war would be inevitable. . . . Therefore let the people of the whole world take emergency action."[51] The second point was made a few days later by the *Chieh-fang-chün pao* (Liberation Army Daily), which argued that the Bloc did not fear war because the "balance of power in our favor has never been so great."[52]

Apart from its confidence that a more favorable balance of forces prevailed at the time of the Middle East crisis of 1958, Peking also believed the Iraqi coup had substantially contributed to deterioration of the Western position there and in other "colonial" areas. On July 14, the very day of the Iraqi coup, Peking contended that it was the "equivalent of an earthquake in the Middle East. . . . " On July 16, a *Jen-min jih-pao* editorial said that the Iraqi coup had broken the backbone of the imperialist position in West Asia. "[It] greatly accelerates the process of complete liquidation of the colonial forces in the Middle East and the world as a whole."[53] On July 17, Politburo member P'eng Chen declared that the victory in Iraq would "undoubtedly impel the national liberation movements in Asia and Africa to a new upsurge."[54]

After implying in the *Jen-min jih-pao* editorials of July 20 and 21 its desire for a more aggressive course of action, Peking on July 22 did endorse Khrushchev's July 19 appeal for an emergency summit meeting—possibly because Khrushchev had indicated to them by this time that he was not prepared to use force unless the West moved into Iraq. Thereafter, from July 23 to July 30, the week preceding Khrushchev's trip to Peking, there was little difference in Soviet and Chinese comment.[55]

That Mao was genuinely distressed at Khrushchev's "soft" response to the Western landings in the Middle East, however, was again to be suggested in Chinese comment after the Mao-Khrushchev meeting in early August.[56] This comment, stressing the inevitability of future Western provocations in the Middle East, the impossibility of "begging for peace," and the need for stern action by all peoples against such Western initiatives, sharply diverged from Soviet comment, which put its emphasis on the assertion that the West was deterred from such initiatives.

CHAPTER 7

KHRUSHCHEV AND THE TAIWAN STRAIT CRISIS: AUTUMN 1958

ON July 31, 1958, Khrushchev arrived in Peking for a three-day visit which had not been advertised and which apparently had been undertaken hurriedly. At the time, most observers related the trip to Khrushchev's July 19 proposal for a summit meeting on the Middle East crisis, and many concluded that the Chinese had forced Khrushchev to withdraw his tentative acceptance of the Western counterproposal for a meeting within the framework of the UN Security Council. As previously noted, Peking had only belatedly endorsed Khrushchev's July 19 proposal, and had done so only after implying a preference for military counteraction. In spite of the Chinese attitude, Khrushchev on the evening of July 23 had conditionally accepted the Western proposal, speaking of a "special meeting" within the Security Council. On July 28, however, even before he flew to Peking, Khrushchev in effect withdrew his acceptance, stating that he had envisaged a five-power meeting, not a regular session of the Security Council, and charging that British Prime Minister Macmillan had abandoned his initial proposal.

Apparently it was not Chinese displeasure alone, or even primarily, that made Khrushchev change his tactics. The most plausible explanation is that, between July 23 and 28, Khrushchev's fear of Western military action in Iraq—the real reason he had called for the summit meeting in the first place—had diminished. At the London meeting of the Council of the Baghdad Pact on July 28, there appeared the first unofficial signs that the West intended to recognize the new Iraqi Government.

If Khrushchev did not intend to go to the Security Council meeting, why then, did he undertake the trip to Peking? Perhaps the most credible reason is to be found in the mounting evidence of a disagreement between the Soviet and Chinese parties on global strategy. This disagreement had already been expressed in the dispute with the Yugoslav Party; it was now again evident during the Middle East crisis. Perhaps most important, the disagreement could result in hostilities at any time in the Taiwan Strait, where the

Chinese Communists had significant military capablities and were not constrained to confine themselves to talk. Sometime in late July the Chinese Communists did in fact begin to make psychological and probably military preparations for their venture in the Strait. In early August there were Chinese Nationalist reports of increasing jet concentrations on airstrips in Fukien and Chekiang provinces— airstrips which could be vital if the Communists wished to secure control of the air over the straits.[1] On July 23, following the end of the two-month meeting of the military committee of the Chinese Communist Party Central Committee, there began a sharp up-surge in propaganda calling for the "liberation" of Taiwan. It was to last one week and then abruptly and strangely cease. During that week—right up to the eve of Khrushchev's sudden visit to Peking— the Taiwan liberation theme was stressed, particularly in meetings in Fukien and Chekiang provinces, opposite the offshore islands. At these meetings citizens pledged readiness to liberate Taiwan "at any time." By July 27, reports of rallies pledging vigilance and affirm-ing readiness to liberate Taiwan were being carried in home service news broadcasts and in NCNA transmissions to the domestic press. Thus it seems almost certain that action in the Strait was already in the planning stage in late July. Khrushchev's sudden trip to Pe-king with Soviet Defense Minister Malinovsky was almost certainly related to the impending Chinese move.

Continuing Disagreement

On the day of Khrushchev's arrival in Peking, *Hung-ch'i* pub-lished an article entitled "A new Upsurge in National Revolution" under the pseudonym "Yu Chao-li," which means "Strength-of-Millions" and which reflects the Chinese emphasis both then and now on the spectacular results to be achieved in domestic and foreign affairs by "reliance on the masses."[2] Yu Chao-li, a name which may represent a Party Politburo member or members, was to become the Party's principal spokesman on imperialism and hence the Party's principal critic of Khrushchev's strategy for dealing with imperialism.

In this first article, Yu significantly took for his text the "national liberation" movement in the Arab countries. He saw a "new chapter" in the story of the movement opening in the Iraqi coup of July 14, and his article embroidered at length his opening

201

declaration that the "independence movement of the 80,000,000 Arab people is flaring like a fire set to dry tinder." Implying strongly that a little Bloc gasoline poured on the fire might ignite other Arab countries besides Iraq, Yu concluded polemically that the significance of the revolutionary movement in colonial areas "must not be underestimated," that Lenin had considered the colonial question of "decisive significance," and that there could be no doubt that "our generation will witness the total destruction of colonialism and imperialism. . . . "

Another of the messages which Yu apparently aimed at Khrushchev stated what had been implied in the *Jen-min jih-pao* editorials of July 20 and 21, and was to be reiterated after Khrushchev left: that the West's action in sending troops to Jordan and Lebanon was a bluff that should have been called: "The U.S. and British imperialists' wanton acts of aggression in the Middle East are to a certain extent an attempt to exploit the people's fear of war. They put on a show as if they wouldn't hesitate to make full-scale war in order to force the peoples to accept a *fait accompli* and thus extend their aggression. The peace-loving people certainly do not want war, but those who really treasure peace will never bow to threats of war. Peace cannot be got by begging from the imperialists. . . . "[3]

Like most intra-Bloc communiqués, the Sino-Soviet communiqué issued on August 3, the day of Khrushchev's departure for home, was ambiguous, phrased in such a way that the two parties could persist in differing positions without flatly contradicting the terms of the "aggreement." The communiqué affirmed, for example, that a new war (a) would be a "disaster" and (b) would permit anti-imperialist forces to "wipe out clean the imperialist aggressors and so establish everlasting world peace." Its most interesting omission was the lack of any reference to the "liberation" of Taiwan—a subject on which Peking's propaganda at the time was concentrated.

Within five days of Khrushchev's departure, two *Jen-min jih-pao* editorials again implicitly rebuked Khrushchev's mild response to the American-British landings in the Middle East. They set forth Mao's thinking on strategy in terms which suggested strongly that Mao not only had not changed his mind about the need for tougher Bloc policies but had felt vindicated by the West's initiative in the Middle East—a result, in Mao's view, of Khrushchev's "soft" policy. The editorial of August 4, the day after Khrushchev's departure, contended that (1) the U.S. and British troops had still not withdrawn; (2) even if they eventually did withdraw, they would soon seek a new opportunity to renew their aggression against the colonial countries; and (3) to prevent local aggressions in the future, it was necessary to demonstrate to the West that the Bloc did not fear the risk of general war:

"The U.S. and British invasion forces are not withdrawing from the Middle East. They are still gravely infringing on the right of the Arab nations to independence. . . . If they are eventually forced to withdraw their troops, they will use their aggressive forces to grasp new privileges and control a series of Middle Eastern countries to create favorable conditions so that they may seek an opportunity to renew and expand their aggression and launch a new war adventure.

"The interests of the U.S. monopoly capitalists are continuously driving Eisenhower and Dulles to carry out so-called 'brink of war' and 'limited war' adventurous policies. Consequently, in order to ease international tension and maintain peace, we must not merely depend on the well-meaning wishes and unilateral efforts of the peace-loving countries and peoples. We stand for peace, but we are by no means afraid of the war provocations of imperialism. We must have firm determination and full confidence to put out the flames of imperialist aggressive war."[4]

The language employed here presumably reflects the position that Mao took with Khrushchev in their three-day meeting. In essence, this appears to have been that Khrushchev's resort to the UN and diplomacy in order to eject the Western troops from the Middle East was tantamount to appeasement and would only encourage the West to make further incursions. To Khrushchev's apparent reply that he was reluctant to take steps which might lead to general war, Mao evidently contended that the Bloc must show "firm determination" and should not "be afraid" of the imperialist provocations.

On August 8, five days after Khrushchev's departure, another editorial in the Chinese Party paper indicated that Mao was more convinced than ever of the need for a "get-tough" policy toward the West. The principal points seemed to be aimed at those, including Khrushchev, with whom Mao had recently been arguing, and they have since reappeared in a number of Chinese pronouncements clearly aimed at Khrushchev. Cast in the form of a commentary on the Sino-Soviet communique of August 3, the Party newspaper's editorial was entitled, "Only Through Resolute Struggle May Peace Be Defended." In a key paragraph reaffirming Mao's view of the importance of armed struggle and of countering Western "brinkmanship," the editorial stated: "The imperialists like to frighten the nervous with the choice between submission or war. Their agents frequently spread the *nonsensical idea that peace can be achieved only by currying favor and compromising with the aggressors. Some soft-hearted advocates of peace even naïvely believe that in order to relax tension at all costs the enemy must not be provoked.* They dare not denounce the war provokers, they are unwilling to trace the responsibility of war and war danger *and to differentiate between right and wrong on the issue of war and peace. Some groundlessly conclude that peace can be gained only when there is no armed resistance* against the attacks of the imperialists and colonialists and when there is no bitter struggle against them" [italics supplied].[5]

The editorial went on to observe that after World War II—i.e., in a period of Western military superiority—the world "several times came close to a major war." But in fact there had not been such a war and indeed "resolute struggle" had forced the imperialists to accept a truce in local wars in Korea and Indochina. More recently, in the Middle East, the resolute struggle of Egypt and Syria, with the "support" of the Bloc, had forced the aggressors to withdraw from Egypt and to refrain from attacking Syria. If general war could be avoided when the Bloc was comparatively weak, it could certainly be avoided now that the Bloc was comparatively strong. In local engagements the West could be repelled. The editorial went on to warn against compromise with the West: "Peace must be fought for. It cannot be begged. . . . Each of the victories in the struggle against aggression and colonialism . . . won by the Asian and African peoples during the decade after the last world war was achieved by resolute struggle. . . . The imperialists are not to be feared. There should be no compromise in dealing with the imperialists, because this will end in submission."[6]

Moreover, the editorial warned against concentrating on

"peace" to the exclusion of preparing the people for wars: "If . . . we allow the people to indulge only in the illusion of peace and the horrors of war, actual war will fill them with panic and confusion. Only . . . by mentally preparing the people with a high morale and confidence in victory and by mobilizing them to fight for peace can peace be effectively defended and aggression stopped. . . . "[7]

By contrast, the *Pravda* editorials of August 5 and 6 on the Mao-Khrushchev meeting emphasized the peace theme. The first editorial, entitled "The Forces of Peace and Socialism Will Score a Great Victory," began by saying that the Khrushchev-Mao meeting "demonstrates the unshakable determination of two great peoples to do everything possible to ease international tension and to prevent the disaster of a new war."[8] The Soviet Union and Communist China were agreed, it went on, that the task at present was to achieve agreement between states, reduce armaments, ban the use of nuclear weapons, and scrap all military alignments and bases. The rest of the editorial was either a paraphrase of the joint communiqué or an innocuous repetition of the unity of views of the two parties. The August 6 editorial, titled "Great Cooperation in the Interests of Peace," began by stressing the deterrent power of the USSR: "Naturally the Soviet Union . . . is a powerful restraining factor for the aggressors." It then quoted approving comment on the Mao-Khrushchev meeting from the Communist press and concluded again on the deterrent note: "The forces of peace have unprecedentedly increased everywhere. They are able to inflict a devastating blow upon aggressors [who have] *gone too far*" [italics supplied].[9]

Various possible interpretations of these divergent Chinese and Soviet editorial lines could be advanced. They could be viewed, for instance, as complementary preparations for the Quemoy crisis. In this interpretation, the Chinese would have been justifying in advance their imminent action in the Strait as part of the need for a much tougher line against the Western "war menace," while the Russians would have been reassuring the Chinese and warning the West that Soviet power would deter its interfering in the Chinese "civil war." It is difficult, however, to read the Chinese editorials without concluding that they meant not to complement but to refute the Soviet position, which had probably been spelled out by Khrushchev in his meeting with Mao. Note, for example, that the editorial of August 8 employs a jargon which is used in communication between Communists but not between them and the West "Some soft-hearted advocates of peace . . . are unwilling . . . *to differentiate between right and wrong on the issue of war and peace*" [italics supplied].[10] It is hard to resist the conclusion that the Chinese were expressing a fundamentally different view of the nature of deterrence from the Soviets—a difference which probably reflected differing views between Mao and Khrushchev.

The Chinese position seems to have been that brinkmanship must be answered in kind, or else the West would get the idea that it could initiate "limited war adventures" with impunity (see the August 4 editorial). The Chinese view further seems to have been that, in order to sober the West, it was necessary to undertake some kind of "armed resistance" and "bitter struggle" (see the August 8 editorial). The best place for such a struggle was the Taiwan Strait.

This view seems not to have prevailed at the Mao-Khrushchev meeting. Otherwise, there would probably have been mention of the Taiwan "liberation" theme in the joint communiqué released on August 3. As we have seen, some kind of preliminary Chinese decision to precipitate the crisis was almost certainly taken in late July. Since, as we shall soon argue, the Chinese intention was not to go to war but rather to exercise intolerable political and psychological pressure on the Quemoy garrison and the Nationalist-American alliance, Mao probably would have desired at least Khrushchev's public acquiescence to the "liberation" of Taiwan. To make this threat fully effective, Mao needed a firm, early, public, and high-level Soviet commitment to give at least moral support to "liberation." He was not to get such a commitment until a month later when the crisis had passed its peak.

The Taiwan Strait Venture[11]

Several elements contributed to the Chinese Communist decision to launch a venture in the Taiwan Strait in August of 1958. First, the West was preoccupied with the Middle East crisis, a fact which was probably central in the timing of the venture. Second, the Chinese believed that they had an unbeatable hand. The evidence strongly suggests they never intended to launch a frontal assault on any of the offshore islands, but believed that, by interdiction, they could force the Quemoy garrison to surrender—a surrender which, in time, would lead to the automatic collapse of the other offshore islands. The Chinese seemed to base their calculations on a judgment widely held in the West: that once air and sea interdiction became effective the offshore islands could not be supplied, unless Nationalist and American forces were prepared to bomb the coastal provinces on the Chinese mainland.

The Chinese Communists probably calculated either (a) that their interdiction attempt would be successful, in which case the islands would fall without an invasion, American prestige would suffer a grave blow, and the U.S.-Nationalist alliance would be seriously weakened; or (b) that to avert the loss of the islands the U.S. and the Nationalists would be forced to bomb the mainland, in which case the USSR would be obliged to come swiftly to Peking's assistance, great pressure would be exerted by America's Western allies to prevent the risk of World War III over a few small offshore islands, and sooner or later the U.S. would force the Nationalists to evacuate the islands. The flaw in the calculation was that the blockade did not work; it did become feasible to supply the offshore islands without bombing the Chinese mainland.

A third Chinese Communist calculation in initiating the venture has already been suggested. Mao probably believed sincerely that the West needed to be given a sobering lesson in brinkmanship in return for its intervention in the Middle East.

Fourth, one of Peking's intentions may have been to extract from Moscow expanded military commitments, including tactical nuclear weapons to oppose those that might be brought to Taiwan.

Fifth, the stimulation of greater popular effort for the leap forward and the commune program may have been expected from military action in the Taiwan Strait.

Sixth, the offshore island venture must also be looked upon as a calculated Chinese Communist probe of U.S. intentions. How far would the Americans go in defending these islands? Until Secretary Dulles' statement at Newport, Rhode Island, on September 4, 1958, there may have been considerable doubt in both Russian and Chinese minds as to what the American response would be. At this time, however, Dulles said that Quemoy was "increasingly related" to the defense of Taiwan and suggested that the U.S. might bomb the Chinese mainland if the Communists attacked

Quemoy. The officer who briefed reporters on the statement added that the U.S. probably would not wait until the situation was "in extremis" before acting.[12] The statement, followed as it was by an American military buildup in the area, must have given Khrushchev and Mao pause.[13] The day following the statement, the Chinese offered to renew the ambassadorial talks with the United States in Warsaw, and the early acute phase of the crisis ended.

A final and not least important Chinese Communist calculation was that the initiation of another crisis over the offshore islands would badly shake the Nationalist confidence in the American alliance and thus serve as a major stepping-stone to the Communists' primary aim of incorporating Taiwan into mainland China and eliminating American forces from the Strait. The Chinese may have miscalculated that the U.S. would not defend the island and that, after several weeks' bombardment, the U.S. would force the Nationalists to withdraw under American pressure. In this manner, they would get the islands and split the American-Nationalist partnership, thus leaving the way open for a Communist-Nationalist deal vis-à-vis Taiwan itself. The offshore islands were, in short, not ends in themselves but pawns in a larger political-psychological game. If one recalls the great pressures in both the United States and Western Europe for an evacuation of the offshore islands, one will see that the Chinese calculation was wrong only in not allowing for the obduracy of Secretary Dulles.

Most analysts now seem agreed that the Chinese Communists never intended to invade the offshore islands. The artillery shelling began immediately before the typhoon season, when amphibious operations would have been precarious. The amphibious lift necessary for an invasion was never brought into the coastal areas. Communist air capability was used with great restraint throughout the crisis. Quemoy, for example, was not bombed by aircraft. In sum, the whole venture seemed to be a classic example of brinkmanship.

Although the evidence suggests that Mao was playing a very well-controlled hand, there were contingencies which he could not foresee that might have led to a widening conflict. The Nationalists might have bombed the mainland without U.S. authorization.[14] American naval vessels convoying Nationalist supply ships might have been hit inadvertently. Communist-Nationalist air battles might have developed into engagements involving Taiwan air space. If the supply situation on Quemoy had really become as desperate as the Chinese Communists evidently thought it would, there would have been the possibility of American intervention in force. The Russians could not be sure that their Chinese allies might not drag them inadvertently into an open military confrontation they did not want, any more than the Americans could be sure that their involvement would be limited.

In the week prior to Khrushchev's sudden arrival in Peking on July 31, Chinese Communist propaganda had built up a small campaign on the theme of "liberating" Taiwan. As already indicated, by July 27 meetings were reported in the coastal provinces of Fukien and Chekiang, at which pledges were made to liberate Taiwan "at any moment."[15] Between July 23 and 29 Peking's central radio broadcast some thirty commentaries on Taiwan. Abruptly on July 29 this "liberation" propaganda ceased and remained dormant until mid-August. It suffered a decline on the eve of Khrushchev's arrival and continued to be minimal after his departure. As mentioned earlier, there was no reference to Taiwan in the Mao-Khrushchev communiqué. Did Khrushchev, it must thus be asked, refuse to go along with the Strait venture on the ground that it was too risky?

A *Sovetskii flot* article on August 7 spoke of the "provocative bustle" in the Taiwan area, caused by "instructions from Washington" and "obviously having aggressive aims." On August 9, Moscow's first radio commentary on the impending crisis condemned the "war preparations" on Taiwan. Neither of these initial Soviet commentaries supported Peking's right to "liberate" Taiwan, although an article in the Czech Party daily, *Rude pravo,* on August 13, quoted by Peking, did explicitly support China's "inviolable right to liberate" Taiwan.

On August 16, Yu Chao-li wrote an article in *Hung ch'i* that may have been intended as the signal of the impending shelling of Quemoy. Beginning from the proposition that "the forces of socialism are overwhelmingly superior to the forces of imperialism," Yu Chao-li contended that "today the last bastions of imperialism are being shaken violently by irrestible popular revolutionary forces."[16] Events since World War II had shown how right Mao was in 1946 in describing the imperialists and their supporters as "truly paper tigers." The United States in particular was "isolated as never before," and the imperialist camp was "overextended on too long a front," lacked the necessary strength, was "vulnerable at many points," and indeed was "shaking in its shoes."[17]

Particularly significant, in the same *Hung ch'i* article, was the revival of Mao's 1946 line that the apparent American fear of Soviet aggression was "in fact a smokescreen" under which the United States was directing its effort toward "invading and enslaving" the countries in the "intermediate region" between the two camps. The U.S., the writer continued, could not start a war against the USSR before it "first brings this capitalist world to its knees."[18] For this reason, and for the further reason that the Russians had military superiority (the "basic condition preventing the outbreak of atomic war"), the author suggested that an increase in Bloc pressure on the West—i.e., an assault on the offshore islands—would not seriously risk a general war. This may well have been the line that Mao took with Khrushchev at their meeting in early August.

On August 19, a Soviet commentary broadcast only in Mandarin gave Moscow's first assurance to the Chinese that they were "not isolated," because the "USSR and the socialist countries stand side by side with People's China."[19] The broadcast condemned the United States for "new provocations" and warned Washington that "it should not take such risks." Had the Russians intended fully to back up the imminent Chinese initiative, it is likely that this warning would have been more widely broadcast or cited a more authoritative Soviet source.

The Chinese venture began in earnest on August 23 with the shelling of the Quemoy complex and naval harassment of Quemoy and the Matsus. Beginning on August 27, Peking's coastal radios (but not the central radio) broadcast warnings to the Quemoy garrison to surrender and threatened an "imminent" landing. Soon thereafter, the coastal radios began a round-the-clock propaganda effort to get the Nationalists on Quemoy to defect. Warnings were addressed to the Quemoy garrison to stop resisting, to "return to the fatherland," to "kill U.S. advisors," and to cross over to the mainland, because the islands were as "hopeless as a pair of turtles trapped in a flask."[20]

It seems likely that this Chinese campaign of late August and early September against the offshore islands was predicated on the assumption of a quick victory. It is pertinent to note that between

August 23, when the shelling began, and September 6, when the Chinese agreed to negotiations, Peking did not let the Chinese public in on the crisis. *Only* the coastal radios, busily trying to subvert the offshore garrisons, played up the adventure. This fact is susceptible of two explanations which are not mutually exclusive: first, that Mao did not wish to arouse public anxiety until he had achieved his quick victory and, second, that he may have been waiting until certain of a Soviet commitment.

On August 24, one day after the Chinese initiated the shelling of the offshore islands, a speech by Khrushchev was reported in *Pravda*. In this speech Khrushchev, surveying the international scene, minimized the possibility of war in the immediate future: "Many ask will there be a war or not. Of course, one cannot vouch for the madmen who exist in the imperialist world; but *at the present time*, it seems to me *there is no cloud from which thunder could roll*" [italics supplied].[21] This de-emphasis of the offshore island crisis was characteristic of the manner in which the Russians minimized it in its early stages, a procedure in sharp contrast to the atmosphere of acute crisis they encouraged in the early stages of other crises, e.g., Suez in 1956 and the Middle East in the summer of 1958.

Illustrative of the low key in which the Russians played the initial stages of the crisis was the meager reporting of it at that time in Soviet media. The Russians ignored the Quemoy developments until August 27 and even then did not take direct notice of the action. The Soviet press cited Tass dispatches from London referring vaguely to action by the CPR shore batteries.[22] On the next day, the Soviet press referred only vaguely to "suspicious maneuvering by the Seventh Fleet."[23]

The first Soviet commitment, when it finally came, was ambiguous. The first authoritative statement of Soviet support, written in the form of an article by "Observer" in *Pravda* for August 31, said merely that anyone threatening an attack against China "must not forget that he is threatening the Soviet Union also," and that the Soviet Union would give China "the necessary moral and material help in its just struggle." The article did not commit the Russians to any specific military response.

On September 4, 1958, Peking claimed a 12-mile limit for its territorial waters. (See *New York Times*, September 5, 1958.) The

United States predictably refused to recognize the claim. American vessels had been escorting Chinese Nationalist supply ships to within 3 miles of the coast in an effort to prevent interdiction of the offshore islands. The Chinese Communist declaration could have markedly increased the danger of a war with the United States because if Chinese Communist coastal batteries fired on U.S. ships in defense of their "territorial sovereignty," intentionally or otherwise, the American reaction might have been to bomb the sites of the coastal batteries on the mainland.

The Soviet reaction to the Chinese declaration was extremely cautious,[24] a caution particularly revealing because the Russians had waged a strong campaign at the 1958 Geneva conference to secure international recognition of the 12-mile limit. Moreover, the Russians in July 1960 would shoot down an American RB-47 because, they contended, it had violated Soviet territorial waters inside the 12-mile limit.

On September 5, a *Pravda* "Observer" article noted statements in the American press to the effect that Washington might use tactical nuclear weapons against the China mainland and might issue a warning that the U.S. Government would not exclude the use of atomic arms by American forces in the Far East. It replied that:

"The Chinese People's Republic has sufficient strength to counter the aggressors fully. . . . The Soviet Union cannot remain inactive in the face of its brave ally. The Soviet Union will not quietly watch U.S. military preparations in the Pacific, whose waters also wash Soviet shores. . . .

"The Soviet people will extend to their brothers, the Chinese people, every kind of aid to bridle the adventurous war provocateurs who have grown insolent and rash. The inspirers and organizers of the new military adventure in the Far East cannot count on the retaliatory blow restricting itself to the area of the offshore islands and the Taiwan Strait. They will receive such a devastating counterblow that an end will be put to U.S. imperialist aggression in the Far East."[25]

As ominous as this statement was, it still contained several ambiguities and loopholes. First, note the statement that the Chinese People's Republic had "sufficient strength" to counter the aggressors, implying that Soviet help was not essential. Second, note the ambiguity of the Soviet threat that it could not "quietly watch" U.S. military preparations. Third, note that it would be the Soviet "people" and not the Soviet Government who would give "every kind of aid" to the Chinese "people." This may have been intended to leave a loophole for Soviet "volunteers" or for some kind of support short of all-out Soviet involvement. Finally, although it was suggested that a nuclear retaliatory blow might be made, this was not made explicit.

It may be of considerable significance that in the first two weeks of the crisis, from August 23 to September 6, Chinese coastal radios (the only Chinese comment there was) avoided virtually all reference to the possibility of nuclear war or to the use of nuclear weapons in the Taiwan Strait crisis. Such references were made *after* Khrushchev's second letter (September 19) to the U.S., in which he warned for the first time that the USSR would reply in kind to an American nuclear attack on China. Obviously, the Chinese did not want to frighten their own people with the specter of American tactical nuclear weapons which they themselves did not have. But it remains a question why, in the period from August 23 to September 6, the Chinese coastal radios did not imply or state that their loyal Soviet allies would answer American nuclear weapons with Soviet nuclear weapons. To give credence to the brinkmanship gambit against the West and to encourage its own populace, Peking almost certainly would have desired to publicize the threat of Soviet nuclear retaliation as early as possible in the crisis. It is just possible that Moscow did not give Peking any concrete assurance of support with tactical nuclear weapons until the Chinese had first taken some of the pressure off the offshore islands and reduced the possibility of an expanding conflict.

The Chinese eased the tension suddenly on September 6, immediately after Secretary Dulles' Newport speech suggesting the U.S. might attack the mainland if there were an attack on Quemoy. Chou En-lai offered to renew ambassadorial talks with the United States. Although this by no means resolved the crisis, it marked the beginning of a new stage. It is most important to note that strong, unequivocal, and high-level Soviet expressions of support for Peking came only *after* Chou En-lai's offer to negotiate. Until the Chinese agreed to ambassadorial talks and reduced the pressure against the offshore islands, Moscow stopped short of committing the USSR to direct military involvement in the event of a clash between American and Chinese Communist forces. It did so only on September 7 (the day *after* Chou En-lai had taken much of the pressure off), when Khrushchev himself wrote President Eisenhower that an attack on the CPR would be regarded as an attack against the USSR.[26]

Khrushchev's two letters to Eisenhower of September 7 and 19 gave various indications of the Soviet attitude toward the Straits venture. It appears that Khrushchev sought to steer a middle course: on the one hand, he wanted to leave the impression that he fully supported the Chinese aspirations and would come to the support of his ally in the event of a showdown with the United States; on the other hand, he clearly wanted to avoid issuing an ultimatum to the West or giving a blank check to China. In his first letter he said that an attack on China "is an attack on the Soviet Union" and that the USSR would "do everything" to defend the security of both countries.[27] He immediately followed this threat by denying that it was a threat at all, contending, "All we want to do is to call your attention to the situation which no one would be able to get out of—neither you, nor we—should a war break out. . . . " In his second letter Khrushchev went further: if China is attacked with atomic weapons, he said, "the aggressor will at once get a rebuff by the same means."[28] He reiterated that an attack on the CPR was an attack on the USSR, and "may none doubt that we shall completely honor our commitments."

Despite these very strong pledges of support, however, both letters contained ambiguous passages which put their emphasis on the Chinese Communist ability to repel Western aggression rather than on the joint ability of the two powers. In his first letter Khrushchev said that if a war were forced on China, "we have not the least doubt that the *Chinese people will strike back* at the aggressor in a fitting manner" [italics supplied]. In his second letter he stated that if American troops did not leave Taiwan and if the American fleet were not recalled from the Taiwan Strait, "*People's China will have no other recourse* but to expel the hostile armed forces from its own territory, which is being converted into a bridgehead for attacking the CPR" [italics supplied]. He thus committed the USSR to give aid immediately if mainland China were attacked by the U.S., but he did not commit the USSR to helping China evict American forces from the Taiwan Strait.

In the week of September 14–21, the tide turned in the off-shore island crisis as the resupply effort proved successful and after a major build-up of U.S. forces. U.S. jet fighters with instructions to fire at Communist aircraft escorted Nationalist transport planes in their first air-dropping of supplies to Quemoy; U.S. technicians rushed completion of missile sites on Taiwan; reinforcements raised the U.S. Seventh Fleet strength to six carriers, three heavy cruisers, and forty destroyers in the Strait.[29]

At about the same time, the U.S. gave the Nationalists side-winder air-to air missiles which were very successful in a September 24 air battle in which ten Chinese Communist MIG's were shot down. Perhaps as a direct reply, the Soviet military paper *Krasnaya zvezda* on September 25 contained the first threat since the crisis began of Soviet "volunteers." The paper recounted how Soviet pilot volunteers had fought in China against Japan and concluded that Soviet pilots are "ready if necessary to come to the aid of their true Chinese friends and crush the interventionists with all the might of their arms." This threat of volunteers did not, however, appear in mass media or in official Soviet government statements.

The Soviet reaction to the American introduction of side-winder missiles was in fact extremely circumspect. On October 1 a Moscow broadcast in English to Southeast Asia merely reported that Nationalist flyers were using "guided missiles" which might at some point have nuclear warheads. No counterthreats were made. On October 3, *Jen-min jih-pao* claimed the crisis had been worsened by U.S. acts of aggression, particularly the introduction of sidewinders. The fact that neither Peking nor Moscow made much propaganda out of the introduction of the sidewinders suggests a Soviet unwillingness to give the Chinese Communist Air Force an equivalent capability. For the Chinese Communists or Russians to call attention to Nationalist sidewinders supplied by the Americans would of course have invited the question why the Russians did not supply the Chinese Communists with air-to-air missiles.

On October 6 the Chinese Communists proclaimed what was tantamount to a cease-fire—the brinkmanship gambit having proved to be a total flop. Two days later the U.S. ordered suspension of the escort service of the Seventh Fleet.

On October 5, a day before the Chinese cease-fire announcement, Khrushchev issued a very unusual reply to a "question" put by a Tass correspondent on the Taiwan crisis:

"The Soviet Government has openly and unambiguously stated, in messages to President Eisenhower, for example, that if the United States starts a war against our friend and ally, the Chinese People's Republic, the USSR will fully honor her commitments under the treaty of friendship, alliance, and mutual aid with the CPR, and that attack on the CPR is an attack on the USSR.

"Does this contain the slightest hint that the USSR is, as President Eisenhower would have it, ready to take part in a civil war in China? No, we have stated and do state something quite different: The *USSR will come to the help of the CPR if the latter is attacked from without; speaking more concretely, if the United States attacks the CPR.*

"The Soviet Government has thought it necessary to make this warning, as the atmosphere in the Far East is such that U.S. interference in Chinese internal affairs has brought the United States to the very brink of a direct military conflict with the CPR. And if the United States steps over this brink, the USSR will not stand aside. *But we have not interfered in and do not intend to interfere in the civil war* which the Chinese people are waging against the Chiang Kai-shek clique.

"The arrangement of their domestic affairs according to their own discretion is the inalienable right of every people. The intention to get back their islands of Quemoy and Matsu and to free Taiwan and the Pescadores is the internal affair of the Chinese people" [italics supplied].[30]

The distinction here made between an American attack on the mainland and the "civil war" between the mainland and Taiwan may seem like obfuscation, but the very fact that Khrushchev made it suggests that all along he had wished to discourage Peking from undertaking too ambitious a venture in the Taiwan Strait.

The question remains as to whether Khrushchev concurred even in a limited venture in the Strait. As noted earlier, Mao had apparently intended only a limited action, one which would not entail an actual invasion of the offshore islands. However, in order to make effective his pressure on the Nationalist garrisons and the Sino-American alliance, he needed a firm and high-level expression of Soviet support in the advancing rather than the retreating stage of the venture. In Mao's view, because Bloc military superiority constituted an absolute deterrent to general war, the deterrent threat could be publicly invoked by Khrushchev without risk to Moscow. Khrushchev evidently did not agree. As it turned out, strong high-level statements of Soviet support were not forthcoming until after the crisis in the Strait had been substantially reduced, and even then these statements were ambiguous as to what Soviet action would be taken against anything short of an American assault on the Chinese mainland. Throughout the crisis, Soviet statements betrayed a genuine concern over the prospects of a nuclear war.

Beyond the general statement that the Russians did not wish to press the Strait venture as far as Peking did, it is difficult to pinpoint the nub of the dispute. It may have been Khrushchev's unwillingness to speak earlier than he did. It may have been his refusal to go beyond the position stated in his letters. The Russians may have imposed constraints on the level of Chinese violence or the area of that violence. The Chinese may have been disappointed in the initial impact of the artillery bombardment, asked for more from the Russians, and got less than they asked. The Chinese may have wanted an earlier and more credible Soviet threat to send "volunteers." Perhaps they even wanted an extension of the territorial limits of conflict in order to expose Chinese Nationalist shipping to severer attacks. Peking may have wanted the crisis to go on through carefully graded increases in brinkmanship and may have been denied this by cool Russian reactions. One or all of these elements may have entered into the Sino-Soviet friction over the Strait venture.

All that can be safely concluded is that Mao Tse-tung, having undertaken a venture on the basis of a calculation of the balance of power which was not shared by Khrushchev, was forced to make a public and humiliating withdrawal. Judging by the secret documents exchanged between the two parties in 1960, there seems good reason to believe that the Russians did fear that the Chinese might drag them into a war and that Peking resented insufficient Soviet support.[31] It seems likely that the Strait venture left much ill feeling on both sides.

The "Paper Tiger" Again

The publication in October 1958 of Mao's *Imperialists and All Reactionaries Are Paper Tigers* marked a significant stage in the development of the Chinese post-ICBM strategic view. The essay was in fact a carefully selected collation of earlier writings designed to illustrate several aspects of Mao's current world view.[32]

First, Mao's cavalier attitude toward the possible consequences of general war was made clear by the repetition of some remarks made by him in February 1957: "firstly, we are against it; secondly, we are not afraid of it. The First World War was followed by the birth of the Soviet Union with a population of 200 million. The Second World War was followed by the emergence of the socialist camp with a combined population of 900 million. If the imperialists should insist on launching a third world war, it is certain that several hundred million more will turn to socialism."[33] Nowhere did Mao even suggest that general war would involve great losses for the Bloc as well as for the West, an admission that was becoming increasingly prominent in Soviet pronouncements.

Second, it was apparent that Mao minimized the possibility of general war and, by implication, maximized the possibility of local war. Included in the collection was a series of replies that Mao had made to Anna Louise Strong, the American journalist, in August 1946. One of Miss Strong's questions was, "What do you think of the possibility of the United States going to war against the Soviet Union?" Mao replied: "Between the United States and the Soviet Union there stretches a vast territory, consisting of many capitalist countries and colonial and semi-colonial countries on the continents of Europe, Asia, and Africa; before the U.S. reactionaries have subjugated these countries, *an attack* against the Soviet Union is out of the question" [italics supplied].[34] At another point in his reply to the same question, Mao said: "Of course, I do not mean to say that the U.S. reactionaries do not intend to attack the Soviet Union. . . . But, today, not long after the end of World War II, the U.S. reactionaries' strident and reckless talk about a U.S.-Soviet war and the foul atmosphere they are creating cannot but make one look at their real aims."[35]

The "real aims" of the United States, according to Mao, were to use the "smokescreen" of a U.S.-Soviet war as a rationale for "oppression" of the American people and for U.S. expansion abroad. It is quite likely that Mao believed this "smokescreen" line, and also believed that the United States would not dare attack the USSR until it had subjugated most of the world. The latter view in particular accords well with his general underemphasis of the strategic revolution which has occurred in the nuclear era and lies at the heart of his advocacy of a more militant Bloc strategy. Since general war is so unlikely, contends Mao, the Bloc can afford greater risks than it is now taking.

If Mao minimized the possibility of an all-out war, it is likely that Moscow did not. Mao's "smokescreen" line was never mentioned by any prominent Soviet leader. Moreover, the Soviet military and political leaders probably dismissed as absurd the Maoist view that the United States, before attacking the USSR, would first have to subjugate much of the vast terriory between the two countries. Beginning in 1955, Soviet military journals had become increasingly preoccupied with the possibilities of preemptive war and surprise attack. Although the Soviet military did not conclude that surprise attack could be decisive in determining the final outcome of a war, they did conclude that the value of surprise in the nuclear age had become immeasurably enhanced. In short, Soviet military and political leaders, like those in the West, were coming increasingly to the view that World War III *might* begin with a sneak nuclear blow. The Soviet military, therefore, were probably not reassured by Mao's dictum that the U.S. would have to subjugate half the world before considering a war with the USSR.

A third important element in Mao's "paper tiger" collection was his implicit call for a more assertive policy against the West. The introduction in the *Jen-min jih-pao* editorial berated many people—including Khrushchev—who fail to "assess the forces of revolution and the forces of reaction in their true light . . . still cherish superstitions and illusions . . . still stand in awe of imperialism, U.S. imperialism in particular [and] remain passive in face of this problem."[36] In addition to these pointed remarks in the introduction, included in the body of Mao's writings were numerous references to those "revolutionaries" who "are apt to be deluded for a while by the enemy's apparent strength," and warnings that "it would be a tremendous error to overestimate the strength of the enemy."

The likelihood that these charges were directed at the Russians as well as to Chinese cadres is suggested by two considerations. First, we have seen how Soviet weapons developments in 1957 led to diverging Chinese and Soviet estimates of the change in the balance of the power between East and West. Peking took a much more optimistic view of this change than did Moscow. It would thus be appropriate for Mao—particularly after Khrushchev failed to give him the support he expected in the Taiwan Strait crisis—to issue a warning to the Soviet leader not to "overestimate the strength of the enemy." Second, some of the remarks about "cherishing illusions" about imperialism and remaining in a state of "passivity" were to be repeated virtually verbatim during and after Khrushchev's visit to the United States in September 1959 in a context which made it quite clear that the Chinese were greatly displeased with Khrushchev's visit in particular and his policy of *détente* in general.

A *Jen-min jih-pao* editorial in early November 1958, about two weeks after the publication of Mao's writings on the "paper tiger," underlined the key points for readers in Moscow.[37] It began with the usual caveat that only by clearly understanding the inner weaknesses of imperialism "can we work out our strategic plans correctly. . . ."[38] In the paragraphs following, there were no fewer than seven references to the misguided or mistaken judgments of "some people" who overestimated the strength of imperialism, mistook superficial calm in the West for stability, were afraid to offend the imperialists lest they become more frenzied, and did not understand that peace could not be secured "without opposing and expelling U.S. imperialism."

Khrushchev's respect for Western weapons capabilities and economic power were, the editorial implied, exaggerated: "There are still people who think that the strength of the West is not to be despised. This is also superstition! . . . In certain fields of military science . . . the United States has lagged far behind the Soviet Union. As to iron and steel, no one is going to be scared by that. It is not only that iron and steel are not the only factors in determining the balance of forces but that the superiority in iron and steel output which the United States and the imperialist camp possess vis-à-vis the Soviet Union and the socialist camp, will soon disappear. The so-called theory of 'weapons decide everything' and 'iron and steel decide everything' is utterly untenable."[39]

In still another paragraph, the editorial obliquely accused Soviet policy of being detrimental to the cause of revolution: "It is the imperialist reactionaries that should fear the revolutionary forces, and not the other way around. But, even now there are many people who still overestimate the strength of the imperialist reactionaries, and underestimate the revolutionary strength of the people. They only see the apparent strength of the imperialist reactionaries, not the fact that they are essentially weak. They only see that the development of the people's strength in certain places for the moment appears to be slow, but fail to see that the people are awakening and rallying together. . . . They only see that certain areas under the rule of the reactionary forces are temporarily quiet on the surface, but fail to see that the flames of the people's revolution are smouldering beneath the surface, that *they will eventually burst forth. . . . All these ideas are badly in error. They only serve to puff up our enemies and lower our own morale; they are of no advantage to the revolutionary cause of the people*" [italics supplied].[40]

The same editorial described Mao's thesis on the "paper tiger" as the Communist world's "sharpest ideological weapon" in the struggle with imperialism and all reactionaries. Moscow apparently did not share this evaluation. Soviet media originated no comment on Mao's thesis. They did not even publish it in full. And at the Moscow Conference in 1960 the Russians are said to have scoffed at the "paper tiger" concept.[41]

PART FOUR

THE BRINK OF SCHISM:
1959–1960

CHAPTER 8

THE NEW BIBLE OF MARXISM-LENINISM

IN THE Communist world, theory is the guide to strategy and strategy is the link between theory and action. As Stalin pointed out in his classic manual of strategy and tactics for the Communist movement, written in 1924, Lenin himself had "uttered and repeated scores of times the well-known thesis that: 'Without a revolutionary theory there can be no revolutionary movement.' "[1] Revolutionary theory was, in Stalin's words, "in indissoluble connection with revolutionary practice" because "theory and theory alone" could give the Communist movement "confidence, the power of orientation, and an understanding of the inner relation of current events; for it, and it alone, can help practice to discern not only how and in which direction classes are moving at the present time, but also how and in which direction they will move in the near future."[2]

To the Communists, theory explains and orders reality at the same time as it provides a program for action. It is both a means of connecting otherwise disparate events and a guide to the strategy and tactics necessary for accelerating the historical process that is "inevitably" moving toward a Communist worldwide victory. The answer to the question often asked in the West as to whether Communist leaders take their ideology "seriously" is contingent upon what is meant by the question. Khrushchev and Mao doubtless do not consult the major theoretical texts before undertaking an important initiative, but the peculiar manner in which they apprehend reality strongly conditions their actions. Moreover, even if theory is sometimes manipulated for pragmatic purposes, it is important to note that whenever practice has changed, the Communists seem to feel compelled to change theory also. To them, the relationship between theory and practice is symbiotic. Consequently, major alterations in Communist ideology provide the non-Communist student with significant clues to changes in estimates of a situation and in strategy and tactics that govern official policy.

While the Western public is right to be suspicious of Khrushchev's 20th Congress emendations of theory and his emphasis on "peaceful coexistence," on the non-inevitability of war, and on the increasing possibility of "peaceful transition to socialism," it is not right to dismiss such changes in Soviet doctrine as meaningless or unimportant, or as deceptions consciously intended to put the West offguard. Such changes in ideology can, and usually do, yield a deeper meaning if the reasons for them are explored.

On September 12, 1959, the most comprehensive ideological work of the post-Stalin era, *Osnovy Marksizma-Leninizma* (*The Fundamentals of Marxism-Leninism*) was signed to the press.[3] This work, 891 pages long in its English version, was evidently designed to replace Stalin's revolutionary handbook. The fourth section, titled "Theory and Tactics of the International Communist Movement," ran to 259 pages and was clearly intended as a directive to the entire international Communist movement on the strategy and tactics for the struggle with the West. A fifth section, encompassing 253 pages, devoted to "The Doctrine Regarding Socialism and Communism," was intended as a directive to ruling Communist parties on the way to build socialism and Communism.

Almost four years in preparation, the *Osnovy* was commissioned by the 20th Congress in 1956 for the evident purpose of codifying the multi-faceted changes in theory that Khrushchev had introduced. Its chief editor was O. V. Kuusinen, the elderly former Comintern official and one of the Presidium's specialists on ideology, who in the summer of 1960 was to deliver the major ideological reply to the Chinese Communist critique of Soviet theory and strategy.

This new revolutionary manual, it might be said, modified Stalinism, in much the same radical way that Stalin had once modified Leninism. It, in fact, signified the adaptation of Communist revolutionary strategy to the nuclear era. We may take this book as a point of departure for a study of the Sino-Soviet conflict over global strategy. We do so for two reasons: first, the book is the single most authoritative ideological guide to Soviet grand strategy that has yet appeared; second, to the extent that the new revolutionary manual represents a retreat from or modification of Stalinist strategy and tactics, it provides an indispensable backdrop to implicit Chinese claims that Khrushchev has "betrayed, revised, and emasculated" Marxism-Leninism. This is not the place to assess the accuracy of those claims or to attempt a comparison between "Khrushchevism," "Leninism," and "Stalinism." I wish here rather to make clear that while some Western scholars might hold modifications made in the Stalinist revolutionary corpus by Khrushchev to be more or less significant, there is little doubt that they are significant. Furthermore, there is little doubt the Communist Chinese think them highly important and believe them to constitute a betrayal of both Communism's and their own worldwide interests. Indeed, *Hung ch'i,* Communist China's major theoretical journal, has not even reviewed the *Osnovy,* and the book has not, so far as I know, been translated into Chinese. In addition, as if to underscore the Soviet betrayal of what Peking considered "pure" Leninist revolutionary doctrine, the Chinese published in the fall of 1960 a series of extracts from Lenin's writings on such subjects as war, the "national liberation movement," and revisionism, all of which, they quite clearly believed, had not been satisfactorily treated by the new Soviet manual. In what follows, I shall attempt merely to sketch some of the points of interest in the *Osnovy* as they bear on the Sino-Soviet conflict.

The Strategy of Flexibility and Caution

Although the new book never explicitly criticizes Stalin's classic treatment of theory and tactics in "The Foundations of Leninism," much of it in effect repudiates or alters the Stalinist doctrine.[4] For example, Part Four of the new strategy bible begins by stressing the similarity rather than the difference between tactics and strategy: "The word tactics is often used to denote the political line pursued for a relatively brief space of time, and determined by certain definite conditions, while the word strategy denotes the line for an entire phase of development. But such distinctions were not always made. In the early stages of the working class movement (before the October Revolution), the word tactics presupposed the entire policy of the party, irrespective of any particular period. It was in this sense that Lenin used it . . . ; *he did not consider it necessary to distinguish strategy from tactics"* [italics supplied].[5] Why did Khrushchev's ideologists, unlike Stalin and Mao, insist on the identity of tactics and strategy? They seem to have done so to justify a maximum of flexibility within any given "stage," so that when Khrushchev decides to try a new tactical approach, he cannot be accused of sacrificing ultimate goals for the sake of transitory tactical goals. The Chinese were in fact arguing that Khrushchev was, by his tactical maneuvering, betraying the long-range goals of the Communist movement.

An alternative and not mutually exclusive explanation of the Soviet contention that strategy and tactics should not be divorced is that it represented an implicit attack on the Maoist "paper tiger" concept which had been brought into new prominence a year earlier, soon after the failure of the offshore island venture. The heart of Mao's dictum, it may be recalled, was that the enemy should be despised strategically (i.e., in the long run) but taken into account and respected tactically (i.e., in any given instance in the short run). One reason the Russians object to this formula is that they do not believe that such a dichotomy is possible. For they probably believe that he who despises the enemy too much strategically is unlikely to be sufficiently prudent tactically. Thus, the way to attack the "paper tiger" concept and the Maoist distinction between the long and the short run was to minimize, if not to deny, Stalin's distinction between strategy and tactics. The enemy, in short, must be respected in both the short and long run.

A second important modification of Stalin's doctrine—similarly designed to increase the capacity for tactical flexibility—was contained in the textbook's warning that political and military strategy cannot be equated or discussed in the same terms. Although the textbook did not specifically mention Stalin's writings in this context, it was plain that it had Stalin in mind, inasmuch as the former Soviet dictator's writings frequently employed military terminology for discussing political strategy. The new textbook contends that "in speaking about the political strategy of the party it is necessary to be on the alert against drawing analogies from the military sphere, for political strategy is vastly different from military strategy."[6] It goes on to explain that the political leader is handicapped because, unlike the military commander, he does not have all the relevant forces under his command. Social classes, for example, in working out the historical process, act not by order of a superior but rather under the influence of their own interests and, what is more, in accordance with their understanding of those interests at any given moment. The task of a political leader in plotting strategy and tactics, then, is more complex than that of a military leader; it requires much more ability to adjust to the complex forces at work in society.

Revolutions and War

In discussing the prospects for revolution in non-Communist countries, the textbook devotes a special sub-section to the question of whether revolution is "necessarily connected with war." In the traditional Leninist-Stalinist view, imperialist wars were the "locomotives" of revolution. It was the task of Communist parties to use imperialist wars to accelerate discontent among the masses and finally to convert the imperialist war into civil war which would offer revolutionary opportunities.

Lenin and Stalin had never said, of course, that revolutions could not take place without war; they merely said that war accelerated the contradictions within capitalist society and thus accelerated the revolutionary process. The conclusion was that imperialist wars—which were in any case inevitable—were in many cases "progressive" in that they hastened the collapse of the imperialist system.

Khrushchev's declarations at the 20th and 21st Congresses of the CPSU that wars are no longer inevitable during the imperialist era naturally raised the question of whether the absence of imperialist wars would not slow down the engine of revolutionary progress. The new textbook explains that, despite the fact that both world wars served as powerful accelerators of the revolutionary movement, "it by no means follows from all this that future revolutionary victories over capitalism presuppose an obligatory premise of war. Although world wars are unthinkable without revolutions, revolutions are fully possible without wars."[7] The implications of this important modification of doctrine are numerous. Above all, it suggests that the Russians are quite serious about avoiding war; otherwise they would have no need to stress to their own Party—and to the other Communist parties—that revolution is possible without war.

Confronted with this Russian view, other Communists, particularly the Chinese, must inevitably ask whether or not the avoidance of war—particularly of local and "liberation" war—will not slow down and perhaps make impossible the further expansion of Communism. Communism, it is quite apparent, has made its biggest gains as a direct result of two world wars. Can it now advance without war? The Chinese Communists have persistently indicated their belief that certain types of local, civil, and "liberation" wars are inevitable and that such wars are powerful accelerators of revolutionary opportunities. They have, for example, quoted Lenin's dictum, "Not a single great revolution in history has been carried out without a civil war, and *no serious Marxist* will believe it possible to make the transition from capitalism to socialism without a civil war" [italics supplied].[8] The Chinese line of thought is directly at variance with the view, implicit in Khrushchev's speeches to the 20th and 21st Congresses and in the 1959 textbook, that Communism can advance without war of any kind.

The Soviet textbook also devotes a special sub-section to the question of what constitutes a revolutionary situation.[9] It dismisses the "naïve" idea that revolutions can be made "according to someone's whims," stressing that they can grow out of "objective conditions." It recalls the three main characteristics ascribed by Lenin to a "revolutionary situation": the inability of the ruling classes to maintain their rule in an immutable form (i.e., a crisis within the ruling classes); the intense aggravation of the misfortunes of the oppressed classes; and a "significant increase" of the "activity of the masses." Without such "objective" changes, the textbook warns, revolution "as a general rule is impossible." In particular, "revolution is impossible without a nationwide crisis," one that envelops both the ruling and the lower classes. Moreover, the book warns, while revolution is impossible without the leadership of the Party, "it is [equally] impossible to win with a vanguard [the Party] alone."

The assessment of when the "objective" conditions for revolution are present is obviously susceptible to varying interpretations. (In November 1917, it will be remembered, many leading Bolsheviks were convinced that the "objective" conditions were not yet ripe for an attempted seizure of power in Russia.) On the basis of Chinese doctrinal writings and the apparent Chinese encouragement of the revolutionary forces in Iraq in the summer of 1959, it is a fair presumption that Peking has in the past seen, and will continue in the future to see, "revolutionary opportunities" somewhat more frequently than the Russians. The Russians tend to think—as they made clear in their reply to Peking's attack in the spring of 1960—that the possibility of "stimulating" revolutions from outside is less than the Chinese believe it to be.

Peaceful Revolution

The textbook goes on to analyze the "possibility of a peaceful path of revolution."[10] At the 20th Congress, Khrushchev had first dwelt on the increasing possibility of a non-violent and parliamentary path to socialism. He did not exclude the possibility of violence but his emphasis was on new elements in the international power balance and the "historical situation" which "made possible a new approach to the question."[11] The textbook takes the Soviet argument for a peaceful transition to socialism an important step further. It contends not only that the non-violent transition is increasingly possible but also, in its very first sentence, that "the peaceful transition to socialism has *great advantages*" because it permits a "radical reorganization of social life" with the "least sacrifices on the part of the laborers" and with "minimum destruction of the productive forces of society" [italics supplied]. The whole question depends, therefore, not on whether the Marxists want a peaceful revolution—a foregone conclusion—but on whether the "objective premises for it exist." The textbook argues that "under certain conditions such premises can arise." The conclusion was thus apparent that peaceful revolution was both desirable and increasingly possible.

In 1960, shortly before the Moscow conference of eighty-one Communist parties, the polemic between Moscow and Peking came increasingly to revolve about this issue of the feasibility of non-violent accession to power by local Communists in non-Communist countries. Some Western analysts have contended that this particular aspect of the polemic is meaningless because both parties, in the final analysis, would agree that violence is necessary if the ruling classes put up firm resistance to a Communist takeover. True, it has always been the classical Leninist justification for Communist violence that it is a necessary response to the inevitable counter-revolutionary violence of the obsolete ruling classes. As the polemic advanced, however, the Russians began to specify the conditions under which the local bourgeoisie in any given country would *prefer* to yield peacefully. The principal condition, it is extremely important to note, was supposedly the increasingly favorable shift in the balance of power between East and West. As *Kommunist* put it in 1960: "The strength of the bourgeoisie and

231

the strength of the working class in every country depends to a considerable degree on the relation of power on the international scale. One must not forget that the bourgeoisie resorts to civil war in case it can count on some substantial inner or outside ally and that the bourgeoisie may prefer to yield its power peacefully if it is convinced that this is the only way it can save its head."[12] In short, the Russians foresaw a time when the East-West balance of power would be so favorable to the Communists that local ruling classes would see the futility of opposing the Communist tide and would peacefully hand over power to local Communist parties. To the Chinese, this view is illusory. They have persistently argued since 1958 that revolutionary violence and civil war are necessary in most cases for the Communists to take power.

Gradual Revolution in the West

In one section of the textbook, Moscow seems to be attempting to provide a new doctrinal rationale for its gradualist revolutionary strategy in the developed capitalist countries: the appearance of a "democracy of a new type." This new "democracy" will be farther to the Left than ordinary "bourgeois democracy," but not yet dominated by the Communists. *Fundamentals of Marxism-Leninism* puts it in these words:

"Today there is a basis for democratic movements not only in the underdeveloped countries and countries with pronounced feudal survivals, but also in the highly developed capitalist countries.

"In the latter case these movements are spearheaded against the ruling bourgeois circles, against imperialism and monopoly domination.

"This does not mean, of course, that all these movements are anti-capitalist by nature. . . . Yet they cannot be characterized as bourgeois-democratic. For *ordinary bourgeois democracy*, even where it has reached its highest development, cannot resolve such issues as ending the menace of war, granting formal and real national liberation, nationalizing the property of the monopolies, and restricting their political power. This can be achieved only under a *democracy of a new type* which expresses the interests of the masses of the working people and the other progressive sections . . . " [italics supplied].[13]

The "democracy of a new type" appears to have close simi-

232

larities to the transitional stage of the "people's democracy" as it was outlined in the very early postwar period—before the Communists seized control of Eastern Europe and then *ex post facto* equated the people's democracy with a "proletarian," i.e. Communist, dictatorship. Soviet scholars between 1945 and 1947 held that the people's democracy was *not* to be confused with a "proletarian" democracy, because in the latter the proletariat did "not share its power with any other class." The people's democracy was, in short, first envisioned as a transitional form of government in Eastern Europe in which the Communists would share power with other parties.[14] It was a hybrid form somewhere between the old bourgeois democratic and the new "socialist" state.

Although, as Brzezinski points out, evidence could be cited to support the argument that the concept of the people's democracy was a sham from the very beginning, ". . . looking more closely at this particular phase, and even at the events preceding it, one notices aspects which suggest that the people's democracy phase, certainly never an end in itself, *was* [italics in original] considered to be a meaningful political expression of the peculiar relationship of domestic and external forces which the Communists felt (in 1945) would exist in postwar Europe. The argument that Soviet domination was the ultimate objective of the people's democracy phase does not in itself mean that the people's democracy did not have content of its own, and it certainly does not prove that this phase had to last the three years that it did, rather than one, five, or ten."[15]

Similarly, the concept of the "democracy of a new type" envisaged in the Soviet textbook of 1959 appears to be a meaningful political expression of the relationship of domestic and external forces which Moscow expects to exist sooner or later in Western Europe and the developed capitalist world. The Russians seem to think of it as a government still dominated by the bourgeoisie which may or may not soon evolve into a socialist government: "Not every democratic revolution will inevitably evolve into a socialist revolution; . . . *it may do so* [italics in original] provided the working class *is able* [italics supplied] to secure the leading position in it."[16] Moreover, this new democracy will be neutral; it will "end the menace of war," rather than ally itself to the Bloc; it will put an end to colonialism ("grant formal and real national liberation") and "nationalize the property of the monopolies and restrict their political power." It would appear to resemble the kind of government that might come into being in Britain under the Left wing of the Labour Party—a government which might at least tolerate if not cooperate with the local Communists and which could be regarded, in the Soviet view, as serving Soviet middle-range interests well. Such governments in the major West European countries would, for example, probably mean the death of NATO. They would also, as far as the Soviets are concerned, provide a better environment for local Communists to operate in without restriction.

It may be objected that Moscow has for many years been encouraging the formation of Left-wing neutralist governments in the West. The point is, however, that for the first time Khrushchev has incorporated into Soviet dogma the existence of a type of non-Communist government with which Moscow is prepared to coexist for an extended period. It is not unlikely that the Chinese Communist polemics on the need for "uninterrupted revolution" were in part a reaction to this Soviet theory of deferred revolution that had been gestating since 1956.[17]

The textbook's directives to Western Communists to work for "democracy of a new type" were quickly implemented in the resolution adopted in Rome on November 25, 1959, by seventeen West European parties.[18] Placing its primary emphasis on the possibility that "war can be eliminated forever," the resolution called for the fullest support in each country to "democratic governments which . . . will be able to carry out a program of democratic advance." The minimum program to which the Communists would lend their full support would be: nationalization of monopolized industry, decentralization of the economy, greater worker initiative and influence in economic life, popular control of economic investment, and agrarian reforms. The resolution also made a plea for working-class unity and concluded that "the perspective of democratic development shows the way forward to socialism." This seems to have been a declaration of open support by Western Communist parties for any Left-wing Western government that introduces the minimum program and at the same time struggles for "peace"—by withdrawing from NATO, for example. Peking never commented on this resolution and its press carried only skimpy versions of the resolution a week later. It is apparent that the Chinese considered the Rome resolution "opportunist" in the sense that it deferred ultimate Communist goals in the interests of short term tactical expediency.[19]

"Democratic" Movements

In encouraging the establishment of Left-wing neutralist governments in the West, the textbook emphasized the need for Communists to support "democratic" movements, not only to prepare the masses for further advances toward Communism, but also in part for their own sake: "It would be wrong to regard the democratic movements as a simple means for bringing the masses to socialist revolution. It would be wrong first of all because they are of tremendous importance as *independent* movements for the working class in particular. Is the struggle for peace, against nuclear destruction, to be regarded solely as a reserve means [i.e., an auxiliary rather than a primary goal]? Is it not one of the *principal* aims of the democrats and progressive mankind as a whole? The same is true of the struggle against fascism and the shameful colonialism from which a large part of humanity suffered only recently."[20] The practical importance of this doctrinal statement was that it amounted to a directive to Communists throughout the world that while supporting wholeheartedly such Communist fronts as the World Peace Council they should not seek to turn them into obvious and immediate tools of Communist strategy. The directive was reiterated in the Rome resolution of seventeen Western parties, which was a joint appeal to "workers and democrats."

On January 30, 1960, the editor of *Fundamentals of Marxism-Leninism,* Presidium member Otto Kuusinen, referred to some of these aspects of Soviet doctrine before a conference on ideological problems in East Berlin. One purpose of the meeting was clearly to reassert Soviet ideological primacy in East Germany after an abortive Peking-Pankow flirtation in 1959. Kuusinen criticized those unnamed "people who tended towards sectarianism," who "were dubious about [supporting] democratic movements," and who believed that it would be "better to spearhead the Communist movement exclusively . . . for the dictatorship of the proletariat."[21] From this it may perhaps be inferred that the opposition argument, openly stated by the Chinese later in 1960, had already condemned the reliance on "democratic" movements as an impediment to revolutionary struggle and progress toward the long-range goals of the Communist movement.

CHAPTER 9

THE DISPUTE ABOUT A *DÉTENTE*
WITH THE WEST

THE YEAR 1959 was notable for deepening Sino-Soviet differences over the possibility and advisability of achieving a *détente* with the West. Khrushchev held such a *détente* to be possible and, for the achievement of short- and middle-range Soviet goals, desirable. He made this clear in his speech to the Soviet 21st Party Congress, the essential point of which was that the Bloc, by using all means short of war, could set the stage for ultimate victory in the struggle with the West if it had sufficient patience and flexibility. Peking, on the other hand, saw a *détente* as impossible and, even if possible, undesirable. It received Khrushchev's gradualist program coolly and began to attack his *détente* tactics in the summer and fall of 1959, the period when the Sino-Soviet conflict began to sharpen.

Khrushchev's 21st Congress Report

Khrushchev, in his report to the 21st CPSU Congress, provided some details of his strategy for the Bloc in the critical five- to fifteen-year period ahead.[1] One of his main points was that Soviet and Bloc economic progress would result in a great political gain for the Bloc at a foreseeable time and that, by implication, a relaxation of tension was essential to realizing this economic program which would increase the Bloc's influence and attractive power. "The fundamental problem of the coming seven years," he said, "is to make the utmost time gain in socialism's economic competition with capitalism." The fulfillment of this aim would "exert a deep influence on the international situation, . . . attract millions of new adherents to the side of socialism, . . . lead to strengthening the forces of peace and weakening the forces of war, and . . . cause tremendous changes not only in our own country, but throughout the world; *there will be a decisive shift in favor of socialism in the economic sphere of the world arena*" [italics supplied].[2] Here was the essence of Khrushchev's strategic conception. When the USSR had outstripped the West in the economic race, he was saying, the uncommitted countries would naturally gravitate toward the USSR and there would be a significant realignment of political power in the world.

What other new factors would be "introduced into the international situation with the fulfillment of the economic plans of the Soviet Union and of all the socialist countries"? Khrushchev answered his own question: "As a result of this *there will be created real possibilities for eliminating war as a means of settling international issues* [italics in original].

"Indeed, when the USSR becomes the world's leading industrial power, when the Chinese People's Republic becomes a mighty industrial power, and when all the socialist countries together will be producing more than half the world's industrial output, the international situation will change radically. . . . One need not doubt that by that time the countries working for the strengthening of peace will be joined by new countries which have freed themselves from colonial oppression. . . . The new balance of forces will be so evident that even the most diehard imperialists will clearly see the futility of any attempt to unleash war against the socialist camp. Relying on the might of the socialist camp, the peace-loving nations will then be able to compel the militant circles of imperialism to abandon plans for a new world war.

"*Thus there will arise a real possibility of excluding world war from the life of society even before the complete triumph of socialism, even with capitalism existing in part of the world*" [italics supplied].[3]

In sum, Khrushchev expected that, by 1970 or shortly thereafter, Bloc economic growth would tip the balance of power decisively in the Communist favor; he believed that behind the Soviet deterrent shield there would develop further nationalist revolts in the underdeveloped areas, similar to those in Iraq and Cuba, in which the West would not dare intervene for fear of military confrontation with the USSR; and he believed that overall Bloc strength would shortly be such that the West would be absolutely deterred from offensive war of any kind.

In his programmatic statement at the 20th Congress in 1956, Khrushchev had taken the first step toward undercutting the Leninist tenet that wars are an inevitable by-product of imperialism when he said that "war is not a fatalistic inevitability." He did leave a loophole, however, asserting that, "as long as imperialism remains," the economic base giving rise to wars would also remain. "That is why we must display the greatest vigilance." In other words, according to the 1956 formulation, the *danger* of war remained so long as imperialism remained, even if war was not inevitable.

Khrushchev's 21st Party Congress speech eroded still further the Leninist-Stalinist dogma on war—and even his own 20th Congress position—largely because on this occasion the loophole was left out. Even while imperialism remained, Khrushchev said, there was a real possibility of eliminating war "from the life of society"— i.e., permanently. Thus he virtually threw out the cherished Leninist thesis that imperialism inevitably breeds war. Peking had gone along with the 20th Congress thesis; it never accepted the 21st Congress revision. It did not do so because it recognized the significance of Khrushchev's 1959 doctrine on war as an ideological justification for the avoidance of all kinds of war and for the pursuance of a low-risk foreign policy.

Khrushchev's description of the strategic situation in or about 1970 contained the implicit assumption that the Bloc's economic and political advantage, *added* to its imposing military might, would be strategically decisive. With war ruled out, the decisive advantage would be held by the side with the most political and economic power.

As of January 1959, it seems, Khrushchev was not confident of achieving the kind of technological breakthrough required to give the USSR an *overwhelming* military advantage by 1970. On the other hand, he may have expected by 1970, that even without such a breakthrough, the West would be completely deterred from the use of military force and the political leverage of the Soviet Union thus greatly enhanced.

To the Chinese, Khrushchev's prospectus was vulnerable to the charge they had been making even before the Soviet Party Congress: that, since the Bloc already *had* decisive military superiority, it was not necessary to wait until 1970 to convert it into absolute political superiority. The prospectus was also open to the charge, which the Chinese began to make later, that while the Bloc military advantage was real, the advantage could be thrown away by disarmament negotiations or forced reductions or by letting the U.S. "buy time" to catch up.

The program must have seemed strangely cautious to the Chinese, then, and not at all befitting professional revolutionaries. The program did not seem to expect the Bloc to enlarge its territory in the five- to fifteen-year period ahead; it held out the hope merely of adding to the "zone of peace" a few more countries, like Iraq and Cuba, which had freed themselves from "colonial and semi-colonial bondage." Reading the program, Mao must certainly have concluded that such leisurely and gentlemanly action, in the short run, offered little hope of realizing China's goals and, in the long run, might result in disaster by giving the non-Communist world sufficient time to stabilize and strengthen itself.

In January 1959 the Chinese Party was at a low point in self-assertiveness. Only the month before it had been forced to revise drastically its commune program, which had been in serious trouble, and under Soviet pressure to withdraw some of the claims for the program. In January and February, in a brief dampness of spirit, the Chinese Party was not prepared to challenge Khrushchev's propositions in its customary clamorous fashion. Even at that time, however, its chief spokesman refrained from supporting them fully. Chou En-lai, the principal Chinese delegate to the Soviet 21st Congress, said on the years ahead, for example, that "The imperialists may run wild for a while." Khrushchev had not said they would "run wild" even for a minute; he had said that conditions were better than ever for deterring the imperialists. As for means of struggling against the imperialists, Chou continued, in a similarly discordant way, the actions of the imperialists would help to awaken and unite "the peoples," forcing them *to cast away their illusions, and take the road of struggle and revolution"* [italics supplied].[4]

Although Soviet Party journals and newspapers found numerous points on which Khrushchev had "creatively" developed Marxist-Leninist theory, an editorial in *Hung ch'i* for February 16 could find only one: "the creative proposition that 'the socialist countries . . . will more or less simultaneously pass to the higher phase of Communist society.' " *Hung ch'i* went so far as to credit Khrushchev with having correctly pointed out the possibility of eliminating world war even before the end of imperialism, but did not hail this proposition as a "creative" addition to Marxism-Leninism. The Chinese press did not discuss the point. Moreover, immediately after mentioning Khrushchev's thesis, *Hung ch'i* declared that "naturally, vigilance against the *war maniacs* can by no means be lessened"; the term "war maniacs," and all that it implies in terms of the irrational element in "imperialist" behavior, had been employed in the 1957 declaration of the Communist parties. Khrushchev had on several occasions in 1957 and 1958 indicated that "one cannot vouch for a madman." (See his interview with UP correspondent Henry Shapiro on November 14, 1957, for example.) But by the fall of 1958, Khrushchev was voicing confidence in the possibility of deterring even "mad" imperialists. In a speech in Krasnodar on October 16, 1958, he said: "The situation is now such that the imperialists will hardly dare to unleash a war against the countries of the socialist camp. . . . Of course, there can be cases of madmen which cannot be guaranteed, but we are confident that a straitjacket can be found for them too."[5]

The Chinese Communists, on the other hand, emphasized the opposite: that even if the West were increasingly deterred by Soviet power, the Bloc could not account for irrationality. This concept of irrationality was also implicit in the metaphor of a "wild beast" that had been cornered, a metaphor used increasingly by the Chinese in 1959 and 1960 to characterize Western behavior.

Hung ch'i endorsed Khrushchev's contention that there were no disputes between the Soviet and Chinese parties. These parties, the journal said, were "bound together by a common ideal and cause."[6] It might have added they were also bound together by strong military and economic considerations. But they had ceased to be bound together by a common view of the means for waging the struggle with the West.

Chinese Attacks on "Détente" Tactics

On April 22, 1959, Secretary Dulles was replaced by Christian Herter. In subsequent months, Moscow almost completely avoided attacks on Secretary Herter, picturing him as one of the moderate elements among American "ruling circles" and suggesting that he was carrying on a more "realistic" American policy, emerging even before Dulles' death, which opened the way for a *détente*. This more "realistic" policy, Moscow contended, had led to the Mikoyan visit to the United States in January, to the foreign ministers' talks in May, and to the Kozlov visit to the United States in July. In

July the *détente* was taken a step further when Eisenhower and Khrushchev began private exchanges, which were followed the next month by an announcement confirming that the two would exchange visits.

As some kind of U.S.-Soviet *rapprochement* appeared imminent, Peking intensified its attacks on American (and by strong implication, Russian) policy, and made it plain that China saw no appreciable shift toward "realism" in the American position. In early June Peking's *Shih-chieh chih-shih* asked the rhetorical question whether Herter would change American policy, answering with a resounding "No."[7] The journal pointed out that the aggressive American policy toward China had remained intact since the turn of the century, despite the fact that there had been nine changes of President and sixteen changes of Secretary of State. The aggressive nature of American imperialism, it warned, would remain. Directly contradicting the Soviet thesis that even Secretary Dulles in his final days had begun to assume a more realistic attitude toward the socialist camp, the journal contended that Dulles continued to be a lackey of American monopolist capital right up to his death. Again, directly contradicting the 21st Congress thesis on war, the article declared that "imperialism remains imperialism forever," and that *so long as imperialism exists, the people cannot avoid the threat of war*"—a line which implied that *détente* was neither possible nor desirable and that was to be the core of Peking's polemics with the Russians in the months to come.

All the Chinese journal was willing to concede was that Herter would "resort to camouflage and appear outwardly more moderate than Dulles . . . ; this is to say, will [probably] be more crafty than Dulles." No matter how imperialism "decks out and disguises itself, it seeks to bite. . . . "[8]

On August 16, after the exchange of visits between Eisenhower and Khrushchev had been formally announced, *Hung ch'i* came forth with its first detailed examination of the possibility—or rather the impossibility—of peaceful coexistence. This article set the tone for others that were to follow.[9] While the forthcoming exchange would contribute to a relaxation of tension, Peking suggested, such a relaxation might not be in the Bloc's interest, because the American policy of creating tensions "can only further stimulate the growth of the national independence movement" [and] indeed frighten away its own allies. Moreover, the policy of tensions served also "to heighten the political understanding of the (American) people at home."

The American Government was not really interested in relaxing tensions. One could no more hope for the U.S. to relax tensions than expect "a cat to keep away from fish."[10] American foreign policy makers were in a quandary. They wanted tension, but were afraid of it; they were forced to turn to relaxation, but at the same time feared it. The implication was that any American policy to relax tension would be subject to change at any moment. The American stratagem could be viewed only as a "trial measure of relaxation," dictated by the fact that American military science and technique lagged far behind that of the USSR. The implication here—later spelled out—was that the U.S. would use the *détente* only to build up its military power so as to reverse the imbalance of power, currently in its disfavor. American intentions would have to be judged solely by actions. If the Americans really wanted coexistence, their military bases would "first of all be withdrawn and the occupation of other people's territories ended." "[The U.S.] must get out and that's all there is to it," said *Hung ch'i*.[11] In other words, no coexistence was possible short of a complete American military withdrawal from Europe and Asia. Understandably skeptical that the United States would meet Peking's conditions for coexistence, the journal concluded with the warning that was to become paramount in the days ahead: the forces of peace must not be deluded, must maintain their vigilance, and must "give unrelenting battle to the war conspiracies of the imperialists" in order to "stay out of the hands of the war maniacs."

This Chinese Communist assessment of the likelihood, desirability, and criteria of peaceful coexistence was clearly at variance with the Soviet view that there was no alternative to coexistence but war and that "realistic" and "sober" American circles were beginning to understand that.

The following day, Chinese Foreign Minister Ch'en Yi, speaking at a reception given by the Indonesian Embassy in Peking to commemorate Indonesian Independence Day, warned that "the imperialists will never give up their policy of war and aggression of their own accord," thus implying that negotiations and talks with the imperialists were not very helpful. He added that the "imperialists" were exploiting the civil war in Laos and trying to "tear up the Geneva agreement" safeguarding peace in Indochina. If this "scheme" were realized, it would jeopardize China's security and would confront all of Southeast Asia with the danger of aggression and intervention.[12] The implication was that negotiations with the West might inhibit the Russians from taking the kind of militant action in Southeast Asia—as well as elsewhere in Asia—that China deemed essential to its security.

On September 16, the very day that Khrushchev arrived in the United States, "Yu Chao-li" launched a bitter and scarcely veiled attack on Khrushchev's negotiatory tactics—the precursor of many to come in the months ahead.[13] This *Hung ch'i* article was cast in the form of a long account of how the Chinese people, under Mao's leadership, had struggled heroically against imperialism and would remain "undaunted" in the struggle until imperialism was finally destroyed. The author asserted that Maoist "revolutionary confidence and determination," "revolutionary far-sightedness and firmness" were the spiritual conditions "indispensable to crushing imperialism"; that if these conditions had been lacking, the revolution could not have won. It is not known whether Yu's article was written before or after the conciliatory one on peaceful coexistence prepared by Khrushchev for the American journal *Foreign Affairs*. In any case, Yu's remarks would apply to it.

Purportedly referring to the bourgeois democrats in China after 1949 who had no faith in the revolutionary viewpoint, Yu seemed actually to have Khrushchev's policy in mind when he said these people "could not clearly perceive the true nature of imperialism and entertained various illusions about it. Hence they often lost their bearings." These naive people thought "the U.S. imperialists would 'lay down their butcher knife and become Buddhas,' that a hard, long-term anti-imperialist struggle was no longer called for, and that the imperialists would no longer proceed with their disruptive schemes."[14] These people were "very much afraid of thoroughly exposing the fundamental nature of imperialism. They feared to meet the imperialists in face-to-face struggle and to 'provoke' the imperialists 'too much,' as if by not 'provoking' them the imperialists would have 'a change of heart.' "[15] This "muddle-headed way of thinking," the author continued, could only serve to make the enemy more arrogant and "bring discouragement to our own ranks, blur the line between the enemy and ourselves, and dull the vigilance of the people vis-à-vis the enemy."[16]

When dealing with the imperialists and their jackals, the author said, Mao had correctly pointed out that "provocation or no provocation, they will remain the same. . . . Only by drawing a sharp line between reactionaries and revolutionaries" could the reactionaries be defeated.[17]

It is important to note that in this first full-scale attack on Khrushchev's *détente* tactics the Chinese were in effect contending that Khrushchev's soft policy toward the West was hazardous primarily because it would dampen the revolutionary spirit of peoples throughout the world. Khrushchev's fear of nuclear war, the author was virtually saying, should not be an excuse for diluting the revolutionary struggle and giving primacy to negotiations. The imperialists would continue to be provocative regardless of the actions of the Communists, so there was no reason to pursue "soft" tactics. Khrushchev was appeasing the West, and such appeasement could lead only to disaster.

The erroneous views about imperialism that Yu Chao-li described had been "convincingly refuted" *en bloc* by Chairman Mao in 1949: "Disrupt, fail, disrupt again, fail again, till their doom— that is the logic of imperialists and all reactionaries in the world. They will certainly go against this logic. This is a Marxist law. We say: 'Imperialism is very vicious.' That is to say that its fundamental nature cannot be changed. Till their doom, the imperialist elements will never lay down their butcher's knife, nor will they ever become Buddhas."[18] In the Chinese view, there could be no breathing space in the struggle against imperialism, no real *détente,* and no genuine peaceful coexistence. The Maoist quotation cited above was reiterated time and again by the Chinese throughout the course of their polemic with the Russians in 1959 and 1960 and as late as the fall of 1961.

CHAPTER 10

THE DISPUTE ABOUT THE "NATIONAL LIBERATION MOVEMENT"

OF THE MANY complex currents which were agitating the Sino-Soviet alliance by 1959, none was potentially more significant than the thinly veiled struggle for power between the two Communist giants which was unfolding in the underdeveloped world. The struggle manifested itself in three forms: a dispute over strategy and tactics for the so-called "national liberation movements" in colonial areas; active competition for favor and influence among the newly independent countries of Asia and Africa, as well as among the countries of Latin America; and a budding rivalry for control of the local Communist movements in all these areas.

While it would be premature to see in these developments an imminent polarization of world Communist leadership in two rival centers, one for the developed areas and the other for the underdeveloped sectors of the world, the potential for such a division is unmistakable. There is considerable evidence indicating that Maoist China regards itself as the appointed leader of the revolutionary movement throughout the underdeveloped world and considers its own revolutionary experience and pattern of "socialist construction" a more suitable model for these areas than the experience and example of the Soviet Union. There is evidence, also, that the Peking leaders are perturbed by what they regard as a softening of the revolutionary militancy of their Soviet ally;[2] that they fear that Moscow's gradualist, Right strategy in the colonial and emergent areas is unnecessarily retarding Communist gains there and could, in the long run, lead to a stalemate for the Communist movement as a whole. Finally, there are evidences of Chinese belief that Moscow, in planning worldwide Communist strategy, is putting Soviet objectives ahead of those of Communist China; that the USSR is failing in the fulfillment of its "proletarian internationalist" obligations to render unequivocal support to the national liberation movements as well as to Communist Bloc countries engaged in active disputes with the West; and that the Soviet Union, as the first country of socialism, should share its resources more generously with the less advanced countries in the Bloc.

The Historical Background

To understand the Sino-Soviet conflict over strategy and tactics for advancing Communism in the underdeveloped areas, it is necessary to review briefly some of the historical background. Since the Bolshevik revolution in 1917, the Communists have been faced with several important questions in their efforts to expedite the revolutionary process in what they call the colonial and semi-colonial areas. First, what should be their attitude toward the national bourgeoisie, i.e., the middle-class leaders of the anti-imperialist revolution? If they ally themselves with the national bourgeoisie and the nationalist parties which they dominate, will they not incur the risk that their nationalist allies will turn on them once they become strong enough or once they achieve power? If they do not ally themselves with the nationalists, will they not find themselves dangerously isolated from the mainstream of the revolutionary process? Second, if the Communists do ally themselves with the national bourgeoisie and the nationalist parties, what should be their relationship with them? Should the Communists cede leadership of the revolutionary movement to the nationalists in the first bourgeois democratic stage of the revolution only to grasp it later when conditions are ripe for the "socialist" revolution? Or is it necessary for the Communists to hold a commanding position in the revolutionary leadership during the first stage as well in order to be certain that their bourgeois allies cannot "steal" the revolution and bring it to a premature end? Third, what is the relationship between the course of the revolutionary process in the advanced capitalist countries and the revolutionary process in the poor, pre-capitalist areas? Is the success of the revolution in the East a pre-requisite for success in the advanced industrial countries? Fourth, can the countries of the East pass over the stage of capitalism and move directly from feudalism to "socialism"? Should the Communists consider state capitalism in the underdeveloped countries "progressive" because it is setting the stage for "socialism"?

The tactical question lying at the root of all of these questions is that of timing. How fast can the revolutionary process be pushed? If one is in a hurry, then it can be argued that the alliance with the national bourgeoisie is unnecessary, that if such an alliance were achieved, the Communists must have the commanding role in it, that the underdeveloped countries can skip the capitalist stage which the USSR itself had to pass through because these countries can avail themselves of Soviet aid *after* the Communists take power. If, on the other hand, one believes that excessive speed would jeopardize the ultimate goal, the counterargument is that the alliance with the national bourgeoisie is essential even if it means temporarily abandoning the leading role to them, that the underdeveloped countries cannot entirely bypass the capitalist stage or they will have no proletariat on which to base the revolution, and so on.

The dilemma is as old as the Second Comintern Congress of 1920, when Lenin and the Indian Communist M. N. Roy, in the first major discussion of the problem, differed over these and related questions.[3] In Lenin's "Explanations" to the Comintern, he told the assembled delegates that "we [in the Commission on the National and Colonial Questions] fought over whether it is proper theoretically and in principle to declare that the Communist International and the Communist parties are bound to support the bourgeois democratic movements in the backward countries." The solution reached was that the Communists should support liberation movements only in cases when these movements are "really revolutionary." If they were not, the Communists were "obliged to fight against the reformist bourgeoisie in those countries."[4]

Roy did not publicly disagree with Lenin, but it was apparent that he wished the adoption of a harder line than Lenin toward the nationalist bourgeoisie in the colonial areas. Roy stressed that the Comintern should not seek to deal with bourgeois nationalist movements in the colonial areas but rather only with the most revolutionary parties and groups. Most important, he contended that even though the colonial revolution in its early stages would not be a Communist revolution, the leadership of the revolution should be from the outset "in the hands of a Communist vanguard."[5]

Roy's view that the Communists should not abandon leadership of the colonial revolution to the nationalists even in the early stages of the revolution was incorporated in Mao's writings in 1939–1940, the period in which he wrote "On New Democracy." Mao's writings in this period suggested, first, that the "new democratic revolution" then developing in China would develop much the same way in all colonial and semi-colonial countries; and, second, that in the early stages of this "new democratic revolution" there would have to be a joint dictatorship of several revolutionary classes. Mao was at great pains to distinguish this new transitional dictatorship both from past democratic revolutions in Western countries and from the "socialist revolution" that had occurred in the USSR. It would differ from the former in that the reins of power would be held not by the bourgeoisie but by a popular front government composed of all revolutionary groups. This would guarantee that even if the Communists could not take power by themselves early in the revolution, they would not be submerged in a nationalist regime or devoured by the nationalists, as the Chinese Communists themselves were in 1927. A "new democratic revolution" would differ from the "socialist revolution" in the USSR in that its initial goal was to fight foreign imperialism, not domestic capitalism. This implied that the Communist alliance with the domestic bourgeoisie in any given colonial country could last for an extended period of time, or as long as it took to rid the country of foreign imperialism. As Mao wrote in an essay on "The Chinese Revolution and the Chinese Communist Party" in December 1939:

"This kind of revolution is developing in China *as well as in all colonial and semi-colonial countries,* and we call it the new democratic revolution. This new democratic revolution . . . politically . . . means the joint dictatorship of several revolutionary classes over the imperialists collaborators and reactionaries and opposition to the transformation of Chinese society into a society under bourgeois dictatorship. Economically, it means nationalization of all big capital and big enterprises of the imperialists, collaborators, and reactionaries, distribution of the land of the landlords among the peasants, and at the same time the general preservation of private capitalist enterprises without the elimination of rich-peasant economy. . . . This kind of new-democratic revolution *differs greatly* from the democratic revolutions in the history of European and American countries, in that it results not in the dictatorship of the bourgeoisie, but in the dictatorship of the united front of all revolutionary classes under the leadership of the proletariat. . . . This kind of new-democratic revolution differs also from a socialist revolution in that *it aims only at overthrowing the rule of the imperialists, collaborators, and reactionaries in China, but not at injuring any capitalist sections which can still take part in the anti-imperialist, anti-feudal struggles"* [italics supplied].[6]

The Maoist claim to have discovered a new type of transitional government valid for all colonial and semi-colonial countries in the period between the democratic and the socialist revolutions was stated even more bluntly in Mao's "On New Democracy" in January 1940. In that work, he identified three types of state systems in the world, classified according to the class character of their political power: (1) republics under bourgeois dictatorship; (2) republics under the dictatorship of the proletariat; and (3) republics under the joint dictatorship of several revolutionary classes. The third kind of government, he said "is the transitional form of state to be adopted by revolutions in colonial and semi-colonial countries. To be sure, revolutions in different colonial and semi-colonial countries necessarily have certain different characteristics, but these constitute only minor differences within a general framework of uniformity."[7]

Mao's writings in this period thus laid the groundwork for the claims to be advanced by the Chinese Communists almost immediately after they took power that China, and by implication not the USSR, was the model for revolution in the underdeveloped countries.[8] Implicit in Mao's analysis was a belief that the underdeveloped countries—for a variety of reasons, chief among which was their primitive stage of economic development—could not move directly from the bourgeois to the socialist stage of the revolution and that there would be a transitional period in which Communist parties in these areas would share power with nationalists and other parties of the Left, but not cede power to them. An important consideration was probably the realization that most of the underdeveloped countries lacked the resources, the working classes, and the level of industrialization to be transferred overnight into "socialist" states. It is most important to note, however, that although Mao seemed well aware that the Communists could not immediately and exclusively take power in the underdeveloped areas and that they would have to forge alliances with nationalists, he would not allow the nationalist parties in the underdeveloped countries by themselves to lead the "new democratic" revolution.

Mao's formula called not for a temporary subordination of the Communists to the nationalists but for the dictatorship of a "united front" in which, presumably, the Communists exercised the leading role and the other groups followed. It was precisely this question of who would lead the revolution in the colonial areas that had haunted the Communists in the past and that lay at the root of Sino-Soviet differences, as we shall presently see.

Both Mao and Stalin were undoubtedly disappointed at the turn of events in the underdeveloped areas after World War II. Conditions did not create opportunities for "new democratic revolutions." Leninist dogma had assumed that the colonial areas would be freed only after bitter struggles, almost inevitably including armed violence and civil war, against the particular imperialist exploiter. Seeking their independence under conditions of bitter and prolonged armed struggle against the "imperialists," the nationalists in colonial countries, it was assumed, could be won over to an alliance with the Communists and ultimately to Communism.

But there was little room in this world-view to explain the major developments after World War II. The Americans kept their promise to free the Philippines. The British withdrew peacefully from India, Pakistan, Ceylon, Burma, and the Middle East. There was in some cases close cooperation, both political and economic, between the former inperialist master and the former imperialist colony. With a few exceptions such as those in Indonesia, Indochina, and Algeria, the nationalist movements in the former imperialist colonies were not forced to fight bitter and prolonged struggles against their Western masters.

This phenomenon presented a critical dilemma to Stalin and to Mao. How were they to behave toward the newly independent countries, such as India, Indonesia, etc., and to the nationalist revolutionary movements in countries which had not yet gained their independence? In the early postwar period, Stalin treated the Nehrus and Sukarnos as nationalist traitors who had sold out the revolutions in their own countries for imperialist pittances and were not genuinely independent. He instructed local Communist parties to make life as difficult as possible for these nationalist governments and not to cooperate with them. In Stalin's inflexible and dichotomic world-view, if the nationalists were not Communist satellites, they could not be trusted.

Having seen the failure of these tactics to make any substantial gains in the postwar years, the Soviet and Chinese leaders—particularly after Stalin's death in March 1953—developed a more subtle strategy in the colonial countries. There was a leap forward in 1955, when Moscow suddenly discovered that the "national bourgeoisie" were not so bad after all, particularly if they pursued neutralist foreign policies. Khrushchev, evidently in the face of opposition from Stalinist die-hards in the Presidium, inaugurated a program of foreign aid to the newly independent countries. China, for its part, inaugurated its "good neighbor" policy at the Bandung Conference. At the 20th Party Congress in 1956, the benevolent attitude toward the neutrals and nationalists still prevailed. The independent countries became part of the "zone of peace" and, although not Communist, were suddenly declared to be on the road to revolutionary progress. The Russians extended the hand of friendship and began sending technicians, artists, and capital in an effort to convince these countries that they sought only their welfare and their genuine independence from the imperialists. At the same time, Communist doctrine, which had already begun in 1951–1952 to play down the concept of armed struggle and civil war in non-Communist countries—due, no doubt, to a failure of these tactics—now began to play up the parliamentary road to socialism. This road was not limited to the more advanced countries. At the 20th Congress Khrushchev specifically said that in "many capitalist and formerly colonial countries "the winning of a parliamentary majority by the proletariat could make possible "fundamental social changes."[9]

By 1959, however, Communist strategy in the underdeveloped areas was increasingly being called into question by the Chinese. In effect, the issue was the same as that which had been at the root of the Lenin-Roy controversy in 1920: to what extent could the Communists cooperate with local nationalists without placing in jeopardy their own ultimate goals? Disappointed with Nasser, Nehru, and Kassim, the Chinese now began to argue in effect for an end to the Communist alliance with and benevolence toward the nationalists. They advanced the arguments that Moscow itself had advanced prior to 1955: that the nationalists could not be trusted, that they might gravitate back toward the West, that they could not and would not make needed social reforms.

The Question of Timing

The central issue in this new strategy debate with Moscow has been one of timing. The controversy over cooperation with bourgeois nationalism has, as we have suggested, never turned on *whether* to form temporary alliances with it, but rather it has turned on *when* to form them and, more important, when to end them. The Chinese seem to fear that time is not necessarily on the Communist side in all colonial and politically emergent areas; that the "liberation" movements may falter or be retarded without strong Bloc support; and that the newly independent governments may stabilize themselves and eventually gravitate back into the Western camp unless increased pressure is put upon them. These apprehensions, coupled with a more sanguine view than Moscow's of the dangers of a global nuclear war, have led the Chinese to advocate a return to the Left startegy: it has led them, in fact, to revive Trotsky's theory of "permanent revolution" and apply it to the "colonial" areas.[10] The Russians, on the other hand, appear genuinely convinced that time and neutralism are working to the Communists' advantage, that in the long run the economic race with the West will be decisive, and that it is needless to assume the risks inherent in a more aggressive strategy.

To define the central strategy issue in the colonial areas as one of timing is not simply to say that the Chinese insist upon, while the Russians oppose, immediate action to foment liberation wars or revolutionary assaults on national bourgeois governments. The issue of timing is actually far more complex, hinging upon questions of how much support can be given to "just" wars of liberation without marring current Soviet diplomatic objectives and incurring the risk of war with the West; how much pressure can and should be exerted by local Communist movements on particular nationalist governments and parties at a particular time; to what extent ultimate Communist goals should be subordinated to the tactical exigencies of alliance with the nationalists and up to what point the latter should be allowed to lead the revolution in its early stages.

With regard to this last question, the Russians and Chinese have stated sharply opposed views. The Chinese reject the Soviet thesis that hegemony can be entrusted to the national bourgeoisie in the post-liberation "democratic" phase of the revolution. The "key" to ensuring a rapid, uninterrupted transition to the socialist revolution, Liu Shao-ch'i said in 1959, "is the firm grasping of hegemony *in the democratic revolution* by the proletariat through the Communist party" [italics supplied].[11] In apparent reply to such views, the dean of Soviet experts on the East, Y. Zhukov, cited Lenin's declaration that "*at the beginning* of any nationalist movement," not the Communists but "the bourgeoisie assumes the role of hegemony" [italics supplied].[12] Zhukov argued that the "main task" in many Asian and African countries for a "comparatively long period" would be the struggle not against capitalism (i.e., the bourgeoisie) but against medieval remnants (i.e., the landlords). Hence, there was a basis for "lengthy cooperation" between the workers and the "progressive" segment of the national bourgeoisie; the day of reckoning could be deferred.

The Chinese position is evidently inspired by apprehension that if the nationalist parties are permitted to continue to command the "democratic" revolution, local Communist chances of gaining power will be deferred and can even be lost entirely. Recollection of the disastrous outcome of the Chinese Party's own Right strategy of collaboration with the Kuomintang in the 1920's strengthens Peking's fears that the nationalist parties—once in firm political control—may turn against and crush the local Communists.[13] The strategic implications of this Chinese view are obvious. In the as yet "unliberated" countries of Africa, for example, the Communists must seek to win the leading role in the national revolutionary movements; and where political independence has already been won under bourgeois nationalist leadership, the Communists must seek sooner rather than later to displace the nationalists at the helm of the revolution's further phases.

The pivotal importance of timing is underscored by Peking's denial that the national bourgeoisie can complete the "democratic" revolution—implying that the Communists must take power to complete it for them—as opposed to Moscow's contention that the national bourgeoisie has not yet exhausted its usefulness. In other words, the Chinese are crystal-clear and doctrinally pure in contending that the national bourgeoisie cannot complete the "democratic" revolution while the Russians are deliberately ambiguous on the point, not so much because they realize they are on weak ideological ground, but rather because the implication of the Chinese formula is that local Communist parties in some under-developed areas must soon take power. If the local Communists were to try to do this, the Soviet alliance with Nasser, Nehru, Sukarno, and the nationalists would be jeopardized. Another indica-tion of the different approach to timing in the underdeveloped areas is the Chinese claim that state capitalism in the newly inde-pendent countries has reached a dead end, whereas Moscow main-tains that it is "playing a progressive role."[14] The implication of the Chinese view is that state capitalism must be replaced by "social-ism" if social "progress" is to be made in the underdeveloped areas; the implication of the Soviet view is that further social progress can be made within the present socio-economic structure of these countries and therefore a Communist-led revolution is not *yet* necessary.

Aid of Liberation Struggles

High on the list of Chinese objections to Soviet strategy in the period under examination was that the Russians were not giving sufficient support to revolutionary nationalist movements engaged in wars of colonial liberation. Algeria, to which we shall return later in this chapter, is an obvious case in point. Although the Rus-sians, apparently bending before Chinese pressure since the col-lapse of the summit, have moved toward an ambiguous *de facto* recognition of the FLN, it is nonetheless remarkable that they have done so little to aid this classical colonial rebellion.

At a January 1959 academicians' conference in Moscow one Chinese representative expressed an annoyance that was typical of numerous Chinese statements on this issue, when he warned: " . . . not to express sympathy with and give assistance to the peoples of countries which are the victims of imperialist aggression and are fighting heroically to win and preserve their national independence, means to lack a sincere desire for the preservation and strengthening of peace."[15] Essentially the same charge was again made, if indirectly, in April 1960, when Peking warned that all "revolutionary" Leninists should support colonial revolutions "without the slightest reservations."[16] In fact, one Chinese journal went so far as to declare that without this support the world revolu-tion "may not finally emerge victorious."[17]

254

The same article insisted on the almost inevitable need for national liberation wars, contending that there had never been any colonial people who achieved independence "without sacrificing thousands of their revolutionary comrades." This was so because "in the face of the powerful and fierce imperialists and colonial powers, national liberation war is necessarily an extremely important means by which peoples in the colonial and semi-colonial areas may achieve the ultimate victory of their national liberation struggle." The article implicitly berated the Russians for their failure to endorse more enthusiastically the need for such liberation wars. It did this by calling attention to the fact that Lenin himself had "never made a general denunciation of war" (as had Khrushchev). Lenin, to the contrary, said the author, had declared in "no uncertain terms" that "our Party must be sympathetic to such wars or insurrections" (i.e. of national liberation). In the choice of one quotation from Lenin, the Chinese journal went so far as to accuse the Russians implicitly of "pacifism" and "nationalism": "To pay lip service to internationalism but to substitute the vulgar nationalism and pacifism for internationalism in their propaganda, agitation, and actual work is a most common phenomenon . . . even in those political parties that profess to be ideologically Communist."

To the Russian contention that civil wars and armed violence in the colonial areas, particularly if supported by the Bloc, might lead to hostilities with the West, the Chinese retorted that active support of armed struggle would strengthen peace because it would weaken imperialism and its capabilities for war: . . . To support the oppressed peoples in the armed struggle against imperialism is an integral part of our struggle for peace. This has been true in the light of facts. During the ten odd years since the war, the rising tide of the struggle against imperialism and for national liberation . . . has seriously weakened the imperialists' capabilities for war and aggression and disturbed their plans for war, thereby contributing most significantly to the defense of world peace. Whoever is genuinely struggling for world peace cannot but link the national liberation movements with the worldwide movement in search of peace and regard it his proper duty to render assistance to the national liberation movements in the colonial and semi-colonial areas. To deny this would not only mean the violation of Lenin's principles of proletarian internationalism, but also may weaken the forces in defense of world peace."

In sum, Khrushchev's strategy not only was a violation of "proletarian internationalism," but it would indirectly strengthen the hand of the West by failing to exploit golden opportunities to weaken it in its colonial underbelly.

Armed Struggle

No one with any sense of history would maintain, of course, that Moscow has permanently renounced armed struggle as a means of seizing power. But in adjusting its strategy to the thermonuclear era, it has—for strategic reasons—put greater stress on political and economic forms of struggle.[18] This emphasis seems to be motivated in part by fear that civil war in any crucially contested area may confront the USSR with a choice between two equally distasteful alternatives: either to take sides with the Communist or pro-Communist group, thus risking Western intervention and a local war, or to stand passively by while the armed uprising is crushed. In part, too, Moscow is well aware that armed Communist uprisings in underdeveloped countries would end the Soviet alliance with the nationalists and its hopes of exploiting nationalism and neutralism.

In *Fundamentals of Marxism-Leninism,* it was contended, as we have seen, that non-violent revolution had great advantages because it permitted a "radical reorganization of social life" with the "least sacrifices on the part of the workers."

Later pronouncements in the Soviet press tied in this new formulation with the bigger problem of East-West coexistence. Early in 1960 a Soviet journal stated quite frankly that in countries where conditions are "ripe" for social change, such change must be brought about in a manner that would not lead "to military clashes of the two antipodal systems."[19] As to how this might be achieved, the journal went on to say: " . . . this situation opens up new, unprecedented horizons for diplomacy. As methods of violence and *diktat* are relegated to the background, methods of negotiation assume even greater importance." Peking has strongly assailed such an assignment of priority to diplomacy and non-violent struggle, standing firm on Lenin's prediction that revolutionary violence will be necessary in a majority of cases because no ruling class ever gives way without a struggle.[20] The Chinese do not, of course, argue that revolutionary violence is the *only* means of advancing the socialist revolution. They appear to believe, however, that a peaceful transition to power is possible only in the rare circumstances when "in a given country a certain local political power is already encircled by revolutionary forces, or when in the world a certain capitalist country is already encircled by socialism."[21]

Response to Western "Intervention"

Not only do the Chinese urge increased emphasis on local "armed struggle" in the "colonial" areas, but they also urge armed responses to any Western military intervention in these areas. In Peking's view, the very fact that Soviet military might deters the Western powers from contemplating global war makes it all the more likely that they will undertake "last-gasp" local wars, particularly in the colonial areas.[22] This contrasts sharply with the USSR's position that its deterrent power discourages Western intervention anywhere, and that local wars are therefore becoming less rather than more likely. Thus, *Kommunist* wrote in late 1960 (No. 13) that it is "really possible to prevent the interference of world reaction in the course of a revolution, at least in the form of open intervention."[23]

Role of the "National Bourgeoisie"

As already indicated, another point at issue between Moscow and Peking has been whether the "national bourgeois" leaderships in the newly independent countries can continue to play a progressive role or, on the contrary, have exhausted their usefulness. Moscow takes a much more optimistic view of the possibilities of further Communist gains through collaboration with these leaderships than do the Chinese, who see in this policy grave risk of imperialist restoration.[24]

In August and September 1959 the *World Marxist Review* published a lengthy "exchange of views" on "The National Bourgeoisie and the Liberation Movement." There were contributions from sixteen Communist parties, including two from the

Soviet Party, but none representing the views of the Chinese Communists appeared—in itself an indication of growing Sino-Soviet disagreement on this question. Although somewhat equivocal, the principal Soviet spokesman, Levihson, generally took the line that further progress could be made via collaboration with the national bourgeoisie. The anti-imperialist and anti-feudal movement could, he said, be carried further "within the framework of the existing regimes," despite bourgeois nationalist "vacillations." Moreover, the final outcome of the revolutionary dilemma in these countries would be decided not only by the strength of the local Communist movements, but also by the course of peaceful competition between East and West. In short, the infant nationalist governments would gradually gravitate toward the socialist camp as the USSR overtakes the West economically.

Chinese objections to this gradualist line emerged most forcefully on October 1, 1959, the tenth anniversary of the People's Republic and the occasion of another Khrushchev visit to Peking. Writing in the anniversary issue of *Hung ch'i,* Wang Chia-hsiang, a secretary of the CCP, voiced impatience with the nationalist leaderships of some Asian and African countries, warning that at any moment they might slide back into the imperialist camp and, in any case could never free themselves from imperialist bondage: "The bourgeoisie which is in power in these countries [in Asia and Africa] has played to a certain degree a historically progressive role. . . . It may to a greater or lesser degree go part of the way in opposing imperialism and feudalism. . . . But after all the bourgeoisie is the bourgeoisie. When in power, it does not follow resolute, revolutionary lines; it oscillates and compromises. Therefore it is out of the question for these countries to pass to socialism, *nor is it possible for them to accomplish in full the tasks of the national-democratic revolution.* What is more, even the national independence they have achieved will not be secure . . . there may emerge bureaucrat-capitalism, which gangs up with imperialism and feudalism. . . . *Thus, in the final analysis, they cannot escape the control and clutches of imperialism*" [italics supplied].[25]

Iraq, a Case Study

Sino-Soviet differences over cooperation with the national bourgeoisie were perhaps best illustrated by the conflicting reactions of the two powers to developments in Iraq during 1959. Shortly after the March uprising in Mosul, which resulted in a sharp increase of their strength, the Iraqi Communists—evidently believing that they had Kassim's backing or at least were in a position where he could not oppose them—launched a campaign demanding Communist participation in the government and removal of the prohibition against political party activity. Kassim, however, countered these demands in a May Day statement which rejected the Communist bid for cabinet representation and declared that although Iraq was on the road to democratic rule, the time was not ripe for restoration of party activities.

The incipient struggle between Kassim and the Communists apparently arose against the background of a split between a militant wing of the Iraqi Party, which favored increased pressure on the government, and a moderate faction which counseled caution until the Party had strengthened its organization and discipline.[26] Several reports in the East European Communists press early in 1959 had intimated the existence of such a division, and the fact that they publicized the viewpoint of the moderates rather than of the militants strongly suggested that it was the former who enjoyed Moscow's support. On July 8–9 the Iraqi Communist Politburo, "after studying present conditions," issued a defiant declaration which seemed to indicate that the militant wing was in the ascendancy. Peking gave prompt publicity to the declaration in its news broadcasts, while Moscow not only pointedly ignored it but continued to voice general approval of the Iraqi government's foreign and domestic policies.

The showdown in Iraq finally came with the Kirkuk uprisings of mid-July. Whether or not the Communists inspired the uprisings, they joined in them and suffered a disastrous setback. The insurrection was quickly put down, and the Communist-infiltrated Popular Resistance Force was disarmed and disbanded. In late July the Communist leadership issued a long *mea culpa* for its "irresponsible acts" and "excessiveness," promising in essence to abandon pressure tactics and cooperate more fully with Kassim. This capitulation no doubt was impelled primarily by the Party's realization of the futility of revolutionary tactics, but it seems also to have been influenced to some degree by Soviet pressure. The Iraqi Party's apologia was carried by *Pravda* on August 17 and by

259

Kommunist at about the same time; it never appeared in the Chinese Communist press.

There is no clear evidence that the Chinese, contrary to Soviet wishes, egged on the Left wing of the Iraqi Party in its abortive revolutionary attempt. But Soviet spokesmen, in the course of more or less open polemics with the Chinese in the summer of 1960, pointedly cited the 1959 tactics of the Iraqi Communists as an example of the issuance of "premature slogans of socialist transformation . . . where conditions for them had not yet matured."[27] They added that the lessons of the Iraqi failure might be "instructive also for some Communist parties of the East and Latin America, if they are faced with basically the same task." The socialist revolution in these areas, the Russians were suggesting, should not be rushed.

Bakdash's Attack on Nasser

With regard to Nasser, one of the most prominent of the "national bourgeois" leaders, there was also indication in the fall of 1959 that the Chinese wished to increase the pressure much beyond that deemed advisable by Moscow. The Bloc's growing disenchantment with Nasser—particularly because of his "persecutions" of Arab Communists—had been reflected in Khrushchev's speech to the 21st CPSU Congress in January 1959, where the Soviet leader made the first direct Bloc criticism of the UAR leader since his assumption to power. Throughout the spring of 1959, Moscow and Cairo exchanged criticisms, with Moscow's largely centered on Nasser's actions against local Communists. Peking echoed these Soviet criticisms.

In the summer, Nasser continued to take the initiative against the Communists. In late June, the Lebanese Communist leader Farajallah al-Hilu was arrested in Damascus. On July 15 Damascus radio broadcast "confessions" by defectors from the Syrian Communist Party and on July 23 Nasser himself attacked Arab Communists as "foreign agents." In September and October, Moscow went so far as to hint that it would withdraw Bloc aid from the UAR, and in October the CPSU anniversary slogans did not contain the customary greetings to the UAR.

Yet, although the Russians were disenchanted, they were evidently not yet ready to impose economic sanctions (e.g., by reneging on the Aswan Dam project) or to force a showdown between Nasser and local Communists. The Soviet line was that further "progress" could be made in the "colonial" areas under the present nationalist leaderships, however vacillating and unreliable they were, and there were no injunctions to local Communists to begin to take a greater revolutionary initiative. The big question for the Bloc was, as in the case of Yugoslavia in the spring of 1958, how great a degree of pressure to bring to bear on Nasser. And, as in 1958, the Chinese seemed to want to exert greater pressures than the Russians. In August, Peking, unlike Moscow, directly protested the arrest of the Lebanese Communist leader in the form of a *Jen-min jih-pao* article saying the Chinese people were "most anxious" about his life and freedom.[28]

More important, on September 28 the Chinese provided a forum for the exiled Syrian Communist leader Khalid Bakdash, head of the Syrian Communist delegation to the Chinese Tenth Anniversary ceremonies, to launch the most violent attack on Nasser and the UAR ever made by any Communist spokesman. This attack on Nasser was given tacit endorsement by Peking when it was broadcast by the Peking radio in Arabic two days later. Moscow did not publish or broadcast this speech. Bakdash called Nasser's government "a terroristic dictatorial regime which applies fascist tactics against all democratic national forces." He warned that Nasser's policies threatened to do away with "all the important victories" of the Arab liberation movements, to effect a *rapprochement* with American imperialism, to disrupt relations with the socialist countries, and to exploit Arab unity for narrow class purposes. Bakdash also charged that Syria, too, was now suffering under a "dictatorial anarchist regime unparalleled in Syrian modern history."

Even before this statement at the Peking anniversary, the UAR reacted sharply to Bakdash's appearance as head of the Syrian Communist delegation; the UAR chargé withdrew from the ceremonies. On September 30, the very same day that Peking broadcast Bakdash's statement, Cairo lodged a formal protest with the Chinese Communist Government and stated that its representatives would take no further part in the anniversary celebrations. Steps were also taken to discourage any local participation in the celebration held by Chinese Communist representatives in Cairo and

Damascus, and it was announced that the new UAR ambassador to Peking would not be departing at the present time for his post and that the chargé in Peking was being recalled. Peking explained blandly that Bakdash had been speaking as the representative of the Syrian Communist Party and was free to make whatever remarks he desired. Even if this explanation were taken at face value, there was clearly no need for Peking to associate itself with Bakdash's remarks—as it did—by broadcasting them to Arab audiences.

In sum, as was the case with Yugoslavia in the spring of 1958, Peking seemed to want to exert greater pressures than Moscow on the opponent whom they both regarded as potentially dangerous. As in spring 1958, Peking moved in such a highhanded manner that it seemed likely that its purpose was to push Moscow onto a more extreme course than Moscow had intended to pursue.

Friction over Soviet Aid

A key element in current Soviet world strategy is the increasing use of economic and financial aid as a means of weaning the newly independent and uncommitted countries away from Western economic influence and thus promoting tendencies toward political neutralism and eventual alignment with the socialist camp. As the British economist Alec Nove has suggested, the Soviet leadership appears to believe that in the long run the uncommitted countries will gravitate toward the Communist Bloc because "an economically mighty bloc will be far better equipped to supply the needs of the underdeveloped world, to outbid the West, and to disorganize 'capitalist' markets at will."[29]

On the other hand, there have been intimations that the Peking leadership takes a jaundiced view of Soviet aid to the new and underdeveloped countries—at least on the scale on which it has been extended. Three plausible motivations for this attitude suggest themselves. The Chinese may believe that extensive Soviet assistance to the existing bourgeois nationalist regimes will impede rather than hasten the "socialist revolution." They may also feel that, since Communist China lacks the resources to match the Soviet aid effort, it is placed at a serious disadvantage in competing with the Soviet Union for favor and influence. Finally, they might feel that the less advanced countries within the Communist Bloc, including China, ought to be given prior claim to Soviet assistance.

Several occurrences last year brought this latent conflict to the surface. Perhaps the most revealing was an incident that took place during Soviet First Deputy Premier Mikoyan's visit to Iraq in April 1960. At a press conference held by Mikoyan, a Chinese correspondent bluntly asked the Soviet leader: "What is the Soviet position on the question of developing the national economy of the Afro-Asian countries, and *how does it differ from the Western position on this question?*"[30] Mikoyan's reply made it evident that he took the question as a provocation: "I can assure the NCNA representative that our position on this question is just as favorable for the Afro-Asian peoples who are building their national economy *as the position of the CPR Government.* We do not regard these countries as raw material appendages of industrially developed countries, as spheres of influence or of capital investment" [italics supplied].[31]

Further discord between Moscow and Peking over the question of economic policy toward the uncommitted countries was manifest at the Afro-Asian Solidarity Conference in Conakry in early April. The Indian secretary on the permanent secretariat of the conference reported that there had been a clash between Moscow and Peking over the formulation of the economic resolution agreed to at the conference.[32] The Chinese wanted to delete a passage which said that Afro-Asian development could be facilitated "the sooner the cold war is ended and international tension is reduced." Peking contended, according to the report, that such a reference would "create illusions among Afro-Asian countries that the imperialists want our economic development and seriously believe in disarmament and world peace." The Chinese attitude reportedly shocked both the Soviet delegate and some observers from the Communist front organization, the World Peace Council. Moscow, for its part, must have been extremely pleased with the wording of the resolution, because it had been contending for some time that the funds saved from disarmament could be used to aid the economic development of the uncommitted countries.

Further evidence of Peking opposition to the Soviet aid program was reflected in the differing Sino-Soviet approaches to the Afro-Asian economic conference in Cairo in early May. A Moscow radio commentary, broadcast to Africa on May 4, stressed that most of the newly liberated countries needed to free themselves from economic dependence on foreign monopolies and that, in order to accomplish that goal, they could "rely" on Soviet aid: "*Relying* on this (Soviet) aid, economically backward countries can develop their economies more quickly and create those branches of industry which they need." The Chinese delegate to the conference, Nan Han-chen, stressed quite to the contrary that the newly developing countries must "rely on their own efforts." Although he drew a distinction between disinterested Soviet aid and that of the West, the burden of his remarks constituted a warning against aid from anywhere, a plea for self-reliance and intra-African and Asian cooperation, and a reminder that Chinese history demonstrated conclusively that foreign aid was not essential to industrialization and economic development. After warning that any country which "relied" on so-called "imperialist aid" would inevitably be forced to surrender national sovereignty, the Chinese delegate said: "We advocate that the Asian and African countries be economically independent and rely on their own efforts, and that we cooperate, aid each other, and develop our trade relations on the basis of equality and mutual benefit. In this respect, the experience of the Chinese people affords powerful proof. In old China, we had to import every year large quantities of wheat and rice from abroad. But today, 10 years after liberation, our grain output has more than doubled."[33] In short, China achieved rapid economic development without a great deal of aid and there was no reason why the newly developing countries could not imitate her.

The same point was made in the July 13, 1960, issue of the Chinese journal *Kuo-chi wen-t'i yen-chiu*, The Chinese People's Republic, an article in this issue affirmed, was economically weaker than "certain newly risen Asian countries which have just won their national independence." Yet the Chinese people, in building up their national economy, "*mainly* relied on their own strength" [italics supplied].[34]

Perhaps the most direct indication of Chinese reservations about Soviet aid programs came in Kuusinen's Lenin Anniversary reply to Chinese attacks on Soviet global strategy. Kuusinen made a strong defense of the Soviet aid policy to the uncommitted countries in polemical terms which left the clear impression that the Chinese opposed such aid. He pointedly contrasted Soviet economic obligations to the Bloc with its "wider understanding of (its) international duty" which included the extending of aid to "any liberated people" even if they were not "members of the world socialist system":

"People who for centuries bore on their shoulders the yoke of colonial exploitation now need not only moral and political support, but also economic aid for development of their national economies.

"As for our relations with countries which joined the socialist camp—the CPR, the SPRK, the DRV, and the Mongolian People's Republic—these relations were determined from the very outset by the principles of socialist internationalism. Close alliance, brotherly friendship, mutual aid, and cooperation in construction of socialism and Communism—such is the basis of these relations. *However, we have a wider understanding of the international duty of our socialist country. We understand that duty to include extending aid to any liberated people even if they are not members of the world socialist system. . . .*

"The road to consolidation of the independence of liberated countries is the road of developing their national economy, advancing their culture, and improving the living standards of their people. Industrialization is of enormous importance for such countries. It is in this matter that young states need support most."[35]

This line of argument ran directly contrary to the line the Chinese had taken in October 1959—that so long as these young countries were led by bourgeois nationalists they could not hope to industrialize, to improve the living standards of their people, or to make much progress towards economic independence from the West.

In the June issue of the Soviet monthly *International Affairs,* Moscow again issued a lengthy defense of its aid policy under the title "Soviet Aid—and Its 'Critics.' " Although the "critics" were identified only as Westerners, it was evident that Moscow had some non-Western critics in mind as well. For example, the author took pains to refute the argument that Soviet assistance to former colonies would impede the revolutionary process—hardly a criticism that had been voiced in the West. The author also pointed out that the struggle in the underdeveloped countries "will not be solely, *or chiefly,* a struggle of the revolutionary proletarians in each country against their bourgeoisie" but would instead be a struggle of all the oppressed countries against international imperialism. It followed from this that exploitation of anti-colonial nationalism should take precedence over promotion of the class struggle, and therefore the Soviet government was "giving economic and technical assistance to the former colonies on an intergovernmental basis *rendering it to nations, and not to some classes within them"* [italics supplied].[36] The counterargument, presumably advanced by Peking, was that Soviet aid should be confined largely to proletarian revolutionary movements.

Soviet or Chinese Model for Underdeveloped Countries

Perhaps at the root of Chinese dissatisfaction with Soviet strategy in the underdeveloped areas was the desire of the Chinese to replace the Russians as leaders of the revolutionary movement there. Such aspirations were best revealed by the bold revival in 1959 and 1960 of Chinese claims that Maoist theory and Chinese revolutionary experience were valid for underdeveloped areas, and, by implication, that Soviet theory and revolutionary experience were not. On the 10th anniversary of the CPR, the Chinese claimed that the Chinese road to power should be regarded as a "typical example" for the underdeveloped countries.[37] Teng Hsiao-ping, writing in *Pravda* on October 2, went so far as to suggest that the Chinese revolution had provided an example not only for the socialist revolution in a backward country but also for "transforming a backward, agricultural country into an advanced industrial country."[38] This emphasis on the Chinese "example" for the underdeveloped countries was put forward even more boldly in *Chung-kuo ch'ing-nien.* The article claimed that because Mao's theories on the "new democratic revolution" were developed from revolutionary experience in a "typical" colonial country, namely China, "they are applicable to other colonial and semi-colonial countries."[39] In fact, it was claimed once again, as in 1949–1951, that Mao's theories "represent a new development and rediscovery of the Marxist-Leninist theory of revolution in colonial and semi-colonial countries." Thus the Chinese were not only voicing critical doubts over Soviet revolutionary strategy in the uncommitted

266

countries but were also laying the groundwork, as in 1949–1951, for Chinese claims to tutelage of the revolutionary movement in all backward areas. To put it another way, the Chinese Communists were telling the Russians not only that they wanted a change in Soviet strategy in the uncommitted countries, but also that the Russians should turn over the revolution in these areas to Peking.

Struggle in the Local Parties

Potentially the most significant aspect of Sino-Soviet conflict in underdeveloped areas is the incipient struggle for power between pro-Soviet and pro-Chinese factions in the Communist parties of Asia, Africa, and Latin America. In some of the older Asian parties, it is true, there have long been divisions between Right elements which wanted to postpone the showdown with bourgeois nationalism and Left elements which sought to hasten it. But as long as Moscow's remained the sole and undisputed voice of world Communist authority, such factionalism was relatively innocuous. What makes the present Left-wing splits in some Communist parties so portentous is the fact that the Leftists now can and do find an ideological rallying point in Peking. So long as the Russians and Chinese continue to vie for influence and to disagree on strategy, such intra-party factionalism cannot be quelled. And if either of the opposing factions manages to wrest control from the other in one or more of these divided parties, the effect can only be to aggravate the strains on the Sino-Soviet axis.[40]

The split in the Indian Communist Party has been so conspicuous that it received wide publicity in the Western press.[41] The Left, pro-Chinese faction, led by B. T. Ranadive, has its strength concentrated largely in West Bengal, Andhra, and the Punjab; the Right, pro-Soviet group, led by Ajoy Ghosh and S. A. Dange, seems to hold a tenuous majority among the party rank-and-file. There is still a third group, led by E. M. S. Namboodiripad, which has sought to remain neutral. The seriousness of the split was evidenced in May 1960 by Ghosh's temporary withdrawal as Party leader in favor of Namboodiripad.

Generally speaking, the Ranadive group would like to lead the Indian Party in a more or less open revolt against Nehru and the Congress Party. While this would probably not mean an actual, immediate attempt to seize power, it would certainly involve a greater resort to strikes and direct action tactics. The Leftists are critical of the Party's failure in Kerala, where the Communists gained and then lost local government control by electoral processes, and are skeptical of Khrushchev's whole thesis of parliamentary take-over. They are also blatantly pro-Chinese on the border question. According to a competent Indian observer, Ranadive is in close contact with the Chinese Communists and transmits their influence to the party.[42] The Rightists, on the other hand, continue to follow the parliamentary path to power laid down in the Amritsar Thesis of 1958. While conceding the increasing domestic conservatism of the Congress Party, they can point to Nehru's neutralist foreign policy and can argue that the Right strategy needs more time to come to fruition.

In the Indonesian Communist Party (PKI), the division is neither so pronounced nor so open, but conflicting pro-Soviet Right and pro-Chinese Left tendencies are nevertheless discernible in the pronouncements of high-ranking Party leaders. The prevailing policies of the PKI are those of its top leader, Secretary-General D. N. Aidit, whose adherence to a Moscow-oriented strategy of "patience" was clearly evident in an article commemorating the 40th Party anniversary last May (*Harian Rajkat*, May 24–25, 1960), which received full publicity in *Pravda*. On the other hand, Sudisman, a member of the Party Politburo, writing in *Harian Rajkat* a week later (May 30), presented an almost pure "Chinese" assessment of the international situation, charging that the "imperialists" regard peace merely as an interval between wars and that real peace can be won only through "struggle." Accusing the "revisionists" of fearing both war and revolution, he concluded by quoting Mao's 1958 statement that an imperialist-provoked third world war would only result in several hundred millions more people turning to socialism.[43] Pro-Chinese views have also been expressed by another member of the Politburo, Njoto.

Cuba, the Congo, and Africa

Sino-Soviet conflicts have, similarly, had reverberations in Latin America and Africa. There is some indication of an incipient Left-Right split in the Cuban Communist Party over an issue which has been a major bone of contention between Moscow and Peking: how fast to move the revolution forward. At a Party congress held in Havana in August 1960, Party leader Blas Roca refrained from mentioning the ultimate "socialist" goals of the Cuban revolution and stressed instead its anti-imperialist and anti-latifundist objectives. Another speaker, Anibal Escalante, put noticeably greater stress on the future stages of the revolution. As the Cuban revolution moves forward, it seems likely that, just as in Iraq in the summer of 1959, Sino-Soviet and local intra-Party differences over timing will arise.

With regard to the Congo, Chinese statements in the summer voiced implied criticism of the Soviet support given in July 1960 to the UN Security Council resolution authorizing the dispatch of a UN force to the Congo. At the time the resolution was under consideration, Soviet propaganda was assailing the UN for procrastination and for not taking firmer action, while the Chinese were taking a quite different tack, accusing the UN of being a U.S.-controlled vehicle for armed intervention.[44] Commenting on the subsequent course of events in the Congo, Chinese newspaper editorials in late November observed with scarcely veiled contempt that "naive people" who "more than four months ago" believed that the United Nations could help the Congolese people were now becoming "fewer and fewer."[45]

Nor has Peking balked at competing with the Russians for influence in Africa. The sheer scope of Chinese political, economic, and ideological overtures to the emergent African states is impressive, particularly in view of China's limited resources. One Western observer reports that of more than 800 foreign groups which travelled to China in 1959 alone, 270 were from Africa—and this figure undoubtedly increased in 1960.[46] Peking radio now broadcasts more extensively to sub-Saharan Africa than does Moscow. At the Afro-Asian Solidarity Conference, held in Conakry in April 1960, the Chinese delegation was the largest and most active, overshadowing the delegation of the USSR.

The Chinese, significantly, are wooing the most radical African leaders. In May 1960, for example, they played host to Odhiambo Okello, from Kenya, whose militancy led him to an open break with the more responsible nationalist leaders in that British colony.[47] Since Peking's unconcealed cultivation of the most militant African nationalists actually prejudices its chances of winning the favor of the more conservative African governments and leaders, its pursuit of this policy seems indicative of a willingness to accept temporary sacrifices for the sake of hastening the eventual Communist take-over.

Chinese Communist propaganda aimed at Africa constantly pledges China's complete support of the African peoples' fight against imperialism and emphasizes the Chinese example as a guide for conducting the liberation struggle. It is quite probable that the Chinese are distributing money, propaganda literature, and guerrilla warfare handbooks in many key areas of Africa. An eyewitness report has attested to such activity in the British Cameroons.[48]

There has already been a direct clash between representatives of Moscow and Peking over African strategy. At the Conakry conference in April, the Soviet and Chinese delegates openly collided over the terms of an economic resolution.[49] The Chinese vigorously opposed a Soviet-approved draft which stated that economic development would be speeded up if the cold war were ended, arguing that such a statement in the resolution would only create the illusion among the Afro-Asian peoples that the imperialists really believed in economic development, disarmament, and peace. According to the Indian secretary of the conference, the Chinese attitude surprised everyone, "especially the Soviet delegate."

Differences over Policy
toward Algeria

The differences between Moscow and Peking over policy toward the "national liberation" movements are nowhere better illustrated than in their respective attitudes toward the Algerian rebellion. For all Communists, the Algerian rebellion is the classical form of the "just" colonial war—a war initiated by a colonial people in order to win independence from an oppressive colonial power.

The Algerian rebellion has never presented any dilemmas to the Chinese Communists. Where Leninist dogma is the sole criterion of policy, the only possible course of action is to recognize the revolutionary government and to aid it with all possible means. The Chinese recognized the FLN immediately after it formed a government in exile in 1958. They have consistently urged a continuation of the war of liberation and have expressed the hope that this war would be an example to other African peoples. Colonial wars, such as the Algerian, present the Chinese with unique opportunities to expand their prestige and influence. They probably calculate that, because the United States will not dare cross its French allies by aiding the nationalist rebellion, the Algerian nationalists will be increasingly driven to look for support in the Communist camp. For these reasons, undoubtedly, the Chinese Communists have never looked with favor on the prospects of a negotiated settlement between the French and the Algerian rebels.

For the Russians, the Algerian rebellion has been the source of a dilemma. Although they are no less eager than the Chinese to spread colonial unrest and revolution, they must balance this long-range goal against their important middle-range aim of splitting the French away from the Western alliance. The departure of the French from NATO would be a bigger prize for the Russians than a free Algeria. Hence the Soviet Union has demonstrated approval of De Gaulle's policy and has never extended *de jure* recognition to the Algerian rebel government. Indeed, it was not until 1960, in the wake of the summit collapse and increasing Chinese rivalry in the colonial areas, that the Russians extended *de facto* recognition.

The argument between Peking and Moscow over Algeria is an argument over tactical priorities within the framework of a common desire to expand Communist power and influence. Because the Chinese have no diplomatic relations with the French, have little to gain from wooing them, and are pessimistic about the possibility of breaking France away from the United States, they want to give unequivocal support to the Algerian rebels and to any other nationalist revolutionary movements in the colonial areas. The Russians, on the other hand, have diplomatic relations with the French, believe they have much to gain from improving those relations, are pleased with De Gaulle's independent attitude toward NATO, and are confident that they can increase the strains between France and the other Western allies.

The differences between Moscow and Peking over Algeria were already smoldering even before October 31, 1959, when Khrushchev suddenly took an important step toward supporting the French position. In his speech to the Supreme Soviet, Khrushchev suddenly reversed the previous Soviet position of hostility to De Gaulle's September 16 proposals for a cease-fire in Algeria.[50] The new Soviet position was that De Gaulle's proposals for self-determination, if supported by concrete steps, "could play an important role in the settlement of the Algerian question." Within this context, Moscow also began to express the hope that French-FLN negotiations would take place and would bring the war to an end. The Soviet reversal was quickly, if embarrassingly, imitated by the French Communist Party, which only a month earlier had denounced De Gaulle's proposals as an attempt to postpone a satisfactory solution.

The reasons why Khrushchev suddenly made his tactical switch on Algeria seem clear. On the eve of his meeting with the French President, scheduled for April, and prior to the summit meeting, Khrushchev was evidently prepared to go far toward showing good will to the French. Khrushchev's switch came ten days after a French Cabinet statement which in effect called for Soviet deeds to substantiate Moscow's alleged interest in *détente*.

It may be objected that the new direction of Khrushchev's policy was more apparent than real and that the Russians must have covertly informed the Algerian rebel leaders not to pay any attention to his words. The rebels, however, had consistently suggested they might turn to the Communists if the French did not grant immediate independence. Hence, even a purely formal and temporary avowal of Russian support for French policy cannot have been encouraging to the Algerians. Indeed, it is not unlikely that Khrushchev's statement undermined the position of rebel extremists who wanted to continue the war, or at least to set a high price on a cease-fire.

The possibility that Khrushchev was and is genuinely prepared to support a cease-fire in Algeria cannot be dismissed. He may have calculated that negotiations leading to a cease-fire were inevitable in any case and that he might as well seek to reap the maximum political advantage from them. At a minimum, his Supreme Soviet speech served notice that he was not prepared to do anything to prevent such negotiations.

The Chinese Communists clearly regarded Khrushchev's tactics in this area as ill-advised and potentially disastrous. They made no comment whatever on any portion of Khrushchev's Supreme Soviet speech, few portions of which could have appealed to them. They did not follow Moscow or the French Communist Party in publicly reversing their hostile attitude toward De Gaulle's proposals. A commentary on November 12 explicitly contradicted the spirit of Khrushchev's statement by denouncing De Gaulle's proposals as "nothing but a trick from A to Z."[51] In the following months Peking continued to indicate its opposition to a negotiated settlement of the Algerian rebellion, encouraged the Algerian rebels to fight through to final victory, and denounced the French proposals as a political maneuver. On November 23, the Peking radio broadcast a statement from an Algerian leader who said flatly: "The Algerian war will continue with greater intensity from now on until independence is achieved." No such statements emanated from Moscow. In celebrating "Imperialists, Quit Africa Day" in late November, Peking referred to French political deceptions and intrigues and said that the Algerian national liberation army was "growing mightier in battle and winning one victory after another."[52] The FLN (the Algerian rebels), said Peking, would "uphold their struggle until they won true independence." The implication, of course, was that anything the French offered in negotiations would not be *true* independence.

The differences between Soviet and Chinese statements on Algerian policy persisted right up to the eve of the abortive summit conference in May 1960. An address of March 3 by De Gaulle on Algerian policy—not attacked by Moscow—was roundly indicted by Peking radio as the statement of an "imperialist" and "reactionary."

Why did the Chinese Communists manifest such hostility toward Khrushchev's tactics? The Chinese Communists looked with disfavor on a negotiated settlement in Algeria not only because they hoped to draw the Algerian rebels closer to themselves but, equally important, because continuation of the war would serve as a vivid illustration of their contention that no colonial people could free itself finally and irrevocably without an armed fight. Algeria, in short, was a lesson in insurrection that the Chinese hoped would spread throughout the remaining colonial territories in Africa, and to the "semi-colonial" countries in Latin America and Asia. A *Hung ch'i* article in mid-March referred to the Algerian example and also to the "massive armed resistance" in the Congo, Nyasaland, Ruanda-Urundi, and Uganda, and concluded that the African people could not be deceived. "There has not been a single case in history," said the writer, "in which the colonialists withdrew from the colonies of their own accord, nor will such a thing ever happen in the future." He summed up the Chinese belief in the importance of the Algerian example succinctly: "This course [war for national liberation] persisted in by the Algerian people is of vital significance to the African national liberation movement as a whole."[53]

On March 20 Peking declared a special "Algeria Day" and marked it by considerable propaganda on Chinese support for the Algerian cause. The statement issued by the Chinese Committee for Afro-Asian solidarity noted that China's Algerian "brothers are now at the forefront of the struggle against imperialism and colonialism," and affirmed that the Algerians had set a "brilliant example" for other African peoples.[54]

One of the principal Soviet problems in handling the Algerian question has been the danger that China, by adopting an irreconcilably anti-French stand in sharp contrast to Moscow's middle-of-the-road stance, would be able to increase its own influence with the Algerian rebels, and ultimately with the independent Algerian government, at the expense of the Russians. The growing Soviet concern over this possibility was evidenced in Mikoyan's April 18 press conference in Baghdad.[55]

Mikoyan replied to a question put to him by the Iraq News Agency correspondent on the Soviet position on Algeria. The correspondent wanted to know why, if the Soviet Union was the staunchest defender of the Algerian people's rights, it had not recognized the Algerian Government, "although there are countries which have done so." There is little doubt that the correspondent meant Peking. Whether the Chinese had put him up to this embarrassing question or whether the Iraqi correspondent simply wished to play the Chinese off against the Russians, Mikoyan quickly replied that "we are giving the greatest possible support to Algeria, *even more so than do some of the countries which have recognized the Algerian government*" [italics supplied].[56]

In response to the next question, as to whether the USSR would send volunteers to fight in Algeria, Mikoyan replied sharply: "Do you understand what this would mean? When you think about it, you will understand that you asked this question to no purpose. Some people who heard your question will hasten to declare that the Bolsheviks want to occupy Algeria by volunteers and make it [their] colony. (Laughter and animation.)"[57]

Peking's mounting interest in the Algerian war was once again illustrated by the extensive publicity given an Algerian rebel delegation which visited China from April 30 to May 20, 1960. It seemed apparent that the Algerians came to Peking in the hopes of receiving commitments for military and financial aid. On May 24, following the delegation's return to Cairo, NCNA reported the leader of the delegation, Vice Premier Krim Balkacem, as having noted that China was "willing to support the Algerian revolution in its struggle against imperialism *with all means.*" An NCNA review of a May 12 article in the FLN organ *El-Mujahid* quoted the paper as stating that "the assistance from the great socialist country [the CPR] is valuable and can contribute to the Algerian revolution in the military and financial spheres."[58] Several newspaper reports from Paris quoted sources there to the effect that the Chinese had prepared to supply immediately 1,000 technicians who would give instructions to FLN fighters on how to handle new Chinese weapons, and that the Chinese had solved the technical problem of delivering arms and other supplies.[59]

Reports to the effect that Krim headed a pro-Chinese faction in the FLN against "Europeans" like Ferhat Abbas were strengthened by the praise accorded the Chinese by Krim in his public statements in Peking.[60] On May 19, in his final banquet speech, he said, "We have been dazzled by what we have seen. The achievements of the big leap forward are evident. Being limited in time . . . we have only seen a tiny part. Yet this suffices to serve as an example for us."[61] The final communiqué signed by the Algerian delegation noted in good Peking fashion that genuine and permanent peace could not be achieved until the colonialist oppressors and imperialist aggressors had been "eliminated" and that the attainment of world peace depended on the "resolute struggles" of the people of the world against imperialism and colonialism.[62] The communiqué also noted that the Algerian Provisional Government "greatly admired the economic and social achievements of the Chinese people in their socialist construction." The Chinese, however, evidently could not get the FLN delegation to go so far as to condemn the United States. "Both sides" agreed to several propositions, but only the "Chinese Government," according to the communiqué, "severely denounced and criticized French imperialism, *aided by U.S. imperialism."* It has long been one of the primary goals of the Chinese to link all the colonial and other problems of the world to the American devil.

The reason why Peking is much more interested than Moscow in stirring up colonial wars such as the Algerian war may lie mainly in Peking's calculation that such wars are the principal means by which it can extend its influence. It cannot compete with the Russian aid program or with the extensive Russian technical assistance to underdeveloped areas. If Peking is to extend its influence in the colonial areas, it can do so only by encouraging civil wars and guerrilla fighting in which the local insurgents will be forced, as the Algerian rebels were, to come to China for aid and advice. The Russians, on the other hand, can exercise their influence by other less risky means.

CHAPTER 11

KHRUSHCHEV IN PEKING:

OCTOBER 1959

A<small>T THE</small> Washington Press Club on September 16, 1959, an American newsman asked Khrushchev what would be the purpose of his visit to Peking after his tour of the United States. "That," he replied hesitatingly before giving an innocuous reply, "is apparently the most 'difficult' question."[1]

As we have seen, Khrushchev was greeted on arrival in Peking with a barrage of articles by CCP leaders which vigorously defended Chinese foreign and domestic policies against Soviet criticism, accused "some people" of "ignorance of Marxism-Leninism," implicitly attacked Soviet policy toward the uncommitted countries, and indirectly warned Khrushchev that the same Russians errors which had led to severe losses for the Chinese Communist movement in the 1920's were now being repeated in the colonial areas. Previously, in fact on the very day Khrushchev had arrived in the United States, Chinese objections to Khrushchev's negotiation tactics had been spelled out in the CCP's leading Party journal.

It should be remembered that Khrushchev was coming to Peking *after* his talks with President Eisenhower. Mao may well have reflected that the President had seen fit to journey to Western Europe to consult with *his* allies before his talks with the Soviet premier. Khrushchev had not emulated Eisenhower. Indeed, he had made the slight to China the more obvious when, in response to a specific question on August 5 as to whether he intended to consult with his allies prior to his American visit, he had cavalierly dismissed the question with these words: "We will probably exchange views with our friends *in one way or another,* but I do not think that we need all gather for any discussions. The question of ensuring world peace is so clear that it is not a controversial one for the socialist countries. That is why we are sure that all the socialist countries will approve our activity in that direction. . . . " [italics supplied].[2] Khrushchev could not have been unaware that the question of "ensuring world peace" was not "so clear" to his Chinese allies. That he was ready to wave them off in this manner suggests he thought that his Chinese comrades, still vitally dependent on the

277

USSR, would have no alternative but to go along with Soviet policies. If this was his belief, it was not borne out by events.

In his two public speeches in Peking, Khrushchev made little effort to meet the objections to Soviet strategy that the Chinese had been voicing for almost two years. In his arrival speech on September 30 he said that "everything must be done to clear the atmosphere and create conditions for friendship among peoples."[3] In his banquet speech the same evening he reasserted his belief that the Bloc would defeat the West in peaceful economic competition.[4] He said that President Eisenhower and other Western leaders had begun to show a more realistic understanding of the world situation and that Eisenhower in particular "understands the need to relax international tension." Therefore, he continued, "we on our part must do all we can to exclude war as a means of settling disputed questions." There was "no other way" than that of peaceful coexistence.

Then, aiming straight at the heart of the Chinese belief that the Bloc could pursue more militant policies all over the world under the shield of the Soviet nuclear deterrent, Khrushchev said: "We must think realistically and understand the contemporary situation correctly. This, of course, does not by any means signify that if we are so strong, then we must test by force the stability of the capitalist system. This would be wrong; the peoples would not understand and would never support those who think of acting in this way."[5] A few sentences later, he seemed to hit at the Chinese exhortations to export revolution: "The socialist countries . . . fire the hearts of men by the *force of their example* in building socialism and *thus lead them to follow in their footsteps*. The question of when this or that country will take the path of socialism is decided by its own people. This, for us, is the holy of holies" [italics supplied].[6]

If Mao had had any hopes of relying on a so-called "China lobby" in the Kremlin, allegedly led by Suslov, the latter's speech in Peking two days earlier cannot have given the Chinese leader much encouragement. Suslov was somewhat less enthusiastic than Khrushchev about the possibilities for relaxing tension, but he nonetheless supported the broad outlines of Khrushchev's global strategy. While he spoke of forces in the West interested in keeping up the cold war, and, discordantly, of the "*projected* relaxation" of tension, he insisted that "wars must be prevented because in our age—the age of the atom and of rocket technology—they threaten *mankind* with countless sufferings and disasters" [italics supplied].[7] This line of reasoning—that the development of military technology threatened civilization and by implication required an adjustment of Soviet strategy—was one vigorously rejected by Mao.

Suslov also made it clear that he supported Khrushchev's long-range policy of seducing the uncommitted countries by trade, aid, and example rather than by the more revolutionary method the Chinese believed necessary for many or most of these countries: "The socialist states resolutely support the strivings of the countries of Asia and Africa to develop their national economies. We are extending help, and, as our possibilities grow, *will extend still more help,* to all countries of Asia and Africa" [italics supplied].[8]

Finally, Suslov defended Khrushchev's trip to the United States as having been accomplished "with honor, dignity and brilliance . . . and with Leninist adherence to principle." In effect, he was disclaiming insinuations in the Chinese press that Khrushchev had watered down Leninist principles in making this trip.

The very fact the Khrushchev allowed Suslov to head a Soviet delegation to Peking before his own arrival and at a time when Sino-Soviet relations were so strained suggests his confidence that Mao would not be able to exploit whatever differences there may have been within the Soviet leadership over foreign policy. The sending of Suslov may even have been intended as a deliberate demonstration to Mao that the Soviet leadership was united on Khrushchev's foreign policy. For it seems likely that one of Mao's calculations may have been that he could force a change in Khrushchev's policy by appealing to Soviet leaders who, he may have believed, shared his dismay over Khrushchev's strategic views and his personal diplomacy with the West.

Whatever arguments Khrushchev and Suslov privately used to defend Soviet strategy, however, it is apparent that the Chinese rejected them. The two sides failed to issue their customary pious joint communiqué and Khrushchev, in his departure speech, made the remarkable statement that "*we Communists of the Soviet Union* consider it our sacred duty, our primary task . . . to utilize all possibilities in order to liquidate the cold war."[9] It seems that Khrushchev could no longer speak for China on this question.

The official Polish Communist delegation to the anniversary celebrations came away convinced, according to a report from the *New York Times* correspondent, that there were important "differences of approach and policy" between Moscow and Peking.[10] The Polish Communists gathered from talks in Peking with both the Russians and the Chinese that Chinese resentment at being left out of the summit talks had been made quite clear to Khrushchev. According to the Poles, the Chinese were also annoyed with Khrushchev for not giving sufficient support to Peking's venture against the offshore islands (see Chapter 4). The Poles also supposed that Chinese Communist resentment at being left out of high-level negotiations was one of the motivations behind Peking's decision to stir up trouble with India over the boundary question. The October incident in Kashmir, where several Indian soldiers were ambushed and killed, was said to be intended as a reminder to India, the Soviet Union, and the West that there were important areas of the world where settlements could be reached only by direct negotiation with Peking.

Khrushchev's Formal Report to the Supreme Soviet, October 31

Khrushchev's speeches in the USSR after returning from Peking reaffirmed his belief in the struggle for peace as "the main task of today" and made oblique attacks on the Chinese Communists for advocating tougher policies toward the West. In these speeches, Khrushchev reaffirmed as well his apparently genuine fear of a nuclear holocaust. Thus, in Vladivostok on October 6, he cautioned that the United States and the USSR could not confront each other like "two cocks ready to lay hold and peck each other."[11] He recalled that, during his meeting with President Eisenhower, the latter had expressed his fear of war, and that he, Khrushchev, had replied, "Only an unreasonable person can be fearless of war in our days." While it was necessary to fight if war was "imposed upon a people," it was "unreasonable to be eager for war. . . . " Khrushchev reaffirmed his confidence in the President as a man of peace and "farsightedness."

Speaking in Novosibirsk on October 10, Khrushchev defined his understanding of peaceful coexistence in a way which suggested he was replying to Chinese criticism that coexistence and revolutionary progress were incompatible: "Peaceful coexistence must be understood correctly. Coexistence means the continuation of the struggle between the two social systems, but of a struggle by peaceful means, without war, without the interference of a state in the domestic affairs of another state. *One should not be afraid*. We must struggle resolutely and consistently for our ideas, for our way of life, for our socialist system. The partisans of capitalism, too, will not, of course, abandon their way of life, their ideology; they will fight. We hold that this struggle must be economic, political, and ideological, but not military" [italics supplied].[12]

Khrushchev's formal report to the Supreme Soviet on October 31 was his first effort to describe the main direction of Soviet policy since his talks with President Eisenhower. This speech was the high point of Khrushchev's climb toward a *détente*.[13] He began by contending that "a more sensible understanding of the relation of forces in the international arena is now beginning to prevail in the West." The West was making a "more sober evaluation of the situation." The new Western evaluation was "bound to lead to the conclusion" that the West could not use its military forces against the socialist world. The factors favoring peace were the increasing strength of the Bloc, the rise of the newly independent countries, the peace-loving forces in the capitalist countries themselves, and the "many statesmen" in the West who "begin to understand" that war threatens destruction.

Peaceful coexistence, continued Khrushchev, was not something to be desired or not desired. It was an "objective necessity" proceeding from the "present situation in the world," namely that both sides "possess weapons which would cause perilous consequences if they were put into action." Moreover, said Khrushchev, coexistence was the existing state of affairs: the question was how to coexist "on a reasonable basis."

Reasonable coexistence, he continued, presupposed "mutual concessions in the interests of peace," a position based on principle which was at the same time "flexible." Lenin had taught that the working class, "before as well as after it has gained power, must be able to pursue a flexible policy, compromise, and come to agreement whenever life and the interests of the cause demand it."[14]

"Mutual concessions," a term which Khrushchev repeated

281

several times, did not mean that there would be any ideological concessions or compromise on "principles." There is, he continued, "no reason to fear that the peoples of the socialist countries will be seduced by the capitalist devil and give up socialism. To think differently means not to believe wholly in the strength of socialism. . . . " A paragraph later, Khrushchev recalled Lenin's "flexible foreign policy" during the period of the Brest peace in 1918: "It was during the period of the Brest peace that Vladimir Ilyich Lenin set the task of concluding peace with Germany in order to insure for the young Soviet state the possibility for peaceful construction of socialism. Lenin and the Party then had to conduct a persistent struggle against Trotsky, who came out then with his Pilate's objections and put forward his *notorious slogan of 'neither peace nor war'* by *which he played into the hands of the German imperialists*. It is known that Trotsky's adventurist policy was used by German imperialism against the Soviet country. . . . Such were the fruits of adventurism in policy" [italics supplied].[15]

By alluding to the Brest peace treaty between Soviet Russia and Germany in which the USSR had agreed to annexation of some of its territory in order to buy time for consolidating the new regime, Khrushchev seemed to be suggesting that the Chinese Communists should emulate Soviet policy in this period and accept a temporary annexation of its territory—i.e. Taiwan—as there was no alternative except war. Moreover, the very mention of Trotsky, the archheretic, is indicative of the seriousness of the charge Khrushchev was, in effect, making against Mao Tse-tung. Trotsky is virtually an "unperson" in Soviet media. Despite the fact that some of the policies advocated by some of the anti-party group in 1957 could have been identified by Khrushchev with Trotskyism, he did not go so far even in indicting his own internal Party opponents. Khrushchev was virtually asserting that, just as Trotsky "played into the hands" of the German imperialists after World War I by refusing to accept an annexationist peace, Mao was now playing into the hands of the Western imperialists by advocating a premature policy of militancy.

After thus severely condemning Mao's policy, Khrushchev went on to assert that the USSR was sincere when it spoke of peaceful coexistence and that it was not advancing the coexistence slogan simply for tactical reasons. He contended that Marxists had "never considered that war among states is necessary for the victory of the working class."

Khrushchev then listed the various indications that a thaw was occurring in international relations. These included the nuclear test ban talks, the foreign ministers' conference, the various exchanges of visits—all of "positive significance." He described his visit with President Eisenhower, as a "particularly important and far-reaching step in the direction of radically improving relations between the USSR and the United States and generally relaxing international tension." Many outstanding American personalities, he said, "with the President at their head," understood the longing of the American people for peace and wanted to find ways to consolidate peace. Moreover, partly because of his visit, there was a better understanding in the United States of the Soviet desire for peace.[16]

In speaking of Taiwan, Khrushchev gave only a mild endorsement of China's rights to the island: "the legal and moral right is on its side." Turning to Korea and Laos, Khrushchev cautioned against the use of force, which Peking had been threatening for some time in both areas. His "impression" was, he said, that the "United States is not seeking a military conflict there [South Korea]," contrary to the Peking contention then and now that the United States was building up for aggression. With regard to Laos, Khrushchev said the USSR was "against the existence of even the smallest source of war in Laos which could give food to the aggressive forces." Given a "sensible approach" there, the "skirmishes taking place could be soon eliminated" and the situation could be "normalized."[17]

Concerning the Sino-Indian border dispute, Khrushchev maintained his neutral attitude: he was grieved that casualties had occurred on "both sides," and he thought the issues could be resolved to the "satisfaction of both sides." This was the first time in Bloc history that the USSR had taken a neutral position in a dispute between a Communist and a non-Communist state, a position which Peking undoubtedly regarded as a betrayal of "proletarian internationalism."

The Soviet leader went on to urge a solution to disarmament, painting a gloomy picture of the consequences of war—consequences not only for the capitalists but for all. A new war, he said

—coming close to Malenkov's heresy of 1954 that civilization would be destroyed—would cause mankind "unprecedented sacrifice, devastation, and suffering."

Khrushchev put himself on record before the Russian people as favoring a long-range accommodation with the West and as prepared to make as well as to receive concessions in order to achieve the accommodation. He attributed sincerity to Western leaders, particularly to President Eisenhower, in their professions of peaceful intentions. Having seen for himself the state of opinion in the United States, he told his listeners, in effect, that he was convinced a long-term stabilization was possible. This is not to say that Khrushchev had overnight abandoned the "world revolution," as the Chinese were in effect maintaining. He did seem to believe, however, that the revolution would be a long-term affair which could not be promoted aggressively in the nuclear era.

To Mao, this speech must have been anathema. The April 1960 *Hung ch'i* and *Jen-min jih-pao* articles[18] indicting the whole theoretical structure of Soviet foreign policy were in large part directed at this speech. The speech probably marked a new downward turn in the increasingly troubled Sino-Soviet relationship. The line between Khrushchev and Mao was now drawn in classical fashion. Khrushchev was calling Mao an adventurist and Trotskyite who was pushing ahead much too fast both in his domestic programs and in his plans for world revolution. Mao was in effect calling Khrushchev an appeaser, and was soon to call him a revisionist, for abandoning the traditional Leninist views on imperialism, war, and peace.

In another speech—to the Hungarian Party Congress on December 1—Khrushchev advanced a long step forward in his ideological indictment of Mao's domestic and foreign policies. This time Khrushchev added a warning that deviation from the Soviet line would not be tolerated—a warning which seems to have had little effect on Mao.[19]

Khrushchev began by reviewing the lessons to be learned from the "mistakes" of the Stalinist Rakosi leadership in Hungary, lessons which, he declared, "other Communist and workers' parties cannot but heed." He decried "armchair leaders" who "order the masses about"; he warned against "disregarding objective conditions" and ruling by "decree" instead of by persuasion; he avowed that, although no Communist leaders were proof against mistakes in socialist construction, "one must have the courage *openly* to admit one's mistakes and to correct them in time" [italics supplied]. In all this, he seemed to be aiming at Mao's headlong economic policies and to be calling on him for a public recantation.

Turning then to a defense of the 20th Congress and the re-evaluation of Stalin, Khrushchev did not agree with "some people" who contended that the de-Stalinization question should "not have been raised so sharply." The Chinese had already indicated their dislike of Khrushchev's handling of this question.

In another series of passages, unmistakably directed at Mao, Khrushchev warned against foolishness and conceit and stressed the need for discipline in the Communist movement: "Even now the enemies of socialism do not abandon their plans of smashing the socialist camp and are, of course, looking for the weak links in it. They want to rout the socialist countries one by one. We must bear this danger in mind, because it is real, and we must do everything to deprive our enemies of these hopes. *In these sinister plans the only ally of imperialist aspirations and hopes can be our foolishness.*

"*If we become conceited, if we commit mistakes in our leadership, if we distort the teaching of Marxism-Leninism on the building of socialism and Communism, these mistakes can be exploited by the enemies of Communism as was done in 1956. . . .*

"Our enemies will attempt to set one socialist country against another in order to weaken the forces of socialism. We must bear in mind that the striving to make the socialist countries quarrel among themselves, to *undermine* the relations of friendship and brotherhood between them, is one of the forms of class struggle employed by our enemy. *This is why the immutable principles of proletarian internationalism are the supreme, irrevocable law of the international Communist movement. . . .*

"We must make sensible use of the great advantages of the socialist system and strengthen the world socialist camp in every way. . . . We must be masters of Leninism. We must not fall behind or go too far ahead. *We must,* figuratively speaking, *synchronize our watches.* If the leadership of this or that country becomes conceited, this can only play into the hands of the enemy. In this case, the socialist countries themselves, the leadership itself, will help the enemy to fight socialism, to fight Communism, *and this cannot be allowed"* [italics supplied].[20]

A little further on in the same speech, Khrushchev was back again refuting Mao's position on peace and war. "No Communist party anywhere, if it really is Communist," he declared, "has ever said that it hopes to achieve its aims through war. Nor indeed, could it say so." Although this was a distortion of the Chinese position, it was a rebuke to Mao's view that armed struggle should be encouraged and supported in many areas of the world.

In these warnings, Khrushchev hinted that Chinese foreign policy was threatening to help the common enemy to "undermine" Sino-Soviet solidarity. Mao's domestic policies, he implied, might lead to insurrection as did Rakosi's in Hungary. Finally, Mao must obey the "supreme irrevocable" law of proletarian internationalism by submitting to Soviet policy. Independent foreign policies in other socialist countries would not be tolerated.

On December 21, the eightieth anniversary of Stalin's birth, *Pravda* and *Jen-min jih-pao* presented divergent interpretations of Stalin's role, and thereby highlighted the strategic and doctrinal differences between the two parties. *Pravda* gave a balanced presentation of Stalin's achievements and failures and avoided his views on war and foreign policy; *Jen-min jih-pao* attended almost exclusively to Stalin's virtues and, in what could only have been a criticism of Khrushchev's *détente* line, reminded its readers that Stalin had urged the need for a "high degree of vigilance against imperialism."[21] The Chinese editorial quoted a 1951 statement by Stalin in which he warned that, "should the warmongers resort to lies to trap and deceive the people in order to drag them into another war, such a war would become inevitable." This statement has been ignored in recent years by Soviet media and was in sharp contrast to Khrushchev's emphasis at the time on the possibility of excluding war from society forever.

In September 1959, then, Khrushchev apparently came to Peking in the mistaken belief that China's dependence on the USSR would force the CCP to accommodate its foreign policies.

His visit seemed only to sharpen the already considerable differences. Khrushchev publicly criticized Mao's thinking as Trotskyist, and as playing into the hands of the enemy. To Mao's dismay, he took a conciliatory attitude toward De Gaulle's proposals for ending the Algerian War. He failed to endorse Chinese positions on several Far Eastern issues. He derided Mao's domestic policies. He accused the Chinese leader of conceit and warned that opposition to fundamental Soviet policies would not be tolerated. By the end of 1959, Khrushchev was suggesting in a fairly open way that the relationship between the two leading Communist parties had deteriorated to a dangerous point.

CHAPTER 12

THE WORSENING OF THE DISPUTE:

EARLY 1960

IN THE first two months of 1960 there was abundant evidence that the Sino-Soviet dispute on strategy, far from being resolved, was becoming more bitter. This was apparent in divergent Chinese and Russian reactions to President Eisenhower's State of the Union message, in the *Hung ch'i* editorial on New Year's day, in the Chinese response to Khrushchev's important January 14 speech, and in a sharp division between the Soviet and Chinese representatives at the Warsaw Pact conference in February.

The President's State of the Union Message

The sharp contrast between Soviet and Chinese views on the possibility and desirability of achieving a *détente* with the United States was well illustrated in the divergent reactions to President Eisenhower's State of the Union message on January 7, 1960. Moscow, in its limited comment, did not criticize the President personally, but chose from the message some of the more hopeful signs (in the Soviet view) that the United States was prepared to ease international tensions, and was in general restrained in what criticism it offered. The Chinese, on the other hand, were unreservedly critical both of the President personally and of what they characterized as a two-faced effort to prepare for war while talking of peace.

The Tass summary of Eisenhower's message began by stating: "The President emphasized in his message that in his final year at the White House he is determined to throw every ounce of his energy into insuring world peace. . . . "[1] Tass further quoted the President as being "always ready to participate with the Soviet Union in serious discussion of [nuclear testing] or any other subjects that may lead to peace with justice." It went on to qualify this, however, by pointing out the President's emphasis on the need to maintain "a high degree" of military effectiveness. In a routine commentary on January 9, Moscow Radio's North American service outlined some of the proposals in the President's speech and commented, "We in the USSR can fully agree with the general trend of the President's suggestions." On the same day, Moscow's European service called attention to the fact that many sections of the American press had interpreted Eisenhower's speech as further evidence of his desire for a further relaxation of international tension.

The Chinese views on the President's message were set forth in more authoritative media and in much more bellicose terms. The *Jen-min jih-pao* editorial of January 21 began its frontal assault by contending that the message was "most convincing evidence of the imperialist nature of the United States."[2] In going through the text of the message, it continued, one could not detect "even a trace" of any concrete steps the United States would take toward relaxing tension; nor did Eisenhower make "any proposal" favorable to peace.

From the State of the Union message, said *Jen-min jih-pao*, "only one conclusion could be drawn": there is no change whatever in the "fundamental policy of arms expansion and war preparations which the United States has long pursued." The Chinese editorial pointed out that the United States (1) was speeding up its programs for the development of intercontinental missiles; (2) was speeding up the construction of two IRBM bases in Italy; (3) was continuing to prepare for war in the Far East, as evidenced by its recently concluded military alliance with Japan, its continued arming of Chinese Nationalist forces, its repeated boasts that it would defend the offshore islands, and its expansion of missile bases in Japan, South Korea, and Taiwan; (4) was threatening to resume nuclear tests at any time; (5) had mapped out in the NATO Council in December 1959 a ten-year program for strengthening NATO and giving it the power to carry on large-scale nuclear warfare as well as greater flexibility in the conduct of local warfare; (6) was stepping up the armament of West Germany with nuclear arms and missiles.[3]

In the Chinese view, America's two-faced policy of talking peace while preparing for war was a maneuver designed to "win time to regain military superiority." To support this view, the Chinese Party newspaper cited a report by an American research group to the effect that the major problem facing the United States in the early 1960's was the need to eliminate the missile gap. Since this task could not be achieved rapidly, according to the report, even if a shock plan were instituted, gaining time was now of the utmost importance.[4]

The Chinese interpretation of American *détente* tactics was that they were nothing more than a maneuver to buy the necessary time to overcome Soviet military superiority. By implication this meant that people like Khrushchev, who thought that any meaningful *détente* could be achieved even for a limited period, were playing into the hands of the West. While the Bloc was making unilateral arms cuts and allowing its vigilance to be undermined by "the spirit of Camp David," the West would be stealthily trying to regain the missile lead and to strengthen its military position.

In the first 1960 issue of *Hung ch'i*, Yu Chao-li reasserted, in terms similar to those cited above, the Chinese argument against a *détente*.[5] The United States was pursuing a two-faced strategy of putting out a smokescreen of peace while continuing to suppress the national liberation movements and building up its military position throughout the world. To strengthen peace it was necessary to continue the struggle against U.S. imperialism. All viewpoints which overestimated the strength of the enemy and underestimated the strength of the people were wrong. Yu Chao-li argued that the socialist forces "had got the upper hand over the imperialist forces," and that Mao had pointed this out at the 1957 Moscow conference, even though "not everyone recognized this new situation clearly when it first appeared."

A subsequent article in the January 21st *Jen-min jih-pao* warned that although "United States double-dealing" was being recognized by more and more people, "from East to West," and although "it may still deceive some people at present, it cannot fool them for long."[6]

Khrushchev's Speech to the Supreme Soviet: Differences over Disarmament

In his long speech to the Supreme Soviet on January 14, 1960, Khrushchev sketched the outlines of a comprehensive doctrine of military strategy, bringing together the ideas about modern war he had been propounding publicly since mid-1957.[7] In essence, this doctrine is based on the dominant role of strategic nuclear weapons in modern war. In contrast to the old battlefield-oriented concept of war prevalent in past Soviet military doctrine, Khrushchev contended that in the future war "there would be little to resemble previous wars," that war would "begin in the heart of the warring countries," and that every strategic area would be subjected to attack during the "first minutes" of war. This was the latest step in the revolution in Soviet military thinking that had been going on since 1955. Khrushchev now proposed a one-third cut in the Soviet armed forces from 3.6 to 2.4 million men. He asserted that this troop reduction would save 16 to 17 billion rubles a year for the Soviet economy and that it would not in the least diminish Soviet fire-power or reduce the effectiveness of its deterrent. Khrushchev further offered the "hope" that "other countries" would follow the road to curtailment of their armed forces, expressed the view that disarmament "would pave the way to a lasting peace and to economic progress in all countries and for all peoples," and contended that the money saved could be used to aid all the economically underdeveloped countries and to reduce taxes in all countries. On June 2, after the collapse of the summit, the USSR offered a new disarmament program in which several of the above-mentioned Khrushchev statements were reiterated.

Whether or not Khrushchev was seriously interested in reaching a disarmament agreement, or an agreement on nuclear test cessations, negotiations concerning which had been going on since 1957, there are various pieces of evidence to suggest that the Chinese feared the Russians were prepared to reach some kinds of agreement with the West which would jeopardize their interests. First of all, there was Khrushchev's own curious statement to the Supreme Soviet that the forthcoming summit talks would not ignore "the views of the states not represented at the conference," that such "apprehensions (were) absolutely groundless," and that the Soviet Government "never had and (did) not have any intention of reaching agreement behind the backs of other countries on matters directly affecting their interests."[8] This statement followed one in which Khrushchev mentioned both the disarmament and test ban issues as requiring negotiation at the summit meeting scheduled for May; it is quite likely that he had China in mind in giving such gratuitous reassurance.

Two days after Khrushchev's Supreme Soviet speech, a *Jen-min jih-pao* editorial applauded it as a manifestation of the Soviet desire for peace and an example of the Soviet Union's confidence in its own strength.[9] At the same time, the Chinese paper contended that the United States was building up its military strength in order to improve its capabilities for both total and limited war, noted that West Germany would soon expand its own troops by one third, and suggested that the United States was not eager for disarmament but only for an "arms drive in preparation for war."

Five days later, on January 21, the Chinese Communists issued a public statement that seemed intended as much for the Russians as for the West. They asserted that "any international agreement concerning disarmament, without the formal participation of the Chinese People's Republic and the signature of her delegate, cannot of course have any binding force on China."[10] No Soviet media acknowledged or supported this statement.

In February the Chinese public refusal to be bound by any international disarmament agreement without its participation was extended to "all other international agreements,"[11] and other Chinese media warned it was "a kind of unpractical fantasy to pin our hope for a lasting world peace on the possibility that the imperialists might agree to, and actually execute, an all-round, thorough disarmament."[12]

A few months later Chinese objections to Soviet disarmament policy became more explicit. On June 7, two days after the new Soviet disarmament proposals had been presented to the West, a *Jen-min jih-pao* editorial insisted that the Bloc must "strengthen" rather than reduce its armed forces: "Confronted by the imperialist bloc headed by U.S. imperialism which is armed to the teeth and filled with wild ambitions, it is entirely necessary for the socialist countries to maintain a high degree of vigilance and *strengthen their armed forces* in order to defend their socialist homelands and world peace" [italics supplied].[13]

The next day the Chinese delegate to the WFTU meeting in Peking, Liu Chang-sheng, a member of the Central Committee, all but openly criticized the Soviet troop cut and Soviet disarmament policy in general. Liu went so far as to extract specific quotations from Khrushchev's January 14 speech and the subsequent Soviet disarmament proposal for purposes of refutation and ridicule. The speech began with these words: "The purpose of putting forward such a proposal is to arouse the people throughout the world to unite and oppose the imperialist scheme for arms drives and war preparations, to unmask the aggressive and bellicose nature of imperialism. . . . But there are people who believe that such a proposal can be realized while imperialism still exists and that the danger of war can be eliminated by relying on such a proposal. This is an unrealistic illusion."[14]

Elsewhere in his speech Liu quoted without attribution, and rejected Khrushchev's view that arms funds could be used for "assisting underdeveloped countries"—a "downright whitewash" of imperialism. Nor could one say—and again he was paraphrasing Khrushchev's January 14 speech—that disarmament would "bring general progress to people as a whole." A world without armament, said Liu, was possible only "when the socialist revolution is victorious throughout the world."[15]

A further indication that the Chinese were annoyed by Soviet disarmament policy was Liu's insistence that "the Soviet Union and the other socialist countries should continue to develop their lead in the sphere of atomic energy," with the implication that a disarmament agreement, particularly a test ban, would hamper them from maintaining and developing that lead and would particularly hinder China's plans to become a nuclear power. Finally, Liu implied that any disarmament agreement was worthless because even after its conclusion imperialism could still "tear it to pieces."[16]

Why should Peking have objected to unilateral Soviet troop cuts and Soviet disarmament proposals? Khrushchev himself provided one possible answer in his January 14 speech when he asked, as a rhetorical question, whether the troop cut would "undermine" the Soviet deterrent.[17] He claimed that it would not do so, because, as he had stated many times before, the West was deterred from both all-out and local war by Soviet strategic weapons. Mao, on the other hand, had been contending for some years that, although the West was deterred for the time being from general war, it was not deterred from local wars. Mao may well have been concerned that the Soviet troop cut would undermine the Soviet capability to fight precisely the kind of war that Mao regarded as "inevitable"—local war.

Mao may also have been concerned with the long-range drift of Soviet disarmament policy. Liu Chang-sheng may have had this in mind in his remarks on June 8 about "people" who think that the danger of war can be eliminated by "relying" on disarmament pro-

posals. Even if Mao exaggerated the "seriousness" of Soviet disarmament proposals, he seems to have felt a real concern that the
USSR might be jeopardizing its military superiority. Last and
certainly not least, Peking may well have feared that the signing of
a test ban with the West would delay if not eliminate its own
chances to become a nuclear power. If the USSR were to sign a test
ban agreement with the West, Peking would be faced with the
alternative dilemmas of acceding to such an agreement and thus renouncing a nuclear capability short of what it could pry from the
USSR or of flouting world opinion by defying such a test ban at a
later date.

Another point in Khrushchev's Supreme Soviet speech must
have been read with great interest, if not dismay, in Peking. In a
key passage on the relative military strength of the two camps,
Khrushchev stated: "Impregnability is a rather relative concept."
The USSR's enemies "will not be marking time [and] can make
good their temporary lagging [in nuclear weapons] . . . and may,
sooner or later, draw even with us."[18] Khrushchev watered down
this possibility a paragraph later when he contended that meanwhile the USSR would not "sit with arms folded," but he nonetheless left open the possibility that the West would reach a state of
nuclear parity with the USSR in the near future. Peking was presumably not pleased by such an admission, for the Chinese had been
arguing since 1957 that the West could never catch up if the USSR
did not fall victim to the spirit of *détente* and reduce its military
program.

The Warsaw Pact Conference:
February 1960

The conference of the political consultative committee of the
member states of the Warsaw Treaty in early February was called
by the Russians probably to demonstrate Bloc unity on the eve of
the forthcoming summit meeting, but, of greater importance, to
discuss the pressing issues of global strategy that divided Moscow
from Peking and threatened to divide the Bloc as a whole.[19]

Before going into the details of the conflict that developed at
the meeting itself, we may find it instructive to examine some of
the evidence that joint Chinese-East German pressure for nuclear
weapons sharing was brought to bear on the Russians on the very

eve of the conference. On January 26, Ulbricht announced in a strongly worded warning to the West Germans that the East German government would "ask our allies to place modern rocket weapons at our disposal" if the atomic armament of West Germany continued. Ulbricht's warning was contained in a 5,000-word letter he sent to Adenauer which was broadcast by the East German radio.[20] The difference between the Soviet and Chinese reactions to this East German threat was striking. Moscow repeated it a few times in foreign language broadcasts to Germany but offered no authoritative comment either approving Ulbricht's suggestion or indicating that Russia might comply. If the Ulbricht threat had been a maneuver coordinated beforehand with the Russians to intimidate the West Germans and to discourage West Germany from seeking nuclear weapons, it is hard to understand why the Russians did not seize on the Ulbricht initiative to dramatize the threat.

In contrast to Moscow's marked restraint, a *Jen-min jih-pao* article of February 4 (the eve of the Warsaw Pact conference) said that the East German request was "not only fully justified but necessary."[21] This Chinese support for the proposal may be compared with the next day's declaration of the Warsaw Treaty states about a "definite change for the better" in the international situation. There was no mention of the possibility that Moscow might transfer rocket weapons to East Germany.[22] In fact, the declaration referred once again to the possibility of a nuclear-free zone in Europe which would include the GDR.

While it might seem improbable that Ulbricht should have been trying, with Chinese support, to force the Soviet hand on the matter, the opposite assumption—that the Russians may have decided to proceed with the atomic armament of East Germany at this moment, six weeks before the ten-power disarmament conference and three months before the summit—looks ever more unlikely.

To the extent that the Chinese encouraged such an East German initiative, it is not hard to see the reason. The Chinese may well have calculated that, if the Russians could be pressed into granting a nuclear capability, however limited and restricted, to the East Germans, the case against such a nuclear capability for China would be drastically weakened.

That the Soviet Union was still resisting pressures to share its nuclear weapons was suggested the following month in an undated letter addressed by Khrushchev to the European Federation Against Atomic Armament and made public by Tass in March.[23] Released about six weeks after President Eisenhower had intimated, at his press conference of February 3, the possibility that the United States would share nuclear weapons with its European allies,[24] the letter seemed calculated to warn that such a step would force the USSR to follow suit. Khrushchev stressed the "undesirability of expansion of the so-called atomic club" and cautioned that American action to supply nuclear weapons to its allies would set off "a kind of chain reaction in the dissemination of nuclear weapons all over the world." Soviet news reports on the President's press conference suggested the unlikelihood that Congress would amend the law in order to permit the diffusion of nuclear weapons, while Chinese reports implied that such nuclear diffusion would take place.[25]

To return to the Warsaw Treaty conference: the February 4 report of the Chinese delegate or "observer," Kang Sheng, an alternate member of the CCP Politburo, was clearly a minority report, since all the Communist states except China refused to publish or broadcast it. It differed notably both in tone and in substance from the much milder declaration issued by the Warsaw Treaty members the next day. Kang acknowledged that "certain procedural agreements had been reached" on disarmament, but he attributed this, not to the good will of the West, but rather to the "repeated struggles" by socialist forces and national revolutionary forces throughout the world.[26] He reiterated the standard Chinese line that American talk about "peace" was merely a stratagem to lull the Bloc. He added the significant new charge that this stratagem was also designed to "dismember the socialist camp," presumably by deliberately fostering revisionism and other centrifugal forces in the individual Communist states.

Kang was most emphatic, in his veiled argument against the Soviet disarmament policy, that the United States would never agree to any real disarmament plan. At the same time, indicating China's own refusal to disarm, he alleged that Chinese forces were less than half their original size.[27] He assumed the position taken by his government on January 21 that the CPR would not be bound by any disarmament agreement in which it did not participate. In contrast, the Warsaw Pact declaration said that the "Warsaw Treaty countries," of which China is not one, had "arrived at the conclusion that the situation [was] now more favorable than ever before for fruitful disarmament talks."[28]

On February 6, a *Jen-min jih-pao* editorial reviewing the Warsaw meeting sniped at Soviet policy. "One cannot but note," it asserted, that the West had in fact stepped up its arms drive.[29] Clearly, the reader would conclude, this was no time for talk of disarmament.

War and Peace

On February 16, the periodical *Chung-kuo ch'ing-nien* published a series of thirteen questions and answers on the subject of war and peace.[30] These constitute one of the frankest and most enlightening Chinese discussions of the question ever published in open media. A brief examination of these questions and answers is essential to an understanding of the fine points of the Chinese view on the likelihood of war and on the possibility and means of averting it.

The thirteen theses may be summarized as follows: (1) it is increasingly difficult for imperialism to provoke a world war, owing to the growing strength of the Bloc, its neutralist friends, and the forces for peace; (3) the principal reason why the United States dares not strike is that the USSR has superiority in missiles; (3) despite the Soviet military lead and despite the fact that time is on the Bloc's side, it is impossible to say that war will not break out, because as long as imperialism exists the danger of war remains; (4) by using peace as a camouflage, the West is trying to gain time to expand its armaments and close the missile gap; (5) the struggle for disarmament is a long and complex one and "no results are possible immediately," because imperialism cannot do away with armaments; for this reason, to rest the hope of lasting peace on the possibility of reaching a disarmament agreement is to indulge in a dream; (6) war is inseparable from class struggle and aggression and wars are the necessary fruits of imperialism; (7) it is possible to strive for a fairly long period of peace, but at the same time we need "to strengthen our own resources, hold fast to Marxist-Leninist policies, ceaselessly expose imperialist schemes, arouse the fighting spirit of the world's people, and maintain a lasting struggle . . . "; (8) a "warless world" can be brought about only by the abolition of imperialism; (9) we seek peace but must never beg it from the imperialists; (10) we must support all "just revolutionary wars" in order to weaken imperialism and secure peace; (11) we cannot seek peace by compromise; (12) there is no foundation to the view that war can never again be the means of settling international disputes, because we can never be sure that imperialism will relinquish war; (13) we oppose war but we do not fear it.

The implications of these theses for Bloc policy are evident: the cold war cannot be abated and, at some points, must become hot; the danger of war will continue to exist and the Bloc must prepare for all contingencies, including all-out war; disarmament negotiations are more or less useless; the Bloc should concentrate first of all, not on negotiations with the West, but on building its own resources and securing its own strength; and the Bloc must actively support all "just" wars.

CHAPTER 13

THE LENIN ANNIVERSARY POLEMICS:

SPRING 1960

THE Chinese Communist indictment of Soviet strategy, which had begun in a low key in the fall of 1957 and had become increasingly shrill in the period shortly before Khrushchev's trip to the United States, reached a new pitch in the spring of 1960. Using the ninetieth anniversary of Lenin's birth (April 22) as a peg, the Chinese launched a comprehensive indictment of Soviet theory, strategy, and tactics in the form of five lengthy and acrimonious doctrinal statements, two in *Hung ch'i* (April 1 and 19), two in *Jen-min jih-pao* (April 22 and 25) and one in a speech on the anniversary itself by Politburo member Lu Ting-i.[1] The Soviet reply came initially in Politburo member Kuusinen's anniversary address on April 22, in articles in *Pravda* and *Sovetskaya rossiya* in June, and finally from Khrushchev himself at the Rumanian Party Congress the same month.

Before the Lenin anniversary articles, the Chinese Communist attacks on Soviet strategy and on the doctrine which was used to justify that strategy had generally been cryptic and moderate. The Chinese articles of April 1960 went so far and so deep that they can be compared in importance only to such watersheds of the post-Stalin era as Khrushchev's secret speech in February 1956. With copious documentation from Lenin and Marx and pointed references to some of Communism's most notorious heretics, the Chinese in effect accused Khrushchev of "revising, emasculating, and betraying" the most fundamental and sacred tenets of Leninism. Such an attack could not avoid having the effect of calling into question Khrushchev's leadership of the Communist movement.[2]

The three principal targets of the Chinese fire were the very three basic ideological innovations which Khrushchev had personally presented to the 20th Party Congress and which provided the doctrinal backdrop for his more flexible post-Stalin global strategy. These were Khrushchev's new doctrines on peaceful coexistence, on the non-inevitability of war, and on the possibility of peaceful roads to power in non-Communist countries. The Chinese articles rejected all three: they advocated a much narrower definition of coexistence which in effect meant that "hot" war could not be altogether avoided; they contended that local and colonial wars were inevitable so long as imperialism remained; and they denied the possibility of peaceful roads to power in the non-Communist world.

In attacking Khrushchev's ideological innovations and the new strategy which went with them, the Chinese were not calling for general war or arguing that general war was inevitable—an interpretation prevalent in the West. They were attacking Khrushchev's gradualist revolutionary conception and putting forth an alternative conception based on the conviction that the West could be defeated sooner than Khrushchev thought if the USSR and the world Communist movement were more aggressive. The Chinese had optimistic estimates of the certainty of success in many areas, particularly in Asia, Africa, and Latin America. They believed that the Soviet deterrent could be invoked to protect revolutionary action in these areas from Western interference. Hence revolutions could be fomented with only a minimal risk of global war. They feared that Soviet gradualism would unnecessarily delay the revolution in the short run and perhaps lead to stagnation in the long run. Mingled with this fear, presumably, was the belief that Khrushchev's gradualism was much too confining for China's aspirations towards Taiwan and for her role as the self-appointed leader of the revolutionary movement in the underdeveloped areas.

The Chinese attack on Soviet strategy, as they conceive it, cannot be understood apart from the actual changes that have taken place in Soviet strategy in recent years. The professed Soviet desire for a *détente* is received in the West with a justifiable skepticism, since few believe that Khrushchev is interested in achieving a lasting peace on the basis of the status quo. He has been quite open about his belief that he can use a *détente* to extend the Soviet sphere of influence and to undermine the Western alliance system. Yet he appeared in the spring of 1960 genuinely to believe that he could achieve these goals without using force or bringing about a war and with a minimum of armed violence on the part of Communist parties throughout the world.

The new and bitter Chinese polemics were probably not a direct attempt to sabotage the summit meeting scheduled for

May. Khrushchev's summit diplomacy was only a symptom and not a root cause of Sino-Soviet strategic differences. Chinese comment on the eve of the summit conference made it evident that Mao was resigned to the talks but expected little "progress" to be made. Rather, the Chinese attack must be viewed as the culmination of two and a half years of frustration over Soviet tactics. In the Chinese view, the Soviet leaders were not only exercising excessive caution, but even where they were exerting the most pressure, as in the Berlin matter, it was in behalf of Soviet and not Chinese aspirations. The Chinese may well have thought that, while Khrushchev was taking steps to clean up his own backyard by "normalizing" the situation in Germany, he should have been willing to exert similar pressure to "normalize" the situation in Communist China's own backyard, Taiwan. Similarly, while Khrushchev's negotiatory tactics were aimed at making gains for the USSR in Europe—through the weakening of the Western alliance system and efforts to induce the West to recognize the status quo in Eastern Europe—these tactics had relatively few advantages, and many disadvantages, for the Chinese. Should a U.S.-Soviet compromise on Berlin, for example, lead to a nuclear test-ban agreement, as seemed one possibility on the eve of the abortive summit, Soviet policy would end by jeopardizing Chinese aspirations to become a nuclear power.

"Peaceful Coexistence" or Continuation of the Cold War

One of the three issues in the debate of April 1960 between Moscow and Peking was the question of peaceful coexistence. Neither side rejected the concept, but the Russians placed their emphasis on the need for something more stable than a mere armed truce, while the Chinese emphasized the impossibility and undesirability of anything more stable than a temporary armed truce. Because the Chinese believed that local wars and armed rebellion were inevitable, they could see no prospect for a genuine *détente* except by sacrificing potential gains.

The question of coexistence was defined by Khrushchev at the 20th Party Congress in 1956 as one of three "fundamental questions" of present-day international development. He told the Congress then, and he has been saying since, that Communism

301

could triumph peacefully, that it was a question of coexistence or "the most destructive war in history," and that the opposing camps must do more than exist side by side: they must "proceed further to improve relations, strengthen confidence, and co-operate."[3]

As of the spring of 1960, Khrushchev appeared to believe he could use a *détente* to wreck the Western alliance system and to seduce the uncommitted countries. He seemed to think that the achievement of these goals would be retarded if the Bloc were to use armed force directly or indiscriminately to promote armed coups on the part of local Communist parties. He believed that Soviet military power exercised a deterrent effect on Western action and could be employed as a shield behind which the revolutionary process in the underdeveloped countries would deepen. He seemed prepared for a long-range political and ideological struggle with the West in which "history" was on his side. His fundamental policy of expansion seemed to some extent tempered by his fear of nuclear war. Moreover, the rigidities and consequent failures of Stalinist foreign policy—even if the post-Stalin Soviet leadership had not been confronted with the nuclear era—would have suggested a more flexible foreign policy which would seek to manipulate the forces of nationalism and neutralism. The coalescence of these various factors in Soviet thinking—the fear of nuclear war, the confidence in peaceful triumph in the long run, the desire for greater flexibility in tactics—helped to explain the Soviet desire for a *détente*.

Soviet awareness of the impact of nuclear technology on revolutionary strategy was expressed in the sharpest terms thus far by Otto Kuusinen on April 22, 1960: "War, using new means of mass destruction, would be madness. Such are the dialectics of military-technical progress that new weapons of war begin to exert pressure on behalf of peace. To Marxists there is nothing puzzling in this. The classics of Marxism have never denied that new weapons not only produce a revolution in the art of war but *can influence policy too.* . . . Lenin, as Krupskaya relates, foresaw that 'the time will come when war will become so destructive as to be impossible' " [italics supplied].[4]

In this remarkable passage the Soviet ideologue elevated nuclear weapons to an importance never anticipated in orthodox doctrine, which held with Lenin that, so long as imperialism remained, war was inevitable. In effect, Kuusinen gave these new weapons the role of an independent agent in the historical process which had produced a revolution so profound that it "could influence policy." That the Russians were hard-pressed to justify this inversion of Marxism-Leninism is apparent from the fact that they were forced to quote, not Lenin or Marx, but Lenin's widow, Krupskaya.

Kuusinen also expressed, in the most cogent terms yet used by any Soviet spokesman, the confidence of the Communists in their ability to triumph eventually over the West with a minimum of revolutionary violence. Quoting from Lenin, Kuusinen said: "Of course the task [of peaceful economic competition] is difficult. But we said and continue to say that socialism has the power of example. Force is of avail in relation to those who want to restore their power. But that exhausts the value of force and after that only influence and example are of avail. We must demonstrate the importance of communism practically, by example."[5]

Elsewhere in the same speech, Kuusinen projected the "main trends of historical progress" in the second half of the twentieth century. The year 2000 would dawn with most or much of the Western world still non-Communist. By the end of the next forty years, he predicted no gains in territory for the Bloc and, in fact, minimized the possibility of successful Communist revolutions in the advanced Western countries.

The need for elasticity in formulating policy and tactics was also strongly defended in the Soviet replies to the Chinese. Matkovskii, deputy director of the Central Committee's Institute for Marxism-Leninism, wrote in *Pravda* that only Left-wing Communists would deny "possible compromises" and, quoting Lenin, asserted that compromises were not to be equated with opportunism.[6] Then he described one of the most essential elements in Soviet strategy: the belief that differences in the Western alliance could be exploited by a readiness to make temporary accommodations: "Lenin taught that one could not wage the most complex struggle for Communism, the struggle against the international bourgeoisie, while rejecting out-of-hand agreements and compromises on individual issues with possible—be it only temporary— allies, and the exploitation of contradictions—be they only temporary ones—among the interests of the enemies. By compromising in some instances, in the interests of the development of the revolutionary movement, Communists are not deviating from their positions of principle."

Kuusinen made the related point that Soviet policy also must differentiate among the various Western leaders and governments: "Division among influential bourgeois circles is undoubtedly significant for the success of the struggle for peace. Lenin has already pointed out that it is not a matter of indifference to us whether we are dealing with those representatives of the bourgeois camp who are attracted to a military solution of the question, or with those representatives of the bourgeois camp who are attracted to pacifism. . . . "[7]

The Chinese rejected all three explanations of Soviet coexistence tactics: that nuclear weapons left no other choice but a more moderate approach to the West, that the Bloc could ultimately triumph with a minimum of revolutionary violence, and that it was necessary to pursue Bloc aims with a maximum of flexibility.[8]

On the question of nuclear weapons, *Hung ch'i* said: "Whichever way you look at it, none of the new techniques like atomic energy, rocketry, and so on has changed . . . the basic characteristics of the epoch of imperialism and proletarian revolution pointed out by Lenin."[9]

On the question of peaceful triumph, the Chinese argued that peaceful coexistence was "conditional," a "temporary breathing space [which could] always come to an end." In the Chinese view, coexistence would have to be interrupted periodically either by imperialist-launched "unjust" wars or by historically inevitable "just" wars for national liberation or emancipation from capitalism, and the Bloc must support these "just" wars and help resist the "unjust" wars.

On the question of flexibility, Peking contended that the Soviet policy of differentiation among capitalist powers was diluting firm Leninist principles and straying toward opportunism. At the Warsaw Pact conference in February 1960, the Chinese strongly objected to Moscow's designating West Germany rather than the United States as the main enemy. Now *Jen-min jih-pao* wrote: "It is entirely necessary to oppose militarism in West Germany and Japan and militarism fostered by the United States in

304

other countries. *But* now it is the war policy of U.S. imperialism that plays the decisive role in all this. *Departing from this point is departing from the heart and essence of the matter.* If the peace-loving people of the world do not concentrate their strength on exposing this war policy of the American authorities and continually wage a serious unflinching struggle against it, the result will inevitably be grievous calamity" [italics supplied].[10]

Lu Ting-yi said: "If the proletariat in the capitalist countries is to win emancipation, if the people of the colonies and semi-colonies are to obtain national liberation, if the people of the world are to defend world peace, *the spearhead of the struggle must be directed against U.S. imperialism"* [italics supplied].[11]

Still another Chinese objection to Moscow's flexible tactics concerned the strategy for the "peace" movement. In the Soviet view, the fight for "peace"—and the disruption of the Western alliance which is the principal goal of this fight—was the most important goal of the present stage. To achieve this goal, Moscow believed that the "peace" movement should concentrate exclusively on peace and should not expose itself as a Communist tool by supporting so-called "just" wars. To the Chinese, putting "peace" before "just" wars was bad tactics. They probably believed that the world Communist movement, and they personally, had more to gain by keeping alive the Algerian rebellion, for example, than by disrupting NATO, a goal which they may well have regarded as illusory in any case. For such reasons, Lu Ting-yi appealed polemically for a "merging" of the struggle for peace with the struggle for liberation:

"In order to oppose the aggressive policy of U.S. imperialism, all the world's revolutionary forces and peace-loving forces must be united. World peace can be further defended and effectively defended only by *linking up the struggle* of the peoples of the socialist countries, the national liberation struggle of the people of the colonies and semi-colonies, the revolutionary struggle of the proletariat in the capitalist countries and of all peoples for peace, forming them into a mighty anti-imperialist front and dealing firm blows at the U.S. imperialist policies of aggression and war. . . . *Separation from the national liberation struggles of colonies and semi-colonies and from the revolutionary struggles of the proletariat and working people in the capitalist countries, will greatly weaken the forces in defense of world peace* and serve the interests of imperialism" [italics supplied].[12]

Peaceful Revolution or Armed
Uprisings and Violence

Throughout Communist history, there has always been controversy between those on the Right who have maximized the possibilities for peaceful acquisition of power and those on the Left who have minimized it. A similar and related controversy has existed between those on the Right who believe that, since revolution is inevitable, it needs little outside stimulation (*podtalkivaniya*) and those on the Left who, agreeing that it is inevitable, nonetheless believe in helping it along.

At the 20th Party Congress in 1956, Khrushchev had taken a big step toward the Rightist position. He deemed it "quite probable" that the forms of transition to socialism would become "more and more varied" and that these forms "need not be associated with civil war under all circumstances." Violence and civil war, he contended, were not the "only way" to remake society. Parliament, particularly in the highly developed capitalist countries where it was a traditional institution, might become an agency of "genuine democracy" for the working people—in other words, a vehicle for Communist control. Khrushchev further implied that the peaceful path to power might be particularly possible in the former colonial countries where capitalism was weak. Capitalist resistance, he seemed to suggest, would be greatest in those countries which were most advanced:

"The winning of a firm parliamentary majority based on the mass revolutionary movement of the proletariat and of the working people would create conditions for the working class of many capitalist and *formerly colonial countries* to make fundamental social changes.

"Of course, *in those countries where capitalism is still strong,* where it possesses a tremendous military and police machine, serious resistance by reactionary forces is inevitable. The transition to socialism *in these countries* will take place amid sharp revolutionary class struggle" [italics supplied].[13]

Despite qualifications, the dominant impression left by the 20th Congress doctrinal revision was that the chances for peaceful takeover in the West were quite good, particularly in the weaker capitalist countries but not excluding the more advanced countries.

As we have seen, the new textbook of Communist strategy issued in the fall of 1959 took another step toward the Right. It deferred indefinitely the question of a Communist takeover in the more advanced countries and strengthened the doctrinal rationalization for achieving power peacefully. The possibility of a peaceful takeover was again emphasized strongly in Kuusinen's reply to the Chinese in April 1960. Even by the year 2000, Kuusinen held out little hope for any kind of a Communist takeover in the advanced capitalist countries and said he could offer no "firm prospects" for the development of these countries. Regarding the colonial and formerly colonial countries, he predicted that the second half of the century would be "marked by a complete liberation of the oppressed peoples and dependent countries."[14] The colonial countries, he said in effect, would completely eliminate Western political and economic influence, but they would not necessarily be Communist. This timetable did not seem predicted on a maximum of direct revolutionary violence.

The Soviet belief that overtaking the West in economic production would provide the key to the future was reflected in the four goals that Kuusinen expected to see reached in the next forty years. He predicted that the USSR would first overtake the West in per capita output, then in the volume of national income, then in the level of labor productivity, and finally in the level of per capital consumption. The "complete liberation" of the colonial countries would be achieved. Also, the "peace forces" would grow to such an extent that "any war" would become impossible. After these goals were achieved, a complete Communist society would be built in the USSR. The other countries of the camp would "march up the hill with the USSR." Gone was Kaganovich's bold prediction of 1955 that the 20th century would see the worldwide victory of Communism.

Khrushchev's defense of this slow revolutionary timetable was that revolutions could not be made without thorough preparation, particularly in the colonial countries where conditions had "not yet matured." Shevlyagin, writing in *Sovetskaya rossiya,* warned against "terrible revolutionaries" eager to spread revolution where conditions are not ripe: "Lenin understood the good intentions of comrades who hasten to race ahead and to speed up the advent of the socialist revolution, but he warned very decidedly against the danger of their transformation into Blanquists. . . . Lenin's teaching on 'compromises' acquires great importance under contemporary conditions, when the Communists, *particularly those in countries where many tasks of the bourgeois-democratic revolution and the winning of national independence have still to be performed,* must be able to conclude alliances, not only with the peasantry, but also with some strata of the national bourgeoisie in the interests of the struggle against the foreign yoke. *Here . . . one must not limp behind events, but one also must not run ahead and prematurely issue slogans of socialist transformation where conditions for it have not yet matured"* [italics supplied].[15]

Shevlyagin thought the failure of the precipitate "Left-wing deviationist" demand of the Iraqi Communist Party in the summer of 1959 for inclusion in the Iraqi Government should be "instructive" to other Communist parties of the underdeveloped countries "if they are faced with basically the same tasks." In short, Moscow was advising Communist parties in the backward areas not to be in a hurry either to enter the government or to seize power. Such tactics could only drive the nationalists closer to the West. Was a Communist takeover in Iraq, for example, worth the alienation of Nasser and Arab nationalism?

Regarding the Chinese desire for a more revolutionary strategy, Soviet Deputy Foreign Minister Zorin, writing in *Kommunist* on the Lenin anniversary, bluntly warned against those Left-wing Communists who demanded the "stimulation" of the world revolution and who argued that the revolution could be brought about "only by war" or through armed struggle:

"[In 1918] Lenin waged a decisive battle with the so-called Left Communists who were attempting to shove Soviet Russia into continuing the war with their arch-revolutionary phrases about 'the victory of the world revolution.' At that time Lenin formulated his well-known position on the impossibility of nudging revolutions and of the inadmissibility of interference in the affairs of other countries for importing revolution from without.

"Lenin wrote: 'It is supposed that the interests of the international revolution demand nudging of it, and that such nudging can be accomplished only by war, not by peace. . . . Such 'theories' have nothing in common with Marxism, which has always denied the nudging of revolutions. The sharpening of class contradictions leads to revolution.'

"So long as the two systems are antagonistic, there will be inevitable struggle between them—economic, political, and ideological. This is the unbreakable law of social development. But from this is does not follow that the battle must lead to armed struggle."[16]

The Chinese View

While Zorin may have exaggerated the Chinese position on revolution, the Chinese polemicists themselves contended that the concept of violent revolution lay "at the root of Marx's and Engel's doctrine," that it was necessary to promote and to "support" such revolutions "without the slightest reservation," that the present epoch was "unprecedently favorable" for them, and that local wars could be salutary in bringing them about. Yu Chao-li put it this way in *Hung ch'i:* "U.S. imperialist aggression is directed primarily against those colonial and semi-colonial countries and those which have won national independence. To achieve world peace, people everywhere should give their *support to national liberation movements in the colonial and semi-colonial countries, to the anti-imperialist struggles of countries which have already won national independence and to the righteous wars for national liberation and against imperialist aggression*" [italics supplied].[17]

Lu Ting-yi said the people of the whole world must "promote" the development of revolution, and continued: "No force on earth can hinder or restrain the people of the colonies and semi-colonies from rising in revolution and smashing the yoke they are under.
. . . All revolutionary Marxist-Leninists should support these just struggles *resolutely and without the slightest reservation*. Similarly, no force on earth can hinder or restrain the proletariat and working people in the capitalist countries from rising in revolution. . . . All revolutionary Marxist-Leninists should likewise support these just struggles, resolutely and without the slightest reservation" [italics supplied].[18]

In another passage he wrote: "The Marxist-Leninists and the modern revisionists, starting from fundamentally different stands and viewpoints, draw fundamentally different conclusions on this situation. The Marxist-Leninists regard this as an unprecedently favorable new epoch for the proletarian revolution in the countries of the world and for the national revolution in the colonies and semi-colonies."[19]

The Chinese strongly implied that local wars would be favorable for the Bloc because they could be turned into revolutionary opportunities in which the local Communists could then seize power. *Jen-min jih-pao* recalled Lenin's warning after World War I that "propaganda for peace was damaging the prospects for protracted war being turned into revolution."[20] Even more blatantly, the April 19 *Hung ch'i* suggested that local wars which involved the use of Bloc forces could be exploited to communize other countries. "Since the armed forces of the socialist countries fight for justice, when these forces have to go beyond their borders to counterattack a foreign enemy, it is only natural that they should exert an influence and have an effect wherever they go. . . . "[21]

The Chinese were concerned, understandably, that without war it would be a difficult task to spread Communism. Since Communist power has in fact been established and extended largely in the conditions created by two world wars, the Chinese had good reason to be more pessimistic than Khrushchev about the prospects for spreading revolution during peacetime.

Inevitability or
Non-Inevitability of War

At the 20th and 21st Soviet Party Congresses Khrushchev had introduced important innovations in Leninist theory on the inevitability of war. At the 20th Congress he said that the present correlation of forces in the world indicated there was "no fatalistic inevitability of wars," and although the danger of war existed the opportunity and conditions had been established for *"ensuring not merely a prolonged but a lasting peace."*[22] At the 21st Congress Khrushchev stated this thesis more sharply when he said that the new balance of forces in the world would engender a "real possibility of excluding world war from the life of society even before the complete triumph of socialism," and that *"any* attempt at aggression" would be stopped short—thus implying that local wars could be avoided as well.[23]

Soviet military and political leaders had for some time before the spring of 1960 been contending that local wars—given the nature of the opposed alliance systems and the nature of nuclear weapons—were bound to escalate. While such statements were and are undoubtedly meant to deter the West from local wars, they probably also reflect a genuine Soviet estimate that the West will not use force to thwart Moscow's aims provided the Communist powers do not initiate aggression and provided local Communists do not attempt to seize power by force themselves but use "front men" like Castro. Kuusinen fortified this impression in his anniversary reply to the Chinese, when he said that the "rapid stream" of historic progress was now flowing in a direction which would finally make "any war" impossible.[24]

Perhaps the frankest statement of Soviet views on the question of local wars came in an article by A. Sovetov in *International Affairs* on the Lenin anniversary. Because the article was analytical rather than propagandistic in nature, it was probably intended as a reply to Chinese assertions on the subject rather than as a warning to the West. The section on war, for example, began not by warning the West against a local war strategy but by stating that the West *was* deterred from local as well as from global war. The balance of forces "exercises a restraining effect on the imperialistic powers as regards so-called local wars." Sovetov then went on to maintain that since 1941 the frequency of local wars had declined by about one-third as compared with past centuries. Moreover, he said, clearly in response to an alternative argument, not one of the local wars since 1945 "has brought a direct gain to the imperialist forces." Although there had been five local wars from 1945 to 1955, only one—the Algerian war—had occurred since 1955. In this quantitative decline of local wars, the "decisive" factor was the might of the socialist system.[25]

The Soviet argument, then, was that local wars were becoming less and less likely because of the might of the Bloc, and that even where local wars had occurred the Bloc had succeeded in preventing the West from improving its position.

Of great interest was Sovetov's statement that the USSR would do all in its power to ensure that revolutions in various countries did not lead to civil wars in which the Bloc might be forced into supporting one side while the West supported the other: "In the atmosphere of rapid social development, characteristic of the present era, peaceful coexistence, while not retarding social changes in countries where these changes are ripe, *must at the same time ensure a situation in which internal processes in particular countries do not lead to military clashes of the two antipodal systems*. The situation is shaping favorably to such a course of events" [italics supplied].[26] If revolutionary gains must be made without risk of expanding violence, how was this to be done? In its next paragraph, the article contended: "This situation opens up new, unprecedented horizons before diplomacy. As methods of violence and *diktat* are relegated to the background, methods of negotiation assume even greater importance." In other words, the USSR hoped to make revolutionary gains via negotiations and without the risk of war.

Soviet views on the non-inevitability of war seemed to be the result of several converging elements in their strategic thinking as of the spring of 1960. First, the Russians had exhibited both in doctrine and in action a belief that the likely costs of general war in the nuclear era are prohibitive. Second, they appeared to believe they could attain their objectives in the middle run without the risk of general *or* local war. Third, Moscow's conservative thinking on war seemed intimately related to the instability of the so-called balance of terror. So long as neither side has an invulnerable nuclear retaliatory force, each must live with the ever-present danger that a deteriorating international situation may at some point encourage the other side to strike first, in order to reap the great advantage of surprise.

The first *Red Flag* article under the imprimatur of Yu Chao-li appeared on April 1 and was almost entirely devoted to refuting Soviet positions on war. Its central thesis was twofold. First, it agreed with the Soviet view that the West was deterred from general war, and it went on to imply that the Russians were acting too timidly under the circumstances. Second, it held that while a two-camp war was unlikely, local wars were inevitable. In contended that the Bloc should support those local revolutionary wars which were "just" and strongly oppose those imperialist-launched local wars which were "unjust."[27]

Some Westerners mistakenly believe the essence of the Chinese position is that general war is inevitable. The Chinese doctrinal articles, like those of the Russians, hold that central war is *possi-*

ble, but they do not consider it either likely or inevitable in the near future. This view is quite explicit in Mao's "smokescreen" line, which was revived in the fall of 1958 and which occupied a central place in the Yu Chao-li article. According to Mao, the imperialist cliques are only "using the rumor that war between the USSR and the United States may break out at any moment as a smokescreen to hide their schemes to control the world." The imperialists are said to be using the threat of a two-camp war in order to apply pressure on their own peoples and as an excuse to expand into the "intermediate zone" between the United States and the USSR.

The "real and direct contradictions" in the world since World War II, said Yu in April 1960, "are not contradictions between the Soviet Union and the United States. The Soviet Union and the United States can and are actually coexisting peacefully." In relation to practical policy decisions, therefore, Chinese public doctrine shows less concern than Soviet public doctrine over the danger of a two-camp war.

The second central element in the Chinese view, closely related to the first, is that while general war is unlikely, local wars are not only likely but inevitable. The "real and direct" contradictions in the world are those "between the reactionary cliques of an imperialist country and its own people, . . . between the imperialist countries and their colonies and semi-colonies, and . . . among the imperialist countries." Such contradictions, say the Chinese, will inevitably lead to civil wars in the capitalist countries, to wars between the capitalist countries and the colonial countries, and to wars among the imperialist countries.

Of these three kinds of inevitable local wars, Yu Chao-li seemed to believe that "colonial" wars were the most likely. "The spearhead of U.S. aggression at present," he said, "is directed primarily against the colonial and semi-colonial states and independent countries." One of the "special features" of international development since World War II has been the surging movement for national independence in colonial areas and the "continual suppression and use of force by imperialism to smother the movement." The imperialists cannot voluntarily give up their plundering of the colonies and semi-colonies, because the very survival of imperialism depends on its obtaining raw-material-producing centers and markets. This being the case, "national liberation wars will remain inevitable."

Yu identified three different kinds of wars that had broken out between imperialism and the colonial areas: (1) wars launched by imperialism to suppress actual colonies; (2) wars of aggression against countries which had achieved national independence, and (3) "national liberation wars" in the form of civil wars to oppose imperialism and "its running dogs." All three kinds, he said, "are still being carried out both separately and simultaneously." He seemed to consider both Western-initiated and Bloc-sponsored or Bloc-supported colonial wars as a continuing feature of the world.

The second type of local war which Yu seemed to hold likely was civil war in a capitalist country. Quoting Lenin, and tacitly discarding Khrushchev's thesis on the possibility of peaceful take-over of power, Yu said: "Civil wars are also wars. Whoever recognizes the class struggle cannot fail to recognize civil wars which in every class of society constitute the natural, and under certain conditions, inevitable continuation, development, and intensification of the class struggle. All the great revolutions prove this. To repudiate civil war, or to forget about it, would mean sinking into extreme opportunism and renouncing the socialist revolution."[28]

Finally, Yu decided there could be no guarantee that World War III would not break out as a result of the irreconcilable contradictions between the capitalist countries: "Who can guarantee that West Germany and Japan will not tread their old path? Again, who can guarantee that West Germany will not launch a new war of aggression in the West and Japan will not launch a new war of aggression in Southeast Asia? Furthermore, who can guarantee that there will not be a recurrence of the Pearl Harbor incident, or that there will not be a new world war among the imperialist countries?"[29]

Chinese views on the inevitability of local war were stated even more revealingly by Central Committee member Liu Chang Sheng on June 8 in his speech to the WFTU meeting in Peking.[30] Liu specified four types of inevitable local wars: imperialist wars of suppression against the colonial countries, imperialist wars of suppression against the people in their own countries, national liberation wars in the colonies, and people's revolutionary wars in the capitalist countries. The first two were "unjust," said Liu, the sec-

314

ond two "just." It was the duty of the Communist Bloc, he said, to uphold just wars and to oppose unjust wars. It was "entirely wrong" to believe that such local wars could be avoided, and it was also wrong to talk indiscriminately (as the Russians did) about opposing war in general without "making a specific analysis of its nature."

The Chinese do not believe, as the Russians evidently do, that the West is deterred from local as well as from general war. The Chinese therefore estimate that the Bloc will have to use force against the West whenever the West initiates local war. Moreover, they believe that local revolutionary wars—whether or not of the Bloc's own making—are inevitable and should be fully supported and exploited. While the Russians have not disavowed "just" wars or aid and support to those fighting "just" wars, their emphasis in the spring of 1960 was on the possibility of eliminating *all* wars, including by implication both the "just" and the "unjust." Their lack of material support for the Algerian rebels indicates they did not believe that their interests would be served as well by stirring up colonial wars as by pursuing their diplomatic objectives *vis-à-vis* the "imperialist" powers.

It is fairly certain the Russians were in 1959–1960 seeking a *détente* which they believed they could utilize to their advantage, and that they were aware they could not have a *détente* and support local wars at the same time. The Chinese, believing as they did that a *détente* would work against both world Communism and their own interests, were interested in stirring up local wars which gave promise of spreading Chinese influence.

The Chinese Communist attack on Soviet ideology and the revolutionary strategy reflected in that ideology virtually accused the Russians of betraying Marxism-Leninism. Such a charge was tantamount to calling into question Khrushchev's leadership of the Communist movement. The three principal targets of the Chinese fire were the very three basic ideological innovations which Khrushchev had personally presented to the 20th Party Congress. They rejected Khrushchev's views on the possibility and advisability of seeking a more or less long-range *détente* with the West and contended that coexistence could mean only an armed truce. They argued that, although general war could be avoided by persistent and defiant revolutionary struggle and a policy of strength, local wars were inevitable so long as imperialism remained, and that it was the Bloc's duty to foster and support "just" wars. They minimized the possibility of peaceful accession to power in the non-Communist world and suggested that those who emphasized this possibility were traitors to the revolution.

The Summit Conference

It is unlikely that China was instrumental in the Soviet decision to wreck the summit conference in May. Although for several years the Chinese had argued that negotiations must not take priority over revolutionary struggle, Chinese public pronouncements on the eve of the summit seemed to reflect resignation rather than opposition. Mao himself was quoted on May 14 as having asserted that "the Chinese supported the holding of the summit conference, no matter whether this sort of conference made achievements or not, or whether the achievements were big or small."[31] The language here could almost be interpreted as an attempt to remove pressure from Khrushchev by saying in effect that the Soviet leader did not necessarily have to gain concessions from the West in order to obtain Mao's *post facto* approval of the conference. In the very next sentence, however, Mao went on to say: *"But* the winning of world peace must depend mainly on the resolute struggle carried out by people of all countries." In short, summitry was all right, provided negotiations did not gain priority over direct action.

This is not to say that Mao did not have reservations about Khrushchev's summitry. Mao could not be certain that his Soviet "comrade" might not reach agreement with the Western leaders adverse to China's interests. In January, as we have seen, Khrushchev had pointedly noted that the Soviet Government did not intend to reach agreement behind the backs of other interested countries at the prospective summit talks.[32] Such earnest protestations that he would not ignore the interests of others suggest that the Chinese had expressed such reservations to Khrushchev privately or that Khrushchev inferred they had such reservations.[33]

If the breakdown of the summit talks cannot, however, be attributed in significant measure to the Chinese, it nonetheless marked a significant turning point in the Sino-Soviet dispute. No sooner had Khrushchev packed his bags in Paris than the Chinese launched a campaign, even more intensive than before, against

Soviet strategic views. The highlight of the renewed Chinese campaign was reached at the WFTU meeting in Peking in June, when the Chinese threw down a challenge to Soviet leadership of the Communist world that the Russians could no longer afford to ignore. The events at the WFTU conference will be discussed in the next chapter. Here it is only important to note that it was evidently the failure of the summit that emboldened Mao to press even more intensely his initiative against Khrushchev's strategy and tactics. Mao probably calculated that the abrupt failure of the summit would deal a severe blow to Khrushchev's prestige throughout the Communist world, particularly among those Stalinist elements which had all along shared Chinese dissatisfaction with the strategy of *détente* and coexistence.

The Chinese post-summit assault on Soviet strategy, however, evidently came as no surprise to Moscow. Just three days after the summit collapse, the Soviet theoretical journal *Kommunist* went to press with an article on the failure of the summit that seemed to be more concerned with refuting the Chinese than with attacking the Western "provocation" at Geneva. The article, an unsigned editorial, seemed to be intended as a preemptive move against anticipated Chinese calls for a fundamental revision of Soviet political strategy: "Some have suggested [said the editorial, that] in the interrelationships between two social systems there is another 'third way out'; neither war, nor peace, that is the maintenance and even strengthening of international tension. . . . The 'third way out' is sheer mockery to the nations which thirst for a stable peace. . . . "[34] The article went on to say that "imperialist wars are inimical to the forces of revolution," that revolutions can be brought about without war, that peaceful coexistence would not dull the vigilance of the people, and that economic power was the key to world revolution. It repeated Khrushchev's significant statement in Paris on May 16: "The Soviet Government is deeply convinced that if not this government of the USA, then another, if not another, then a third, will understand that there is no alternative except peaceful coexistence of the two systems."[35] Finally, the article reaffirmed the Soviet Union's confidence in its disarmament policy, contending—in direct contradiction to Peking—that disarmament would free funds to assist the underdeveloped countries.

This article, and others like it which appeared in the Soviet press shortly after the summit collapse, seemed designed to serve notice to the Communist world that the summit failure did not presage a radical shift in Soviet foreign policy and world Communist strategy. In fact no such shift occurred at that time. *Kommunist* seemed to be taking an almost quiescent line. If Eisenhower did not wish to negotiate with the Russians, they would wait for Kennedy or Nixon. If the new President was not inclined to negotiate, the Russians would wait still another four years. This pacific Soviet attitude, now clashing head-on with intensified Chinese pressures for a radical change in Soviet policy, almost inevitably led to a showdown at the June conference in Bucharest.

CHAPTER 14

THE SOVIET COUNTEROFFENSIVE:

JUNE TO SEPTEMBER 1960

At the conference of Communist parties in Bucharest in late June,[1] the Russians moved to the offensive for the first time in the three-year-old dispute with China. At that conference, a lengthy secret letter from Moscow to Peking, in which the Russians indicted various Chinese policies, was tabled before Communist leaders from all over the world. The conference was also the scene of a bitter exchange between Khrushchev and the Chinese representative, P'eng Chen.

Following the conference, more than a dozen increasingly severe and explicit attacks on Chinese Communist policies and leadership appeared in the Soviet press, and a Soviet Central Committee plenum attacked Left-wing sectarianism and "narrow nationalism" in the Communist movement. Soviet spokesmen, still without naming the Chinese, accused Peking obliquely of "disorienting" Bloc parties and Communist front organizations and of putting its own interests above those of the entire Communist world. The August issue of *Problems of Peace and Socialism* contained previously unpublished letters written by Lenin in 1915. In a series of footnotes to the letters, the journal pointedly noted that Lenin's Leftist opponents, such as Karl Radek, Trotsky, and the Dutch Communists Gorter and Pannekuk, had either left or been expelled from the Communist movement. In early August the Russian press, by warning that those who were one-sided in their views of the contemporary international situation were "not Marxists,"[2] suggested the possibility of Chinese exclusion from the world Communist movement. By mid-August, the Soviet press warned even more openly that China might face exclusion from the Communist Bloc and, by implication, loss of Soviet economic support and military protection. For the first time, Communist China was the explicit object of a thinly veiled threat. No "great country like, let us say, China" could build socialism if it were in an "isolated position," said one Soviet writer.[3] At this time all, or almost all, Soviet technical specialists were withdrawn from China. In September the North Vietnamese (DRV) Party Congress was the scene of another bitter

319

confrontation between Soviet and Chinese delegates. Meanwhile, the Russians were taking unusual measures to acquaint the Soviet Party with the gravity of the dispute. There were increasingly explicit charges of divisive activities by the "dogmatists," increasing stress on the danger of "dogmatism" to the Communist world, and implicit calls for a public recantation by the Chinese Communists of their errors.

The Chinese, although quiet in July and early August and evidently awaiting the outcome of top-level Party meetings, issued a number of statements in August and September suggesting that they had no intention of backing down. Moreover, they began in August increased emphasis on the need for "self-reliance" and "painstaking struggle," and explicit statements that although "we hope for foreign aid, [but] we cannot rely on it."[4] These themes, prominent in provincial as well as central media, suggested an expectation of reduced economic support from the European Bloc countries.

The period between the Bucharest Conference in June and the Moscow Conference in November was without question the most strained in the long history of the Sino-Soviet alliance. Both parties were seeking to convey to each other their intentions not to yield to pressure. Khrushchev made a personal and vindictive attack on Mao, and Mao's spokesmen replied in kind. Neither side seemed willing to adjust its policies and strategy in the manner advocated by the other. One of the most severe sanctions available to the Russians—the withdrawal of technical specialists—had been applied without the desired effect. It may even have stiffened Chinese resistance.

The WFTU Meeting in Peking

On June 5–9, 1960, there was a meeting in Peking of the General Council of the World Federation of Trade Unions (WFTU), one of the most important front organizations of the Communist movement.[5] It marked the beginning of the most acute phase of the Sino-Soviet conflict. Evidently calculating that the collapse of the summit had served to discredit Khrushchev's policies, which put such emphasis on the possibility of negotiation, the Chinese Communists used the WFTU meeting to deliver both publicly and privately a comprehensive indictment of Soviet strategy. Liu Chang-sheng, the Chinese Vice-President of the WFTU, publicly attacked Khrushchev's 21st Congress thesis, about the possibility of eliminating war while imperialism remained, as a dangerous "illusion" which would lead to "evil consequences of a serious nature which, in fact, we can already see at present."[6] Liu restated the Chinese position: eliminating world war was only a "possibility"; local wars of varying kinds, particularly in the colonial areas, were "unavoidable"; it was wrong to "talk indiscriminately" about opposing war in general, because only "unjust" wars must be opposed and "just" wars must be supported; to believe that "just" wars of liberation should be opposed would be tantamount to leaving the oppressed peoples in a state of enslavement; it was an "unrealistic illusion" to believe that disarmament could be attained while imperialism remained. Regarding disarmament, Liu cited, without attribution, portions of Khrushchev's proposals of June 2 and proceeded to refute them as a "downright whitewash and embellishment of imperialism."

It is quite likely that this public speech by Liu Chang-sheng was part of a Chinese attempt to use the WFTU meeting as the scene for a massive assault on Soviet policies before selected members of the world Communist movement and Left-wing trade union groups. (The meeting was attended by 64 delegations from 58 countries.) Various observers have reported that the Chinese privately assembled certain leaders of the Communist movement then present in Peking for the specific purpose of attacking Soviet policies.[7] Agostino Novella, the Italian Communist who presided over the trade union federation, was one of the main speakers at the WFTU meeting. He observed after his return home that the WFTU discussions produced "differences of opinion" which "even became impassioned." He openly admitted that the Chinese were unwilling to accept the Soviet coexistence line, and thus made the first public disclosure of Sino-Soviet differences by a Communist source: "A few divergences from the line presented by the WFTU secretariat were expressed by the Chinese delegation, with some agreement by the Indonesian delegation. Some doubts were expressed as to the realism and coherence of the present struggle for disarmament and international relaxation. There was a tendency, in substance, to make achievement of these objectives dependent on the end of capitalist society and the [victory] of socialist society."[8] A correspondent in Peking of the Italian Socialist Party paper, *Avanti,* wrote two months later that "the violence of the [Chinese] attack against Khrushchev amazed the delegates."[9]

Vittoria Foa, an Italian socialist who attended the WFTU meeting as one of a five-man Italian trade union delegation, on returning home wrote that the discussion was "emotionally prolonged for many days" and that the final resolution was "far from satisfactory." He described the Chinese positions at the WFTU meeting as follows: "We cannot talk of disarmament so long as imperialism exists and to talk about it demoralizes the working masses and the people especially in those countries still under the colonial yoke. It is an illusion to think that armaments expenditures can be devoted to the development of underdeveloped countries because in no case would the capitalist countries accept such a reallocation of the armaments resources. The unions must not deceive the workers on the possibility of improving their conditions as long as imperialism predominates. The only objective of the unions must therefore be that of a total struggle against imperialism in order to eradicate it with revolutionary action creating socialism."[10]

Foa contended that the adoption of such a line would end by "isolating the [trade union] movement," liquidate any hope for "unity of action" with non-WFTU trade unions, and thus constitute a "radical reversal of the line painstakingly developed so far." A month later, the Soviet trade union chairman, V. Grishin, himself the Soviet representative at the meeting, in an article dealing partly with the WFTU conference, criticized unspecified people who "sow a lack of faith among the masses of the working class" and who "disorganize the ranks of the progressive trade unions."[11] Moreover, leaks from the Indian Communist Party suggest that one of the "gravest" Soviet charges against the Chinese at the Bucharest Conference in late June was the alleged Chinese attempt to "break up the unity" of such "non-Party" mass organizations as the WFTU.[12]

The WFTU meeting seems to have produced a division of opinion between the European delegations and some of those in Asia and the underdeveloped countries. While this is not the place to enter into a discussion of how much support the Chinese had from other Communist parties or trade union groups at the

WFTU meeting, Novella's implication that only the Indonesians supported the Chinese is demonstrably untrue.[13] A careful study of those portions of the speeches by foreign delegates published in the Chinese press, making necessary allowances for Chinese tendentiousness in selecting extracts of the speeches, shows that of the fifty-five speeches made by international delegates at the meeting at least eleven gave varying degrees of support to Chinese positions.[14] On some issues, particularly strong support for the Chinese came from the representatives of Japan, Burma, North Vietnam, Ceylon, Zanzibar, Sudan, Somalia, and Argentina, as well as from Indonesia.[15] The Argentine delegate, Rubens Iscaro, used such Chinese phrases as "paper tiger" to describe the United States. His speech led all the rest in Peking's broadcasts to Latin America on June 9. Further indication that the WFTU meeting was divided to some extent between the representatives of the European and those of the underdeveloped countries can be found in a report from the Peking correspondent of *Avanti:* "The Chinese did not want the final WFTU council resolution to mention disarmament or the utilization for purposes of peace of the funds diverted from armaments. The Soviets, Italians, French, Germans, Poles, Czechs, Hungarians, and Indians fought instead to have this resolution emphasize the support of the labor union world for Khrushchev's foreign policy. At the end, there was issued a resolution of compromise, which set aside the problem. . . . but the final resolution is far from satisfying, *especially to European trade union people*" [italics supplied].[16] Foa, describing those delegations who were "together with the Italian delegation" against the positions taken by the Chinese, listed "the French, the Indians, the Russians, the Poles, the Czechs, the Germans, and all the countries of Eastern Europe."[17]

The apparently active Chinese lobbying against Soviet policy within one of the main arms of the Communist movement may have been the straw that broke the back of Khrushchev's patience. The day after the WFTU meeting concluded, it was evident that the Russians had decided to move to the offensive. The newspaper *Sovetskaya rossiya* warned that "Leftism, sectarianism, and dogmatism" had not yet been overcome in the international Communist movement and added pointedly: "It happens that not only groups of Communists, but also *the leaderships of individual parties* prove incapable of solving . . . problems, and lose their Marxist-Leninist bearings, veering off into Left-wing deviationism or Right-wing opportunism [italics supplied].[18]

While the Russians had previously attacked "leaders" of unspecified Communist parties for "conceit," they had never before accused such leaders of "veering" toward the path of "deviationism." As if to leave no doubt about the target of attack, the author stated that "even *large* Communist parties which have been tempered in class struggles encounter remnants of Leftism and the erroneous views of comrades whom V. I. Lenin has already characterized, in an ironical manner, as the 'terrible revolutionaries' " [italics supplied].

Two days later an article in *Pravda,* ostensibly commenting on Lenin's book, *Left-Wing Communism: an Infantile Disorder,* rebuked "contemporary Leftists in the international Communist movement" who wished to skip historical stages and who wrongly evaluated the policy of peaceful coexistence, the struggle to end the arms race, and the possibility of talks between East and West as "some kind of retreat from Marxism-Leninism."[19] The main point of this article was to make it abundantly clear that Moscow would not tolerate any challenge to Soviet hegemony within the Communist world. Ostensibly referring to the past, *Pravda* wrote: "Lenin stressed that *the Russian model teaches* ALL *countries something, and something very important, about their inevitable and none-too-distant future"* [italics, and capitals in original].[20] Still another sentence in heavy type seemed to make the same point: that Moscow would not tolerate diffusion of its ideological authority. Referring to the early years of the Bolshevik Party, *Pravda* said: *"Mastering Bolshevism was the most important task of the young Communist parties.* In those stormy years there was not a single party, with the exception of the Bolshevik Party, which possessed such profound knowledge of Marxist theory and had such revolutionary experience as our Party, which became an example for the Communist parties of other countries" [italics in original].[21] In the traditional manner of Communist communication, the paragraph conveyed a directive by positing the desirable as something already achieved. In this case, what was desired was unconditional loyalty to the Soviet line. The justification was superior Soviet knowledge and experience. The implication was

324

that the mastering of Bolshevism was a difficult business for younger parties and that it was therefore best to trust to the wisdom of the Russians.

The very fact that the Russians so provocatively raised the crucial issue of ideological authority indicated both that they intended to force a showdown and the ground on which they were prepared to stand. A *Pravda* editorial on the eve of the Bucharest Conference stated bluntly that "among Socialist countries, there cannot be two opinions on the question of peace or war."[22] *Pravda* also included a quotation from Khrushchev's speech in December 1959 to the Hungarian Party Congress on the need for all Communist parties to "synchronize their watches," and his warning that leaders of socialist countries who "would set themselves up to be above the rest" could only "play into the hands of the enemy."

The Bucharest Conference

The Russians evidently came to the Bucharest Conference in late June with the intention of forcing a Chinese retreat. The idea probably was to demonstrate to the Chinese that they were isolated in the Communist world and that the vast majority of the Communist leaders agreed with Soviet policies and, in any case, would support the Russians in a test of Soviet authority. The Russians evidently brought with them to the conference a lengthy letter which had originally been sent to Peking on June 12.[23] From accounts of the letter that have appeared in print, it seems to have been a restatement of Soviet strategic views and a criticism of those Chinese views that had been in contention for several years.[24]

The Bucharest Conference was also the scene of a bitter exchange between Khrushchev and the Chinese representative, P'eng Chen, a Politburo member close to Mao. In this exchange, Khrushchev is reported by Edward Crankshaw to have attacked Mao personally and to have compared him to Stalin in being oblivious of any interests but his own and in spinning theories detached from the realities of the modern world. Khrushchev reportedly added that the Chinese knew little about the realities of modern war. P'eng is said to have replied with a bitter attack on the Soviet Party and on Khrushchev personally. He charged that Khrushchev had confused the basic issues and said that the Chinese Party did not trust Khrushchev's analysis of the international situation. He further charged that Khrushchev had called the Bucharest meeting for the sole purpose of undermining Chinese prestige, a further indication that the Russians probably took the initiative against Peking at the conference. He replied to Khrushchev's allegation that the Chinese lacked sophistication about modern war by saying the Chinese had already shown in Korea and against the Japanese that they knew more about war than most people.

Khrushchev's public speech to the Bucharest Conference also implicitly attacked Mao for an inability to apply Marxist doctrine "creatively." On June 21, Khrushchev used these words: "On the basis of Marxism-Leninism, we must think for ourselves, profoundly study life, analyze the present situation, and draw conclusions which benefit the common cause of Communism. One must not only be able to read but must also correctly understand what one has read and apply it to specific conditions of the time in which we live, taking into consideration the situation and the *real balance of forces. A political leader* acting in this manner shows that he not only can read but also can creatively apply revolutionary teaching. If he does not do this, he resembles a man about whom people say: 'He looks into a book but sees nothing' " [italics supplied].[25]

Here Khrushchev was reiterating the Soviet view that Mao overestimated the change in the balance of forces in the Bloc's favor and did not sufficiently appreciate the complex problems of the contemporary international scene. The essence of the passage was that it was necessary to adapt Leninist revolutionary doctrine to new conditions. In a striking departure from normal practice, *Jen-min jih-pao* failed to publish the full text of Khrushchev's speech to the Bucharest Conference, and the excerpt quoted above was not included in the abbreviated version carried in the Chinese Party paper.[26] The Bucharest meeting did not end in complete disorder, although there is no evidence that the Chinese retreated an inch. A very short and uninformative joint communiqué was signed by the Russians and Chinese, as well as by the other Communist parties in attendance, evidently for the sake of presenting at least a façade of unity.[27] That it was only a façade was evident within a week of the conclusion of the meeting when *Pravda* and *Jen-min jih-pao* presented divergent views on the significance of the communiqué.[28]

326

It was evidently at Bucharest that it was decided to convene a meeting of all eighty-one Communist parties in Moscow in November to make another attempt to bridge the rapidly growing gulf between Moscow and Peking.

The Soviet Offensive
After Bucharest

At a mid-July plenum of the Soviet Central Committee, Kozlov gave the report on the Bucharest Conference, despite the fact that he had not attended it, perhaps in order to demonstrate to Peking that the Soviet Party was united. The Chinese may have calculated that Khrushchev's position in the Soviet hierarchy was such that sufficient pressure from them might at least severely restrict his freedom of action. According to the plenum resolution after Kozlov's report on Bucharest, "The plenum completely approved the political line of the activity of the CPSU delegation headed by Comrade Khrushchev."[29] This desire of the CPSU to present a united front to the Chinese and the rest of the Communist world may also have been one reason for the resurgence of the "collective leadership" line and the propagation of a new collective image of the Presidium in Soviet media in the remaining months of 1960.

The plenum resolution contained the most serious formal charges against the Chinese that had yet been made by the Russians, although they still refrained from mentioning the Chinese by name. The Communist movement, the resolution said, had decided to rebuff "Left-wing sectarian deviation" and "manifestations of narrow nationalistic tendencies." In Soviet journal articles after the plenum, an additional charge was stressed: namely, that the Chinese were undermining international proletarian solidarity. This combination of charges was similar to, although not as strong as, the Cominform Resolution of June 28, 1948, that expelled the Yugoslav Party from the organization for "seceding from the united socialist front against imperialism, . . . betraying the cause of international solidarity of the working people, and [taking] up a position of nationalism."[30]

Another parallel with the 1948 situation was the order which evidently went out some time in early July to Soviet media to boycott or play down Communist China. There were some news

327

items but no commentaries about China on the Moscow radio Home Service from July 11 to late August, the longest period of editorial silence in recent years. At about the same time, the Russians suspended the distribution in the Soviet Union of the Chinese-originated Russian-language magazine, *Druzhba* (Friendship), organ of the Sino-Soviet Friendship Society. This prohibition signified that the conflict had affected state as well as Party relations.

In late July there appeared in the Indian pro-Communist paper *Blitz* an article—possibly written at the behest of the Russians—that strongly criticized the Chinese by name as "Trotskyite" and claimed they were completely isolated in the Communist movement.[31] Moscow itself evidently wished to refrain from openly calling the Chinese "deviationists," thus avoiding an open schism. Instead, it left the task to Indian subordinates. This Soviet technique of employing fraternal parties to criticize other Communist parties when the Russians would prefer not to do it themselves is a familiar one. Stalin used the French Communist leader, Maurice Thorez, to criticize the American Communist leader, Earl Browder, soon after the end of World War II. In 1957, the East Germans and Czechs led the Soviet-inspired attack against Gomulka.

The headline of the *Blitz* article was "Moscow 'Boxes The Ears' of Peking Trotskyites." The initial paragraph said that the Soviet July plenum was "the beginning of a massive Soviet challenge to the isolationist, self-defeating Left-sectarian line which the Chinese Communists, with their newly acquired pride in power and arrogance of might, have been pursuing for the last two years." The purpose of the article was evidently to impress on Communist parties, particularly in Asia, the intention of the CPSU to force a Chinese retreat and the potential danger to other parties of taking sides with Peking, a possibility that Moscow had good reason to fear.

Perhaps the most significant development in July, however, was the indication that the Russians were informing the lower as well as higher levels of the Soviet Party on the acute state of the Sino-Soviet relationship. The Moscow correspondent of the Italian Socialist paper, *Avanti,* in an uncensored dispatch from Moscow on August 5, wrote: "Immediately following the Bucharest conference an internal event occurred in the USSR which cannot be underestimated: the dispute with China went from the higher levels to the lower levels. The Central Committee turned the dispute over to the entire Party. It is true that Kozlov's speech to the Central Committee concerning the Bucharest conference has not been published, nor has that of Suslov to the Moscow party *Aktiv;*[32] however, one highly significant fact can be observed; whereas up to a few months ago it was unusual to find a Soviet who would admit that the impersonal attacks of *Pravda,* of *Sovetskaya rossiya* and *Kommunist* against the dogmatists and extremists were directed at the Chinese, today this fact has become public knowledge."[33]

The Italian correspondent reported that it was not known how the question was passed to the lower levels but that he had "the impression that Suslov spoke very firmly and without mincing words." He speculated also that this meant "we are not faced with a tactical maneuver but rather with an intention to maintain a certain policy to the very end." Thus he implied that the Russians would stick to their position even if it meant an open split with the Chinese.

It is quite likely that Suslov was the Presidium member charged with acquainting the Soviet Party apparatus of the critical state of Sino-Soviet relations after the Bucharest meeting. In a public report of July 28 to the Leningrad Oblast Party meeting, Suslov voiced sharp criticism of dogmatism.[34] In late July *Pravda* reported Party meetings in various parts of the USSR, most of which concluded with endorsements of the Central Committee plenum resolution.[35]

Meanwhile, throughout July and August, the Soviet press continued to step up the intensity of its anti-"dogmatist" campaign. The most detailed Soviet reply to the Chinese views came in an article in *Kommunist* by Chief Editor F. Konstantinov and editorial board member Kh. Momdzhyan. The article ridiculed any attempt to take Leninist doctrines on war and imperialism as literally applicable to the present day and insisted again that Leninist doctrine must be adapted to changing conditions.[36] A Marxist dialectician could not abstract himself from the growing forces of socialism and peace without the risk of departing from the ground of reality.[37] Quoting Lenin, *Kommunist* argued that the decisive battle between East and West would be in the sphere of economic production:" Now, [Lenin] wrote, we influence the international revolution primarily by our economic policy. . . .

In this field the struggle is being waged on a worldwide scale. Let us solve this task, and we will have won on a worldwide scale, for sure and definitely."[38]

Repeating Kuusinen's emphasis, in his Lenin anniversary speech, on the impact of modern technology on the contemporary international scene, *Kommunist* quoted the same passage Kuusinen had cited from Krupskaya's memoirs to demonstrate that even Lenin foresaw the time when military technology would become so destructive as to preclude war.[39] The article went on to note the three major areas of Soviet policy about which the Chinese Communists had raised objections: peaceful coexistence, peaceful transition to socialism, and negotiation and compromise with the West. On the first, *Kommunist* argued that peaceful coexistence was "the alternative to a nuclear atomic war which is fraught with disastrous consequences for the peoples";[40] on peaceful transition to socialism, it contended that the changes in the balance of forces between capitalism and socialism would make it increasingly possible;[41] on compromise with the West, it quoted Lenin as authority for the view that such compromises were permissible under certain circumstances.[42]

In late July *Pravda* published, and Radio Moscow broadcast to Soviet listeners, a portion of a speech that Italian Communist Party leader Togliatti had delivered to a joint plenum of the Italian Party Central Committee and Central Control Commission.[43] Togliatti contended that the collapse of the summit meeting should cause, not an abandonment of the search for relaxation of tension, but rather an intensification of this search. He expressed publicly what may well have been the private rationale of the Soviet leaders for renewing pressure tactics against the West after the collapse of the summit conference. "New public pressure," Togliatti said, was "essential" in order to convene a new summit conference. He conceded that "debates" were taking place over the Bloc's "long-term aims" and he implied that sections of the Communist world, including some in the Italian Party, believed that the summit failure meant abandonment of the policy of coexistence. This was not so, Togliatti indicated. He spoke more vividly of the dangers and destructiveness of a nuclear war than any Communist leader before him. He said a modern war could be "suicidal" for those who began it and "might" lead to "complete destruction of the centers of civilization." He continued: "Woe to him who does not understand the new nature war has acquired. He risks being at least a generation behind in his views on war and peace."[44] The new nature of war, Togliatti continued, "impels us to bring a new attitude to bear on our views on war and peace." While "our distinction between just and unjust wars remains fully in force," the "assumption of total destruction . . . applying to both sides" makes it obvious "that other considerations [beyond the cause for which the war is fought] should be added to the definition of the just nature of a war." The implication was clear that even "just wars" might have to be avoided if they carried the risk of escalation to global war.

Togliatti also contradicted the Chinese view that revolutionary wars, and even a world war, would accelerate the triumph of socialism: "Let us assume that our country were hit by the 20 or 30 nuclear charges which would suffice to cause total destruction and transform everything into a desert. Would it be possible to build socialism in those conditions? We should be lying to the people if we said that one could bring socialism nearer through war. We must speak the truth; that is, if we want the way to socialism opened up for the Italian people, we must do everything necessary to avoid war."[45]

Togliatti went on to argue that the Soviet coexistence line did not hinder but aided the struggle against imperialism. Avoiding war and struggling against imperialism "are closely interconnected [and] only he who argues schematically, divorced from reality, can fail to notice this connection."

On August 7, a long *Pravda* article by Yu. Frantsev accused unidentified "Leftist phrasemongers" of wanting to nudge forward the world revolution by means of war and said the Leftist views represented an "absolute departure" from Marxism. On August 13, *Izvestiya* charged that "some people" drew "absolutely absurd conclusions" from recent "international complications," implied that these unidentified "people" were trying to mislead others, and warned that the substitution of "dead dogma" for living Marxist teachings was a "blasphemy."

At about this time, it may be remembered, the Russians moved from polemics to economic sanctions and ordered a withdrawal of Soviet technicians from China. It is reasonably certain that the

Russians, not the Chinese, took the initiative in this action.[46] Moreover, it seems likely that most, if not all, Soviet technicians were withdrawn.[47] The Russians justified the withdrawal on the ground that the Chinese were filling Soviet advisors with political propaganda.

Throughout July and early August the Chinese, apparently awaiting the outcome of top-level Party meetings, had been quiet on the polemical front. The top CCP leadership was absent from Peking between August 2 and 13. By the latter date a basic policy decision had evidently been made. Chou En-lai addressed Party and government cadres that day on the "domestic and international" situation, though the speech was never released. On the same day, a *Jen-min jih-pao* editorial, apparently responding directly to the Frantsev article in *Pravda* for August 7, contended that "modern revisionists" were "parroting" the imperialist slander about China's wanting to push forward the world revolution by means of war, that in doing so they had virtually become "apologists for imperialism," and that their charges would "do China no harm at all but [would] put [these] modern revisionists in a pretty fix." The idea that China would not suffer, but that Russia would be in a "pretty fix" if it continued its present offensive was an extraordinary assertion of Chinese independence and an indication that a policy of defiance had been sanctioned by the top-level CCP meeting in early August. The editorial, notably, made no reference whatever to the USSR and did not even include routine references to Soviet leadership of the camp or to Sino-Soviet solidarity. Moreover, it strongly hinted that the Chinese had support from other Communist parties and would continue to support the worldwide revolutionary movement even if the Russians did not.

The same issue of *Jen-min jih-pao* carried the reprint of an article that had appeared a week earlier in a Shanghai paper.[48] The basic theme of the article was that no matter how great the foreign and domestic difficulties, the Chinese Communist revolutionary will could not be weakened. It called for a bitter, self-reliant, and stubborn struggle for socialism, urged reliance "on our own strength," and warned against stretching out "our hands . . . for help."[49] In a clear allusion to Stalin's China policy, the article spoke of reactionaries "at home and abroad" who said the Chinese revolution could never succeed. It declared that imperialists and "reactionaries in a number of countries" were seeking to "isolate us" and "they do not permit us to speed up the pace of our socialist construction and our preparations for transition to Communism." These people, it said, "dream of . . . forcing our revolution to a halt." But China would respond with "rage" and "heroism" and after eight or ten more years or "even slightly longer," let "them see us then and they will be surprised."[50] Although enemies may suppress and curse us, and "some of the less enlightened people" may "call us stupid fellows and charge us with attempting something we are not capable of, we shall nevertheless carry out our revolutionary goal," the article continued.[51]

Although the revolutionary struggle would be replete with setbacks and even "great sacrifices," China would never be dispirited. It would "stand undaunted" and would continue the revolutionary struggle, "no matter how severe the setback is": "We want the kind of work and effort that proceeds with full speed. . . . Also we must work practically. Unless we do this, we cannot surge ahead of others. Of course, when we say that we want to surge ahead, we do not mean that we shall allow none to catch up with us or even overtake us. If we have that idea, we are not Communists. While striving to get ahead, we want the others to surpass us, and as this takes place, we shall try to catch up with and surpass them. Under the impetus of this emulation, the socialist-Communist cause develops without interruption, society advances steadily and science and culture grows."[52] In other words, there must be competition for first place in the Communist world, and the mere fact that the Russian revolution occurred before the Chinese revolution does not mean that Russia would lead the Communist camp for all time.

In the one conciliatory note struck in the entire article, the author assured his potential Soviet readers that China still recognized Soviet leadership of the Communist Bloc and that all her actions were designed only to strengthen the Bloc: "The steadily growing socialist camp headed by the Soviet Union is the reliable guarantee of success in checking imperialist aggression and defending world peace. China is a socialist country and is a big country. We exert ourselves primarily for the purpose of strengthening the socialist camp and checking imperialist aggression and defending world peace."[53]

Three days later, a long *Hung ch'i* editorial by economic

333

planner Li Fu-ch'un repeated the emphasis on self-sufficiency: "Although the greatest possible help from abroad should be obtained in socialist construction, the Party has consistently held that we should *mainly rely on our own efforts*. This was so in the past and will be *more so in the future*. . . . We are very confident that we can rely on our own efforts to build our country into a great, rich, strong, socialist power" [italics supplied].[54]

The polemical emphasis on "self-reliance" in articles published after the CCP meetings in early August suggests that one of the major issues before the Chinese leaders was how far they could go in their quarrel with Moscow without provoking Soviet economic sanctions. There is evidence that some members of the Chinese hierarchy were in favor of a retreat. On March 30 the influential Kwantung provincial first secretary, T'ao Chu, noted in a speech published in a Canton theoretical journal that the USSR had given China "an enormous amount of material and spiritual assistance" and that such "mutual assistance . . . must be strengthened before the building of socialism can be carried out by us at a faster rate."[55] T'ao went on to say: "Because of this, *our basic interest* lies in strengthening the solidarity of the socialist camp headed by the Soviet Union and the international solidarity of the proletariat. *We must make our utterances and action beneficial to international solidarity*. The conspiracy of imperialism to provoke and wreck this solidarity must be exposed and hit with vigor. This is the *only way* to insure the smooth progress of our socialist construction" [italics supplied].[56]

In the same article T'ao warned that "international solidarity" must be strengthened because it was "the condition *essential* to the smooth progress of socialist construction" in China [italics supplied]. In effect, T'ao seemed to be calling for conciliation of the Russians since Soviet support and trade were indispensable to the progress of the Chinese revolution. The sentence emphasized above, saying that Chinese utterances and actions must be tailored to the exigencies of international solidarity, was, to my knowledge, unique. But the thinly veiled views of T'ao probably represented the views of a considerable number of the Chinese Communist "realists."

A revised version of T'ao's speech in the August 5 *Jen-min jih-pao*,[57] which issued a ringing call for "self-reliance," an article with a similar emphasis on August 13, and the concurrent assault on "reactionaries" in other countries were firm evidence that the Right-wing views had been overcome and that a decision had been made to stand firm even in the face of massive Soviet pressure.

Throughout August evidence accumulated of an accelerating deterioration of relations between Moscow and Peking, a deterioration that was fast reaching the point of no return. The Chinese failed to attend the opening of the Orientalist Congress in Moscow on August 9. Mikoyan, in his opening speech to the Congress, did not once mention China, a remarkable omission in a conference devoted to problems of Orientology.

In mid-August a widely reprinted article in the Soviet regional press for the first time dropped all euphemisms, specifically referred to China in a polemical tone, and issued the unprecedented warning that if China were outside the socialist camp she would suffer an economic blockade and military blows from the West: "Is it possible to imagine the successful construction of socialism under contemporary conditions even in such a great country as, let us say, China, if that country were in an isolated position, not depending on the cooperation and mutual aid of all other socialist countries? While being subjected to an economic blockade on the part of the capitalist countries, such a country would simultaneously be subjected to military blows from without. It would experience the very greatest difficulties even in the event that it withstood the furious onslaught of the enemy."[58]

The author of this article, S. Titarenko, clearly held out the possibility of an open schism between Moscow and Peking in which China would be expelled from the socialist camp much as Yugoslavia had been in 1948. In this event, he was suggesting, Russia would withdraw its deterrent shield and economic support, and the West would be free to intensify its economic and military pressure on an isolated China. In an ascending order of gravity, this warning was clearly the gravest in the long history of the Sino-Soviet polemic. Nevertheless, it did not appear in any central Soviet media, but only in several regional papers. This suggests that Moscow wished to convey to the Chinese and to selected portions of the Russian people the clear warning that an open Sino-Soviet split was now possible, but that it did not wish to put the warning in the form of an outright ultimatum that could be picked up and

335

amplified in the Western press.[59] Had a veiled threat of this kind appeared in *Pravda,* for example, it would undoubtedly have been widely reported in the West and, moreover, it would have caused a much bigger stir in Communist countries than it in fact did. The Russians, it seems, were intent on maximizing the credibility of their threat to banish China from the Communist camp while leaving themselves room to back down if the Chinese showed signs of retreating.

The Titarenko article was only one of many surface indicators of the severe strains agitating the Sino-Soviet alliance in August and early September of 1960. Another such indicator was an article in the Bulgarian agricultural paper, *Kooperativno selo.*[60] The Bulgarian article did not, like the Titarenko one, mention China directly, but it again raised the possibility of an open break by citing the Yugoslav case in 1948 as an indication that "separation" from the "world socialist system" carried "mortal danger": "The Yugoslav case clearly shows that today, *as in the future,* the separation of peoples from the world socialist system carries and will carry mortal danger for the national, economic, and cultural development of the peoples, and for the socialist system" [italics supplied].[61] Such a "mortal danger" would in fact "doom" and "destroy" any socialist nation which left the Bloc: this was so because "Imperialism would inevitably attack with all its political, military, economic, ideological, and other weapons, and would suppress and *destroy as a progressive force* any social force that separates itself from the common course of the world revolutionary movement. . . . " [italics supplied].[62] Thus, the article added to the Titarenko warning of imperialist blockade and military attack a prediction of inevitable catastrophe for China if it left the Bloc.

The fact that this obscure Bulgarian paper, rather than *Pravda,* was chosen to issue such a blunt warning was again indicative of the Soviet desire to add credibility to its campaign of massive pressure without arousing public opinion throughout the world to the acute nature of the conflict.

The Hanoi Meeting in Early September

The third North Vietnamese (DRV) Party Congress in early September was, like the Rumanian Party Congress in June, dominated by the Sino-Soviet conflict. Just as the Bucharest Conference had broken up with little agreement between the Soviet and Chinese delegations, so the Hanoi meeting was also a failure and may even have contributed to a further sharpening of the conflict. On September 11 Tass reported tersely that "on the day before, a CPR delegation visited the Soviet delegation in its residence; an exchange of opinions on many questions took place between the delegations." Tass did not indicate that any kind of accord between the two sides was reached. The day after this meeting, on September 11, the leader of the CPSU delegation to the congress, N. I. Mukhitdinov, addressed a rally in Hanoi and in the course of it assailed unnamed Bloc "dogmatists" in unusually specific terms: "They at times oppose their local narrow national interests to the international tasks of the world proletariat or deem them superior. Their sectarian activities in international public organizations harm the democratic forces of the world and interests of the socialist camp."[63] Mukhitdinov added that the "dogmatists" wanted to pass off their erroneous ideas as Marxist-Leninist truths and to "force them on the other side," a clear indication that the Chinese were not retreating. Although the usual Soviet practice is to condemn revisionism as the "main danger," Mukhitdinov called dogmatism "no less harmful" than revisionism.

The Chinese used the Hanoi meeting to continue their efforts to convince the Communist world that their strategic views were sounder than those of the Russians. They evidently believed, with some justification, that the Russians had presented a false interpretation of the Sino-Soviet differences to other Communist parties, and they were apparently anxious to get their own case across. The Chinese as well as the Russians, of course, were distorting the arguments of the other side and had been doing so for some time. The Russians sought to create the false impression that the Chinese were pressing for a global war, and the Chinese sought to create the equally false impression that the Russians had given up the struggle for world revolution.

At the Hanoi conference the Chinese evidently were particularly anxious to get their true views across to the Indians. We have available a firsthand report from one of the two Indian Communist Party representatives at the meeting. He states that he was chosen by the Chinese to lead the attack in the Communist Party of India on the Soviet positions. This Indian Communist, Harekrishna Konar, told the Calcutta District committee of his Party, after his return from the Congress, that after talking to the CCP representatives in Hanoi he was now in a position to place the Chinese point of view before the Indian Party, even if his doing so amounted to a breach of proper Party conduct.[64] Konar reported that the Chinese told him their differences with the Russians started soon after Stalin's death. Peking did not like the CPSU's handling of the Beria case. The Chinese described the Soviet attitude toward Yugoslavia as "cringing." They considered that the Soviet leaders had vacillated during the Hungarian revolution, that Khrushchev had been on the point of withdrawing Soviet troops, and that they themselves persuaded the Russian leaders to take a firm stand. The Chinese also complained bitterly about the withdrawal of "almost all" the Russian technicians before their contract had ended.

As if this were not enough, Peking continued implicitly to press its accusations that Khrushchev was a revisionist whose policies would lead to disaster.[65] A massive propaganda campaign was inaugurated in late September on the occasion of the publication of the fourth volume of the *Selected Works of Mao Tse-tung,* during which the "Cult of Mao" reached new heights. Portions of Mao's writings were employed to demonstrate that Mao's assessments of strategy and tactics had consistently been right in the period covered in the volume (1945–1949), and, by thinly veiled allusion, to demonstrate that Mao's recent assessments, disputed by Khrushchev, were also correct. Authoritative comment on the fourth volume, which included historical references to "impractical illusions about the imperialists cherished by some of the people," promised that the volume would "become a powerful ideological weapon for expediting the socialist revolution and socialist construction of our country and for *intensifying the struggle against* imperialism and *modern revisionism*" [italics supplied].[66]

One of the articles rhetorically inquired: "Why do some people always take a wrong view while Chairman Mao takes a very correct view of the situation, the nature of the enemy, the strategy and tactics of struggle against the enemy, and the forces to be relied upon for beating the enemy?"[67] The answer was that while Chairman Mao took a "proletarian world view of things," the unidentified "people take a bourgeois view of things."[68] The same article

338

suggested that Stalin had held back the Chinese Communists in 1946 out of fear of a world war and, by implication, that Khrushchev was repeating this error.[69] At the time, it was alleged, Chairman Mao's "brilliant" and "penetrating analysis" of the postwar situation had dealt a "strong rebuff" to the "Rightist thinking" which overestimated the strength of the enemy and the danger of world war. Chairman Mao had indicated that the peace forces could prevent the outbreak of a third world war, that the U.S. "paper tiger" was not so powerful, and that the military superiority of the enemy was only temporary. The implication was clear that the same "penetrating" analysis of the current scene was available in Peking now and had only to be adopted by Khrushchev. The victory of the Chinese revolution, it was explicitly stated, was a victory of *both* Marxism Leninism and "the thought of Mao Tsetung."[70] The conclusion, all but stated, was that the victory of the world revolution would result from a similar combination.

It is possible to argue that the uncompromising positions taken by both sides in the months preceding the Moscow conference were advanced for tactical reasons. In this perspective, both sides stated maximum demands and acted as if nothing else but a substantial retreat on the part of the other would avert a break. In this view, the task of both parties was to convince the other that it would not itself back down. Just as the Communists are wont to practice blackmail against the West, so they practice it against each other. In this view, the maximum demands of each Party concealed minimum demands, or fallback positions, which both parties had from the beginning.

It is also possible to argue that the uncompromising positions taken by both sides was not merely a tactical maneuver designed to gain the best possible bargain, but was the result of a calculated decision to force a retreat from the other.[71] In this perspective, both parties were prepared to denounce the other publicly if the other did not back down. The reason why such a schism did not occur, in this view, is that the Russians, at the last moment and for reasons difficult to discern with precision, decided against forcing matters. There may, in this view, have been division within the Soviet ruling elite on how far to go. Alternatively, the Russians may have underestimated the amount of support for China throughout the world Communist movement or they may have underestimated the pressures for a settlement. Or Khrushchev may simply have reversed course at the last moment.

Whichever of the two views stated above is correct, or more nearly correct, both the Russians and the Chinese evidently came to the conference table willing to strike a bargain.

PART FIVE

NEITHER SPLIT
NOR SOLUTION

Someone [at the Moscow conference] has raised the question as to who is the one who determines what is truth and what complies with the principles of Marxist-Leninist doctrine."

—Ulbricht's report on the Moscow
Conference, *Neues Deutschland,*
December 18, 1960.

"As usual, ecclesiastical history has a precedent. In 1439, dignitaries of the Eastern Orthodox and Roman Catholic Churches came together in Florence to try to heal the division between them. After long debate, they agreed on a union-document which seemed even to have got over the great stumbling-block of 'filioque' (compared with which the interpretation of 'coexistence' is a simple matter). But Eastern and Western Churches read different things in the decree; and went their own ways. In 1472, Patriarch Gennadius II of Constantinople renounced the union. We may not have to wait so long."

—*Manchester Guardian,* commenting
on the Moscow Declaration,
December 7, 1960.

CHAPTER 15

THE MOSCOW CONFERENCE:

THE AMBIGUOUS COMPROMISE

THE Moscow Conference of eighty-one Communist parties in November 1960 was probably the most important gathering of its kind in the entire history of Communism. It is certain to be remembered as a landmark by students of Communist history, both those within the Communist movement itself and those in the West.

The conference was convened at a climactic moment. By the fall of 1960 a real question had arisen whether the Sino-Soviet alliance could survive in any meaningful sense. Relations between the Russians and Chinese had reached a point where they could barely, if at all, have absorbed further strain and where open schism between the two partners—and hence between the two major segments of the Communist camp—was quite possible. The conference gave an opportunity to decide whether the breach would be healed, whether it would merely be papered over, or whether in fact it would crystallize into an open Sino-Soviet split.

The questions at issue were great in scope and their implications fundamental. Critical issues of Communist strategy and policy had already come between the two powers. At a time when increasing political leverage was being acquired by newly independent and less-developed countries, and when the West was making renewed efforts in the military and political spheres, the Communist camp was faced with the need to hammer out a revised set of guidelines for pursuing its struggle to attain world hegemony. Whether it could bridge the gap between Soviet and Chinese views on what these guidelines should be was very much an open question.

The conference provided the first international forum for a direct confrontation of Russian and Chinese views that had diverged increasingly during the preceding three years. It gathered together representatives of the whole Communist movement. It put before the movement's eighty-one parties the entire range of points at issue between Russia and China and forced them for the first time formally to take sides. It was likely to reflect, therefore, the

343

extent of Soviet, as compared to Chinese, influence in the Communist world.

On the eve of the conference it was plain that Mao and Khrushchev no longer had full confidence in one another. Both, through intermediaries, had exchanged insults and abuse. For three years the Chinese Communists had found fault with the Soviet line on strategy and had failed to modify it significantly in the direction they desired. They were beginning to form, or try to form, anti-Soviet factions in Communist parties and front organizations throughout the world, and blatantly justified this action to the Russians on the grounds that Lenin, too, had created factions when he was convinced he was right and the majority wrong.[1]

In response, beginning in June of 1960, the Russians had mounted a campaign designed to combat Chinese pressures. They even indirectly warned China that if she left the Bloc she would be destroyed by the imperialists. The Chinese reacted by continuing to promote Mao as the wisest strategist and ideologist of the Communist world, and by intensifying their attacks on "revisionism," the euphemism which by now all but a few Communists as well as most informed analysts in the West knew referred to Khrushchev's policies.

Cooperation on many practical levels had also been breaking down. The Russians had apparently resisted Chinese pressures for nuclear weapons sharing, and there is evidence to suggest that there were other snags in military relations.[2] The Russians, in August, had abruptly withdrawn their technical advisers and specialists, and in doing so must have caused severe dislocations in an already ailing Chinese economy. There were indications of border frictions.[3] Cultural cooperation was on the wane.[4] Coverage of each country by the media of the other was unprecedentedly meagre.[5] Reports of petroleum shortages in China suggested that the Russians, the principal suppliers of Chinese oil, had imposed sanctions.

Sometime in September the Russians evidently prepared the preliminary draft of a declaration for submission to the Moscow Conference. It was reviewed in October by an editorial commission representing twenty-six parties, including the twelve in the Communist Bloc.[6] The formulation of a joint declaration thus lasted two months in all—most of October, when the preparatory commission was in session, and part of November and early December when the eighty-one-party conference itself met. The very length of the meeting was thus in itself testimony to the gulf between Soviet and Chinese views. The declaration was a masterpiece of ambiguity. It noted the differences of view without, in any but the most superficial sense, resolving them. Indeed, after the preparatory committee had met and presumably agreed to a draft declaration that would be put before the conference, which was then in session, there were major differences of emphasis in the Soviet and Chinese press. The former emphasized coexistence,[7] the latter the primacy of revolutionary struggle.[8] The Chinese warned that although it was necessary to "enrich" Marxism-Leninism with "new summations to guide revolutionary struggles," nevertheless "under no circumstances should we depart from the fundamental principles and methods of Marxism-Leninism and disregard the facts. Otherwise it would be a fundamental violation of Marxism-Leninism."[9] It may be assumed from this polemical language that the conference was not proceeding to Peking's liking.[10]

For purposes of analysis we can separate the major issues taken up in the Moscow Declaration into two categories: first, those affecting the locus of authority within the Communist camp; second, those relating to the strategy and tactics to be employed in the struggle against the West. It will be useful for us to examine what the declaration says in these areas, and to try to deduce from this evidence which of the parties to the Sino-Soviet conflict prevailed.

The Question of Authority

Premier Ulbricht's revealing report on the Moscow Conference acknowledged what a number of Western analysts had already suspected concerning the question of authority in the Communist camp—namely, that the Chinese were contesting the very claim of the Russians to lay down binding policy. "Someone," Ulbricht said, had raised the question of "who is the one who determines what is truth and what complies with the principles of Marxist-Leninist doctrine."[11] Someone had even raised objections to the very concept of a general line. In view of the heat and course of the Sino-Soviet dialogue that had gone before, these challenges could have come only from Peking. Although China probably did not make them with the aim of displacing Russia as leader of the Communist movement, she certainly aimed at setting strict limits on, if not cutting back, Soviet leadership.

Numerous indications both before and after the Moscow Conference suggested that it failed to resolve the question of authority within the Bloc. The day after the conference declaration was issued, for instance, *Jen-min jih-pao* clearly implied that, while China continued to recognize what the paper called the "position of prime importance of the great Soviet Union in the whole socialist camp and of the great CPSU in the entire international Communist movement," she claimed special prerogatives just as the Soviet Union did. "China and the Soviet Union," said the *Jen-min jih-pao* writer, "are the two biggest countries in the socialist camp and the Communist parties of China and the Soviet Union are the two biggest parties in the international Communist movement."[12] From the fact that other authoritative Chinese comment on the conference carried this exact statement, while no parallel thought was expressed either in the declaration or in Soviet media immediately after the conference, it seems highly likely that the symbolic implications of the above analogy were clear to both sides. Perhaps the Chinese, in an effort to give symbolic recognition to their demands for parity in Bloc leadership, sought unsuccessfully to insert such a statement in the declaration itself and, having failed, turned to their own press to record it.

The tortuous language of the declaration on the crucial question of Bloc leadership and Soviet prerogatives indicates that no clear settlement was reached. It also suggests that much maneuvering and some give-and-take took place before the statement was acceptable to both sides.

Russia was called the "universally recognized vanguard" of the world Communist movement, not the "head" as in 1957.[13] (It will be remembered that Khrushchev, in his report on the conference, conceded that it was "neither possible nor necessary" for leadership to be exercised from "any center at all," and it is likely that the Russians did not even press for the use of the term "head." It will also be recalled that at the November 1957 conference the Russians did not insist on being designated as the "center" of the Communist movement and such a formulation was put in the declaration only at Chinese insistence.) The experience of the CPSU was held to be of "fundamental significance for the entire international Communist movement"; the Soviet Union was acknowledged as the "first country in history to be blazing a trail to Communism." These formulations begged the question of how significant Soviet experience was and who would reach Communism first. The "historic decisions" of the 20th Congress of the CPSU were acknowledged to have "initiated a new stage in the world Communist movement and to have promoted its development on the basis of Marxism-Leninism."[14] But the 21st Congress —which, the Russians had consistently claimed, creatively contributed to the treasury of Marxism-Leninism, and which the Chinese implied had produced heresies—was not mentioned in this connection.

In endorsing the "Leninist principle of peaceful coexistence," the declaration called it the "unshakable basis of the foreign policy of the socialist countries," not the "general line" as the Russians had done before the conference.

The remaining key clauses on Party relations were double-edged and subject to predictably divergent interpretations. One of these asserted, for example, that every Communist Party is responsible "to the working class, to the working people of its country, to the international working class and Communist movement as a whole."[15] This wording, perhaps, indicates that the Russians hoped to subject China to the will of the "Communist movement as a whole," a movement in which the Russians at present enjoy a dominant position. On the other hand, the Chinese could interpret the wording to mean that they had a "higher" responsibility to their own working people, and that the Soviet Union ought to be guided by the views and interests of the "working class" throughout the Bloc.

The "true equality" of Bloc members, the declaration said, could be found in a "correct combination of the principles of socialist internationalism and socialist patriotism," but nothing was said about how this combination could be achieved in the absence of a recognized arbiter of Bloc policy. Indeed, the declaration said the interests of the Communist movement require adherence by every Party "to the estimates and conclusions concerning the common tasks in the struggle against imperialism, for peace, democracy and socialism, *jointly* reached by the fraternal parties at their meetings" [italics supplied]."[16] To the Russians, this probably meant that the Chinese should adhere to Soviet estimates and conclusions; the Chinese could just as well interpret the passage to mean that conclusions should be jointly reached after Bloc consultation and discussion.

Another key clause, equally ambiguous, said: "Whenever a Party wants to clear up questions relating to the activities of another fraternal Party, its leadership approaches the leadership of the Party concerned; if necessary, they hold meetings and consultations."[17] In other words, the Chinese should direct questions about the wisdom of Soviet strategy to the Russians themselves instead of appealing to third parties within the Bloc. The Russians, for their part, obligated themselves to hold consultations when questions involving Soviet activities were raised by other Communist states. The question of who was to be the final arbiter remained untouched.

Questions of Strategy: the "Nature of the Era"

Of all the politically charged issues that divided Moscow and Peking at the time of the Moscow Conference, none was more central than the deceptively abstract one concerning "the nature of the era." The Russians had contended that the distinguishing feature of the present historical period was a world socialist system already capable, or soon to be capable, of influencing the development of world society through its manifest economic strength and prosperity. The Chinese had held, on the other hand, that the period was still one of imperialism and proletarian revolution. The Russian view suggested that, because the world Communist system counted for so much in world politics, its influence, example, and power of attraction were the principal revolutionary agents; it maximized the ability of the Communist camp to exert a decisive influence on world affairs without resort to violence. The Chinese view implied that the era had not changed much from what it had been forty years earlier when Lenin outlined his revolutionary strategy. In this Leninist—and Chinese—view, imperialism by its very nature gives birth to wars and violent revolution because it is bound to resist its own doom and the dawn of a Communist age.

Therefore, either revolutionary violence to advance the historical process, or counter-revolutionary violence to restrain it, is the distinguishing characteristic of the age. In the Chinese view, local and civil wars are one of the principal means by which the world revolution will be advanced.

Several things indicate that the Moscow Conference did not achieve much success in bridging the gap between these differing views of the role of violence. First of all, the text of the declaration leaned heavily toward the Soviet viewpoint, with a nod to the Chinese:

"Our time, whose main content is the transition from capitalism to socialism initiated by the Great October Socialist Revolution, is a time of struggle between the two opposing social systems, a time of socialist revolutions and national liberation revolutions, a time of the breakdown of imperialism, of the abolition of the colonial system, a time of transition of more peoples to the socialist path, of the triumph of socialism and Communism on a worldwide scale.

"It is the principal characteristic of our time that the world socialist system is becoming the decisive factor in the development of society [italics in original]. . . .

"The course of social development proves right Lenin's prediction that the countries of victorious socialism would influence the development of world revolution chiefly by their economic construction."[18]

The first paragraph quoted above is in part a watered-down version of the Chinese view that the era is marked by a fierce struggle of imperialism and socialism, characterized by socialist revolution and national liberation war. (Note that there is no reference to national liberation "war" but only to "revolution.") The description of the "main content" of the era is a compromise. The second and third paragraphs embody the Soviet view that the transition from socialism to Communism will be promoted mainly by the impact of the world socialist system, particularly of its economic strength, rather than by violent revolution and war.

In the Soviet and Chinese comment on the declaration, both sides continued to emphasize their special views. The Chinese took care to avoid repeating the contents of the second and third paragraphs in this section of the declaration.[19]

Premier Ulbricht, to whose post-conference report we can look

349

for many interesting observations, also provided evidence of the continuing dispute about the "nature of the era" and the role of violence. He noted that "some comrades" held a view which "disregards the most important element of our time, the world socialist system." He said that these unidentified "comrades" had given an "obsolete" definition to the era.[20] Moreover, Khrushchev himself, in his post-conference speech, made a special point of stating that, while world imperialism was still strong, the world socialist system was increasingly determining the "nature, methods, and ways of international relations."[21] No Chinese commentaries conceded the truth of this statement.

The Question of
Local War

In the realm of warfare, the central issue between the Russians and Chinese concerned the probability and desirability of local wars. The Chinese position on the eve of the Moscow Conference had been that local wars of varying kinds were inevitable and even desirable. They were inevitable in the colonial areas, for example, because "national liberation" movements, like those in Algeria and Laos, would have to resort to arms in almost every case. When they did so, the Bloc must support them, even if it meant risking war with the West. Furthermore, the West itself would not tolerate the gradual erosion of its position in the Middle East, Africa, Asia, and Latin America and would probably intervene militarily to restore or preserve the status quo. The Anglo-French invasion of Suez in 1956 and the Anglo-American landings in Lebanon and Jordan in 1958 were repeatedly cited by the Chinese as two prime examples of such imperialist intervention. In such cases, they argued, the Bloc must respond to force with force.

While arguing that local wars were inevitable, the Chinese minimized the possibility of such wars escalating into a large-scale or general war. It had been the core of their position since the Soviet weapons developments of 1957 that these developments marked a decisive turning point in the balance of power and that the Bloc had acquired strategic superiority. This superiority was not sufficient to prevent the West from intervening in the revolutionary process, but it was sufficient to deter the West from raising the stakes in any local war. In the Chinese view, the West would

350

accept local defeats. Communist "brinkmanship," therefore, would not carry excessive risks of world war and was, in any case, essential for the furtherance of the revolutionary process.

The Russians, on the other hand, viewed local war in the context of their overall assessment of the catastrophic consequences of a general war. They repeatedly expressed the view that there was a grave danger of local wars spreading into a global conflict and that revolutionary gains must and could be made without taking such risks. They argued that Soviet power was sufficient to deter the West from intervening to curb the revolutionary process.

This semantic dispute between Moscow and Peking about the likelihood of imperialist intervention in the revolutionary process has more than academic or theoretical interest. Behind Soviet confidence in the camp's ability to deter Western intervention, apparently, lies a high confidence in the political leverage of Soviet deterrent power *and* a recognition of the need to proceed carefully in order to avoid provocation that might reasonably be expected to invite a strategic Western military response. Coupled with the Chinese belief that the West will intervene locally, but that local wars can be contained, is a conviction that, behind the shield of Soviet deterrent power, Communists in many underdeveloped areas should make bold thrusts to expel Western interests. The real question, indeed, seems to be over how far to go in exploiting Soviet deterrent power.

The Moscow Conference treated the many facets of this critical issue in an ambiguous way. In a single breath, so to speak, it stated both the Chinese view that the imperialists would continue to start local wars and the Soviet view that such local wars could be deterred: "Experience shows that it is possible to combat effectively the local wars started by the imperialists and to stamp out successfully the hotbeds of such wars."[22] The same pair of incompatible contentions were evident in two earlier juxtaposed sentences. One stated that "more than once in the past years the imperialists have brought mankind to the brink of world catastrophe by starting local wars." Here the implication was the Chinese one that such approaches to the "brink" had not been decreasing and would continue. The sentence immediately following stressed the Soviet ability either to prevent local wars altogether or to end them quickly once begun. "The resolute stand of the Soviet Union . . .

put an end to the Anglo-French-Israeli intervention in Egypt, and averted a military invasion of Syria, Iraq, and some other countries by the imperialists."[23]

The Moscow Declaration was also ambiguous with regard to the amount and kinds of support that the Bloc would give to national liberation movements at war with Western powers. In the specific case of Algeria, there was a vague pledge of "regards and support" to the Algerian people, coupled with a demand for "an immediate cessation of the aggressive war against Algeria." In more general terms, there was a pledge of the "fullest moral and material assistance" to the peoples struggling for independence, but the "struggling" could be taken to indicate political as well as military conflict. The Chinese, but not the Russians, interpreted it to mean the latter.[24]

The declaration equivocated, too, about the important question of whether national liberation wars were, as the Chinese thought, "inevitable," or whether they might occur, as the Russians maintained, "in some cases."[25] It said merely that "Communists have always recognized the progressive, revolutionary significance of national liberation wars." It thus begged the question to which such bitter pre-conference debate had been directed.

In a post-conference speech on January 6, Khrushchev moved somewhat closer to the Chinese view than he had been willing to do in the declaration itself. He specifically said that the Soviet Party had "assured the participants in the conference" that the Soviet Union would "spare no effort to fulfill its international obligations" but that, "at the same time, the CPSU delegation proposed that this wording should not be included in the declaration or other documents of the Communist movement."[26] It may be supposed that Khrushchev had assured the Communist parties he would not default on his "obligations" to revolutionary movements throughout the world, but he chose not to define those obligations so precisely as to limit his freedom to determine the action he would take in any given case. Nevertheless, in this same speech, Khrushchev conceded to the Chinese what he had not conceded in the declaration itself, that liberation wars were not only admissible but also inevitable. On January 6 he had this to say: "Now a word about national liberation wars. The armed struggle by the Vietnamese people or the war of the Algerian people, which is already in its seventh year, serve as the latest examples of such wars. These wars began as an uprising by the colonial peoples against their oppressors and changed into guerrilla warfare. Liberation wars will continue to exist as long as imperialism exists, as long as colonialism exists. These are revolutionary wars. *Such wars are not only admissible but inevitable,* since the colonialists do not grant independence voluntarily" [italics supplied].[27]

Khrushchev's willingness to make such a flat statement after the conference but not to include it in the declaration itself, as the Chinese would no doubt have done enthusiastically, probably again indicates his desire to retain flexibility. To commit himself to the view that liberation wars were "inevitable" in an official Party declaration would imply obligations and raise questions of Soviet support that Khrushchev preferred to leave open.

In this connection, one of the most important elements in Khrushchev's post-conference speech was the distinction he now drew for the first time between local wars, which he defined as wars between states, and liberation wars, which "began as an uprising by the colonial peoples against their oppressors and changed into guerrilla warfare."[28] With regard to the former, he argued that while they could not be excluded, "opportunities for imperialists to unleash these wars, too, are becoming fewer and fewer." He again warned of the danger that such wars between states could grow into "a world thermonuclear rocket war" and concluded, "We must therefore combat both world wars and local wars." With regard to liberation wars, while he conceded that they were "inevitable," he was as ambiguous as the declaration itself about the scope and kind of support that the Russians would provide, and he strongly implied at one point that the USSR would not intervene directly in such wars with its own military forces. In referring to the Cuban war of "liberation," he said: "Or let us take Cuba's example. A war took place there too. But it also started as an uprising against the internal tyrannical regime supported by U.S. imperialism. Batista was a protégé of the United States. The latter rendered active assistance to him. *However, the United States did not interfere in that war directly with its armed forces.* The Cuban people, under the leadership of Fidel Castro, have won" [italics supplied].[29]

In this important statement, and elsewhere in his speech, Khrushchev seemed to be suggesting that while the USSR would render to liberation movements assistance of a scope and kind which would depend on the circumstances, it would not intervene directly with its own military forces unless the West did so. This, of course, left open the question as to what Khrushchev would do if the West did intervene in a war of "liberation."

From Khrushchev's fancy dialectical footwork, we may draw several conclusions. First, it is apparent that Khrushchev desired to maintain maximum flexibility on the critical question of Soviet involvement in situations that might lead to direct military involvement with the West, while the Chinese sought to push him toward an advance commitment to such involvement. Second, Khrushchev was willing to go further in his post-conference speech than he was in the declaration itself toward meeting some of the Chinese objections. Third, the Chinese had forced him into clarifying his views on local wars. This clarification resulted in a new distinction between liberation wars, which were now declared to be inevitable, and wars between states, which could be prevented. Fourth, Soviet statements continued to be vague on the nature of the assistance they would provide to insurgent groups engaged in war with the West, and on the extent to which Moscow would order local Communists to push armed insurrections.

Khrushchev continued to appear confident that the Bloc could avoid direct military confrontations with the West, and he refused to make any clear commitment to a strategy that would make such a conflict inevitable. Unless he was very badly misinformed about Western intentions, it seems unlikely that he believed the Communist camp could provoke armed insurrection in many areas with impunity. It is more likely that his confidence sprang from an intention to avoid any blatant challenge to the West and to sanction armed struggle only in exceptional cases, as in Laos early in 1961, where Moscow could effectively control the risk, or as in Cuba, where the armed struggle was led by self-proclaimed nationalists rather than by the local Communist Party. Such a policy could not possibly satisfy the Chinese Communists, who continued to believe that Khrushchev would avoid a direct military confrontation with the West only at the cost of defaulting on his "obligations" to the world revolution.

The reader might ask at this point where Khrushchev's pressure on Berlin since the fall of 1958 fits into the author's interpretation of Soviet policy advanced above. First of all, it must be stated that Khrushchev has moved very slowly in pushing his Berlin gambit. Two and one-half years after he first gave the West what was in effect a six-month ultimatum, the West still had not budged and Khrushchev still had not signed a separate peace treaty. Second, there are a number of steps that Khrushchev can take even after the signing of a peace treaty that will fall short of a blatant challenge to the Western presence in Berlin. There can be continual harassment tactics designed to obtain Western recognition of East Germany but no single one of these tactics will, it can be presumed, in itself be sufficient to provoke Western military action. The West is likely to fight in Berlin only if its access rights are threatened; as long as Khrushchev stops short of denying that access, he can control the level of risk of a military confrontation while still seeking his goal through bluff and bluster.

The Question of World War

Behind the Sino-Soviet polemics on world war lie three critical questions: what is the likelihood of world war, and in the light of the answer to this question what levels of defense expenditure and what measures are called for in Communist states? What would be the likely cost of world war, and if this were unacceptable, should Communist worldwide tactics aim to avoid the risk of world war at all costs? What are the psychological effects on the Communist side of stressing the dangers of world war, and do the gains accruing from the Communist peace campaign and Communist support of neutralism and pacifism outweigh what is lost through the restraints that must concomitantly be placed on more militant policies? The Moscow meeting provided no real answers to these questions, any more than it had to previous ones, though once again, it seems, the Soviet voice was dominant.

Concerning the likelihood of world war, the Moscow Declaration reiterated, with one significant addition, the 21st Congress thesis that there was a "real possibility" of excluding world war from the life of society even before socialism had achieved complete victory and while capitalism still existed in a part of the world. The Chinese acceptance of this formula represented a concession inasmuch as they had repeatedly implied, even after the 21st Congress, that the danger of world war would disappear only *after* the final and complete triumph of the Communists. The CPSU, however, in outlining the conditions necessary for the elimination of world war, made a significant concession to the Chinese. According to Khrushchev at the 21st Congress, the elimination of world war would be possible when the USSR had become the "foremost" industrial power and China a "mighty industrial power," when the socialist system was turning out more than half of all industrial production, and when there were "new countries, freed of colonial oppression." The Moscow Declaration added to this list the "complete disintegration of the colonial system."[30] Thus, the possibility of eliminating world war was pushed further into the future. The Communists, however, have never defined the criteria of the "complete disintegration of the colonial system." Is the mere political independence of all the colonies enough, or must they also achieve economic independence? It can be expected that the Chinese will interpret the "disintegration" clause more broadly than the Russians. If "neo-colonialism" has to be eliminated, as the Chinese are likely to require, then the elimination of world war may not be theoretically possible for an indefinite period.

Another Chinese argument concerning the likelihood of world war was that the Communists could not predict the behavior of the imperialist general staffs, and that the West, despite the pronounced military superiority of the Bloc, might unleash a world war. The Chinese argued in this way while clinging to the seemingly contrary position that the danger of world war was but a "smokescreen" put up by the imperialists to unnerve the fainthearted. Depending on their immediate purposes, the Chinese emphasized one or the other side of their argument. If they sought to encourage the Russians to undertake a more militant policy in a given area, they argued that the Russians overestimated the dangers of world war. On the other hand, when Khrushchev began to talk about the possibility of eliminating world war altogether, to make unilateral cuts in his troop strength, and to seek a relaxation of tensions, the Chinese argued that the danger of world war was always present so long as imperialism remained.

The Moscow Declaration did little to clear up this confusion. Conflicting Chinese and Soviet arguments were placed side by side with no attempt at reconciliation. The declaration stated that the war menace had grown; two paragraphs later, it contended that the time was past "when the imperialists could decide at will whether there should or should not be war."[31]

Perhaps a more significant polemical issue concerned the consequences of global war. The Chinese had minimized the consequences of a world war and contended that, if one were forced upon the camp, the Communists would win and go on to build a beautiful Communist civilization on the ashes of imperialism. Khrushchev's statements, and those of other Communist leaders,[32] betrayed the fear that after a global war there might well be Communist as well as imperialist ashes. Khrushchev had spoken of hundreds of millions of casualties, of human progress set back by decades, and of the leading centers of world civilization in ruin. Even at his gloomiest moment, however, Khrushchev had never literally repeated the Malenkov line of 1954, that world war would "destroy civilization." Khrushchev, understandably enough, had never abandoned his insistence that the Soviet Union could achieve a meaningful victory in a world war.[33]

The operative political conclusion that the Chinese seem to have drawn from their minimizing of the consequences of world war was that Communist policy should free itself of the inhibitions and restraints that affected Khrushchev. They did not conclude, however, that the Bloc should start a global war against the West. The conclusion drawn by the Russians from their maximizing of the consequences of world war was that the pursuit of revolutionary goals must be cautious. They were far from concluding that those goals should be abandoned.

The Moscow Declaration adopted the Soviet view of the consequences of war. It warned that a new war could cause "unheard-of destruction to entire countries" and would bring death to "hundreds of millions of people, among them people in countries [e.g., China?] not involved in it."[34] Another Soviet victory in the section on world war was the categorical repetition of the Soviet line that there was no alternative to peaceful coexistence except a "destructive war." The Chinese had been arguing that there *was* an alternative, a so-called "third way" involving protracted conflict, sometimes cold, sometimes inevitably hot, but never boiling up into world war or subsiding into peace.

The Possibility of Negotiations

While the Chinese had not ruled out the possibility of occasional negotiations with the West, they had implied that such negotiations were merely another vehicle for pursuing the offensive and could not, in and of themselves, contribute much to the pursuit of Communist aims. The Chinese position was that the West could only be forced into making concessions, not cajoled or maneuvered into making them. Moreover, the Chinese argued that negotiations created illusions in the minds of the militant revolutionaries throughout the world and undermined their fighting spirit.

The Russians, on the other hand, evinced confidence that they could make gains through negotiations, in part because there were "sober circles" among the Western bourgeoisie with whom they could "do business." The Russians stressed that these "sober circles," unlike their adventurist colleagues in the West, feared war, implying that the danger of war could be used to extract concessions from them. The Chinese generally dismissed the idea of "sober circles" in the Western ruling classes.

On this point, too, the Moscow Declaration supported the Russian position. It stated that "the policy of peaceful coexistence is also favored by a definite section of the bourgeoisie of the developed capitalist countries, which takes a sober view of the relationship of forces and of the dire consequence of a modern war."[35] That the Russians wanted to go further, and the Chinese much less far, than this was suggested by subsequent comment from Moscow and Peking. A *Pravda* editorial of December 13 argued that peaceful coexistence would make possible "a more active role" for the "sober" bourgeois circles. Peking's subsequent comment foresaw no such possibility.

Disarmament

The principal Chinese objections to Soviet disarmament initiatives seem to have been, first, that the Russians were overestimating the chances of obtaining agreement on disarmament through negotiations and could reach such agreements only after severely weakening the Western position. The Chinese attitude toward disarmament negotiations, as to all other negotiations with the West, was that the West would have to be "forced" into disarmament agreements.

The Russians began verbally to agree to this general Chinese view even before the Moscow Conference. Like the Chinese, they began to stress in their propaganda that the imperialists could be

358

"forced" into disarmament agreements. Nevertheless, Soviet and Chinese statements before the Moscow Conference give the impression that the Russians expected more tangible results from disarmament talks than the Chinese. The Russians put their emphasis both on obtaining results and on using disarmament as a tactic. The Chinese put their emphasis almost exclusively on the latter. The Moscow Declaration seems to bow in both the Soviet and the Chinese directions at once. Take this passage, for example: "It is essential to wage an active and determined struggle against the aggressive imperialist forces with the aim of carrying this program [general and complete disarmament] into practice. It is necessary *to wage this struggle on an increasing scale* and *to strive perseveringly to achieve tangible results*—the banning of the testing and manufacture of nuclear weapons, the abolition of military blocs and war bases on foreign soil, and a substantial reduction of armed forces and armaments, all of which should pave the way to general disarmament" [italics supplied].[36]

Taking this along with other evidence, we can speculate that the Russians and Chinese disagreed at the Moscow Conference on the possibility and desirability of reaching accord on partial disarmament measures, such as a test ban. A *Hung ch'i* article in December avowed support for Soviet disarmament initiatives but added that it was "entirely correct" for the declaration to specify the need to "force" an agreement, since the imperialists would not easily accept "*even* partial disarmament" [italics supplied].[37]

Strategy in the Underdeveloped Areas

Before the Moscow Conference, the Russians had advanced various reasons for moving slowly toward Communism in the underdeveloped areas. They argued that revolutions must proceed through stages; that state capitalism in the underdeveloped countries was progressive and sowed the seeds of change; that the present nationalist governments were, despite vacillations, on the whole eliminating Western influence, pursuing a neutralist foreign policy, and making domestic reforms; that the local Communist parties in many areas were weak; that the newly independent countries would in any case slowly gravitate toward the Bloc as it won the economic race with the West.

The Chinese had been much less sanguine. The evolution of

359

the emergent states after World War II, they believed, demonstrated that nationalism and neutralism might be, not stepping-stones toward Communism, but rather obstacles in its path. They seem to have felt that only a direct seizure of power by each local Communist Party, preferably at the head of a popular-front alliance, would ensure a permanent victory. They did not trust the newly independent governments and considered their political independence a sham. They did not believe that the existing governments could carry much further the "democratic" revolution, and pointed to increasing Western investment in these areas as a means by which the West was seeking successfully to bring them into economic dependence.

On this crucial question of the timing of revolutions in the emergent states, the Moscow Declaration contained some clauses that would partially satisfy both sides but fully satisfy neither. Other statements were so ambiguous that both sides could and did interpret them to their own choosing. The single most significant element in the treatment of the "national liberation movement" was the new concept of "national democracy," which was said to be the model for a transitional form of government halfway between bourgeois nationalism and Communism. The "national democratic" state, said the declaration, is one which "consistently upholds its political and economic independence, fights against imperialism and its military blocs, against military bases on its territory; a state which fights against the new forms of colonialism and the penetration of imperialist capital; a state which rejects dictatorial and despotic methods of government; a state in which the people are ensured broad democratic rights and freedoms (freedom of speech, press, assembly, demonstrations, establishment of political parties and social organizations), the opportunity to work for the enactment of an agrarian reform and other democratic and social changes, and for participation in shaping government policy. The formation and consolidation of national democracies enables the countries concerned to make rapid social progress and play an active part in the people's struggle for peace, against the aggressive policies of the imperialist camp, for the complete abolition of the colonial yoke."[38]

Translated from Bolshevik jargon into English, this meant that Communists in underdeveloped areas must work, in the middle run, for the establishment, not of a Communist state, but a state that was somewhere in limbo between a neutral "bourgeois democracy" and an outright Communist satellite. A "national democracy" would have a government which allowed complete freedom of action to local Communists, allowed the Communists a prominent voice in determining policy, rejected military relations with the West, accepted Soviet but not Western aid, and enacted land reforms. This was a government which, in Communist jargon, would set out to complete both the "democratic revolution" and the process of "national liberation," tasks which are viewed by the Communists as way-stations on the road to a Communist seizure of power. As one East German Communist said after the meeting, Cuba is "today the model type of such a national democratic state."[39] Such a state would provide the ideal environment for the Communists to build up their strength and await the opportune time to take over, possibly even without the need for physical violence.

It should not be assumed that the term "national democracy" was a euphemism for a state that would be Communist in all but name.[40] There were no provisions in the definition for "proletarian hegemony." The "national democracy" was, like the "democracy of a new type" prescribed for mature capitalist countries, a transitional stage *before* the Communist takeover, and it represented a realistic assessment of the political forms the Communists hoped to see and intended to work for in the underdeveloped countries in the future. The term "*national* democracy" was preferred to the term "*people's* democracy," it has been said, because the struggle for national freedom and independence is the first and most important anti-imperialist action.[41] In other words, of the two goals implied in the concept of "national democracy," the "national" goal—independence from "imperialism"—was regarded as more important in the early stages than the "democratic" goal, pressures for nationalization, land reform, and so on. The Russians were well aware that the implementation of the anti-imperialist aspect of the program would be much less likely to cause a rupture in their relations with the emergent states than the implementation of the "democratic" aspects of the program which implied radical social and economic reforms that, in many cases, would be undesirable to the nationalist governments. As for the Chinese, the longer the "democratic" revolution was deferred, the greater their fear that it might never be realized.

Although "national democracy" was a formula designed to satisfy both the patient Russians and the nervous Chinese, on balance it was a victory for Soviet gradualism. It was, in fact, the Russians who proposed the concept in the draft declaration they submitted to the 26-party editorial committee in October.[42] Moreover, the day after the 81-party conference ended, *Pravda,* but not *Jen-min jih-pao,* hailed it as a "new Marxist-Leninist thesis."[43] The transitional character of the proposed state satisfied the Russians because, while it bowed in the direction of Chinese demands to move faster, it did not mean an end to the Soviet gradualist strategy in the underdeveloped areas or a rupture in diplomatic relations with Nasser, Kassim, Nehru, Sukarno etc. Such a rupture would almost certainly follow the adoption of the Chinese strategy. The tactical goal implicit in the concept was not the overthrow of the neutralist governments but an increase of pressure on them. The pressure was in fact increased shortly after the conference, and by the spring of 1961 it had brought about a new worsening of relations between Moscow and the UAR.

The Chinese, who wanted to replace the nationalist governments with new revolutionary regimes in which the Communists would play a leading role, must have regarded the Soviet policy of increased pressure as a mere palliative which could not hope to cure the disease of "bourgeois nationalism." Thus, the Russians moved just far enough to the left to injure their relations with Nasser but not nearly far enough to satisfy Peking.

The "compromise" completely avoided the central issue of the timing of the final revolution. Nowhere did the declaration indicate how much time should be allotted for the emergence of "national democracies" or how long it would be before such democracies, once achieved, were ready for "socialist revolution." One post-conference report said that the transition from the colonial state to the socialist revolution, by way of the national democracy, was "possible even without a lengthy process of capitalist development,"[44] which implied that the process would not be as "lengthy" as had been believed but still left the question open.

Another "theoretical" issue between Moscow and Peking that had obvious practical implications for strategy in the underdeveloped areas was the question of how "progressive" were the national bourgeoisies. In ideological terms, the argument was whether or not the nationalist leaders could carry out the "democratic" revolution. If the answer were "no," then the Communists must carry it out for them, and hence must take power sooner rather than later. The Chinese Communists had explicitly stated that the national bourgeoisie could not carry out all the tasks of the "democratic" revolution; the Russians said that whether or not they could was an open question, but that in any case they could go further than they had. Progress, said the Russians, could be made within the framework of the existing regimes.

The Moscow Declaration reached a dead end on this question. The national bourgeoisie, it said, "retains the capacity" to make further progress in the "democratic" struggle, but whether it will "depends on concrete conditions, on changes in the relationship of class forces, on the sharpness of the contradictions between imperialism, feudalism, and the people, and on the depth of the contradictions between imperialism, feudalism, and the national bourgeoisie."[45] Hence, the question whether the nationalists would make further "progress" depended on how Moscow and Peking chose to interpret the "concrete conditions" in any given country.

Other Issues

Of the various other issues which divided the Russians from the Chinese, the Moscow Conference resolved few. On the question of the parliamentary versus the revolutionary path to power, the declaration reached a meaningless compromise that both sides could interpret to their own choosing. It said that the "forms" of development of the socialist revolution "will depend on the specific balance of the class forces in the country concerned, on the organization and maturity of the working class and its vanguard, and on the extent of the resistance put up by the ruling classes."[46] It thus begged the question of whether peaceful evolution toward socialism was increasingly likely (the Russian view) or very unlikely (the Chinese view) and settled for the old 1957 formula that both violent and non-violent paths to power were possible.

On the question of Yugoslavia and revisionism, the declaration went much further than the Russians probably desired to go when it condemned the Yugoslavs for "subversive work" against the socialist camp. Although it was stated that dogmatism and sectarianism might become the main danger, revisionism continued for the present to be accorded that distinction. This probably represented a defeat for the Russians, who in the months before the conference had been emphasizing the threat from the dogmatists rather than that from the revisionists.

The section of the Moscow Declaration dealing with domestic policy for Bloc states was almost the only one that constituted an unequivocal Soviet victory. "Lenin's cooperative plan," not the communes, was said to have great vitality in both advanced and underdeveloped countries. A "material base" was said to be necessary for the transition to Communism. Higher productivity, the declaration pointed out, must be achieved through technical progress, economic planning, and strict observance of material incentives. All these were Soviet views. Only a slight bow was made in the Chinese direction, in the statement that higher productivity could be achieved by "heightening the political consciousness of the people."

We know from Ulbricht's speech after the conference that there was a controversy over the chronic problem of how far "national peculiarities" justified modifying the "universal laws." In 1957 the Poles and Hungarians sought to emphasize national peculiarities as justification for greater domestic autonomy. In 1960 the Chinese almost certainly joined them. The conference declaration reflected an impasse when it reiterated the 1957 equivocation that there must be neither "undue emphasis" on national peculiarities nor "mechanical copying" of the policies of other countries. The 1960 declaration, however, added a condemnation of "nationalism and national narrowmindedness"—exactly the same charge implicitly leveled against the Chinese by the Russians in July 1960 after the Bucharest Conference.

On the question of strategy toward the developed capitalist countries, the Moscow Declaration once again reflected the Soviet viewpoint. It set forth a list of "democratic" goals comparable to that issued by the Rome conference of West European Communist parties in November 1959. The Chinese had evidently attacked the Rome list of "democratic" goals as tending "to distract the workers from the struggle for socialist goals."[47] A *Jen-min jih-pao* editorial of December 7 did not mention "democratic" objectives in the advanced capitalist countries but said instead that it was "the task of the Communists" in those countries "to bring it home gradually to the masses of people that socialism alone provides a real way out for them." The issue here, as in the underdeveloped areas, again concerned the rate of advance toward Communism. The Chinese evidently believed that emphasis on short- and middle-range objectives, rather than on ultimate ones, would defer the day of Communist victory.

The Balance of Forces
at Moscow

The Moscow Declaration constituted, in boxing terms, a victory on points for the Soviet Party. It was *essentially* a Soviet document in the sense that the Soviet grand strategy—aiming at the worldwide triumph of Communism without war—remained intact. The Chinese succeeded in qualifying and hardening certain Soviet theses, in leaving several crucial ones open to varying interpretations, and, in general, moving the manifesto further to the Left than it would have been if drafted by the Russians alone. They did not succeed, however, in establishing any of their principal points: that peaceful coexistence was a mirage, that local wars were inevitable, that the Bloc must lend military support to "colonial" wars even at the risk of local war with the West, that the newly independent governments in Asia and Africa were unreliable and must be overturned soon; and that the possibilities for peaceful accession to power of any Communist Party were extremely rare.

The document was *essentially* Soviet because its overall tone and contents, however qualified, continued to adhere to the Soviet view that the Bloc had not yet reached a decisive strategic superiority over the West and must therefore move cautiously; that, in any case, time was on the side of the Communist movement; that the economic race with the West would in the end be decisive; that the newly independent countries could be gradually alienated from the West politically and economically by Soviet aid, trade, and example; that the value of violence should not be overestimated; and that the dangers and likely consequences of war were great.

For three years the Chinese had been urging a radical departure from the Bloc strategy laid down by the Soviet leaders. The Chinese views were explicitly based on the belief that the Bloc had achieved a decisive strategic superiority over the West. In any case, the Chinese argued, time was not necessarily on the side of Communism; the economic race with the West would not be decisive as Moscow thought; the role of violence in advancing Communist aims had been underestimated by the Russians; and the likely consequences of war were not as bad as Moscow believed.

The Moscow Conference ended one phase of Communist history and began another which will have a lasting impact on Soviet policy, Sino-Soviet relations, and the future evolution of relations within the Communist movement. With regard to Soviet policy, the single most important upshot of the conference was that the Chinese seemed to have succeeded in part in their intention to rob Soviet diplomacy of some of its flexibility and room for maneuver. The signs of this were numerous both in the proceedings of the conference and in the international behavior of the Russians after the conference concluded. First, there was the fact that for the first time in recent Communist history, a Soviet leader recognized Soviet "obligations" to the world Communist movement. During the Stalin era and most of the Khrushchev era, the only "obligations" had been those of the Communist movement throughout the world to defend and to obey the Soviet center. By 1960 the Chinese and other parties had brought so much pressure to bear on the Russians that the latter not only recognized their reciprocal obligations to those other parties but also stated publicly that they would not evade their responsibilities. While Khrushchev successfully fought to retain some flexibility in deciding how to meet those "obligations," the very recognition of them has forced Soviet diplomacy to take risks that have heretofore been avoided. Even before the conference convened, Khrushchev had begun to take a tougher line on international policy as early as June 1960, at the very time when he was moving toward a showdown with the Chinese. No sooner had the summit meeting collapsed than he shot down an American plane, scuttled the ten-power disarmament talks at Geneva, accused all the Western powers of backing Belgian military intervention in the Congo, made ICBM threats to the U.S. with regard to Cuba, gave *de facto* recognition to the Algerian rebels, and took to banging his shoes on the desk at the UN. While not all of these tactics can be explained solely as reactions to Chinese pressure, none of them, particularly the recognition of the

Algerian rebels, can be explained without taking that pressure into consideration.

After the Moscow Conference had concluded, Khrushchev moved even further towards a "hard" policy toward the West, undertaking a large-scale airlift to supply the Laotian Communist rebels and renewing his ultimatum on Berlin. In both these instances, while they did not yet signal adoption of the Chinese strategy, the Soviet leader nonetheless moved closer towards the risk of local wars with the West that the Chinese had persistently argued were inevitable and that he had argued could be avoided. Although both of these actions can in part be understood in terms of Khrushchev's own strategic conception, there is little doubt but that he assumed greater risks than he otherwise might. He was seeking to fend off Chinese accusations that he was reneging on his duties to support worldwide revolution and other Communist states in their struggle with the West. Khrushchev is well aware of the danger to the Soviet position of allowing China to appear as the only ardent champion of the Communist revolution: militant parties and anti-Western nationalist insurgents would be driven into the hands of Peking.

Another indication of decreasing Soviet flexibility was the implied Soviet promise in the Moscow Declaration to give greater weight to the views and interests of the Chinese Communists both before and during any future negotiations with the West, and also in the general conceptualization of Bloc strategy and tactics. If such a promise is observed in practice, it may not prevent East-West negotiation, but it will clearly make it more difficult.

With specific regard to Sino-Soviet relations, the significance of the Moscow Conference and its declaration was that the Russians and Chinese could not, even after two months of negotiation and with the help of seventy-nine other parties, resolve their differences. Neither the question of the locus of authority in the Communist world nor the complex issues of strategy and tactics were defined with precision. The declaration represented, not a real compromise of Soviet and Chinese views, but a collation of them. While the document, in its broad outlines, must be regarded as a Soviet "victory," its ambiguities and qualifications were so numerous that it could hardly serve as a guide for any of the Communist parties. Both Russia and China could and did derive different conclusions from it. The ostensible Soviet victory was thus bought at the very heavy price of an unworkable compromise which served clearly to demonstrate that the Russians were no longer able unilaterally to dictate law for the entire international Communist movement.

The hollowness of the Sino-Soviet "compromise" achieved at the Moscow Conference would be demonstrated before the next twelve months had run their course. At the 22nd Congress of the Soviet Communist Party in October 1961, Khrushchev seemed determined to exact the Chinese surrender that he was not able to get in 1960.

In the light of this later blatant attempt by Khrushchev to force a Chinese retreat, the question must be asked why he did not choose to do so a year earlier at the Moscow Conference? There are several possible explanations. First, it is possible that Khrushchev genuinely hoped his willingness to accede to some Chinese demands, particularly by hardening his line toward the West, would relieve some of the Chinese pressure. Second, there may have been in 1960 a division within the Soviet Presidium on how far to go in risking an open break with China. Although it seems dubious that there is an internal opposition to Khrushchev strong enough to oust him from the leadership, there is abundant evidence of policy disputes within the Soviet hierarchy and some indication that Khrushchev has not been able to get his own way or has been reversed on certain matters affecting Soviet agriculture and military policy. Third, there is the possibility, mentioned earlier, that the Russians expected all of the Communist parties to support them in a show of strength with Peking but found that many parties, particularly those in Asia, would not do so. In such a situation, Khrushchev would almost certainly have been reluctant to force a showdown that might result not only in a Sino-Soviet schism but in a breakup of the world Communist movement into two wings, one of which would be led by China.

Whatever the reasons for Khrushchev's caution in 1960, these reasons apparently were not so compelling a year later. At this time, Khrushchev must have seen a good opportunity. China was in the midst of economic crisis so severe that it was forced to turn to Canada and Australia for grain. There were increasing reports of perilously low food supplies on the mainland. The commune system had been all but abandoned and the Left-wing economic policies that Khrushchev had condemned now seemed to be in disgrace. Surely Khrushchev felt he could now restore Soviet authority in the international Communist movement to a preeminent position. What better target, therefore, than the tiny Balkan Communist state, Albania, which had—with Chinese economic and political support—increasingly defied the Kremlin throughout 1960 and early 1961?

CHAPTER 16

KHRUSHCHEV'S ATTACK ON ALBANIA
AT THE 22ND CONGRESS

ALBANIA'S defiance of the Kremlin, which goes back to 1956 but which became "especially distinct" in the middle of 1960,[1] according to Khrushchev himself, could scarcely have endured so long if China had not given the Balkan country considerable political and economic support. Khrushchev's open attack on the Albanian Party leadership at the 22nd Party Congress in October 1961 was, of course, an attack on the Chinese Communist leadership as well. Khrushchev made his principal target plain enough in his opening speech when he said that the course laid down by the Russians at the 20th Congress in 1956 would not be changed because they could not yield on a question of principle "either to the Albanian leaders or to anyone else." None in the Communist world could have any doubts about who the "anyone else" was after Chinese Premier Chou En-lai had failed to applaud Khrushchev's attack on the Albanians, implicitly condemned it two days later,[2] and abruptly returned home before the Congress had concluded. Moreover, less than twenty-four hours after the Soviet leader's attack on Albania, the Chinese Communists made public a speech delivered several days earlier by a Chinese delegate to the fifth congress of the Women's Union of Albania in Tirana; he pointedly noted that "the friendship between the Chinese and Albanian peoples, based on the principles of Marxism-Leninism and proletarian internationalism, is unbreakable and no force can destroy it."[3]

It thus appeared likely that the Chinese Communists were not prepared to give in easily to the pressure of their Russian allies and that a protracted struggle over Albania was in the offing. This would put even more strain on an uneasy alliance.

It seems quite probable that Khrushchev's attack on the Albanians was a surprise to Peking.[4] This is suggested principally by Chou En-lai's sudden departure, which must be considered a walkout. The Soviet news agency gave as the reason for Chou's departure "the coming session of the National People's Congress,"[5] but the Chinese news agency offered no reason at

370

all.[6] Indeed, Peking has nowhere mentioned a forthcoming NPC meeting.

If Peking had previously been aware of Khrushchev's intentions, it is unlikely that it would have sent the kind of delegation it did. The very composition of that delegation indicated that Peking was not girding for a showdown. In addition to the moderate Chou, who is probably more inclined to conciliation than Liu Shao-ch'i and other Chinese militants, the delegation included T'ao Chu, the influential Kwantung First Secretary, who had previously made clear his views on the need for patching up the Sino-Soviet dispute because of overriding economic necessity. In the spring of 1960, shortly before Peking launched a major polemical assault against the Russians, T'ao indicated his disapproval of the impending assault in a speech which argued that "the condition essential to the smooth progress of socialist construction" was to "make our utterances and action beneficial to international solidarity."[7] This unprecedented statement, in effect calling upon the Chinese Party to swallow its pride and to patch up its quarrel with the Russians as the only way out of its worsening domestic economic crisis, probably represented the views of a considerable number of the Chinese moderates.

On the other hand, the remaining two members of the Chinese delegation, P'eng Chen and Kang Sheng, had in the past identified themselves with the more militant wing of the CCP. P'eng reportedly launched a bitter attack in the summer of 1960 on both the Soviet Party and Khrushchev personally.[8] Kang delivered the polemical assault on Soviet policy at the Warsaw Pact meeting early in 1960. It seems likely that the Chinese delegation was deliberately balanced between the "conciliators" and the "militants," a common Communist practice when there is a division of opinion at the top.[9] If such was actually the case, the mixed Chinese delegation must have come to Moscow prepared neither for pressing the initiative nor for making a substantial retreat. A mounting domestic economic crisis and an apparent division of opinion within the Chinese Party on how far it would be wise to flout Moscow were among the factors which ruled out an aggressive attitude. Yet too much was at stake to accept a humiliating surrender.

Such a balance of conflicting influences was evident in Chinese public statements from the time of the Moscow Conference in the fall of 1960 right up to the eve of the 22nd Party Congress. But there were a number of indications that the conflict continued to smolder. There were visible differences between Moscow and Peking over Laos,[10] Yugoslavia,[11] Albania,[12] the new U.S. administration,[13] and strategy and tactics in the underdeveloped areas.[14] The Chinese continued implicitly to challenge Soviet authority by building up the cult of Mao Tse-tung and calling for the Sinification of Marxism-Leninism.[15] They published a collection of ancient Chinese stories about ghosts in which the preface warned against those "ghost-fearing men of the 20th century" who are "frightened out of their wits by imperialism and reaction."[16] On the very eve of the 22nd Congress, a high-ranking Chinese spokesman went so far as to reject in unmistakable, if still veiled, language the Soviet concept of a "national democracy" for the underdeveloped countries.[17] The concept had been endorsed by the Moscow Conference and subsequently hailed by the Russians, but not by the Chinese, as a "creative" contribution to Marxism-Leninism.

Moreover, one month before the Soviet Draft Party Program was released, and presumably after the Chinese had seen it, Peking made it quite clear that while the program was valid for the Soviet Union it had no binding effect on the Chinese Communists. *Hung ch'i* said: "In analyzing a social problem, the absolute demand of Marxist theory is to place the problem within a definite historical limit. In addition, if a certain country (or, for example, the national program of this country) is referred to, the concrete characteristics of this country that distinguish it from other countries in the same historical era must be taken into account."[18] The clear implication was that the Soviet program could be valid for other Communist states only within certain limits. The same point was made in effect by Teng Hsiao-p'ing, who, in a speech to the North Korean Party Congress, made the first mention of the Soviet program by any Chinese leader. Referring to it in a rather offhand manner, he said that the Soviet space ships and the draft program, "which outlines the gigantic plan of the *Soviet* people," were "strong proof" of the superiority of the socialist system.[19] Although *Jen-min jih-pao* published the full text of the CPSU program on August 5, there was no comment whatever, an unusual omission for a document of such importance.

The Chinese effort before the Congress to delimit the appli-

372

cability of the Soviet program was in marked contrast to the Russian and East European effort to universalize it. An unsigned editorial-article in *Pravda* on August 2 noted that the program testified to the "leading role" of the CPSU in the further development of Marxism-Leninism and bluntly stated: "The CPSU Central Committee is the true center of theoretical thought." This marked contrast between Soviet and Chinese attitudes toward the Draft Program continued at the Congress itself. Chou En-lai told the Congress that the new program "set forth *for the Soviet people* a grand plan for building communism. . . . " Khrushchev himself called the program "a new stage in the revolutionary theory of Marx, Engels, and Lenin," and he noted pointedly: "We can proudly say to those who want to know what communism is, 'Read our Party program.' "

In spite of these and other indications that the Sino-Soviet conflict had by no means been bridged, on the eve of the 22nd Congress neither Party seemed prepared to force matters to a head. The "compromise" that had been worked out at Moscow in 1960 showed an ambiguity that perhaps reflected the awareness of both sides that an impasse was preferable to a break-up of the world Communist movement. The fact that the Chinese had modified many aspects of their ambitious "leap-forward" and commune program, even if this were for domestic reasons and not owing to Soviet pressure, could only help to improve matters. While the Chinese continued their veiled polemics against the Russians, they did so somewhat less clamorously than in 1960. The Russians, for their part, gave no signs that they were preparing a major offensive against Peking. It is true that the Draft Party Program released in late July warned against "national narrow-mindedness" and the "reactionary and politically dangerous" course of socialist construction "in isolation,"[20] but these warnings had been made earlier and the Draft Program, on the whole, went easy on the Chinese.

Viewed in this perspective, what may have been the calculations behind Khrushchev's surprise attack on Albania? First of all, it is necessary to point out an obvious but significant fact— that Khrushchev has not directly attacked the Chinese themselves, despite the fact that they are the real source of his problem. The Albanians could not hope to defy a united Sino-Soviet axis. But

Khrushchev has not yet been willing to engage the Chinese frontally. He prefers, for the time being, to launch an indirect assault on the Chinese through their Albanian proxies, perhaps the weakest link in their chain, because Albania is so far away from China and because there is undoubtedly much less sympathy in the international Communist movement for Albania than for China. The similarity in this respect between Khrushchev's pressure on China through Albania and his pressure on the West in Berlin is worth noting. In both cases, he has skillfully found an exposed and vulnerable point in the opponent's position and has begun to apply the scalpel rather than the axe. In both cases, it is questionable how far Khrushchev will go if his "salami tactics" do not work. Would he risk war over Berlin, a break with China over Albania?

Khrushchev's precise calculations in launching the attack on Albania are difficult to gauge. His action was undoubtedly fraught with grave risk inasmuch as it meant that if the Chinese did not back down, the possibility of an open rift would be greatly enhanced. Why then did he take in 1961 the portentous step that he refrained from taking in 1960?

First of all, Khrushchev may have calculated that he could obtain a Chinese surrender. China in 1961 was in the midst of a severe economic crisis which threatened mass starvation. The Left-wing domestic policies of the preceding three years had been proved unsound much as the Russians had warned. The Chinese were more than ever in dire need of Soviet trade, credit, and assistance, meager as it was. What better time then for the Soviet leader to expect that he could succeed in blackmailing his Chinese ally into submission? That it was indeed intended blackmail and deliberately designed to humiliate China was apparent from the forum in which Khrushchev made his surprise attack. The Russian leader knew very well that China's delegate to the Soviet Party Congress, Chou En-lai, would have to speak to the 22nd Congress two days after Khrushchev attacked the Albanians. By his timing, he presented Chou with a 48-hour ultimatum. His maximum hope, of course, was not that Chou would support his attack on Albania but rather that Chou would remain silent. Thus, before the assembled delegates from throughout the Soviet Union and the international Communist world, Khrushchev would have made clear that he had sought and obtained a Chinese surrender. In short,

Khrushchev may have miscalculated by underestimating the fierce pride of the Chinese Communist leadership.

Secondly, Khrushchev may have calculated that neglecting to take action to ward off the Peking-Tirana axis would be a sign of weakness and, in potential consequence, of greater danger than the risks of action. Then, too, Khrushchev was faced with serious problems both at home and abroad. At home, there was obvious dissatisfaction in the Party with some of his military and domestic economic policies. Abroad, there were not only the Chinese and Albanian parties more or less openly flouting his will, but many other parties either sympathetic to the Chinese or with factions inclined toward Peking. Although no single one of these threats in and of itself probably represented a danger to Khrushchev's power position, taken in combination they gave promise of sooner or later posing such a threat.

Finally, it must be pointed out that Khrushchev's action against Albania was a response to Chinese-Albanian initiatives. From the very day that the Moscow conference of 1960 closed, China and Albania demonstrated by word and deed that neither was prepared to accept Soviet dictates. The Chinese continued to challenge Soviet policy and, by supporting Albania both politically and economically, to demonstrate that they intended to keep on trying to build up a pro-Chinese faction within the international Communist movement.

If Khrushchev, for any or all of these reasons, launched his attack in expectation of a Chinese retreat, he seemed—at the end of 1961—uncertain of getting it. After the Soviet attack on Albania the Chinese began to negotiate new economic agreements with that country.[21] They republished Albanian statements accusing Khrushchev of "anti-Marxist" conduct, of resorting to "lies, pressure and threats, slanders and inventions," of "opportunism," "revisionism," and "treachery." They even went so far as to print the slashing attack on Khrushchev made by Communist Party First Secretary Hoxha, on the November 7 anniversary of the Bolshevik revolution. The Chinese waited nine days before printing this speech, a fact which suggests the Party deliberated over it at some length. By publishing the speech, which was not picked up anywhere else in the Communist Bloc, they took the most provocative action they could take short of openly attacking Moscow itself.

375

Moreover, on the 20th anniversary of the Albanian Party on November 8, the Chinese Party sent the Albanian Party a message in which it referred to the "correct guidance" of its "tested leader" Enver Hoxha, the man who Khrushchev all but read out of the Communist world. And in sharp contrast to Soviet and East European Bloc statements which began after the Congress to exclude Albania from the camp, the Chinese continued pointedly to refer to the "twelve socialist countries" in the Bloc.

The Russians, for their part, broke diplomatic relations with Albania early in December and published in their own press explicit criticisms of "our Chinese friends" by various East European satellite leaders.[22] On December 10, Tass published a comprehensive ideological indictment of Albania which had appeared in the Soviet theoretical journal *Kommunist*. This article said that dogmatism might become the main danger in "some parties" and that it had already become the main danger in the Albanian Party, an obvious warning to Peking. More blatantly, *Pravda* on December 14 warned that there were no exceptions for any Party, "large or small," to the duty to show fidelity to Marxism-Leninism or "break" with it. The Russians had issued similar warnings to Peking in 1960, as the reader will recall. Would they now be followed by more stringent actions?

In many respects, Khrushchev's open denunciation of the Albanians may in fact have been more an admission of weakness rather than an indication of strength. During the year and a half preceding the 22nd Congress, the Russians had imposed economic sanctions on Albania,[23] and may even have attempted a coup.[24] They had withdrawn (or been forced to withdraw) part or all of their submarine fleet. The Albanian Party continued to side with the Chinese on most outstanding issues of intra-bloc and global policy, evidently fearing above all that Khrushchev's *rapprochement* with Yugoslavia might ultimately lead to political annexation by Tito. In February, at the 4th Congress of the Albanian Party, there were defiant attacks on the "revisionists" who were trying to turn Albania's geographic encirclement "into an economic blockade and make effective the political isolation of our socialist country." They would not succeed in this attempt, however, because "socialist Albania is not alone."[25]

In April, China and Albania signed three economic protocols, one of which provided for Chinese equipment and technical assistance for building twenty-five chemical, metallurgical, electrical, and other plants. At the same time, it was revealed that the agreements signed in February had included one for a Chinese loan to Albania worth 112.5 million rubles, bringing Chinese aid to Albania since 1956 over the Soviet figure.[26] Albania was not represented by her Party First Secretary either at the March or the August Warsaw Pact meeting in Moscow. She was not represented at all at the meeting in May of most European Bloc leaders in Prague for the fortieth anniversary of the Czech Communist Party.[27] Whether this absence was self-imposed or forced upon them by Moscow, the fact remains that the Albanians in effect had partially severed Party and military relations with the European Bloc and had as yet been able to get away with it.[28]

The serious problem with which the Albanians faced Moscow stemmed from their example to the Communist world that the tiniest of all Bloc countries, if supported by Peking, could defy the Russians with impunity. For all of Khrushchev's insistence that no party could dictate to another, it must have become clear to him that if he allowed the Peking-Tirana axis to continue without a frontal attack upon it, it might soon become the basis of a much larger group of dissidents within the international Communist movement—a group that Peking clearly sought to form and to head. In launching a frontal attack, therefore, Khrushchev was in effect saying that all else had failed in his attempt to bring Albania to heel and that the only way left was an open threat of expulsion from the Communist Bloc.

It is important to note that the resolution adopted at the conclusion of the 22nd Congress was notably milder on the Albanians than Khrushchev had been in his speech of October 27. In that speech, Khrushchev in effect called for the resignation of Shehu, Hoxha, "and others . . . in the commanding posts in the Party and the State." The resolution, on the other hand, merely expressed the hope that "the Albanian leaders . . . will renounce their erroneous views and return to the road of unity and cooperation with all socialist countries. . . . "[29] This restraint could have stemmed from a division within the Soviet leadership over how far to go in pushing the matter[30] or it could have reflected the fact that one-third of the parties represented at the Congress refused to go along with the Russians. Possibly, too, Moscow wanted to give the Albanian leaders a last opportunity to confess their "sin."

Perhaps the most intriguing aspect of the 22nd Congress was the revival of the attacks on the anti-Party group and particularly on Molotov. Although it is quite likely that there were internal compulsions for such attacks, their relation to the Sino-Soviet conflict has been made quite explicit by Soviet spokesmen. Kuusinen accused Molotov of "fishing in foreign waters,"[31] and Mikoyan said that Molotov's rejection of peaceful coexistence "was close to that of the foreign opponents of peaceful coexistence, treating it as a variant of the cold war, as a state of armed peace."[32] Mikoyan also referred to Molotov's opposition to Khrushchev's personal diplomacy. Pospelov accused Molotov of "slanderously alleging" that the Party line laid down at the 20th Congress was "in complete contradiction to the revolutionary essence of Marxism-Leninism,"[33] a position also taken by Peking. Khrushchev himself, in his concluding speech, said that "only the hopeless dogmatists," Molotov and "his like," did not understand the changes that had taken place in the world situation.[34]

Did the anti-Party group in general, and Molotov in particular, seek to make common cause with the Chinese in an effort to unseat Khrushchev? On the basis of available evidence it is impossible to answer this question. It is apparent, however, that as early as June 1957, when Khrushchev defeated the anti-Party group, Peking had serious reservations about the purge. Its comment on the removals from the Presidium was the least enthusiastic of the entire Bloc. It is likely, but again undemonstrable, that Peking had earlier supported Khrushchev against Malenkov, for Malenkov's emphasis on light industry would have meant fewer Soviet capital goods for China. If Peking did in fact support Khrushchev at this juncture, it must have been bitterly disappointed when Khrushchev stole some of Malenkov's thunder by adopting a semi-moderate position towards the West and towards the relative priorities to be accorded heavy and light industry. After the fall of 1957, there can be little doubt that the views of the Peking Left, both on foreign and domestic policy, were much closer to those of the fallen Molotov than to those of Khrushchev. That Peking would have preferred a change in Soviet leadership is a fairly safe inference; but what precisely it did to bring this change about must remain a matter for speculation. It is noteworthy that Soviet leaders, after the Bucharest confrontation in June 1960, began placing heavy stress on the collective leadership of the USSR, as if to demonstrate to Peking that there was no possibility of splitting it.

Khrushchev's unexpected attack on Stalin at the Congress—considering all the obvious liabilities for the Communist world that such an attack carries with it—raises another crucial question: what was the motivation for it? Hoxha, in a very revealing speech on the October Revolution anniversary, suggests that the Stalin question was in part being "used as a bogey for putting pressure on the other parties and for liquidating the leaders who do not please N. Khrushchev."[35] Although Hoxha is obviously not a disinterested observer in this matter, it does in fact seem likely that—whatever the internal compulsions for the move against Stalin—Khrushchev is also consciously using the "personality cult" issue to blacken those leaders in the Communist movement, such as Mao and Hoxha, who have refused in recent years to accept his dictates. Khrushchev would much prefer to deal with collective leaderships in some parties so that he could play one faction off against another and thus minimize the ability of one powerful leader to defy him. While Stalin was alive, the existence of "little Stalins" throughout the Communist world did not hinder the exercise of Soviet authority because none of the little Stalins would have dared to defy the *vozhd*. But now that authority in the international Communist world has become more diffuse and the means of control more subtle, Communist leaders with unlimited power in their own parties can be a severe limitation on Khrushchev's freedom of maneuver.

The Sino-Soviet struggle over Albania implies and illustrates the rivalry over power and authority in the Communist world that has been at the heart of the Sino-Soviet conflict since 1956. Had Sino-Soviet differences been limited to mere matters of policy, one might have supposed that the hardening of Soviet foreign policy since the summer of 1960, combined with the radical domestic retreat of the Chinese, would have gone some way toward removing or decreasing the causes of conflict. After all, the enthusiasm with which Peking seconded the Soviet government decision to resume nuclear testing[36] and its prompt support of the Soviet stand on Berlin[37] revealed a satisfaction with Soviet foreign policy that was missing in 1958 and 1959. At the very time, however, when there was this slight narrowing of the political gulf between the two powers, the yawning gap over authority and power was shown to be unresolved.

The Albanian Party has not been the only cat's-paw in what has become in part a struggle for power and for spheres of influence within the international Communist movement. In July 1961, Moscow demonstrated a rare benevolence to all three of the Asian satellite countries, extending massive aid to continue through 1965. There were new credits as well as debt cancellations. In the same month, the Russians sent no less a person than Suslov to the Mongolian Party Congress, where he made a curious reference to the "firm security" of the Outer Mongolia borders on both the Chinese and Soviet sides. In this he may have been reassuring the Outer Mongolian Party that Moscow would not tolerate Chinese attempts at border adjustments.[38] (Chinese Communist maps, unlike Soviet ones, have persistently shown the Sino-Mongolian border as undelimited.) There were also clear signs of a Sino-Soviet tug-of-war in North Korea. In early July, Kim Il-song made brief visits to both Moscow and Peking. In a joint communiqué signed in Moscow, Kim came out against "deviations from the principles of socialist internationalism,"[39] phraseology which in this context could have been aimed only at Peking. In a communiqué issued a few days later (July 15), following his visit to Peking, there was no reference to such "deviations" but instead there was a vigorous attack on "Yugoslav revisionism," the euphemism that Peking has employed since 1958 to denote "soft" Soviet policies.[40] In both Moscow and Peking, Kim got formal assurances of support in case of trouble with the West. In sum, Kim was dexterously reaping the advantages of being wooed by rival suitors. This was safe ground for him as it was for both Moscow and Peking, each of which would prefer to keep the Asian parties in the middle rather than see them openly allied with the other.

If Albania, too, had decided to play the middle, it is quite likely that Khrushchev would not have launched his frontal assault. For what the Russians must seek to avoid at all costs is the creation of an Asian Cominform led by Peking and supported by other parties throughout the Communist movement. The Chinese, on the other hand, must seek at all costs to avoid isolation within the Communist world. In this connection, it is important to consider the reaction of the various delegations at the 22nd Congress to the Soviet attack on Albania. This was the first issue between Moscow and Peking that was put to a vote, as it were, in the international Communist movement. The reaction of the eighty-odd parties obviously indicates a great deal about the relative strength of Moscow and Peking in world Communism. The Russians carried with them nearly all the parties in Europe, the Middle East, and Latin America, most of whom joined in the condemnation of Albania. The Chinese were tacitly supported by all the Asian parties which, with the single exception of the Ceylonese, refrained from mentioning Albania.[41] It is difficult to say to what extent this line-up disappointed either Moscow or Peking. It has long been apparent that the European parties would support the Russians right up to the brink of an open schism, despite the fact that there are elements sympathetic to Chinese positions in many of those European parties. It has also been apparent for some time that most of the Asian parties have been very careful to stay in the middle of the Sino-Soviet dispute. Before the Congress met, there had been some question about the Latin American and Middle Eastern parties, many of which might have been expected to favor the more militant Chinese tactics for gaining power, but which, on the other hand, were disinclined to defy the Russians because of geographical propinquity, financial dependence, or Moscow-trained leaderships. Some of these parties, moreover, desire to continue a hitherto successful non-violent policy.

It is extremely important also to qualify the Asian parties' "support" for Peking. Abstention is after all a middle-of-the-road position. None of the Asian parties followed Chou En-lai's example by criticizing the Russians implicitly for their attack on Albania. The Congress, therefore, made it plain that the depth of commitment of the European, Middle Eastern, and Latin American parties to the Russians is for the most part greater than the depth of commitment of the Asian parties to Peking. This suggests that, were an open break between Moscow and Peking to occur, Moscow could probably count on the support of all those parties which joined it in condemning Albania; while it is not at all certain that

Peking could count on the support of all those parties who refrained from mentioning Albania. The results of this Soviet-sponsored "poll" of the international Communist movement will undoubtedly be pondered by the Chinese, who are manifestly fearful of isolation.

On the other hand, it is an impressive fact that *all* but one of the Asian parties refused to attack Albania. This is a fact that will undoubtedly be pondered well by the Russians. It certainly suggests that geography plays an unexpectedly large role in Communist Bloc politics. And it brings somewhat closer to reality the nightmare that must haunt Moscow—the possibility of a breakup of the Communist world into Eastern and Western empires.

The Implications of the Struggle over
Albania

The Albanian incident demonstrated how profound and far-reaching the Sino-Soviet conflict had become by 1961. The situation had reached the point where it was increasingly difficult for both parties to avoid an open rift on some issues. Moreover, a wider rift was not to be precluded.

The struggle over Albania had acquired a momentum of its own. The prestige of both the Russians and Chinese was heavily engaged. In such a situation compromise becomes extremely difficult. Moreover, on Albania and on other similar tests of strength in the future, Khrushchev and Mao may miscalculate one another's intentions, each believing that the other is bluffing and not prepared to go to the brink. Mao may believe that if he gives in to Khrushchev on Albania, other demands will follow, while Khrushchev may conclude that if he does not force Mao to retreat now, the Chinese challenge to Soviet hegemony may soon grow stronger. Finally, there is the unpredictable role of irrationality in a conflict where·much depends on the whims of two powerful leaders.

On the other hand, the struggle over Albania and all that it reflects of deep-seated tensions within the Sino-Soviet alliance should not obscure the fact that the two Communist allies continue to share a number of common goals and interests and are especially bound by a common hostility to the United States, the principal pillar of the non-Communist world standing in the way of both Russia's and China's ambitions.

382

The rift over Albania merely culminates a long and bitter dispute waged obliquely for several years. This dispute has profoundly altered the relationship between Moscow and Peking and it has had important consequences for the entire Communist world as well as for the West. It is to these considerations of great import for the future that we now turn.

CHAPTER 17

SOME GENERAL IMPLICATIONS

THE Sino-Soviet conflict has already had considerable impact on Sino-Soviet relations, the relations within the Communist world, and the relations between East and West. It is my purpose in this concluding chapter to consider how the conflict has already affected each of these areas and to try to project these developments into the future. I shall also mention some of the implications of the conflict for the West. First, however, I should like to restate some of the cohesive factors in the Sino-Soviet alliance and then to consider those factors which have driven the allies to the point of near open split.

Some Limitations
on Sino-Soviet Conflict

It is easy either to overstate or to understate the gravity of the Sino-Soviet conflict. We need some perspective in which to view the conflict, in order both to assess the past and to hazard some judgments about the future. Perhaps the most important question that can be asked in this connection is: what are the limits of the Sino-Soviet conflict? Are those limits predictable? Can they contract or expand? What are the conditions under which they are likely to shrink or to expand? Let me state what I believe to be the *present* limits of conflict, that is, those limits which are likely to hold for the foreseeable future.[1]

First, both parties are very much aware of the weaker position they would assume relative to the non-Communist West if they were to split apart completely. China would be reduced to the role of a third-rate power without the ability to wage nuclear war or to defend herself against such a war, and without the protection of the Soviet deterrent shield. While Soviet strategic and military power would not be affected, the political power of the USSR would be seriously weakened, its southern and eastern boundaries would be less secure, and its influence in Asia would be severely diminished.

Second, both parties are aware that a split would drastically, perhaps mortally, weaken the international Communist movement. Some parties, particularly those in Asia, would be split wide open

384

and rendered correspondingly ineffective; others would gravitate into either the Soviet or the Chinese sphere of influence, but would suffer from the activities of dissident factions wanting to go in the other direction. It can hardly be doubted that the international revolutionary process, by which both parties hope to see Communism dominate the earth, would be severely retarded. Clearly, from this viewpoint alone, both parties have a tremendous stake in avoiding a total break.

Third, the goal of the Chinese Communists, so far as it is possible to deduce that goal, is not now to replace the Soviet Party at the head of the Communist movement but rather to obtain parity in leadership, particularly in the leadership of the revolutionary movement in the underdeveloped countries; to push Soviet policies in a more militant direction; to increase their own power and prestige in the Communist Bloc at the expense of the Russians; to undermine Khrushchev's position in the Soviet Party so as to encourage a change in Soviet leadership[2]; and to pressure the Russians into pooling the resources of the more and less developed Bloc countries more equitably.

Fourth, it is unlikely that either Russia or China will change partners in the foreseeable future. A Soviet-American alliance directed against China, a subject of occasional speculation in the West, is extremely unlikely. There is no indication whatever at the present time that such a consideration enters Soviet thinking. The prospect of a Chinese-American alliance directed against Moscow is even more remote.

The Divisive Factors

The tensions that were impossible to conceal in the Sino-Soviet relationship by the end of 1961 stem from a number of factors: their uneven stages of socio-economic development; their divergent revolutionary expectations and aspirations; the strong element of nationalism and anti-white imperialism in the Chinese Communist revolution.

There is also little question but that what began as a dispute over alternative revolutionary strategies had soon developed into an incipient struggle for power in the international Communist movement. This is amply indicated by the controversy over Al-

385

bania, which occurred despite the fact that the Russians were moving somewhat closer to the tougher global line desired by Peking. This struggle is also reflected in obvious Russian efforts in late 1960 and 1961 to consolidate their positions in Outer Mongolia, North Korea, North Vietnam, efforts which indicated preparations for a long-term struggle for power with China within the Communist movement. Even if Soviet and Chinese policies change in the direction of greater compatibility, the struggle for power within the Communist movement will probably continue. This struggle has already led to the appearance of more or less open pro-Chinese and pro-Russian factions in various parties throughout the world.

This should not be taken to mean that policy disputes between Russia and China have been merely incidents in a Machiavellian struggle for power, or that they will be so in the future. It is idle to attempt to speculate on whether the Chinese leaders genuinely believe that more militant policies are required in certain areas of the world or whether they are using the desire for more militant policies on the part of local Communist parties as a means of exercising leverage on the Russians. Considerations of both power and principle are undoubtedly present. In the 1927 dispute between Stalin and Trotsky over revolutionary strategy in China, Stalin probably began by believing that the best interests of the USSR required a strong alliance with the Chinese Nationalists. Trotsky probably believed with equal sincerity that such an alliance would prove disastrous. Yet each of them seems to have consciously employed his China policy as a stick with which to beat the other in the intra-party struggle then going on. The same mixed motives are present in the Sino-Soviet conflict today.

The Chinese Communist leaders, or at least the dominant group within the Chinese leadership, believe in pursuing a more militant revolutionary strategy than the Russians choose to follow. So long as Communist China remains internationally isolated, anxious to regain territories to which she lays historical claim, and without all the instrumentalities possessed by the Russians for waging a more subtle worldwide revolutionary policy, China is likely to remain the more militant of the two Communist powers.

At the same time, the Chinese Communists are doubtless very much aware that being more radical than the Russians increases their influence in the underdeveloped areas of the world, where

Communist and proto-Communist parties will be less inclined toward moderate strategies, such as Khrushchev's, based on a parliamentary path to power, and more inclined toward direct revolutionary action. By advocating more radical policies than the Russians, the Chinese Communists increase their bargaining power vis à vis the Russians. Their weakness in terms of national power is thus converted into strength in the worldwide Communist movement.

Since, in more than four years, the two Communist powers have not succeeded in reconciling divergent policies, it is a fair presumption that the causes of these differences run deep into their history, ideological preconceptions, national environments, and interest calculations. It is instructive to recall that differences between the two began in 1956–1957, when China was pursuing a relatively moderate Right strategy, and continued after 1958 when the Chinese Communists shifted to a Left strategy both at home and abroad. Moreover, these differences intensified from year to year despite attempts that must have been made to eliminate them. This suggests that much more is involved than differences in policy.

So long as alternative courses of action are open to the Communist Bloc in a changing and complex world, differing assessments of priority, interest, opportunities, and risks are bound to occur between the two principal partners in the Bloc. There is a rough parallel in certain respects between Eastern and Western experience. London constantly pulls American policy in one direction, while Taipei and Bonn pull it in another, less moderate direction. A similar phenomenon is observable in the Communist world. Belgrade and Warsaw have tried to pull Soviet policy toward moderation, while Peking, Pankow, and Tirana have sought more or less consistently in recent years to pull it in the other direction. Because such differences in perspective are intimately bound up with each Party's sense of its own security and best interests, they are not likely to disappear. Taiwan will remain for China a more pressing goal than it is for Moscow and one for which the Chinese will want to risk more than the Russians. The Chinese attitude toward arms control or disarmament or any kind of negotiation with the West is likely to remain quite different from the Soviet attitude so long as China does not have a nuclear capability and a delivery system and so long as it is excluded from the community of nations. So long as such differences in environments and in

387

priority of aims remain, there are likely to be differences in strategy.

It is beside the point to contend, as is occasionally done in the West, that all alliances have their problems and that Sino-Soviet differences are no more nor no less serious than those between, say, Washington and Paris. Neither the United States nor France is intent on establishing worldwide hegemony. The Communist movement has long insisted on iron discipline for good reason. The seizure and consolidation of power in any given country is impossible without such discipline. The more ambitious goal of expediting and controlling a worldwide revolutionary process requires even greater discipline.

Soviet and Chinese assessments of their interests and priorities in the underdeveloped areas will probably diverge in the future as frequently as they have in the past. In 1958–1959 the Chinese Communists came to the conclusion that their "soft" policies toward the emerging nations had proved unsuccessful. Despite the good neighbor policy which the Chinese Communists inaugurated in 1954, few of the new nations made any dramatic moves toward supporting China's foreign policy objectives. The Chinese accordingly changed that policy and began to take a more hostile attitude toward the Nehrus, Nassers, and Kassims. Their maximum purpose was to overthrow the "bourgeois nationalist" governments in favor of more responsive regimes; their minimum purpose was to increase the pressure on them so as to influence their policies in a more favorable direction. The Russians, on the other hand, were not so dissatisfied as Peking with the "soft" policy toward the nationalists. The new governments pursued for the most part neutralist foreign policies, and in some cases even supported Soviet foreign policy. The urge to replace ruling classes of these states was therefore not so great in Moscow as it was in Peking. Such differences are likely to continue in the future, in part because the Russians have much greater resources and opportunities than the Chinese for influencing the course of development in the new countries. The Russians can cooperate on a state-to-state level by moving in with technicians and machines and trade, the very things that the underdeveloped countries most want. The Chinese, on the other hand, do not have the instrumentalities available to compete on this level.

When the new governments do not act in accord with Chinese

wishes, Peking can resort only to a combination of threat and blandishment. The threat is primarily that of getting the local revolutionary movement to step up pressure on the troublesome nationalist regime. This threat, of course, cannot be made to any effect unless the Chinese control the local revolutionary movement. Hence, one of their basic aims in the period under discussion was to take over control of the revolutionary movements in all underdeveloped areas. To the extent that this aim is realized, however, conflict with Moscow will result whenever the Chinese seek to use a local revolutionary movement for what Moscow regards as a premature assault on a given nationalist government. A good example was the experience of Iraq in the summer of 1959. The Russians cannot be indifferent to Chinese-led Communist assaults on the very governments the Russians are trying to woo.

One of the basic differences between Moscow and Peking in the period from 1957 to 1960 concerned the level of risk that could be assumed in protecting and abetting local revolutionary movements, which both believe it is their duty to aid and which both believe are the precursors of inevitable Communist-led revolution throughout the world. The Russians accused the Chinese of minimizing the dangers of all-out nuclear war; the Chinese accused the Russians of exaggerating those dangers. The Russians said local wars could be avoided; the Chinese argued that they could not. While Moscow seemed prepared to use its strategic power to deter the West from interference in the revolutionary process throughout the world, it was reluctant to use that power in a manner inviting large risk of war. Even when the USSR seemingly ran some small risks of war with the West, as in Berlin or in Laos, its leaders took great care to maintain control over those risks.

The reasons for this significant divergence between the risk calculations of Moscow and Peking are undoubtedly complex. In part it results from the fact that Peking has an outstanding unredeemed territory in Taiwan which, the Chinese may calculate, can be regained only by taking risks of a local war with the West. Moscow has no such unredeemed lands. In part, the divergence may be attributable to the simple fact that China does not have nuclear weapons and can afford the luxury of rattling someone else's missiles. (The corollary is that when China does develop a nuclear delivery capability—and not until then—it may become more responsible.) In part, China may feel that the Bloc can avoid war risks only by not supporting local revolutionary movements. Finally, the Chinese Communists may well calculate that a third world war, if it were to come, would leave China as the predominant world power. Chou En-lai is reported to have said as early as 1956 that after the next war there will be "twenty million Americans, five million Englishmen, fifty million Russians, and three hundred million Chinese left," a prospect not likely to appeal to the Kremlin.[3] Whatever the reasons, and whatever shifts in Chinese policy may occur in the foreseeable future, the deep-seated causes which produced the divergence are likely to remain.

Then, too, so long as Mao and Khrushchev live, the possibility of a Sino-Soviet *rapprochement* seems remote. There seems no doubt that the conflict between the parties has been greatly exacerbated by the personal rivalry and animosity between the two leaders. In the fall of 1959 and subsequently, Khrushchev and the Russian press occasionally referred to the "conceit" and arrogance of some leaders of large Communist parties. At the Bucharest conference in June 1960, as we have already seen, a bitter exchange took place between Khrushchev and the Chinese representative, an exchange in which Khrushchev hurled abuse at Mao and the Chinese delegate responded by launching a personal attack on the Soviet chief. The prestige of both leaders has become deeply engaged.

A Partial Bridging
of the Gap

Although a restoration of complete harmony between Moscow and Peking is unlikely, there are certain developments that could bring the Russians and Chinese closer together sometime in the future. As we have suggested, to the extent that the personal rivalry between Mao and Khrushchev aggravates the conflict, it is possible that the death of one or both would open the way for compromise. Although an arrangement for divided authority nowhere seems on the horizon, such a possibility cannot be precluded. A huge step-up in Soviet economic and military assistance to the Chinese could also have a mitigating effect on their tensions. A real or imagined Western threat to the survival of either regime would have a similar effect.

Moreover, the effects of the continuing economic crisis in China should have a restraining influence on the Chinese Communist leadership and make it less anxious for a showdown with Moscow that could lead to even more drastic economic sanctions than the Russians have yet taken.[4] The economic crisis has already led to a major policy shift. The communes have become almost an empty shell; industrial investment has been severely cut back; there is a new emphasis on farm mechanization; "regularization and rationalization," which were "bourgeois" words in 1958–1959, have now become more respectable; there is a new emphasis on balance and "rationality," on improving statistical work and investigating "concrete conditions"; there is a suggestion that more wages will be paid in money and less in kind; there has been a revival of the "hundred flowers" policy designed to allow greater freedom to China's 100,000 intellectuals and scientists; finally, the program for the "socialist transformation" of Tibetan agriculture has been postponed for at least five years.[5]

The radical economic policies instituted in 1958 went awry for a number of reasons. First of all, the regime's frenetic policies, particularly in agriculture, lowered productivity, much as the Russians had warned. The peasantry would not increase agricultural output so long as it had no tangible rewards for harder work. Second, the communes overcentralized the economy and proved to be organizationally unsound. Third, there appears to have been a serious miscalculation about the 1958 harvest, which was thought to be a bumper harvest and which led the regime into a fanciful belief that China's food problem had been solved. This miscalculation led to a cutback in sown acreage and helps explain the gross overoptimism expressed by the Chinese leaders in 1958. Fourth, the new farming methods, such as "deep plowing," proved ineffective. Fifth, poor weather, particularly in 1960, contributed to the food shortages, though probably not as much as the regime has subsequently claimed. Additional reasons were the lack of chemical fertilizer, the shortage of draft animals, and lack of tractors, of technicians to repair them, and of oil to fuel them.

The seriousness of the food shortages is borne out by the following facts. Grain purchases from Canada, Australia, and Burma already amount to 160 million dollars and, according to some estimates, may reach 500 million. The scale of these grain deals, moreover, suggests that the Chinese expect a continued shortage through 1963. In this connection it is significant that Chinese repayments on their debts to the USSR are not to reach more than a token level until 1963.[6] It seems quite likely, then, that the swing back to the Right is calculated to last for at least three and perhaps more years. There have been reports of famine in certain areas of China; of the execution of some Party secretaries at the commune level for allowing local conditions to get too bad; of black markets in some cities; of anti-regime peasant organizations appearing in the countryside; and of widespread apathy. Most of the refugees flowing into Hong Kong are said to be in poor health. The number of food parcels from Hong Kong to relatives and friends on the mainland has risen markedly.[7]

It is an open question whether the policies adopted hastily by the CCP in early 1961 will be enough to restore the economy to a sound footing. There are signs that the Chinese Communists have come very close to using up foreign exchange reserves and that the land-population ratio is getting worse rather than better.

If economic considerations were decisive in the calculations of the Chinese leadership as to how far they could go in defying the Kremlin, they would not have continued to support tiny Albania as they did in 1961. But even if these considerations are not decisive, they are certainly critical. There is some evidence to suggest the existence of a faction within the Chinese Party which advocates making concessions to the Russians on the basis of such considerations. Their argument surely must be that China must first build itself into a modern industrial power before it can afford a split with Moscow. To what extent such arguments will temper Chinese policies in the future is difficult to assess because they must be weighed in the balance with the fierce pride and nationalism of China's leaders—which the Russians dare not underestimate.

In the final analysis, the Sino-Soviet dilemma is whether or not it is possible to divide ideological authority in a revolutionary movement that has historically required a single leader to interpret the ideology and to dictate the strategy and tactics in a shifting and complex world. A closely related dilemma is whether it is possible to carve up the world into spheres of influence. The history of Communism thus far suggests that it is not compatible with shared authority.[8]

Searching the past for guide-lines for the future, one is struck by the similarities between the Sino-Soviet conflict and the Bolshevik-Menshevik controversy in the decade before the 1917 Revolution. Serious issues of doctrine and tactics separated the two wings of the Russian Social Democratic Party even though both shared a common Marxist ideology and a common enemy. While the Bolsheviks insisted on the need for a general staff of insurrection, the Mensheviks emphasized political activity as the precursor for insurrection. For the Bolsheviks, participation in the elections to the First Duma in 1906 merely encouraged "constitutional illusions"; genuine revolutionaries, they argued, should be actively preparing for revolution. Charges and countercharges of "treason" to the revolution, "opportunism," and conciliation" were made. The Bolsheviks contended, with little justification, that the Mensheviks were seeking to confine Social Democratic tactics solely to legal activity and were restricting their aims to reform. Throughout most of the factional infighting, Lenin maintained an intransigent attitude, insisting that the Mensheviks accept his conditions for unity or that a *rapprochement* was out of the question. Several "unity" congresses and meetings served only to paper over the differences, not to bridge them, e.g. the Fourth Congress in 1906, a Central Committee plenum in Paris in 1910, and the Brussels unification Congress in 1914. Intermediary groups such as the Bund, Trotsky's group, and the Socialist International all urged compromise and conciliation. At the Brussels Congress, a resolution was adopted calling for unity upon five conditions, one of which was that the minority should always accept the decisions of the majority. Lenin never accepted this verdict.[9]

Without pushing this historical analogy too far, the similarity between Lenin's position from 1905 to the eve of the October Revolution and that of the Chinese from 1956 to 1961 is, in some respects, striking. Both acted as if they believed that only they could be relied upon to lead the revolution forward successfully. Both seemed contemptuous of Communists with whom they disagreed. Both seemed prepared to risk a split rather than to give in to a majority they believed to be in error. In both cases, differences of tactics, temperament, and doctrine were intertwined with aspirations for power. In both cases, the conflict ebbed and flowed over a number of years but was not completely breached.

One can also find suggestive parallels between the views of the Chinese Communist leaders in recent years and those of the Bolsheviks in the years of the first Five Year Plan when the Russians themselves were intent on turning their backward country into a major industrial power overnight. In the 1930's, the Bolsheviks too were obsessed with speed of development even at the cost of imbalance; Soviet academicians too argued that "there are no fortresses which Bolsheviks cannot storm"; there was during this hectic period of forced collectivization and rapid industrialization a swing to the Left in foreign policy which lasted until the shadow of fascism drove the Russians back to a Popular Front strategy. The implication would seem to be that uneven development is as great if not greater a problem for the Communists as Lenin imagined it would be for the West.

The Emergence of Polycentrism

One of the most significant accompaniments of the Sino-Soviet conflict has been the tendency towards polycentrism[10] in the international Communist movement. With the Russians and Chinese unable to agree on many critical issues of domestic and foreign policy, the smaller Communist parties have been able to pick and choose from each side those policies which they believe to be most in their own interests and to adapt these policies to their own national perspectives and environments. So long as China continues to set herself up as a rival arbiter of doctrine in the Communist world, local Communist parties will enjoy greater domestic autonomy and more flexibility in foreign policy. In the words of Richard Lowenthal, the old doctrine of Moscow *locuta causa finita* is no longer valid. In time the Russians may more and more have to adjust to other viewpoints and interests. The international Communist movement may gradually change from a Soviet rubber stamp to a genuine forum for reconciling differences of opinion and interest.

To the extent that Chinese policy remains to the Left of Soviet policy, it will provide a rallying ground for the Communist world's neo-Stalinists, of whom there are some in every party, and for those parties, such as the Albanian, whose interests lie in intensifying the East-West struggle. Even in the unlikely event that Chinese policy moves to the Right of Soviet policy, where it was in 1956–

1957, China will still be a focal point for dissidents, in this case the Bloc "liberals" and those Communists and "revisionists" throughout the world who would like to pursue moderate policies at home and abroad. Since it is unlikely that Soviet and Chinese policies on all controversial issues will be exactly the same, the very existence of a rival center—irrespective of the policies it pursues—will encourage the growth of centrifugal tendencies.

Since the very outset of the Sino-Soviet conflict in 1956, the smaller Communist parties have sought to exploit the conflict in their own interests, and to play off one big power against the other. In 1956 and 1957, for example, the Poles saw in China an ally against Soviet pressure. By 1960 Gomulka had swung around to become one of the staunchest supporters of Khrushchev against Peking, for the simple reason that Khrushchev was then more moderate than Mao. The Poles benefit from a moderate Bloc foreign policy because it enables them to keep channels open to the West, which in turn reduces domestic dissatisfaction and enables them to get badly needed aid. They benefit from a tolerant line on "revisionism" because it creates a climate in which the "special" Polish road to Communism can be pursued with a minimum of outside interference. The Poles support Khrushchev, one supposes, because he will find it difficult to mount pressure on them so long as he needs Communist allies against Mao. Similarly, those Communist parties not in power that wish to pursue united front strategies, in order to gain respectability and influence in their own countries, will take the Russian side as long as the Russians stay to the Right of Peking. Togliatti, the Italian Party leader and the original advocate of polycentrism, for example; has supported the Russians against the Chinese because the more moderate Russian policy makes the Italian Party look more "respectable" and thus increases its chances of making headway with the socialists and other parties of the non-Communist left.

At the other end of the spectrum there are parties both inside and outside the Bloc, or minority factions within the parties, which for a variety of reasons would like to run faster than the Russians. The Albanian Party, for example, evidently convinced that Khrushchev's sporadic flirtations with Yugoslavia may one day endanger its very existence, sided with Peking principally because the Chinese offered a tougher line toward Yugoslavia.[11]

395

The Albanian leaders may have believed that Khrushchev, in his anxiety to reach an understanding with Tito, might one day offer the Yugoslav leader a Balkan federation under Yugoslav control which would mean Tito's swallowing up of Albania. Since Tito was demanding a cleaning out of all Stalinist leaders, they may also have feared for their own power positions.

The unstable allegiances within the Communist Bloc are illustrated also by the case of East Germany. In late 1958 and early 1959 there was considerable evidence of an incipient Peking-Pankow axis. East German spokesmen took a much more sympathetic attitude than the Russians to the communes and the "great leap forward," supported the Chinese, as Moscow did not, on the Indian border crisis, and in general displayed approval of China's tougher foreign policy stand. There were several reasons for this temporary closeness of China and East Germany. Both countries had territorial claims which were primary objectives to them but secondary to the Russians. Hence they had a common interest in seeking to force Soviet policy to the Left. There was also some common ground in the approach to domestic problems. Although East Germany's domestic economic problems were in no way similar to those of China, some of the German neo-Stalinists and some of the more ideologically oriented cadres believed that in the commune and leap forward program the CCP had succeeded in mobilizing mass initiative and revolutionary fervor, which were sadly lacking in their own country. The Peking-Pankow axis was abruptly broken only in 1960. One may suppose that Khrushchev tightened the screws on Ulbricht and also offered some positive inducement. The inducement may have been some sort of promise to renew the Berlin crisis. The fact that since then Ulbricht has been supporting the Russians in their conflict with China suggests that he believes he can exercise leverage on the Russians to take a stronger stand over Berlin by this means. Throughout the Berlin crisis, Ulbricht's speeches and threats have generally been more blatant than Khrushchev's. While this may be a calculated division of labor, it is also possible that Ulbricht seeks consciously to bring pressure on the Kremlin for a faster and fuller settlement of the Berlin crisis than the Russians would like to risk. There can be little doubt, at any rate, that Ulbricht plays his own game and that there are limits to the Soviet ability to force him into line.

Another Bloc party which is using the Sino-Soviet conflict to further its own interests is that of North Korea. Long thought to be a Soviet satellite by some and a Chinese satellite by others, North Korea now openly talks about adapting Marxism-Leninism "creatively" to the specific conditions of North Korea.[12] This formula implies that the North Korean Party believes that, so long as Russia and China cannot agree on the proper model for socialist and Communist constructions in Asian countries, it will have greater freedom to find its own model. In foreign policy, the North Koreans will tend to support whichever major party offers them the best hope of achieving Korean unification.

The Sino-Soviet conflict has given the smaller parties unprecedented opportunities to increase their freedom of action. Examples could be multiplied almost indefinitely. This does not mean that any have yet achieved, or will soon achieve, sovereign independence. The Russians have a considerable amount of economic and political influence on the European Communist parties and the Chinese have similar influence on the Asian. The lineup of parties on the Albanian controversy at the 22nd Congress demonstrated that geography plays a large role in Bloc politics. But it would be a mistake to regard geography as decisive. The Albanian, Polish, and East German examples demonstrate that some European parties may sometimes regard Chinese policy as better serving their interests than Soviet policy.

The increased opportunity for smaller Communist parties to maneuver between Moscow and Peking has important implications for Communist-led or Communist-supported revolutionary and nationalist movements. In African countries like Guinea, Mali, and Ghana, which the Russians now view as on the way to becoming "national democracies," there will be opportunities to play off Moscow against Peking.

This will help them to achieve a distinctively African type of Communism ("Afro-Communism") if they decide they want to do so.[13] Both Moscow and Peking will be wary of imposing their wills too blatantly on these emergent countries and on local revolutionary movements, because if one of them antagonizes a third party, the latter can always threaten to go to the other, as well as to the West. Moscow and Peking will be competing for favor and influence in most of these areas, and the result may well be that the target country or revolutionary movement will borrow a little from each but go its own way. Such may be the ultimate development in Cuba, for example, where the Russians have the initial foothold. Nevertheless, to the extent that Castro wants to move faster than the Russians, he can look for Chinese support. Hence we may yet see Castro, and the Latin American Leftist groups generally, taking aid from the Russians, talking and acting like the Chinese, and striving for independence from both. The Russians have already hedged their bets on Castro, being very careful not to accept him wholeheartedly into the socialist family. Castro's Cuba is merely a "national democracy" on the way to the "socialist" revolution but still not there. This caution signifies that Moscow is not yet sure that Castro is completely reliable. Although he may well have passed the point of no return, the Russians cannot be sure that he may not one day make a deal with the United States, or embarrass them by pushing too fast in Latin America against governments with whom the Russians want to do business.

In many areas of the world where "bourgeois nationalists" come to power, the Russians will face the problem that the nationalist revolutions are potentially dangerous to them unless they can establish an effective degree of control over them. The Sino-Soviet conflict will make it more, not less, difficult for the USSR to achieve this control, and will thus make it easier for Communist or pro-Communist revolutionaries in the emergent areas to pursue policies distinct from those of both the Russians and the Chinese.

In the long run the international Communist movement could both reap advantages and suffer grave disadvantages from polycentrism. The principal disadvantage is that diversity threatens unity. Communists have long condemned "separate roads to socialism" and "deviations" in foreign policy as "revisionist" heresies. The Communist credo claims to be universal, not national. The politics of nationalism must not be allowed to replace the supranational Communist goals. Yet as long as Russia and China continue to disagree on important issues of domestic and foreign policy, there will be a tendency for "Polish," "North Korean," and other variants of socialism and Communism to appear. While this is by no means an insurmountable problem for the Communist Bloc and although it certainly does not diminish the very real challenge that Communism presents to the Western world, it could lead to a vastly different Communist world from the one with which we are familiar. Ideological ties may become increasingly general and hence less binding, and authority may become increasingly diffused. The Russians may have to govern the Bloc within the limits of something like an international Communist consensus. Already they are no longer able to enforce their dictates unilaterally. The international Communist movement will be able both to push Soviet policy in some directions and to restrain it from taking other directions. This will deprive it of flexibility. The Russians will have to recognize more and more their "obligations" to other parties —both those wielding state power and those seeking it. The parties in power will seek greater independence of Moscow and may have greater opportunities to bargain with the Russians. Increasingly, the Communist world might turn into a loose "commonwealth of nations" bound together primarily by a common enemy in the West.

Communism will gain from polycentrism in that local Communist parties, in adapting themselves to local conditions and sentiments, will be better able to gain the genuine support of their own peoples. It is significant that the Yugoslav and Chinese parties, both of which came to power essentially through their own efforts, and in the Chinese case against Soviet advice, probably enjoyed much greater mass support than the Eastern European satellites which were imposed by Soviet arms. It would not be surprising if in the long run Gomulka's relatively moderate brand of Communism, tailored to peculiar Polish circumstances, struck deeper roots than the Czech, East German, and other European brands.

The growth of diversity within the Communist world, an important result of the Sino-Soviet conflict, will almost certainly continue and have long-range effects. To Western policymakers, this diversity opens up new problems and new opportunities.

Sino-Soviet Conflict
and the West[14]

The ramifications of the Sino-Soviet conflict for the Western world are numerous and complex. I should like to discuss only briefly a few of them that seem to me most important.

First, it should not be assumed that the conflict inevitably benefits the West. In 1960 and 1961, at the very same time that

Khrushchev's relations with Mao were deteriorating, so were his relations with the West. This is no accident. So long as the Chinese remain on his left, accusing him of going soft on the West, Khrushchev, and any successor, will find it necessary to demonstrate to the Communist world that such charges are without foundation, that the Russians are just as militant in advancing Communist international aims as the Chinese. The Chinese have succeeded and may continue to succeed in forcing the Russians to pursue the offensive more forcefully and to take greater risks than they otherwise might, particularly in the underdeveloped areas, where the Russians, a white and European power, are at a disadvantage in competing with China for the loyalty of the local Communists.

This leads to a second point. One reason the Russians have in the past not pursued the offensive as vigorously as they might is their fear of a nuclear war. The Sino-Soviet conflict seems to demonstrate that the Russians are extremely reluctant to become directly involved in local wars with the West or to take risks of such wars. Weak Western responses to Communist initiatives encourage the Russians to raise the margin of risk and deprive Khrushchev of the argument he has used with Mao, that the danger of world war is considerable. Conversely, Western strength would give Khrushchev the argument that he needs to convince Mao, and other like-minded Communists, that the danger of world war is greater than they believe it to be.

We are not dealing, as is sometimes suggested in the Western world, with another Hitler when we deal with Khrushchev or Mao. The Communists, Chinese and Russian alike, are professional revolutionaries, capable of bluster and bluff but also of extreme caution and circumspection, depending on their assessment of objective reality. Where, as in Berlin, the Soviet leaders were quite confident that the balance of forces was thoroughly in their favor, they acted with less caution than they did, for example, in the Quemoy-Matsu and Lebanon crisis of 1958, where they recognized a less favorable balance. They were and are capable of retreat in the face of a superior enemy, or even a seemingly determined one. Clearly the West must step up its efforts to convince Moscow and Peking, and indeed the world as a whole, that the balance of power is not shifting in the Communist favor. Success in this task may depend as much on firmer and more rapid political responses as on the development of greater military capabilities.

At almost every key juncture in recent times, the Communists have made a careful assessment of the balance of power and framed their strategy accordingly. As I have argued, different Soviet and Chinese assessments of this balance were in part responsible for the origin of the conflict. The Chinese evidently concluded in 1957 that the balance of power had shifted decisively to the East. The Russians expect such a shift sometime in the future. Both the Chinese conclusion and the Russian expectation must be shown to be illusory.

In all Communist states, the ally of the West is nationalism. It is a suggestive fact that the three Communist parties with which Moscow has had the most trouble in the postwar era—the Chinese, the Yugoslav and the Albanian—all waged partisan warfare and liberated or played a large part in liberating their own countries. This experience seems to have made for a party with indigenous roots, a sense of independence, and a strong tide of nationalism. In Eastern Europe and in the Asian Bloc, there will arise increasing opportunity to encourage national distinctiveness.

In the coming decade, the challenge to the West of the Sino-Soviet alliance can be expected to be many times more potent than it has been in the past. Communist China will have nuclear weapons, and, in time, a delivery capability. The military balance of power in Asia may be expected to change accordingly. By 1965, China's industrial production may, according to some estimates, reach about twenty-five percent of that of the USSR, thereby providing China an industrial base for an expanded foreign aid program in support of the Bloc's overall foreign economic policies. Under such conditions, Communism's already potent attractive power is likely to increase substantially. Pressures for accommodation with the Communists will increase in the underdeveloped and developed countries of the world alike. Such success is very likely to maintain if not to increase the element of universalist messianism in the motivation of both Soviet and Chinese Communist policy.

NOTES

INTRODUCTION

1. See, for example, the puerile supplement to the *National Review,* "Bear and Dragon, What Is the Relation between Moscow and Peking?" November 5, 1960. In an introduction, Mr. James Burnham writes that "the Sino-Soviet conflict" seems "to be a subject of conversation much favored by Communist hosts, and has been frequently featured in the reports of statesmen and journalists on return from visits to Peking or Moscow." Mr. Burnham finds that the "operational consequences" of much of the newspaper discussion of this subject are "to divert non-Communists . . . from a line of action aiming at the defeat of the Communist enterprise." He is not sure whether any of the formulas with regard to Sino-Soviet conflicts are "deliberate deception by the Communists, wishful thinking by non-Communists," or a fusion of both. One of the contributors to the supplement, Natalie Grant, makes the rather astonishing statement that "a careful study of the material forming the alleged grounds for concluding that there is a serious Sino-Soviet conflict proves the absence of any objective foundation for such a belief." In fact, it turns out, "all statements regarding the existence of disagreement between Moscow and Peking on foreign policy, war, peace, revolution, or attitude toward imperialism are an invention. All are the fruit of fertile imagination and unbased unspeculation." She says that much of the "misinformation" on Sino-Soviet relations is "Communist-inspired" and "reminiscent of that almost forgotten era dominated by the Institute of Pacific Relations." Mr. Peter H. S. Tang takes the view elsewhere that the dispute is greatly exaggerated.

2. For a fuller discussion of some of these views and a critique of them, see Marshall D. Shulman, *Prelude to Policy: Understanding,* The RAND Corporation, Santa Monica, California, June 9, 1961.

3. See Ferdinand Lundberg's comment on an article by this author in *The New Leader,* May 15, 1961, pp. 29–30. He believes that my findings justify conclusions more far-reaching than I cared to venture.

4. Clearly one has to define what is meant by a "break." In drawing the distinction above between a "break" which I can envision under some circumstances and one which I cannot, I mean that I can foresee an open, public Soviet denunciation of Chinese "deviation" and a subsequent break in Party but not state relations. This would be on the order of the second, not the first, Soviet-Yugoslav rift. A total break of diplomatic, economic, and military relations is a possibility that seems remote.

5. Of course, the ideology tends to divide as well as to bring together.

6. For the Declaration of the twelve Communist parties, see *Pravda,* November 22, 1957.

7. Oleg Hoeffding, *Sino-Soviet Economic Relations in Recent Years,* The Rand Corporation, Santa Monica, California, August 26, 1960, p. 1. In a

series of agreements since 1950, the USSR has agreed to provide China with complete installations for 291 major projects that are the very core of China's industrialization program. Some 11,000 Soviet engineers, plant and machinery designers, planning advisers, and other experts were employed in Communist China in the first decade of the Sino-Soviet alliance.

8. George Kennan, "Stalin and China," *The Atlantic*, May 1961, pp. 35–42. For a detailed study of Stalin's China policy in the mid-1920's, see Conrad Brandt, *Stalin's Failure in China, 1924–1927*, Harvard University Press, Cambridge, Massachusetts, 1958. Another indispensable source is Harold Isaacs, *The Tragedy of the Chinese Revolution*, Stanford University Press, Palo Alto, California, 1951.

9. The best evidence of Stalin's caution in China in the early postwar years is contained in a Yugoslav account of his statement in February 1948 to a group of Yugoslav leaders. He is quoted as having said: "It is true, we also have made mistakes. For instance, after the war we invited the Chinese comrades to come to Moscow and we discussed the situation in China. We told them bluntly that we considered the development of the uprising in China had no prospects, that the Chinese comrades should seek a *modus vivendi* with Chiang Kai-shek, and that they should join the Chiang Kai-shek government and dissolve their army. The Chinese comrades . . . acted quite otherwise. They mustered their forces, organized their armies, and now, as we see, they are beating Chiang Kai-shek's army. Now, in the case of China, we admit we were wrong. It has proved that the Chinese comrades and not the Soviet comrades were right." (V. Dedijer, *Tito Speaks*, Simon and Schuster, London, 1953, p. 331.) For what amounts to recent Chinese confirmation of this, see footnote 11.

10. Liu Shao-ch'i, "The Victory of Marxism-Leninism in China," written for *The World Marxist Review* in celebration of the tenth anniversary of the CPR in October 1959. See the book which includes this and other tenth anniversary articles, *Ten Glorious Years, 1949–1959*, Foreign Languages Press, Peking, 1960, pp. 3–4 where Liu pointedly mentions Russian Menshevik and Trotskyite sources of deviation in the Chinese Communist Party during the 1920's and 1930's. The Chinese Communists had generally attributed Left and Right deviations to the mistakes of errant Chinese Communist leaders. See, for example, Ho Kan-chih, *A History of the Modern Chinese Revolution*, Foreign Languages Press, Peking, 1959, passim.

11. The full quotation was: "When Chiang Kai-shek removed his mask of false peace and in July 1946 launched a civil war unprecedented in the history of China, some people lacked sufficient belief in our ability to defeat the enemy because its forces were about 3.5 times greater than ours and were equipped with superior arms while being backed by U.S. imperialism, most imperialist in the world. Moreover, some people took a pessimistic view of the international situation at that time, that is, they were afraid of the outbreak of the third world war and were afraid of U.S. imperialism. Because of this, they dare not oppose counter-revolutionary war by revolutionary war." *Chung-kuo ch'ing nien*, 19, October 1, 1960; *Selections from*

China Mainland Magazines, hereinafter cited as *Selections,* 233, October 31, 1960, p. 2.

12. Anna Louise Strong, "The Thought of Mao Tse-tung," *Amerasia,* 6, June 1947, p. 161.

13. Philip Bridgham, Arthur Cohen, Herb Jaffe, "Chinese and Soviet Views on Mao as a Marxist Theorist and on the Significance of the Chinese Revolution for the Asian Revolutionary Movement," an unpublished manuscript, Washington, D.C., 43 pp.

14. Italian and Swiss students studying at Peita (Peking) University in 1960 were told, according to information available to the author, that Mao's theory was an advance of Marxism-Leninism, while Stalin had made only secondary contributions. When they inquired about Khrushchev's contributions, they were told he had not made any. Such information is consonant with the rare acknowledgments in the Chinese press since 1958 of any Khrushchev contributions to the "treasury" of Marxism-Leninism.

15. One historian of Chinese Communism writes in this connection: "In Peking there was current a story, said to come from Communist sources, that after the war in Europe was over Stalin sent Mao Tse-tung a Russian book on partisan warfare, the fruit of Russian experience during the German invasion. Mao read it, and showed it to Lin Piao, his best military commander, and the greatest expert on guerrilla warfare in China. Liu remarked: 'If we had had this as our textbook we should have been annihilated ten years ago.' Whether founded on fact or not, it is certainly true that Russia did not appreciate the meaning of guerrilla warfare as the Chinese Communists practiced it." See Charles Patrick Fitzgerald, *Revolution in China,* Frederick A. Praeger, New York, 1952, p. 97.

16. *Daily Telegraph and Morning Post* (London), December 6, 1960.

17. It is true that Mao maintained to a British Labor Party delegation that some Scandinavian countries had colonies in Africa, but similar errors have been made by Western leaders without the conclusion being drawn that they were ignorant of the world scene.

18. Richard Lowenthal, "The Changed Antagonist," *Encounter,* January 1961, p. 49, and passim.

19. At the Moscow Conference of 1960, Khrushchev had to promise other Communist parties that the USSR would not renege on its international "obligations." See his post-conference speech, Soviet Home Service, January 19, 1961.

20. The evidence for this proposition, it must be conceded, is circumstantial. Khrushchev and Bulganin journeyed to Peking in the fall of 1954, at a time when the struggle between Khrushchev and Malenkov was still going on. There are a number of reasons why Mao might have preferred Khrushchev to Malenkov. It is unlikely, for example, that Mao would have approved of Malenkov's premature espousal of a mutual deterrence line as reflected in his famous statement that world war would destroy civilization. Nor could Mao have approved of Malenkov's emphasis on light over heavy industry, a policy which must have contributed to the Chinese view, hinted

at in recent years, that the Russians are putting excessive emphasis on raising their own standards of living at the expense of their "obligations" to less developed Communist countries.

A NOTE ON METHODOLOGY

1. See, for example Robert Conquest, *Power and Policy in the USSR, St. Martin's Press*, New York, 1961; Allen S. Whiting, *China Crosses the Yalu*, The Macmillan Co., New York, 1960; Herbert S. Dinerstein, *War and the Soviet Union*, Frederick A. Praeger, New York, 1959; and Myron Rush, *The Rise of Khrushchev*, Public Affairs Press, Washington, D.C., 1958.

2. This is one reason for the appearance of symbolic evidence stressed by both Conquest and Rush. See Conquest's chapter 3 on "Questions of Evidence" and Rush's "The Role of Esoteric Communication in Soviet Politics" in their works as cited above in footnote 1.

3. The first phase is Brzezinski's, the second Nathan Leites'. Leites' *A Study of Bolshevism* (The Free Press, Glencoe, Illinois, 1953) was a truly pioneering work in the study of Bolshevik political strategy and tactics. While Leites conceded that the "operational code" was highly ambiguous, inconsistent, incomplete, and far from static, he placed his emphasis, correctly in this author's view, on the "significant measure of continuity in Bolshevism." For some of the factors which account for this conservatism with regard to operational doctrine, see Leites' Introduction, p. 19.

4. A Polish columnist, J. Kisielewski, writes: "In our public, political, and intellectual life, in our organizations and newspapers, there exists a special figurative speech. It consists of the usage of certain turns of phrase. . . . All that is needed is a clue. Those who have guessed that clue are able to read public utterances as if they were an open book and thus learn a lot of things. It goes without saying that one has to read between the lines, to follow hidden ideas. And this reading between the lines is not illegitimate: on the contrary, the texts are construed in such a way that reading between the lines is the only way to grasp their meaning. To be able to follow the figurative speech one has to possess many years' training in reading it, one must have lived for years in milieus indulging in this form of speech, one must have lived for many years in our country. Those who cannot read our special language are as naïve as little children. . . . " (*Tygodnik powszechny*, July 6, 1958, cited by Conquest, *op. cit.*, p. 51.)

5. Compare the language and argumentation employed by the Russians in an alleged secret letter to the Chinese Party in June 1960 with articles in *Kommunist*. The alleged extracts from the letter appeared in *Deutsche zeitung*, September 30, 1960. (See Appendix I.) Other examples can be found in Fainsod's examination of the Smolensk archives captured by the Germans in World War II and now in American hands, *Smolensk under Soviet Rule*, Harvard University Press, Cambridge, Massachusetts, 1959.

6. It has been called to my attention by Alexander George, author of a voluminous study on the content analysis of Nazi propaganda, that similar observations were made after World War II with regard to the unexpected

similarity between the "propagandistic" communications of the Nazi leaders and the private communications which came to light after their defeat. See George's *Propaganda Analysis: A Study of Inferences made from Nazi Propaganda in World War II*, Row, Peterson and Co., Evanston, Illinois, 1959.

7. New China News Agency, hereinafter cited as *NCNA*, August 8, 1958.

8. Yu Chao-li, "On Imperialism as the Source of War in Modern Times and on the Way for all Peoples to Struggle for Peace," *Hung ch'i*, 7, April 1, 1960; NCNA, March 30, 1960.

9. Liu Shao-ch'i, "The Victory of Marxism-Leninsm in China," in *Ten Glorious Years, 1949–1959*, Foreign Languages Press, Peking, 1960, p. 31. Another article by Teng Hsiao-p'ing used the same phrase for purposes of refutation, a possible indication that both Liu and Teng were citing an oppositionist document. See Teng's 10th Anniversary article in *Ten Glorious Years*, p. 99.

10. *Ibid.*, p. 33.

11. For the Chinese view, see Liu Shao-ch'i, "The Victory of Marxism-Leninism in China," *op. cit.*, p. 4. For the Soviet view, see Y. Zhukov, *Pravda*, August 26, 1960.

12. *Rabotnichesko delo*, October 18, 1958.

13. *Izvestiya*, October 1, 1958.

14. *Jen-min jih-pao* editorial, February 4, 1959; NCNA, February 4, 1959.

15. For an idea of how such evidence can be used both with restraint and insight to shed light on many obscurities in postwar Soviet history, see Conquest, *op. cit.*

16. Myron Rush, "Esoteric Communication in Soviet Politics," *World Politics*, July 1959, p. 615.

17. *Voprosy istorii*, 7, 1960, pp. 160–162.

CHAPTER ONE

1. Edward Crankshaw, "The Moscow-Peking Clash," *Observer* (London), February 12 and 19, 1961.

2. For the text of Khrushchev's speech at the 20th Congress, see *Pravda*, February 15, 1956.

3. Crankshaw, *op. cit.*

4. "On Historical Experience concerning the Dictatorship of the Proletariat," *Jen-min jih-pao*, April 5, 1956; *Current Background*, hereinafter cited as CB, 403, July 25, 1956, p. 1.

5. *Ibid.*, p. 3.

6. Palmiro Togliatti, "9 Domande sullo Stalinismo," *Nuovo Argomenti*, 20, June 16, 1956. In *The Anti-Stalin Campaign and International Communism*, The Russian Institute, Columbia University (ed.), Columbia University Press, New York, 1956, p. 215.

7. See the author's "The Spectre of Revisionism," *Problems of Communism*, July-August 1958, pp. 15–21.

8. "On Historical Experience concerning the Dictatorship of the Proletariat," *op. cit.*, pp. 4–5.

9. On April 7, *Pravda* published what it called a "somewhat abbreviated" version of the article which deleted all references to "contradictions" between the individual and the collective in socialist societies. However, these passages of the Chinese article were restored in reprints of the editorial subsequently issued by the *Pravda* publishing house in 200,000 copies and signed for the press on June 1, 1956. Moreover, *Pravda* did reprint the full text of the Chinese statement of December 29, 1956, which contained a number of passages dealing with internal contradictions in socialist society, including contradictions between the government and the people. This did not mean approval of the Chinese line on "contradictions," for, as we shall subsequently see, in comment initiated by the Russians, the Maoist "contradictions" thesis was handled with considerable circumspection.

10. See, for example, the June 30, 1956, resolution in *The Anti-Stalin Campaign and International Communism, op. cit.*, pp. 275–307.

11. "On Historical Experience concerning the Dictatorship of the Proletariat," *op. cit.*, pp. 2–3.

12. *Ibid.*, p. 2.

13. *Jen-min jih-pao*, July 12, 1956; NCNA, July 12, 1956.

14. *Jen-min jih-pao*, November 5, 1956; NCNA, November 5, 1956. For the Soviet view, see "Collapse of the Antipopular Adventure in Hungary," editorial in *Pravda*, October 28, 1956, in *National Communism and Popular Revolt in Eastern Europe;* a selection of documents on events in Poland and Hungary, February-November 1956, Paul E. Zinner (ed.), Columbia University Press, New York, 1956, pp. 435–440.

15. Zbigniew Brzezinski, *The Soviet Bloc: Unity and Conflict,* Harvard University Press, Cambridge, Massachusetts, 1960, passim.

16. *Pravda*, February 15, 1956.

17. See the Soviet-Yugoslav Declaration of June 20, 1956, in *National Communism and Popular Revolt in Eastern Europe, op. cit.*, p. 13.

18. See *The Anti-Stalin Campaign and International Communism, op. cit.*

19. See particularly the June 30th resolution in *The Anti-Stalin Campaign and International Communism, op. cit.* The CPSU resolution said that although the Comintern and Cominform had ceased activity, "it does not follow from this, however, that international solidarity and the need for contacts among revolutionary fraternal parties adhering to positions of Marxism-Leninism have lost their significance . . . the Marxist parties . . . must retain and strengthen their ideological unity and international fraternal solidarity . . . " (p. 303).

20. The June 30, 1956, CPSU resolution wrote typically in the manner of a Bolshevik directive, positing what is directed as being already achieved: "all Communist parties . . . are rallying together and *strengthening* their ties. . . . The ideological unanimity and fraternal solidarity of Marxist parties of the working class of various countries is all the more necessary

because capitalist monopolies are creating their own international aggressive unions and blocs . . . " [italics supplied], *ibid.*, p. 304. And *Pravda*, June 22, 1956, said "the socialist countries are developing as independent socialist states but the greater their unity the stronger their independence."

21. *Sovetsko-Kitayaskiye Otnosheniya, 1917–1957,* Eastern Languages Publishing House, Moscow, 1959, document 207, pp. 318–321. At the same time, the new concept of the "socialist commonwealth," as opposed to the "socialist camp," came into greater prominence.

22. *Pravda,* November 7, 1956.

23. *Ibid.,* November 19, 1956.

24. For Tito's speech, see *National Communism and Popular Revolt in Eastern Europe, op. cit.,* pp. 516–541.

25. *Rude pravo,* December 30, 1956.

26. See the article by Azizyan in *Pravda,* December 23, 1956. He wrote, *inter alia:* "If the Communist parties are to proceed according to the prescription proposed on the pages of *Nowa kultura,* then instead of a firm front of revolutionary forces connected by undivided unity, of conscious discipline and voluntary mutual obligations and a common aim, there will be a sum total of parties proceeding along lone paths."

27. Belgrade, Tanyug, December 29, 1956.

28. *Izvestiya,* July 9, 1957.

29. *Pravda,* July 12, 1957.

30. Czechoslovak Radio Home Service, July 14, 1957.

31. *Ibid.,* July 16, 1957.

32. *L'Unità* (Rome), June 26, 1956. In *The Anti-Stalin Campaign and International Communism, op. cit.,* p. 215.

33. "On Historical Experience concerning the Dictatorship of the Proletariat," *op. cit.,* p. 4.

34. Flora Lewis, *A Case History of Hope,* Doubleday and Co., New York, 1958, p. 182. Miss Lewis is the wife of Sydney Gruson, former *New York Times* correspondent in Poland.

35. *Ibid.,* p. 183.

36. *Ibid.*

37. For further details on Mao's sympathetic attitude toward Gomulka in the struggle with Moscow, see the excellent dispatches from Gruson, throughout October 1956. In particular, see Gruson's story reporting "reliable sources" in Warsaw, on October 16, 1956.

38. Gruson, *New York Times,* January 11, 1957. Mao allegedly informed Warsaw of this stand in his telegram of support in January 1957. Gruson's knowledge of the telegram apparently came from a firsthand source. In a secret letter to the Russians on September 10, 1960, the Chinese, in recounting the origins of the Sino-Soviet conflict, said that they objected strongly to the Soviet mobilization plan against Poland in 1956, which they claim they effectively restrained, and also to an alleged Russian plan to have the Polish Party collectively condemned by all Communist parties. See

Crankshaw, *op. cit.* The author has been told that similar stories, claiming Chinese intervention against Soviet plans to use force against Gomulka, were in circulation in Warsaw.

39. NCNA dispatch from Warsaw, October 25, 1956.

40. *Ibid.*

41. *Sovetsko-Kitayaskiye Otnosheniya, op. cit.,* document 208, pp. 321–322.

42. *Jen-min jih-pao,* November 21, 1956; NCNA, November 21, 1956.

43. *Rude pravo,* December 8, 1956, cited by Brzezinski, *The Soviet Bloc, op. cit.,* p. 275.

44. *National Communism and Popular Revolt in Eastern Europe, op. cit.,* pp. 516–541.

45. "More on the Historical Experience of the Dictatorship of the Proletariat," *Jen-min jih-pao,* December 29, 1956; NCNA, December 29, 1956.

46. *Ibid.*

47. *Ibid.*

48. Gruson, *New York Times,* December 9, 1956.

49. Speech at a Budapest rally, NCNA, January 16, 1957.

50. *Ibid.*

51. Speech at a Moscow mass rally, NCNA, January 18, 1957.

52. NCNA, March 5, 1957.

53. The author has greatly benefited in the discussion that follows from an internal working paper of The Rand Corporation written by Allen S. Whiting, "Strategic Implications of the Sino-Soviet Attack on Yugoslavia," July 21, 1958.

54. *Ibid.*

55. *Jen-min jih-pao,* November 3, 1956; NCNA, November 3, 1956.

56. *Hsueh-hsi,* January 3, 1957; *Extracts,* 73, March 11, 1957, p. 9.

57. For the Soviet position, see *The Soviet-Yugoslav Dispute,* Royal Institute of International Affairs, London, 1948. For Chinese comment, see Liu Shao-ch'i, *Internationalism and Nationalism,* Foreign Languages Press, Peking, 1951 (written November 1948).

58. *Pravda,* July 12, 1957.

59. For the text of Mikoyan's September 17, 1956 speech, see *Pravda,* September 18, 1956.

60. NCNA, April 11, 1957.

61. A member of the Polish Government delegation to Peking in April told the *New York Times* in May that he was told by Chinese "comrades" that "contradictions" in the Communist world must be solved by persuasion rather than by force, and that "internal contradictions" between the leaders and the masses had replaced the traditional class struggle in importance. The Polish delegate, Stanislaw Brodzki, a former member of the editorial board of *Trybuna Ludu,* the Polish Party paper, said also that the "entire attack and entire power" of the Chinese Communists was directed against "dogmatism and sectarianism" (*New York Times,* May 14, 1957).

410

Chapter Two

1. Some of the arguments in this chapter are based on Roderick Mac-Farquhar's excellent article on the Chinese Communist leadership, "Communist China's Intra-Party Dispute," *Pacific Affairs,* December 1958, pp. 323–335. MacFarquhar describes in detail the change in economic policy which took place between June and September 1957.

2. The terms "Left" and "Right" will be employed throughout this book as they are used by the Communists. The terms are useful not only because the Communists themselves employ them, but also because they are essential to an understanding of the radical shifts and turns in Communist behavior that have been a cause of so much confusion in the West. The Left policy, either at home or abroad, has been marked by revolutionary slogans, by uncompromising actions, by a desire for rapid gains. It is generally practiced when revolutionary opportunities are believed to be ripe. It can also be, however, like Stalin's forced collectivization drive in 1928, a product of desperation. The Right strategy has generally been marked by slogans and gestures of compromise either to domestic or foreign class enemies, and by cautious advance, consolidation, or even retreat in the pursuit of revolutionary aims. It is generally adopted in periods of adversity, although, as the example cited above indicates, this is not always the case. The domestic or foreign strategy of any Communist party could be written in terms of these two divergent syndromes of behavior. What frequently causes disharmony between Moscow and any given Communist party is conflict between the Soviet desire to pursue a Rightist strategy throughout the world, and the belief of the local party that the time is ripe for rapid revolutionary advance. Local parties, of course, can also be to the Right of Moscow.

3. Roderick MacFarquhar, *The Hundred Flowers Campaign and the Chinese Intellectuals,* Frederick A. Praeger, New York, 1960. The book is a selection of documentary material from the "hundred flowers" period with brief introductory and analytical remarks by the author.

4. For this explanation of the "hundred flowers" episode, I am indebted to MacFarquhar, *The Hundred Flowers Campaign and the Chinese Intellectuals, op. cit.*

5. MacFarquhar, "Communist China's Intra-Party Dispute," *op. cit.*

6. Address to a conference of cadres in Chungking on May 16, 1957, NCNA, May 17, 1957.

7. Speech to the National People's Congress, "Working for the National Economic Plan for 1956 and Draft National Economic Plan for 1957," NCNA, July 1, 1957.

8. See Liu Shao-ch'i's speech to the second session of the 8th Party Congress on May 5, 1958, *Peking Review,* 14, June 3, 1958, pp. 6–22.

9. Liu Shao-ch'i wrote on the 10th anniversary of the CPR: "It goes without saying that we must do a good job of economic planning to enable, as far as possible, the various branches of the national economy to spurt ahead in harmony. We want both high speed and overall balance. This is

not easy to achieve; in high-speed development, it is more likely that certain imbalances will occur. We should not, however, give way to 'fear of the wolf in front and the tiger behind,' vainly hoping for a haven of peace by adopting the method of reducing speed unjustifiably to achieve a balance." See his article, "The Victory of Marxism-Leninism in China," in *Ten Glorious Years, 1949–1959,* Foreign Languages Press, Peking, 1960, pp. 26–27.

10. Yang Ying-chieh, "Study the Experience of the Soviet Union in Construction," *Hsueh-hsi,* 21, November 3, 1957; Extracts, 120, February 24, 1958, pp. 5–6.

11. See MacFarquhar, "Communist China's Intra-Party Dispute," *op. cit.* See also his "The Leadership in China," *The World Today,* August 1959, pp. 210–323.

12. See his speech to the Congress, *op. cit.*

13. MacFarquhar, "Communist China's Intra-Party Dispute," *op. cit.*

14. For more details on the Chinese Communist intra-party struggle, see "Mao Leads Attack on 'Rightists,'" *The Daily Telegraph* (London), November 16, 1959.

15. For this report, see CB, 463, July 2, 1957.

16. CB, 413, October 5, 1956, p. 6.

17. See MacFarquhar, "Communist China's Intra-Party Dispute," *op. cit.,* pp. 327–328.

18. Speech to the 8th Party Congress, *op. cit.*

19. *Jen-min jih-pao,* November 21, 1957; NCNA, November 21, 1957.

20. *Jen-min jih-pao,* December 12, 1957; NCNA, December 12, 1957.

Chapter Three

1. *Peking Review,* 14, June 3, 1958, pp. 15 and 12.

2. Y. Bugachev and B. Liebson, "Guiding Force in the Advance to Communism," *Problems of Peace and Socialism,* April 1959, p. 3.

3. *Peking Review,* 29, September 16, 1958, p. 23. The commune resolution was published on September 10, 1958; for this quotation, see *Peking Review,* 29, September 16, 1958, p. 23.

4. For one of the few discussions, see Stuart R. Schram, "La 'revolution permanente' en Chine," *Revue française de science politique,* September 1960. Reprinted by the Centre d'Etude des Relations Internationales, Fondation Nationale des Sciences Politiques, Paris.

5. The same term, "buduan geming," is employed by the Chinese to translate Trotsky's "heresy" and to label Mao's own version of "permanent revolution." *Peking Review,* a weekly English language publication from Peking, translates the term as "uninterrupted revolution."

6. It is important to note here that the use of the term "permanent revolution" is not, as is generally imagined, a heresy in the Soviet Union. What is a heresy is the Trotskyite definition. In its restricted Marxist sense— i.e., the need for a rapid transition from the bourgeois democratic to the socialist revolution—the term can be found in *Bolshaya sovetskaya*

entsiklopediya, vol. 32, pp. 508–509 (State Publishing House, Moscow, 1955). The Russians seem to prefer "uninterrupted" (*neprerivniy*) to "permanent," but the two terms are used interchangeably.

7. The phrase "socialist and Communist construction" is used throughout this book in the same sense in which the Communists use it. It denotes the social, economic, and political processes of building first a "socialist" society and finally a "Communist" society.

8. *Peking Review,* 14, June 3, 1958, p. 14.

9. *Ibid.,* p. 15.

10. *Hsueh-hsi,* October 10, 1958.

11. Wu Chiang, "A partisan of the permanent revolution theory must be a consistent dialectic materialist," *Che-hsueh yen-chiu,* 8, 1959, cited by Schram, *op. cit.* In 1960, Wu Chiang, a prominent CCP philosopher, would write again that "there is a theory which maintains that development need not pass through struggle and qualitative leap." This theory, Wu wrote, although it is "well-intentioned" in order to "protect" socialism, in fact impedes the development of socialism because it would lead to a "lifeless society." See *Selections,* 225, September 6, 1960, pp. 10–11. Wu criticized the "long-bankrupt 'productive force theory' " which held that it was necessary only to carry out technical revolution and not to "revolutionize" the social system in socialist and even Communist societies.

12. "Unite Under Lenin's Revolutionary Banner!" in *Long Live Leninism,* Foreign Languages Press, Peking, 1960, pp. 94–95.

13. J. V. Stalin, *Marxism and Linguistics,* International Publishers, New York, 1951.

14. See Gustav A. Wetter's *Dialectical Materialism,* a history and systematic survey of philosophy in the Soviet Union, Routledge and Kegan Paul, London, 1958, chapter 10, "Stalin as a Philosopher," pp. 209–230.

15. *Pravda,* February 15, 1956.

16. *Ibid.,* November 8, 1957. Khrushchev's speech on the 40th Anniversary of the Revolution.

17. *Forty Years, 1917–1957; Theses of the Propaganda Department of the CPSU and the Marxist-Leninist Institute on the 40th Anniversary of the Great October* Revolution, September 15, 1957, Soviet News Booklet, 16, London, November 1957.

18. For some of the analysis and information in this section, the author is indebted to an excellent unpublished study of the origins of the Chinese communes by Philip Bridgham. For additional information, see "Communes and Communism," Radio Free Europe, Background Information (ad hoc reports), Munich, April 27, 1950. There are also two very suggestive and perceptive essays, "The People's Commune" and "Some Remarks on the Economic Aspect," by A. V. Sherman and Alfred Zauberman respectively in *The Chinese Communes,* Soviet Survey, London, 1960. See also Albert Ravenholt's "People's Communes," American Universities

Field Staff report from Hongkong, AB-8-1858; "China's 'Uninterrupted Revolution,'" articles by Stanley Rich, David Rousset, and Richard Lowenthal in *Problems of Communism*, January-February 1959, pp. 1–24; and Robert Carin, China's Land Problem Series, vols. 3 and 4 on the communes, P.O. Box 5217, Kowloon, Hongkong (no other identification given).

19. Bridgham, *op. cit.*

20. *Ibid.*

21. Zauberman, *op. cit.*, p. 62.

22. In 1961, the pendulum swung back to the Right in economic policy but the Left-wing leaders seemed unscathed.

23. Zauberman, *op. cit.*, p. 66.

24. See Oleg Hoeffding, "Sino-Soviet Economic Relations in Recent Years," The Rand Corporation, Santa Monica, California, August 26, 1960, pp. 16–26. Paper delivered at the Third International Conference of Sovietologists at Lake Kawaguchi, Japan, September 1960. The author cautions that "with information at hand, one cannot exclude the possibility that China has not asked for additional credits." He also points out that the three "economic assistance" agreements since 1954 (April 1956, August 1958, and February 1959) provide for Soviet deliveries of equipment for Chinese plants but do not appear to include any Soviet credit features.

25. *Jen-min jih-pao* editorial, November 11, 1957; NCNA, November 11, 1957.

26. Bridgham, *op. cit.*

27. Wilson, *op. cit.* Ravenholt, *op. cit.*, writes: ". . . almost every able-bodied peasant man and woman not critically needed elsewhere was mustered out with a hoe, a shovel, wheelbarrow, carrying basket, or cart drawn by a mule or draft cow . . . ," p. 4.

28. *Jen-min jih-pao*, September 12, 1958; NCNA, September 12, 1958.

29. *Jen-min jih-pao*, June 11, 1958; NCNA, June 11, 1958.

30. *Jen-min jih-pao*, October 1, 1958; NCNA, October 1, 1958.

31. See, for example, V. Trifonov, "Voprosy industrial'nogo razvitiya KNR v gody pervoi pyatiletki," *Voprosy ekonomiki*, 7, July 1958, pp. 82–93.

32. See article by Stadnichenko in *Sovetskoye kitayavedeniye*, 2, signed to the press September 27, 1958.

33. *Ibid.*

34. After the communes were formed, Soviet economic journals and other media in fact occasionally called them "higher-type cooperatives." This distortion, concealing the radical nature of the communes, probably also reflected a Soviet belief that Peking should have stopped short at such a higher-type cooperative organization.

35. Mao Tse-tung, "Introducing a Cooperative," *Hung ch'i*, June 1, 1958; NCNA, May 31, 1958.

36. *Ibid.*

37. As Richard Lowenthal has suggested, Mao's decision to call one of the prototype communes "Sputnik" should be viewed against the background of his statement in November 1957 that the Soviets should lead the Bloc inasmuch as they had two sputniks and China did not even have one-fourth of a sputnik. He may in 1958 have been suggesting that while the Russians had the technological lead, the Chinese had the ideological. Another of the prototype communes in Honan Province, created on April 20, 1958, was called *Weihsing* or "Satellite."

38. See Wu Chi-pu, First Secretary of Honan Provincial Committee, CCP, "From APC's to People's Communes," *Hung ch'i*, 8, September 16, 1958.

39. *Pravda*, June 4, 1958.

40. See Yu. Vasil'yev, "A Scientific Conference on the Theoretical Problems of the Building of Communism in the USSR," *Voprosy istorii*, 9, 1958, pp. 176–195. For full proceedings of the conference, see *Voprosy stroitel'stva kommunizma v SSSR*, Soviet Academy of Sciences, Moscow, 1959. The *Voprosy istorii* summary was translated in Joint Publications Research Service, hereinafter cited as JPRS, 471-D, January 13, 1959. The quotation above is on p. 84 of this translation.

41. *Sovetskoye kitayavedeniye*, 2, 1958.

42. See "Long Live People's Communes," *Jen-min jih-pao*, August 29, 1959; *Survey of China Mainland Press*, hereinafter cited as SCMP, 2090, September 4, 1959, p. 15.

43. "Under the Banner of Comrade Mao Tse-tung," *Hung ch'i*, 4 (July 16), 1958; *Extracts from China Mainland Magazines*, hereinafter cited as *Extracts*, 138, August 11, 1958, p. 13.

44. This journal, an official organ of the Central Committee, published by *Pravda's* publishing house, is one of the principal propaganda and agitational organs in the USSR, designed to furnish background on current topics for Party propagandists and Party schools throughout the USSR.

45. V. Akshinskii, "Uspekhi general'noi linii kommunisticheskoi partii Kitaya v stroitel'stve sotsializma," *V pomoshch' politicheskomu soobrazovaniyu*, August 5, 1958, p. 12.

46. *Kazakhstanskaya pravda* on August 16, *Leningradskaya pravda* on August 17, *Kommunist tadzhikistana* on August 21, *Sovetskaya litva* on August 20, and *Sovetskaya Moldavia* on August 29, 1958.

47. *Ibid.*

48. *Pravda*, August 18, 1958.

49. Liu Yi-hsing, "People's Communes, A New Stage," *China Reconstructs*, December 1958, p. 9.

50. *Peking Review*, 29, September 16, 1958, p. 23.

51. *Ibid.*, p. 22.

52. *Hung ch'i*, 7 (September 1), 1958; *Peking Review*, 28, September 9, 1958, p. 11.

53. N. Khrushchev, "Za tesnuyu svyaz' literatury i iskusstva s zhizn'yu naroda," *Kommunist*, 12, August 21, 1957.

54. *Pravda,* November 14, 1958.

55. *Ibid.,* January 28, 1959.

56. V. I. Lenin, *State and Revolution,* International Publishers, New York, 1932, p. 78.

57. *Pravda,* January 28, 1959.

58. See *Voprosy stroitel'stva kommunizma v SSSR, op. cit.*

59. *Ibid.,* pp. 32–36.

60. The new Soviet Party program issued in July 1961 postpones distribution according to "need" to the distant future, saying only that in the coming two decades the groundwork for such distribution will be laid. For the text of the program, see the *New York Times,* August 1, 1961.

61. Article in *Jen-min jih-pao,* October 13, 1958, by the editor of the Shanghai *Chieh-fang;* NCNA, October 13, 1958. The author is a member of the Shanghai Municipal Party Committee.

62. On October 17 two articles in *Jen-min jih-pao,* replying to the one cited above, were titled, "The Wage System Was Necessary after Liberation," and "Do Not Deny the Historical Significance of the Wage System"; NCNA, October 17, 1958.

63. *Jen-min jih-pao,* October 22, 1958; NCNA, October 22, 1958.

64. For the text of the resolution, see *Peking Review,* 43, December 23, 1958, pp. 10–19.

65. *Extracts,* 149, December 1, 1958, p. 35.

66. NCNA, September 9, 1959.

67. See Richard L. Walker, "Chairman Mao and the Cult of Personality," *Encounter,* June 1960, p. 33.

68. Liu Lan-t'ao, "The Communist Party of China is the High Command of the Chinese People in Building Socialism," *Jen-min jih-pao,* September 28, 1959; in *Ten Glorious Years, 1949–1959,* Foreign Language Press, Peking, 1960, p. 296.

69. SCMP, 2118, October 16, 1959, p. 23.

70. "Mao Tse-tung's Ideology Glows 100,000 Feet High," Peking Radio (Home Service), January 24, 1960.

71. *Chung-kuo ch'ing-nien,* 3, 1960.

72. "Arm the Workers and Peasants with Mao Tse-tung's Thinking," *Sheng-si jih-pao* February 1, 1960; SCMP, 2209, March 4, 1960, p. 12.

73. On January 4, 1960, *Jen-min jih-pao* said "the ideas of Mao, from world outlook to methods of thought and methods of work, constitute a developing and ever-improving Sinified Marxism, a scientific theory of socialist revolution and socialist construction" (NCNA, January 4, 1960).

74. NCNA, December 15, 1958.

75. Chinese evangelism was largely limited to statements in Party journals. However, there were other more active examples. In late September, for example, there appeared in *Literarni noviny,* the organ of the Czech Writers Union, a curious and unprecedented letter "to a friend abroad" from the Chinese Minister of Culture Mao Tun. Purportedly about recent developments in Chinese art and literature, Mao Tun's letter also

416

ranged over the entire complex of economic programs in China, including the communes, stressed the speed and scope of these economic programs, the "revolutionary romanticism" with which they were imbued, and clearly suggested that the Czechoslovaks could find much of value in Chinese experience. Not once in the course of this curious 3,000-word document was there a reference to the USSR.

It is necessary to quote a few paragraphs from this remarkable document to enable the reader to savor its flavor:

Dear friend,

In answer to your interesting suggestion I would like to say a few words about the recent development of art and literature in our country. In order to get to the heart of the matter, it will be necessary, dear friend, to first have a good look at the tremendous changes in the life of our people, which have taken place during the past year. . . .

Should you have ever read about the construction of the Ming Tomb Dam, you must have noticed that the whole project is permeated with revolutionary romanticism. You are quite right in thinking that this revolutionary romanticism has become one of our characteristic features. . . . In present-day China, miracles happen constantly. Things which our ancestors did not even dare to think of, are being carried out by the thousands. Our production of pig iron will increase by 20 million tons this year. You will certainly agree when I say that this is not an unimportant matter. . . . It was possible to construct so many furnaces in so short a time because the production of iron and steel is a matter of concern to our whole nation. . . . Why? Because the strong light of the general line has illuminated the human mind. People have discarded the myth that the metallurgical industry is something of a mystery and they have done away with the old ideas on expanding industrialization. . . . They acquired the courage to think and to act. In short, they manifested a spirit of revolutionary romanticism. This is the principal force underlying the Great Leap Forward.

I think, dear friend, that I should end my long and extensive letter. In conclusion I would like to say a few words still and ask you to give them some thought. Workers become intellectuals, and intellectuals become workers, and thus we eliminate the divergencies between physical and mental work. This is our great goal.

The letter was widely commented on in Czech but particularly in Slovak journals. A writer in the Bratislava *Kulturny zivot* wrote that he had discussed the open letter with Czechoslovak engineers, physicians, workers, and workers in the public administration who "understand very well its meaning." "We, too, in Eastern Slovakia," he continued, are overtaking centuries within the limits of "our possibilities." The writer concluded that Mao's letter "tells of things we can learn from the Chinese people" and that it constituted "one of the most serious contributions to our unending discussions." A Czech writer in a subsequent issue of *Literarni noviny* concluded that his previous skepticism toward Chinese plans was unfounded and that "we in Czechoslovakia are following with much interest everything which takes place in your country."

This exchange between Mao Tun and writers in Czechoslovakia in the early fall of 1958 was significant for two reasons. First, it underlined the Chinese interest in spreading Chinese ideas and experience to other fraternal Bloc parties, even those in Eastern Europe. Secondly, and perhaps more important, it indicated a receptivity on the part of Czechoslovak Communist writers who presumably reflected higher elements in the Czech and Slovak parties. It is unlikely that Mao Tun's letter could have been published in the official organ of the Czech Writers Union unless it had been sanctioned by higher Party authorities.

76. *Extracts,* 138, August 11, 1958, p. 14.

77. *Ibid.,* pp. 6–7. In Communist writings, the "East" includes all underdeveloped countries in Latin America as well as in Asia and Africa.

78. There were no fraternal Party delegates at this Congress, a unique occurrence in recent Chinese Communist history.

79. This claim appeared in both *Hsueh-hsi* and *Jen-min jih-pao* immediately after the Congress, according to Bridgham, *op. cit.* Bridgham also says that Tan Ch'en-lin in east China in June contended that there was an increase in grain production of 50 per cent in 1958 which was a victory of "historical significance" and would basically solve China's food problem, and that the mass line underlying this constituted a "new development of Marxism on the question of socialist construction."

80. Quoted by Davis Binder, "More Contagious than the Asiatic Flu Mao Bug Bites Reds in East Reich," *Chicago Daily News,* March 24, 1954.

81. *Pravda,* March 1, 1958.

82. See, for example, the article by M. Mitin, in *Pravda,* March 6, 1958.

83. As late as June 1959, Khrushchev continued to dismiss with heavy sarcasm attempts by lecturers to discuss in detail the forthcoming Communist society. He told a Central Committee plenum that it would be more worthwhile to work on such problems as improving faulty components manufactured in Soviet factories: "What will be the thoughts of people about a hundred years after the victory of Communism? This is indeed a fine subject for a lecture, and please don't think I am against good lectures, but we can wait for such lectures and reports for another 50 or 80 years (Laughter, applause)." (*Pravda,* July 21, 1959.) The transition to Communism was the subject of a special session of the departments of social sciences of the USSR Academy of Sciences in June 1958, following the initial announcement in connection with the 40th Anniversary of the Revolution in November 1957 that Communism was the "immediate practical aim" of the Soviet people. (See *Forty Years, 1917–1957; Theses of the Propaganda Department of the CPSU and the Marxist-Leninist Institute on the 40th Anniversary of the Great October Revolution, op. cit.*) Even without Chinese pressure, there was thus *some* reason for the CPSU to take

greater interest in the subject. However, the Academy of Sciences session was not very optimistic about introducing Communism in the near future in the USSR and the 40th Anniversary slogan that Communism was the "immediate practical aim" was not repeated throughout 1958. It was only beginning in 1959 and 1960, after the Chinese challenge, that the USSR began to turn out about 100 books and countless articles on the subject. See Erich Goldhagen, "The Glorious Future, Realities and Chimeras," *Problems of Communism,* November-December 1960, p. 12.

84. In June 1958, Khrushchev told the Bulgarian Party Congress that theory is gray, whereas the "tree of life is green." *Pravda,* June 4, 1958.

85. For reflections of this view, see particularly Paul Wandel in *Einheit,* December 1958 and December 1959. Wandel, East Germany's ambassador to Communist China, wrote in 1958 that the key to the Chinese successes was the fact that they had "sought and found" a solution to their immense tasks in mobilizing the masses. There were enormous "spiritual forces" inherent in the masses; the socialist consciousness of the masses was growing and "becoming a factor surpassing all expectations." Wandel also was the first and only Bloc spokesman known to the writer to accept the heretical Chinese redefinition of "uninterrupted revolution." Wandel implied that the Maoist version of the concept was valid because it derived from China's "own abundant experience" and from the "theoretical evaluation of that experience by Comrade Mao." Wandel also predicted that "new 'miracles' " of socialist development were forthcoming in China and he quoted Liu Shao-ch'i to the effect that a rapid pace of economic advance would not lead to unnecessary social tensions, as some critics contended, but was in fact required by "objective conditions."

86. See his speech in Peking, *Jen-min jih-pao,* October 30, 1958, and subsequently on Chinese developments in *Rabotnichesko delo,* January 15, 1959.

87. The Brigades of Communist Labor, a "spontaneous" mass movement designed to increase labor productivity and efficiency, were initiated in October 1958. By June 1960 they were said to have rallied over 5,000,000 workers in more than 40,000 brigades (*Pravda,* June 1, 1960). One of the most important goals of the labor brigades was to "guard the norms of socialist society" and to combat the "vestiges of the past in the consciousness of the people" (*Voprosy filosofii,* 10, 1959, p. 135).

The other "public" organization begun in the fall of 1958 was the people's militia (*druzhiny*), designed to help perform the functions of safeguarding public order. The initiative for this organization was credited to a "workers' militia group" in Leningrad in November 1958. Early in 1959 the militia's role was formalized in a joint party-government decree published on March 10, 1959. For a discussion of these developments, see Herbert Ritvo, "Totalitarianism without Coercion?" *Problems of Communism,* November-December 1960, pp. 19–30.

88. *Pravda,* September 7, 1958.

89. It is true that in November 1957, Khrushchev had announced the

impending entry of the USSR into a new stage of Communist construction and that the Congress of the builders of Communism might have been called in any event to ratify and publicize the entry into this new stage.

90. For an account of the 21st Congress proceedings in the context of the Sino-Soviet conflict, see Richard Lowenthal, "Khrushchev's 'Flexible Communism'—The 21st Congress in Moscow," *Commentary,* April 1959, pp. 277–284. See also Seweryn Bialer, "The 21st Congress and Soviet Policy," *Problems of Communism,* March-April 1959, pp. 1–9.

91. "Navstrechu XXI syezdu kommunisticheskoi partii Sovetskogo Soyuza," *Kommunist,* 12, 1958, p. 3. It is worth noting that, as the article clearly implies, the Russians have never announced the final completion of socialist construction. They do contend that socialism has *triumphed* finally and fully but this refers only to the triumph in an international context. It means, as the Soviets have said, that restoration of a capitalist system in Russia is no longer possible because of the might of the Soviet state. They also say that socialism has been "built," but this is not equated with the completion of socialist construction. Khrushchev clearly implied to the July 1959 Central Committee plenum that the building of socialism was still going on, together with the building of Communism.

92. V. Zhamin, "Velikii Kitai stroit sotsializm," *Voprosy ekonomiki,* 10, 1958, pp. 6–7.

93. *Ibid.,* p. 15. *Voprosy istorii,* KPSS, 5, 1959, also called the communes cooperatives. See also *Leningradskaya pravda,* October 23, 1958, which called the communes a "new low-level form of organization of socialist society in China."

94. Ts. A. Stepanyan, "Oktyabrskaya revolyutsiya i stanovlenie kommunisticheskoi formatsii," *Voprosy filosofii,* 10, 1958, p. 34.

95. *Pravda,* October 19, 1958. Bulgarian media, in reporting the CPSU slogans, distorted the greeting to China. While Moscow had the CPR, along with the East European and Asian satellites, "building socialism," the Bulgarian Party organ had the CPR alone "finishing the building of socialism." See *Rabotnichesko delo, October* 18, 1958.

96. NCNA, November 6 and 7, 1958.

97. As of the date of this writing, fall 1961, no Soviet Presidium member has publicly referred to the Chinese communes.

98. V. Trifonov, *op. cit.,* p. 89. (See note 31.)

99. *Ibid.,* pp. 87–88.

100. V. K. Kurbatov, "Nekotorie voprosy mekhanizatsii sel'skogo khozyaistva Kitaya," *Sovetskoye kitayavedeniye,* 3, 1958, p. 56.

101. A. V. Meliksetov, "Bolshoi skachok v ekonomicheskom i kulturnom razvitii KNR," *Sovetskoye kitayavedeniye,* 4, 1958, p. 12.

102. V. Zhamin, *op. cit.,* p. 17. The second issue of *Problemy vostokavedeniya,* 1959, in a more detailed review of the great leap, also went out of its way to stress the economic problems facing the Chinese that made the commune organization inevitable. A correct understanding of the "numerous and diverse" origins of the leap, it wrote, was essential for "an

understanding of the perspective of development of our great friend and ally." The article stressed that China was an agrarian country in which the peasantry constituted more than 80 per cent of the population and that it was therefore necessary to develop industry and agriculture simultaneously. Such a course, it continued, provided the opportunity to mobilize "the largest labor army in the world" for the development of grain production and various secondary good products, and to harness "astonishing labor power to produce enormous wealth. . . . " A great role in the speeding up of socialist construction was being played by the communes, which allowed a "much larger and more rational use of labor power." It was "clear," the article concluded, that although much work was necessary to perfect the communes, "already the first months of practice show that this form in the conditions of China contains many possibilities for stepping up the tempo of development of production in the Chinese countryside."

103. V. Berezhkov, "Year of a 'Great Leap,'" *New Times,* 1, January 1959, p. 12.

104. Tass, September 30, 1958.

105. Moscow Radio Home Service, September 30, 1958.

106. *Pravda,* September 30, 1958.

107. Information made available to the author by USIA.

108. The preceding account is based on the following works: Naum Jasny, *The Socialized Agriculture of the USSR,* Stanford University Press, Palo Alto, California, 1959; Harry Schwartz, *Russia's Soviet Economy,* Prentice-Hall, Inc., New York, 1950; Bienstock, Schwarz, and Yugow, *Management in Russian Industry and Agriculture,* Oxford University Press, London, 1944.

109. A regional Party secretary wrote in *Pravda* on January 15, 1930, that since it was impossible to move directly from individual farming to the commune, "we shall reach that stage (the commune) at a later time."

110. J. V. Stalin, "Report on the Work of the Central Committee to the 17th Congress of the CPSU," *Selected Writings,* International Publishers, New York, 1942, p. 343.

111. *Ibid.*

112. Speech to the Hungarian Party Congress in Budapest, December 1, 1959. See *Pravda,* December 2, 1959.

113. V. Molotov, "The Third Five Year Plan for the National Economic Development of the USSR," *The Land of Socialism Today and Tomorrow* (proceedings of the 18th Congress), Foreign Languages Publishing House, Moscow, 1939, p. 167.

114. S. G. Strumulin, "Nekotorye problemy dal'neishego razvitiya kolkhoznogo stroya," *Voprosy ekonomiki,* 5, May 1958.

115. I. Glotov, "Reorganizatsiya MTS i kolkhoznaya sobstvennost," *Kommunist,* April 1958, p. 54.

116. SCMP, 1894, November 14, 1958, p. 34.

117. SCMP, 1902, November 26, 1958, p. 2.

118. *Jen-min jih-pao,* November 22, 1958; NCNA, November 22, 1958.

119. *Peking Review,* 43, December 23, 1958, p. 11.

120. *Politicheskaya ekonomiya uchebnik,* State Publishing House for Political Literature, Moscow, signed to the press September 15, 1958.

121. *Peking Review,* 43, December 23, 1958, p. 13.

122. *Ibid.*

123. *Ibid.*

124. NCNA, December 31, 1958.

125. *Rabotnichesko delo* editorial, October 16, 1958. See also Zhivkov's report of November 11, Bulgarian Home Service, November 14, 1958, in which he called for a "great leap forward" every year. For a round-up of the accelerated Bulgarian economic development program which began in the fall of 1958, see Boris A. Christoff, "The Bulgarian 'Leap Forward,'" *Problems of Communism,* September-October 1959, pp. 15–20.

126. Higher economic targets in Hungary were announced by Party leader Karoly Kiss on December 9. See *East Europe,* January 1959. For the sudden increase in Hungarian collectivization in early 1959, see also the Current Developments sections of *East Europe,* March, April, and June 1959.

127. A Central Committee meeting decided upon higher economic targets in late November. See *Scinteia* (Bucharest), December 2, 1958.

128. The author was unable to find any reference to the Albanian decision in the Soviet press of that period.

129. *Pravda,* February 6, 1959.

130. *Ibid.,* February 8, 1959.

131. For these figures, and for the material in the following paragraph, I am indebted to Oleg Hoeffding, "Sino-Soviet Economic Relations in Recent Years," *op. cit.*

132. *Pravda,* January 28, 1959.

133. I. V. Zhegalin, *Pravda,* February 5, 1959.

134. *Izvestiya,* January 29, 1959.

135. Khrushchev's protégé, D. Polyanski, said: "The conclusion about the nature of the advance of society towards Communism, the ways and means of developing and bringing closer together collective farms and state farms of property, the merger of these farms into a single Communist property, constitute a long-range program not only for us, *but for all our friends abroad"* [italics supplied], *Pravda,* January 29, 1959.

136. *Ibid.,* February 6, 1959.

137. *Ibid.,* January 28, 1959.

138. *Ibid.*

139. *Peking Review,* 43, December 23, 1958, p. 13.

140. *Pravda,* January 28, 1959.

141. *Ibid.*

142. *Ibid.*

143. *Pravda,* February 6, 1959.

144. P. Fedoseev and I. Pomelov, "O Razvitii mirovoi sotsialisticheskoi sistemy k kommunizmu," *Kommunist*, 5, April 1959, p. 36.

145. *Pravda*, January 28, 1959.

146. Senator Hubert H. Humphrey, "My Marathon Talk with Russia's Boss," *Life*, January 12, 1959, pp. 80–91.

147. *Pravda*, January 28, 1959.

148. *Ibid.*, February 6, 1959. To avoid mentioning the communes, Yudin resorted to a clumsy circumlocution; he referred to the "socialist reform in rural communities" going on throughout the country.

149. *Jen-min jih-pao*, February 5, 1959; *Peking Review*, 6, February 10, 1959, pp. 6–8.

150. *Hung ch'i* editorial, February 16, 1959; *Peking Review*, 8, February 24, 1959, pp. 7–11.

151. *Ibid.*, p. 10.

152. Moscow Home Service, July 21, 1959.

153. *Ibid.*

154. V. Mikheev, "Vydayushchiisya uspekhi kitaiskogo naroda," *Kommunist*, 8, June 1959, p. 103.

155. V. Berezhkov, "The People's Communes and the Paper Tigers," *New Times*, 12, March 1959, p. 14.

156. Lenin was attacking undisciplined bourgeois revolutionaries who struck out in all directions at once and had no logical revolutionary program.

157. See Wilson, *op. cit.*, pp. 94–99. *Hung ch'i* of September 1, 1959, lists the Rightist heresies; *Peking Review*, 39, October 1, 1959, pp. 20–22.

158. "The Communist Party of China is the High Command of the Chinese People in Building Socialism," *op. cit.*, pp. 287–288. (See note 68.)

159. *Pravda*, September 29, 1959.

160. *Ibid.*, October 2, 1959.

161. *Ibid.*, October 1, 1959.

162. Teng Hsiao-p'ing in *Pravda*, October 1, 1959 (written for the 10th Anniversary of the CPR); in *Ten Glorious Years*, *op. cit.*, pp. 98–99. This article is also in *Peking Review*, 39, October 1, 1959.

163. On the 10th anniversary of the CPR, Liu Shao-ch'i wrote in the international Communist journal, *Problems of Peace and Socialism:* "Of course, revolution and construction in China have features peculiar to this country. But it is also possible that some of these important special features may reappear in some other countries. In this sense, Chinese experience is to a certain extent of international significance." See *Ten Glorious Years*, *op. cit.*, pp. 33–34; Article also in *Peking Review*, 39, October 1, 1959. On September 20, immediately prior to Khrushchev's arrival in Peking, *Jen-min jih-pao* wrote that Chinese experience "has also greatly enriched the *general treasury* of Marxism-Leninism and played a positive role in the revolution and construction of our fraternal countries" [italics supplied], NCNA, September 20, 1959.

164. Liu Lan-t'ao, "The Communist Party of China is the High Command of the Chinese People in Building Socialism," *op. cit.*, pp. 295–296.

165. "Forward Along the Path of the Great Lenin!" *Jen-min jih-pao* editorial, April 22, 1960, and Lu Ting-yi, "Unite Under Lenin's Revolutionary Banner!" both in *Long Live Leninism, op. cit.,* pp. 60–63, 94–96. (These articles are also in the "Long Live Leninism" issue of *Peking Review,* 17, April 26, 1960.)

CHAPTER FOUR

1. *New York Times,* January 12, 1957.

2. *Jen-min jih-pao,* November 20, 1957; SCMP, 1656, November 21, 1957. The speech was summarized by NCNA on November 18, 1957.

3. *Jen-min jih-pao,* November 25, 1957; NCNA, November 25, 1957.

4. Tass, November 18, 1957.

5. East German Home Service, July 11, 1958.

6. *New York Times,* June 15 and July 15, 1958.

7. NCNA, November 6, 1957.

8. "Report on Visits to Eleven Countries in Europe and Asia," in CB, 439, March 8, 1957, p. 7.

9. See the speech cited in footnote 7.

10. *Ibid.*

11. "More on the Historical Experience of the Dictatorship of the Proletariat," *Jen-min jih-pao,* December 29, 1956; CB, 433, January 2, 1957, p. 11.

12. Speech of November 6 to the Supreme Soviet, *op. cit.*

13. Mao Tse-tung, *On the Correct Handling of Contradictions among the People,* Foreign Languages Press, Peking, 1958, p. 54.

14. See the account by the West Bengal Communist, Harekrishna Konar in the Indian news magazine *Link,* October 16, 1960.

15. NCNA, April 11, 1957.

16. *Kuang-ming jih-pao,* February 2, 1958.

CHAPTER FIVE

1. For an excellent discussion of the relation between ideology and strategy, see Zbigniew Brzezinski, "Communist Ideology and International Affairs," *The Journal of Conflict Resolution,* September 1960, pp. 266–291.

2. *Jen-min jih-pao,* August 30, 1957; NCNA, August 30, 1957.

3. See Khrushchev's interview with Hearst, *Pravda,* November 29, 1957.

4. See, for example, *Ta kung pao,* October 6, 1957, in SCMP, 1627, October 9, 1957, p. 25; *Kuang-ming jih-pao,* October 7, 1957, in SCMP, 1628, October 10, 1957, p. 41; and *Jen-min jih-pao,* October 7, 1957, also in SCMP, 1628, pp. 40–41.

5. See chapter 3, "The Soviet View of Deterrence," in Herbert S. Dinerstein's *War and the Soviet Union,* Frederick A. Praeger, New York, 1950.

6. See *Kommunist* (Yerevan), March 12, 1954 for Mikoyan's full speech and *Pravda,* of the same date, for an abbreviated text.

7. *Pravda,* March 13, 1954.

8. *Ibid.*, April 27, 1954.

9. Maj. Gen. N. Talenskii, "On Atomic and Conventional Weapons," *International Affairs*, 1, 1955, p. 20.

10. *Pravda*, February 15, 1956.

11. *Ibid.*, September 8, 1957.

12. *Ibid.*, November 22, 1957.

13. *Ibid.*, January 26, 1958.

14. See Khrushchev's interview with the Paris *Figaro* on March 19, 1958.

15. Speech in Krasnodar, *Pravda*, October 16, 1958.

16. Speech in Vlore, Albania, May 31, 1959, Moscow Radio Home Service, June 1, 1959.

17. Arnold Horelick and Myron Rush, The RAND Corporation, Santa Monica, California, work in progress on Soviet military strategy.

18. Maj. Gen. N. Talenskii, "Military Strategy and Foreign Policy," *International Affairs*, 3, 1958, pp. 28–29.

19. Prof. L. Ilyichov, "The Sputniks and International Relations," *International Affairs*, 3, 1958, p. 7.

20. *Ibid.*, p. 11.

21. *Ibid.*

22. In Khrushchev's 40th Anniversary report to the Supreme Soviet on November 6, 1957, an occasion which could have provided the perfect backdrop for a dramatic announcement of the superiority of the Bloc over the West, Khrushchev appraised the year 1957 not as a turning point but as a year of "outstanding victories." One Soviet writer, in assessing the impact of the sputnik on the balance of forces, wrote that the balance was now *"tipping* still further in (the Bloc's) favor . . . " [italics supplied]. See V. Korinov, "The Crisis of the 'Positions of Strength' Policy," *International Affairs*, 3, 1958, p. 34. As late as March 4, 1959, Khrushchev told an East German audience that if it were possible to invent an instrument which would measure with precision the political and military strength of the Bloc and the West, it "would show that both sides are sufficiently strong at present." *Pravda*, March 5, 1959.

23. See, for example, his interview with UP correspondent Shapiro, *Pravda*, November 19, 1957; see also his speech to the Supreme Soviet on November 6th in which he said the use of atomic and ballistic weapons would bring tremendous disaster to *all* mankind, *Pravda*, November 7, 1957.

24. *Jen-min jih-pao*, November 20, 1957; SCMP, 1656, November 21, 1957.

25. This excerpt from Mao's November 18, 1957, speech in Moscow is contained in his *Imperialism and All Reactionaries Are Paper Tigers*, Foreign Languages Press, Peking, 1958, p. 28. It is also in *Peking Review*, 37, November 11, 1958.

26. For the latest reiteration of this formula, see the Moscow Declaration of December 6, 1960, *Pravda*, December 6, 1960. Also in *Peking Review*, 49–50, December 13, 1960, p. 9.

27. Mao Tse-tung, *Imperialism and All Reactionaries Are Paper Tigers,* *op. cit.,* p. 27.

28. *Ibid.*

29. These articles included a *Jen-min jih-pao* editorial on November 24; an article in *Shih-chieh chih-shih* on December 5 and another in the same journal on December 20; an article in *Hsueh-hsi* on January 3, 1958; and articles in *Kuang-ming jih-pao* on December 8, 1957, and February 9, 1958.

30. *Jen-min jih-pao* (November 24), for instance, noted that the socialist world "has superiority in the entire balance of forces" (SCMP, 1660, November 27, 1957, p. 27). And in the words of *Shih-chieh chih-shih* (December 20), "the strength of the socialist camp is now ahead of the strength of the imperialist camp" (Hu Pin, "The New World Situation," in JPRS, 507-D, January 27, 1959, Chinese Communist Articles on World Situation).

31. JPRS, DC-263, August 22, 1958, translations of political articles from the China Mainland Press, p. 44.

32. Hu Pin, "The New World Situation," *op. cit.,* p. 3.

33. Speech to the Supreme Soviet, January 14, 1961, Moscow Radio Home Service, January 14, 1961.

34. See Khrushchev's interview with James Reston in the *New York Times,* October 10, 1957.

35. *Kuang-ming jih pao,* December 8, 1957; SCMP, 1669, December 11, 1957, p. 45.

36. "The Great Revolutionary Declarations," *Jen-min jih-pao,* November 25, 1957; SCMP, 1660, November 27, 1957, p. 28.

37. *Ibid.*

38. "The East Wind Overpowers the West Wind (Chief Characteristic of the Current International Situation)," *Hsueh-hsi,* 1, January 3, 1958; JPRS, 507-D, January 27, 1959, p. 20.

39. *Pravda,* January 28, 1959.

40. SCMP, 1660, November 27, 1957, pp. 27–28.

41. *Ibid.*

42. Hu Pin, "The World Situation," *op. cit.,* p. 8.

43. *Ibid.,* pp. 15–16.

44. Chi Lung, "U.S. Strategy is in a Blind Alley," *Shih-chieh chih-shih,* December 5, 1957; *Extracts,* 121, March 3, 1958, pp. 1–6.

45. *Ibid.* p. 1.

46. *Ibid.,* p. 4.

47. See the message from Bulganin to President Eisenhower, *Pravda,* December 12, 1957.

48. Bulganin's message to Turkish Premier Menderes, September 10, in *Pravda,* September 14, 1957; see also Gromyko's statement to the press on the same date in which he spoke of the danger of escalation (*Pravda,* September 11, 1957), as well as Khrushchev's interview with a Brazilian newspaper on November 21, 1957, when he said, "We must not think that under present conditions minor wars would be localized. Should such wars break out, they could soon grow into a world war" (Tass, December 5, 1957).

49. The writer is indebted for this formulation to Hans Speier, "The Soviet Threat to Berlin," The RAND Corporation, Santa Monica, California, April 15, 1961.

50. Chi Lung, "U.S. Strategy Is in a Blind Alley," *op. cit.,* p. 4.

51. Speech to the National People's Congress, July 27, 1955, in CB, 347, August 23, 1955, p. 30.

52. Article by General Liu Ya-lou, Commander of the PLA Air Force, "Seriously Study Mao Tse-tung's Military Thinking," *Chieh-fang-chün pao,* May 23, 1958; SCMP, 1900, November 24, 1958, p. 10. See also Alice L. Hsieh's "Communist China and Nuclear Warfare," *The China Quarterly,* April–June 1960, pp. 1–15.

53. Marshal Ho Lung, *Jen-min jih-pao,* August 1, 1958; NCNA, August 1, 1958.

54. Tass, November 27, 1957.

55. *Ibid.*

Chapter Six

1. "Full Steam Ahead," *Jen-min jih-pao,* January 1, 1958; NCNA, January 1, 1958.

2. *Ibid.*

3. *Ibid.*

4. NCNA, February 10, 1958.

5. *Ibid.*

6. *Ibid.*

7. *Ibid.*

8. Richard Lowenthal, "Tito's Gamble," *Encounter,* October 1958, pp. 56–65.

9. For an excellent discussion of what each sought from the other, see Seweryn Bialer, "Moscow vs. Belgrade; A Key to Soviet Policy," *Problems of Communism,* July–August 1958, pp. 1–8.

10. Lowenthal, "Tito's Gamble," *op. cit.,* p. 62.

11. *Ibid.,* p. 63.

12. *New York Times,* July 15, 1958, cited in *The Soviet-Yugoslav Controversy, 1948–1958,* Robert Bass and Elizabeth Marbury (eds.), Prospect Books, New York, 1959, p. 107.

13. See the author's "The Spectre of Revisionism," *Problems of Communism,* July–August 1958, pp. 15–21.

14. Bass and Marbury, eds., *op. cit.,* p. 107.

15. *Ibid.*

16. P. Fedoseev, I. Pomelov, V. Cheprakov, "O proekte programmy Soyuza Kommunistov Yugoslavii," *Kommunist,* 6, 1958, p. 39.

17. *New York Times,* April 25, 1958.

18. "Modern Revisionism Must be Condemned," *Jen-min jih-pao,* May 5, 1958; SCMP, 1767, May 8, 1958. This article also in *Peking Review,* 11, May 13, 1958.

19. *Kuang-ming jih-pao,* February 2, 1958.

20. That the plenum discussed the Yugoslav issue was subsequently revealed by Lithuanian Party secretary Snieckus in *Sovetskaya litva,* May 17, 1958.

21. Bass and Marbury, eds., *op. cit.,* pp. 189–190.

22. *Hung ch'i,* 1, June 1, 1958; *Peking Review,* 16, June 17, 1958, p. 9.

23. Bass and Marbury, eds., *op. cit.,* p. 190.

24. *Ibid.,* p. 201.

25. *Ibid.,* p. 214.

26. *Jen-min jih-pao,* June 26, 1958; *Peking Review,* 18, July 1, 1958, p. 7.

27. *For Victory in Peaceful Competition with Capitalism,* collection of speeches by Khrushchev, E. P. Dutton and Co., Inc., New York, 1960, p. 575.

28. *Ibid.,* p. 578.

29. Chang Hsiang-shan, "The Same Stuff from One Basket—the Tito Clique and Djilas," *Hsueh-hsi,* September 10, 1958; *Extracts,* 146, October, 27, 1958, pp. 1–5.

30. For an excellent account of Sino-Soviet-Yugoslav relationships, see Richard Lowenthal, "Shifts and Rifts in the Russo-Chinese Alliance," *Problems of Communism,* January-February 1959, pp. 14–24.

31. *Jen-min jih-pao,* May 5, 1958; *Peking Review,* 11, May 13, 1958, p. 8.

32. SCMP, 1787, June 9, 1958, pp. 49–51.

33. *Ibid.,* p. 50.

34. *For Victory in Peaceful Competition with Capitalism, op. cit.,* pp. 394–433.

35. *Ibid.*

36. NCNA, July 25, 1958.

37. For the background in the following paragraph, the author is indebted to a study by Alice Hsieh, *Communist China in the Nuclear Era,* Prentice-Hall, Inc., Englewood Cliffs, New Jersey, 1962.

38. "People's Army, People's War," CB, 514, August 6, 1958, pp. 1–4.

39. *Chieh-fang-chün pao,* August 1, 1958; SCMP, 1881, October 24, 1958, p. 2.

40. *Chieh-fang-chün pao,* July 1, 1958; SCMP, 1881, October 24, 1958, p. 4.

41. "Seriously Study Mao Tse-tung's Military Thinking," *Chieh-fang-chün pao,* May 23, 1958; SCMP, 1900, November 24, 1958, pp. 9–10.

42. *Ibid.*

43. *Jen-min jih-pao,* August 1, 1958; NCNA, August 1, 1958.

44. Lowenthal, "Shifts and Rifts in the Russo-Chinese Alliance," *op. cit.,* p. 19.

45. *Ibid.*

46. See, for instance, Sobelev's statement to the Security council on July 15 (Tass, July 15, 1958); the Soviet Government statement of July 16

(Tass, July 16, 1958); and the Izvestiya article "Vooruzhenniya agressiya SSHA na Arabskom vostoke," signed "Observer," July 17, 1958.

47. *Jen-min jih-pao,* July 20, 1958; *Peking Review,* 22, July 29, 1958, p. 5.

48. *Jen-min jih-pao,* July 21, 1958; NCNA, July 21, 1958. The USSR had earlier warned in an official government statement of July 18 that Soviet Moslems might go to the aid of their co-religionists. The Chinese may have been calling for action rather than threat.

49. See the text of Khrushchev's letter in the *New York Times,* July 20, 1958.

50. *For Victory in Peaceful Competition with Capitalism, op. cit.,* p. 612.

51. NCNA, July 17, 1958.

52. *Chien-fang-chün pao,* July 25, 1958; SCMP, 1822, July 30, 1958, p. 12.

53. NCNA, July 16, 1958.

54. SCMP, 1817, July 23, 1958, p. 34.

55. See Herbert Ritvo, "Sino-Soviet Relations and the Summit," *Problems of Communism,* September-October 1958, pp. 47–49. Ritvo demonstrates that the Chinese and Soviet press reacted similarly both to Khrushchev's original acceptance of Macmillan's proposals (July 23) and to his subsequent charges against the alleged modifications of the original plan. (Khrushchev's letters to the heads of Western governments on July 28, published in *Pravda,* July 29, 1958.) This weakens the popular thesis that Mao forced Khrushchev to withdraw from the summit inasmuch as Khrushchev was clearly withdrawing even before his visit to Peking. It does not weaken the thesis advanced here, however, that in the week preceding July 23 there was considerable evidence of Peking's dissatisfaction with Khrushchev's political response to the Western troop landings. It probably became apparent in the week after July 23 both to Mao and to Khrushchev that the West was not going to move on Iraq. Greece recognized the new Iraqi government on July 30 and Britain and the United States followed suit on August 1 and 2.

56. See footnotes 2–10 in the next chapter.

CHAPTER SEVEN

1. *New York Times,* August 4, 1958.

2. *Hung ch'i,* 5, 1958; *Peking Review,* 26, August 26, 1958, pp. 8–9.

3. *Ibid.*

4. *Jen-min jih-pao,* August 4, 1958; NCNA, August 4, 1958.

5. *Jen-min jih-pao,* August 8, 1958; NCNA, August 8, 1958.

6. *Ibid.*

7. *Ibid.*

8. *Pravda,* August 5, 1958.

9. *Ibid.,* August 6, 1958.

10. See note 5.

11. There are two good studies of the Quemoy crisis: *The Embroilment over Quemoy: Mao, Chiang, and Dulles,* by Tang Tsou, Institute of International Affairs, University of Utah Press, Salt Lake City, Utah, 1959; and a chapter in a work by Alice L. Hsieh (see footnote 37, Chapter 6). There is also an as yet unpublished study of Soviet behavior in the Quemoy crisis by John Thomas, formerly of The RAND Corporation, Santa Monica, California.

12. *New York Times,* Sept. 5, 1958.

13. A good indication of the sobering effect on Khrushchev of Dulles' "brinkmanship" tactics was provided by Khrushchev himself in an interview with Drew Pearson in 1961. At this time, the Soviet leader said: "I came to have admiration for Dulles before he died. He would disagree with you, but *you knew exactly where he stood.* And he did not want war. He would go up to the edge of war, or as he called it 'brinkmanship', but he stopped before war" [italics supplied]. *Los Angeles Mirror,* August 29, 1961.

14. It is Tang Tsou's contention that Chiang sought deliberately to involve the United States in war with Communist China.

15. Peking coastal radios, July 27, 1958.

16. "The Forces of the New are bound to Defeat the Forces of Decay," in *Peking Review,* 25, August 19, 1958, p. 8.

17. *Ibid.,* p. 9.

18. *Ibid.*

19. Moscow radio in Mandarin, August 19, 1958.

20. Peking coastal radios, in Mandarin to Taiwan, August 27–29, 1958. The defection appeals ceased abruptly on September 2, and two such previously announced appeals were dropped without explanation.

21. *Pravda,* August 24, 1958. It is important to note that Khrushchev was reported to have delivered the speech containing this passage on August 13. An 11-day delay in the publication of a Khrushchev speech is quite unusual. It seems unlikely that Khrushchev would have been unaware of the impending crisis even on August 13, ten days after his hurriedly arranged meeting with Mao which had included the Soviet Defense Minister. It is more likely that Khrushchev was well aware of the impending Chinese action. One of his purposes in the timing of publication, then, may have been to put Mao on notice that the USSR would not take very large risks in support of Chinese objectives.

22. *Sovetskii flot* and *Pravda,* August 27, 1958.

23. *Sovetskaya aviatzia,* August 28, 1958.

24. In the only major Soviet comment on the CPR declaration prior to the official Soviet Government response, *Izvestiya* said on September 6, 1958, that it had the "full understanding of the Soviet public." The official Soviet Government statement on September 9, published in the Soviet press on the following day, said the USSR took "note" of the declaration and "would fully respect it." There were no threats to other countries which would not respect it nor even statements of Soviet support, in contrast to

"respect," for the declaration. (For the four references cited above, the author is indebted to Thomas, *op. cit.*)

25. *Pravda*, September 5, 1958.

26. Khrushchev message of September 7, 1958, to President Eisenhower, text in the *New York Times*, September 9, 1958. It is fairly consistent Soviet practice to rattle missiles *after* the peak of a crisis is passed. This enables them to take credit for having deterred the U.S. while at the same time avoiding high risk.

27. *Ibid.*

28. For the text of this letter, see the *New York Times*, September 20, 1958.

29. *New York Times*, September 14–21, 1958.

30. *Pravda*, October 6, 1958.

31. See Edward Crankshaw, "The Moscow-Peking Clash Exposed," *Observer* (London), February 12 and 19, 1961. Thomas, *op. cit.*, concludes after a more detailed investigation of Soviet behavior during the crisis than is possible here, that "the Soviets spoke softly particularly when the danger of conflict was greatest" and that Soviet threats grew more menacing as the crisis shifted into a political phase. He also makes the perceptive observation that Soviet awareness of the ineffectiveness of their support of the Chinese in the Quemoy crisis may be deduced from their modesty in describing their role subsequently. The Soviets have made sweeping claims about their decisive role in deterring the West in other crises. They claim to have saved Nasser from being overthrown by Britain and France in 1956; to have saved Syria from being overwhelmed by Turkey, with U.S. backing, in 1957; and to have saved Iraq from U.S. intervention in 1958. In sharp contrast, Mikoyan, shortly after the Quemoy crisis was over, gave credit to *China* for having "succeeded in not allowing the outbreak of conflict in the region of Taiwan." (Speech on the 41st Anniversary of the Bolshevik Revolution, *Pravda*, November 7, 1958.)

32. See the editor's note in *Imperialism and All Reactionaries Are Paper Tigers*, Foreign Languages Press, Peking, 1958.

33. *Ibid.*, pp. 29–30.

34. *Ibid.*, p. 18.

35. *Ibid.*, p. 19.

36. *Ibid.*, p. 3.

37. "Scorn Imperialism and all Reactionaries," *Jen-min jih-pao*, November 12, 1958; *Peking Review*, 38, November 18, pp. 11–12.

38. *Ibid.*, p. 11.

39. *Ibid.*, p. 12.

40. *Ibid.*, pp. 11–12.

41. Crankshaw, *op. cit.*

CHAPTER EIGHT

1. J. Stalin, *Problems of Leninism*, Foreign Languages Publishing House, Moscow, 1953, p. 31.

2. *Ibid.*

3. A second printing was signed to the press on October 5, 1959, and a slightly revised edition, not announced as such, appeared shortly thereafter with a signed to the press date of November 26, 1959. An English-language edition appeared in 1960; citations following are taken from this edition.

4. See particularly subsection, "Strategy and Tactics," pp. 80–91, in J. Stalin, *Problems of Leninism, op. cit.* The 1953 edition is the eleventh and most recent.

5. *The Fundamentals of Marxism-Leninism*, Foreign Languages Publishing House, Moscow, 1960, pp. 424–425.

6. *Ibid.*, p. 425.

7. *Ibid.*, p. 606.

8. *Long Live Leninism*, Foreign Languages Press, Peking, 1960, p. 36.

9. *The Fundamentals of Marxism- Leninism, op. cit.*, p. 607.

10. *Ibid.*, p. 614.

11. *Pravda*, February 15, 1956.

12. A. Butenko and V. Plechin, "Sovremennaya epokha i tvorcheskoe razvitie Marksizma-Leninizma," *Kommunist*, 12, 1960, p. 15.

13. *The Fundamentals of Marxism-Leninism, op. cit.*, p. 591.

14. See Z. Brzezinski, *The Soviet Bloc: Unity and Conflict,* Harvard University Press, Cambridge, Massachusetts, 1960, p. 31. Brzezinski's introductory chapters on the people's democracy are the fullest and best discussion of this subject in English known to the author.

15. *Ibid.*, p. 47.

16. *The Fundamentals of Marxism-Leninism, op. cit.*, p. 596.

17. The current Soviet emphasis on transitional forms of government— i.e., governments not yet under Communist domination—was to be illustrated again in the fall of 1960 when the concept of a "national democracy" was evolved for the underdeveloped areas. Like the "democracy of a new type," the "national democracy" was envisioned as a government more hospitable to local Communists and to middle-range Soviet interests, but not yet dominated by the Communists.

18. *World Marxist Review*, January 1960, pp. 47–50.

19. The program of the Rome Conference, according to A. Belyakov and F. Burlatskii in *Kommunist*, 13, 1960, has been attacked by "dogmatists" within the Communist movement as tending to "distract the workers from the struggle for socialist goals."

20. *The Fundamentals of Marxism-Leninism, op. cit.*, p. 603.

21. *Neues Deutschland*, February 5, 1960.

CHAPTER NINE

1. *Pravda*, January 28, 1959.

2. *Ibid.*

3. *Ibid.*

4. SCMP, 1948, February 4, 1959, p. 5.

5. *Pravda*, October 16, 1958.

6. See *Peking Review*, 8, February 24, 1959, pp. 7–11, for the above contentions.

7. *Shih-chieh chih-shih*, June 1959.

8. *Ibid.*

9. Yu Chao-li, "Peaceful Competition: an Inevitable Trend," *Hung ch'i*, August 16, 1959; *Peking Review*, 33, August 18, 1959, pp. 6–8.

10. *Ibid.*, p. 6.

11. *Ibid.*, p. 8.

12. Report of Ch'en Yi speech, NCNA, August 17, 1959.

13. *Peking Review*, 38, September 22, 1959, pp. 6–11 (somewhat abridged).

14. *Ibid.*, p. 7.

15. *Ibid.*

16. *Ibid.*

17. *Ibid.*

18. *Ibid.*

CHAPTER TEN

1. This chapter is an enlarged version of the author's article "Sino-Soviet Friction in Underdeveloped Areas," *Problems of Communism*, March-April 1961, pp. 1–13.

2. Several Yugoslav academicians, one of whom spent two years in China, told this writer in February 1960 that the Chinese Communists cannot understand why so much emphasis is placed on raising living standards in the Communist Bloc countries of Europe. They further indicated that the Chinese believe that the USSR, in seeking to raise its own living standards, is defaulting on its obligations to the less advanced Bloc countries. At the Chinese Communist Writers' Congress in July 1960, there were pointed warnings against "bourgeois theories of human nature" which deny the class struggle and revolution and "spread illusions about imperialism." For an analysis of the anti-Soviet overtones of the Congress, see Ernest Kux, "The Chinese Writers' Congress," *Thought* (Delhi, India), October 15, 1960. (The article first appeared in the *Neue zuercher zeitung*.)

3. For an excellent account of these differences, see Allen S. Whiting, *Soviet Policies in China, 1917–1924*, Columbia University Press, New York, 1954, chapter 3, "The Second Comintern Congress." See also Walter Z. Laqueur, "The 'National Bourgeoisie,' A Soviet Dilemma in the Middle East," *International Affairs*, July 1959, pp. 324–331, for an account of the controversy with respect to the underdeveloped areas, particularly the Middle East. For a good summary of the shifts in the Communist line on the national bourgeoisie, see Milton Kovner, *The Challenge of Coexistence*, Public Affairs Press, Washington, D.C., 1961, chapter 5.

4. Xenia J. Eudin and Robert C. North, *Soviet Russia and the East, 1920–1927: a Documentary Survey*, Stanford University Press, Palo Alto, California, 1957, pp. 68–69.

5. *Ibid.*, p. 67.

6. *Selected Works of Mao Tse-tung,* vol. 3, People's Publishing House, Ltd., Bombay, 1954, pp. 96–97.

7. *Ibid.,* p. 119.

8. See Liu Shao-ch'i's speech of November 16, 1949, NCNA, November 23, 1949; and Lu Ting-yi, "The World Significance of the Chinese Democratic United Front," July 1, 1951, CB, 89, July 5, 1951, pp. 29–33.

9. *Pravda,* February 15, 1956.

10. Since 1958, the Chinese have revived the concept of "permanent revolution" both internally (there should be no long gaps between the domestic stages of building communism) and internationally (there can be no long gaps between the "democratic" and "socialist" revolutions in non-Communist countries). Liu Shao-ch'i, for example, in a 10th Anniversary article, spoke of the need to ensure the rapid, uninterrupted transition to the socialist revolution "immediately after" the victory of the democratic revolution. See "The Victory of Marxism-Leninism in China," in *Ten Glorious Years, 1949–1959,* Foreign Languages Press, Peking, 1960, p. 4. For the specific application of the theory of "permanent revolution" to the colonial countries, see Wang Chia-hsiang's article in *Ten Glorious Years,* op. cit., pp. 271–282.

11. Liu Shao-ch'i, "The Victory of Marxism-Leninism in China," *op. cit.,* p. 4.

The importance attached by the Chinese to the question of the leading role for the Communists in the first phase of the revolutionary process was emphasized in another article in *Kuo-chi wen-t'i yen chiu* on January 3, 1960. Explaining why the Cuban revolution was such a "good example" of national democratic revolutions in Asia, Africa, and Latin America, it said this was the case in part because the Cuban worker-peasant movement "was under the leadership and influence of the Cuban Communist Party." It was for this reason, the article asserted, that the "strong Communist leadership" in the Cuban revolutionary movement was able to promote the "correct 'united-front' policy." Thus, the Chinese strategy was not against "united fronts" with the bourgeoisie in the underdeveloped areas *if* the Communists occupied a prominent role in the leadership of the united front.

12. Yu. Zhukov, "Znamenatel'nyi faktor nashego vremeni," *Pravda,* August 26, 1960.

13. In criticizing Soviet strategy, the Chinese have obliquely referred several times to the diaster that overtook their Party in 1927. See footnote 11 above.

14. *The Fundamentals of Marxism-Leninism,* Foreign Languages Publishing House, Moscow, 1960, states that "in the countries of the East, state capitalism in its present form is not a tool of the imperialist monopolies; on the contrary, it stimulates an anti-imperialist movement and is objectively directed against the expansion of these monopolies in the East. . . . All this is basis for concluding that state capitalism in the countries of the East is playing a progressive role" (pp. 511–512). On the contrary, *Hung ch'i* (October 1, 1959) declared that by following the road of state capitalism,

the newly independent states "will not be able to rid themselves of the exploitation and oppression by imperialism and feudalism." Wang Chiahsiang, in *Ten Glorious Years, op. cit.*, p. 279.

15. See remarks by Hsun Fu in the Soviet journal *International Affairs*, 3, 1959, p. 84.

16. Lu Ting-yi, "United Under Lenin's Revolutionary Banner!" in *Long Live Leninism*, Foreign Languages Press, Peking, 1960, pp. 103–104.

17. "The Fundamental Path for the Liberation Movements in Colonial and Semi-Colonial Areas," *Kuo-chi wen-t'i yen-chiu*, 5, May 3, 1960.

18. Zhukov, for example, did not mention armed struggle at all in his lead article on the January 1959 joint Sino-Soviet "seminar on the colonial question" in Moscow. See "The Bankruptcy of the Imperialist Colonial System and International Relations," *International Affairs*, 3, 1959, pp. 65–68.

19. A. Sovetov, "Leninist Foreign Policy and International Relations," *International Affairs*, 4, 1960, p. 9.

20. *Long Live Leninism, op. cit.*, p. 36.

21. *Ibid.*, p. 39. Such reasoning might explain why the Chinese Communists seem to pursue a more patient strategy in small countries in close proximity to China, e.g., Cambodia and Nepal. It would also help to explain why they are less optimistic about the possibilities of peaceful revolution in countries such as the UAR, India, Indonesia, and Iraq, which are either larger or not "encircled by socialism."

22. See the articles in *Long Live Leninism, op. cit.*

23. A. Belyakov and F. Burlatski, "Leninskaya teoriya sotsialisticheskoi revolyutsii i sovremennost," *Kommunist*, 13, 1960, p. 14.

24. The controversy over the national bourgeoisie apparently also played a large part in the reported exchange of letters between the Chinese and Soviet parties in the summer of 1960. According to one report, a Soviet letter read at Bucharest in June 1960 "rejects Chinese charges that the CPSU had commenced a flirtation with the national bourgeoisie" and defends such ties with the argument that this fosters neutralism and thereby weakens imperialism. For purported extracts from the letter, see *Deutsche zeitung*, September 30, 1960, Appendix I.

The point that the national bourgeoisie in a colonial and semicolonial country "cannot be depended upon for the complete overthrow of the imperialist and feudal forces in the new democratic revolution" was made by *Chung-kuo ch'ing-nien*, no. 9, May 1, 1960. This was, in fact, a "scientific conclusion of Chairman Mao." Furthermore, the danger was great that the present national bourgeois governments in many of these countries might be replaced by a "dictatorship of the upper bourgeois class," a development which could set back the newly independent country to the status of a "temporary semi-colony."

25. *Ten Glorious Years, op. cit.*, pp. 276–279.

26. The controversy between the Left and Right groups in the Iraqi CP was recently brought into the open. The Warsaw *Glos pracy* of January 28,

1961, summarized a recent undated Iraqi Communist document criticizing the Left wing for "trying to push the Party on the road of adventurism" and the Right wing for "rejecting the revolutionary struggle." The fight, which apparently began early in 1959, appears to hinge on how much pressure should be brought against the government and how soon to strike for power. On February 17, 1959, the Polish paper *Zycie warszawy* quoted an Iraqi Communist publicist, Aziz Al-Hadj, as saying that his Party "does not proclaim the necessity to create a Communist society now" and that "an antigovernment conspiracy would be a crime in any Arab state struggling against imperialism, *even if communism were persecuted*" [italics supplied].

27. D. Shevlyagin, in *Sovetskaya rossiya*, June 19, 1960.

28. Shen Chun-ju article in *Jen-min jih-pao*, August 27, 1959, SCMP, 2089, September 3, 1959, p. 49.

29. *Communist Economic Strategy: Soviet Growth and Capabilities*, National Planning Association, Washington, D.C. October 1959, p. 2.

30. Moscow Radio Home Service, April 18, 1960.

31. *Ibid.*

32. For comments on the clash, see statement by H. D. Malaviya, Indian member of the secretariat of the Afro-Asian Solidarity Council, reported by the Indian news agency PTI on May 5, 1960.

33. NCNA, May 4, 1960.

34. *Kuo-chi wen-t'i yen-chiu*, 7, July 13, 1960, pp. 2–7.

35. *Pravda*, April 23, 1960.

36. L. Stepanov, "Soviet Aid and Its Critics," *International Affairs*, 6, 1960, p. 22.

37. Wang Chia-hsiang, "The International Significance of the Chinese People's Victory," *op. cit.*, p. 276.

38. "The Great Unity of the Chinese People and the Great Unity of the Peoples of the World," in *Ten Glorious Years, op. cit.*, p. 100.

39. "Study Chairman Mao's Dialogue on Questions of Democracy in Colonial and Semi-colonial Countries," *Chung-kuo ch'ing-nien*, 9, May 1, 1960.

40. For remarks on this jurisdictional question, see Leonard Schapiro, "The Chinese Ally from the Soviet Point of View," paper delivered at the Third International Conference of Sovietologists, held in Tokyo, Japan, September 18–25, 1960.

41. See the *Christian Science Monitor*, September 10, 1960; "Indian Communists Divided," *The Times* (London), December 6, 1960; *Times of India*, August 18, 1960; Rajani Mukherje, "Emergence of 'Maoism' in India's Communist Party," *The Commoner* (Katmandu, Nepal), August 10, 1960; *The Hindustan Times*, September 2 and 5, 1960, and August 6, 1960.

42. Mukherje, *op. cit.*

43. See "The Fortieth Anniversary of the Indonesian Communist Party," JPRS 35544, September 28, 1960.

44. NCNA, August 6, 1960.

45. *Ta kung pao*, November 28, 1960, excerpted in SCMP, 2390,

December 5, 1960; see also "Aggressive Countenance of U.S. Imperialism Exposed," *Ta kung pao*, November 26, 1960, in SCMP, 2388, December 1, 1960, p. 19.

46. See Fritz Schatten, "Peking's Growing Influence in Africa," *Swiss Review of World Affairs*, August 1960.

47. *Asian Analyst*, June 1960; for a further list of African extreme nationalists and radicals entertained in Peking in the past year or two, see *The Interpreter*, September 1960, and the *Economist*, July 16, 1960.

48. *Daily Telegraph* (London), November 12, 1960.

49. Malaviya statement, *op. cit.*

50. *Pravda*, November 1, 1959.

51. Peking radio broadcast in Indonesian, November 12, 1959.

52. NCNA, November 30. 1959.

53. "Victory Belongs to the Great African People, "*Hung ch'i*, March 16, 1960; SCMP, 2221, March 22, 1960, pp. 34–37.

54. NCNA, March 29, 1960.

55. Moscow Radio Home Service, April 18, 1960.

56. *Ibid.*

57. *Ibid.*

58. NCNA, May 28, 1960.

59. See the *Washington Post and Times Herald*, June 26 and July 20, 1960.

60. In August 1961, Benyoussef Ben Khedda replaced Abbas as Premier of the Algerian Provisional Government and there were several reports that he was more favorably disposed towards accepting Chinese aid than Abbas. A UAR source told the *New York Times* that Ben Khedda might open the way to increasing Chinese influence. He asserted that 5,000 Algerian "volunteers" who had been trained in China were ready to fight the French and that Nasser was concerned over the possible arrival of Chinese "volunteers" in Algeria. Ben Khedda, according to an unidentified Algerian, was alleged to believe that "colonialism and imperialism" were so entrenched in the West that Algeria "must look elsewhere for salvation" (*New York Times*, August 30, 1961).

61. SCMP, 2265, May 25, 1960, p. 33. Ben Khedda made similar statements when he headed a delegation to Peking in 1959.

62. *Peking Review*, 21, May 24, 1960, p. 17.

Chapter Eleven

1. *Let us Live in Peace and Friendship*. The visit by N. S. Khrushchev to the USA, September 15–27, 1959; Foreign Languages Publishing House, Moscow 1959, p. 74.

2. *Ibid.*, p. 17.

3. *Pravda*, October 1, 1959.

4. *Ibid.*

5. *Ibid.*

6. *Ibid.*

7. *Pravda*, September 29, 1959.

8. *Ibid.*

9. *Pravda*, October 5, 1959.

10. *New York Times*, November 27, 1959.

11. *Pravda*, October 7, 1959.

12. *Ibid.*, October 11, 1959.

13. *Ibid.*, November 1, 1959.

14. *Ibid.*

15. *Ibid.*

16. *Ibid.*

17. *Ibid.*

18. See *Peking Review*, 17, April 26, 1960, pp. 6–23 and pp. 23–32 respectively.

19. *Pravda*, December 2, 1959.

20. *Ibid.*

21. *Jen-min jih-pao*, December 21, 1959.

CHAPTER TWELVE

1. Tass, January 8, 1960.

2. "What the Messages of the U.S. President Show," *Peking Review*, 4, January 26, 1960, p. 21.

3. *Ibid.*, p. 22.

4. *Ibid.*, p. 23.

5. "Excellent Situation for the Struggle for Peace," *Hung ch'i*, 1, 1960; *Peking Review*, 1, January 5, 1960, pp. 15–19.

6. "What the Messages of the U.S. President Show," *op. cit.*, p. 25.

7. *Pravda*, January 15, 1960.

8. *Ibid.*

9. *Jen-min jih-pao*, January 16, 1960; NCNA, January 16, 1960.

10. Resolution of the National People's Congress Standing Committee, January 21, 1960; *Peking Review*, 4, January 26, 1960, p. 19.

11. Kang Sheng to the Warsaw Pact members, February 4, 1960; *Peking Review*, 6, February 9, 1960, p. 7.

12. Sung Tu, "Answers to Readers' Queries on War and Peace," *Chung-kuo ch'ing-nien*, 4, February 16, 1960; *Extracts*, 207, April 11, 1960, p. 4.

The Chinese were probably very much concerned, for example, that Khrushchev might reach a test-ban agreement with the West which would not only make it difficult for China to test its own nuclear weapons, except at the cost of flouting world opinion, but which would provide for control posts on Chinese territory despite the fact that China itself had not been a party to the original agreement. In this connection, it is of interest to note that the Soviet test-ban proposal tabled on August 11, 1960, provided for twelve inspection posts in Asia (exclusive of the USSR) in the first five years after the treaty was signed. Some of these posts undoubtedly would have had to be installed on Chinese territory. Yet there was nothing in the Soviet draft treaty providing for Chinese accession before the inspection posts were installed. Chinese opposition to a test-ban agreement between the USSR and the United States can be inferred from the following statement by Khrushchev in August 1961 after the USSR resumed testing. " . . . merely an agreement on stopping nuclear weapons tests cannot by itself put an end to the arms race. . . . The states which do not yet possess thermonuclear weapons will in their turn try to create them despite the agreement that prohibits atomic tests. *By the way, they can advance arguments which the champions of nuclear disarmament will have difficulty in parrying.* Indeed is it realistic to expect that a situation will continue for long where some states that are far advanced in developing atomic power for war purposes will continue to manufacture mountains of atomic and hydrogen bombs on the basis of experiments carried out, while others would . . . lag more and more behind the nuclear powers in their military might and consequently in the capacity of insuring their security. Experience proves the contrary" [italics supplied]. *New York Times,* August 31, 1961.

13. *Peking Review,* 24, June 14, 1960, p. 8.

14. NCNA, June 8, 1960.

15. *Ibid.*

16. *Ibid.*

17. This may have reflected fears of some in the Soviet military, who wanted more ground troops for possible local war.

18. *Pravda,* January 15, 1960.

19. The Warsaw Pact conference was preceded by an unusual conference of all Bloc members, with the exception of China and North Vietnam, "to exchange experience in developing agriculture." The first official and perfunctory communiqué of the conference, released by Tass on February 2, 1960, said that the European Bloc members were "participating" in the conference and North Korean and Mongolian Party representatives had "expressed the desire to attend." The clear implication was that China and North Vietnam, the remaining Bloc members, had not expressed such a desire. The fact that such a high-level conference on agriculture took place at all—it was attended by all the Party first secretaries— suggests that it was in part employed by the Russians to attack the Chinese communes. The final communiqué issued on February 3, 1960, stressed the successes in the "socialist countries of Europe" in reorganizing agriculture, developing agricultural production, the "advantages of collective forms of agriculture," and the need for "exchanges of experience." There was no mention of the Chinese communes.

20. *New York Times,* January 27, 1960.

21. NCNA, February 4, 1960.

22. Full text of the Declaration of the Member States of the Warsaw Treaty, *Pravda,* February 5, 1960.

23. Tass, March 18, 1960.

24. For the text of Eisenhower's press conference, see the *New York Times*, February 4, 1960.

25. NCNA, February 7, 1960, quoted *Ta kung pao* as having said "The United States *is planning* to place nuclear weapons directly in the hands of more member countries of aggressive military blocs . . . " [italics supplied]; Moscow Radio Home Service, February 6, 1960, by contrast, quoted Anne Wheaton to the effect that nuclear sharing was under consideration in the U.S. but that Congress was neither discussing nor preparing to discuss it, and the President had not made any proposals along that line.

26. *Peking Review*, 6, February 9, 1960, pp. 6–9.

27. *Ibid.*, p. 7.

28. See the Warsaw Treaty states' declaration, *op. cit.*

29. "A Decisive Force to Safeguard Peace, *"Jen-min jih-pao,* February 6, 1960; *Peking Review*, 6, February 9, 1960, p. 10.

30. Sung Tu, "Answers to Readers' Queries on War and Peace," *Chung-kuo ch'ing-nien*, 4, February 16, 1960; *Extracts*, 207, April 11, 1960, pp. 1–7.

CHAPTER THIRTEEN

1. The CCP has described the articles as both a development of Marxism-Leninism and a defense of it against the "major menace in the international Communist movement, modern revisionism." See "Protect Leninism—the Powerful Weapon against Modern Revisionism," *Chung-kuo ch'ing-nien*, 9, May 1, 1960, pp. 2–3 (translated in JPRS, 3915, September 13, 1960). The same article contended that the "modern revisionists" utilized "all dirty tactics to show contempt for China, our Party, and our great leader."

2. The Chinese claimed that not only the CCP but also "Marxists of other countries" were determined to "wage a struggle against modern revisionism," thus suggesting they would encourage factional opposition to the CPSU in other Communist parties (*ibid.*, p. 4). Crankshaw reports that the Chinese claimed the right to form anti-Soviet factions in other parties on the ground that Lenin himself, when in a minority, had followed similar tactics. See Edward Crankshaw, "The Moscow-Peking Clash Exposed," *Observer* (London), February 12 and 19, 1961.

3. *Pravda*, February 15, 1956.

4. *Ibid.*, April 23, 1960. (See also the pamphlet, *Realization of Lenin's Ideas*, published by the USSR Embassy in Canada, for a quasi-official version in English.)

5. *Ibid.*

6. *Pravda*, June 12, 1960.

7. *Ibid.*, April 23, 1960. Soviet media have persistently claimed that there was a struggle in the United States between the more moderate elements of the bourgeoisie and those bent on a military solution.

8. While the Chinese granted the need for flexibility, they implied that

Khrushchev had abandoned revolutionary principle by lapsing into opportunism, or, to put it another way, that he was sacrificing long-term interests for questionable short-term goals.

9. *Long Live Leninism,* Foreign Languages Press, Peking, 1960, p. 22.

10. "Forward Along the Path of the Great Lenin," article by the editorial department of *Jen-min jih-pao,* April 22, 1960, in *Peking Review,* 17, April 26, 1960, pp. 29–30.

11. "Unite Under Lenin's Revolutionary Banner!" Long Live Leninism, *op. cit.,* p. 103.

12. *Ibid.*

13. *Pravda,* February 15, 1956.

14. *Ibid.,* April 23, 1960.

15. *Sovetskaya rossiya,* June 10, 1960.

16. "Leninskie printsipy vneshnei politiki SSSR," *Kommunist,* 6, 1960, p. 142.

17. *Hung ch'i,* April 1, 1960; *Peking Review,* 15, April 12, 1960, p. 23.

18. "Unite Under Lenin's Revolutionary Banner!" *op. cit.,* pp. 103–104.

19. *Ibid.,* p. 97.

20. *Jen-min jih-pao,* April 25, 1960; NCNA, April 25, 1960.

21. *Long Live Leninism, op. cit.,* p. 34.

22. *Pravda,* February 15, 1956.

23. *Ibid.,* January 28, 1961.

24. *Ibid.,* April 23, 1960.

25. "Leninist Foreign Policy and International Relations," *International Affairs,* 4, 1960, p. 8.

26. *Ibid.,* p. 9.

27. *Peking Review,* 15, April 21, 1960, pp. 17–24. In this period the Russians generally avoided discussing the Bloc's duty to support "just" wars, or were equivocal.

28. *Ibid.,* p. 20.

29. *Ibid.,* p. 22.

30. *Peking Review,* 24, June 14, 1960, pp. 13–14.

31. *Peking Review,* 20, May 17, 1960, p. 5.

32. Speech to the Supreme Soviet, January 14, 1960, Moscow Radio Home Service, January 16, 1960.

33. One specific issue may have concerned the nuclear test ban. See note 12, Chapter 12. When the Russians resumed testing in 1961, Khrushchev suggested that the Chinese could "advance arguments" for testing that the nuclear disarmers would "have difficulty in parrying." Of course, Khrushchev clearly had an interest in justifying Soviet resumption of testing by alluding in this manner to his difficulties with China, but it is not difficult to believe that while he sought to take advantage of those difficulties, they were in fact the cause of considerable friction.

34. "Sovetskii soyuz-glavnaya opora mirolyubivogo chelovechestva," *Kommunist,* 8, 1960, p. 15.

35. *Ibid.*

Chapter Fourteen

1. This was not a formal conference such as those held in Moscow in November 1957 and again in November-December 1960 but rather an impromptu gathering. Communist leaders were assembled in Bucharest for the Rumanian Party Congress, and the Russians evidently decided at the very last moment to use the occasion for an assault against Peking.

2. Yu. Frantsev, "Problemy voiny i mira v sovremennikh usloviyakh," *Pravda*, August 7, 1960.

3. S. Titarenko, "Lenin's Teachings on the Victory of Socialism and the Present Day," published simultaneously on August 16 in the Baku daily, *Bakinskii rabotchii*, and in *Sovetskaya latvia*. The article reappeared in *Leningradskaya pravda* on August 23, in *Sovetskaya litva* and *Kommunist tadzhikstana* on August 24, and in *Sovetskaya kirghizia* on August 27. It is interesting that the strong warnings to China were deleted from the version of the article in *Leningradskaya pravda*.

4. "Firmly Establish Self-reliance, Arouse Ambitious Thought," *Kung-jen jih-pao*, September 11, 1960.

5. No reason was given for a delay in opening the meeting. Although most of the delegates had arrived in Peking for the expected opening on May 30, the meeting did not begin until June 5. It seems likely that the delay was caused by hurried and unsuccessful attempts to heal the serious breach between the Russian and Chinese delegations that was subsequently brought to light. One of the intriguing aspects of the meeting was the fact that Louis Saillant, the French Secretary-General of the WFTU, was reported to have been taken ill en route and was unable to attend the meeting. His report was read by Marcel Bras. Some speculation, which is impossible to corroborate, suggests that Saillant had thrown his weight on the side of the Chinese prior to the meeting and that the Russians prevented him from attending.

6. NCNA, June 8, 1961; CB, 621, June 27, 1960, p. 621. This issue also contains some of the speeches to the WFTU meeting and all of the WFTU resolutions.

7. See, for example, Richard Lowenthal, "The Sino-Soviet Dispute," *Commentary*, May 1961, p. 383. Lowenthal does not cite the source of this information.

8. Interview with Agostino Novella in Rome, *L'Unità*, the Italian Communist Party daily, June 19, 1960. Novella's interview was broadcast on June 20, 1960, by "Oggi in Italia," radio organ of the Italian Communist Party which broadcasts from Prague.

9. *Avanti*, August 14, 1960.

10. *Ibid.*, June 14, 1960.

11. *Trud*, July 7, 1960.

12. *Link*, October 30, 1960.

13. This assertion has been accepted uncritically even by very acute Western observers.

14. For summaries of the speeches, see *Jen-min jih-pao,* June 7, 8 and 9, 1960; NCNA, June 7, 8 and 9, 1960.

15. It must be noted that these delegations did not represent the Communist parties of the countries from which they came but the trade union federations which, in some cases, notably the Indonesian, are far to the Left of the corresponding local parties.

16. *Avanti,* August 14, 1960.

17. *Ibid.,* June 14, 1960.

18. D. Shevlyagan, "A Militant Weapon of the Communist Parties: On the Occasion of the 40th Anniversary of the Publication of V. I. Lenin's book, *Left-wing Communism; an Infantile Disorder,"* *Sovetskaya rossiya,* June 10, 1960.

19. N. Matkovskii, "An Ideological Weapon of Communism," *Pravda,* June 12, 1960.

20. *Ibid.*

21. *Ibid.*

22. *Pravda,* June 20, 1960.

23. Edward Crankshaw, "The Moscow-Peking Clash Exposed," *Observer* (London), February 12 and 19, 1961; see also Crankshaw's article "Khrushchev and China," in *Atlantic Monthly,* May 1961, pp. 43–47.

24. Crankshaw's articles contain various references to charges made in the letters although it is often difficult to separate Crankshaw's own remarks from those of the Russians.

25. *Pravda,* June 22, 1960.

26. During 1959 and 1960, *Jen-min jih-pao* had published the full texts of previous Khrushchev speeches that contained veiled criticisms of China. For example, it published the full texts of Khrushchev's Supreme Soviet speech of October 31, 1959, his speech to the Hungarian Party Congress on December 1, 1959, and his speech to the Supreme Soviet on January 14, 1960.

27. *Pravda,* June 28, 1960. The communiqué of June 24, 1960, was signed by the twelve Bloc parties.

28. For the Chinese reaction, see the *Jen-min jih-pao* editorial, June 29, 1960, in *Peking Review,* 27, July 5, 1960, pp. 6–9; for the Russian reaction, see the *Pravda* editorial, June 27, 1960.

29. *Pravda,* July 17, 1960.

30. *New York Times,* June 29, 1948.

31. See the Indian weekly *Blitz,* July 30, 1961, pp. 10–11.

32. Pietro Nenni, leader of the Italian Partito Socialista Italiano (PSI), also wrote in *Avanti* of August 21, 1960, that "there has been a speech by Suslov to the Moscow *Aktiv* and similar speeches in the various Soviet Republics." Suslov's speech in Moscow was never published.

33. *Avanti,* August 6, 1960.

34. *Leningradskaya pravda,* July 30, 1960; a shorter summary of his remarks is in *Pravda* for the same day.

35. *Pravda,* July 29 and 30, 1960.

36. "Dialektika i sovremennost," *Kommunist*, 10, 1960, signed to the press July 19, 1960, p. 43.

37. *Ibid.*

38. *Ibid.*, p. 45.

39. *Ibid.*, p. 47.

40. *Ibid.*, pp. 45–46.

41. *Ibid.*, p. 48.

42. *Ibid.*, p. 46.

43. *Pravda*, July 28, 1960.

44. *Ibid.*

45. *Ibid.*

46. See the account by the West Bengal Communist leader, Harekrishna K. Konar, published in the Indian weekly *Link* and quoted by Boris Nikolaevsky in *The New Leader* of January 16, 1961, p. 16.

47. See *Link*, October 16, 1960, for an account given by the Chinese to an Indian Communist.

48. "To be a Revolutionary, One Must have the Revolutionary Will," *Jen-min jih-pao*, August 13, 1960; SCMP, 2335, September 12, 1960, pp. 4–9.

49. *Ibid.*, p. 6.

50. *Ibid.*, p. 5.

51. *Ibid.*, p. 8.

52. *Ibid.*, p. 6.

53. *Ibid.*, p. 9.

54. *Hung ch'i*, 16, August 16, 1960, in *Peking Review*, 34, August 23, 1960, p. 15.

55. *Shang-yu* (Canton), 9, April 1960. The article was subsequently republished in a number of Chinese regional papers. See SCMP, 2287, June 29, 1960, p. 16, taken from *Nan-fang jih-pao*, May 13, 1960.

56. *Ibid.*

57. An edited version of T'ao Chu's article appeared in the August 5 *Jen-min jih-pao;* this version watered down T'ao's original stress on the need for Soviet aid, and it quoted him as saying that socialist construction should be pursued "by relying on our own efforts in the main," a statement not ascribed to T'ao in the original article published in *Shang-yu*.

58. S. Titarenko, *op. cit.*

59. It is quite likely that one function of the Chinese Embassy in Moscow is to scan the leading Soviet republican, as well as central, newspapers. The former Polish Communist Seweryn Bialer has indicated that the Polish Communist Party has an internal bulletin which includes extracts from important articles in the world Communist press and which circulates only in the highest circles of the Party. It is probable that all Communist parties have a similar bulletin. The Russians could therefore be reasonably sure that articles in their leading republican papers would reach the Chinese without acquiring world notice.

60. *Kooperativno selo* (Sofia), August 25, 1960.

61. *Ibid.*

62. *Ibid.*

63. Tass, September 11, 1960.

64. *Link,* October 16, 1960.

65. In September, for example, the Chinese published in English a series of booklets in "commemoration of the 90th Anniversary of the birth of Lenin," each of which was designed, by a careful collation of Lenin's writings on subjects at issue between Moscow and Peking, to offer "scriptural" support for the Chinese position. The booklets were titled: "Lenin on the National Liberation Movement," "Lenin on War and Peace," "Lenin on the Struggle Against Revisionism," "Lenin on Proletarian Revolution and Proletarian Dictatorship," "Lenin on Imperialism, on the Eve of the Proletarian Social Revolution," and "Lenin on the Revolutionary Proletarian Party of a New Type." A second edition of these booklets was published in October. All were published by the Peking Foreign Languages Press "in conformity with the Chinese edition," the original date of which is not available but which must have been published sometime between April and September.

66. "An Introduction to the 4th Volume of *Selected Works of Mao Tse-tung," Hung ch'i* 19, October 1, 1960; *Selections,* 233, October 31, 1960, pp. 14–15.

67. "Study Seriously the Fourth Volume of Selected Works of Mao Tse-tung," *Chung-kuo ch'ing-nien,* 19, October 1, 1960; *Selections,* 233, October 31, 1960, p. 4.

68. *Ibid.,* pp. 4–5.

69. *Ibid.,* p. 2. The article wrote: "When Chiang Kai-shek removed his mask of false peace and in July 1946 launched a civil war unprecedented in the history of China, some people lacked sufficient belief in our ability to defeat the enemy because its forces were about 3.5 times greater than ours. . . . Moreover, some people took a pessimistic view of the international situation at that time, that is, they were afraid of the outbreak of the third world war and were afraid of U.S. imperialism."

70. "Slighting the Enemy Strategically and Taking Full Account of Him Tactically," editorial, *Hung ch'i,* 19, October 1, 1960; *Selections,* 231, October 18, 1960, p. 1.

71. There were several hints in the Soviet press in the summer and fall of 1960 that the Russians would settle for nothing less than public Chinese recantation. One Soviet journal pointedly remarked that a Communist party must maintain a critical attitude toward "its mistakes" and that a "serious party" would "admit a mistake openly, realize its causes," and "analyze the circumstances that fostered it." The journal recalled the CPSU's "frank statement" on the Stalin cult as an example of such "bold self-criticism," the implication being that bold self-criticism on the Chinese part was now the only way out. See B. N. Ponamarev, "Istoricheskii opyt KPSS—na sluzhby kommunisticheskomu stroitel'stvu," *Voprosy istorii KPSS,* 4, 1960, signed to the press, July 19, 1960, pp. 19–20.

Chapter Fifteen

1. Edward Crankshaw, "The Moscow-Peking Clash," *Observer* (London), February 12 and 19, 1961.

2. Crankshaw, *op. cit.*, reports the breakdown of a scheme for a unified Pacific naval command, for example.

3. The Soviet journal *Voprosy istorii* wrote in July of unprovoked Chinese attacks on Russian border settlements in the Amur during the 17th century. See that journal, 7, 1960, pp. 160–162. More recently, the press of Russia's Kazakhstan republic has been calling for increased vigilance among the border guards. (Kazakhstan's only border is with China.)

4. In December, Chinese Foreign Minister Ch'en Yi admitted to a British MP that "the training of students in Russia was costly and the numbers were being reduced" *Daily Telegraph and Morning Post* (London), December 6, 1960.

5. Communist China's press coverage of the Soviet Union began to drop sharply in June. During the first quarter of 1960, about 16 per cent of the foreign news in *Jen-min jih-pao* was devoted to the USSR. In the second quarter, the percentage fell to 6 per cent. In prominence of placement, Soviet affairs also suffered a setback. In April, the USSR was the fourth most prominently reported country in *Jen-min jih-pao;* it was the fourteenth in June and tenth in July. During the first three weeks of August, only one front-page news item was primarily devoted to the Soviet Union. For these and other statistics, see *Current Scene,* Research Report, "Press Attention Given to USSR in the Foreign News Section of *Jen-min jih-pao* and NCNA during January-July 1960," undated. *Current Scene* is published at 26 Garden Road, Hongkong. Soviet press and radio coverage of Communist China throughout the summer of 1960 was similarly sparse.

6. See Hermann Matern's report on the Moscow Conference in the East German Party paper, *Neues deutschland, December* 23, 1960. Matern is a Politburo member.

7. *Pravda,* November 23, 1960.

8. "Give Full Play to the Revolutionary Spirit of the 1957 Moscow Declarations," *Jen-min jih-pao* editorial, November 21, 1960; NCNA, November 21, 1960.

9. *Ibid.*

10. Perhaps the Chinese, having seen that the draft approved by the editorial commission was unacceptable in certain respects, wished to warn Moscow that they were determined to air their case in public unless the Russians took more account of China's views in framing the final declaration. For an analogous interpretation, see Victor Zorza, "Peking Jumps the Gun—and Warns Mr. K.," *The Guardian* (London), November 22, 1960.

11. See speech by Walter Ulbricht, first secretary of the East German Party, after he returned from the Moscow Conference. The report was published in *Neues deutschland,* December 18, 1960.

12. *Jen-min jih-pao,* December 7, 1960; NCNA, December 6, 1960.

13. For the November 1957 Declaration, see *Pravda*, November 22, 1957.

14. The declaration appeared in *Pravda* on December 6, 1960.

15. *Ibid.*

16. *Ibid.*

17. *Ibid.*

18. *Ibid.*

19. See, for example, the *Jen-min jih-pao* editorial of December 7, 1960, in NCNA, December 6, 1960, and the resolution on the Moscow Conference adopted by the Ninth Plenary Session of the CCP Central Committee, in *Peking Review*, 4, January 27, 1961, pp. 7–9. For Soviet comment, see *Pravda*, December 7, 1960.

20. *Neues deutschland*, December 18, 1960.

21. Khrushchev's report on the Moscow Conference, Moscow Radio Home Service, January 19, 1961.

22. *Pravda*, December 6, 1960.

23. *Ibid.*

24. The *Hung ch'i* editorial of December 15, 1960, said "the conference expressed sympathy with and support for armed struggle waged by suppressed people to liberate themselves." NCNA, December 15, 1960. No such statement was in the Declaration itself or in subsequent Soviet comment.

25. A Belyakov and F. Burlatskii, "Leninskaya teoriya sotsialisticheskoi revolyutsii i sovremennost," *Kommunist* 13, September 10, 1960, p. 17.

26. Moscow Radio Home Service, January 19, 1961.

27. *Ibid.*

28. *Ibid.*

29. *Ibid.*

30. *Pravda*, December 6, 1960.

31. *Ibid.*

32. See particularly Togliatti's statement in the July 28, 1960, *Pravda*.

33. See his January 14, 1960, speech to the Supreme Soviet.

34. *Pravda*, December 6, 1960.

35. *Ibid.*

36. *Ibid.*

37. *Hung ch'i*, December 15, 1960; NCNA, December 15, 1960.

38. *Pravda*, December 6, 1960.

39. See Matern's report, *op. cit.*

40. Subsequent Soviet discussions of the "national democracy" have hinted that Mali and Guinea as well as Cuba come under that category.

41. Matern's report, *op. cit.*

42. *Ibid.*

43. *Pravda*, December 7, 1960.

44. Matern's report, *op. cit.*

45. *Pravda*, December 6, 1960.

46. *Ibid.*

47. A. Belyakov and F. Burlatskii, *op. cit.*, p. 21. The writers accused "dogmatists" within the Communist movement of making such an accusation.

CHAPTER SIXTEEN

1. The text of Khrushchev's Central Committee report was broadcast by the Moscow Radio Home Service on October 18, 1961.

2. The text of Chou En-lai's speech was released by NCNA on October 19, 1961. He said: "We hold that if a dispute or difference unfortunately arises between fraternal parties or fraternal countries, it should be resolved patiently in the spirit of proletarian internationalism and on the principles of equality and unanimity through consultation. Any public, one-sided censure of any fraternal party does not help unity and is not helpful in resolving problems."

3. *New York Times,* October 19, 1961.

4. Hoxha, in a speech on the October revolution anniversary, referred to Khrushchev's "putschist" methods and "surprise tactics" at the 22nd Congress. Tirana radio, November 7, 1961.

5. Moscow Radio Home Service, October 24, 1961.

6. NCNA, October 24, 1961.

7. Speech of T'ao Chu at the political economy class of the Kwantung CCP Provincial Committee on March 30, 1960, as published in the Canton *Nan-fang jih-pao* on May 13, 1960, *Survey of the China Mainland Press* (*SCMP*), no. 2287, June 29, 1960, p. 16.

8. Edward Crankshaw, "The Moscow-Peking Clash Exposed," *The Observer,* London, February 12, 1961.

9. When Khrushchev and Malenkov flew to Warsaw in the hectic days after Gomulka came to power in 1956, for example, they took with them Molotov and Kaganovich, who represented a hard line on intra-bloc relations.

10. In the early stages of the Laotian crisis, there were indications of differences over the relative priorities to be assigned to negotiations and a cease-fire. The Russians seemed willing, but the Chinese did not, to accede to the Western demand that a cease-fire precede negotiations. More recently, there have been indications of a Chinese reluctance to agree to an integration of Pathet Lao with Laotian government troops.

11. For Chinese attacks on Yugoslavia which were quite inconsonant with the relatively softer Soviet line, see "Yugoslav Agriculture on the Capitalist Road," *Peking Review,* no. 23, June 9, 1961, pp. 10–13, and "The Tito Clique's 'Self-Management of Enterprises,'" *Peking Review,* no. 29, July 21, 1961, pp. 11–14.

12. Almost immediately after the 1960 Moscow Conference, at which there was a violent argument between Albanian Party leader Hoxha and Khrushchev, the Chinese moved to strengthen political, economic, and cultural ties with the Albanians. For an excellent account of the Peking-

Tirana-Moscow tug-of-war, see William E. Griffith, "An International Communism?" *East Europe,* July 1961.

13. Even Khrushchev's militant speech on the twentieth anniversary of the German invasion of the USSR, widely broadcast by Moscow Radio on June 21, was not enough for Peking. A *Jen-min jih-pao* editorial on June 28 praised that speech and then went on to add criticism of the U.S. administration that went far beyond Khrushchev. At the 22nd Congress itself, Khrushchev and other Soviet speakers suggested that the West was now coming to its senses on Berlin while Chou warned against the "deceptive" Kennedy administration which was "decorating itself with olive branches." NCNA, October 19, 1961.

14. It is true that the Russians began to stiffen their line toward the national bourgeoisie immediately following the Moscow conference. There were direct attacks in Soviet journals on the governments of India, Burma, Indonesia, Pakistan, the UAR, the Sudan, and other countries for pursuing domestic policies that retarded social progress. The accusation was made that the national bourgeoisie in some countries had saved the landowning class from liquidation from below, that it sought to isolate the workers from the peasant movement, and that its attitude towards foreign capital was inconsistent. For a good round-up of this material, see "Renewed Attacks on the National Bourgeoisie," *Bulletin of the Institute for the Study of the USSR,* VIII (August 1961), pp. 3–9. Nevertheless, throughout 1961 Peking published long theoretical articles on the "democratic" revolution in China whose purpose was manifestly to suggest (1) that the Chinese revolutionary model, and not Khrushchev's imaginary one, was valid for revolution in the underdeveloped areas, (2) that the Communist Party and the proletariat must engage in armed struggle as a means of forcing the national bourgeoisie into a "patriotic" front, (3) that prolonged cooperation with the weak and vacillating national bourgeoisie would prove to be disastrous, and (4) that only the Communist Party could lead the "democratic" revolution —i.e., the stage before the socialist revolution—to a successful conclusion. See, for example, "The Distinction and Link-up Between the Two Stages of the Chinese Revolution," *Hung ch'i,* January 1, in *Peking Review,* January 20, 1961, pp. 9–18; "The Peasant Question in the Democratic Revolution," *Hung ch'i,* March 1, in *Peking Review,* March 31, 1961, pp. 5–13; "The Role of the United Front in the Chinese Revolution," *Hung ch'i,* June 1, 1961, published serially in *Peking Review,* June 9, 1961, pp. 13–16 and June 16, 1961, pp. 17–21; "The Chinese People's Democratic United Front," *Hung ch'i,* published serially in *Peking Review,* August 18, 1961, pp. 11–15, August 25, 1961, pp. 12–18, and September 1, 1961, pp. 10–14. The Russians, for all the toughening of their line, continued to take the view, expressed in the Party program, that the national bourgeoisie could make further progress.

15. See particularly "The Thought of Mao Tse-tung Opens the Way for the Development of China's Science of History," by Teng T'o, *Selections,* no. 264, June 5, 1961, pp. 1–14, in which Chinese historians are

urged to abolish European-centered historiography and put more emphasis on the "several-thousand-year-old" history of China. Historians were also told in this article that blind observance of foreign rules must be abolished, that Marxism-Leninism must be made to assume Chinese features, and that the thought of Mao represents "the key to the gate of the science of history."

16. "Preface to 'Stories About Not Being Afraid of Ghosts,'" *Peking Review,* March 10, 1961, p. 7.

17. Vice Chairman Tung Pi-wu, speaking at a meeting held to commemorate the fiftieth anniversary of the 1911 revolution, suggested that this revolution failed because it was led by the Chinese national bourgeoisie and went on to say: "As everyone knows, in the epoch of imperialism, there is no country in which the national and democratic revolution can achieve complete victory under the leadership of the bourgeoisie; neither the plan for a bourgeois republic *nor that for any other form of bourgeois-state* can enable these countries to embark on the road of completely independent development. In the present epoch, only under the leadership of the proletariat, and by obtaining the help of the socialist countries, will it be possible for any country to win complete victory in its national and democratic revolution. . . . " [italics supplied.]

18. *Hung ch'i,* July 1, 1961.

19. NCNA, September 12, 1961.

20. For text of the Draft Program, see *New York Times,* August 1, 1961.

21. An Albanian trade delegation arrived in China on Nov. 17.

22. Gomulka, Novotny, and Ulbricht criticized China.

23. The Russians and the other East European Bloc countries apparently pulled out their technicians from Albania in 1961. An AP correspondent who made a three-week tour of Albania reported that the deported Bloc experts were being replaced by Chinese. The East Germans were reported to have received an order to leave by August 31 even if it meant breaking contracts. The same report said that not one tourist from any Soviet-Bloc nation had come to spend a vacation on the Adriatic coast since mid-June. Security restrictions were at a maximum and the Albanians were apparently fearful of a Soviet attack or a Soviet staged uprising. See *New York Times,* October 22, 1961. According to Hoxha, *op. cit.,* Moscow cut all credits to Albania, demanded repayment of old credits, and withdrew its technicians.

24. See Griffith, *op. cit.*

25. See *East Europe,* April 1961, p. 3.

26. *The Interpreter,* June 1961, p. 24.

27. *Ibid.,* p. 25.

28. At the 22nd Congress, Ulbricht suggested that Albania had taken unspecified actions which were not in keeping with its Warsaw Pact obligations.

29. Moscow Radio Home Service, November 1, 1961.

30. The Albanian issue was not mentioned in the Congress speeches of Furtseva, Podgorny, Shvernik, and Voronov. Moreover, some of the Con-

gress speakers' criticism of the Albanians was weaker in tone than that of others.

31. Moscow Radio Home Service, October 27, 1961.

32. Moscow Radio Home Service, October 21, 1961.

33. TASS, October 26, 1961.

34. TASS, October 27, 1961. In the same context, Khrushchev referred to "some people" who accuse us of contradicting Lenin's appraisal of imperialism.

35. Tirana radio, November 7, 1961.

36. "A Timely Warning to War Plotters," *Peking Review*, September 8, 1961.

37. "China Fully Supports the Warsaw Treaty Countries' Stand on the German Question," *Peking Review*, August 18, 1961.

38. Moscow Radio Home Service, July 4, 1961.

39. TASS, July 10, 1961.

40. *Peking Review*, July 21, 1961, p. 7.

41. Of the 68 foreign delegates whose speeches were published in *Pravda*, 44 attacked Albania and 24 refrained. The following non-Asian parties did not attack Albania: Canada, Sweden, Switzerland, Norway, Iceland, Northern Ireland, Luxemburg, Belgium, Denmark, Dominican Republic, Algeria, South Africa, Guadelupe, and Martinique. Many of the above parties abstained, probably not so much as a symbol of support for Peking as a sign of neutrality. The Russians carried with them all the principal parties in Europe, Latin America, the Middle East, and Tunis and Morocco in North Africa.

Chapter Seventeen

1. For some very suggestive remarks on the pattern of bargaining between Moscow and Peking, see Zbigniew Brzezinski, "Patterns and Limits of the Sino-Soviet Dispute," *Problems of Communism*, September-October 1960.

2. That this was one of Peking's intentions, or at least that Moscow believed it to be, can be inferred from the great effort made by the Russians in the period from July 1960 up to and during the Moscow Conference to stress that Khrushchev spoke for a united party.

3. *Brzezinski*, The Soviet Bloc, *op. cit.*, p. 403. Brzezinski says the remark was reported to him by a high-ranking Communist who had heard it from Koca Popovic, to whom the remark has been made. The view is quite consistent with numerous public Chinese Communist statements to the effect that the Communist world can go on to build a beautiful future on the ashes of a dead imperialism. The remark should not, however, be taken as an indication of Chinese Communist advocacy of a nuclear war but rather as an expectation of the consequences of such a war.

4. The Chinese are almost entirely dependent on the Russians for petroleum and jet aviation fuels.

5. See H. F. Schurmann, "The Dialectic in Action—Vicissitudes in In-

dustrial Management in China," *Asian Survey,* May 1961, pp. 3–19; also "Technocrats on the Way Up," *Far Eastern Economic Review,* May 25, 1961, p. 346; "Back to Planning," *Far Eastern Economic Review,* April 6, 1961, p. 14; Yuan-li Wu, "An Interpretation of the Industrial Cutback in Communist China," *Current Scene,* August 8, 1961, pp. 1–6; for the revival of the "hundred flowers" policy, see "Peking Weeds the Intellectual Garden, *Current Scene,* May 31, 1961; for the new emphasis on material incentives, see *Jen-min jih-pao* editorial, April 2, 1961, "Implement in Earnest All the Various Policies of Rural People's Communes"; according to this same editorial, measures have been taken "to assure that the supply portion will not be more than 30 per cent and the wage portion not less than 70 per cent so that commune members having greater labor power and achieving better work results receive more income; there have been numerous suggestions that the return to free markets for the sale of produce grown on private plots will be long-term policy. For the key article spelling out the new policy, see the speech by Po I-po, chairman of the National Economic Commission, in *Hung ch'i,* 3–4, 1961, extracts of which are contained in *Peking Review,* No. 8, February 24, 1961, pp. 5–8. It is instructive that while Liu Shao-chi announced the original leap forward at the Party Congress in May 1958, it was Po, one of the top economic planners, who announced what is tantamount to a reversal of that policy. For the reversal of Tibetan policy, see "Peking Postpones Socialist Transformation of Tibet in Major Policy Shift," *Current Scene,* May 15, 1961.

6. The author is indebted to Oleg Hoeffding for this observation.

7. According to the Postmaster General of Hong Kong, during the second quarter of 1961 some 3,500,000 two-pound food packets were sent by people in Hong Kong and Macao to relatives and friends in mainland China. This was in addition to the reportedly larger number sent through commercial stores. *The Peking Informers,* August 1, 1961, p. 5.

8. In 1959, Gen. Liu Ya-Lou, Commander of the PLA Air Force, wrote that in fifteen years, when China had a modern industry and was capable of producing its own atomic bombs, there would be another turning point in the international situation. While he had reference to a turning point in the balance of power between East and West, one cannot help but wonder if he might also not have had in mind a new turning point in the balance of power between Russia and China. I have in Chapter 14 cited a Chinese Communist article which suggested that Communist countries should not fear competition with each other for top place.

9. For a discussion of the Bolshevik-Menshevik dispute, see Leonard Schapiro, *The Communist Party of the Soviet Union,* Random House, New York, 1960, pp. 1–141.

10. The word "polycentrism" may not be entirely appropriate for the set of relationships now emerging in the Communist world inasmuch as there are not many but only two centers: Moscow and Peking. The point is that so long as the two centers cannot agree on fundamental issues, the smaller parties can pursue policies of their own choosing. The concept of poly-

centrism is employed here because it was first suggested by the Italian Party leader Togliatti in 1956 to describe a situation in which Moscow would no longer dictate to other Communist parties. The concept of duo-centrism might be a better one except for the fact that it would imply a stable division of labor between Moscow and Peking in which the lines of authority and the spheres of influence would be clear.

11. For an excellent discussion of the Peking-Tirana-Moscow relationship in particular and the emergence of polycentrism in general see William E. Griffith, "An International Communism?" *East Europe*, July 1961.

12. See John Bradbury, "Sino-Soviet Competition in North Korea," *The China Quarterly*, April–June 1961.

13. In the July 1961 issue of *Foreign Affairs* (No. 4), Walter Laqueur, in a perceptive analysis of what he calls Afro-Communism, argues that while many Africans such as Sekôu Touré of Guinea use Marxist jargon and accept many Marxist views, they have nevertheless transposed Marxism to an African setting where nationalism, pan-Africanism, and the concept of negritude are more important than the classical ideology which is European in origin. Touré's recent moves to put down Communist-inspired agitation in his country is indicative of the dilemma which Moscow faces in Guinea.

14. The implications of the Sino-Soviet conflict for Western policy involve a number of considerations going beyond the Sino-Soviet relationship itself. Western policy toward the underdeveloped countries will, for example, have a profound impact on the Sino-Soviet conflict, one element of which concerns Communist strategy in those areas. Western military strategy, particularly regarding local or limited war, will also inevitably affect the conflict, inasmuch as it is the brunt of the Chinese argument that such wars cannot be avoided. Whether or not the West chooses to intervene in critical third areas threatened by Communist takeovers will be of considerable relevance because it is the essence of the Soviet position that the West can be deterred from intervention. Western disarmament policy will similarly play a role because the Russians have seemed to be more interested in negotiations on this matter than the Chinese, no doubt in part because China has not been and is not likely to be a party to such negotiations. In view of the complexity of these issues, and the fact that they need be decided on the basis of many considerations of which the Sino-Soviet conflict is but one, I have chosen at this time to avoid a detailed discussion of policy implications.

APPENDIX I

The following item appeared in the West Berlin newspaper *Deutsche zeitung* on September 30, 1960. It purports to be an extract from a secret letter circulated by the Communist Party of the Soviet Union to other Communist parties at the Bucharest Conference in June 1960. Circumstantial evidence leads me to believe that both it and the item following are generally accurate. Similar evidence suggests that other "secret" documents circulating in the West may be forgeries.

Deutsche Zeitung, 30 September 1960

"PEKING GOES BEHIND MOSCOW'S BACK"

Experts on Soviet Russia have worked out a comprehensive report on the content of a letter which the Communist Party of the Soviet Union circulated and had read at the conference of Communist Party leaders in Bucharest in June 1960. This letter concerns itself with the ideological differences of opinion between Moscow and Peking. According to information from absolutely reliable sources, the report of the Sovietologists, copies of which exist in a number of Western capitals, has generally the following text:

It is reportedly stated in the letter that a definition of the present epoch is of the greatest importance; varying definitions lead to varying conclusions about the fundamentals of foreign policy strategy and tactics. The Chinese reject the Soviet definition, according to which the present epoch is distinguished by the transition from capitalism to socialism, and by the extension and consolidation of a world socialist system. Instead of this, they erroneously claim that we are living the epoch of imperialism, of wars and revolutions. In this they misinterpret Lenin; they do not take into consideration the changes in the world and in the balance of forces since the October Revolution. The letter rejects the Chinese charges that the Soviets deny the aggressive character of imperialism. According to the Soviet view, imperialism is even yet aggressive by nature, but the position of imperialism in the world, and especially its ability to take aggressive action, have radically changed.

PAPER TIGER IMPERIALISM

Although the Chinese did at one time support the thesis of the 20th Congress of the CPSU on the avoidability of war, they now deviate from this thesis and maintain that it leads only to illusions. The Chinese believe that the imperialists can unleash war with impunity. This view is not objective, since it underestimates the strength of the socialist system and of the peace movement, through which wars can be prevented. The Chinese views are contradictory; on the one hand, imperialism is a paper tiger, on the other hand it is all-powerful. One should neither underestimate nor overestimate imperialism. The theory that war is unavoidable as long as capitalism exists impedes the active struggle of the people against imperialism. Being against war does not mean, as the Chinese claim it does, being against wars of liberation. When necessary, the CPSU supports just wars.

The letter asserts that peaceful coexistence is not a tactical slogan, but the general foreign policy line of all socialist countries. The letter then attacks an article in the [Ed: Chinese Communist] *People's Daily*, which in effect contested the possibility of peaceful co-existence. . . . In the letter it is further argued that peace is vitally necessary for the socialist system, that a modern war would wipe out whole nations, that a socialist victory can be won in 10 to 15 years of peaceful coexistence, through the achievement of industrial superiority, and that peaceful coexistence, which is a definite form of the class struggle, would increase the contradictions between the imperialists and assist the revolutionary struggle in all countries.

FLIRTATION WITH THE BOURGEOISIE

The letter rejects Chinese charges that the CPSU has commenced a flirtation with the national bourgeoisie. Ties with the national bourgeoisie are defended with the argument that this fosters neutralism and thereby weakens imperialism. Marxists should not skip stages in the revolutionary struggle.

According to reports at hand, the letter rejects as false and unfounded Chinese charges that disarmament is an illusion, and that the slogan of disarmament makes the masses defenseless and converts them to pacifism.

Disarmament is now possible, since the Soviet Union has the lead in armaments. If the disarmament question is raised, it will be harder for the Pentagon to carry out its measures for arming; thereby a blow is struck against Western military bases and military pacts.

At the congress of the World Federation of Trade Unions, the Chinese spoke of a third path, that is the coexistence of the two systems with the possibility of local wars and of a cold war, but without a world war. (With their reference to a third path, the Chinese clearly are thinking of Khrushchev's statement that the only alternative to peaceful coexistence is a world war.) That is wrong. A local war can easily become a world war. Besides, this thesis signifies lasting cold war, the continuation of the arms race, and political difficulties for the socialist countries in connection with their policy of peace.

The letter takes up and opposes Chinese claims that the CPSU favors peaceful means as the only means of attaining power. The letter repeats the Soviet view that either a peaceful or a forcible seizure of power may be attempted by Communist parties in the imperialist countries, depending on the circumstances. The letter attacks the Chinese because they have given up their earlier support of this position.

The letter charges that the Chinese have deviated from the principles of the Moscow Declaration and of the Peace Manifesto of 1957, which they had previously supported. Moreover the letter contains an extended defence of the de-Stalinization campaign of 1956. It asserts that the Chinese had originally supported this campaign, and then attacks the recent questioning of this campaign by China. It is argued, rather mysteriously, that the Chinese position obstructs the conclusion of the de-Stalinization of several other parties.

In the Declaration of Moscow, the necessity of international solidarity had been underlined. There should be no criticism by one party of another behind its back, since this undermines proletarian internationalism.

Many of the actions of the Chinese in the recent past have been disloyal and uncomradely toward the CPSU. While the Chinese say that the USSR should be the leader of the socialist camp, they attack the CPSU and criticize it. They have violated the principles of proletarian internationalism.

The friendship with the Chinese people is important. Everything must be done to overcome the difficulties without a surrender of principles. The Chinese must take account of the interests of the communist movement throughout the world. The differences of opinion between the USSR and China directly benefit imperialism.

APPENDIX II

On December 3, 1960, the *Daily Telegraph* of London published a brief account taken from the Indian journal *Link* of an 84-page Soviet letter allegedly sent to all Communist parties after the Bucharest meeting and of the Chinese Communist reply, said to be a document of 160 pages.

Daily Telegraph, 3 December 1960

"COMMUNISTS MAINTAIN FACADE OF UNITY"

How little cordiality there has been in Russo-Chinese relations for the last three years was made clear yesterday in the first reliable accounts to be received of the documents exchanged between the two parties. They formed the basis of the discussions at the Moscow conference and were given in an Indian Left-wing journal *Link*.

The journal gave a summary of the 84-page letter which the Russian Communists sent to all Communist parties after the Bucharest meeting of last June.

BREACH WIDENING—Leaders Differed

The Russians were reported to have appealed to the other Communist parties in writing only because it had been found that the longer Mr. Khrushchev and Mao Tse-tung talked together the wider their differences became.

The more striking charges levelled against the Chinese were:

1. They had not accepted the decisions of the 1957 conference in Moscow:
2. They had taken up positions fundamentally opposed to those agreed at international conferences:
3. They had resented Russian criticism of their policies over Tibet and their "communes":
4. The Russians considered Chinese interference in the affairs of two East European Communist parties "unfriendly."

459

FRICTION IN CHINA—Soviet Retaliation

5. The Chinese had prevented Russian political instructors from working among Russians in China and had tried to subvert Russian Communists working in China; that was why the Russian technicians had been withdrawn:

6. The Chinese had closed down the Russian periodical appearing in Peking. After this the Russians had been obliged to ban the Chinese journal published in Moscow, which had been attacking Soviet positions:

7. The Chinese had tried to turn the international "mass" organizations, like the World Federation of Trade Unions and the Peace Movements, into purely Communist bodies. The letter said that the Chinese had withdrawn their representatives from the headquarters of the World Peace Movement.

CHINESE REPLY—Main Points

The Chinese Communists' reply to the Russian charges was a document of 160 pages. The main points were:

1. The Russians' denigration of Stalin after his death was "obnoxious."

2. The Soviet attitude towards the Jugoslavs was "cringing."

3. The Russian attitude at the time of the Hungarian revolt of 1956 had been "vacillating." Mr. Khrushchev was said by the Chinese to have been on the point of withdrawing the Russian troops. The Chinese had had great difficulty in persuading the Russians to take a firm line and "go to the defence of the Hungarian revolution."

4. The Russians did not regard Jugoslav "revisionism" as the main danger at the 1959 conference in Moscow. That was because they were themselves taking a revisionist line. The Chinese warned them: "If you do not fight revisionism we shall have to take up the battle single-handed against all distortions of Marxism.

460

5. The Russians had gone back on the agreed decisions of the 1957 declaration.
6. The Chinese complained that the Russians had withdrawn nearly all their technicians from China. The reason given was that they did not like the "political education" arranged for them by the Chinese Communists.
7. The Russians were only scaring people by saying that the alternative to peaceful co-existence was world war. The alternative was cold war. Russians were sowing illusions by insisting that peaceful co-existence was possible.

BIBLIOGRAPHY

THE FOLLOWING BIBLIOGRAPHY is intended primarily to be a selective guide to the Western and Communist literature pertaining to the Sino-Soviet conflict since 1956. It also includes some Western literature on the analytical method employed in this book and on the broad question of Communist strategy.

NON-COMMUNIST MATERIALS

I. SELECTED BOOKS

Barnett, A. Doak. *Communist China and Asia: Challenge to American Policy*. Harper & Brothers for the Council on Foreign Relations, New York, 1960.

Brzezinski, Zbigniew. *The Soviet Bloc: Unity and Conflict*. Harvard University Press, Cambridge, Massachusetts, 1960.

Conquest, Robert. *Power and Policy in the USSR*. St. Martin's Press, New York, 1961.

Dinerstein, Herbert S. *War and the Soviet Union*. Frederick A. Praeger, New York, 1959.

George, Alexander. *Propaganda Analysis: a Study of Inferences made from Nazi Propaganda*. Row, Peterson and Co., Evanston, Illinois, 1959.

Hsieh, Alice L. *Communist China's Strategy in the Nuclear Era*. Prentice-Hall, Inc., Englewood Cliffs, New Jersey, 1962.

Kautsky, John H. *Moscow and the Communist Party of India: A Study in the Postwar Development of International Communist Strategy*. The Technology Press (M.I.T.) and John Wiley and Sons, Inc., New York, 1956.

Kovner, Milton. *The Challenge of Coexistence*. Public Affairs Press, Washington, D.C. 1961.

Leites, Nathan. *A Study of Bolshevism*. The Free Press, Glencoe, Illinois, 1953.

Lewis, Flora. *A Case History of Hope*. Doubleday and Co., New York, 1958.

MacFarquhar, Roderick. *The Hundred Flowers Campaign and the Chinese Intellectual*. Frederick A. Praeger, New York, 1960.

Rush, Myron. *The Rise of Khrushchev*. Public Affairs Press, Washington, D.C., 1958.

Whiting, Allen S. *China Crosses the Yalu*. The Macmillan Co., New York, 1960.

463

————. *Soviet Policies in China, 1917–1924.* Columbia University Press, New York, 1954.

II. COLLECTIONS, MONOGRAPHS, PAMPHLETS

The Anti-Stalin Campaign and International Communism. The Russian Institute, Columbia University, ed., Columbia University Press, New York, 1956.

Bass, Robert and Marbury, Elizabeth, eds. *The Soviet-Yugoslav Controversy, 1948–1958.* Prospect Books, New York, 1959.

Bridgham, Philip L. Unpublished study of the origins of the Chinese communes. Washington, D.C.

————, Cohen, Arthur, and Jaffe, Herb. "Chinese and Soviet Views on Mao as a Marxist Theorist and the Significance of the Chinese Revolution for the Asian Revolutionary Movement." Unpublished manuscript, Washington, D.C.

Carin, Robert. China's Land Problem Series, vols. 1–4. P.O. Box 5217, Kowloon, Hongkong.

The Chinese Communes: A Documentary Review and Analysis of the "Great Leap Forward." Soviet Survey, London, 1960.

"Communes and Communism" (ad hoc reports). Radio Free Europe, Munich. (See particularly the one dated April 27, 1960.)

Dallin, Alexander. "International Movements." Paper delivered to a Conference on "A Century of Russian Foreign Policy: Studies in Historical Perspective." New Haven, Connecticut, April 6–8, 1961.

"Economics and Ideology in Sino-Soviet Relations." Panel discussion on September 19, 1958, chaired by William Griffith and including Peter Wiles, Werner Klatt, Wolfgang Leonhard, and Herbert Ritvo. Radio Free Europe, Munich, September 29, 1958.

Halpern, A. M. "Communist China's Demands on the World." Paper presented to a meeting of the American Political Scientists Association in St. Louis, Missouri, September 6–9, 1961.

————. "The Chinese Communist Line on Neutralism." Paper presented to the Third International Conference of Sovietologists in Tokyo, September 18–25, 1960.

————. "The Foreign Policy Uses of the Chinese Revolutionary Model." Paper delivered at a meeting of the Association of Asian Studies in Chicago, Illinois, March 27, 1961.

Hoeffding, Oleg. "Sino-Soviet Economic Relations in Recent Years." The Rand Corporation, Santa Monica, California, August 26, 1960.

Loh, Pichon P. Y. "Sino-Soviet Ideological Differences on Peaceful Co-existence." Paper read before the 1961 Convention of the Association for Asian Studies, Chicago, Illinois, March 29, 1961.

Meissner, Boris. "The Conception of the People's Commune as a Manifestation of the Ideological Differences between Peking and Moscow." Paper presented to the Third International Conference of Sovietologists in Tokyo, September 18–25, 1960.

National Communism and Popular Revolt in Eastern Europe: a selection of documents on events in Poland and Hungary, February-November 1956. Paul E. Zinner, ed. Columbia University Press, New York, 1956.

North, Robert C. "Soviet and Chinese Goal Values (A Study in Communism as a Behavior System)." Paper presented to the Third International Conference of Sovietologists in Tokyo, September 18–25, 1960.

Ravenholt, Albert. "People's Communes (China's Peasants take 'the Ultimate Step')." American Universities Field Staff report, Hongkong, AR-8-'58.

Schapiro, Leonard. "The Chinese Ally from the Soviet Point of View." Paper presented to the Third International Conference of Sovietologists, Tokyo, September 18–25, 1960.

Seton-Watson, Hugh. "The Role of the 'National Bourgeoisie' in Afro-Asian Independence Movements: Theory and Practice in Soviet Strategy." Paper presented to the Third International Conference of Sovietologists, Tokyo, September 18–25, 1960.

Shulman, Marshall D. "Prelude to Policy: Understanding." The Rand Corporation, Santa Monica, California, June 9, 1961.

III. PUBLISHED ARTICLES

Bialer, Seweryn. "Moscow vs. Belgrade; A Key to Soviet Policy." *Problems of Communism,* July-August 1958.

———. "The 21st Congress and Soviet Policy." *Problems of Communism,* March-April 1959.

Brzezinski, Zbigniew. "The Challenge of Change in the Soviet Bloc." *Foreign Affairs,* April 1961.

———. "Communist Ideology and International Affairs." *Journal of Conflict Resolution,* September 1960.

———. "Patterns and Limits of the Sino-Soviet Dispute." *Problems of Communism,* September-October 1960.

————. "Political Developments in the Sino-Soviet Bloc." *Annals* (of the Academy of Political and Social Science), July 1961.

Crankshaw, Edward. "Khrushchev and China." *Atlantic,* May 1961.

————. "The Moscow-Peking Clash." *Observer* (London), February 12 and 19, 1961.

Dallin, Alexander. "Commune Controversy." *The New Leader,* April 20, 1959.

Deutscher, Isaac. "Khrushchev, Mao and Stalin's Ghost." *The Reporter,* February 19, 1959.

————. "Uneasy Allies in Algeria." *The Reporter,* November 10, 1960.

Essler, Martin. "Peking-Pankow Axis?" *The China Quarterly,* July-September 1960.

Griffith, William E. "An International Communism? (Peiping, Tirana and Moscow: Polycentrism in Practice)." *East Europe,* July 1961.

Halpern, A. M. "Communist China and Peaceful and Coexistence." *The China Quarterly,* July-September 1960.

Herber, Robert C. "Mao and Polycentric Communism." *Orbis,* 2, Summer, 1958.

Hinton, Harold C. "Intra-Party Politics and Economic Policy in Communist China." *World Politics,* July 1960.

————. "The Succession Problem in Communist China." *Current Scene,* July 19, 1961.

Hudson, G. F. "Mao, Marx and Moscow." *Foreign Affairs,* July 1959.

————. "Moscow and Peiping: Seeds of Conflict?" *Problems of Communism,* November-December 1956.

————. "The Peking-Moscow Axis: Who Is Top Dog?" *Commentary,* December 1958.

————. "Russia and China: the Dilemmas of Power." *Foreign Affairs,* October 1960.

Kennan, George. "Stalin and China." *Atlantic,* May 1961.

Labedz, Leopold. "The Growing Sino-Soviet Dispute." *The New Leader,* September 12, 1960.

Ladejinsky, Wolf. "More than Mao can Chew (A Report on China's Rural Communes)." *The Reporter,* October 27, 1960.

Laqueur, Walter Z. "Soviet Views on Africa." *Survey,* April-June 1959.

————. "The 'National Bourgeoisie,' A Soviet Dilemma in the Middle East." *International Affairs* (London), July 1959.

————. "Towards National Democracy (Soviet Doctrine and the New Countries)." *Survey,* July-September 1961.

Lindsay, Michael (Lord of Birker). "Is Cleavage between Russia and China Inevitable?" *Annals,* July 1961.

Lowenthal, Richard. "The Changed Antagonist." *Encounter*, January 1961.

―――. "Diplomacy and Revolution: The Dialectics of a Dispute." *The China Quarterly*, January-March 1961. (A later version of this article appeared in *Commentary*, May 1961.)

―――. "Khrushchev's 'Flexible Communism'—The 21st Congress in Moscow." *Commentary*, April 1959.

―――. "Shifts and Rifts in the Russo-Chinese Alliance." *Problems of Communism*, January-February 1959.

―――. "Three Roads to Power." *Problems of Communism*, July-August 1956.

―――. "Tito's Gamble." *Encounter*, October 1958.

MacFarquhar, Roderick. "China and Russia: The First Decade." *Commentary*, May 1960.

―――. "Communist China's Intra-Party Dispute." *Pacific Affairs*, December 1958.

―――. "The Leadership in China." *The World Today*, August 1959.

Ravenholt, Albert. "Chinese Communes: Big Risks for Big Gains." *Foreign Affairs*, July 1959.

Rich, Stanley. "The Communes—Mao's Big Family." *Problems of Communism*, January-February 1959.

Rousset, David. "The New Tyranny in the Countryside." *Problems of Communism*, January-February 1959.

Rupen, Robert A. "Sino-Soviet Rivalry in Outer Mongolia." *Current Scene*, August 31, 1961.

Rush, Myron. "Esoteric Communication in Soviet Politics." *World Politics*, July 1959.

Schatten, Fritz. "Peking's Growing Influence in Africa." *Swiss Review of World Affairs*, August 1960.

Schram, Stuart R. "La 'revolution permanente' en Chine." *Revue française de science politique*, September 1960. (Reprinted as a pamphlet by the Centre d'Etude des Relations Internationales, Fondation Nationale des Sciences Politiques, Paris.)

Schwartz, Benjamin. "New Trends in Maoism." *Problems of Communism*, July-August 1957.

Seton-Watson, Hugh. "Soviet Foreign Policy on the Eve of the Summit." *International Affairs* (London), July 1960.

Sherman, A. V. "The People's Commune," in *The Chinese Communes*.

Thornton, Thomas P. "Peking, Moscow and the Underdeveloped Areas." *World Politics*, July 1961.

Tucker, Robert C. "Russia, the West, and World Order." *World Politics*, October 1959.

Walker, Richard L. "Chairman Mao and the Cult of Personality." *Encounter,* June 1960.

Whiting, Allen S. "Contradictions in the Moscow-Peking Axis." *Journal of Politics,* February 1958.

———. "Dynamics of the Moscow-Peking Axis." *Annals,* January 1959.

———. "Moscow and Peking: Suspended Dialogue?" *Current Scene,* June 21, 1961.

———. "Sino-Soviet Stresses and Strains." *The New Leader,* October 19, 1959.

Zagoria, Donald S. "The Future of Sino-Soviet Relations." *Asian Survey,* April 1961.

———. "The Sino-Soviet Conflict over the Transition to Communism." *Survey,* October-December, 1961.

———. "Sino-Soviet Friction in Underdeveloped Areas." *Problems of Communism,* March-April 1961.

———. "Strains in the Sino-Soviet Alliance." *Problems of Communism,* May-June 1960.

Zauberman, Alfred. "Some Remarks on the Economic Aspect," in *The Chinese Communes.*

Zorza, Victor. See the numerous articles in *The Guardian* (London), from 1956 to 1961.

COMMUNIST MATERIALS

I. SELECTED BOOKS

The Fundamentals of Marxism-Leninism. Foreign Languages Publishing House, Moscow, 1960.

Ho Kan-chih. *A History of the Modern Chinese Revolution.* Foreign Languages Press, Peking, 1959.

Kapelinskii, Yu N., Kisvyantsev, L. A., Pankin, M. S., Nekshev, Yu. A., Senin, V. P., and Sychev, V. G. *Development of the Economy and Foreign Economic Contacts of the People's Republic of China.* Translated from the Russian by JPRS, 3234, May 23, 1960.

Kapitsa, M. S. *Sovetsko-kitaiskie otnosheniya.* Gosudarstvennoe Izdatel'stvo Politicheskoi Literatury, Moskva, 1958.

Politicheskaya ekonomiya uchebnik. Gosudarstvennoe Izdatel'stvo Politicheskoi Literatury, Moskva. Signed to the press September 15, 1958.

Stalin, J. *Problems of Leninism.* Foreign Languages Publishing House, Moscow, 1953.

II. COLLECTIONS, MONOGRAPHS, PAMPHLETS

Akademiya nauk, SSSR. Institut kitaevedeniya. *Sovetsko-kitaiskiye otnosheniya, 1917–57:* Sbornik dokumentov. Izdatel'stvo Vostochnoi Literatury, Moskva, 1959.

For Victory in Peaceful Competition with Capitalism, collection of speeches by Khrushchev. E. P. Dutton and Co., Inc., New York, 1960.

Forty Years, 1917–57: Theses of the Propaganda Department of the CPSU and the Marxist-Leninist Institute on the 40th Anniversary of the Great October Revolution. September 15, 1957, Soviet News Booklet, 16, London, November 1957.

Lenin on Imperialism on the Eve of the Proletarian Social Revolution. Foreign Languages Press, Peking, September 1960.

Lenin on the National Liberation Movement. Foreign Languages Press, Peking, September 1960.

Lenin on Proletarian Revolution and Proletarian Dictatorship. Foreign Languages Press, Peking, September 1960.

Lenin on the Revolutionary Proletarian Party of a New Type. Foreign Languages Press, Peking, September 1960.

Lenin on the Struggle Against Revisionism. Foreign Languages Press, Peking, September 1960.

Lenin on War and Peace. Foreign Languages Press, Peking, September 1960.

Let Us Live in Peace and Friendship. The visit by N. S. Khrushchev to the U.S.A. September 15–27, 1959. Foreign Languages Publishing House, Moscow, 1959.

Long Live Leninism. Foreign Languages Press, Peking, 1960.

Mao Tse-tung. *Imperialism and All Reactionaries Are Paper Tigers.* Foreign Languages Press, Peking, 1958. (Also in *Peking Review,* 37, November 11, 1958.)

———. *On the Correct Handling of Contradictions Among the People.* Foreign Languages Press, Peking, 1958.

Skachkov, P. E. *Bibliografia kitaya. Izdatel'stvo Vostochnoi Literatury,* Moskva, 1960.

Ten Glorious Years, 1949–1959. Foreign Languages Press, Peking, 1960.

Ten Years of the People's Republic of China. Moscow, 1959, translated from the Russian by JPRS, 2825, June 22, 1960.

Voprosy stroitel'stva kommunizma v SSSR. Izdatel'stvo Akademii Nauk, SSSR, Moskva, 1959.

III. DOCUMENTS, ARTICLES, REPORTS, ETC.
(listed chronologically)

Khrushchev, Speech to the 20th Congress. *Pravda,* February 15, 1956.

"On Historical Experience Concerning the Dictatorship of the Proletariat." *Jen-min jih-pao,* April 5, 1956; CB, 403, July 25, 1956.

Togliatti, Palmiro, "9 Domande sullo Stalinismo." *Nuovo Argomenti,* 20, June 16, 1956, in *The Anti-Stalin Campaign and International Communism.*

Soviet-Yugoslav Declaration of June 20, 1956, in *National Communism and Popular Revolt in Eastern Europe.*

CPSU resolution of June 20, 1956, in *The Anti-Stalin Campaign and International Communism.*

Jen-min jih-pao on Poland and Hungary, July 12, 1956; NCNA, July 12, 1956.

"Collapse of the Antipopular Adventure in Hungary." *Pravda* editorial, October 28, 1956.

Soviet Government Declaration of October 30, 1956, in *Sovetsko-kitaiskiye otnosheniya.*

Chinese Government Statement of November 1, 1956, in *Sovetsko-kitaiskiye otnosheniya.*

Jen-min jih-pao on the Hungarian revolution, November 5, 1956; NCNA, November 5, 1956.

Suslov, October Revolution Anniversary Speech. *Pravda,* November 7, 1956.

Azizyan, Rebuttal of Tito speech. *Pravda,* December 23, 1956.

"More on the Historical Experience of the Dictatorship of the Proletariat." *Jen-min jih-pao,* December 29, 1956; NCNA, December 29, 1956.

Khrushchev, Reply to questions submitted by Czech newspaper. *Rude pravo,* December 30, 1956.

Hsueh-hsi on the Hungarian rebellion, January 3, 1957; *Extracts,* 73, March 3, 1957.

Chou En-lai. Speech at a Budapest rally. NCNA, January 16, 1957.

————. Speech at a Moscow mass rally. NCNA, January 18, 1957.

Polish-CPR communiqué, April 11, 1957. NCNA, April 11, 1957.

Chou En-lai. Report to the National People's Congress, June 1957. CB, 463, July 2, 1957.

Khrushchev, Speech in Czechoslovakia on national peculiarities, July 11, 1957. *Pravda,* July 12, 1957.

Soviet-Czech communiqué. *Pravda,* July 16, 1957.

Yang Ying-chieh. "Study the Experience of the Soviet Union in Construction." *Hsueh-hsi,* 21, November 2, 1957; *Extracts,* 120, February 24, 1958.

Khrushchev, Speech on the 40th Anniversary of the Revolution. *Pravda,* November 8, 1957.

Mao Tse-tung. November 17 speech at Moscow University. *Jen-min jih-pao,* November 20, 1957; SCMP, 1656, November 21, 1957.

Declaration of 12 Communist parties. *Pravda,* November 22, 1957.

"The Great Revolutionary Declarations." *Jen-min jih-pao* editorial, November 25, 1957; NCNA, November 25, 1957.

Chi Lung. "U.S. Strategy is in a Blind Alley." *Shih-chieh chih-shih,* 23, December 5, 1957; *Extracts,* 121, March 3, 1958.

Jen-min jih-pao editorial indicating triumph of Left economic policy, December 12, 1957. NCNA, December 12, 1957.

Hu Pin. "The World Situation." *Shih-chieh chih-shih,* 24, December 20, 1957; JPRS, 507-D, January 27, 1959.

"Full Steam Ahead," *Jen-min jih-pao* editorial. January 1, 1958; NCNA, January 1, 1958.

"The East Wind Overpowers the West Wind (Chief Characteristic of the Current International Situation)." *Hsueh-hsi,* January 3, 1958; JPRS, 507-D, January 27, 1958.

Talenskii, Maj. Gen. N. "Military Strategy and Foreign Policy." *International Affairs,* 3, 1958.

Fedoseev, P., Pomelov, I., and Cheprakov, V. "O proekte programmy soyuza kommunistov Yugoslavii" (On the Draft Program of the Yugoslav Party Congress). *Kommunist,* 6, April 15, 1958.

Glotov, I. "Reorganizatsiya MTS i kolkhoznaya sobstvennost'" (The Reorganization of the MTS and Kolkhoz Property). *Kommunist,* 6, April 15, 1958.

Liu Shao-ch'i. Speech to the 2nd Session of the Eighth Party Congress, May 5, 1958. *Peking Review,* 14, June 3, 1958.

"Modern Revisionism Must be Condemned." *Jen-min jih-pao* editorial, May 5, 1958; SCMP, 1767, May 8, 1958. (Article also in *Peking Review,* 11, May 13, 1958.)

Strumulin, S. G. "Nekotorye problemy dal'neishego razvitiya kolkhoznogo stroya" (Some Problems of the Further Development of the Kolkhoz Regime). *Voprosy ekonomiki,* 5, May 20, 1958.

Khrushchev, Report to the Warsaw Pact, May 24, 1958, in *For Victory in Peaceful Competition with Capitalism.*

Ch'en Yün. Speech to the Warsaw Pact, May 27, 1958. SCMP, 1787, June 9, 1958.

Khrushchev, Speech to the Bulgarian Party Congress. *Pravda,* June 4, 1958.

471

Ch'en Po-ta. "Under the Banner of Comrade Mao Tse-tung." *Hung ch'i,* 4, July 16, 1958; *Extracts,* 138, August 11, 1958.

"The Countries of the World Who Love Peace and Freedom Cannot Stand Idly By." *Jen-min jih-pao,* July 20, 1958; Peking Radio, July 20, 1958.

Yu chao-li. "A New Upsurge in National Revolution." *Hung ch'i,* 5, August 1, 1958.

Mao-Khrushchev communiqué, August 3, 1958, in *Sovetsko-kitaiskiye otnosheniya.*

Yu Chao-li. "The Forces of the New are Bound to Defeat the Forces of Decay." *Hung ch'i,* August 16, 1958; *Peking Review,* 25, August 19, 1958.

Chinese commune resolution, August 29, 1958 (published September 10, 1958). *Peking Review,* 29, September 16, 1958.

Vasil'yev, Yu. "A Scientific Conference on the Theoretical Problems of the Building of Communism in the USSR." *Voprosy istorii,* 9, 1958; translated by JPRS, 471-D, January 13, 1959.

Zhamin, V., "Velikii Kitai stroit sotsializm" (Great China Builds Socialism). *Voprosy ekonomiki,* 10, 1958.

Stepanyan, Ts. A. "Oktyabrskaya revolyutsiya i stanovlenie kommunist-icheskoi formatsii" (The October Revolution and the Growth of Communist Formation). *Voprosy filosofii,* 10, 1958.

Yudin, Pavel. Speeches in Peking on the building of communism, November 6 and 7, 1958. NCNA, November 6 and 7, 1958.

"Scorn Imperialism and All Reactionaries." *Jen-min jih-pao* editorial, November 12, 1958; *Peking Review,* 38, November 18, 1958.

Khrushchev, November 14 "Theses" on Soviet Seven-Year Plan. *Pravda,* November 14, 1958.

Chu Teh. Speech at a conference of young activists, November 21, 1958. SCMP, 1902, November 26, 1958.

Wu Chiang. "A Partisan of the Permanent Revolution Theory must be a Consistent Dialectic Materialist." *Che-hsueh yen-chiu,* 8, December 1958.

CCP Resolution of December 10, 1958 on the communes. *Peking Review,* 43, December 23, 1958.

Khrushchev, Report to the 21st CPSU Congress. *Pravda,* January 28, 1959.

Jen-min jih-pao editorial commenting on Khrushchev's propositions to the 21st CPSU Congress, February 5, 1958. *Peking Review,* 6, February 10, 1959.

Yudin, Pavel. Speech to the 21st CPSU Congress. *Pravda,* February 6, 1959.

Hung ch'i editorial on Khrushchev's propositions to the 21st CPSU Congress, February 16, 1959. *Peking Review,* 8, February 24, 1959.

Bugachev, Y., and Liebson, B. "Guiding Force in the Advance to Communism." *Problems of Peace and Socialism,* April 1959.

Fedoseev, P. and Pomelov, I. "O razvitii mirovoi sotsialisticheskoi sistemy k kommunizmu" (On the Progress of the World Socialist System toward Communism). *Kommunist,* 5, April 14, 1959.

Khrushchev, Speech in Poland, "The Cooperative Way is the Surest Way for the Peasant," July 18, 1959. Moscow Radio Home Service, July 21, 1959.

Yu Chao-li. "Peaceful Competition: an Inevitable Trend." *Hung ch'i,* August 16, 1959; *Peking Review,* 33, August 18, 1959.

Articles presented at a symposium on the "national bourgeoisie." *World Marxist Review,* August and September 1959.

Liu Shao-ch'i. "The Victory of Marxism-Leninism in China." September 14, 1959; in *Ten Glorious Years.*

Yu Chao-li. "The Great Victory of the Chinese People's Anti-Imperialist Struggle." *Jen-min jih-pao,* September 16, 1959; CB, 595, October 5, 1959.

Liu Lan-t'ao. "The Communist Party of China is the High Command of the Chinese People in Building Socialism." *Jen-min jih-pao,* September 28, 1959; in *Ten Glorious Years.*

Wang Chia-hsiang. "The International Significance of the Chinese People's Victory." *Hung ch'i,* 10, October 1, 1959; in *Ten Glorious Years.* (Also in JPRS, 1013-D.)

Li Ching-chuan. "The People's Communes are the Inevitable Outcome of China's Social Development." In *Ten Glorious Years.*

Li Fu-ch'un. "On the Big Leap Forward in China's Socialist Construction." In *Ten Glorious Years.*

Chou En-lai. "A Great Decade," October 1, 1959. In *Ten Glorious Years.*

Ch'en Yi. "Ten Years of Struggle for World Peace and Human Progress." (Written for *Izvestiya.*) In *Ten Glorious Years.*

Teng Hsiao-p'ing. "The Great Unity of the Chinese People and the Great Unity of the Peoples of the World." *Pravda,* October 1, 1959; in *Ten Glorious Years.*

Khrushchev, Speech in Peking on the occasion of the October Revolution Anniversary. *Pravda,* October 1, 1959.

Resolution on "democracy of new type" adopted in Rome, November 25, 1959, by 17 West European parties. *World Marxist Review,* December 1959.

Khrushchev, Speech to the Hungarian Party Congress, Budapest, December 1, 1959. *Pravda,* December 2, 1959.

Yu Chao-li. "Excellent Situation for the Struggle for Peace. "*Hung ch'i,* 1, (January 1), 1960; *Peking Review,* 1, January 5, 1960.

Khrushchev, Speech to the Supreme Soviet, January 14, 1960. *Pravda,* January 15, 1960.

Hu Hsi-kuei. "Mao Tse-tung's Ideology Glows 100,000 Feet High." Peking Radio Home Service, January 1, 24, 1960.

Resolution of the National People's Congress Standing Committee, January 21, 1960. *Peking Review,* 4, January 26, 1960.

"What the Messages of the U.S. President Show." *Jen-min jih-pao* editorial, January 21, 1960; *Peking Review,* 4, January 26, 1960.

"Arm the Workers and Peasants with Mao Tse-tung's Thinking." *Sheng-si jih-pao,* February 1, 1960; SCMP, 2209, March 4, 1960.

Kang Sheng. "On the Current International Situation," Speech on February 4, 1960, to the Political Consultative Committee of the Warsaw Treaty Organization. *Peking Review,* 6, February 9, 1960.

"A Decisive Force to Safeguard Peace." *Jen-min jih-pao* editorial, February 6, 1960; *Peking Review,* 6, February 9, 1960.

Sung Tu. "Answers to Readers' Queries on War and Peace." *Chung-kuo ch'ing-nien,* February 16, 1960; *Extracts,* 207, April 11, 1960.

Sovetov, A. "Leninist Foreign Policy and International Relations." *International Affairs,* 4, March 21, 1960.

Yu Chao-li. "On Imperialism as the Source of War in Modern Times, and on the Way for All Peoples to Struggle for Peace." *Hung ch'i,* April 1, 1960; March 30, 1960.

Zorin, V. "Leninskie printsipy vneshnei politiki SSSR" (Leninist Principles of the Foreign Policy of the USSR). *Kommunist,* 6, April 14, 1960.

"Long Live Leninism!" *Hung ch'i* editorial, 8, April 16, 1960, in *Long Live Leninism.*

Lu Ting-yi. "Unite Under Lenin's Revolutionary Banner!" Report delivered at a meeting of the Central Committee of the CCP, April 22, 1960, on the 90th Anniversary of the Birth of Lenin. In *Long Live Leninism.*

"Forward Along the Path of the Great Lenin!" *Jen-min jih-pao* editorial, April 22, 1960. In *Long Live Leninism.* (Also in *Peking Review,* 17, April 26, 1960.)

Kuusinen, O. V. Report at a celebration meeting, Moscow, April 22, 1960, on the 90th Anniversary of the Birth of Lenin. Tass, April

22, 1960. (Also available as the *Realization of Lenin's Ideas,* The Press Office, USSR Embassy, Canada.)

Hu Hse-huei. "Lenin's Theory on Peace and War." *Jen-min jih-pao,* April 25, 1960.

Chang Hsiang-shan. "Study Chairman Mao's Dialogue on Questions of Democracy in Colonial and Semi-colonial Countries." *Chung-kuo ch'ing-nien,* 9, May 1, 1960.

"Protect Leninism—The Powerful Weapon Against Modern Revisionism." *Chung-kuo ch'ing-nien,* 9, May 1, 1960; JPRS, 3915, September 13, 1960.

"The Fundamental Path for the Liberation Movements in the Colonial and Semi-colonial Areas." *Kuo-chi wen-t'i yen chiu,* 5, May 3, 1960.

"Sovetskii soyuz—glavnaya opora mirolyubivogo chelovechestva" (The Soviet Union—Chief Support of Peace-Loving Humanity). *Kommunist,* 8, May 18, 1960.

Stephonon, L. "Soviet Aid—and Its 'Critics.'" *International Affairs,* 6, May 20, 1960.

Wu Chiang. "Victory for Historical Dialectics." *Che-hsueh yen-chiu,* 6, June 10, 1960; *Selections,* 225, September 6, 1960.

Matkovskii, N. "Ideinoe oruzhie kommunizma: K sorokaletiyu vykhoda v svet knigi V. I. Lenina 'Detskaya bolezn' Levizny v Kommunizme'" (An Ideological Weapon of Communism: On the Occasion of the 40th Anniversary of the Publication of V. I. Lenin's Book "Leftwing Communism, an Infantile Disorder"). *Pravda,* June 12, 1960.

Shih Tung-hsiang. "Refuting the Fallacy that the Nature of Imperialism has Changed." *Hung ch'i,* June 16, 1960; NCNA, June 15, 1960.

Konstantinov, F. and Momdzhyan, Kh. "Dialektika i sovremennost" (Dialectics and Our Times). *Kommunist,* 10, July 19, 1960.

Togliatti, Palmiro, Address to the Italian Communist Party Central Committee, *l'Unita* (Rome). July 24, 1960.

"To Be a Revolutionary, One Must Have the Revolutionary Will." *Jen-min jih-pao,* August 13, 1960 (from the Shanghai *Chieh-fang,* August 5, 1960); SCMP, 2335, September 12, 1960.

Frantsev, Yu. "Problemy voiny i mira v sovremennikh usloviyakh" (Problems of War and Peace in Present Conditions). *Pravda,* August 7, 1960.

Li Wei. "Raise High the Red Flag of the Thought of Mao Tse-tung, Write More and Better Memoirs of the Revolutionary Struggles." *Jen-min jih-pao,* August 10, 1960; SCMP, 2328, August 31, 1960.

Ponomarev, B. "Mirnoe sosvshchestvovanie zhizhennaya neobkhodimost' " (Peaceful Coexistence Is a Vital Necessity). *Pravda,* August 12, 1960.

"Refuting the Statement of the U.S. State Department." *Jen-min jih-pao* editorial, August 13, 1960; NCNA, August 13, 1960.

Titarenko, S. "Lenin's Teachings on the Victory of Socialism and the Present Day." *Bakinskii rabochii,* and *Sovetskaya latvia* August 16, 1960; *Leningradskaya pravda,* August 23, 1960; *Sovetskaya litva,* and *Kommunist Tadzhikistana,* August 24, 1960; and *Sovetskaya Kirghiziya,* August 27, 1960.

Li Fu-ch'un. "Raise High the Red Flag of the General Iine and Continue to March Forward." *Hung ch'i,* 16, August 16, 1960; *Peking Review,* 34, August 23, 1960.

Butenko, A., and Pchelin, V. "Sovremennaya epokha i tvorcheskoe razvitie Marksizma-Leninizma" (The Present Epoch and the Creative Development of Marxism-Leninism). *Kommunist,* 12, August 23, 1960.

Zhukov, Yu. "Znamenatel'nyi faktor nashego vremeni" (Outstanding Factor of Our Time). *Pravda,* August 26, 1960.

Belyakov, A., and Burlatski, F. "Leninskaya teoriya sotsialisticheskoi revolyutsii i sovremennost" (The Leninist Theory of Socialist Revolution and the Present Time). *Kommunist,* 13, September 10, 1960.

"Firmly Establish Self-reliance, Arouse Ambitious Thought." *Kung-jen jih-pao,* September 11, 1960.

"An Introduction to the Fourth Volume of 'Selected Works of Mao Tse-tung.' " *Hung ch'i,* 19, October 1, 1960; *Selections,* 233, October 31, 1960.

"Slighting the Enemy Strategically and Taking Full Account of Him Tactically." *Hung ch'i* editorial, 19, October 1, 1960; *Selections,* 231, October 18, 1960.

Chang Ming-yang. "Use Two Tactics of Revolution to Oppose Two Tactics of Counter-Revolution (Notes on Study of the "Selected Works of Mao Tse-tung," Volume 4.) *Shih-chieh chih-shih,* 20, October 20, 1960; *Selections,* 239, December 12, 1960.

"A Basic Summary of the Victorious Experience of the Chinese People's Revolution." *Hung ch'i* editorial, November 1, 1960; NCNA, October 30, 1960.

Teng, Li-ch'ün, and Wu Chiang. "Dialectics is the Algebra of Revolution (After Reading the Fourth Volume of 'Selected Works of Mao Tse-tung')." *Hung ch'i,* 20–21, November 1, 1960; *Selections,* 237, November 28, 1960.

Fedoseev, P. "Sotsialisticheskaya revolyutsiya i sotsial'nye problemy

XX veka" (The Socialist Revolution and the Social Problems of the 20th Century). *Pravda,* November 4, 1960.

"Hold High the Red Banner of the October Revolution; March from Victory to Victory." *Jen-min jih-pao* editorial, November 7, 1960; NCNA, November 7, 1960.

Hsiao Shu, and Yang Fu. "Party's Policy is a Guarantee for Victory in Revolution." *Hung ch'i,* 22, November 16, 1960; *Selections,* 238, December 5, 1960.

"Give Full Play to the Revolutionary Spirit of the 1957 Moscow Declarations." *Jen-min jih-pao* editorial, November 21, 1960; NCNA, November 21, 1960.

"Marksizm-Leninizm—pobedônosnaya znamya nashei epokhi" (Marxism-Leninism Is the Triumphant Banner of Our Epoch). *Pravda* editorial, November 28, 1960.

Jen Hui-po. "The Reactionary Clique Will Never Change Its Character." *Hung ch'i,* 23, December 1, 1960.

"A Great Anti-Imperialist Call." *Hung ch'i* editorial, 24, December 16, 1960; *Selections,* 241, December 28, 1960.

Ulbricht, W. Report on the Moscow Conference statement. *Neues deutschland,* December 18, 1960.

Matern, Hermann. Report on the Moscow Conference. *Neues deutschland,* December 23, 1960.

Khrushchev's Report on the Moscow Conference, World Marxist Review, No. 1, 1961.

Chinese Communist Party Resolution on the Moscow Conference, NCNA, January 20, 1961.

Hoxha's speech on the anniversary of the Bolshevik Revolution, Tirana radio, November 7, 1961.

(For a more complete listing of the relevant articles and speeches in 1961, see notes to Chapter 16.)

INDEX

DONALD S. ZAGORIA is a member of the Political Science faculty and Fellow in the Research Institute on Communist Affairs at Columbia University. Formerly a member of the Social Science Division of the RAND Corporation, he was from 1951 to 1961 an analyst of Communist Bloc politics for the United States government.

Atheneum Paperbacks

HISTORY—AMERICAN

Atheneum Paperbacks

HISTORY

HISTORY—ASIA

THE NEW YORK TIMES BYLINE BOOKS

Atheneum Paperbacks

STUDIES IN AMERICAN NEGRO LIFE

LAW AND GOVERNMENT

Atheneum Paperbacks

DIPLOMACY AND INTERNATIONAL RELATIONS

ECONOMICS AND BUSINESS

PSYCHOLOGY AND SOCIOLOGY

Atheneum Paperbacks

Atheneum Paperbacks

THE WORLDS OF NATURE AND MAN

LITERATURE AND THE ARTS